Contents

Micr

V

B

Microsoft

PUBLISHED BY
Microsoft Press
A Division of Microsoft Corporation
One Microsoft Way
Redmond, Washington 98052-6399

Library of Congress Cataloging-in-Publication Data
Microsoft Visual Basic 6.0 Programmer's Guide / Microsoft Corporation.
p. cm.
Includes index.
ISBN 1-57231-863-5
1. Microsoft Visual BASIC. 2. BASIC (Computer program language)
I. Microsoft Corporation.
QA76.73.B3M5589 1998
005.26'8--dc21 98-14786
CIP

Printed and bound in the United States of America.

2 3 4 5 6 7 8 9 WCWC 3 2 1 0 9 8

Distributed in Canada by ITP Nelson, a division of Thomson Canada Limited.

A CIP catalogue record for this book is available from the British Library.

Microsoft Press books are available through booksellers and distributors worldwide. For further information about international editions, contact your local Microsoft Corporation office or contact Microsoft Press International directly at fax (425) 936-7329. Visit our Web site at mspress.microsoft.com.

Acquisitions Editor: Eric Stroo
Project Editor: Maureen Williams Zimmerman

Document Conventions

This manual uses the following typographic conventions.

Example of convention	Description
Sub, If, Case Else, Print, True, BackColor, Click, Debug, Long	Words with initial letter capitalized indicate language-specific keywords.
setup	Words you're instructed to type appear in bold.
event-driven	In text, italic letters can indicate defined terms, usually the first time they occur in the book. Italic formatting is also used occasionally for emphasis.
variable	In syntax and text, italic letters can indicate placeholders for information you supply.
[*expressionlist*]	In syntax, items inside square brackets are optional.
{**While** | **Until**}	In syntax, braces and a vertical bar indicate a choice between two or more items. You must choose one of the items unless all of the items also are enclosed in square brackets.

`Sub HelloButton_Click()`
`Readout.Text = _`
`"Hello, world!"`
`End Sub`
	This font is used for code.

ENTER	Capital letters are used for the names of keys and key sequences, such as ENTER and CTRL+R.
ALT+F1	A plus sign (+) between key names indicates a combination of keys. For example, ALT+F1 means to hold down the ALT key while pressing the F1 key.
DOWN ARROW	Individual direction keys are referred to by the direction of the arrow on the key top (LEFT, RIGHT, UP, or DOWN). The phrase "arrow keys" is used when describing these keys collectively.
BACKSPACE, HOME	Other navigational keys are referred to by their specific names.
c:\Vb\Samples\Calldlls.vbp	Paths and file names are given in mixed case.

Programming Style in This Manual

The following guidelines are used in writing programs in this manual. For more information, see Chapter 5, "Programming Fundamentals."

- Keywords appear with initial letters capitalized:

```
' Sub, If, ChDir, Print, and True are keywords.
Print "Title Page"
```

- Line labels are used instead of line numbers. The use of line labels is restricted to error-handling routines:

```
ErrorHandler:
   Power = conFailure
End Function
```

- An apostrophe (') introduces comments:

```
' This is a comment; these two lines
' are ignored when the program is running.
```

- Control-flow blocks and statements in Sub, Function, and Property procedures are indented from the enclosing code:

```
Private Sub cmdRemove_Click ()
   Dim Ind As Integer

   Ind = lstClient.ListIndex   ' Get index.
   ' Make sure list item is selected.
   If Ind >= 0 Then
      lstClient.RemoveItem Ind ' Remove it
                               ' from list box.
      ' Display number.
      lblDisplay.Caption = lstClient.ListCount
   Else
      Beep           ' If nothing selected, beep.
   End If
End Sub
```

- Lines too long to fit on one line (except comments) may be continued on the next line using a line-continuation character, which is a single leading space followed by an underscore (_):

```
Sub Form_MouseDown (Button As Integer, _
Shift As Integer, X As Single, Y As Single)
```

- Intrinsic constant names are in a mixed-case format, with a two-character prefix indicating the object library that defines the constant. Constants from the Visual Basic (VB) and Visual Basic for applications (VBA) object libraries are prefaced with a "vb"; constants from the data access (DAO) object library are prefaced with a "db"; constants from the Microsoft Excel object library are prefaced with an "xl." For example:

```
vbTileHorizontal
dbAppendOnly
xlDialogBorder
```

Throughout this book, user-defined constants are usually prefaced with "con" and are mixed case. For example:

```
conYourOwnConstant
```

When using Windows API constants, however, the code examples still follow the same conventions as in previous versions of Visual Basic. For example:

```
EM_LINESCROLL
```

Programmer's Guide

Welcome to the *Microsoft Visual Basic 6.0 Programmer's Guide*, a comprehensive manual on programming with Visual Basic. To accommodate the wealth of features and capabilities in Visual Basic, the *Microsoft Visual Basic 6.0 Programmer's Guide* is divided into two parts.

The first part covers the basic concepts, providing a foundation for programmers new to Visual Basic. Part 2 covers more advanced programming concepts and techniques. Additional information helpful in using the product is presented in the appendices.

Part 1 Visual Basic Basics

An introduction to programming in Visual Basic.

Part 2 What You Can Do with Visual Basic

Advanced topics on Visual Basic programming.

Appendix A Visual Basic Specifications, Limitations, and File Formats

Technical details for Visual Basic.

Appendix B Visual Basic Coding Conventions

Suggested guidelines for consistent and readable code.

Appendix C Native Code Compiler Switches

Details on command line switches for compiling to native code.

Appendix D Adding Help to Your Application

Guidelines for adding online Help to a Visual Basic application.

PART 1

Visual Basic Basics

Many of the things that you can do with Visual Basic really aren't very basic at all. The Visual Basic language is quite powerful — if you can imagine a programming task, it can probably be accomplished using Visual Basic. As you might guess, there's a lot to be learned before you can consider yourself a guru; but once you understand the basics of Visual Basic you'll find that you are productive in no time at all.

The first five chapters of the *Microsoft Visual Basic 6.0 Programmer's Guide* cover the basics, providing the foundation that you will need for anything you want to do in Visual Basic.

Chapter 1 Introducing Visual Basic

Explains how to install Visual Basic and get assistance while you work.

Chapter 2 Developing an Application in Visual Basic

An introduction to the integrated development environment and the process of creating your first application.

Chapter 3 Forms, Controls, and Menus

An introduction to the objects that you can put together to create an application.

Chapter 4 Managing Projects

An introduction to the tools used to organize your work in Visual Basic.

Chapter 5 Programming Fundamentals

An introduction to the nuts and bolts of the Visual Basic language.

CHAPTER 1

Introducing Visual Basic

This chapter contains information on installing Microsoft Visual Basic on your system, adding or removing Visual Basic components, and resources for learning or getting additional help with Visual Basic.

Contents

Welcome to Visual Basic

Welcome to Microsoft Visual Basic, the fastest and easiest way to create applications for Microsoft Windows. Whether you are an experienced professional or brand new to Windows programming, Visual Basic provides you with a complete set of tools to simplify rapid application development.

So what is Visual Basic? The "Visual" part refers to the method used to create the graphical user interface (GUI). Rather than writing numerous lines of code to describe the appearance and location of interface elements, you simply put prebuilt objects into place on screen. If you've ever used a drawing program such as Paint, you already have most of the skills necessary to create an effective user interface.

The "Basic" part refers to the BASIC (Beginners All-Purpose Symbolic Instruction Code) language, a language used by more programmers than any other language in the history of computing. Visual Basic has evolved from the original BASIC language and now contains several hundred statements, functions, and keywords, many of which relate directly to the Windows GUI. Beginners can create useful applications by learning just a few of the keywords, yet the power of the language allows professionals to accomplish anything that can be accomplished using any other Windows programming language.

The Visual Basic programming language is not unique to Visual Basic. The Visual Basic programming system, Applications Edition included in Microsoft Excel, Microsoft Access, and many other Windows applications uses the same language. The Visual Basic Scripting Edition (VBScript) is a widely used scripting language and a subset of the Visual Basic language. The investment you make in learning Visual Basic will carry over to these other areas.

Whether your goal is to create a small utility for yourself or your work group, a large enterprise-wide system, or even distributed applications spanning the globe via the Internet, Visual Basic has the tools you need.

- Data access features allow you to create databases, front-end applications, and scalable server-side components for most popular database formats, including Microsoft SQL Server and other enterprise-level databases.
- ActiveX technologies allow you to use the functionality provided by other applications, such as Microsoft Word word processor, Microsoft Excel spreadsheet, and other Windows applications. You can even automate applications and objects created using the Professional or Enterprise editions of Visual Basic.
- Internet capabilities make it easy to provide access to documents and applications across the Internet or intranet from within your application, or to create Internet server applications.
- Your finished application is a true .exe file that uses a Visual Basic Virtual Machine that you can freely distribute.

Visual Basic Editions

Visual Basic is available in three versions, each geared to meet a specific set of development requirements.

- The Visual Basic Learning edition allows programmers to easily create powerful applications for Microsoft Windows and Windows NT. It includes all intrinsic controls, plus grid, tab, and data-bound controls. Documentation provided with this edition includes the Learn VB Now CD plus the Microsoft Developer Network (MSDN) Library CDs containing full online documentation.
- The Professional edition provides computer professionals with a full-featured set of tools for developing solutions for others. It includes all the features of the Learning edition, plus additional ActiveX controls, the Internet Information Server Application Designer, integrated Visual Database Tools and Data Environment, Active Data Objects, and the Dynamic HTML Page Designer. Documentation provided with the Professional edition includes the Visual Studio Professional Features book plus Microsoft Developer Network CDs containing full online documentation.
- The Enterprise edition allows professionals to create robust distributed applications in a team setting. It includes all the features of the Professional edition, plus Back Office tools such as SQL Server, Microsoft Transaction Server, Internet Information Server, Visual SourceSafe, SNA Server, and more. Printed documentation provided with the Enterprise edition includes the Visual Studio Enterprise Features book plus Microsoft Developer Network CDs containing full online documentation.

Installing Visual Basic

You install Visual Basic on your computer using the Setup program. The Setup program installs Visual Basic and other product components from the CD-ROM to your hard disk. It also installs the files necessary to view the documentation on the Microsoft Developer Network CD. If you choose, you can install only the Visual Basic documentation and samples to your machine.

Important You cannot simply copy files from the CD-ROM to your hard disk and run Visual Basic. You must use the Setup program, which decompresses and installs the files in the appropriate directories.

- Before You Run Setup   Things to check prior to installation.
- Setting Up Visual Basic   Instructions for installing Visual Basic.

Before You Run Setup

Before you install Visual Basic, make sure that your computer meets the minimum requirements, and read the Readme file, located at the root directory on your installation disc.

Check the Hardware and System Requirements

To run Visual Basic, you must have certain hardware and software installed on your computer. The system requirements include:

- Microsoft Windows 95 or later, or Microsoft Windows NT Workstation 4.0 (Service Pack 3 recommended) or later.
- 486DX/66 MHz or higher processor (Pentium or higher processor recommended), or any Alpha processor running Microsoft Windows NT Workstation.
- A CD-ROM disc drive.
- VGA or higher-resolution screen supported by Microsoft Windows.
- 16 MB of RAM for Windows 95, 32 MB of RAM for Windows NT Workstation.
- A mouse or other suitable pointing device.

For More Information For more details about requirements, see "System Requirements for Visual Basic Applications" in Appendix A, "Visual Basic Specifications, Limitations, and File Formats."

Read the Readme File

The Readme file lists any changes to the Visual Basic documentation since its publication. It can be found by selecting Read Me First from the initial setup screen, or in the root directory of the CD-ROM. It can also be accessed from the Visual Basic Start Page in the documentation. Check the first section of the file for details and new information about installing Visual Basic.

Setting Up Visual Basic

When you run the Setup program, a directory is created for Visual Basic; you can then select the components of Visual Basic that you want to install.

With the exception of the operating system files in the \Os directory, files on the compact disc are not compressed, so they're usable directly from the disc. For example, there are numerous tools and components in the \Tools directory that can be run or installed directly from the CD-ROM.

To set up from compact disc

1. Insert the compact disc in the CD-ROM drive.
2. Use the appropriate command in your operating environment to run the Setup program, which is available in the root directory on Disk 1. If AutoPlay is enabled on your system, the Setup program will automatically load when you insert the compact disc.
3. Select **Install Visual Basic 6.0**.
4. Follow the setup instructions on the screen.

For More Information See the Readme file for detailed information on issues related to installing Visual Basic.

Adding or Removing Components of Visual Basic

You can run Setup as many times as necessary. For example, you can run Setup to reinstall Visual Basic in another directory, or to install other portions of Visual Basic.

To add or remove components of Visual Basic

1. Insert the compact disc in the CD-ROM drive.
2. Use the appropriate command in your operating environment to run the Setup program, which is available in the root directory on the compact disc. If AutoPlay is enabled on your system, the Setup program will automatically load when you insert the compact disc.
3. Select the **Custom** button in the **Microsoft Visual Basic 6.0 Setup** dialog box.

4. Select the components to be installed (or deselect the components to be removed) in the **Options** list box of the **Custom** dialog box.
5. Follow the setup instructions on the screen.

Starting Visual Basic

Once you have completed the Setup procedure, you can start Visual Basic by using the Start button on the Windows taskbar. If AutoPlay is enabled on your system, you can also start Visual Basic by inserting the Visual Basic compact disc.

For More information See Chapter 2, "Developing an Application in Visual Basic."

Getting Assistance While You Work

The online documentation system references nearly all aspects of Visual Basic. It includes:

- All of the Visual Basic books, providing conceptual information on using the multitude of features in Visual Basic.
- Language Reference, containing extensive information on the Visual Basic programming environment and language.
- Visual Basic online links, providing pointers to sources of Visual Basic information on the Web.
- Microsoft Product Support Services, with information on obtaining technical support.

Note You can view the documentation from the MSDN CDs (you must go through the MSDN installation process) or you can custom install the Visual Basic documents and samples to your machine during MSDN installation.

Getting the Most Out of Help Content

Help content includes several features designed to make finding information easier.

- What's New in Visual Basic 6.0?

  Use this section to go quickly to information on new and enhanced features of Visual Basic. Organized by feature category, it provides close to 200 described links to more information.

- Find It Fast

  Use this section to sort out subject areas covered throughout the documentation. Debugging information, for example, comes in a variety of flavors, depending on the kind of project you're working on. The described links in this section make the search easier.

- Overview topics

  Use these to get information about topics in a book or chapter before you go to the topics themselves. By providing a glimpse of content in each topic, the described links in overviews at the head of books, parts, and chapters save time.

- See Also links

  Click the See Also link under the topic title to view the titles of topics you can go to for more or related information.

Context-Sensitive Help

Many parts of Visual Basic are *context sensitive*. Context sensitive means you can get help on these parts directly without having to go through the Help menu. For example, to get Help on any keyword in the Visual Basic language, place the insertion point on that keyword in the Code window and press F1.

You can press F1 from any context-sensitive part of the Visual Basic interface to display Help information about that part. The context-sensitive parts are:

- Every window in Visual Basic (Properties window, Code window, and so on)
- Controls in the Toolbox
- Objects on a form or document object
- Properties in the Properties window
- Visual Basic keywords (statements, functions, properties, methods, events, and special objects)
- Error messages

Running Code Examples from Help

Many of the language topics in Help contain code examples that you can run from Visual Basic. The following procedures show you how to copy and run a code example from Help.

> **Note** The following procedure is for code examples that do not contain public declarations.

To copy a code example from Help

1. Create a new form by choosing **Add Form** from the **Project** menu, or use an existing form. (For more information on creating and using forms, see Chapter 2, "Developing an Application in Visual Basic.")
2. Choose **Index** from the **Help** menu.

3. In Help, search for *graphics*, and go to the topic called "FillColor Property."
4. In the FillColor Property topic, click the **Example** jump, located in the nonscrolling region near the top of the window. (A *jump* is a word that you can click to go to another topic. Jumps are underlined and the jump text is colored.)

   Select the subroutine portion of the example. Note that the first "Sub" marks the beginning of the procedure and the last "End Sub" marks the end of the procedure.
5. Right-click the selected text and select **Copy** from the context menu. The text is copied onto the Clipboard.
6. Return to the form you created and double-click the form to display the Code window.
7. Place the insertion point below any existing code in the Code window.
8. From the **Edit** menu, choose **Paste**. The example now appears in the Code window.
9. From the **Run** menu, choose **Start**, or press F5.
10. Click the form to run the example code.

    Note Some code examples require you to draw controls on the form. For more information on drawing controls, see Chapter 3, "Forms, Controls, and Menus."

Visual Basic Online Links

If you have a modem or other means of access, additional information about Visual Basic is available on the Web.

Microsoft Web Site

Microsoft's Web site contains several areas of interest to Visual Basic programmers. The Visual Basic home page is located at http://www.microsoft.com/vbasic/. Information available at this site includes:

- Updates on new features, product releases, related products, seminars and special events.
- Additional information on Visual Basic features, including white papers, tips and tutorials, and training resources.
- New product downloads including updates to program files, help updates, drivers, and other Visual Basic related files.

  Tip The Visual Basic Web site also contains a special Owner's Area for registered owners that contains many free samples, components, tools, and much more. Why not go to http://www.microsoft.com/vbasic/owners/ and register your copy of Visual Basic right now?

To access the Microsoft Visual Basic Web site

1. Choose **Microsoft on the Web** from the **Help** menu.
2. Select the appropriate option from the submenus.

Note You must have a Web browser installed and you must be connected to the Internet for these options to work. Some of the content on the Microsoft Web site is optimized for Microsoft Internet Explorer and may not be fully visible to other browsers. You can download the latest version of Internet Explorer from the Web site.

Microsoft Product Support Services

Microsoft offers a variety of support options to help you get the most from Visual Basic.

If you have a question about the product, first look in the online documentation. If you can't find the answer, contact Microsoft Product Support Services.

Support services are available both within the United States and through subsidiary offices worldwide. For complete details, see Technical Support under the Visual Basic Help menu.

Tell Us What You Think

Microsoft is committed to providing the best possible products to our customers. With each new version, Visual Basic has evolved in order to meet the changing needs of Windows programmers.

We're always interested in hearing from our customers. If you have any suggestions or comments regarding improvements or features that you would like to see in future versions of Visual Basic, let us know. You can send your suggestions via e-mail to *vbwish@microsoft.com*, or by calling (425) 936-WISH.

CHAPTER 2

Developing an Application in Visual Basic

It takes just a few minutes to build your first Visual Basic application. You create the user interface by "drawing" controls, such as text boxes and command buttons, on a form. Next, you set properties for the form and controls to specify such values as captions, color, and size. Finally, you write code to bring the application to life. The basic steps you take in creating your first application will show you principles that you'll use with every other application you develop.

This chapter provides an overview of the application development process, describes the terms and skills you need to use Visual Basic, and takes you step by step through several simple applications.

Contents

Sample Application: Firstapp.vbp

Some of the code examples in this chapter are taken from the Firstapp.vbp sample application which is listed in the Samples directory.

Visual Basic Concepts

In order to understand the application development process, it is helpful to understand some of the key concepts upon which Visual Basic is built. Because Visual Basic is a Windows development language, some familiarity with the Windows environment is necessary. If you are new to Windows programming, you need to be aware of some fundamental differences between programming for Windows versus other environments.

How Windows Works: Windows, Events and Messages

A complete discussion of the inner workings of Windows would require an entire book. A deep understanding of all of the technical details isn't necessary. A simplified version of the workings of Windows involves three key concepts: windows, events and messages.

Think of a window as simply a rectangular region with its own boundaries. You are probably already aware of several different types of windows: an Explorer window in Windows 95, a document window within your word processing program, or a dialog box that pops up to remind you of an appointment. While these are the most common examples, there are actually many other types of windows. A command button is a window. Icons, text boxes, option buttons and menu bars are all windows.

The Microsoft Windows operating system manages all of these many windows by assigning each one a unique id number (window handle or hWnd). The system continually monitors each of these windows for signs of activity or events. Events can occur through user actions such as a mouse click or a key press, through programmatic control, or even as a result of another window's actions.

Each time an event occurs, it causes a message to be sent to the operating system. The system processes the message and broadcasts it to the other windows. Each window can then take the appropriate action based on its own instructions for dealing with that particular message (for example, repainting itself when it has been uncovered by another window).

As you might imagine, dealing with all of the possible combinations of windows, events and messages could be mind-boggling. Fortunately, Visual Basic insulates you from having to deal with all of the low-level message handling. Many of the messages are handled automatically by Visual Basic; others are exposed as Event procedures for your convenience. This allows you to quickly create powerful applications without having to deal with unnecessary details.

Understanding the Event-Driven Model

In traditional or "procedural" applications, the application itself controls which portions of code execute and in what sequence. Execution starts with the first line of code and follows a predefined path through the application, calling procedures as needed.

In an event-driven application, the code doesn't follow a predetermined path — it executes different code sections in response to events. Events can be triggered by the user's actions, by messages from the system or other applications, or even from the application itself. The sequence of these events determines the sequence in which the code executes, thus the path through the application's code differs each time the program runs.

Because you can't predict the sequence of events, your code must make certain assumptions about the "state of the world" when it executes. When you make assumptions (for example, that an entry field must contain a value before running a procedure to process that value), you should structure your application in such a way as to make sure that the assumption will always be valid (for example, disabling the command button that starts the procedure until the entry field contains a value).

Your code can also trigger events during execution. For example, programmatically changing the text in a text box cause the text box's Change event to occur. This would cause the code (if any) contained in the Change event to execute. If you assumed that this event would only be triggered by user interaction, you might see unexpected results. It is for this reason that it is important to understand the event-driven model and keep it in mind when designing your application.

Interactive Development

The traditional application development process can be broken into three distinct steps: writing, compiling, and testing code. Unlike traditional languages, Visual Basic uses an interactive approach to development, blurring the distinction between the three steps.

With most languages, if you make a mistake in writing your code, the error is caught by the compiler when you start to compile your application. You must then find and fix the error and begin the compile cycle again, repeating the process for each error found. Visual Basic interprets your code as you enter it, catching and highlighting most syntax or spelling errors on the fly. It's almost like having an expert watching over your shoulder as you enter your code.

In addition to catching errors on the fly, Visual Basic also partially compiles the code as it is entered. When you are ready to run and test your application, there is only a brief delay to finish compiling. If the compiler finds an error, it is highlighted in your code. You can fix the error and continue compiling without having to start over.

Because of the interactive nature of Visual Basic, you'll find yourself running your application frequently as you develop it. This way you can test the effects of your code as you work rather than waiting to compile later.

Elements of the Integrated Development Environment

The working environment in Visual Basic is often referred to as the integrated development environment or IDE because it integrates many different functions such as design, editing, compiling, and debugging within a common environment. In most traditional development tools, each of these functions would operate as a separate program, each with its own interface.

Starting the Visual Basic IDE

When you run the Visual Basic Setup program, it allows you to place the program items in an existing program group or create a new program group and new program items for Visual Basic in Windows. You are then ready to start Visual Basic from Windows.

To start Visual Basic from Windows

1. Click **Start** on the Taskbar.
2. Select **Programs**, and then **Microsoft Visual Basic 6.0**.

   – or –

   Click **Start** on the Taskbar.

   Select **Programs**.

   Use the **Windows Explorer** to find the Visual Basic executable file.
3. Double-click the Visual Basic icon.

You can also create a shortcut to Visual Basic, and double-click the shortcut.

When you first start Visual Basic, you see the interface of the integrated development environment, as shown in Figure 2.1.

Figure 2.1 The Visual Basic integrated development environment

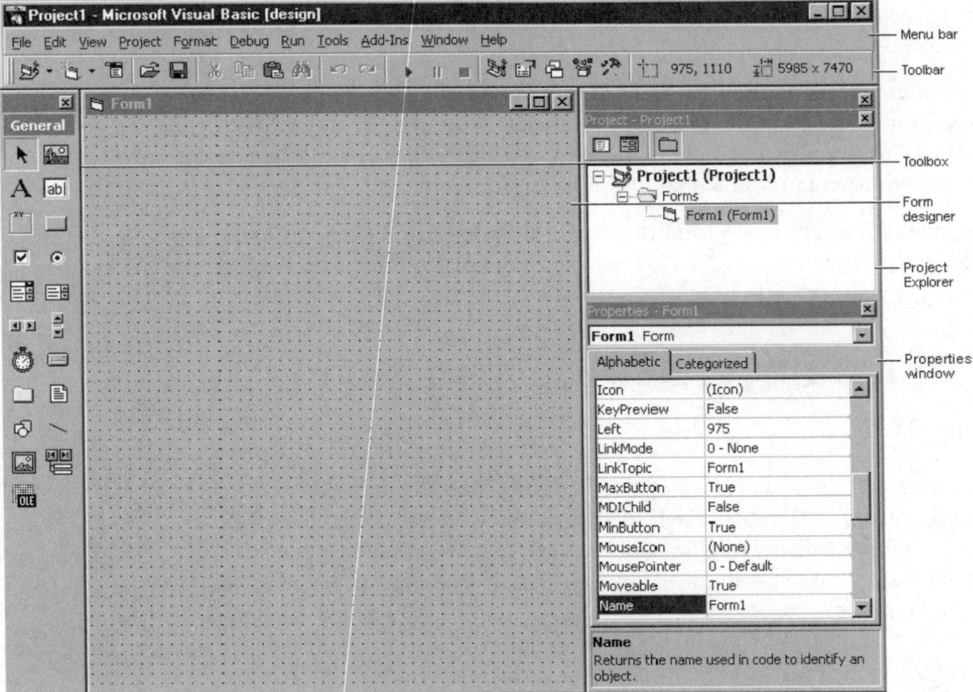

Integrated Development Environment Elements

The Visual Basic integrated development environment (IDE) consists of the following elements.

Menu Bar

Displays the commands you use to work with Visual Basic. Besides the standard File, Edit, View, Window, and Help menus, menus are provided to access functions specific to programming such as Project, Format, or Debug.

Context Menus

Contain shortcuts to frequently performed actions. To open a context menu, click the right mouse button on the object you're using. The specific list of shortcuts available from context menus depends on the part of the environment where you click the right mouse button. For example, the context menu displayed when you right click on the Toolbox lets you display the Components dialog box, hide the Toolbox, dock or undock the Toolbox, or add a custom tab to the Toolbox.

Toolbars

Provide quick access to commonly used commands in the programming environment. You click a button on the toolbar once to carry out the action represented by that button. By default, the Standard toolbar is displayed when you start Visual Basic. Additional toolbars for editing, form design, and debugging can be toggled on or off from the Toolbars command on the View menu.

Toolbars can be docked beneath the menu bar or can "float" if you select the vertical bar on the left edge and drag it away from the menu bar.

Toolbox

Provides a set of tools that you use at design time to place controls on a form. In addition to the default toolbox layout, you can create your own custom layouts by selecting Add Tab from the context menu and adding controls to the resulting tab.

For More Information To learn more about specific controls, see Chapter 3, "Forms, Controls, and Menus," and Chapter 7, "Using Visual Basic's Standard Controls." For information on how to add controls to the Toolbox, see "Adding Controls to a Project" in Chapter 4, "Managing Projects."

Project Explorer Window

Lists the forms and modules in your current project. A *project* is the collection of files you use to build an application.

For More Information For information on projects, see Chapter 4, "Managing Projects."

Properties Window

Lists the property settings for the selected form or control. A *property* is a characteristic of an object, such as size, caption, or color.

For More Information For information on properties, see "Understanding Properties, Methods, and Events" in Chapter 3, "Forms, Controls, and Menus."

Object Browser

Lists objects available for use in your project and gives you a quick way to navigate through your code. You can use the Object Browser to explore objects in Visual Basic and other applications, see what methods and properties are available for those objects, and paste code procedures into your application.

For More Information For more information on using the Object Browser to view procedures, see "Finding Out About Objects" in Chapter 9, "Programming with Objects." For details on using add-ins to extend the Visual Basic programming environment, see "Using Wizards and Add-Ins" in Chapter 4, "Managing Projects."

Form Designer

Serves as a window that you customize to design the interface of your application. You add controls, graphics, and pictures to a form to create the look you want. Each form in your application has its own form designer window.

For More Information To learn how to add controls to an application, see "Your First Visual Basic Application" later in this chapter. To learn more about designing an interface, see Chapter 6, "Creating a User Interface."

Code Editor Window

Serves as an editor for entering application code. A separate code editor window is created for each form or code module in your application.

For More Information To learn more about entering code and using the code editor, see Chapter 5, "Programming Fundamentals."

Form Layout Window

The Form Layout window (Figure 2.2) allows you to position the forms in your application using a small graphical representation of the screen.

Figure 2.2 The Form Layout window

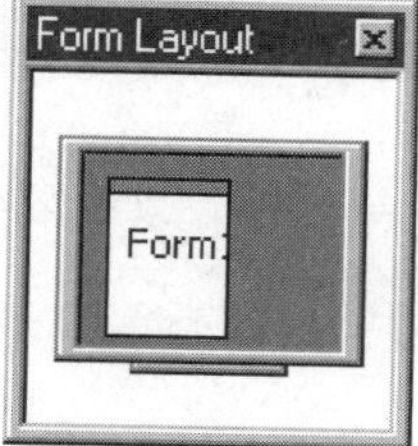

Immediate, Locals, and Watch Windows

These additional windows are provided for use in debugging your application. They are only available when you are running your application within the IDE.

For More Information To learn more about debugging and using the debug windows, see Chapter 13, "Debugging Your Code and Handling Errors."

> **Note** You can also add features to the Visual Basic interface by using a program called an *add-in*. Add-ins, which are available from Microsoft and third-party developers, can provide features like source code control, which allows you to support group development projects.

Environment Options

Visual Basic provides a great deal of flexibility, allowing you to configure the working environment to best suit your individual style. You can choose between a single or multiple document interface, and you can adjust the size and positioning of the various Integrated Development Environment (IDE) elements. Your layout will persist between sessions of Visual Basic.

SDI or MDI Interface

Two different styles are available for the Visual Basic IDE: single document interface (SDI) or multiple document interface (MDI). With the SDI option, all of the IDE windows are free to be moved anywhere on screen; as long as Visual Basic is the current application, they will remain on top of any other applications. With the MDI option, all of the IDE windows are contained within a single resizable parent window.

To switch between SDI and MDI modes

1. Select **Options** from the **Tools** menu.

   The **Options** dialog box is displayed.

2. Select the **Advanced** tab.

3. Check or uncheck the **SDI Development Environment** check box.

   The IDE will start in the selected mode the next time you start Visual Basic.

   – or –

   Run Visual Basic from the command line with a /sdi or /mdi parameter.

Docking Windows

Many of the windows in the IDE can be docked, or connected, to each other or to the edge of the screen. These include the Toolbox, Form Layout Window, Project Explorer, Properties window, Color Palette, and Immediate, Locals, and Watch windows.

With the MDI option, windows can be docked to any side of the parent window; with SDI they can only be docked beneath the menu bar. Docking capabilities can be toggled on or off for a given window by selecting the appropriate check box on the Docking tab of the Options dialog box, available from the Options command on the Tools menu.

To dock or undock a window

1. Select the window you wish to dock or undock.
2. Drag the window to the desired location by holding down the left mouse button.
3. The outline of the window will be displayed as you drag.
4. Release the mouse button.

Your First Visual Basic Application

Creating an application in Visual Basic is simple. How simple? For the answer, try out the Hello, Visual Basic and Firstapp applications that follow.

Hello, Visual Basic

There are three main steps to creating an application in Visual Basic:

1. Create the interface.
2. Set properties.
3. Write code.

To see how this is done, use the steps in the following procedures to create a simple application that consists of a text box and a command button. When you click the command button, the message "Hello, world!" appears in the text box.

Creating the Interface

Forms are the foundation for creating the interface of an application. You can use forms to add windows and dialog boxes to your application. You can also use them as containers for items that are not a visible part of the application's interface. For example, you might have a form in your application that serves as a container for graphics that you plan to display in other forms.

The first step in building a Visual Basic application is to create the forms that will be the basis for your application's interface. Then you draw the objects that make up the interface on the forms you create. For this first application, you'll use two controls from the Toolbox.

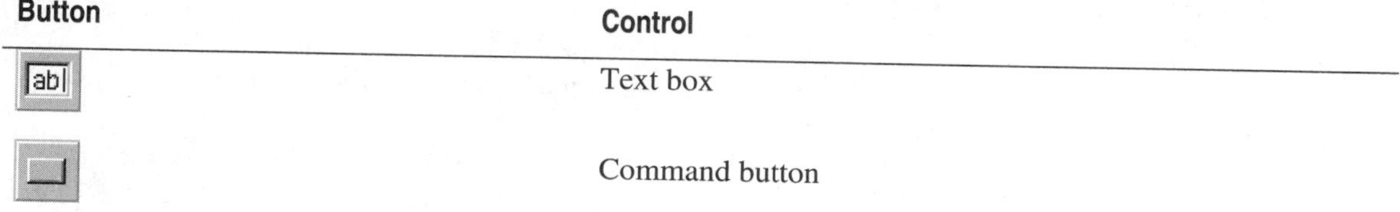

Button	Control
abl	Text box
	Command button

To draw a control using the Toolbox

1. Click the tool for the control you choose to draw — in this case, the **text box**.
2. Move the pointer onto your form. The pointer becomes a cross hair, as shown in Figure 2.3.

Figure 2.3 Drawing a text box with the Toolbox

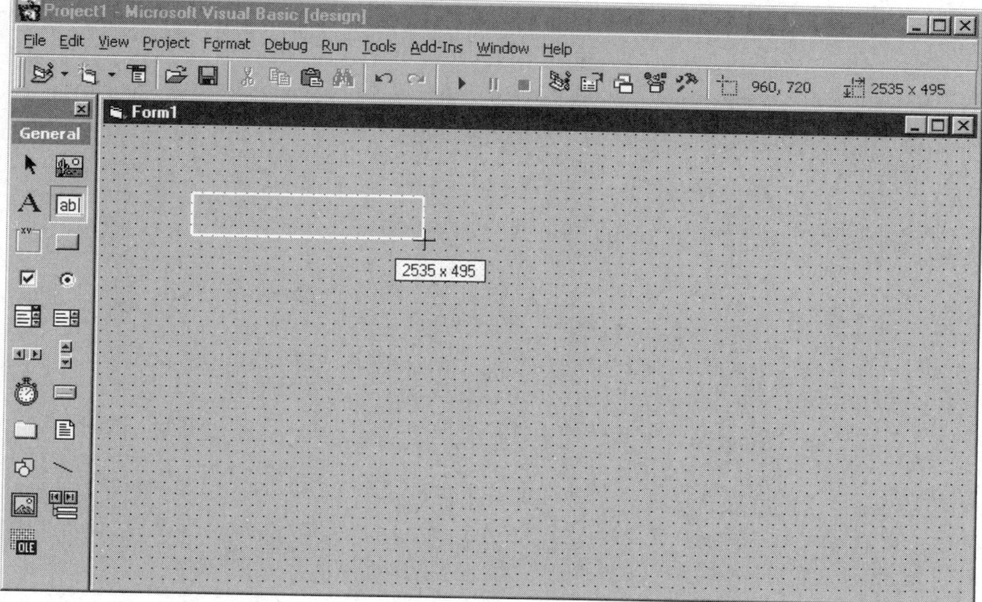

3. Place the cross hair where you want the upper-left corner of the control.
4. Drag the cross hair until the control is the size you want. (*Dragging* means holding the left mouse button down while you move an object with the mouse.)
5. Release the mouse button.

   The control appears on the form.

Another simple way to add a control to a form is to double-click the button for that control in the Toolbox. This creates a default-size control located in the center of the form; then you can move the control to another location on the form.

Resizing, Moving, and Locking Controls

Notice that small rectangular boxes called *sizing handles* appear at the corners of the control; you'll use these sizing handles in the next step as you resize the control. You can also use the mouse, keyboard, and menu commands to move controls, lock and unlock control positions, and adjust their positions.

To resize a control

1. Select the control you intend to resize by clicking it with the mouse.

   Sizing handles appear on the control.
2. Position the mouse pointer on a sizing handle, and drag it until the control is the size you choose.

   The corner handles resize controls horizontally and vertically, while the side handles resize in only one direction.
3. Release the mouse button.

   – or –

   Use SHIFT with the arrow keys to resize the selected control.

To move a control

- Use the mouse to drag the control to a new location on the form.

  – or –

  Use the Properties window to change the **Top** and **Left** properties.

When a control is selected, you can use CTRL with the arrow keys to move the control one grid unit at a time. If the grid is turned off, the control moves one pixel at a time.

To lock all control positions

- From the **Format** menu, choose **Lock Controls**.

  – or –

  Click the **Lock Controls Toggle** button on the Form Editor toolbar.

This will lock all controls on the form in their current positions so that you don't inadvertently move them once you have them in the desired location. This will lock controls only on the selected form; controls on other forms are untouched. This is a toggle command, so you can also use it to unlock control positions.

To adjust the position of locked controls

- You can "nudge" the control that has the focus by holding CTRL down and pressing the appropriate arrow key.

  – or –

  You can change the control's **Top** and **Left** properties in the Property window.

You now have the interface for the "Hello, world!" application, as shown in Figure 2.4.

Figure 2.4 The interface for the "Hello, world!" application

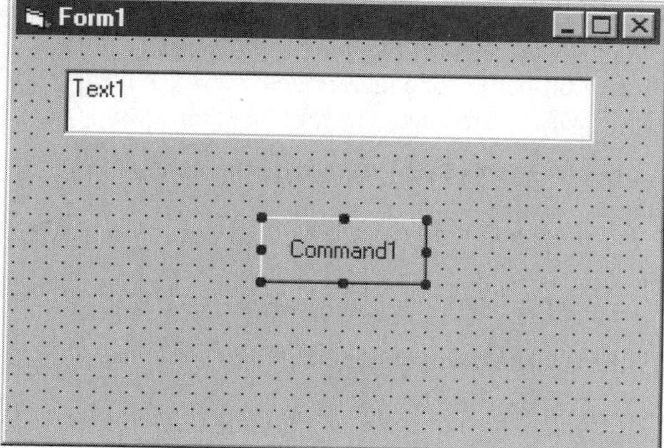

Setting Properties

The next step is to set properties for the objects you've created. The Properties window (Figure 2.5) provides an easy way to set properties for all objects on a form. To open the Properties window, choose the Properties Window command from the View menu, click the Properties Window button on the toolbar, or use the context menu for the control.

Figure 2.5 The Properties window

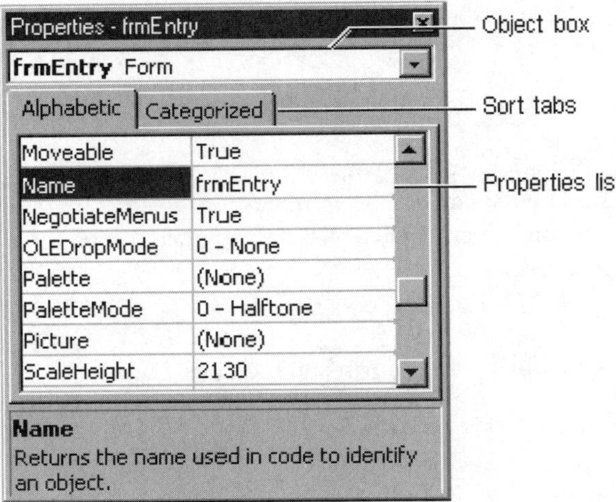

The Properties window consists of the following elements:

- Object box — Displays the name of the object for which you can set properties. Click the arrow to the right of the object box to display the list of objects for the current form.
- Sort tabs — Choose between an alphabetic listing of properties or a hierarchical view divided by logical categories, such as those dealing with appearance, fonts, or position.
- Properties list — The left column displays all of the properties for the selected object. You can edit and view settings in the right column.

To set properties from the Properties window

1. From the **View** menu, choose **Properties**, or click the **Properties** button on the toolbar.

   The Properties window displays the settings for the selected form or control.

2. From the **Properties** list, select the name of a property.
3. In the right column, type or select the new property setting.

   Enumerated properties have a predefined list of settings. You can display the list by clicking the down arrow at the right of the Settings box, or you can cycle through the list by double-clicking a list item.

For the "Hello, world!" example, you'll need to change three property settings. Use the default settings for all other properties.

Object	Property	Setting
Form	Caption	Hello, world!
Text box	Text	(Empty)
Command button	Caption	OK

Setting the Icon Property

All forms in Visual Basic have a generic, default icon that appears when you minimize that form. However, you will probably change this icon to one that illustrates the use of the form or your application. To assign an icon to a form, set the Icon property for that form. You can use 32 x 32 pixel icons that were standard in 16-bit versions of Microsoft Windows and are also used in Windows 95 and Windows NT, as well as the 16 x 16 pixel icons used in Windows 95.

Writing Code

The *Code Editor window* is where you write Visual Basic code for your application. Code consists of language statements, constants, and declarations. Using the Code Editor window, you can quickly view and edit any of the code in your application.

To open the Code window

- Double-click the form or control for which you choose to write code.

  – or –

  From the Project Explorer window, select the name of a form or module, and choose the **View Code** button.

Figure 2.6 shows the Code Editor window that appears when you double-click the Command button control, and the events for that command.

Figure 2.6 The Code Editor window

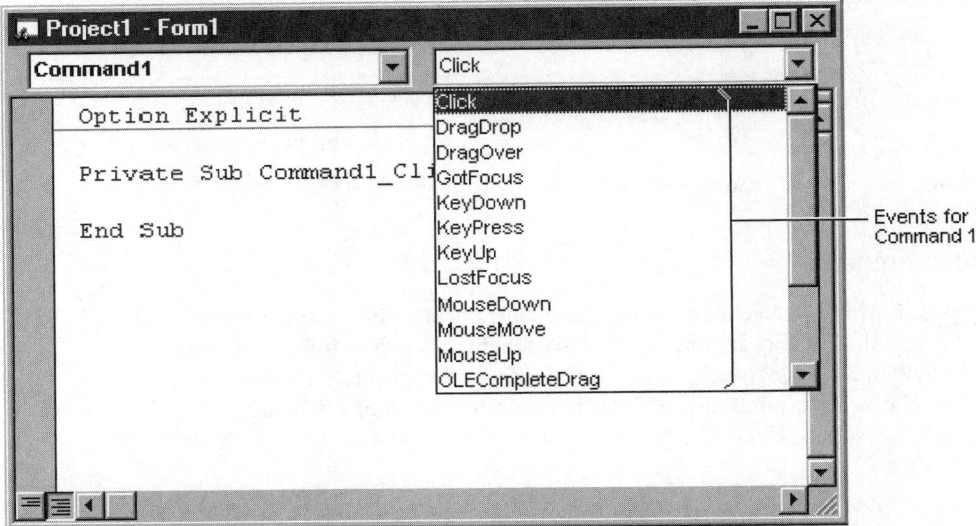

You can choose to display all procedures in the same Code window, or display a single procedure at a time.

To display all procedures in the same Code window

1. From the **Tools** menu, select the **Options** dialog box.
2. On the **Editor** tab in the **Options** dialog box, select the check box to the left of **Default to Full Module View**. The check box to the left of **Procedure Separator** adds or removes a separator line between procedures.

   – or –

   Click the **Full Module View** button in the lower left corner of the Code Editor window.

To display one procedure at a time in the Code window

1. From the **Tools** menu, select the **Options** dialog box.
2. On the **Editor** tab in the **Options** dialog box, clear the check box to the left of **Default to Full Module View**.

   – or –

   Click the **Procedure View** button in the lower left corner of the Code Editor window.

The Code window includes the following elements:

- Object list box — Displays the name of the selected object. Click the arrow to the right of the list box to display a list of all objects associated with the form.
- Procedure list box — Lists the procedures, or events, for an object. The box displays the name of the selected procedure — in this case, Click. Choose the arrow to the right of the box to display all the procedures for the object.

Creating Event Procedures

Code in a Visual Basic application is divided into smaller blocks called *procedures*. An *event procedure*, such as those you'll create here, contains code that is executed when an event occurs (such as when a user clicks a button). An event procedure for a control combines the control's actual name (specified in the Name property), an underscore (_), and the event name. For example, if you want a command button named Command1 to invoke an event procedure when it is clicked, use the procedure Command1_Click.

To create an event procedure

1. In the **Object** list box, select the name of an object in the active form. (The *active* form is the form that currently has the focus.)

   For this example, choose the command button, **Command1**.

2. In the **Procedure** list box, select the name of an event for the selected object.

   Here, the **Click** procedure is already selected, because it's the default procedure for a command button. Note that a *template* for the event procedure is now displayed in the Code window.

3. Type the following code between the **Sub** and **End Sub** statements:

   ```
   Text1.Text = "Hello, world!"
   ```

   The event procedure should look like this:

   ```
   Private Sub Command1_Click ()
      Text1.Text = "Hello, world!"
   End Sub
   ```

You'll note here that the code is simply changing the Text property of the control named Text1 to read "Hello, world!" The syntax for this example takes the form of *object.property,* where `Text1` is the object and `Text` is the property. You can use this syntax to change property settings for any form or control in response to events that occur while your application is running.

For More Information For information on creating other types of procedures, see "Introduction to Procedures" in Chapter 5, "Programming Fundamentals."

Running the Application

To run the application, choose Start from the Run menu, or click the Start button on the toolbar, or press F5. Click the command button you've created on the form, and you'll see "Hello, world!" displayed in the text box.

The Firstapp Sample Application

Visual Basic provides you with a wealth of tools beyond the ones used in this first application, so you'll soon use many other features to manage and customize your applications. Reviewing sample applications can be an excellent way to learn more about Visual Basic. The following example illustrates how easy it can be to create a useful application in Visual Basic.

The Firstapp application demonstrates how a *data control* and a *grid control* can be used to display a table of information from a database. Visual Basic makes it easy to access database information from within your application. The data control provides the ability to navigate through the database *recordset*, synchronizing the display of records in the grid control with the position in the recordset.

The application consists of a data control, a MSFlexGrid control, a list box control, and two command buttons. The grid displays a table of information about products retrieved from the Northwind database. As the user selects an item by using the navigation buttons on the data control, the name of the selected product is displayed in the data control. The user can also add items to a "shopping list" in the list box control by double-clicking the current selection in the grid.

To add items to the list box, you use the AddItem method. (A *method* is a Visual Basic function that acts on a particular object, in this case a ListBox object.) The syntax for specifying a method (*object.method*) is similar to the syntax for setting a property (*object.property*). The AddItem method allows you to dynamically add items to the list box while the application is running. Conversely, the Clear method is used to remove all items from the list box.

For More Information To learn more about methods, see "Understanding Properties, Methods, and Events" in Chapter 3, "Forms, Controls, and Menus."

Creating a Project

You begin creating this application by choosing New Project from the File menu, then selecting Standard EXE in the New Project dialog box (when you first start Visual Basic, the New Project dialog box is presented). Visual Basic creates a new *project* and displays a new form. To draw the interface, you use a data control, a MSFlexGrid control, a list box control, and two command buttons. The MSFlexGrid control isn't in the default toolbox, so you'll need to add it:

To add a control to the toolbox

1. Select **Components** from the context menu for the toolbox. (You can right-click within the toolbox window to display the context menu.)

   The **Components** dialog box will be displayed.

2. Find the MSFlexGrid (Microsoft Flex Grid 6.0) in the **Controls** list box and select the check box to its left.

3. Click the **OK** button.

   The icon for the **MSFlexGrid** control will appear in the toolbox.

Use the Toolbox to draw a data control, an MSFlexGrid control, a list box control, and two command buttons on the form. If you don't remember how, check out "Creating the Interface" earlier in this chapter.

Setting Properties

In the Properties window, set properties for the objects according to the following table. Use the default settings for all other properties.

Object	Property	Setting
Form	Caption	Products
Data1	DatabaseName RecordSource	*path* \Biblio.mdb All Titles
DataGrid1	DataSource	Data1
Command1	Caption	Clear
Command2	Caption	Exit

The DatabaseName property of the data control must include the actual path to the database. By default, the Nwind.mdb database is installed in the same directory as Visual Basic. When you select the DatabaseName property in the Properties window, you can click the button to the right of the property to display a standard FileOpen dialog box to browse for the file. Once the DatabaseName property has been set, the RecordSource property in the Properties window will contain a list of tables or recordsets for the selected database. Setting the DataSource property of the MSFlexGrid control to Data1 automatically links the grid to the data control.

Writing Event Code

All the code for the application is contained in the Command1_Click, Command2_Click, Data1_Reposition, and MSFlexGrid1_DblClick event procedures. Double-click the form or control to display the Code window, and then type the code for each event procedure.

Add this code to the Command1_Click event procedure to clear the list box when the user clicks the button:

```
Private Sub Command1_Click ()
   List1.Clear              ' Clears the list box.
End Sub
```

In the above statement, you are invoking the Clear method of the list box, List1. The Clear method deletes the contents of the list box.

Add this code to the Command2_Click event procedure to unload the form from memory and end the application:

```
Private Sub Command2_Click ()
   Unload Form1
   End                      ' Ends application.
End Sub
```

In the above procedure, the first statement invokes the Unload event for the form. If you needed to perform a function at shutdown, such as saving a file, you could place that code in the form's Unload event procedure. The second statement calls the End function, which ends the application.

Add this code to the Data1_Reposition event procedure to update the caption each time a record is selected:

```
Private Sub Data1_Reposition ()
   Data1.Caption = Data1.Recordset("Title")
End Sub
```

In the above statement, you are assigning the value on the right (the contents of the Title field in the Recordset of the data control) to the property on the left (the Caption property of the data control object).

Add this code to the MSFlexGrid_DblClick event procedure to add an item to the list box when the user double-clicks a selected row:

```
Private Sub MSFLexGrid1_DblClick ()
   List1.AddItem MSFlexGrid1.Text
End Sub
```

In the above statement, you are invoking the AddItem method of the list box (List1). The text to be added to the list box is contained in the *argument* of the method, in this case, the value of the title field in the recordset of the data control. Passing a value to an argument is similar to assigning a value to a property; unlike the assignment statement, the equal sign isn't required.

Saving a Project

You finish your work on the application by choosing Save Project from the File menu. Visual Basic will prompt you separately to save the form and then the project. One possible name for the project is "Northwind Shopping List." Both Windows 95 and Windows NT allow you to use file names up to 255 characters in length, and file names can include spaces. Older versions of Microsoft Windows limited you to file names of eight characters, with a three-character extension.

Enhancing Your Application

You have just completed your first Visual Basic application: one that performs a simple but useful function. You can use this application as a basis for adding similar functionality in your own applications, substituting your own data instead of Biblio.mdb. Of course, to make this application truly useful, you might want to add functionality to save or print the contents of the list box, to add additional information such as price and availability, and even to gather credit card information and transmit an order across the Internet. As you continue on through the rest of the *Microsoft Visual Basic 6.0 Programmer's Guide*, you will find examples of doing all that and a lot more.

CHAPTER 3

Forms, Controls, and Menus

The first step to creating an application with Visual Basic is to create the interface, the visual part of the application with which the user will interact. Forms and controls are the basic building blocks used to create the interface; they are the objects that you will work with to build your application.

Forms are objects that expose properties which define their appearance, methods which define their behavior, and events which define their interaction with the user. By setting the properties of the form and writing Visual Basic code to respond to its events, you customize the object to meet the requirements of your application.

Controls are objects that are contained within form objects. Each type of control has its own set of properties, methods and events that make it suitable for a particular purpose. Some of the controls you can use in your applications are best suited for entering or displaying text. Other controls let you access other applications and process data as if the remote application was part of your code.

This chapter introduces the basic concepts of working with forms and controls and their associated properties, methods, and events. Many of the standard controls are discussed, as well as form-specific items such as menus and dialog boxes.

Contents

Sample Application: Controls.vbp

The code examples in this chapter are taken from the Controls.vbp sample application which is listed in the Samples directory.

Understanding Properties, Methods, and Events

Visual Basic forms and controls are objects which expose their own properties, methods and events. Properties can be thought of as an object's attributes, methods as its actions, and events as its responses.

An everyday object like a child's helium balloon also has properties, methods and events. A balloon's properties include visible attributes such as its height, diameter and color. Other properties describe its state (inflated or not inflated), or attributes that aren't visible such as its age. By definition, all balloons have these properties; the settings of these properties may differ from one balloon to another.

A balloon also has inherent methods or actions that it might perform. It has an inflate method (the action of filling it with helium), a deflate method (expelling its contents) and a rise method (if you were to let go of it). Again, all balloons are capable of these methods.

Balloons also have predefined responses to certain external events. For instance, a balloon would respond to the event of being punctured by deflating itself, or to the event of being released by rising into the air.

Figure 3.1 Objects have properties, respond to events, and perform methods

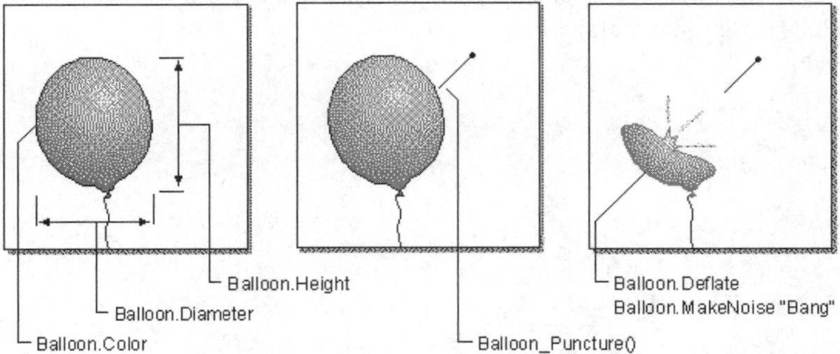

If you were able to program a balloon, the Visual Basic code might look like the following. To set the balloon's properties:

```
Balloon.Color = Red
Balloon.Diameter = 10
Balloon.Inflated = True
```

Note the syntax of the code — the object (Balloon) followed by the property (.Color) followed by the assignment of the value (Red). You could change the color of the balloon from code by repeating this statement and substituting a different value. Properties can also be set in the Properties window while you are designing your application.

A balloon's methods are invoked like this:

```
Balloon.Inflate
Balloon.Deflate
Balloon.Rise 5
```

The syntax is similar to the property — the object (a noun) followed by the method (a verb). In the third example, there is an additional item, called an *argument*, which denotes the distance to rise. Some methods will have one or more arguments to further describe the action to be performed.

The balloon might respond to an event as follows:

```
Sub Balloon_Puncture()
   Balloon.Deflate
   Balloon.MakeNoise "Bang"
   Balloon.Inflated = False
   Balloon.Diameter = 1
End Sub
```

In this case, the code describes the balloon's behavior when a puncture event occurs: invoke the Deflate method, then invoke the MakeNoise method with an argument of "Bang" (the type of noise to make). Since the balloon is no longer inflated, the Inflated property is set to False and the Diameter property is set to a new value.

While you can't actually program a balloon, you can program a Visual Basic form or control. As the programmer, you are in control. You decide which properties should be changed, methods invoked or events responded to in order to achieve the desired appearance and behavior.

Designing a Form

Form objects are the basic building blocks of a Visual Basic application, the actual windows with which a user interacts when they run the application. Forms have their own properties, events, and methods with which you can control their appearance and behavior.

Figure 3.2 Forms and controls have their own properties, events, and methods

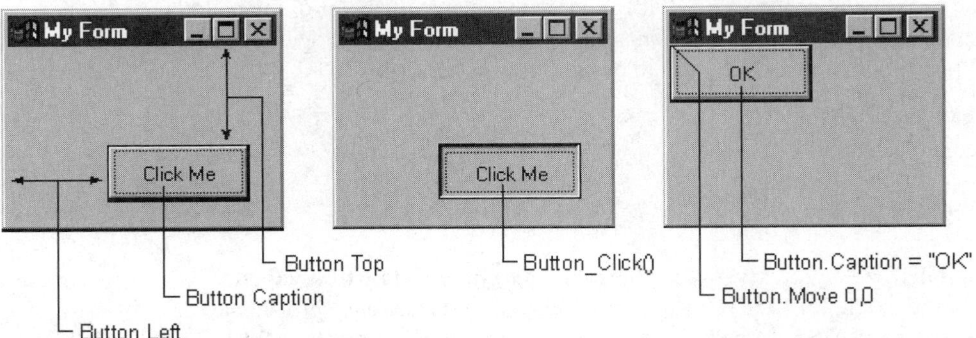

The first step in designing a form is to set its properties. You can set a form's properties at *design time* in the Properties window, or at *run time* by writing code.

> **Note** You work with forms and controls, set their properties, and write code for their events at *design time*, which is any time you're building an application in the Visual Basic environment. *Run time* is any time you are actually running the application and interacting with the application as the user would.

Setting Form Properties

Many of a form's properties affect its physical appearance. The Caption property determines the text that is shown in the form's title bar; the Icon property sets the icon that is displayed when a form is minimized. The MaxButton and MinButton properties determine whether the form can be maximized or minimized. By changing the BorderStyle property, you can control the resizing behavior of the form.

Height and Width properties determine the initial size of a form; Left and Top properties determine the form's location in relation to the upper left-hand corner of the screen. The WindowState property can be set to start the form in a maximized, minimized, or normal state.

The Name property sets the name by which you will refer to the form in code. By default, when a form is first added to a project, its name is set to Form1, Form2, and so forth. It's a good idea to set the Name property to something more meaningful, such as "frmEntry" for an order entry form.

The best way to familiarize yourself with the many form properties is to experiment. Change some of the properties of a form in the Properties window (Figure 3.3), then run the application to see their effect. You can learn more about each property by selecting it and pressing F1 to view the context-sensitive Help.

Figure 3.3 The Properties window

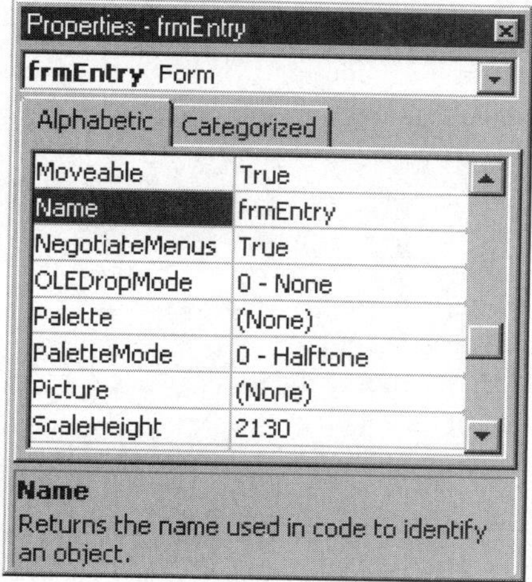

Form Events and Methods

As objects, forms can perform methods and respond to events.

The Resize event of a form is triggered whenever a form is resized, either by user interaction or through code. This allows you to perform actions such as moving or resizing controls on a form when its dimensions have changed.

The Activate event occurs whenever a form becomes the active form; the Deactivate event occurs when another form or application becomes active. These events are convenient for initializing or finalizing the form's behavior. For example, in the Activate event you might write code to highlight the text in a particular text box; in the Deactivate event you might save changes to a file or database.

To make a form visible, you would invoke the Show method:

```
Form2.Show
```

Invoking the Show method has the same effect as setting a form's Visible property to True.

Many of a form's methods involve text or graphics. The Print, Line, Circle, and Refresh methods are useful for printing or drawing directly onto a form's surface. These methods and more are discussed in Chapter 12, "Working with Text and Graphics."

For More Information For additional information on forms, see "More About Forms" in Chapter 6, "Creating a User Interface."

Clicking Buttons to Perform Actions

The easiest way to allow the user to interact with an application is to provide a button to click. You can use the command button control provided by Visual Basic, or you can create your own "button" using an image control containing a graphic, such as an icon.

Using Command Buttons

Most Visual Basic applications have command buttons that allow the user to simply click them to perform actions. When the user chooses the button, it not only carries out the appropriate action, it also looks as if it's being pushed in and released. Whenever the user clicks a button, the Click event procedure is invoked. You place code in the Click event procedure to perform any action you choose.

There are many ways to choose a command button at run time:

- Use a mouse to click the button.
- Move the focus to the button by pressing the TAB key, and then choose the button by pressing the SPACEBAR or ENTER. (See "Understanding Focus" later in this chapter.)
- Press an access key (ALT+ the underlined letter) for a command button.
- Set the command button's Value property to True in code:

  ```
  cmdClose.Value = True
  ```

- Invoke the command button's Click event in code:

  ```
  cmdClose_Click
  ```

- If the command button is the *default command button* for the form, pressing ENTER chooses the button, even if you change the focus to a different control other than a command button. At design time, you specify a default command button by setting that button's Default property to True.
- If the command button is the default *Cancel button* for the form, then pressing ESC chooses the button, even if you change the focus to another control. At design time, you specify a default Cancel button by setting that button's Cancel property to True.

All these actions cause Visual Basic to invoke the Click event procedure.

The Test Buttons Application

You use the Caption property to display text on the button to tell the user what the button does. In Figure 3.4, the Test Buttons example from the Controls sample application contains a command button with its Caption property set to "Change Signal." (For a working version of this example, see Button.frm in the Controls.vbp sample application.)

Notice that 'S' is the access key for this button, denoted by an underline. Inserting an ampersand (&) in the text of the Caption property makes the character following it the access key for that button (for example, Change &Signal).

Figure 3.4 Command button with a caption

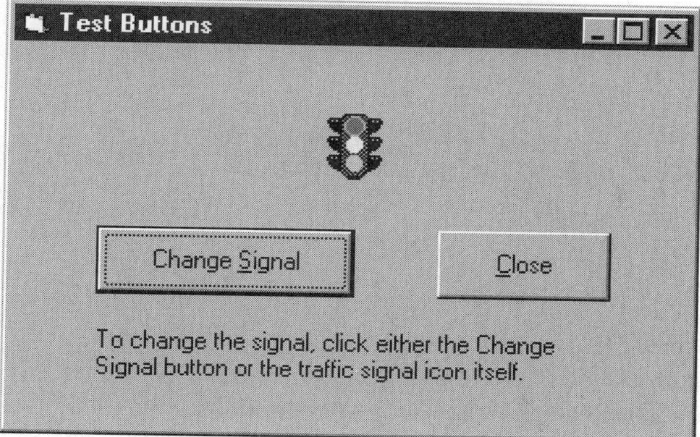

When a user clicks the command button, the code in the command button's Click event procedure is executed. In the example, a different traffic light icon is displayed each time the button is clicked.

For More Information For information on additional properties of the command button, see Chapter 7, "Using Visual Basic's Standard Controls."

Controls for Displaying and Entering Text

Label and text box controls are used to display or enter text. Use labels when you want your application to display text on a form, and text boxes when you want to allow the user to enter text. Labels contain text that can only be read, while text boxes contain text that can be edited.

To provide this feature	Use this control
Text that can be edited by the user, for example an order entry field or a password box	Text box
Text that is displayed only, for example to identify a field on a form or display instructions to the user	Label

Using Labels to Display Text

A label control displays text that the user cannot directly change. You can use labels to identify controls, such as text boxes and scroll bars, that do not have their own Caption property. The actual text displayed in a label is controlled by the Caption property, which can be set at design time in the Properties window or at run time by assigning it in code.

By default, the caption is the only visible part of the label control. However, if you set the BorderStyle property to 1 (which you can do at design time), the label appears with a border — giving it a look similar to a text box. You can also change the appearance of the label by setting the BackColor, BackStyle, ForeColor, and Font properties.

Sizing a Label to Fit Its Contents

Single-line label captions can be specified at design time in the Properties window. But what if you want to enter a longer caption, or a caption that will change at run time? Labels have two properties that help you size the controls to fit larger or smaller captions: AutoSize and WordWrap.

The AutoSize property determines if a control should be automatically resized to fit its contents. If set to True, the label grows horizontally to fit its contents, as shown in Figure 3.5.

Figure 3.5 AutoSize example

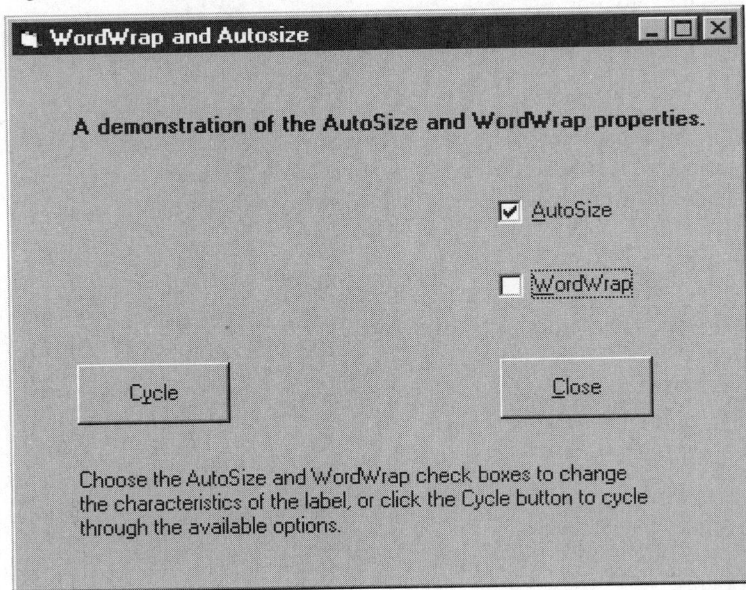

The WordWrap property causes the label to grow vertically to fit its contents, while retaining the same width, as shown in Figure 3.6. For a working version of this example, see Wordwrap.frm in the Controls.vbp sample application.

Figure 3.6 WordWrap example

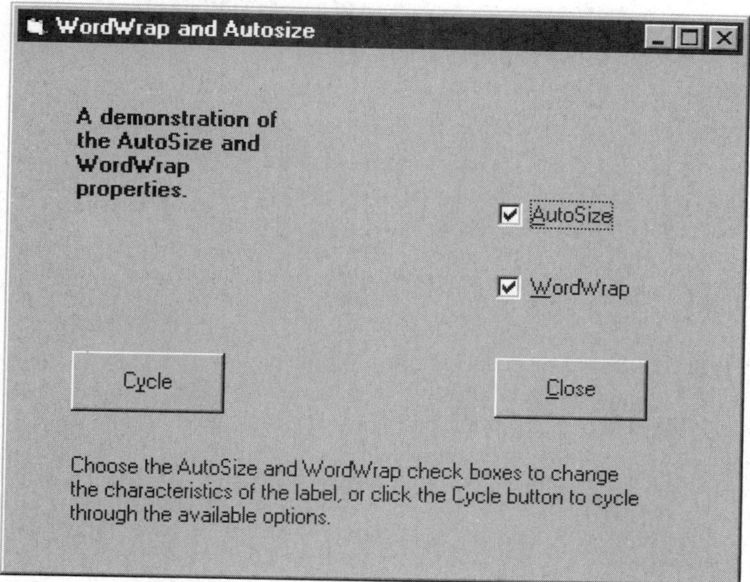

> **Note** If you run the AutoSize example from Controls.vbp, you'll notice that for the WordWrap example to actually work, both check boxes must be selected. This is because, for the label's WordWrap property to take effect, AutoSize must be set to True. The width of the label is increased only if the width of a single word exceeds the current width of the control.

For More Information For additional information on the label control's properties, see Chapter 7, "Using Visual Basic's Standard Controls."

Working with Text Boxes

Text boxes are versatile controls that can be used to get input from the user or to display text. Text boxes should not be used to display text that you don't want the user to change, unless you've set the Locked property to True.

The actual text displayed in a text box is controlled by the Text property. It can be set in three different ways: at design time in the Property window, at run time by setting it in code, or by input from the user at run time. The current contents of a text box can be retrieved at run time by reading the Text property.

Multiple-Line Text Boxes and Word Wrap

By default, a text box displays a single line of text and does not display scroll bars. If the text is longer than the available space, only part of the text will be visible. The look and behavior of a text box can be changed by setting two properties, MultiLine and ScrollBars, which are available only at design time.

> **Note** The ScrollBars property should not be confused with scroll bar controls, which are not attached to text boxes and have their own set of properties.

Setting MultiLine to True enables a text box to accept or display multiple lines of text at run time. A multiple-line text box automatically manages word wrap as long as there is no horizontal scroll bar. The ScrollBars property is set to 0–None by default. Automatic word wrap saves the user the trouble of inserting line breaks at the end of lines. When a line of text is longer than what can be displayed on a line, the text box wraps the text to the next line.

Line breaks cannot be entered in the Properties window at design time. Within a procedure, you create a line break by inserting a carriage return followed by a linefeed (ANSI characters 13 and 10). You can also use the constant vbCrLf to insert a carriage return/linefeed combination. For example, the following event procedure puts two lines of text into a multiple-line text box (Text1) when the form is loaded:

```
Sub Form_Load ()
   Text1.Text = "Here are two lines" _
   & vbCrLf & "in a text box"
End Sub
```

Working with Text in a Text Box

You can control the insertion point and selection behavior in a text box with the SelStart, SelLength and SelText properties. These properties are only available at run time.

When a text box first receives the focus, the default insertion point or cursor position within the text box is to the left of any existing text. It can be moved by the user from the keyboard or with the mouse. If the text box loses and then regains the focus, the insertion point will be wherever the user last placed it.

In some cases, this behavior can be disconcerting to the user. In a word processing application, the user might expect new characters to appear after any existing text. In a data entry application, the user might expect their typing to replace any existing entry. The SelStart and SelLength properties allow you to modify the behavior to suit your purpose.

The SelStart property is a number that indicates the insertion point within the string of text, with 0 being the left-most position. If the SelStart property is set to a value equal to or greater than the number of characters in the text box, the insertion point will be placed after the last character, as shown in Figure 3.7. For a working version of this example, see Text.frm in the Controls.vbp sample application.

Figure 3.7 Insertion point example

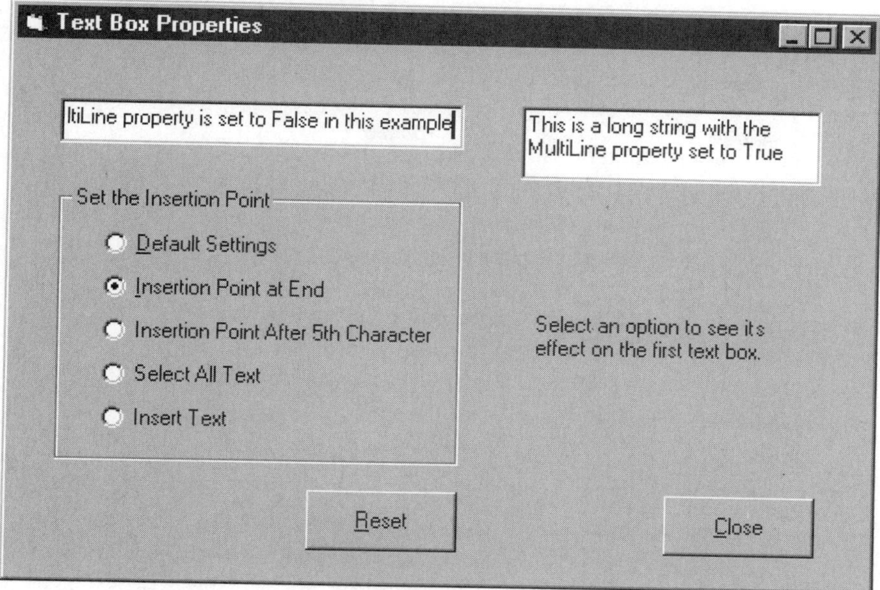

The SelLength property is a numeric value that sets the width of the insertion point. Setting the SelLength to a number greater than 0 causes that number of characters to be selected and highlighted, starting from the current insertion point. Figure 3.8 shows the selection behavior.

Figure 3.8 Selection example

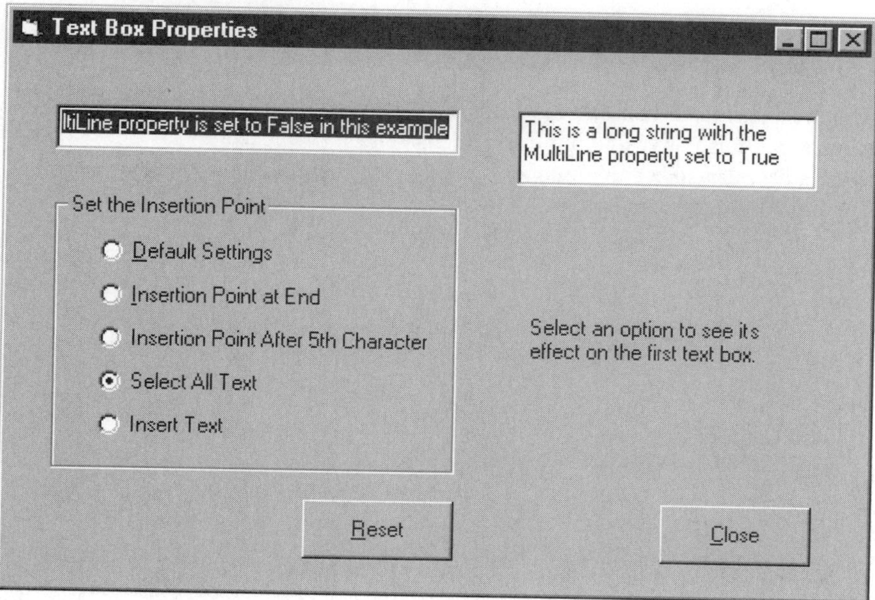

If the user starts typing while a block of text is selected, the selected text will be replaced. In some cases, you might want to replace a text selection with new text by using a paste command. The SelText property is a string of text that you can assign at run time to replace the current selection. If no text is selected, SelText will insert its text at the current insertion point.

For More Information For additional information on the text box control's properties, see Chapter 7, "Using Visual Basic's Standard Controls."

Controls That Present Choices to Users

Most applications need to present choices to their users, ranging from a simple yes/no option to selecting from a list containing hundreds of possibilities. Visual Basic includes several standard controls that are useful for presenting choices. The following table summarizes these controls and their appropriate uses.

To provide this feature	Use this control
A small set of choices from which a user can choose one or more options.	Check boxes
A small set of options from which a user can choose just one.	Option buttons (use frames if additional groups are needed)
A scrollable list of choices from which the user can choose.	List box
A scrollable list of choices along with a text edit field. The user can either choose from the list or type a choice in the edit field.	Combo box

Selecting Individual Options with Check Boxes

A check box indicates whether a particular condition is on or off. You use check boxes in an application to give users true/false or yes/no options. Because check boxes work independently of each other, a user can select any number of check boxes at the same time. For example in Figure 3.9, Bold and Italic can both be checked.

Figure 3.9 Check boxes

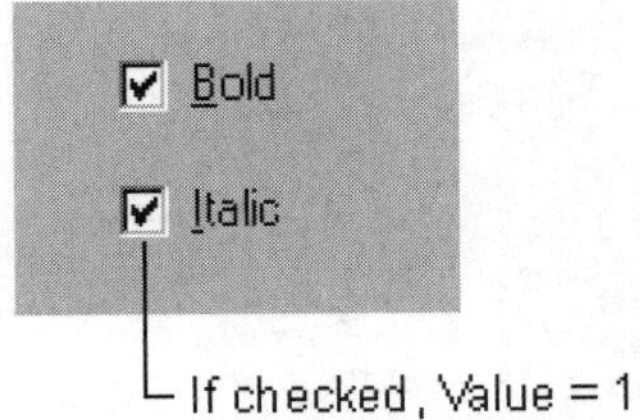

The Check Box Application

The Check Box example uses a check box to determine whether the text is displayed in regular or italic font. For a working version of this example, see Check.frm in the Controls.vbp sample application.

The application has a text box, a label, a command button, and two check boxes, as shown in Figure 3.10.

Figure 3.10 Check box example

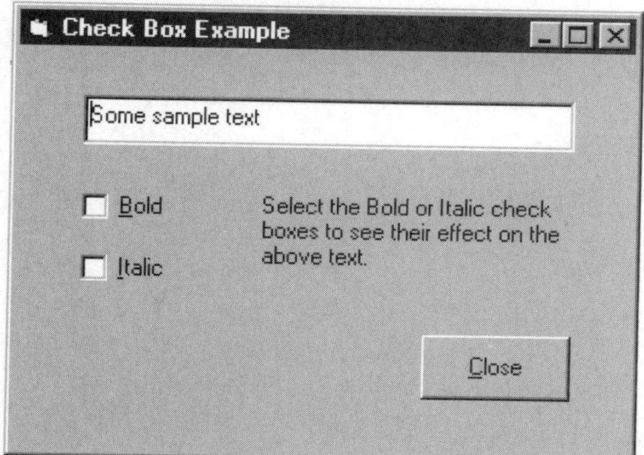

The following table lists the property settings for the objects in the application.

Object	Property	Setting
Form	Name Caption	frmCheck Check Box Example
Text box	Name Text	txtDisplay Some sample text
First Check box	Name Caption	chkBold &Bold
Second Check box	Name Caption	chkItalic &Italic
Command button	Name Caption	cmdClose &Close

When you check Bold or Italic, the check box's Value property is set to 1; when unchecked, its Value property is set to 0. The default Value is 0, so unless you change Value, the check box will be unchecked when it is first displayed. You can use the constants vbChecked and vbUnchecked to represent the values 1 and 0.

Events in the Check Box Application

The Click event for the check box occurs as soon as you click the box. This event procedure tests to see whether the check box has been selected (that is, if its Value = vbChecked). If so, the text is converted to bold or italic by setting the Bold or Italic properties of the Font object returned by the Font property of the text box.

```
Private Sub chkBold_Click ()
   If ChkBold.Value = vbChecked Then  ' If checked.
      txtDisplay.Font.Bold = True
   Else                               ' If not checked.
      txtDisplay.Font.Bold = False
   End If
End Sub

Private Sub chkItalic_Click ()
   If ChkItalic.Value = vbChecked Then   ' If checked.
      txtDisplay.Font.Italic = True
   Else                                 ' If not checked.
      txtDisplay.Font.Italic = False
   End If
End Sub
```

Grouping Options with Option Buttons

Option buttons present a set of two or more choices to the user. Unlike check boxes, however, option buttons should always work as part of a group; selecting one option button immediately clears all the other buttons in the group. Defining an option button group tells the user, "Here is a set of choices from which you can choose one and only one."

For example, in the option button group shown in Figure 3.11, the user can select one of three option buttons.

Figure 3.11 Selecting an option button

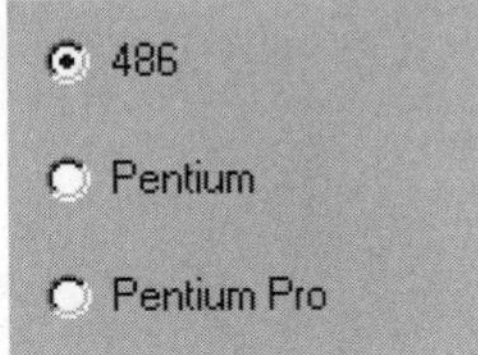

Creating Option Button Groups

All of the option buttons placed directly on a form (that is, not in a frame or picture box) constitute one group. If you want to create additional option button groups, you must place some of them inside frames or picture boxes.

All the option buttons inside any given frame constitute a separate group, as do all the option buttons inside a picture box. When you create a separate group this way, always draw the frame or picture box first, and then draw the option buttons on top of it. Figure 3.12 shows a form with two option button groups.

Figure 3.12 Option button groups

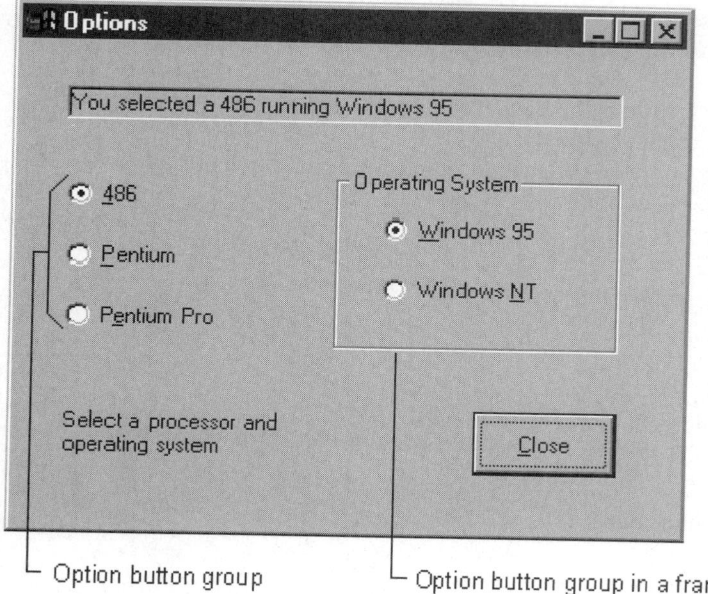

A user can select only one option button in the group when you draw option buttons in a frame.

To group controls in a frame

1. Select the frame control from the toolbox and draw the frame on the form.
2. Select the option button control from the toolbox and draw the control within the frame.
3. Repeat step 2 for each additional option button you wish to add to the frame.

Drawing the frame first and then drawing each control on the frame allows you to move the frame and controls together. If you try to move existing controls onto a frame, the controls will not move with the frame.

> **Note** If you have existing controls that you want to group in a frame, you can select all the controls and cut and paste them into a frame or picture control.

Containers for Controls

While controls are independent objects, a certain *parent and child relationship* exists between forms and controls. Figure 3.12 demonstrates how option buttons can be contained within a form or within a frame control.

To understand the concept of containers, you need to understand that all controls are children of the form on which they are drawn. In fact, most controls support the read-only Parent property, which returns the form on which a control is located. Being a child affects the placement of a control on the parent form. The Left and Top properties of a control are relative to the parent form, and controls cannot be moved outside the boundaries of the parent. Moving a container moves the controls as well, and the control's position relative to the container's Left and Top properties does not change because the control moves with the container.

Selecting or Disabling Option Buttons

An option button can be selected by:

- Clicking it at run time with the mouse.
- Tabbing to the option button group and then using the arrow keys to select an option button within the group.
- Assigning its Value property to True in code:

  ```
  optChoice.Value = True
  ```

- Using a shortcut key specified in the caption of a label.

To make a button the default in an option button group, set its Value property to True at design time. It remains selected until a user selects a different option button or code changes it.

To disable an option button, set its Enabled property to False. When the program is run it will appear dimmed, meaning that it is unavailable.

The Options Application

The form shown in Figure 3.13 uses option buttons to determine the processor type and operating system for a fictional computer. When the user selects a option button in either group, the caption of the label is changed to reflect the current choices. For a working version of this example, see Options.frm in the Controls.vbp sample application.

Figure 3.13 Option button example

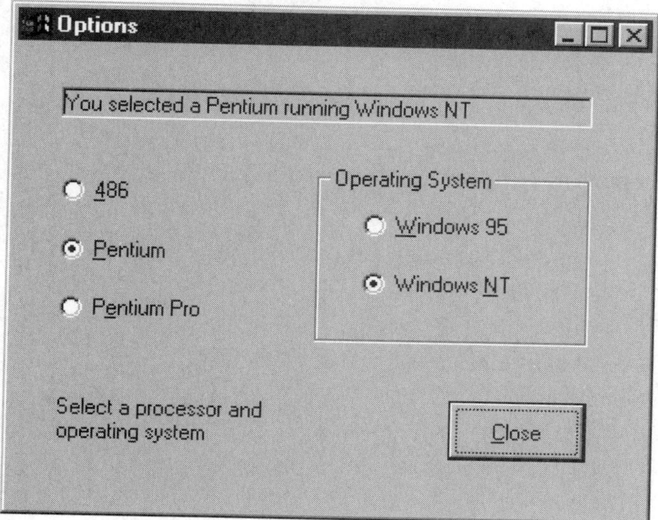

The following table lists the property settings for the objects in the application.

Object	Property	Setting
Label	Name Caption	lblDisplay (Empty)
Command button	Name Caption	cmdClose &Close
First option button	Name Caption	opt486 &486
Second option button	Name Caption Value	opt586 &Pentium True
Third option button	Name Caption	opt686 P&entium Pro
Frame	Name Caption	fraSystem &Operating System
Fourth option button	Name Caption	optWin95 Windows 95
Fifth option button	Name Caption Value	optWinNT Windows NT True

Events in the Options Application

The Options application responds to events as follows:

- The Click events for the first three option buttons assign a corresponding description to a form-level string variable, strComputer.
- The Click events for the last two option buttons assign a corresponding description to a second form-level variable, strSystem.

The key to this approach is the use of these two form-level variables, strComputer and strSystem. These variables contain different string values, depending on which option buttons were last selected.

Each time a new option button is selected, the code in its Click event updates the appropriate variable:

```
Private Sub opt586_Click()
   strComputer = "Pentium"
   Call DisplayCaption
End Sub
```

It then calls a sub procedure, called DisplayCaption, that concatenates the two variables and updates the label's Caption property:

```
Sub DisplayCaption()
   lblDisplay.Caption = "You selected a " & _
   strComputer & " running " & strSystem
End Sub
```

A sub procedure is used because the procedure of updating the Caption property is essentially the same for all five option buttons, only the value of the variables change from one instance to the next. This saves you from having to repeat the same code in each of the Click events.

For More Information Variables and sub procedures are discussed in detail in Chapter 5, "Programming Fundamentals."

Using List Boxes and Combo Boxes

List boxes and combo boxes present a list of choices to the user. By default, the choices are displayed vertically in a single column, although you can set up multiple columns as well. If the number of items exceeds what can be displayed in the combo box or list box, scroll bars automatically appear on the control. The user can then scroll up and down or left to right through the list. Figure 3.14 shows a single-column list box.

Figure 3.14 Single-column list box

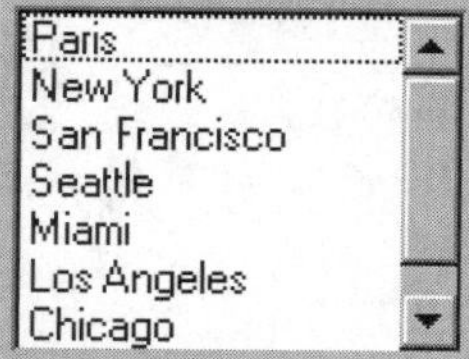

A combo box control combines the features of a text box and a list box. This control allows the user to select either by typing text into the combo box or by selecting an item from its list. Figure 3.15 shows a combo box.

Figure 3.15 Combo box

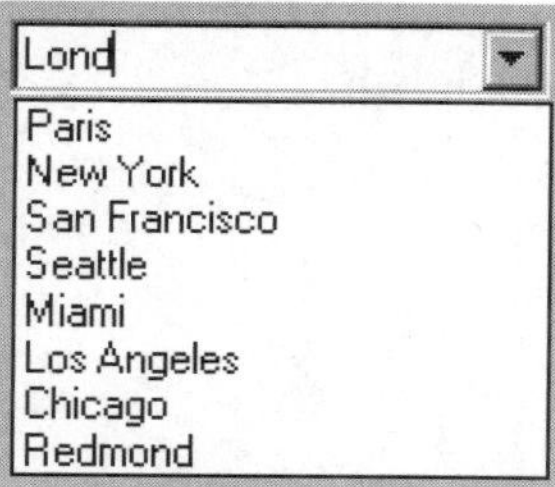

In contrast to some other controls that contain a single value; for example the label's Caption property or the text box's Text property, list boxes and combo boxes contain multiple values or a collection of values. They have built-in methods for adding, removing and retrieving values from their collections at run time. To add several items to a list box named List1, the code would look like this:

```
List1.AddItem "Paris"
List1.AddItem "New York"
List1.AddItem "San Francisco"
```

List boxes and combo boxes are an effective way to present a large number of choices to the user in a limited amount of space.

For More Information For additional information on the list box and combo box controls, see Chapter 7, "Using Visual Basic's Standard Controls."

Using Scroll Bars as Input Devices

Although scroll bars are often tied to text boxes or windows, you'll sometimes see them used as input devices. Because these controls can indicate the current position on a scale, scroll bar controls can be used individually to control program input — for example, to control the sound volume or to adjust the colors in a picture. The HScrollBar (horizontal) and VScrollBar (vertical) controls operate independently from other controls and have their own set of events, properties, and methods. Scroll bar controls are not the same as the built-in scroll bars that are attached to text boxes, list boxes, combo boxes, or MDI forms (text boxes and MDI forms have a ScrollBars property to add or remove scroll bars that are attached to the control).

Windows interface guidelines now suggest using slider controls as input devices instead of scroll bars. Examples of slider controls can be seen in the Windows 95 control panel. A Windows 95 style slider control is included in the Professional and Enterprise editions of Visual Basic.

For More Information For additional information on scroll bar controls, see Chapter 7, "Using Visual Basic's Standard Controls."

Controls That Display Pictures and Graphics

Because Windows is a graphical user interface, it's important to have a way to display graphical images in your application's interface. Visual Basic includes four controls that make it easy to work with graphics: the picture box control, the image control, the shape control, and the line control.

The image, shape and line controls are sometimes referred to as "lightweight" graphical controls. They require less system resources and consequently display somewhat faster than the picture box control; they contain a subset of the properties, methods and events available in the picture box. Each is best suited for a particular purpose.

To provide this feature	Use this control
A container for other controls.	Picture box
Printing or graphics methods.	Picture box
Displaying a picture.	Image control or picture box
Displaying a simple graphical element	Shape or line control

Working with the Picture Box Control

The primary use for the picture box control is to display a picture to the user. The actual picture that is displayed is determined by the Picture property. The Picture property contains the file name (and optional path) for the picture file that you wish to display.

> **Note** Form objects also have a Picture property that can be set to display a picture directly on the form's background.

To display or replace a picture at run time, you can use the LoadPicture function to set the Picture property. You supply the name (and optional path) for the picture and the LoadPicture function handles the details of loading and displaying it:

```
picMain.Picture = LoadPicture("VANGOGH.BMP")
```

The picture box control has an AutoSize property that, when set to True, causes the picture box to resize automatically to match the dimensions of its contents. Take extra care in designing your form if you plan on using a picture box with the AutoSize enabled. The picture will resize without regard to other controls on the form, possibly causing unexpected results, such as covering up other controls. It's a good idea to test this by loading each of the pictures at design time.

Using the Picture Box as a Container

The picture box control can also be used as a container for other controls. Like the frame control, you can draw other controls on top of the picture box. The contained controls move with the picture box and their Top and Left properties will be relative to the picture box rather than the form.

A common use for the picture box container is as a toolbar or status bar. You can place image controls on it to act as buttons, or add labels to display status messages. By setting the Align property to Top, Bottom, Left, or Right, the picture box will "stick" to the edge of the form. Figure 3.16 shows a picture box with its Align property set to Bottom. It contains two label controls which could be used to display status messages.

Figure 3.16 Picture box used as a status bar

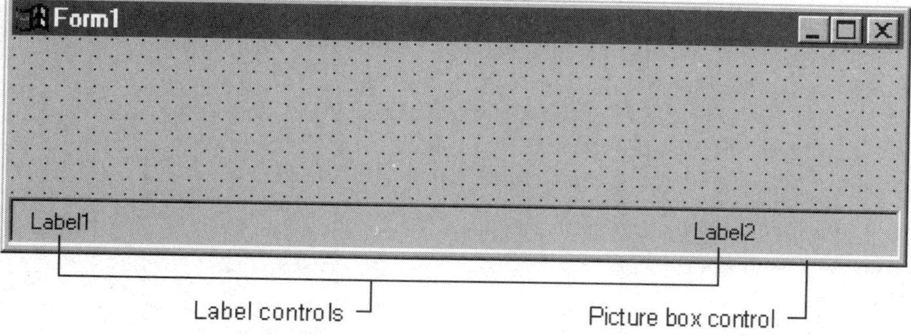

Other Uses for the Picture Box

The picture box control has several methods that make it useful for other purposes. Think of the picture box as a blank canvas upon which you can paint, draw or print. A single control can be used to display text, graphics or even simple animation.

The Print method allows you to output text to the picture box control just as you would to a printer. Several font properties are available to control the characteristics of text output by the Print method; the Cls method can be used to erase the output.

Circle, Line, Point and Pset methods may be used to draw graphics on the picture box. Properties such as DrawWidth, FillColor, and FillStyle allow you to customize the appearance of the graphics.

Animation can be created using the PaintPicture method by moving images within the picture control and rapidly changing between several different images.

For More Information For additional information on the picture box control, see Chapter 7, "Using Visual Basic's Standard Controls."

Lightweight Graphical Controls

The image, shape and line controls are considered to be lightweight controls; that is, they support only a subset of the properties, methods, and events found in the picture box. Because of this, they typically require less system resources and load faster than the picture box control.

Using Image Controls Instead of Picture Boxes

The image control is similar to the picture box control but is used only for displaying pictures. It doesn't have the ability to act as a container for other controls, and it doesn't support the advanced methods of the picture box.

Pictures are loaded into the image control just as they are in the picture box: at design time, set the Picture property to a file name and path; at run time, use the LoadPicture function.

The sizing behavior of the image control differs from that of the picture box. It has a Stretch property while the picture box has an AutoSize property. Setting the AutoSize property to True causes a picture box to resize to the dimensions of the picture; setting it to False causes the picture to be cropped (only a portion of the picture is visible). When set to False (the default), the Stretch property of the image control causes it to resize to the dimensions of the picture. Setting the Stretch property to True causes the picture to resize to the size of the image control, which may cause the picture to appear distorted.

For More Information For additional information on the image control, see Chapter 7, "Using Visual Basic's Standard Controls."

Using an Image Control to Create Your Own Buttons

An image control also recognizes the Click event, so you can use this control anywhere you'd use a command button. This is a convenient way to create a button with a picture instead of a caption. Grouping several image controls together horizontally across the top of the screen — usually within a picture box — allows you to create a toolbar in your application.

For instance, the Test Buttons example shows an image control that users can choose like they choose a command button. When the form is first displayed, the control displays one of three traffic icons from the Icon Library included with Visual Basic. Each time the image control is clicked, a different icon is displayed. (For a working version of this example, see Button.frm in the Controls.vbp sample application.)

If you inspect the form at design time, you will see that it actually contains all three icons "stacked" on top of each other. By changing the Visible property of the top image control to False, you allow the next image (with its Visible property set to True) to appear on top.

Figure 3.17 shows the image control with one of the traffic icons (Trffc10a.ico).

Figure 3.17 Image control with a traffic icon

To create a border around the image control, set the BorderStyle property to 1-Fixed Single.

> **Note** Unlike command buttons, image controls do not appear pushed in when clicked. This means that unless you change the bitmap in the MouseDown event, there is no visual cue to the user that the "button" is being pushed.

For More Information For information on displaying a graphic image in an image control, see Chapter 7, "Using Visual Basic's Standard Controls."

Using Shape and Line Controls

Shape and line controls are useful for drawing graphical elements on the surface of a form. These controls don't support any events; they are strictly for decorative purposes.

Several properties are provided to control the appearance of the shape control. By setting the Shape property, it can be displayed as a rectangle, square, oval, circle, rounded rectangle, or rounded square. The BorderColor and FillColor properties can be set to change the color; the BorderStyle, BorderWidth, FillStyle, and DrawMode properties control how the shape is drawn.

The line control is similar to the shape control but can only be used to draw straight lines.

For More Information For additional information on the shape and line controls, see Chapter 7, "Using Visual Basic's Standard Controls."

The Images Application

The form shown in Figure 3.18 uses four image controls, a shape control, a picture box, and a command button. When the user selects a playing card symbol, the shape control highlights the symbol and a description is displayed in the picture box. For a working version of this example, see Images.frm in the Controls.vbp sample application.

Figure 3.18 Image and shape control example

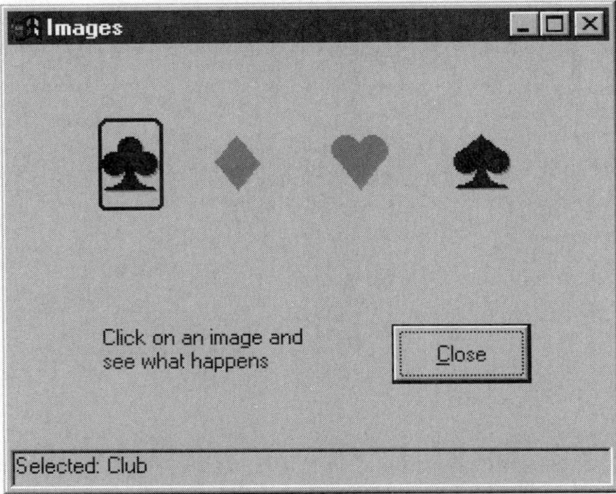

The following table lists the property settings for the objects in the application.

Object	Property	Setting
Picture box	Name Align	picStatus Bottom
First image control	Name Picture	imgClub Spade.ico
Second image control	Name Picture	imgDiamond Diamond.ico
Third image control	Name Picture	imgHeart Heart.ico
Fourth image control	Name Caption	imgSpade Spade.ico

Object	Property	Setting
Shape control	Name Shape BorderWidth	shpCard 4 - Rounded Rectangle 2
	Height	735
	Width	495
Command button	Name Caption	cmdClose &Close

Events in the Images Application

The Images application responds to events as follows:

- The Click event in each of the image controls sets the Left property of the shape control equal to its own Left property, moving the shape on top of the image.
- The Cls method of the picture box is invoked, clearing the current caption from the status bar.
- The Print method of the picture box is invoked, printing the new caption on the status bar.

The code in the image control Click event looks like this:

```
Private Sub imgHeart_Click()
    shpCard.Left = imgClub.Left
    picStatus.Cls
    picStatus.Print "Selected: Club"
    shpCard.Visible = True
End Sub
```

Note that the first line in the Click event code assigns a value (the Left property of the image control) to the Left property of the shape control using the = operator. The next two lines invoke methods, so no operator is needed. In the third line, the value ("Selected: Club") is an argument to the Print method.

There is one more line of code in the application that is of interest; it is in the Form Load event.

```
shpCard.Visible = False
```

By setting the Visible property of the shape control to False, the shape control is hidden until the first image is clicked. The Visible property is set to True as the last step in the image control Click event.

For More Information For additional information on properties, methods, and events see Chapter 5, "Programming Fundamentals."

Additional Controls

Several other standard controls are included in the Visual Basic toolbox. Some controls are useful for working with large amounts of data contained in an external database. Other controls can be used to access the Windows file system. Still other controls defy categorization, but are useful nonetheless.

You can also use ActiveX controls, previously called custom or OLE controls, in a Visual Basic application in the same way that you use the standard controls. The Professional and Enterprise editions of Visual Basic include several ActiveX controls as well as the capability to build your own controls. Additional ActiveX controls for just about any purpose imaginable are available for purchase from numerous vendors.

For More Information For additional information on using ActiveX controls, see Chapter 4, "Managing Projects."

Data Access Controls

In today's business, most information is stored in one or more central databases. Visual Basic includes several data access controls for accessing most popular databases, including Microsoft Access and SQL Server.

- The ADO Data control is used to connect to a database. Think of it as a pipeline between the database and the other controls on your form. Its properties, methods, and events allow you to navigate and manipulate external data from within your own application.
- The DataList control is similar to the list box control. When used in conjunction with an ADO Data control, it can be automatically filled with a list of data from a field in an external database.
- The DataCombo control is like a combination of the DataList control and a text box. The selected text in the text box portion can be edited, with the changes appearing in the underlying database.
- The DataGrid control displays data in a grid or table. When used in conjunction with an ADO Data control, it presents fully editable data from multiple fields in an external database.
- The Microsoft Hierarchical FlexGrid control is a unique control for presenting multiple views of data. Think of it as a combination of a grid and a tree or outline control. At run time, the user can rearrange columns and rows to provide different views of the data.

For More Information For additional information on data access controls, see Chapter 7,"Using Visual Basic's Standard Controls." For more information on working with external data, see the *Visual Basic Data Access Guide* online.

File System Controls

Visual Basic includes three controls for adding file handling capabilities to your application. These controls are normally used together to provide a view of drives, directories and files; they have special properties and events that tie them together.

- The DriveListBox control looks like a combo box. It provides a drop-down list of drives from which the user can select.
- The DirListBox is similar to a list box control, but with the built-in capability of displaying a list of directories in the currently selected drive.
- The FileListBox control also looks like a list box with a list of file names in a selected directory.

> **Note** These controls are provided primarily for backward compatibility with applications created in earlier versions of Visual Basic. The common dialog control provides an easier method of working with file access. For more information on common dialog control, see "Miscellaneous Controls" below.

Miscellaneous Controls

Several other standard controls are included in Visual Basic. Each serves a unique purpose.

- The timer control can be used to create an event in your application at a recurring interval. This is useful for executing code without the need for user interaction.
- The OLE container control is an easy way to add capabilities like linking and embedding to your application. Through the OLE container control, you can provide access to the functionality of any OLE-enabled application such as Microsoft Excel, Word and many others.
- The common dialog control adds built-in dialog boxes to your application for the selection of files, colors, fonts, and printing functions.

For More Information For additional information on any of the standard controls, see Chapter 7, "Using Visual Basic's Standard Controls."

Understanding Focus

Focus is the ability to receive user input through the mouse or keyboard. When an object has the focus, it can receive input from a user. In the Microsoft Windows interface, several applications can be running at any time, but only the application with the focus will have an active title bar and can receive user input. On a Visual Basic form with several text boxes, only the text box with the focus will display text entered by means of the keyboard.

The GotFocus and LostFocus events occur when an object receives or loses focus. Forms and most controls support these events.

Event	Description
GotFocus	Occurs when an object receives focus.
LostFocus	Occurs when an object loses focus. A LostFocus event procedure is primarily used for verification and validation updates, or for reversing or changing conditions you set up in the object's GotFocus procedure.

You can give focus to an object by:

- Selecting the object at run time.
- Using an access key to select the object at run time.
- Using the SetFocus method in code.

You can see when some objects have the focus. For example, when command buttons have the focus, they appear with a highlighted border around the caption (see Figure 3.19).

Figure 3.19 A command button showing focus

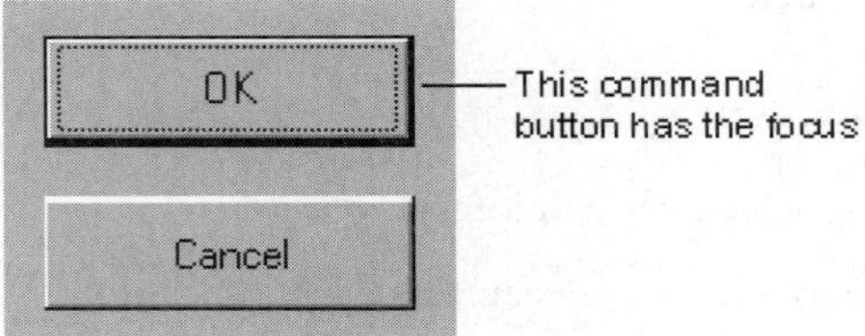

An object can receive focus only if its Enabled and Visible properties are set to True. The Enabled property allows the object to respond to user-generated events such as keyboard and mouse events. The Visible property determines whether an object is visible on the screen.

> **Note** A form can receive focus only if it doesn't contain any controls that can receive the focus.

Validate Event of Controls

Controls also have a Validate event, which occurs before a control loses focus. However, this event occurs only when the CausesValidation property of the control that is about to receive the focus is set to True. In many cases, because the Validate event occurs before the focus is lost, it is more appropriate than the LostFocus event for data validation. For more information, see "Validating Control Data by Restricting Focus" in Chapter 7, "Using Visual Basic's Standard Controls."

Controls That Can't Receive Focus

Some controls, such as the lightweight controls, cannot receive focus. Lightweight controls include the following:

- Frame control
- Image control
- Label control
- Line control
- Shape control

Additionally, controls that are invisible at run time, such as the Timer control, cannot receive focus.

Setting the Tab Order

The *tab order* is the order in which a user moves from one control to another by pressing the TAB key. Each form has its own tab order. Usually, the tab order is the same as the order in which you created the controls.

For example, assume you create two text boxes, Text1 and Text2, and then a command button, Command1. When the application starts, Text1 has the focus. Pressing TAB moves the focus between controls in the order they were created, as shown in Figure 3.20.

Figure 3.20 Tab example

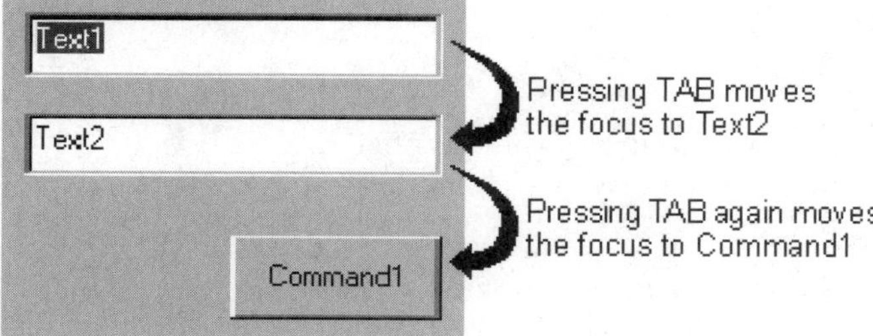
Text1
Text2
Command1
Pressing TAB moves the focus to Text2
Pressing TAB again moves the focus to Command1

To change the tab order for a control, set the TabIndex property. The TabIndex property of a control determines where it is positioned in the tab order. By default, the first control drawn has a TabIndex value of 0, the second has a TabIndex of 1, and so on. When you change a control's tab order position, Visual Basic automatically renumbers the tab order positions of the other controls to reflect insertions and deletions. For example, if you make Command1 first in the tab order, the TabIndex values for the other controls are automatically adjusted upward, as shown in the following table.

Control	TabIndex before it is changed	TabIndex after it is changed
Text1	0	1
Text2	1	2
Command1	2	0

The highest TabIndex setting is always one less than the number of controls in the tab order (because numbering starts at 0). Even if you set the TabIndex property to a number higher than the number of controls, Visual Basic converts the value back to the number of controls minus 1.

Note Controls that cannot get the focus, as well as disabled and invisible controls, don't have a TabIndex property and are not included in the tab order. As a user presses the TAB key, these controls are skipped.

Removing a Control from the Tab Order

Usually, pressing TAB at run time selects each control in the tab order. You can remove a control from the tab order by setting its TabStop property to False (0).

A control whose TabStop property has been set to False still maintains its position in the actual tab order, even though the control is skipped when you cycle through the controls with the TAB key.

Note An option button group has a single tab stop. The selected button (that is, the button with its Value set to True) has its TabStop property automatically set to True, while the other buttons have their TabStop property set to False.

Menu Basics

If you want your application to provide a set of commands to users, menus offer a convenient and consistent way to group commands and an easy way for users to access them.

Figure 3.21 Illustrates the elements of a menu interface on an untitled form.

Figure 3.21 The elements of a menu interface on a Visual Basic form

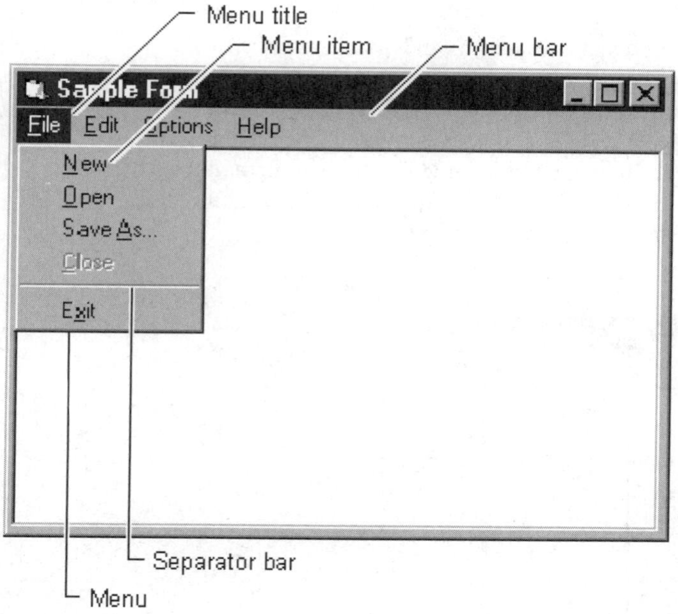

The *menu bar* appears immediately below the *title bar* on the form and contains one or more *menu titles*. When you click a menu title (such as File), a menu containing a list of menu items drops down. Menu items can include commands (such as New and Exit), separator bars, and submenu titles. Each menu item the user sees corresponds to a menu control you define in the Menu Editor (described later in this chapter).

To make your application easier to use, you should group menu items according to their function. In Figure 3.21, for example, the file-related commands New, Open, and Save As… are all found on the File menu.

Some menu items perform an action directly; for example, the Exit menu item on the File menu closes the application. Other menu items display a *dialog box* — a window that requires the user to supply information needed by the application to perform the action. These menu items should be followed by an ellipsis (…). For example, when you choose Save As… from the File menu, the Save File As dialog box appears.

A menu control is an object; like other objects it has properties that can be used to define its appearance and behavior. You can set the Caption property, the Enabled and Visible properties, the Checked property, and others at design time or at run time. Menu controls contain only one event, the Click event, which is invoked when the menu control is selected with the mouse or using the keyboard.

For More Information For additional information on menu controls, see "Creating Menus with the Menu Editor" in Chapter 6, "Creating a User Interface."

Pop-up Menus

A *pop-up menu* is a floating menu that is displayed over a form, independent of the menu bar, as shown in Figure 3.22. The items displayed on the pop-up menu depend on the location of the pointer when the right mouse button is pressed; therefore, pop-up menus are also called *context menus*. (In Windows 95, you activate context menus by clicking the right mouse button.) You should use pop-up menus to provide an efficient method for accessing common, contextual commands. For example, if you click a text box with the right mouse button, a contextual menu would appear, as shown in Figure 3.22.

Figure 3.22 A pop-up menu

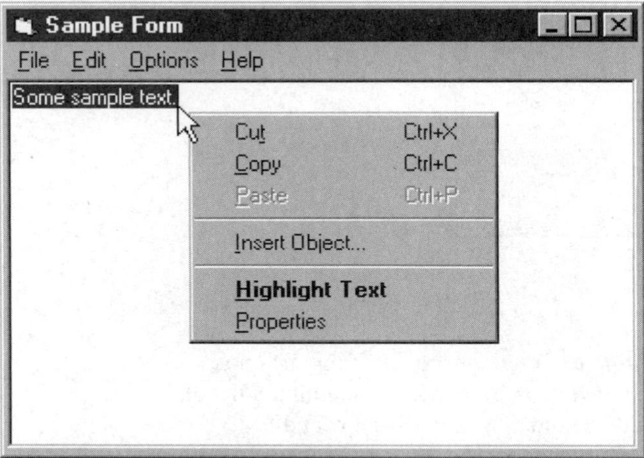

Any menu that has at least one menu item can be displayed at run time as a pop-up menu. To display a pop-up menu, use the PopupMenu method.

For More Information For additional information on creating pop-up menus, see "Creating Menus with the Menu Editor" in Chapter 6, "Creating a User Interface."

Using the Menu Editor

With the Menu Editor, you can add new commands to existing menus, replace existing menu commands with your own commands, create new menus and menu bars, and change and delete existing menus and menu bars. The main advantage of the Menu Editor is its ease of use. You can customize menus in a completely interactive manner that involves very little programming.

To display the Menu Editor

- From the **Tools** menu, choose **Menu Editor**.

This opens the Menu Editor, shown in Figure 3.23

Figure 3.23 The Menu Editor

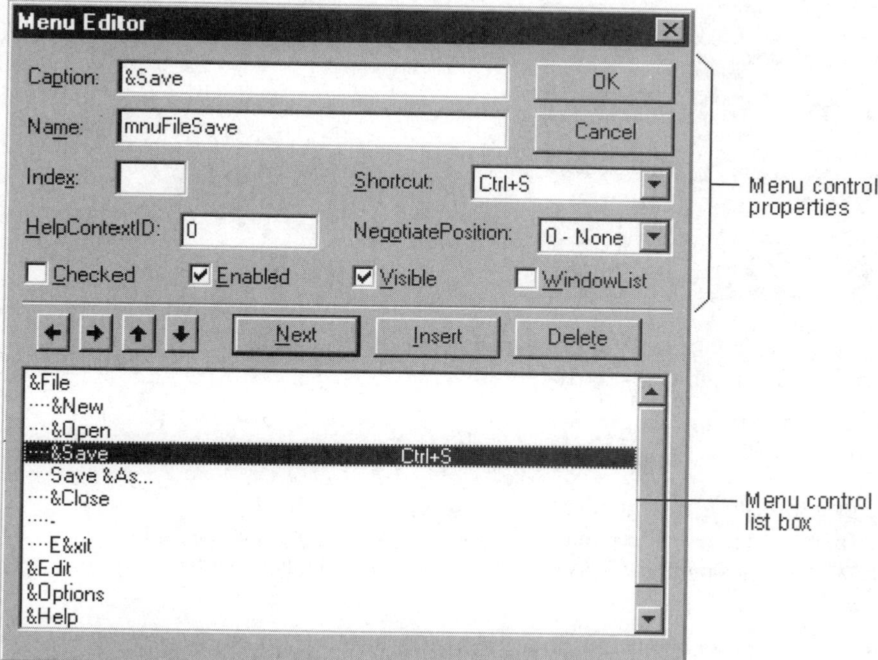

While most menu control properties can be set using the Menu Editor; all menu properties are also available in the Properties window. You would normally create a menu in the Menu Editor; however, to quickly change a single property, you could use the Properties window.

For More Information For additional information on creating menus and using the Menu Editor, see "Creating Menus with the Menu Editor" in Chapter 6, "Creating a User Interface."

Prompting the User with Dialog Boxes

In Windows-based applications, dialog boxes are used to prompt the user for data needed by the application to continue or to display information to the user. Dialog boxes are a specialized type of form object that can be created in one of three ways:

- *Predefined* dialog boxes can be created from code using the MsgBox or InputBox functions.
- *Customized* dialog boxes can be created using a standard form or by customizing an existing dialog box.
- *Standard* dialog boxes, such as Print and File Open, can be created using the common dialog control.

Figure 3.24 shows an example of a predefined dialog box created using the MsgBox function.

Figure 3.24 A predefined dialog box

This dialog is displayed when you invoke the MsgBox function in code. The code for displaying the dialog box shown in Figure 3.24 looks like this:

```
MsgBox "Error encountered while trying to open file," & vbCrLf & "please retry.",
➥ vbExclamation, "Text Editor"
```

You supply three pieces of information, or arguments, to the MsgBox function: the message text, a constant (numeric value) to determine the style of the dialog box, and a title. Styles are available with various combinations of buttons and icons to make creating dialog boxes easy.

Because most dialog boxes require user interaction, they are usually displayed as modal dialog boxes. A modal dialog box must be closed (hidden or unloaded) before you can continue working with the rest of the application. For example, a dialog box is modal if it requires you to click OK or Cancel before you can switch to another form or dialog box.

Modeless dialog boxes let you shift the focus between the dialog box and another form without having to close the dialog box. You can continue to work elsewhere in the current application while the dialog box is displayed. Modeless dialog boxes are rare; you will usually display a dialog because a response is needed before the application can continue. From the Edit menu, the Find dialog box in Visual Basic is an example of a modeless dialog box. Use modeless dialog boxes to display frequently used commands or information.

For More Information For additional information on creating dialog boxes, see Chapter 6, “Creating a User Interface.”

CHAPTER 4

Managing Projects

To create an application with Visual Basic, you work with projects. A *project* is the collection of files you use to build an application. This chapter describes how to build and manage projects.

When you create an application, you will usually create new forms; you might also reuse or modify forms that were created for previous projects. The same is true for other modules or files that you might include in your project. ActiveX controls and objects from other applications can also be shared between projects.

After all of the components in a project have been assembled and the code written, you compile your project to create an executable file.

Contents

Working with Projects

As you develop an application, you work with a project to manage all the different files that make up the application. A project consists of:

- One project file that keeps track of all the components (.vbp).
- One file for each form (.frm).
- One binary data file for each form containing data for properties of controls on the form (.frx). These files are not editable and are automatically generated for any .frm file that contains binary properties, such as Picture or Icon.

- Optionally, one file for each class module (.cls).
- Optionally, one file for each standard module (.bas).
- Optionally, one or more files containing ActiveX controls (.ocx).
- Optionally, a single resource file (.res).

The project file is simply a list of all the files and objects associated with the project, as well as information on the environment options you set. This information is updated every time you save the project. All of the files and objects can be shared by other projects as well.

When you have completed all the files for a project, you can convert the project into an executable file (.exe): From the File menu, choose the Make *project.exe* command.

> **Note** With the Professional and Enterprise editions of Visual Basic, you can also create other types of executable files such as .ocx and .dll files. References in this chapter assume a standard .exe project; for additional information related to other project types see the *Microsoft Visual Basic 6.0 Component Tools Guide* volume of the *Microsoft Visual Basic 6.0 Reference Library.*

For More Information For more details about creating executables, see "Making and Running an Executable File," later in this chapter. For information about binary data files and project files, see Appendix A, "Visual Basic Specifications, Limitations, and File Formats."

The Project Explorer

As you create, add, or remove editable files from a project, Visual Basic reflects your changes in the Project Explorer window, which contains a current list of the files in the project. The Project Explorer window in Figure 4.1 shows some of the types of files you can include in a Visual Basic project.

Figure 4.1 The Project Explorer window

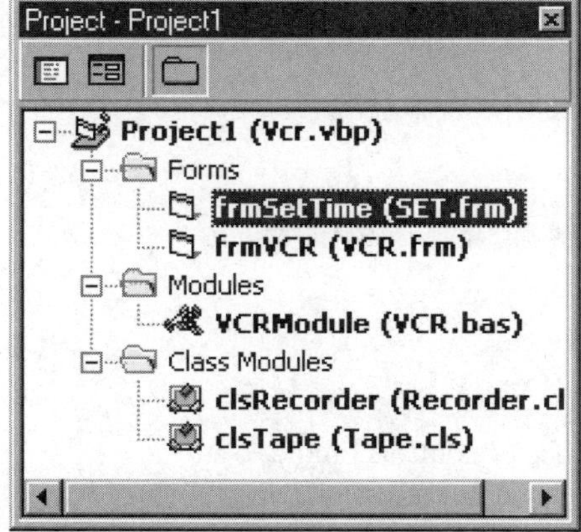

The Project File

Each time you save a project, Visual Basic updates the project file (.vbp). A project file contains the same list of files that appears in the Project Explorer window, as well as references to the ActiveX controls and insertable objects that are used in the project.

You can open an existing project file by double-clicking its icon, by choosing the Open Project command from the File menu, or by dragging the file and dropping it on the Project Explorer window.

For More Information The specific format of information stored in the .vbp file is described in Appendix A, "Visual Basic Specifications, Limitations, and File Formats."

The Structure of a Visual Basic Project

The following sections describe the different types of files and objects that you can include in a project.

Form Modules

Form modules (.frm file name extension) can contain textual descriptions of the form and its controls, including their property settings. They can also contain form-level declarations of constants, variables, and external procedures; event procedures; and general procedures.

For More Information For more about creating forms, see Chapter 2, "Developing an Application in Visual Basic," and Chapter 6, "Creating a User Interface." For information about the format and content of form files, see Appendix A, "Visual Basic Specifications, Limitations, and File Formats."

Class Modules

Class modules (.cls file name extension) are similar to form modules, except that they have no visible user interface. You can use class modules to create your own objects, including code for methods and properties.

For More Information For information about writing code in class modules, see "Creating Your Own Classes" in Chapter 9, "Programming with Objects."

Standard Modules

Standard modules (.bas file name extension) can contain public or module-level declarations of types, constants, variables, external procedures, and public procedures.

For More Information For information about using modules, see Chapter 5, "Programming Fundamentals," and Chapter 9, "Programming with Objects."

Resource Files

Resource files (.res file name extension) contain bitmaps, text strings, and other data that you can change without having to re-edit your code. For example, if you plan to localize your application in a foreign language, you can keep all of the user-interface text strings and bitmaps in a resource file, which you can then localize instead of the entire application. A project can contain no more than one resource file.

For More Information For more information on using resource files, see "Using Resource Files for Localization," later in this chapter, and Chapter 16, "International Issues."

ActiveX Documents

ActiveX documents (.dob) are similar to forms, but are displayable in an Internet browser such as Internet Explorer. The Professional and Enterprise editions of Visual Basic are capable of creating ActiveX documents.

For More Information For more information on ActiveX documents, see "Creating ActiveX Components" in the *Microsoft Visual Basic 6.0 Component Tools Guide.*

User Control and Property Page Modules

User Control (.ctl) and Property Page (.pag) modules are also similar to forms, but are used to create ActiveX controls and their associated property pages for displaying design-time properties. The Professional and Enterprise editions of Visual Basic are capable of creating ActiveX controls.

For More Information For more information on ActiveX control creation, see "Creating an ActiveX Control" in "Creating ActiveX Components" in the *Microsoft Visual Basic 6.0 Component Tools Guide,* volume of the *Microsoft Visual Basic 6.0 Reference Library*.

Components

In addition to files and modules, several other types of components can be added to the project.

ActiveX Controls

ActiveX controls (.ocx file name extension) are optional controls which can be added to the toolbox and used on forms. When you install Visual Basic, the files containing the controls included with Visual Basic are copied to a common directory (the \Windows\System subdirectory under Windows 95). Additional ActiveX controls are available from a wide variety of sources. You can also create your own controls using the Professional or Enterprise editions of Visual Basic.

For More Information For more information on using the included ActiveX controls, see "Using the ActiveX Controls" in the *Microsoft Visual Basic 6.0 Component Tools Guide*.

Insertable Objects

Insertable objects, such as a Microsoft Excel Worksheet object, are components you can use as building blocks to build integrated solutions. An *integrated solution* can contain data in different formats, such as spreadsheets, bitmaps, and text, which were all created by different applications.

For More Information For more information on using other applications' objects, see Chapter 10, "Programming with Components."

References

You can also add references to external ActiveX components that may be used by your application. You assign references by using the References dialog, accessed from the References menu item on the Project menu.

For More Information For more information on references, see "Using Other Applications' Objects" later in this chapter.

ActiveX Designers

ActiveX designers are tools for designing classes from which objects can be created. The design interface for forms is the default designer. Additional designers may be available from other sources.

For More Information For more information about ActiveX designers, see "ActiveX Designers" in Chapter 9, "Programming with Objects."

Standard Controls

Standard controls are supplied by Visual Basic. Standard controls, such as the command button or frame control, are always included in the toolbox, unlike ActiveX controls and insertable objects, which can be removed from or added to the toolbox.

For More Information For more information on standard controls, see Chapter 3, "Forms, Controls, and Menus," and Chapter 7, "Using Visual Basic's Standard Controls."

Creating, Opening, and Saving Projects

Four commands on the File menu allow you to create, open, and save projects.

Menu command	Description
New Project	Closes the current project, prompting you to save any files that have changed. You can select a type of project from the New Project dialog. Visual Basic then creates a new project with a single new file.
Open Project	Closes the current project, prompting you to save any changes. Visual Basic then opens an existing project, including the forms, modules, and ActiveX controls listed in its project (.vbp) file.
Save Project	Updates the project file of the current project and all of its form, standard, and class modules.
Save Project As	Updates the project file of the current project, saving the project file under a file name that you specify. Visual Basic also prompts you to save any forms or modules that have changed.

It is also possible to share files between projects. A single file, such as a form, can be part of more than one project. Note that changes made to a form or module in one project will be propagated amongst all projects that share that module.

For More Information For more information about sharing files, see "Adding, Removing, and Saving Files" later in this chapter.

Working with Multiple Projects

In the Professional and Enterprise editions of Visual Basic, it is possible to have more than one project open at a time. This is useful for building and testing solutions involving user-created controls or other components. When more than one project is loaded, the caption of the Project Explorer window will change to Project Group and the components of all open projects will be displayed.

To add an additional project to the current project group

1. From the **File** menu, choose **Add Project**.

   The **Add Project** dialog box is displayed.

2. Select an existing project or a new project type, and choose **Open**.

To remove a project from the current project group

1. Select a project or a component of a project in the Project Explorer.
2. From the **File** menu, choose **Remove Project**.

For More Information To learn more about working with multiple projects, see "Creating ActiveX Components" in the *Microsoft Visual Basic 6.0 Component Tools Guide*.

Adding, Removing, and Saving Files

Working with files within a project is similar to working with the projects themselves.

To add a file to a project

1. Select **Project, Add** *filetype* (where filetype is the type of file).

   The **Add** *filetype* dialog box (Figure 4.2) is displayed.

2. Select an existing file or a new file type, and choose **Open**.

Figure 4.2 The Add Form dialog box

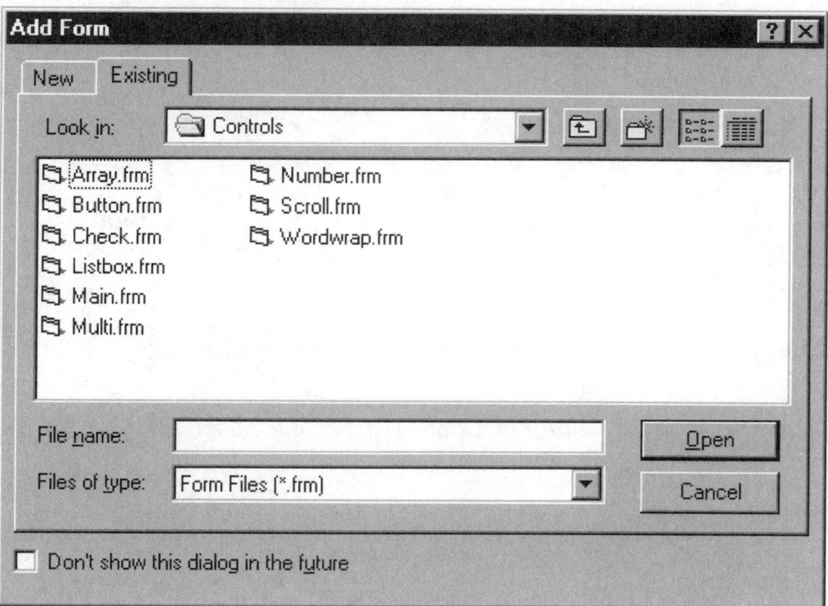

When you add a file to a project, you are simply including a reference to the existing file in the project; you are not adding a copy of the file. Therefore, if you make changes to a file and save it, your changes will affect any project that includes the file. To change a file without affecting other projects, select the file in the Project Explorer, choose Save *filename* As from the File menu, and then save the file under a new file name.

> **Note** You can drag and drop files from the Windows Explorer, File Manager, or Network Neighborhood into the Project window to add them to a project. You can also drag and drop .ocx files onto the toolbox to add new controls.

To remove a file from a project

1. Select the file in the Project Explorer.
2. From the **Project** menu, choose **Remove** *filename*.
3. The file will be removed from the project but not from the disk.

If you remove a file from a project, Visual Basic updates this information in the project file when you save it. If you delete a file outside of Visual Basic, however, Visual Basic cannot update the project file; therefore, when you open the project, Visual Basic displays an error message warning you that a file is missing.

To save an individual file without saving the project

1. Select the file in the Project Explorer.
2. From the **File** menu, choose **Save** *filename*.

Merging Text

You can also insert existing text from other files into one of your code modules. This is useful for adding a list of constants or for adding snippets of code that you might have saved in text files.

To insert a text file into your code

1. From the Project window, select the form or module into which you want to insert code.
2. Choose the **View Code** button, and move the cursor to the point in the Code Editor where you want to insert code.
3. From the **Edit** menu, choose **Insert File**.
4. Select the name of the text file you want to insert, and choose **Open**.

   Note If you edit Visual Basic source files using a text or code editor other than Visual Basic, be careful not to change settings of the attribute VB_PredeclaredId. In particular, changing this attribute may cause serious problems with the GlobalMultiUse and GlobalSingleUse classes.

   In general, you should not edit attributes manually, as doing so may put the module into an internally inconsistent state.

Adding Controls to a Project

The set of controls available in the toolbox can be customized for each project. Any given control must be in the toolbox before you can add it to a form in the project. The basic set of standard controls that always appear in the toolbox is described in Chapter 3, "Forms, Controls, and Menus."

Adding ActiveX Controls to a Project

You can add ActiveX controls and insertable objects to your project by adding them to the toolbox.

To add a control to a project's toolbox

1. From the **Project** menu, choose **Components**.

   The **Components** dialog box is displayed, as shown in Figure 4.3. The items listed in this dialog box include all registered ActiveX controls, insertable objects, and ActiveX designers.

2. To add a control (.ocx file name extension) or an insertable object to the toolbox, select the check box to the left of the control name.

   To view controls with .ocx file name extensions, select the **Controls** tab. To view insertable objects, such as a Microsoft Excel Chart, select the **Insertable Objects** tab.

3. Choose **OK** to close the **Components** dialog box. All of the ActiveX controls that you selected will now appear in the toolbox.

Figure 4.3 The Components dialog box

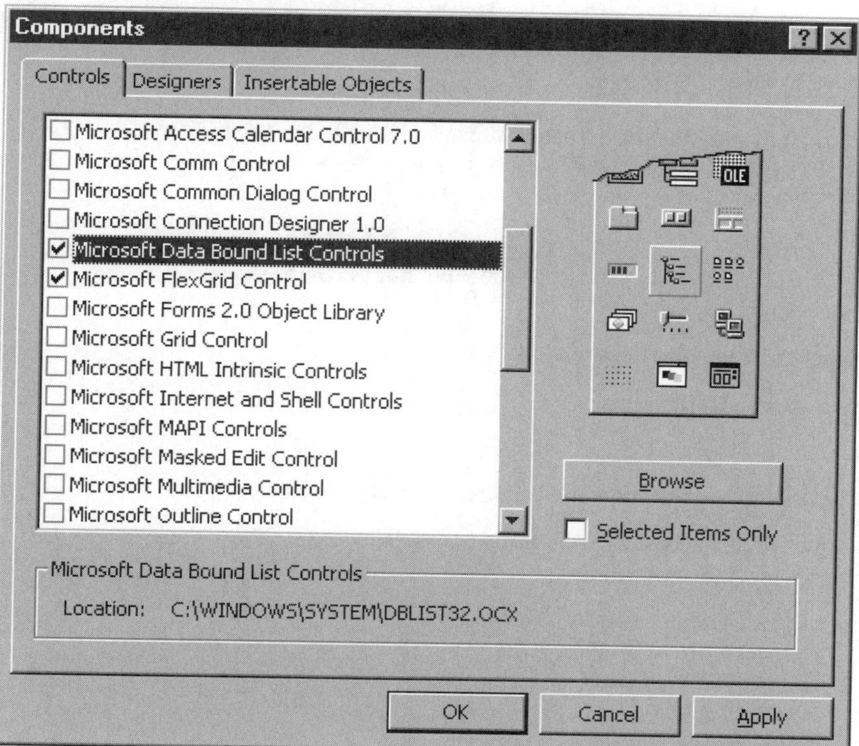

To add ActiveX controls to the Components dialog box, choose the Browse button, and search other directories for files with a .ocx file name extension. When you add an ActiveX control to the list of available controls, Visual Basic automatically selects the check box.

Note Each ActiveX control is accompanied by a file with an .oca extension. This file stores cached type library information and other data specific to the control. The .oca files are typically stored in the same directory as the ActiveX controls and are recreated as needed (file sizes and dates may change).

Removing Controls from a Project

To remove a control from a project

1. From the **Project** menu, choose **Components**.

   The **Components** dialog box is displayed.

2. Clear the check box next to each control you want to remove.

   The control icons will be removed from the toolbox.

   Note You cannot remove any control from the toolbox if an instance of that control is used on any form in the project.

Using Other Applications' Objects

You can also use objects from other applications, such as those included in the Microsoft Excel object library, either as controls in the toolbox or as programmable objects in your code. To add objects to the toolbox, see "Adding Controls to a Project" earlier in this chapter.

To make another application's objects available in your code, but not as controls, set a reference to that application's object library.

To add a reference to another application's object library

1. From the **Project** menu, choose **References**.

   The **References** dialog box is displayed, as shown in Figure 4.4.

2. Select the check box next to each reference you want to add to your project.

   To add references to applications not listed in the **References** dialog box, choose the **Browse** button, and then select the application.

3. Choose **OK** to add the selected references to your project.

Figure 4.4 The References dialog box

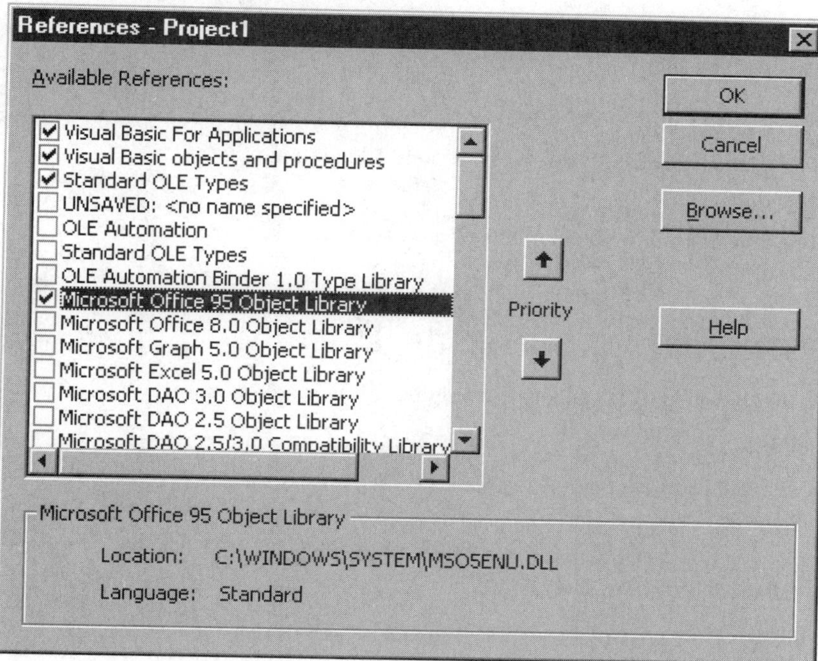

If you are not using any objects in a referenced library, you should clear the check box for that reference to minimize the number of object references Visual Basic must resolve, thus reducing the time it takes your project to compile.

Once you have set references to the object libraries you want, you can find a specific object and its methods and properties in the Object Browser by choosing Object Browser from the View menu. You can use any object listed in the Object Browser in your code.

For More Information For information on the Object Browser, see "Finding Out About Objects" in Chapter 9, "Programming with Objects."

Using a Resource File

A resource file allows you to collect all of the version-specific text and bitmaps for an application in one place. This can include constant declarations, icons, screen text, and other material that may change between localized versions or between revisions or specific configurations.

To add a file to a project

1. From the **Project** menu, select **Add File**.

   The **Add File** dialog box is displayed.

2. Select an existing resource file (.res) and choose **Open**.

A single project can have only one resource file; if you add a second file with a .res extension, an error occurs.

For More Information For more information on the contents of a resource file, see Chapter 16, "International Issues."

Making and Running an Executable File

You can make an executable file (.exe) from Visual Basic using the following procedure.

To make an executable file in Visual Basic

1. From the **File** menu, choose **Make** *projectname* **.exe** where projectname is the application name for the project.
2. Type a file name, or browse through the directories and select an existing file name to overwrite an existing executable with a newer version.
3. By clicking the **Options** button, you can also specify a number of version-specific details about the executable file in the **Project Properties** dialog box.
4. If you want to modify the version number of the project, set the appropriate **Major**, **Minor**, and **Revision** numbers. Selecting **Auto Increment** will automatically step the **Revision** number each time you run the **Make** *projectname* **.exe** command for this project.
5. To specify a new name for the application, under **Application**, type a new name in the **Title** box. If you want to specify a new icon, choose one from the list.
6. You can also enter version-specific commentary on a variety of issues under the **Version Information** box (comments, company name, trademark and copyright information, and so on) by selecting a topic from the list box and entering information in the text box.
7. Choose **OK** to close the **Project Properties** dialog box, and then choose **OK** in the **Make** *appname* **.exe** dialog box to compile and link the executable file.

You can run the executable file like any other Windows-based application: double-click the icon for the executable file.

> **Note** Building an executable file from the command line in a DOS session can be useful when you want to compile a project programmatically. In a batch file, type:
>
> **Vb6 /make** *projectname***[.vbp] [***exename***]**
>
> For *projectname*, type the name of the project file. Use the variable *exename* to rename the resulting executable file.

Conditional Compilation

Conditional compilation lets you selectively compile certain parts of the program. You can include specific features of your program in different versions, such as changing the date and currency display filters for an application distributed in several different languages.

For More Information To learn more about conditional compilation, see "Using Conditional Compilation" in Chapter 8, "More About Programming."

Setting Project Options

Visual Basic allows you to customize each project by setting a number of properties. Use the Project Properties dialog box, accessible through the Project Properties command on the Project menu. Property settings are saved to the project (.vbp) file.

The following table describes some of the options you can set.

Option	Description
Startup Object	The first form that Visual Basic displays at run time, or Sub Main ( ).
Project Name	Identifies the project in code. It can't contain periods (.), spaces, or start with a nonalphabetic character. For a public class name, the project name and class name cannot exceed a total of 37 characters.
Help File	The name of the Help file associated with the project.
Project Help Context ID	The context ID for the specific Help topic to be called when the user selects the "?" button while the application's object library is selected in the Object Browser.
Project Description	A user-friendly name for the project. Displayed in the References and Object Browser dialog boxes.

Many other options are also available, including those for compiling, components, and multithreading. When you're ready to access some of the more advanced options, you can find more information by searching Help.

For More Information To learn about setting environment options that affect all projects, see Chapter 2, "Developing an Application in Visual Basic."

Using Wizards and Add-Ins

Visual Basic allows you to select and manage *add-ins*, which are extensions to Visual Basic. These extensions add capabilities to the Visual Basic development environment, for example, special source code control capabilities.

Microsoft and other developers have created add-ins you can use in your applications. Wizards are a type of add-in that can simplify certain tasks, such as creating a form. Several wizards are included in Visual Basic.

To have an add-in appear on the Add-In Manager dialog box, the developer of the add-in must ensure that it is installed properly.

Using the Add-In Manager

You can add or remove an add-in to your project by using the Add-In Manager, which is accessible from the Add-Ins menu. The Add-In Manager dialog box lists the available add-ins.

To install an add-in

1. From the **Add-Ins** menu, choose **Add-In Manager**.
2. Highlight an add-in from the list and click the desired behaviors in Load Behavior. To unload an add-in or prevent it from loading, clear all Load Behavior boxes.
3. When you are finished making your selections, choose **OK**.

   Depending upon your Load Behavior selections, Visual Basic connects the selected add-ins and disconnects the cleared add-ins.

Visual Basic saves your add-in selections between editing sessions.

> **Note** Selecting an add-in may add menu items to the Visual Basic Add-Ins menu.

Using Wizards

Wizards make working with Visual Basic even easier by providing task-specific assistance. For example, the Application Wizard included in Visual Basic helps you to create the framework for an application by presenting a series of questions or choices. It generates the forms and the code behind the forms based on your choices; all you need to do is add code for your own specific functionality.

The Professional and Enterprise editions of Visual Basic include other wizards, including a Data Form Wizard for creating forms to be used with databases, and an ActiveX Document Wizard for converting forms for use in Internet applications.

Wizards are installed or removed using the Add-in Manager. Once installed, they will appear as selections on the Add-Ins menu. Some of the wizards also appear as icons in the related dialog boxes; for example, the Application Wizard can also be accessed using its icon in the New Project dialog box.

To start the Application Wizard

- From the **Add-Ins** menu, choose **Application Wizard**.

  –or–

1. From the **File** menu, choose **New Project**.
2. Select the Application Wizard icon.

CHAPTER 5

Programming Fundamentals

This chapter introduces the essential components of the Visual Basic language. After creating the interface for your application using forms and controls, you will need to write the code that defines the application's behavior. As with any modern programming language, Visual Basic supports a number of common programming constructs and language elements.

Visual Basic is an object-based programming language. The mere mention of objects may cause undue anxiety in many programmers. Don't worry: whether you realize it or not, you've been dealing with objects most of your life. Once you understand a few basic concepts, objects actually help to make programming easier than ever before.

If you've programmed in other languages, much of the material covered in this chapter will seem familiar. While most of the constructs are similar to other languages, the event-driven nature of Visual Basic introduces some subtle differences. Try and approach this material with an open mind; once you understand the differences you can use them to your advantage.

If you're new to programming, the material in this chapter will serve as an introduction to the basic building blocks for writing code. Once you understand the basics, you will be able to create powerful applications using Visual Basic.

Contents

Sample Application: Vcr.vbp

Many of the code samples in this chapter are taken from the Vcr.vbp sample application which is listed in the Samples directory.

The Structure of a Visual Basic Application

An application is really nothing more than a set of instructions directing the computer to perform a task or tasks. The structure of an application is the way in which the instructions are organized; that is, where the instructions are stored and the order in which instructions are executed.

Simple applications such as the classic "hello world" example have a simple structure; organization isn't very important with a single line of code. As applications become more complex, the need for organization or structure becomes obvious. Imagine the chaos that would result if your application's code was allowed to execute in random order. In addition to controlling the execution of an application, the structure is important to the programmer: how easily can you find specific instructions within your application?

Because a Visual Basic application is based on objects, the structure of its code closely models its physical representation on screen. By definition, objects contain data and code. The form that you see on screen is a representation of the properties that define its appearance and intrinsic behavior. For each form in an application, there is a related *form module* (with file name extension .frm) that contains its code.

Figure 5.1 A form and its related form module

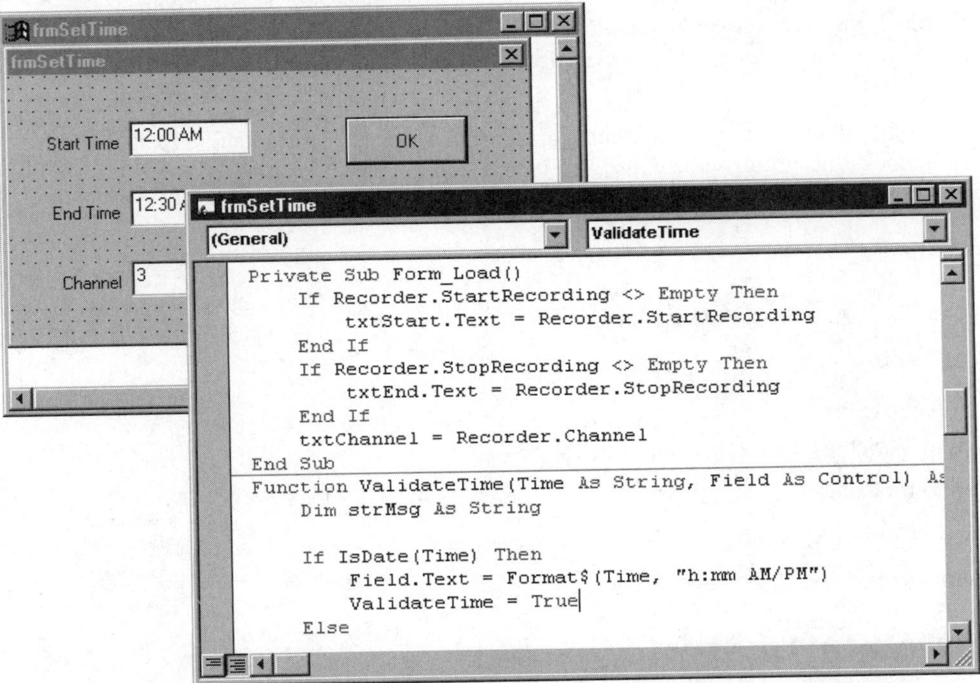

Each form module contains *event procedures* — sections of code where you place the instructions that will execute in response to specific events. Forms can contain controls. For each control on a form, there is a corresponding set of event procedures in the form module. In addition to event procedures, form modules can contain general procedures that are executed in response to a call from any event procedure.

Code that isn't related to a specific form or control can be placed in a different type of module, a *standard module* (.BAS). A procedure that might be used in response to events in several different objects should be placed in a standard module, rather than duplicating the code in the event procedures for each object.

A *class module* (.CLS) is used to create objects that can be called from procedures within your application. Whereas a standard module contains only code, a class module contains both code and data — you can think of it as a control without a physical representation.

While Chapter 4, "Managing Projects," describes which components you can add to an application, this chapter explains how to write code in the various components that make up an application. By default, your project contains a single form module. You can add additional form, class, and standard modules, as needed. Class modules are discussed in Chapter 9, "Programming with Objects."

How an Event-Driven Application Works

An event is an action recognized by a form or control. Event-driven applications execute Basic code in response to an event. Each form and control in Visual Basic has a predefined set of events. If one of these events occurs and there is code in the associated event procedure, Visual Basic invokes that code.

Although objects in Visual Basic automatically recognize a predefined set of events, it is up to you to decide if and how they will respond to a particular event. A section of code — an event procedure — corresponds to each event. When you want a control to respond to an event, you write code in the event procedure for that event.

The types of events recognized by an object vary, but many types are common to most controls. For example, most objects recognize a Click event — if a user clicks a form, code in the form's Click event procedure is executed; if a user clicks a command button, code in the button's Click event procedure is executed. The actual code in each case will most likely be quite different.

Here's a typical sequence of events in an event-driven application:

1. The application starts and a form is loaded and displayed.
2. The form (or a control on the form) receives an event. The event might be caused by the user (for example, a keystroke), by the system (for example, a timer event), or indirectly by your code (for example, a Load event when your code loads a form).
3. If there is code in the corresponding event procedure, it executes.
4. The application waits for the next event.

Note Many events occur in conjunction with other events. For example, when the DblClick event occurs, the MouseDown, MouseUp, and Click events also occur.

Before You Start Coding

Perhaps the most important (and often overlooked) part of creating an application in Visual Basic is the design phase. While it's obvious that you need to design a user interface for your application, it may not be as obvious that you need to design the structure of the code. The way you structure your application can make a difference in its performance as well as in the maintainability and usability of your code.

The code in a Visual Basic application is organized in a hierarchical fashion. A typical application consists of one or more modules: a form module for each form in the application, optional standard modules for shared code, and optional class modules. Each module contains one or more procedures that contain the code: event procedures, Sub or Function procedures, and Property procedures.

Determining which procedures belong in which module depends somewhat on the type of application that you are creating. Because Visual Basic is based on objects, it helps to think of your application in terms of the objects that it represents. The design of the sample application for this chapter, Vcr.vbp, is based on the objects that comprise a video cassette recorder and a television. The VCR application consists of two form modules, a standard module, and two class modules. You can use the Object Browser to examine the structure of the project (Figure 5.2).

Figure 5.2 The structure of the VCR project is shown in the Object Browser

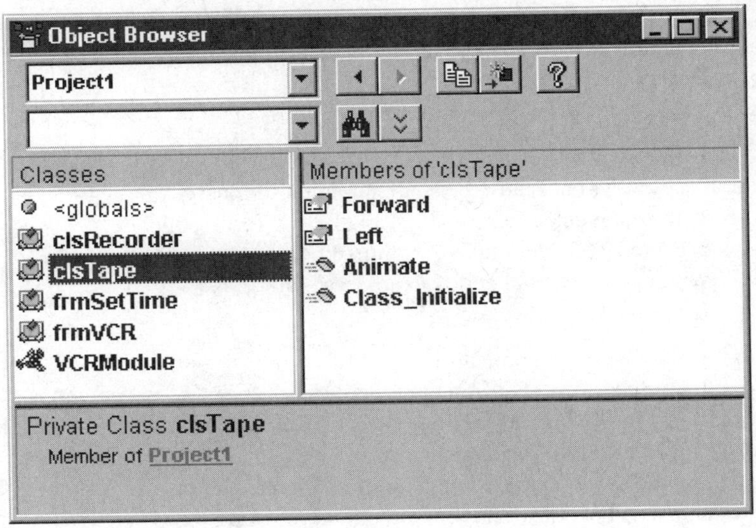

The main form for the VCR application (frmVCR) is a visual representation of a combination VCR and television screen (Figure 5.3). It is composed of several objects that model those found in the real world version. A group of Command buttons (cmdPlay, cmdRecord, and so on) mimic the buttons used to operate a VCR. The software VCR also contains a clock (lblTime), a channel indicator (lblChannel), function indicators (shpPlay, shpRecord, and so on), and a "picture tube" (picTV). The event procedures for all of these objects are contained in the Vcr.frm form module.

Figure 5.3 The main form for the VCR application

In many cases there are repetitive procedures that are shared by more than one object. For example, when the Play, Rewind, or Record buttons are "pushed," the Pause and Stop buttons need to be enabled. Rather than repeat this code in each button's Click event procedure, it's better to create a shared Sub procedure that can be called by any button. If these routines need to be modified in the future, all of the modifications can be done in one place. This and other shared procedures are contained in the standard module, Vcr.bas.

Some parts of a VCR aren't visible, such as the tape transport mechanism or the logic for recording a television program. Likewise, some of the functions of the software VCR have no visual representation. These are implemented as two class modules: Recorder.cls and Tape.cls. Code to initiate the "recording" process is contained in the clsRecorder module; code to control the direction and speed of the "tape" is contained in the clsTape module. The classes defined in these modules have no direct references to any of the objects in the forms. Because they are independent code modules, they could easily be reused to build an audio recorder without any modifications.

In addition to designing the structure of your code, it's important to establish naming conventions. By default, Visual Basic names the first form in a project Form1, the second Form2, and so on. If you have several forms in an application, it's a good idea to give them meaningful names to avoid confusion when writing or editing your code. Some suggested naming conventions are presented in Appendix B, "Visual Basic Coding Conventions."

As you learn more about objects and writing code, you can refer to the VCR sample application for examples of various different coding techniques.

Code Writing Mechanics

Before you begin, it's important to understand the mechanics of writing code in Visual Basic. Like any programming language, Visual Basic has its own rules for organizing, editing, and formatting code.

Code Modules

Code in Visual Basic is stored in modules. There are three kinds of modules: form, standard, and class.

Simple applications can consist of just a single form, and all of the code in the application resides in that form module. As your applications get larger and more sophisticated, you add additional forms. Eventually you might find that there is common code you want to execute in several forms. You don't want to duplicate the code in both forms, so you create a separate module containing a procedure that implements the common code. This separate module should be a standard module. Over time, you can build up a library of modules containing shared procedures.

Each standard, class, and form module can contain:

- Declarations. You can place constant, type, variable, and dynamic-link library (DLL) procedure declarations at the module level of form, class or standard modules.
- Procedures. A Sub, Function, or Property procedure contains pieces of code that can be executed as a unit. These are discussed in the section "Introduction to Procedures" later in this chapter.

Form Modules

Form modules (.FRM file name extension) are the foundation of most Visual Basic applications. They can contain procedures that handle events, general procedures, and form-level declarations of variables, constants, types, and external procedures. If you were to look at a form module in a text editor, you would also see descriptions of the form and its controls, including their property settings. The code that you write in a form module is specific to the particular application to which the form belongs; it might also reference other forms or objects within that application.

Standard Modules

Standard modules (.BAS file name extension) are containers for procedures and declarations commonly accessed by other modules within the application. They can contain global (available to the whole application) or module-level declarations of variables, constants, types, external procedures, and global procedures. The code that you write in a standard module isn't necessarily tied to a particular application; if you're careful not to reference forms or controls by name, a standard module can be reused in many different applications.

Class Modules

Class modules (.CLS file name extension) are the foundation of object-oriented programming in Visual Basic. You can write code in class modules to create new objects. These new objects can include your own customized properties and methods. Actually, forms are just class modules that can have controls placed on them and can display form windows.

For More Information For information about writing code in class modules, see Chapter 9, "Programming with Objects."

> **Note** The Professional and Enterprise editions of Visual Basic also include ActiveX Documents, ActiveX Designers, and User Controls. These introduce new types of modules with different file name extensions. From the standpoint of writing code, these modules should be considered the same as form modules.

Using the Code Editor

The Visual Basic Code Editor is a window where you write most of your code. It is like a highly specialized word processor with a number of features that make writing Visual Basic code a lot easier. The Code Editor window is shown in Figure 5.4.

Figure 5.4 The Code Editor window

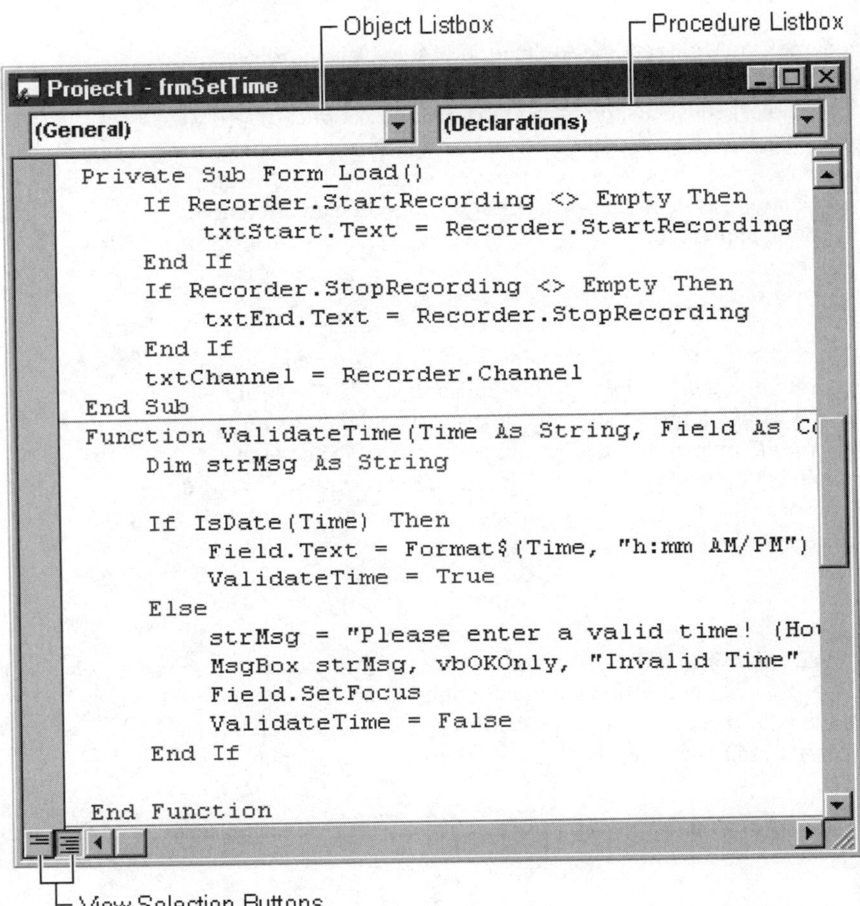

Because you work with Visual Basic code in modules, a separate Code Editor window is opened for each module you select from the Project Explorer. Code within each module is subdivided into separate sections for each object contained in the module. Switching between sections is accomplished using the Object Listbox. In a form module, the list includes a general section, a section for the form itself, and a section for each control contained on the form. For a class module, the list includes a general section and a class section; for a standard module only a general section is shown.

Each section of code can contain several different procedures, accessed using the Procedure Listbox. The procedure list for a form module contains a separate section for each event procedure for the form or control. For example, the procedure list for a Label control includes sections for the Change, Click, and DblClick events, among others. Class modules list only the event procedures for the class itself — Initialize and Terminate. Standard modules don't list any event procedures, because a standard module doesn't support events.

The procedure list for a general section of a module contains a single selection — the Declarations section, where you place module-level variable, constant, and DLL declarations. As you add Sub or Function procedures to a module, those procedures are added in the Procedure Listbox below the Declarations section.

Two different views of your code are available in the Code Editor window. You can choose to view a single procedure at a time, or to view all of the procedures in the module with each procedure separated from the next by a line (as shown in Figure 5.4). To switch between the two views, use the View Selection buttons in the lower left-hand corner of the editor window.

Automatic Code Completion

Visual Basic makes writing code much easier with features that can automatically fill in statements, properties, and arguments for you. As you enter code, the editor displays lists of appropriate choices, statement or function prototypes, or values. Options for enabling or disabling these and other code settings are available on the Editor tab of the Options dialog, accessed through the Options command on the Tools menu.

When you enter the name of a control in your code, the Auto List Members feature presents a drop-down list of properties available for that control (Figure 5.5). Type in the first few letters of the property name and the name will be selected from the list; the TAB key will complete the typing for you. This option is also helpful when you aren't sure which properties are available for a given control. Even if you choose to disable the Auto List Members feature, you can still access it with the CTRL+J key combination.

Figure 5.5 The Auto List Members feature

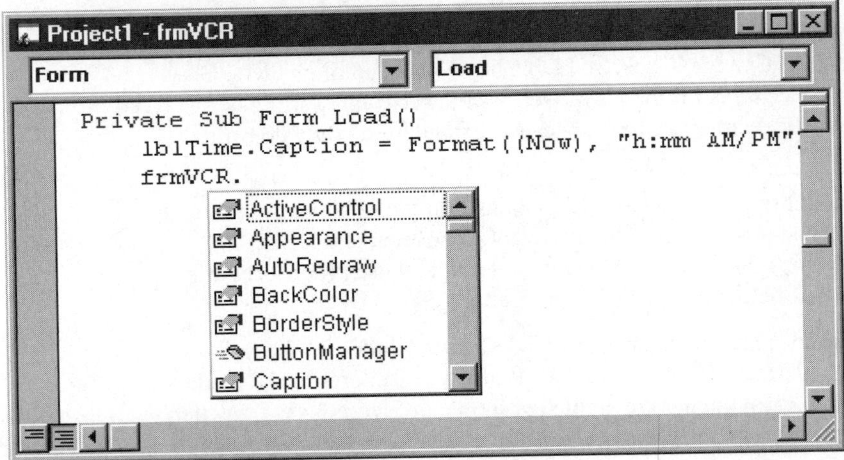

The Auto Quick Info feature displays the syntax for statements and functions (Figure 5.6). When you enter the name of a valid Visual Basic statement or function the syntax is shown immediately below the current line, with the first argument in bold. After you enter the first argument value, the second argument appears in bold. Auto Quick Info can also be accessed with the CTRL+I key combination.

Figure 5.6 Auto Quick Info

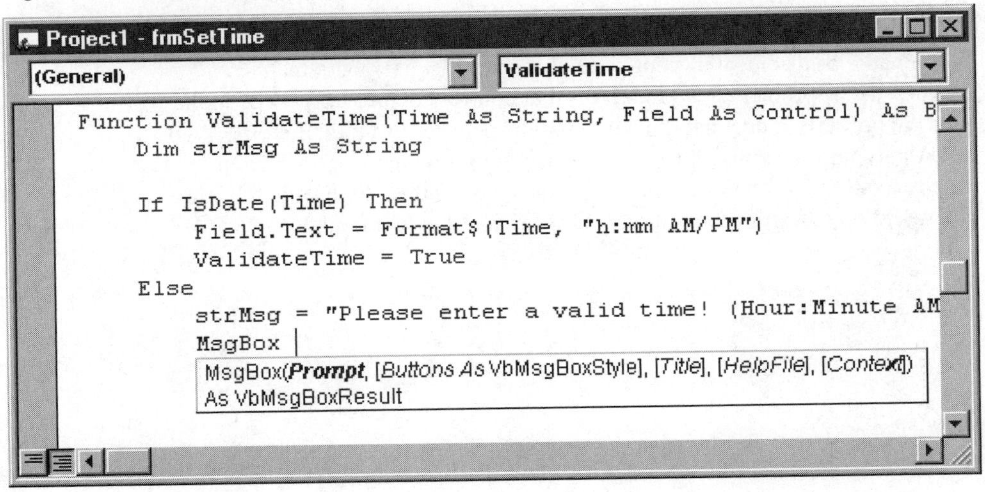

Project1 - frmSetTime

(General) | ValidateTime

```
Function ValidateTime(Time As String, Field As Control) As B
    Dim strMsg As String

    If IsDate(Time) Then
        Field.Text = Format$(Time, "h:mm AM/PM")
        ValidateTime = True
    Else
        strMsg = "Please enter a valid time! (Hour:Minute AM
        MsgBox |
```

MsgBox(***Prompt***, [*Buttons As* VbMsgBoxStyle], [*Title*], [*HelpFile*], [*Context*]) As VbMsgBoxResult

Bookmarks

Bookmarks can be used to mark lines of code in the Code Editor so that you can easily return to them later. Commands to toggle bookmarks on or off as well as to navigate existing bookmarks are available from the Edit, Bookmarks menu item, or from the Edit toolbar.

Code Basics

This section presents information on code writing mechanics, including breaking and combining lines of code, adding comments to your code, using numbers in code, and following naming conventions in Visual Basic.

Breaking a Single Statement into Multiple Lines

You can break a long statement into multiple lines in the Code window using the *line-continuation character* (a space followed by an underscore). Using this character can make your code easier to read, both online and when printed. The following code is broken into three lines with line-continuation characters (_):

```
Data1.RecordSource = _
"SELECT * FROM Titles, Publishers" _
& "WHERE Publishers.PubId = Titles.PubID" _
& "AND Publishers.State = 'CA'"
```

You can't follow a line-continuation character with a comment on the same line. There are also some limitations as to where the line-continuation character can be used.

Combining Statements on One Line

There is usually one Visual Basic statement to a line, and there is no statement terminator. However, you can place two or more statements on a line if you use a colon (:) to separate them:

```
Text1.Text = "Hello" : Red = 255 : Text1.BackColor = _
Red
```

In order to make your code more readable, however, it's better to place each statement on a separate line.

For More Information For more information, see Appendix A, "Visual Basic Specifications, Limitations, and File Formats."

Adding Comments to Your Code

As you read through the examples in this guide, you'll often come across the comment symbol ('). This symbol tells Visual Basic to ignore the words that follow it. Such words are remarks placed in the code for the benefit of the developer, and other programmers who might examine the code later. For example:

```
' This is a comment beginning at the left edge of the
' screen.
Text1.Text = "Hi!"     ' Place friendly greeting in text
                       ' box.
```

Comments can follow a statement on the same line or can occupy an entire line. Both are illustrated in the preceding code. Remember that comments can't follow a line-continuation character on the same line.

> **Note** You can add or remove comment symbols for a block of code by selecting two or more lines of code and choosing the Comment Block or Uncomment Block buttons on the Edit toolbar.

Understanding Numbering Systems

Most numbers in this documentation are decimal (base 10). But occasionally it's convenient to use hexadecimal numbers (base 16) or octal numbers (base 8). Visual Basic represents numbers in hexadecimal with the prefix &H and in octal with &O. The following table shows the same numbers in decimal, octal, and hexadecimal.

Decimal	Octal	Hexadecimal
9	&O11	&H9
15	&O17	&HF
16	&O20	&H10
20	&O24	&H14
255	&O377	&HFF

You generally don't have to learn the hexadecimal or octal number system yourself because the computer can work with numbers entered in any system. However, some number systems lend themselves to certain tasks, such as using hexadecimals to set the screen and control colors.

Naming Conventions in Visual Basic

While you are writing Visual Basic code, you declare and name many elements (Sub and Function procedures, variables, constants, and so on). The names of the procedures, variables, and constants that you declare in your Visual Basic code must follow these guidelines:

- They must begin with a letter.
- They can't contain embedded periods or type-declaration characters (special characters that specify a data type.
- They can be no longer than 255 characters. The names of controls, forms, classes, and modules must not exceed 40 characters.
- They can't be the same as restricted keywords.

A *restricted keyword* is a word that Visual Basic uses as part of its language. This includes predefined statements (such as If and Loop), functions (such as Len and Abs), and operators (such as Or and Mod).

For More Information For a complete list of keywords, see the *Microsoft Visual Basic 6.0 Language Reference* volume of the *Microsoft Visual Basic 6.0 Reference Library.*

Your forms and controls can have the same name as a restricted keyword. For example, you can have a control named Loop. In your code you cannot refer to that control in the usual way, however, because Visual Basic assumes you mean the Loop keyword. For example, this code causes an error:

```
Loop.Visible = True         ' Causes an error.
```

To refer to a form or control that has the same name as a restricted keyword, you must either qualify it or surround it with square brackets: [ ]. For example, this code does not cause an error:

```
MyForm.Loop.Visible = True ' Qualified with the form
                           ' name.
[Loop].Visible = True      ' Square brackets also
                           ' work.
```

You can use square brackets in this way when referring to forms and controls, but not when declaring a variable or defining a procedure with the same name as a restricted keyword. Square brackets can also be used to force Visual Basic to accept names provided by other type libraries that conflict with restricted keywords.

> **Note** Because typing square brackets can get tedious, you might want to refrain from using restricted keywords as the name of forms and controls. However, you can use this technique if a future version of Visual Basic defines a new keyword that conflicts with an existing form or control name when you update your code to work with the new version.

Introduction to Variables, Constants, and Data Types

You often need to store values temporarily when performing calculations with Visual Basic. For example, you might want to calculate several values, compare them, and perform different operations on them, depending on the result of the comparison. You need to retain the values if you want to compare them, but you don't need to store them in a property.

Visual Basic, like most programming languages, uses *variables* for storing values. Variables have a name (the word you use to refer to the value the variable contains) and a *data type* (which determines the kind of data the variable can store). *Arrays* can be used to store indexed collections of related variables.

Constants also store values, but as the name implies, those values remain constant throughout the execution of an application. Using constants can make your code more readable by providing meaningful names instead of numbers. There are a number of built-in constants in Visual Basic, but you can also create your own.

Data types control the internal storage of data in Visual Basic. By default, Visual Basic uses the Variant data type. There are a number of other available data types that allow you to optimize your code for speed and size when you don't need the flexibility that Variant provides.

Variables

In Visual Basic, you use variables to temporarily store values during the execution of an application. Variables have a name (the word you use to refer to the value the variable contains) and a data type (which determines the kind of data the variable can store).

You can think of a variable as a placeholder in memory for an unknown value. For example, imagine you are creating a program for a fruit stand to track the sales of apples. You don't know the price of an apple or the quantity sold until the sale actually occurs. You can use two variables to hold the unknown values — let's name them ApplePrice and ApplesSold. Each time the program is run, the user supplies the values for the two variables. To calculate the total sales and display it in a Textbox named txtSales, your code would look like this:

```
txtSales.txt = ApplePrice * ApplesSold
```

The expression returns a different total each time, depending on what values the user provides. The variables allow you to make a calculation without having to know in advance what the actual inputs are.

In this example, the data type of ApplePrice is Currency; the data type of ApplesSold is an integer. Variables can represent many other values as well: text values, dates, various numeric types, even objects.

Storing and Retrieving Data in Variables

You use assignment statements to perform calculations and assign the result to a variable:

```
ApplesSold = 10    ' The value 10 is passed to the
                   ' variable.
ApplesSold = ApplesSold + 1 ' The variable is
                            ' incremented.
```

Note that the equal sign in this example is an assignment operator, not an equality operator; the value (10) is being assigned to the variable (ApplesSold).

Declaring Variables

To declare a variable is to tell the program about it in advance. You declare a variable with the Dim statement, supplying a name for the variable:

Dim *variablename* [**As** *type*]

Variables declared with the Dim statement within a procedure exist only as long as the procedure is executing. When the procedure finishes, the value of the variable disappears. In addition, the value of a variable in a procedure is *local* to that procedure — that is, you can't access a variable in one procedure from another procedure. These characteristics allow you to use the same variable names in different procedures without worrying about conflicts or accidental changes.

A variable name:

- Must begin with a letter.
- Can't contain an embedded period or embedded type-declaration character.
- Must not exceed 255 characters.
- Must be unique within the same *scope,* which is the range from which the variable can be referenced — a procedure, a form, and so on.

The optional As *type* clause in the Dim statement allows you to define the data type or object type of the variable you are declaring. Data types define the type of information the variable stores. Some examples of data types include String, Integer, and Currency. Variables can also contain objects from Visual Basic or other applications. Examples of Visual Basic object types, or classes, include Object, Form1, and TextBox.

For More Information For more information on objects see Chapter 9, "Programming with Objects," and Chapter 10, "Programming with Components." Data types are discussed in detail in the section, "Data Types," later in this chapter.

There are other ways to declare variables:

- Declaring a variable in the Declarations section of a form, standard, or class module, rather than within a procedure, makes the variable available to all the procedures in the module.
- Declaring a variable using the Public keyword makes it available throughout your application.
- Declaring a local variable using the Static keyword preserves its value even when a procedure ends.

Implicit Declaration

You don't have to declare a variable before using it. For example, you could write a function where you don't need to declare `TempVal` before using it:

```
Function SafeSqr(num)
   TempVal = Abs(num)
   SafeSqr = Sqr(TempVal)
End Function
```

Visual Basic automatically creates a variable with that name, which you can use as if you had explicitly declared it. While this is convenient, it can lead to subtle errors in your code if you misspell a variable name. For example, suppose that this was the function you wrote:

```
Function SafeSqr(num)
   TempVal = Abs(num)
   SafeSqr = Sqr(TemVal)
End Function
```

At first glance, this looks the same. But because the `TempVal` variable was misspelled on the next-to-last line, this function will always return zero. When Visual Basic encounters a new name, it can't determine whether you actually meant to implicitly declare a new variable or you just misspelled an existing variable name, so it creates a new variable with that name.

Explicit Declaration

To avoid the problem of misnaming variables, you can stipulate that Visual Basic always warn you whenever it encounters a name not declared explicitly as a variable.

To explicitly declare variables

- Place this statement in the Declarations section of a class, form, or standard module:

  ```
  Option Explicit
  ```

  – or –

  From the **Tools** menu, choose **Options**, click the **Editor** tab and check the **Require Variable Declaration** option. This automatically inserts the Option Explicit statement in any new modules, but not in modules already created; therefore, you must manually add Option Explicit to any existing modules within a project.

Had this statement been in effect for the form or standard module containing the SafeSqr function, Visual Basic would have recognized `TempVal` and `TemVal` as undeclared variables and generated errors for both of them. You could then explicitly declare `TempVal`:

```
Function SafeSqr(num)
   Dim TempVal
   TempVal = Abs(num)
   SafeSqr = Sqr(TemVal)
End Function
```

Now you'd understand the problem immediately because Visual Basic would display an error message for the incorrectly spelled `TemVal`. Because the Option Explicit statement helps you catch these kinds of errors, it's a good idea to use it with all your code.

> **Note** The Option Explicit statement operates on a per-module basis; it must be placed in the Declarations section of every form, standard, and class module for which you want Visual Basic to enforce explicit variable declarations. If you select Require Variable Declaration, Visual Basic inserts Option Explicit in all subsequent form, standard, and class modules, but does not add it to existing code. You must manually add Option Explicit to any existing modules within a project.

Understanding the Scope of Variables

The scope of a variable defines which parts of your code are aware of its existence. When you declare a variable within a procedure, only code within that procedure can access or change the value of that variable; it has a scope that is local to that procedure. Sometimes, however, you need to use a variable with a broader scope, such as one whose value is available to all the procedures within the same module, or even to all the procedures in your entire application. Visual Basic allows you to specify the scope of a variable when you declare it.

Scoping Variables

Depending on how it is declared, a variable is scoped as either a procedure-level (local) or module-level variable.

Scope	Private	Public
Procedure-level	Variables are private to the procedure in which they appear.	Not applicable. You cannot declare public variables within a procedure.
Module-level	Variables are private to the module in which they appear.	Variables are available to all modules.

Variables Used Within a Procedure

Procedure-level variables are recognized only in the procedure in which they're declared. These are also known as local variables. You declare them with the Dim or Static keywords. For example:

```
Dim intTemp As Integer
```

– or –

```
Static intPermanent As Integer
```

Values in local variables declared with Static exist the entire time your application is running while variables declared with Dim exist only as long as the procedure is executing.

Local variables are a good choice for any kind of temporary calculation. For example, you can create a dozen different procedures containing a variable called `intTemp`. As long as each `intTemp` is declared as a local variable, each procedure recognizes only its own version of `intTemp`. Any one procedure can alter the value in its local `intTemp` without affecting `intTemp` variables in other procedures.

Variables Used Within a Module

By default, a module-level variable is available to all the procedures in that module, but not to code in other modules. You create module-level variables by declaring them with the Private keyword in the Declarations section at the top of the module. For example:

```
Private intTemp As Integer
```

At the module level, there is no difference between Private and Dim, but Private is preferred because it readily contrasts with Public and makes your code easier to understand.

Variables Used by All Modules

To make a module-level variable available to other modules, use the Public keyword to declare the variable. The values in public variables are available to all procedures in your application. Like all module-level variables, public variables are declared in the Declarations section at the top of the module. For example:

```
Public intTemp As Integer
```

> **Note** You can't declare public variables within a procedure, only within the Declarations section of a module.

For More Information For additional information about variables, see "Advanced Variable Topics."

Advanced Variable Topics

Using Multiple Variables with the Same Name

If public variables in different modules share the same name, it's possible to differentiate between them in code by referring to both the module and variable names. For example, if there is a public Integer variable `intX` declared in both Form1 and in Module1, you can refer to them as `Module1.intX` and `Form1.intX` to get the correct values.

To see how this works, insert two standard modules in a new project and draw three command buttons on a form.

One variable, `intX`, is declared in the first standard module, Module1. The Test procedure sets its value:

```
Public intX As Integer     ' Declare Module1's intX.
Sub Test()
   ' Set the value for the intX variable in Module1.
   intX = 1
End Sub
```

The second variable, which has the same name, `intX`, is declared in the second standard module, Module2. Again, a procedure named Test sets its value:

```
Public intX As Integer     ' Declare Module2's intX.
Sub Test()
   ' Set the value for the intX variable in Module2.
   intX = 2
End Sub
```

The third intX variable is declared in the form module. And again, a procedure named Test sets its value.

```
Public intX As Integer   ' Declare the form's intX
                         ' variable.

Sub Test()
   ' Set the value for the intX variable in the form.
   intX = 3
End Sub
```

Each of the three command buttons' Click event procedures calls the appropriate Test procedure and uses MsgBox to display the values of the three variables.

```
Private Sub Command1_Click()
   Module1.Test            ' Calls Test in Module1.
   MsgBox Module1.intX     ' Displays Module1's intX.
End Sub

Private Sub Command2_Click()
   Module2.Test            ' Calls Test in Module2.
   MsgBox Module2.intX     ' Displays Module2's intX.
End Sub

Private Sub Command3_Click()
   Test                    ' Calls Test in Form1.
   MsgBox intX             ' Displays Form1's intX.
End Sub
```

Run the application and click each of the three command buttons. You'll see the separate references to the three public variables. Notice in the third command button's Click event procedure, you don't need to specify Form1.Test when calling the form's Test procedure, or Form1.intX when calling the value of the form's Integer variable. If there are multiple procedures and variables with the same name, Visual Basic takes the value of the more local variable, which in this case, is the Form1 variable.

Public vs. Local Variables

You can also have a variable with the same name at a different scope. For example, you could have a public variable named Temp and then, within a procedure, declare a local variable named Temp. References to the name Temp within the procedure would access the local variable; references to Temp outside the procedure would access the public variable. The module-level variable can be accessed from within the procedure by qualifying the variable with the module name.

```
Public Temp As Integer
Sub Test()
   Dim Temp As Integer
   Temp = 2               ' Temp has a value of 2.
   MsgBox Form1.Temp      ' Form1.Temp has a value of 1.
End Sub
```

```
Private Sub Form_Load()
   Temp = 1              ' Set Form1.Temp to 1.
End Sub
Private Sub Command1_Click()
   Test
End Sub
```

In general, when variables have the same name but different scope, the more local variable always *shadows* (that is, it is accessed in preference to) less local variables. So if you also had a procedure-level variable named `Temp`, it would shadow the public variable `Temp` within that module.

Shadowing Form Properties and Controls

Due to the effect of shadowing, form properties, controls, constants, and procedures are treated as module-level variables in the form module. It is not legal to have a form property or control with the same name as a module-level variable, constant, user-defined type, or procedure because both are in the same scope.

Within the form module, local variables with the same names as controls on the form shadow the controls. You must qualify the control with a reference to the form or the Me keyword to set or get its value or any of its properties. For example:

```
Private Sub Form_Click ()
Dim Text1, BackColor
' Assume there is also a control on the form called
' Text1.
   Text1 = "Variable"    ' Variable shadows control.
   Me.Text1 = "Control"  ' Must qualify with Me to get
                         ' control.
   Text1.Top = 0         ' This causes an error!
   Me.Text1.Top = 0      ' Must qualify with Me to get
                         ' control.
   BackColor = 0         ' Variable shadows property.
   Me.BackColor = 0      ' Must qualify with Me to get
                         ' form property.
End Sub
```

Using Variables and Procedures with the Same Name

The names of your private module-level and public module-level variables can also conflict with the names of your procedures. A variable in the module cannot have the same name as any procedures or types defined in the module. It can, however, have the same name as public procedures, types, or variables defined in other modules. In this case, when the variable is accessed from another module, it must be qualified with the module name.

While the shadowing rules described above are not complex, shadowing can be confusing and lead to subtle bugs in your code; it is good programming practice to keep the names of your variables distinct from each other. In form modules, try to use variables names that are different from names of controls on those forms.

Static Variables

In addition to scope, variables have a *lifetime*, the period of time during which they retain their value. The values in module-level and public variables are preserved for the lifetime of your application. However, local variables declared with Dim exist only while the procedure in which they are declared is executing. Usually, when a procedure is finished executing, the values of its local variables are not preserved and the memory used by the local variables is reclaimed. The next time the procedure is executed, all its local variables are reinitialized.

However, you can preserve the value of a local variable by making the variable *static*. Use the Static keyword to declare one or more variables inside a procedure, exactly as you would with the Dim statement:

```
Static Depth
```

For example, the following function calculates a running total by adding a new value to the total of previous values stored in the static variable `Accumulate`:

```
Function RunningTotal(num)
   Static ApplesSold
   ApplesSold = ApplesSold + num
   RunningTotal = ApplesSold
End Function
```

If `ApplesSold` was declared with Dim instead of Static, the previous accumulated values would not be preserved across calls to the function, and the function would simply return the same value with which it was called.

You can produce the same result by declaring `ApplesSold` in the Declarations section of the module, making it a module-level variable. Once you change the scope of a variable this way, however, the procedure no longer has exclusive access to it. Because other procedures can access and change the value of the variable, the running totals might be unreliable and the code would be more difficult to maintain.

Declaring All Local Variables as Static

To make all local variables in a procedure static, place the Static keyword at the beginning of a procedure heading. For example:

```
Static Function RunningTotal(num)
```

This makes all the local variables in the procedure static regardless of whether they are declared with Static, Dim, Private, or declared implicitly. You can place Static in front of any Sub or Function procedure heading, including event procedures and those declared as Private.

Constants

Often you'll find that your code contains constant values that reappear over and over. Or you may find that the code depends on certain numbers that are difficult to remember — numbers that, in and of themselves, have no obvious meaning.

In these cases, you can greatly improve the readability of your code — and make it easier to maintain — by using constants. A *constant* is a meaningful name that takes the place of a number or string that does not change. Although a constant somewhat resembles a variable, you can't modify a constant or assign a new value to it as you can to a variable. There are two sources for constants:

- *Intrinsic* or *system-defined* constants are provided by applications and controls. Visual Basic constants are listed in the Visual Basic (VB) and Visual Basic for applications (VBA) object libraries in the Object Browser. Other applications that provide object libraries, such as Microsoft Excel and Microsoft Project, also provide a list of constants you can use with their objects, methods, and properties. Constants are also defined in the object library for each ActiveX control. For details on using the Object Browser, see Chapter 9, "Programming with Objects."
- *Symbolic* or *user-defined* constants are declared using the Const statement. User-defined constants are described in the next section, "Creating Your Own Constants."

In Visual Basic, constant names are in a mixed-case format, with a prefix indicating the object library that defines the constant. Constants from the Visual Basic and Visual Basic for applications object libraries are prefaced with "vb" — for instance, vbTileHorizontal.

The prefixes are intended to prevent accidental collisions in cases where constants have identical names and represent different values. Even with prefixes, it's still possible that two object libraries may contain identical constants representing different values. Which constant is referenced in this case depends on which object library has the higher priority.

To be absolutely sure you avoid constant name collisions, you can qualify references to constants with the following syntax:

[*libname.*][*modulename.*]*constname*

Libname is usually the class name of the control or library. *Modulename* is the name of the module that defines the constant. *Constname* is the name of the constant. Each of these elements is defined in the object library, and can be viewed in the Object Browser.

Creating Your Own Constants

The syntax for declaring a constant is:

[Public|Private] Const *constantname*[**As** *type*] = *expression*

The argument *constantname* is a valid symbolic name (the rules are the same as those for creating variable names), and *expression* is composed of numeric or string constants and operators; however, you can't use function calls in *expression*.

A Const statement can represent a mathematical or date/time quantity:

```
Const conPi = 3.14159265358979
Public Const conMaxPlanets As Integer = 9
Const conReleaseDate = #1/1/95#
```

The Const statement can also be used to define string constants:

```
Public Const conVersion = "07.10.A"
Const conCodeName = "Enigma"
```

You can place more than one constant declaration on a single line if you separate them with commas:

```
Public Const conPi = 3.14, conMaxPlanets = 9, _
conWorldPop = 6E+09
```

The expression on the right side of the equal sign (=) is often a number or literal string, but it can also be an expression that results in a number or string (although that expression can't contain calls to functions). You can even define constants in terms of previously defined constants:

```
Const conPi2 = conPi * 2
```

Once you define constants, you can place them in your code to make it more readable. For example:

```
Static SolarSystem(1 To conMaxPlanets)
If numPeople > conWorldPop Then Exit Sub
```

Scoping User-Defined Constants

A Const statement has scope like a variable declaration, and the same rules apply:

- To create a constant that exists only within a procedure, declare it within that procedure.
- To create a constant available to all procedures within a module, but not to any code outside that module, declare it in the Declarations section of the module.

- To create a constant available throughout the application, declare the constant in the Declarations section of a standard module, and place the Public keyword before Const. Public constants cannot be declared in a form or class module.

For More Information For more information regarding scope, see "Understanding the Scope of Variables" earlier in this chapter.

Avoiding Circular References

Because constants can be defined in terms of other constants, you must be careful not to set up a *cycle*, or circular reference between two or more constants. A cycle occurs when you have two or more public constants, each of which is defined in terms of the other.

For example:

```
' In Module 1:
Public Const conA = conB * 2    ' Available throughout
                                ' application.
' In Module 2:
Public Const conB = conA / 2    ' Available throughout
                                ' application.
```

If a cycle occurs, Visual Basic generates an error when you attempt to run your application. You cannot run your code until you resolve the circular reference. To avoid creating a cycle, restrict all your public constants to a single module or, at most, a small number of modules.

Data Types

Variables are placeholders used to store values; they have names and data types. The data type of a variable determines how the bits representing those values are stored in the computer's memory. When you declare a variable, you can also supply a data type for it. All variables have a data type that determines what kind of data they can store.

By default, if you don't supply a data type, the variable is given the Variant data type. The Variant data type is like a chameleon — it can represent many different data types in different situations. You don't have to convert between these types of data when assigning them to a Variant variable: Visual Basic automatically performs any necessary conversion.

If you know that a variable will always store data of a particular type, however, Visual Basic can handle that data more efficiently if you declare a variable of that type. For example, a variable to store a person's name is best represented as a string data type, because a name is always composed of characters.

Data types apply to other things besides variables. When you assign a value to a property, that value has a data type; arguments to functions also have data types. In fact, just about anything in Visual Basic that involves data also involves data types.

You can also declare arrays of any of the fundamental types.

For More Information For more information, see the section, "Arrays," later in this chapter. Selecting data types to improve your application's performance is discussed in Chapter 15, "Designing for Performance and Compatibility."

Declaring Variables with Data Types

Before using a non-Variant variable, you must use the Private, Public, Dim or Static statement to declare it As *type*. For example, the following statements declare an Integer, Double, String, and Currency type, respectively:

```
Private I As Integer
Dim Amt As Double
Static YourName As String
Public BillsPaid As Currency
```

A Declaration statement can combine multiple declarations, as in these statements:

```
Private I As Integer, Amt As Double
Private YourName As String, BillsPaid As Currency
Private Test, Amount, J As Integer
```

> **Note** If you do not supply a data type, the variable is given the default type. In the preceding example, the variables `Test` and `Amount` are of the Variant data type. This may surprise you if your experience with other programming languages leads you to expect all variables in the same declaration statement to have the same specified type (in this case, Integer).

Numeric Data Types

Visual Basic supplies several numeric data types — Integer, Long (long integer), Single (single-precision floating point), Double (double-precision floating point), and Currency. Using a numeric data type generally uses less storage space than a variant.

If you know that a variable will always store whole numbers (such as 12) rather than numbers with a fractional amount (such as 3.57), declare it as an Integer or Long type. Operations are faster with integers, and these types consume less memory than other data types. They are especially useful as the counter variables in For...Next loops.

For More Information To read more about control structures, see "Introduction to Control Structures" later in this chapter.

If the variable contains a fraction, declare it as a Single, Double, or Currency variable. The Currency data type supports up to four digits to the right of the decimal separator and fifteen digits to the left; it is an accurate fixed-point data type suitable for monetary calculations. Floating-point (Single and Double) numbers have much larger ranges than Currency, but can be subject to small rounding errors.

Note Floating-point values can be expressed as *mmm***E***eee* or *mmm***D***eee*, in which *mmm* is the mantissa and *eee* is the exponent (a power of 10). The highest positive value of a Single data type is 3.402823E+38, or 3.4 times 10 to the 38th power; the highest positive value of a Double data type is 1.79769313486232D+308, or about 1.8 times 10 to the 308th power. Using **D** to separate the mantissa and exponent in a numeric literal causes the value to be treated as a Double data type. Likewise, using **E** in the same fashion treats the value as a Single data type.

The Byte Data Type

If the variable contains binary data, declare it as an array of the Byte data type. (Arrays are discussed in "Arrays" later in this chapter). Using Byte variables to store binary data preserves it during format conversions. When String variables are converted between ANSI and Unicode formats, any binary data in the variable is corrupted. Visual Basic may automatically convert between ANSI and Unicode when:

- Reading from files
- Writing to files
- Calling DLLs
- Calling methods and properties on objects

All operators that work on integers work with the Byte data type except unary minus. Since Byte is an unsigned type with the range 0–255, it cannot represent a negative number. So for unary minus, Visual Basic coerces the Byte to a signed integer first.

All numeric variables can be assigned to each other and to variables of the Variant type. Visual Basic rounds off rather than truncates the fractional part of a floating-point number before assigning it to an integer.

For More Information For details on Unicode and ANSI conversions, see Chapter 16, "International Issues."

The String Data Type

If you have a variable that will always contain a string and never a numeric value, you can declare it to be of type String:

```
Private S As String
```

You can then assign strings to this variable and manipulate it using string functions:

```
S = "Database"
S = Left(S, 4)
```

By default, a string variable or argument is a *variable-length string*; the string grows or shrinks as you assign new data to it. You can also declare strings that have a fixed length. You specify a *fixed-length string* with this syntax:

String * *size*

For example, to declare a string that is always 50 characters long, use code like this:

```
Dim EmpName As String * 50
```

If you assign a string of fewer than 50 characters, `EmpName` is padded with enough trailing spaces to total 50 characters. If you assign a string that is too long for the fixed-length string, Visual Basic simply truncates the characters.

Because fixed-length strings are padded with trailing spaces, you may find the Trim and RTrim functions, which remove the spaces, useful when working with them.

Fixed-length strings in standard modules can be declared as Public or Private. In forms and class modules, fixed-length strings must be declared Private.

For More Information See "Ltrim, RTrim and Trim Functions" in the *Microsoft Visual Basic 6.0 Language Reference* volume of the *Microsoft Visual Basic 6.0 Reference Library*.

Exchanging Strings and Numbers

You can assign a string to a numeric variable if the string represents a numeric value. It's also possible to assign a numeric value to a string variable. For example, place a command button, text box, and list box on a form. Enter the following code in the command button's Click event. Run the application, and click the command button.

```
Private Sub Command1_Click()
   Dim intX As Integer
   Dim strY As String
   strY = "100.23"
   intX = strY     ' Passes the string to a numeric
                   ' variable.
   List1.AddItem Cos(strY) ' Adds cosine of number in
                           ' the string to the listbox.
   strY = Cos(strY)        ' Passes cosine to the
                           ' string variable.
   Text1.Text = strY       ' String variable prints in
                           ' the text box.
End Sub
```

Visual Basic will automatically coerce the variables to the appropriate data type. You should use caution when exchanging strings and numbers; passing a non-numeric value in the string will cause a run-time error to occur.

The Boolean Data Type

If you have a variable that will contain simple true/false, yes/no, or on/off information, you can declare it to be of type Boolean. The default value of Boolean is False. In the following example, `blnRunning` is a Boolean variable which stores a simple yes/no setting.

```
Dim blnRunning As Boolean
   ' Check to see if the tape is running.
   If Recorder.Direction = 1 Then
   blnRunning = True
End if
```

The Date Data Type

Date and time values can be contained both in the specific Date data type and in Variant variables. The same general characteristics apply to dates in both types.

For More Information See the section, "Date/Time Values Stored in Variants," in "Advanced Variant Topics," later in this chapter.

When other numeric data types are converted to Date, values to the left of the decimal represent date information, while values to the right of the decimal represent time. Midnight is 0, and midday is 0.5. Negative whole numbers represent dates before December 30, 1899.

The Object Data Type

Object variables are stored as 32-bit (4-byte) addresses that refer to objects within an application or within some other application. A variable declared as Object is one that can subsequently be assigned (using the Set statement) to refer to any actual object recognized by the application.

```
Dim objDb As Object
Set objDb = OpenDatabase("c:\Vb5\Biblio.mdb")
```

When declaring object variables, try to use specific classes (such as `TextBox` instead of `Control` or, in the preceding case, `Database` instead of `Object`) rather than the generic Object. Visual Basic can resolve references to the properties and methods of objects with specific types before you run an application. This allows the application to perform faster at run time. Specific classes are listed in the Object Browser.

When working with other applications' objects, instead of using a Variant or the generic Object, declare objects as they are listed in the Classes list in the Object Browser. This ensures that Visual Basic recognizes the specific type of object you're referencing, allowing the reference to be resolved at run time.

For More Information For more information on creating and assigning objects and object variables, see "Creating Objects" later in this chapter.

Converting Data Types

Visual Basic provides several conversion functions you can use to convert values into a specific data type. To convert a value to Currency, for example, you use the CCur function:

```
PayPerWeek = CCur(hours * hourlyPay)
```

Conversion function	Converts an expression to
Cbool	Boolean
Cbyte	Byte
Ccur	Currency
Cdate	Date
CDbl	Double
Cint	Integer
CLng	Long
CSng	Single
CStr	String
Cvar	Variant
CVErr	Error

Note Values passed to a conversion function must be valid for the destination data type or an error occurs. For example, if you attempt to convert a Long to an Integer, the Long must be within the valid range for the Integer data type.

For More Information See the *Microsoft Visual Basic 6.0 Language Reference* for a specific conversion function.

The Variant Data Type

A Variant variable is capable of storing all system-defined types of data. You don't have to convert between these types of data if you assign them to a Variant variable; Visual Basic automatically performs any necessary conversion. For example:

```
Dim SomeValue       ' Variant by default.
SomeValue = "17"    ' SomeValue contains "17" (a two-
                    ' character string).
SomeValue = SomeValue - 15   ' SomeValue now contains
                             ' the numeric value 2.
SomeValue = "U" & SomeValue ' SomeValue now contains
                     ' "U2" (a two- character string).
```

While you can perform operations on Variant variables without much concern for the kind of data they contain, there are some traps you must avoid.

- If you perform arithmetic operations or functions on a Variant, the Variant must contain something that is a number. For details, see the section, "Numeric Values Stored in Variants," in "Advanced Variant Topics," later in this chapter.
- If you are concatenating strings, use the & operator instead of the + operator. For details, see the section, "Strings Stored in Variants," in "Advanced Variant Topics," later in this chapter.

In addition to being able to act like the other standard data types, Variants can also contain three special values: Empty, Null, and Error.

The Empty Value

Sometimes you need to know if a value has ever been assigned to a created variable. A Variant variable has the Empty value before it is assigned a value. The Empty value is a special value different from 0, a zero-length string (""), or the Null value. You can test for the Empty value with the IsEmpty function:

```
If IsEmpty(Z) Then Z = 0
```

When a Variant contains the Empty value, you can use it in expressions; it is treated as either 0 or a zero-length string, depending on the expression.

The Empty value disappears as soon as any value (including 0, a zero-length string, or Null) is assigned to a Variant variable. You can set a Variant variable back to Empty by assigning the keyword Empty to the Variant.

The Null Value

The Variant data type can contain another special value: Null. Null is commonly used in database applications to indicate unknown or missing data. Because of the way it is used in databases, Null has some unique characteristics:

- Expressions involving Null always result in Null. Thus, Null is said to "propagate" through expressions; if any part of the expression evaluates to Null, the entire expression evaluates to Null.
- Passing Null, a Variant containing Null, or an expression that evaluates to Null as an argument to most functions causes the function to return Null.
- Null values propagate through intrinsic functions that return Variant data types.

You can also assign Null with the Null keyword:

```
Z = Null
```

You can use the IsNull function to test if a Variant variable contains Null:

```
If IsNull(X) And IsNull(Y) Then
   Z = Null
Else
   Z = 0
End If
```

If you assign Null to a variable of any type other than Variant, a trappable error occurs. Assigning Null to a Variant variable doesn't cause an error, and Null will propagate through expressions involving Variant variables (though Null does not propagate through certain functions). You can return Null from any Function procedure with a Variant return value.

Variables are not set to Null unless you explicitly assign Null to them, so if you don't use Null in your application, you don't have to write code that tests for and handles it.

For More Information For information on how to use Null in expressions, see "Null" in the *Microsoft Visual Basic 6.0 Language Reference*.

The Error Value

In a Variant, Error is a special value used to indicate that an error condition has occurred in a procedure. However, unlike for other kinds of errors, normal application-level error handling does not occur. This allows you, or the application itself, to take some alternative based on the error value. Error values are created by converting real numbers to error values using the CVErr function.

For More Information For information on how to use the Error value in expressions, see "CVErr Function" in the *Microsoft Visual Basic 6.0 Language Reference*. For information on error handling, see Chapter 13, "Debugging Your Code and Handling Errors." For additional information about the Variant data type, see "Advanced Variant Topics," below.

Advanced Variant Topics

Internal Representation of Values in Variants

Variant variables maintain an internal representation of the values that they store. This representation determines how Visual Basic treats these values when performing comparisons and other operations. When you assign a value to a Variant variable, Visual Basic uses the most compact representation that accurately records the value. Later operations may cause Visual Basic to change the representation it is using for a particular variable. (A Variant variable is not a variable with no type; rather, it is a variable that can freely change its type.) These internal representations correspond to the explicit data types discussed in "Data Types" earlier in this chapter.

Note A variant always takes up 16 bytes, no matter what you store in it. Objects, strings, and arrays are not physically stored in the Variant; in these cases, four bytes of the Variant are used to hold either an object reference, or a pointer to the string or array. The actual data are stored elsewhere.

Most of the time, you don't have to be concerned with what internal representation Visual Basic is using for a particular variable; Visual Basic handles conversions automatically. If you want to know what value Visual Basic is using, however, you can use the VarType function.

For example, if you store values with decimal fractions in a Variant variable, Visual Basic always uses the Double internal representation. If you know that your application does not need the high accuracy (and slower speed) that a Double value supplies, you can speed your calculations by converting the values to Single, or even to Currency:

```
If VarType(X) = 5 Then X = CSng(X)' Convert to Single.
```

With an array variable, the value of VarType is the sum of the array and data type return values. For example, this array contains Double values:

```
Private Sub Form_Click()
   Dim dblSample(2) As Double
   MsgBox VarType(dblSample)
End Sub
```

Future versions of Visual Basic may add additional Variant representations, so any code you write that makes decisions based on the return value of the VarType function should gracefully handle return values that are not currently defined.

For More Information For information about the VarType function, see "VarType Function" in the *Microsoft Visual Basic 6.0 Language Reference*. To read more about arrays, see "Arrays" later in this chapter. For details on converting data types, see "Data Types" earlier in this chapter.

Numeric Values Stored in Variants

When you store whole numbers in Variant variables, Visual Basic uses the most compact representation possible. For example, if you store a small number without a decimal fraction, the Variant uses an Integer representation for the value. If you then assign a larger number, Visual Basic will use a Long value or, if it is very large or has a fractional component, a Double value.

Sometimes you want to use a specific representation for a number. For example, you might want a Variant variable to store a numeric value as Currency to avoid round-off errors in later calculations. Visual Basic provides several conversion functions that you can use to convert values into a specific type (see "Converting Data Types" earlier in this chapter). To convert a value to Currency, for example, you use the CCur function:

```
PayPerWeek = CCur(hours * hourlyPay)
```

An error occurs if you attempt to perform a mathematical operation or function on a Variant that does not contain a number or something that can be interpreted as a number. For example, you cannot perform any arithmetic operations on the value U2 even though it contains a numeric character, because the entire value is not a valid number. Likewise, you cannot perform any calculations on the value 1040EZ; however, you can perform calculations on the values +10 or –1.7E6 because they are valid numbers. For this reason, you often want to determine if a Variant variable contains a value that can be used as a number. The IsNumeric function performs this task:

```
Do
   anyNumber = InputBox("Enter a number")
Loop Until IsNumeric(anyNumber)
MsgBox "The square root is: " & Sqr(anyNumber)
```

When Visual Basic converts a representation that is not numeric (such as a string containing a number) to a numeric value, it uses the Regional settings (specified in the Windows Control Panel) to interpret the thousands separator, decimal separator, and currency symbol.

Thus, if the country setting in the Windows Control Panel is set to United States, Canada, or Australia, these two statements would return true:

```
IsNumeric("$100")
IsNumeric("1,560.50")
```

While these two statements would return false:

```
IsNumeric("DM100")
IsNumeric("1.560,50")
```

However, the reverse would be the case — the first two would return false and the second two true — if the country setting in the Windows Control Panel was set to Germany.

If you assign a Variant containing a number to a string variable or property, Visual Basic converts the representation of the number to a string automatically. If you want to explicitly convert a number to a string, use the CStr function. You can also use the Format function to convert a number to a string that includes formatting such as currency, thousands separator, and decimal separator symbols. The Format function automatically uses the appropriate symbols according to the Regional Settings Properties dialog box in the Windows Control Panel.

For More Information See "Format Function" and topics about the conversion functions in the *Microsoft Visual Basic 6.0 Language Reference*. For information on writing code for applications that will be distributed in foreign markets, see Chapter 16, "International Issues."

Strings Stored in Variants

Generally, storing and using strings in Variant variables poses few problems. As mentioned earlier, however, sometimes the result of the + operator can be ambiguous when used with two Variant values. If both of the Variants contain numbers, the + operator performs addition. If both of the Variants contain strings, then the + operator performs string concatenation. But if one of the values is represented as a number and the other is represented as a string, the situation becomes more complicated. Visual Basic first attempts to convert the string into a number. If the conversion is successful, the + operator adds the two values; if unsuccessful, it generates a `Type mismatch` error.

To make sure that concatenation occurs, regardless of the representation of the value in the variables, use the & operator. For example, the following code:

```
Sub Form_Click ()
   Dim X, Y
   X = "6"
   Y = "7"
   Print X + Y, X & Y
   X = 6
   Print X + Y, X & Y
End Sub
```

produces this result on the form:

```
67    67
13    67
```

> **Note** Visual Basic stores strings internally as Unicode. For more information on Unicode, see Chapter 16, "International Issues."

Date/Time Values Stored in Variants

Variant variables can also contain date/time values. Several functions return date/time values. For example, DateSerial returns the number of days left in the year:

```
Private Sub Form_Click ()
   Dim rightnow, daysleft, hoursleft, minutesleft
   rightnow = Now ' Now returns the current date/time.
   daysleft = Int(DateSerial(Year(rightnow) _
   + 1, 1, 1) - rightnow)
   hoursleft = 24 - Hour(rightnow)
   minutesleft = 60 - Minute(rightnow)
   Print daysleft & " days left in the year."
   Print hoursleft & " hours left in the day."
   Print minutesleft & " minutes left in the hour."
End Sub
```

You can also perform math on date/time values. Adding or subtracting integers adds or subtracts days; adding or subtracting fractions adds or subtracts time. Therefore, adding 20 adds 20 days, while subtracting 1/24 subtracts one hour.

The range for dates stored in Variant variables is January 1, 0100, to December 31, 9999. Calculations on dates don't take into account the calendar revisions prior to the switch to the Gregorian calendar, however, so calculations producing date values earlier than the year in which the Gregorian calendar was adopted (1752 in Britain and its colonies at that time; earlier or later in other countries) will be incorrect.

You can use date/time literals in your code by enclosing them with the number sign (#), in the same way you enclose string literals with double quotation marks (""). For example, you can compare a Variant containing a date/time value with a literal date:

```
If SomeDate > #3/6/93# Then
```

Similarly, you can compare a date/time value with a complete date/time literal:

```
If SomeDate > #3/6/93 1:20pm# Then
```

If you do not include a time in a date/time literal, Visual Basic sets the time part of the value to midnight (the start of the day). If you do not include a date in a date/time literal, Visual Basic sets the date part of the value to December 30, 1899.

Visual Basic accepts a wide variety of date and time formats in literals. These are all valid date/time values:

```
SomeDate = #3-6-93 13:20#
SomeDate = #March 27, 1993 1:20am#
SomeDate = #Apr-2-93#
SomeDate = #4 April 1993#
```

For More Information For information on handling dates in international formats, see Chapter 16, "International Issues."

In the same way that you can use the IsNumeric function to determine if a Variant variable contains a value that can be considered a valid numeric value, you can use the IsDate function to determine if a Variant contains a value that can be considered a valid date/time value. You can then use the CDate function to convert the value into a date/time value.

For example, the following code tests the Text property of a text box with IsDate. If the property contains text that can be considered a valid date, Visual Basic converts the text into a date and computes the days left until the end of the year:

```
Dim SomeDate, daysleft
If IsDate(Text1.Text) Then
   SomeDate = CDate(Text1.Text)
   daysleft = DateSerial(Year(SomeDate) + _
   1, 1, 1) - SomeDate
   Text2.Text = daysleft & " days left in the year."
Else
   MsgBox Text1.Text & " is not a valid date."
End If
```

For More Information For information about the various date/time functions, see "Date Function" in the *Microsoft Visual Basic 6.0 Language Reference*.

Objects Stored in Variants

Objects can be stored in Variant variables. This can be useful when you need to gracefully handle a variety of data types, including objects. For example, all the elements in an array must have the same data type. Setting the data type of an array to Variant allows you to store objects alongside other data types in an array.

Arrays

If you have programmed in other languages, you're probably familiar with the concept of arrays. Arrays allow you to refer to a series of variables by the same name and to use a number (an index) to tell them apart. This helps you create smaller and simpler code in many situations, because you can set up loops that deal efficiently with any number of cases by using the index number. Arrays have both upper and lower bounds, and the elements of the array are contiguous within those bounds. Because Visual Basic allocates space for each index number, avoid declaring an array larger than necessary.

> **Note** The arrays discussed in this section are arrays of variables, declared in code. They are different from the control arrays you specify by setting the Index property of controls at design time. Arrays of variables are always contiguous; unlike control arrays, you cannot load and unload elements from the middle of the array.

All the elements in an array have the same data type. Of course, when the data type is Variant, the individual elements may contain different kinds of data (objects, strings, numbers, and so on). You can declare an array of any of the fundamental data types, including user-defined types (described in the section, "Creating Your Own Data Types," in Chapter 8, "More About Programming") and object variables (described in Chapter 9, "Programming with Objects").

In Visual Basic there are two types of arrays: a *fixed-size array* which always remains the same size, and a *dynamic array* whose size can change at run-time. Dynamic arrays are discussed in more detail in the section "Dynamic Arrays" later in this chapter.

Declaring Fixed-Size Arrays

There are three ways to declare a fixed-size array, depending on the scope you want the array to have:

- To create a *public array*, use the Public statement in the Declarations section of a module to declare the array.
- To create a *module-level array*, use the Private statement in the Declarations section of a module to declare the array.
- To create a *local array*, use the Private statement in a procedure to declare the array.

Setting Upper and Lower Bounds

When declaring an array, follow the array name by the upper bound in parentheses. The upper bound cannot exceed the range of a Long data type (-2,147,483,648 to 2,147,483,647). For example, these array declarations can appear in the Declarations section of a module:

```
Dim Counters(14) As Integer     ' 15 elements.
Dim Sums(20) As Double          ' 21 elements.
```

To create a public array, you simply use Public in place of Dim:

```
Public Counters(14) As Integer
Public Sums(20) As Double
```

The same declarations within a procedure use Dim:

```
Dim Counters(14) As Integer
Dim Sums(20) As Double
```

The first declaration creates an array with 15 elements, with index numbers running from 0 to 14. The second creates an array with 21 elements, with index numbers running from 0 to 20. The default lower bound is 0.

To specify a lower bound, provide it explicitly (as a Long data type) using the To keyword:

```
Dim Counters(1 To 15) As Integer
Dim Sums(100 To 120) As String
```

In the preceding declarations, the index numbers of `Counters` range from 1 to 15, and the index numbers of `Sums` range from 100 to 120.

Arrays that Contain Other Arrays

It's possible to create a Variant array, and populate it with other arrays of different data types. The following code creates two arrays, one containing integers and the other strings. It then declares a third Variant array and populates it with the integer and string arrays.

```
Private Sub Command1_Click()
   Dim intX As Integer  ' Declare counter variable.
   ' Declare and populate an integer array.
   Dim countersA(5) As Integer
      For intX = 0 To 4
         countersA(intX) = 5
      Next intX
   ' Declare and populate a string array.
      Dim countersB(5) As String
         For intX = 0 To 4
            countersB(intX) = "hello"
         Next intX
   Dim arrX(2) As Variant   ' Declare a new two-member
                            ' array.
      arrX(1) = countersA()' Populate the array with
                            ' other arrays.
      arrX(2) = countersB()
      MsgBox arrX(1)(2) ' Display a member of each
                        ' array.
      MsgBox arrX(2)(3)
End Sub
```

Multidimensional Arrays

Sometimes you need to keep track of related information in an array. For example, to keep track of each pixel on your computer screen, you need to refer to its X and Y coordinates. This can be done using a multidimensional array to store the values.

With Visual Basic, you can declare arrays of multiple dimensions. For example, the following statement declares a two-dimensional 10-by-10 array within a procedure:

```
Static MatrixA(9, 9) As Double
```

Either or both dimensions can be declared with explicit lower bounds:

```
Static MatrixA(1 To 10, 1 To 10) As Double
```

You can extend this to more than two dimensions. For example:

```
Dim MultiD(3, 1 To 10, 1 To 15)
```

This declaration creates an array that has three dimensions with sizes 4 by 10 by 15. The total number of elements is the product of these three dimensions, or 600.

> **Note** When you start adding dimensions to an array, the total storage needed by the array increases dramatically, so use multidimensional arrays with care. Be especially careful with Variant arrays, because they are larger than other data types.

Using Loops to Manipulate Arrays

You can efficiently process a multidimensional array by using nested For loops. For example, these statements initialize every element in `MatrixA` to a value based on its location in the array:

```
Dim I As Integer, J As Integer
Static MatrixA(1 To 10, 1 To 10) As Double
For I = 1 To 10
   For J = 1 To 10
      MatrixA(I, J) = I * 10 + J
   Next J
Next I
```

For More Information For information about loops, see "Loop Structures" later in this chapter.

Dynamic Arrays

Sometimes you may not know exactly how large to make an array. You may want to have the capability of changing the size of the array at run time.

A dynamic array can be resized at any time. Dynamic arrays are among the most flexible and convenient features in Visual Basic, and they help you to manage memory efficiently. For example, you can use a large array for a short time and then free up memory to the system when you're no longer using the array.

The alternative is to declare an array with the largest possible size and then ignore array elements you don't need. However, this approach, if overused, might cause the operating environment to run low on memory.

To create a dynamic array

1. Declare the array with a Public statement (if you want the array to be public) or Dim statement at the module level (if you want the array to be module level), or a Static or Dim statement in a procedure (if you want the array to be local). You declare the array as dynamic by giving it an empty dimension list.

   ```
   Dim DynArray()
   ```

2. Allocate the actual number of elements with a ReDim statement.

   ```
   ReDim DynArray(X + 1)
   ```

The ReDim statement can appear only in a procedure. Unlike the Dim and Static statements, ReDim is an executable statement — it makes the application carry out an action at run time.

The ReDim statement supports the same syntax used for fixed arrays. Each ReDim can change the number of elements, as well as the lower and upper bounds, for each dimension. However, the number of dimensions in the array cannot change.

```
ReDim DynArray(4 to 12)
```

For example, the dynamic array `Matrix1` is created by first declaring it at the module level:

```
Dim Matrix1() As Integer
```

A procedure then allocates space for the array:

```
Sub CalcValuesNow ()
   .
   .
   .
   ReDim Matrix1(19, 29)
End Sub
```

The ReDim statement shown here allocates a matrix of 20 by 30 integers (at a total size of 600 elements). Alternatively, the bounds of a dynamic array can be set using variables:

```
ReDim Matrix1(X, Y)
```

> **Note** You can assign strings to resizable arrays of bytes. An array of bytes can also be assigned to a variable-length string. Be aware that the number of bytes in a string varies among platforms. On Unicode platforms the same string contains twice as many bytes as it does on a non-Unicode platform.

Preserving the Contents of Dynamic Arrays

Each time you execute the ReDim statement, all the values currently stored in the array are lost. Visual Basic resets the values to the Empty value (for Variant arrays), to zero (for numeric arrays), to a zero-length string (for string arrays), or to Nothing (for arrays of objects).

This is useful when you want to prepare the array for new data, or when you want to shrink the size of the array to take up minimal memory. Sometimes you may want to change the size of the array without losing the data in the array. You can do this by using ReDim with the Preserve keyword. For example, you can enlarge an array by one element without losing the values of the existing elements using the UBound function to refer to the upper bound:

```
ReDim Preserve DynArray(UBound(DynArray) + 1)
```

Only the upper bound of the last dimension in a multidimensional array can be changed when you use the Preserve keyword; if you change any of the other dimensions, or the lower bound of the last dimension, a run-time error occurs. Thus, you can use code like this:

```
ReDim Preserve Matrix(10, UBound(Matrix, 2) + 1)
```

But you cannot use this code:

```
ReDim Preserve Matrix(UBound(Matrix, 1) + 1, 10)
```

For More Information For information about dynamic arrays, see "ReDim Statement" in the *Microsoft Visual Basic 6.0 Language Reference*. To learn more about object arrays, see Chapter 9, "Programming with Objects."

Introduction to Procedures

You can simplify programming tasks by breaking programs into smaller logical components. These components — called *procedures* — can then become building blocks that let you enhance and extend Visual Basic.

Procedures are useful for condensing repeated or shared tasks, such as frequently used calculations, text and control manipulation, and database operations.

There are two major benefits of programming with procedures:

- Procedures allow you to break your programs into discrete logical units, each of which you can debug more easily than an entire program without procedures.
- Procedures used in one program can act as building blocks for other programs, usually with little or no modification.

There are several types of procedures used in Visual Basic:

- Sub procedures do not return a value.
- Function procedures return a value.
- Property procedures can return and assign values, and set references to objects.

For More Information Property procedures are discussed in Chapter 9, "Programming with Objects."

Sub Procedures

A Sub procedure is a block of code that is executed in response to an event. By breaking the code in a module into Sub procedures, it becomes much easier to find or modify the code in your application.

The syntax for a Sub procedure is:

[Private|Public][Static]Sub *procedurename* (*arguments*)
statements

End Sub

Each time the procedure is called, the *statements* between Sub and End Sub are executed. Sub procedures can be placed in standard modules, class modules, and form modules. Sub procedures are by default Public in all modules, which means they can be called from anywhere in the application.

The *arguments* for a procedure are like a variable declaration, declaring values that are passed in from the calling procedure.

In Visual Basic, it's useful to distinguish between two types of Sub procedures, *general procedures* and *event procedures*.

General Procedures

A general procedure tells the application how to perform a specific task. Once a general procedure is defined, it must be specifically invoked by the application. By contrast, an event procedure remains idle until called upon to respond to events caused by the user or triggered by the system.

Why create general procedures? One reason is that several different event procedures might need the same actions performed. A good programming strategy is to put common statements in a separate procedure (a general procedure) and have your event procedures call it. This eliminates the need to duplicate code and also makes the application easier to maintain. For example, the VCR sample application uses a general procedure called by the click events for several different scroll buttons. Figure 5.7 illustrates the use of a general procedure. Code in the Click events calls the ButtonManager Sub procedure, which runs its own code, and then returns control to the Click event procedure.

Figure 5.7 How general procedures are called by event procedures

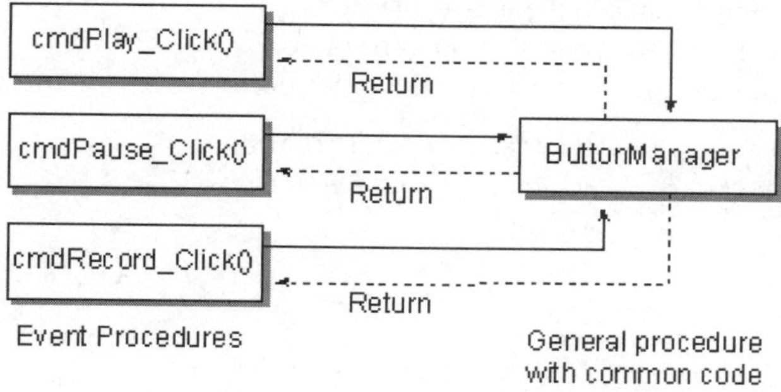

Event Procedures

When an object in Visual Basic recognizes that an event has occurred, it automatically invokes the event procedure using the name corresponding to the event. Because the name establishes an association between the object and the code, event procedures are said to be attached to forms and controls.

- An event procedure for a control combines the control's actual name (specified in the Name property), an underscore (_), and the event name. For instance, if you want a command button named cmdPlay to invoke an event procedure when it is clicked, use the procedure cmdPlay_Click.
- An event procedure for a form combines the word "Form," an underscore, and the event name. If you want a form to invoke an event procedure when it is clicked, use the procedure Form_Click. (Like controls, forms do have unique names, but they are not used in the names of event procedures.) If you are using the MDI form, the event procedure combines the word "MDIForm," an underscore, and the event name, as in MDIForm_Load.

All event procedures use the same general syntax.

Syntax for a control event	**Syntax for a form event**

Private Sub *controlname_eventname* (*arguments*)
  statements
End Sub
	Private Sub Form_*eventname* (*arguments*)
	  statements
	End Sub

Although you can write event procedures from scratch, it's easier to use the code procedures provided by Visual Basic, which automatically include the correct procedure names. You can select a template in the Code Editor window by selecting an object from the Object box and then selecting a procedure from the Procedure box.

It's also a good idea to set the Name property of your controls before you start writing event procedures for them. If you change the name of a control after attaching a procedure to it, you must also change the name of the procedure to match the new name of the control. Otherwise, Visual Basic won't be able to match the control to the procedure. When a procedure name does not match a control name, it becomes a general procedure.

For More Information Visual Basic recognizes a variety of events for each kind of form and control. For explanations of all events, see the *Microsoft Visual Basic 6.0 Language Reference*.

Function Procedures

Visual Basic includes built-in, or intrinsic functions, like Sqr, Cos or Chr. In addition, you can use the Function statement to write your own Function procedures.

The syntax for a Function procedure is:

[Private|Public][Static]Function *procedurename* (*arguments*) [**As** *type*]
statements

End Function

Like a Sub procedure, a Function procedure is a separate procedure that can take arguments, perform a series of statements, and change the value of its arguments. Unlike a Sub procedure, a Function procedure can return a value to the calling procedure. There are three differences between Sub and Function procedures:

- Generally, you call a function by including the function procedure name and arguments on the right side of a larger statement or expression (*returnvalue* = *function()*).
- Function procedures have data types, just as variables do. This determines the type of the return value. (In the absence of an As clause, the type is the default Variant type.)
- You return a value by assigning it to the *procedurename* itself. When the Function procedure returns a value, this value can then become part of a larger expression.

For example, you could write a function that calculates the third side, or hypotenuse, of a right triangle, given the values for the other two sides:

```
Function Hypotenuse (A As Integer, B As Integer) _
As String
   Hypotenuse = Sqr(A ^ 2 + B ^ 2)
End Function
```

You call a Function procedure the same way you call any of the built-in functions in Visual Basic:

```
Label1.Caption = Hypotenuse(CInt(Text1.Text), _
CInt(Text2.Text))
strX = Hypotenuse(Width, Height)
```

For More Information For additional details about the Function procedure, see "Function Statement" in the *Microsoft Visual Basic 6.0 Language Reference*. The techniques for calling all types of procedures are discussed in the section, "Calling Procedures," later in this chapter.

Working with Procedures

Creating New Procedures

To create a new general procedure

- Type a procedure heading in the Code window and press ENTER. The procedure heading can be as simple as Sub or Function followed by a name. For example, you can enter either of the following:

  ```
  Sub UpdateForm ()
  Function GetCoord ()
  ```

  Visual Basic responds by completing the template for the new procedure.

Selecting Existing Procedures

To view a procedure in the current module

- To view an existing general procedure, select "(General)" from the Object box in the Code window, and then select the procedure in the Procedure box.

  – or –

  To view an event procedure, select the appropriate object from the Object box in the Code window, and then select the event in the Procedure box.

To view a procedure in another module

1. From the **View** menu, choose **Object Browser**.
2. Select the project from the **Project/Library** box.
3. Select the module from the **Classes** list, and the procedure from the **Members of** list.
4. Choose **View Definition**.

Calling Procedures

The techniques for calling procedures vary, depending on the type of procedure, where it's located, and how it's used in your application. The following sections describe how to call Sub and Function procedures.

Calling Sub Procedures

A Sub procedure differs from a Function procedure in that a Sub procedure cannot be called by using its name within an expression. A call to a Sub is a stand-alone statement. Also, a Sub does not return a value in its name as does a function. However, like a Function, a Sub can modify the values of any variables passed to it.

There are two ways to call a Sub procedure:

```
' Both of these statements call a Sub named MyProc.
Call MyProc (FirstArgument, SecondArgument)
MyProc FirstArgument, SecondArgument
```

Note that when you use the Call syntax, arguments must be enclosed in parentheses. If you omit the Call keyword, you must also omit the parentheses around the arguments.

Calling Function Procedures

Usually, you call a function procedure you've written yourself the same way you call an intrinsic Visual Basic function like Abs; that is, by using its name in an expression:

```
' All of the following statements would call a function
' named ToDec.
Print 10 * ToDec
X = ToDec
If ToDec = 10 Then Debug.Print "Out of Range"
X = AnotherFunction(10 * ToDec)
```

It's also possible to call a function just like you would call a Sub procedure. The following statements both call the same function:

```
Call Year(Now)
Year Now
```

When you call a function this way, Visual Basic throws away the return value.

Calling Procedures in Other Modules

Public procedures in other modules can be called from anywhere in the project. You might need to specify the module that contains the procedure you're calling. The techniques for doing this vary, depending on whether the procedure is located in a form, class, or standard module.

Procedures in Forms

All calls from outside the form module must point to the form module containing the procedure. If a procedure named SomeSub is in a form module called Form1, then you can call the procedure in Form1 by using this statement:

```
Call Form1.SomeSub(arguments)
```

Procedures in Class Modules

Like calling a procedure in a form, calling a procedure in a class module requires that the call to the procedure be qualified with a variable that points to an instance of the class. For example, DemoClass is an instance of a class named Class1:

```
Dim DemoClass as New Class1
DemoClass.SomeSub
```

However, unlike a form, the class name cannot be used as the qualifier when referencing an instance of the class. The instance of the class must be first be declared as an object variable (in this case, DemoClass) and referenced by the variable name.

For More Information You can find details on object variables and class modules in Chapter 9, "Programming with Objects."

Procedures in Standard Modules

If a procedure name is unique, you don't need to include the module name in the call. A call from inside or outside the module will refer to that unique procedure. A procedure is unique if it appears only in one place.

If two or more modules contain a procedure with the same name, you may need to qualify it with the module name. A call to a common procedure from the same module runs the procedure in that module. For example, with a procedure named CommonName in Module1 and Module2, a call to CommonName from Module2 will run the CommonName procedure in Module2, not the CommonName procedure in Module1.

A call to a common procedure name from another module must specify the intended module. For example, if you want to call the CommonName procedure in Module2 from Module1, use:

```
Module2.CommonName(arguments)
```

Passing Arguments to Procedures

Usually the code in a procedure needs some information about the state of the program to do its job. This information consists of variables passed to the procedure when it is called. When a variable is passed to a procedure, it is called an *argument*.

Argument Data Types

The arguments for procedures you write have the Variant data type by default. However, you can declare other data types for arguments. For example, the following function accepts a string and an integer:

```
Function WhatsForLunch(WeekDay As String, Hour _
As Integer) As String
   ' Returns a lunch menu based on the day and time.
   If WeekDay = "Friday" then
      WhatsForLunch = "Fish"
   Else
      WhatsForLunch = "Chicken"
   End If
   If Hour > 4 Then WhatsForLunch = "Too late"
End Function
```

For More Information Details on Visual Basic data types are presented earlier in this chapter. You can also see the *Microsoft Visual Basic 6.0 Language Reference* for specific data types.

Passing Arguments by Value

Only a copy of a variable is passed when an argument is passed by value. If the procedure changes the value, the change affects only the copy and not the variable itself. Use the ByVal keyword to indicate an argument passed by value.

For example:

```
Sub PostAccounts(ByVal intAcctNum as Integer)
   .
   . ' Place statements here.
   .
End Sub
```

Passing Arguments by Reference

Passing arguments by reference gives the procedure access to the actual variable contents in its memory address location. As a result, the variable's value can be permanently changed by the procedure to which it is passed. Passing by reference is the default in Visual Basic.

If you specify a data type for an argument passed by reference, you must pass a value of that type for the argument. You can work around this by passing an expression, rather than a data type, for an argument. Visual Basic evaluates an expression and passes it as the required type if it can.

The simplest way to turn a variable into an expression is to enclose it in parentheses. For example, to pass a variable declared as an integer to a procedure expecting a string as an argument, you would do the following:

```
Sub CallingProcedure()
   Dim intX As Integer
   intX = 12 * 3
   Foo(intX)
End Sub

Sub Foo(Bar As String)
   MsgBox Bar  'The value of Bar is the string "36".
End Sub
```

Using Optional Arguments

You can specify arguments to a procedure as optional by placing the Optional keyword in the argument list. If you specify an optional argument, all subsequent arguments in the argument list must also be optional and declared with the Optional keyword. The two pieces of sample code below assume there is a form with a command button and list box.

For example, this code provides all optional arguments:

```
Dim strName As String
Dim strAddress As String

Sub ListText(Optional x As String, Optional y _
As String)
   List1.AddItem x
   List1.AddItem y
End Sub

Private Sub Command1_Click()
   strName = "yourname"
   strAddress = 12345' Both arguments are provided.
   Call ListText(strName, strAddress)
End Sub
```

This code, however, does not provide all optional arguments:

```
Dim strName As String
Dim varAddress As Variant

Sub ListText(x As String, Optional y As Variant)
   List1.AddItem x
   If Not IsMissing(y) Then
      List1.AddItem y
   End If
End Sub
```

```
Private Sub Command1_Click()
   strName = "yourname" ' Second argument is not
                        ' provided.
   Call ListText(strName)
End Sub
```

In the case where an optional argument is not provided, the argument is actually assigned as a variant with the value of Empty. The example above shows how to test for missing optional arguments using the IsMissing function.

Providing a Default for an Optional Argument

It's also possible to specify a default value for an optional argument. The following example returns a default value if the optional argument isn't passed to the function procedure:

```
Sub ListText(x As String, Optional y As _
Integer = 12345)
   List1.AddItem x
   List1.AddItem y
End Sub

Private Sub Command1_Click()
   strName = "yourname" ' Second argument is not
                        ' provided.
   Call ListText(strName)  ' Adds "yourname" and
                           ' "12345".
End Sub
```

Using an Indefinite Number of Arguments

Generally, the number of arguments in the procedure call must be the same as in the procedure specification. Using the ParamArray keyword allows you to specify that a procedure will accept an arbitrary number of arguments. This allows you to write functions like Sum:

```
Dim x As Integer
Dim y As Integer
Dim intSum As Integer

Sub Sum(ParamArray intNums())
   For Each x In intNums
      y = y + x
   Next x
   intSum = y
End Sub
```

```
Private Sub Command1_Click()
   Sum 1, 3, 5, 7, 8
   List1.AddItem intSum
End Sub
```

Creating Simpler Statements with Named Arguments

For many built-in functions, statements, and methods, Visual Basic provides the option of using *named arguments* as a shortcut for typing argument values. With named arguments, you can provide any or all of the arguments, in any order, by assigning a value to the named argument. You do this by typing the argument name plus a colon followed by an equal sign and the value (MyArgument:= "SomeValue") and placing that assignment in any sequence delimited by commas. Notice that the arguments in the following example are in the reverse order of the expected arguments:

```
Function ListText(strName As String, Optional strAddress As String)
   List1.AddItem strName
   List2.AddItem strAddress
End Sub

Private Sub Command1_Click()
   ListText strAddress:="12345", strName:="Your Name"
End Sub
```

This is especially useful if your procedures have several optional arguments that you do not always need to specify.

Determining Support for Named Arguments

To determine which functions, statements, and methods support named arguments, use the AutoQuickInfo feature in the Code window, check the Object Browser, or see the *Microsoft Visual Basic 6.0 Language Reference*. Consider the following when working with named arguments:

- Named arguments are not supported by methods on objects in the Visual Basic (VB) object library. They are supported by all language keywords in the Visual Basic for applications (VBA) object library, and by methods in the data access (DAO) object library.
- In syntax, named arguments are shown as bold and italic. All other arguments are shown in italic only.

  Important You cannot use named arguments to avoid entering required arguments. You can omit only the optional arguments. For Visual Basic (VB) and Visual Basic for applications (VBA) object libraries, the Object Browser encloses optional arguments with square brackets [ ].

Introduction to Control Structures

Control structures allow you to control the flow of your program's execution. If left unchecked by control-flow statements, a program's logic will flow through statements from left to right, and top to bottom. While some very simple programs can be written with only this unidirectional flow, and while some flow can be controlled by using operators to regulate precedence of operations, most of the power and utility of any programming language comes from its ability to change statement order with structures and loops.

Decision Structures

Visual Basic procedures can test conditions and then, depending on the results of that test, perform different operations. The decision structures that Visual Basic supports include:

- If...Then
- If...Then...Else
- Select Case

If...Then

Use an If...Then structure to execute one or more statements conditionally. You can use either a single-line syntax or a multiple-line *block* syntax:

If *condition* **Then** *statement*

If *condition* **Then**
    statements
End If

The *condition* is usually a comparison, but it can be any expression that evaluates to a numeric value. Visual Basic interprets this value as True or False; a zero numeric value is False, and any nonzero numeric value is considered True. If *condition* is True, Visual Basic executes all the *statements* following the Then keyword. You can use either single-line or multiple-line syntax to execute just one statement conditionally (these two examples are equivalent):

```
If anyDate < Now Then anyDate = Now

If anyDate < Now Then
   anyDate = Now
End If
```

Notice that the single-line form of If...Then does not use an End If statement. If you want to execute more than one line of code when *condition* is True, you must use the multiple-line block If...Then...End If syntax.

```
If anyDate < Now Then
   anyDate = Now
   Timer1.Enabled = False   ' Disable timer control.
End If
```

If...Then...Else

Use an If...Then...Else block to define several blocks of statements, one of which will execute:

If *condition1* **Then**
   [*statementblock-1*]
[**ElseIf** *condition2* **Then**
   [*statementblock-2*]] ...
[**Else**
   [*statementblock-n*]]
End If

Visual Basic first tests *condition1*. If it's False, Visual Basic proceeds to test *condition2*, and so on, until it finds a True condition. When it finds a True condition, Visual Basic executes the corresponding statement block and then executes the code following the End If. As an option, you can include an Else statement block, which Visual Basic executes if none of the conditions are True.

If...Then…ElseIf is really just a special case of If...Then...Else. Notice that you can have any number of ElseIf clauses, or none at all. You can include an Else clause regardless of whether you have ElseIf clauses.

For example, your application could perform different actions depending on which control in a menu control array was clicked:

```
Private Sub mnuCut_Click (Index As Integer)
   If Index = 0 Then          ' Cut command.
      CopyActiveControl       ' Call general procedures.
      ClearActiveControl
   ElseIf Index = 1 Then     ' Copy command.
      CopyActiveControl
   ElseIf Index = 2 Then     ' Clear command.
      ClearActiveControl
   Else                       ' Paste command.
      PasteActiveControl
   End If
End Sub
```

Notice that you can always add more ElseIf parts to your If...Then structure. However, this syntax can get tedious to write when each ElseIf compares the same expression to a different value. For this situation, you can use a Select Case decision structure.

For More Information See "If...Then...Else Statement" in the *Microsoft Visual Basic 6.0 Language Reference*.

Select Case

Visual Basic provides the Select Case structure as an alternative to If...Then...Else for selectively executing one block of statements from among multiple blocks of statements. A Select Case statement provides capability similar to the If...Then...Else statement, but it makes code more readable when there are several choices.

A Select Case structure works with a single test expression that is evaluated once, at the top of the structure. Visual Basic then compares the result of this expression with the values for each Case in the structure. If there is a match, it executes the block of statements associated with that Case:

Select Case *testexpression*
    [**Case** *expressionlist1*
        [*statementblock-1*]]
    [**Case** *expressionlist2*
        [*statementblock-2*]]
        .
        .
        .
    [**Case Else**
        [*statementblock-n*]]
End Select

Each *expressionlist* is a list of one or more values. If there is more than one value in a single list, the values are separated by commas. Each *statementblock* contains zero or more statements. If more than one Case matches the test expression, only the statement block associated with the first matching Case will execute. Visual Basic executes statements in the Case Else clause (which is optional) if none of the values in the expression lists matches the test expression.

For example, suppose you added another command to the Edit menu in the If...Then...Else example. You could add another ElseIf clause, or you could write the function with Select Case:

```
Private Sub mnuCut_Click (Index As Integer)
   Select Case Index
      Case 0                  ' Cut command.
         CopyActiveControl    ' Call general procedures.
         ClearActiveControl
      Case 1                  ' Copy command.
         CopyActiveControl
      Case 2                  ' Clear command.
         ClearActiveControl
```

```
      Case 3              ' Paste command.
         PasteActiveControl
      Case Else
         frmFind.Show     ' Show Find dialog box.
   End Select
End Sub
```

Notice that the Select Case structure evaluates an expression once at the top of the structure. In contrast, the If...Then...Else structure can evaluate a different expression for each ElseIf statement. You can replace an If...Then...Else structure with a Select Case structure only if the If statement and each ElseIf statement evaluates the same expression.

Loop Structures

Loop structures allow you to execute one or more lines of code repetitively. The loop structures that Visual Basic supports include:

- Do...Loop
- For...Next
- For Each...Next

Do...Loop

Use a Do loop to execute a block of statements an indefinite number of times. There are several variations of the Do...Loop statement, but each evaluates a numeric condition to determine whether to continue execution. As with If...Then, the *condition* must be a value or expression that evaluates to False (zero) or to True (nonzero).

In the following Do...Loop, the *statements* execute as long as the *condition* is True:

Do While *condition*
  statements

Loop

When Visual Basic executes this Do loop, it first tests *condition*. If *condition* is False (zero), it skips past all the statements. If it's True (nonzero), Visual Basic executes the statements and then goes back to the Do While statement and tests the condition again.

Consequently, the loop can execute any number of times, as long as *condition* is nonzero or True. The statements never execute if *condition* is initially False. For example, this procedure counts the occurrences of a target string within another string by looping as long as the target string is found:

```
Function CountStrings (longstring, target)
   Dim position, count
   position = 1
```

```
    Do While InStr(position, longstring, target)
       position = InStr(position, longstring, target)_
        + 1
       count = count + 1
    Loop
    CountStrings = count
End Function
```

If the target string doesn't occur in the other string, then InStr returns 0, and the loop doesn't execute.

Another variation of the Do...Loop statement executes the statements first and then tests *condition* after each execution. This variation guarantees at least one execution of *statements*:

Do
statements

Loop While *condition*

Two other variations are analogous to the previous two, except that they loop as long as *condition* is False rather than True.

Loop zero or more times	Loop at least once

Do Until *condition*
  statements
Loop
	Do
	  statements
	Loop Until *condition*

For...Next

Do loops work well when you don't know how many times you need to execute the statements in the loop. When you know you must execute the statements a specific number of times, however, a For...Next loop is a better choice. Unlike a Do loop, a For loop uses a variable called a counter that increases or decreases in value during each repetition of the loop. The syntax is:

For *counter* = *start* **To** *end* [**Step** *increment*]
statements

Next [*counter*]

The arguments *counter*, *start*, *end*, and *increment* are all numeric.

Note The *increment* argument can be either positive or negative. If *increment* is positive, *start* must be less than or equal to *end* or the statements in the loop will not execute. If *increment* is negative, *start* must be greater than or equal to *end* for the body of the loop to execute. If Step isn't set, then *increment* defaults to 1.

In executing the For loop, Visual Basic:

1. Sets *counter* equal to *start*.
2. Tests to see if *counter* is greater than *end*. If so, Visual Basic exits the loop.

   (If *increment* is negative, Visual Basic tests to see if *counter* is less than *end*.)
3. Executes the *statements*.
4. Increments *counter* by 1 or by *increment*, if it's specified.
5. Repeats steps 2 through 4.

This code prints the names of all the available Screen fonts:

```
Private Sub Form_Click ()
   Dim I As Integer
   For i = 0 To Screen.FontCount
      Print Screen.Fonts(i)
   Next
End Sub
```

In the VCR sample application, the HighlightButton procedure uses a For...Next loop to step through the controls collection of the VCR form and show the appropriate Shape control:

```
Sub HighlightButton(MyControl As Variant)
   Dim i As Integer
   For i = 0 To frmVCR.Controls.Count - 1
      If TypeOf frmVCR.Controls(i) Is Shape Then
         If frmVCR.Controls(i).Name = MyControl Then
            frmVCR.Controls(i).Visible = True
         Else
            frmVCR.Controls(i).Visible = False
         End If
      End If
   Next
End Sub
```

For Each...Next

A For Each...Next loop is similar to a For...Next loop, but it repeats a group of statements for each element in a collection of objects or in an array instead of repeating the statements a specified number of times. This is especially helpful if you don't know how many elements are in a collection.

Here is the syntax for the For Each...Next loop:

For Each *element* **In** *group*
    statements

Next *element*

For example, the following Sub procedure opens Biblio.mdb and adds the name of each table to a list box.

```
Sub ListTableDefs()
   Dim objDb As Database
   Dim MyTableDef as TableDef
   Set objDb = OpenDatabase("c:\vb\biblio.mdb", _
   True, False)
   For Each MyTableDef In objDb.TableDefs()
      List1.AddItem MyTableDef.Name
   Next MyTableDef
End Sub
```

Keep the following restrictions in mind when using For Each...Next:

- For collections, *element* can only be a Variant variable, a generic Object variable, or an object listed in the Object Browser.
- For arrays, *element* can only be a Variant variable.
- You cannot use For Each...Next with an array of user-defined types because a Variant cannot contain a user-defined type.

Working with Control Structures

Nested Control Structures

You can place control structures inside other control structures (such as an If...Then block within a For...Next loop). A control structure placed inside another control structure is said to be *nested.*

Control structures in Visual Basic can be nested to as many levels as you want. It's common practice to make nested decision structures and loop structures more readable by indenting the body of the decision structure or loop.

For example, this procedure prints all the font names that are common to both the Printer and Screen:

```
Private Sub Form_Click()
   Dim SFont, PFont
   For Each SFont In Screen.Fonts()
      For Each PFont In Printer.Fonts()
         If SFont = PFont Then
            Print SFont
         End If
      Next PFont
   Next SFont
End Sub
```

Notice that the first Next closes the inner For loop and the last For closes the outer For loop. Likewise, in nested If statements, the End If statements automatically apply to the nearest prior If statement. Nested Do...Loop structures work in a similar fashion, with the innermost Loop statement matching the innermost Do statement.

Exiting a Control Structure

The Exit statement allows you to exit directly from a For loop, Do loop, Sub procedure, or Function procedure. The syntax for the Exit statement is simple: Exit For can appear as many times as needed inside a For loop, and Exit Do can appear as many times as needed inside a Do loop:

For *counter* = *start* **To** *end* [**Step** *increment*]
    [*statementblock*]
    [**Exit For**]
    [*statementblock*]

Next [*counter*[, *counter*] [,...]]

Do [{**While** | **Until**} *condition*]
    [*statementblock*]
    [**Exit Do**]
    [*statementblock*]

Loop

The Exit Do statement works with all versions of the Do loop syntax.

Exit For and Exit Do are useful because sometimes it's appropriate to quit a loop immediately, without performing any further iterations or statements within the loop. For example, in the previous example that printed the fonts common to both the Screen and Printer, the code continues to compare Printer fonts against a given Screen font even when a match has already been found with an earlier Printer font. A more efficient version of the function would exit the loop as soon as a match is found:

```
Private Sub Form_Click()
   Dim SFont, PFont
   For Each SFont In Screen.Fonts()
      For Each PFont In Printer.Fonts()
         If SFont = PFont Then
            Print Sfont
            Exit For        ' Exit inner loop.
         End If
      Next PFont
   Next SFont
End Sub
```

As this example illustrates, an Exit statement almost always appears inside an If statement or Select Case statement nested inside the loop.

When you use an Exit statement to break out of a loop, the value of the counter variable differs, depending on how you leave the loop:

- When you complete a loop, the counter variable contains the value of the upper bound plus the step.
- When you exit a loop prematurely, the counter variable retains its value subject to the usual rules on scope.
- When you iterate off the end of a collection, the counter variable contains Nothing if it's an Object data type, and contains Empty if it's a Variant data type.

Exiting a Sub or Function Procedure

You can also exit a procedure from within a control structure. The syntax of Exit Sub and Exit Function is similar to that of Exit For and Exit Do in the previous section, "Exiting a Control Structure." Exit Sub can appear as many times as needed, anywhere within the body of a Sub procedure. Exit Function can appear as many times as needed, anywhere within the body of a Function procedure.

Exit Sub and Exit Function are useful when the procedure has done everything it needs to do and can return immediately. For example, if you want to change the previous example so it prints only the first common Printer and Screen font it finds, you would use Exit Sub:

```
Private Sub Form_Click()
   Dim SFont, PFont
   For Each SFont In Screen.Fonts()
      For Each PFont In Printer.Fonts()
         If SFont = PFont Then
            Print Sfont
            Exit Sub         ' Exit the procedure.
         End If
      Next PFont
   Next SFont
End Sub
```

Working with Objects

When you create an application in Visual Basic, you work with objects. You can use objects provided by Visual Basic — such as controls, forms, and data access objects. You can also control other applications' objects from within your Visual Basic application. You can even create your own objects, and define additional properties and methods for them.

What Is an Object?

An object is a combination of code and data that can be treated as a unit. An object can be a piece of an application, like a control or a form. An entire application can also be an object. The following table describes examples of the types of objects you can use in Visual Basic.

Example	Description
Command button	Controls on a form, such as command buttons and frames, are objects.
Form	Each form in a Visual Basic project is a separate object.
Database	Databases are objects, and contain other objects, like fields and indexes.
Chart	A chart in Microsoft Excel is an object.

Where Do Objects Come From?

Each object in Visual Basic is defined by a *class*. To understand the relationship between an object and its class, think of cookie cutters and cookies. The cookie cutter is the class. It defines the characteristics of each cookie — for instance, size and shape. The class is used to create objects. The objects are the cookies.

Two examples of the relationship between classes and objects in Visual Basic may make this clearer.

- The controls on the Toolbox in Visual Basic represent classes. The object known as a control doesn't exist until you draw it on a form. When you create a control, you're creating a copy or *instance* of the control class. That instance of the class is the object you refer to in your application.
- The form you work with at design time is a class. At run time, Visual Basic creates an instance of the form's class.

The Properties window displays the class and Name property of objects in your Visual Basic application, as shown in Figure 5.8.

Figure 5.8 Object and class names shown in the Properties window

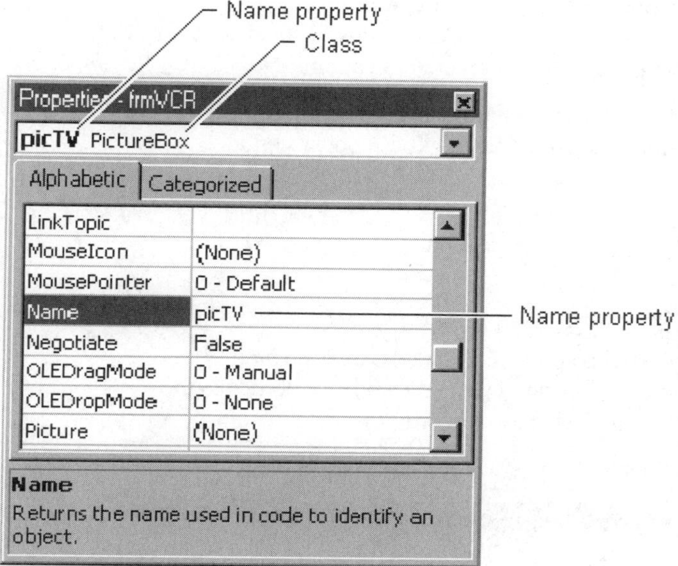

All objects are created as identical copies of their class. Once they exist as individual objects, their properties can be changed. For example, if you draw three command buttons on a form, each command button object is an instance of the CommandButton class. Each object shares a common set of characteristics and capabilities (properties, methods, and events), defined by the class. However, each has its own name, can be separately enabled and disabled, can be placed in a different location on the form, and so on.

For simplicity, most of the material outside of this chapter won't make many references to an object's class. Just remember that the term "list box control," for example, means "an instance of the ListBox class."

What Can You Do with Objects?

An object provides code you don't have to write. For example, you could create your own File Open and File Save dialog boxes, but you don't have to. Instead, you can use the common dialog control (an object) provided by Visual Basic. You could write your own scheduling and resource management code, but you don't have to. Instead, you can use the Calendar, Resources, and Task objects provided by Microsoft Project.

Visual Basic Can Combine Objects from Other Sources

Visual Basic provides the tools to allow you to combine objects from different sources. You can now build custom solutions combining the most powerful features of Visual Basic and applications that support Automation (formerly known as OLE Automation). *Automation* is a feature of the *Component Object Model* (COM), an industry standard used by applications to expose objects to development tools and other applications.

You can build applications by tying together intrinsic Visual Basic controls, and you can also use objects provided by other applications. Consider placing these objects on a Visual Basic form:

- A Microsoft Excel Chart object
- A Microsoft Excel Worksheet object
- A Microsoft Word Document object

You could use these objects to create a checkbook application like the one shown in Figure 5.9. This saves you time because you don't have to write the code to reproduce the functionality provided by the Microsoft Excel and Microsoft Word objects.

Figure 5.9 Using objects from other applications

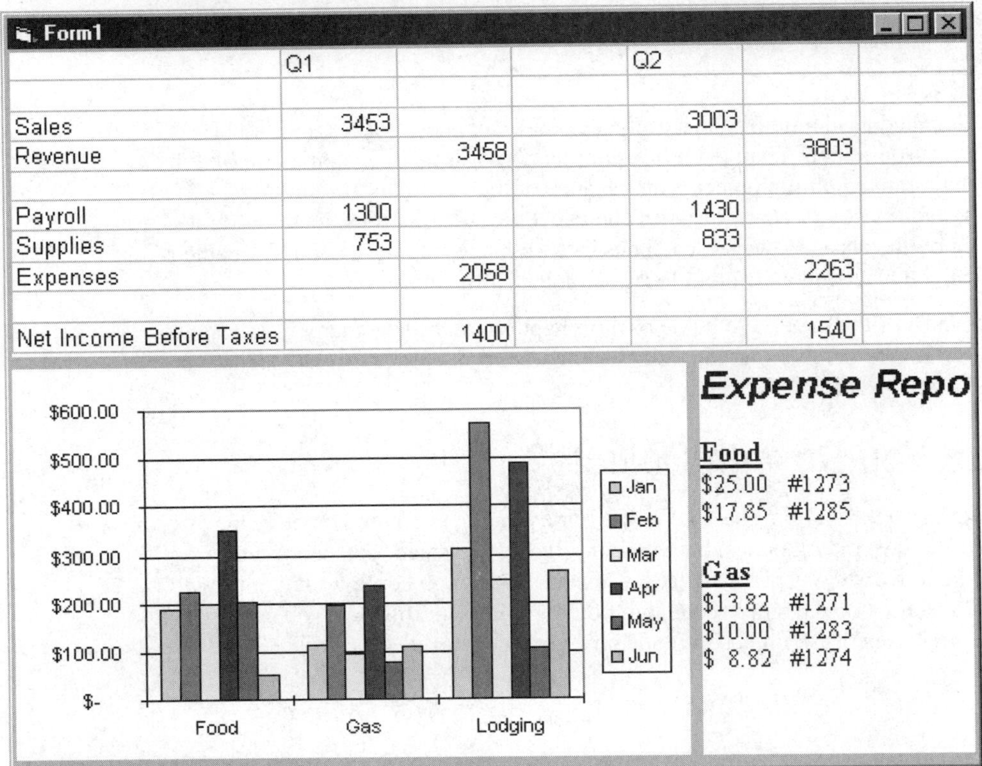

	Q1			Q2		
Sales	3453			3003		
Revenue		3458			3803	
Payroll	1300			1430		
Supplies	753			833		
Expenses		2058			2263	
Net Income Before Taxes		1400			1540	

The Basics of Working with Objects

Visual Basic objects support properties, methods, and events. In Visual Basic, an object's data (settings or attributes) are called properties, while the various procedures that can operate on the object are called its methods. An event is an action recognized by an object, such as clicking a mouse or pressing a key, and you can write code to respond to that event.

You can change an object's characteristics by changing its properties. Consider a radio: One property of a radio is its volume. In Visual Basic, you might say that a radio has a "Volume" property that you can adjust by changing its value. Assume you can set the volume of the radio from 0 to 10. If you could control a radio with Visual Basic, you might write code in a procedure that changes the value of the "Volume" property from 3 to 5 to make the radio play louder:

```
Radio.Volume = 5
```

In addition to properties, objects have methods. Methods are a part of objects just as properties are. Generally, methods are actions you want to perform, while properties are the attributes you set or retrieve. For example, you dial a telephone to make a call. You might say that telephones have a "Dial" method, and you could use this syntax to dial the seven-digit number 5551111:

```
Phone.Dial 5551111
```

Objects also have events. Events are triggered when some aspect of the object is changed. For example, a radio might have a "VolumeChange" event. A telephone might have a "Ring" event.

Controlling Objects with Their Properties

Individual properties vary as to when you can set or get their values. Some properties can be set at design time. You can use the Properties window to set the value of these properties without writing any code at all. Some properties are not available at design time; therefore, you must write code to set those properties at run time.

Properties that you can set and get at run time are called *read-write properties*. Properties you can only read at run time are called *read-only properties*.

Setting Property Values

You set the value of a property when you want to change the appearance or behavior of an object. For example, you change the Text property of a text box control to change the contents of the text box.

To set the value of a property, use the following syntax:

object.property = *expression*

The following statements demonstrate how you set properties:

```
Text1.Top = 200' Sets the Top property to 200 twips.
Text1.Visible = True        ' Displays the text box.
Text1.Text = "hello" ' Displays 'hello' in the text
                     ' box.
```

Getting Property Values

You get the value of a property when you want to find the state of an object before your code performs additional actions (such as assigning the value to another object). For example, you can return the Text property of a text box control to determine the contents of the text box before running code that might change the value.

In most cases, to get the value of a property, you use the following syntax:

variable = object.property

You can also get a property value as part of a more complex expression, without assigning the property to a variable. In the following code example, the Top property of the new member of a control array is calculated as the Top property of the previous member, plus 400:

```
Private Sub cmdAdd_Click()
   ' [statements]
   optButton(n).Top = optButton(n-1).Top + 400
   ' [statements]
End Sub
```

> **Tip** If you're going to use the value of a property more than once, your code will run faster if you store the value in a variable.

Performing Actions with Methods

Methods can affect the values of properties. For example, in the radio analogy, the SetVolume method changes the Volume property. Similarly, in Visual Basic, list boxes have a List property, which can be changed with the Clear and AddItem methods.

Using Methods in Code

When you use a method in code, how you write the statement depends on how many arguments the method requires, and whether the method returns a value. When a method doesn't take arguments, you write the code using the following syntax:

object.method

In this example, the Refresh method repaints the picture box:

```
Picture1.Refresh   ' Forces a repaint of the control.
```

Some methods, such as the Refresh method, don't have arguments and don't return values.

If the method takes more than one argument, you separate the arguments with a comma. For example, the Circle method uses arguments specifying the location, radius, and color of a circle on a form:

```
' Draw a blue circle with a 1200-twip radius.
Form1.Circle (1600, 1800), 1200, vbBlue
```

If you keep the return value of a method, you must enclose the arguments in parentheses. For example, the GetData method returns a picture from the Clipboard:

```
Picture = Clipboard.GetData (vbCFBitmap)
```

If there is no return value, the arguments appear without parentheses. For example, the AddItem method doesn't return a value:

```
List1.AddItem "yourname"    ' Adds the text 'yourname'
                            ' to a list box.
```

For More Information See the *Microsoft Visual Basic 6.0 Language Reference* for the syntax and arguments for all methods provided by Visual Basic.

How Are Objects Related to Each Other?

When you put two command buttons on a form, they are separate objects with distinct Name property settings (*Command1* and *Command2*), but they share the same class — CommandButton.

They also share the characteristic that they're on the same form. You've seen earlier in this chapter that a control on a form is also contained by the form. This puts controls in a hierarchy. To reference a control you may have to reference the form first, in the same way you may have to dial a country code or area code before you can reach a particular phone number.

The two command buttons also share the characteristic that they're controls. All controls have common characteristics that make them different from forms and other objects in the Visual Basic environment. The following sections explain how Visual Basic uses collections to group objects that are related.

Object Hierarchies

An object hierarchy provides the organization that determines how objects are related to each other, and how you can access them. In most cases, you don't need to concern yourself with the Visual Basic object hierarchy. However:

- When manipulating another application's objects, you should be familiar with that application's object hierarchy. For information on navigating object hierarchies, see Chapter 10, "Programming with Components."
- When working with data access objects, you should be familiar with the Data Access Object hierarchy.

There are some common cases in Visual Basic where one object contains others. These are described in the following sections.

Working with Collections of Objects

Collection objects have their own properties and methods. The objects in a collection object are referred to as *members* of the collection. Each member of the collection is numbered sequentially beginning at 0; this is the member's *index number*. For example, the Controls collection contains all the controls on a given form, as shown in Figure 5.10. You can use collections to simplify code if you need to perform the same operation on all the objects in a collection.

Figure 5.10 Controls collection

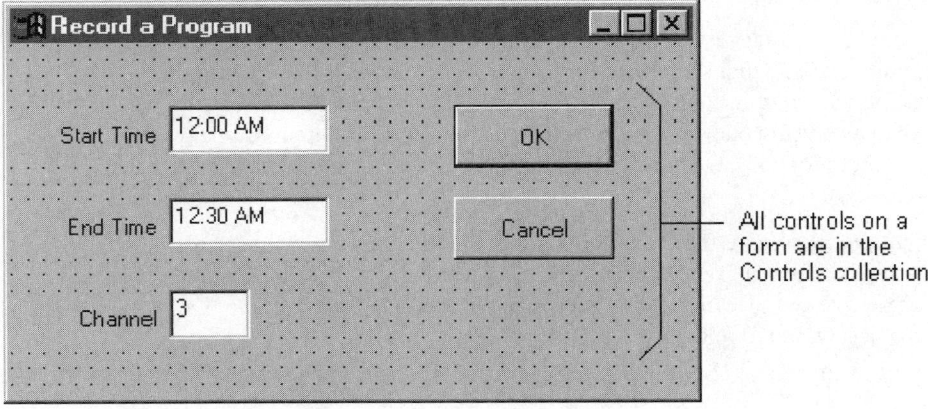

For example, the following code scrolls through the Controls collection and lists each member's name in a list box.

```
Dim MyControl as Control
For Each MyControl In Form1.Controls
   ' For each control, add its name to a list box.
   List1.AddItem MyControl.Name
Next MyControl
```

Applying Properties and Methods to Collection Members

There are two general techniques you can use to address a member of a collection object:

- Specify the name of the member. The following expressions are equivalent:

  ```
  Controls("List1")
  Controls!List1
  ```

- Use the index number of the member:

  ```
  Controls(3)
  ```

Once you're able to address all the members collectively, and single members individually, you can apply properties and methods using either approach:

```
' Set the Top property of the list box control to 200.
Controls!List1.Top = 200
```

– or –

```
Dim MyControl as Control
For Each MyControl In Form1.Controls()
   ' Set the Top property of each member to 200.
   MyControl.Top = 200
Next MyControl
```

Objects That Contain Other Objects

Some objects in Visual Basic contain other objects. For example, a form usually contains one or more controls. The advantage of having objects as containers for other objects is that you can refer to the container in your code to make it clear which object you want to use. For example, Figure 5.11 illustrates two different forms you could have in an application — one for entering accounts payable transactions, and the other for entering accounts receivable transactions.

Figure 5.11 Two different forms can contain controls that have the same name

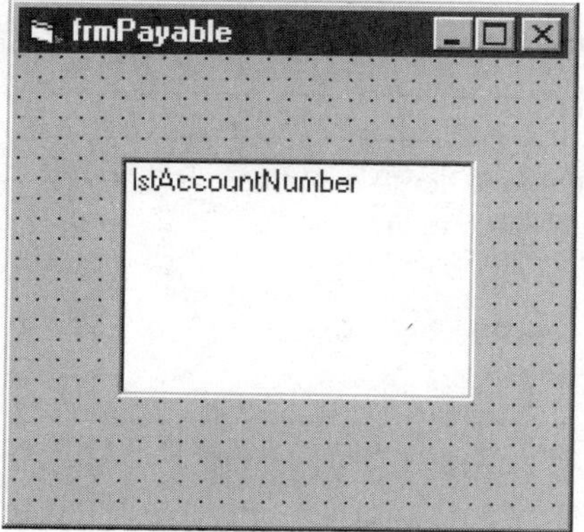

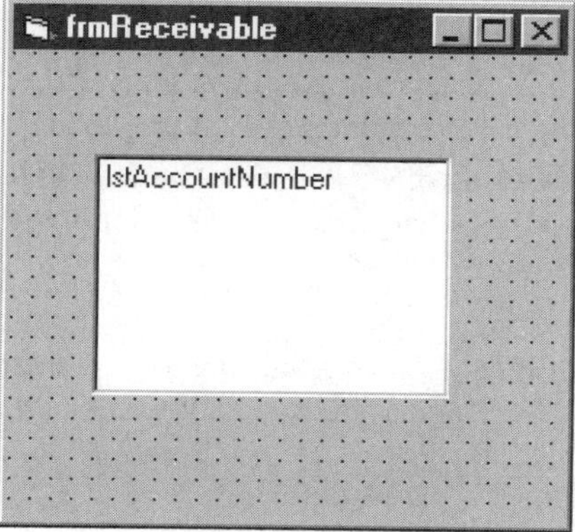

Both forms can have a list box named lstAcctNo. You can specify exactly which one you want to use by referring to the form containing the list box:

```
frmReceivable.lstAcctNo.AddItem 1201
```

– or –

```
frmPayable.lstAcctNo.AddItem 1201
```

Common Collections in Visual Basic

There are some common cases in Visual Basic where one object contains other objects. The following table briefly describes the most commonly used collections in Visual Basic.

Collection	Description
Forms	Contains loaded forms.
Controls	Contains controls on a form.
Printers	Contains the available Printer objects.

You can also implement object containment in Visual Basic.

For More Information For information about object containment, see "Using Collections as an Alternative to Arrays" in Chapter 8, "More About Programming." For information on the Printers collection, see Chapter 12, "Working with Text and Graphics." For details on the forms and controls collections, see the *Microsoft Visual Basic 6.0 Language Reference* volume and the *Microsoft Visual Basic 6.0 Controls Reference* volume of the *Microsoft Visual Basic 6.0 Reference Library.*

The Container Property

You can use the Container property to change an object's container within a form. The following controls can contain other controls:

- Frame control
- Picture box control
- Toolbar control (Professional and Enterprise editions only)

This example demonstrates moving a command button around from container to container on a form. Open a new project, and draw a frame control, picture box control and a command button on the form.

The following code in the form's click event increments a counter variable, and uses a Select Case loop to rotate the command button from container to container.

```
Private Sub Form_Click()
    Static intX as Integer
    Select Case intX
        Case 0
        Set Command1.Container = Picture1
        Command1.Top= 0
        Command1.Left= 0

        Case 1
        Set Command1.Container = Frame1
        Command1.Top= 0
        Command1.Left= 0

        Case 2
        Set Command1.Container = Form1
        Command1.Top= 0
        Command1.Left= 0

    End Select
    intX = intX + 1
End Sub
```

For More Information See "Container Property" in the *Microsoft Visual Basic 6.0 Language Reference.*

Communicating Between Objects

In addition to using and creating objects within Visual Basic, you can communicate with other applications and manipulate their objects from within your application. The ability to share data between applications is one of the key features of the Microsoft Windows operating system. With Visual Basic, you have great flexibility in how you can communicate with other applications.

For More Information For details on using and communicating with other applications' objects, see Chapter 10, "Programming with Components."

Creating Objects

The easiest way to create an object is to double-click a control in the Toolbox. However, to realize the full benefit of all the objects available in Visual Basic and from other applications, you can use Visual Basic's programmability features to create objects at run time.

- You can create references to an object with object variables.
- You can create your own objects "from scratch" with class modules.
- You can create your own collections with the Collection object.

For More Information Other chapters show you how to access objects. The CreateObject and GetObject functions, for example, are discussed in Chapter 10, "Programming with Components."

Using Object Variables

In addition to storing values, a variable can refer to an object. You assign an object to a variable for the same reasons you assign any value to a variable:

- Variable names are often shorter and easier to remember than the values they contain (or, in this case, the objects they refer to).
- Variables can be changed to refer to other objects while your code is running.
- Referring to a variable that contains an object is more efficient than repeatedly referring to the object itself.

Using an object variable is similar to using a conventional variable, but with one additional step — assigning an object to the variable:

- First you declare it:

  Dim *variable* As *class*

- Then you assign an object to it:

  Set *variable* = *object*

Declaring Object Variables

You declare an object variable in the same way you declare other variables, with Dim, ReDim, Static, Private, or Public. The only differences are the optional New keyword and the *class* argument; both of these are discussed later in this chapter. The syntax is:

{**Dim** | **ReDim** | **Static** | **Private** | **Public**} *variable* **As** [**New**] *class*

For example, you can declare an object variable that refers to a form in the application called frmMain:

```
Dim FormVar As New frmMain ' Declare an object
                           ' variable of type frmMain.
```

You can also declare an object variable that can refer to any form in the application:

```
Dim anyForm As Form        ' Generic form variable.
```

Similarly, you can declare an object variable that can refer to any text box in your application:

```
Dim anyText As TextBox     ' Can refer to any text box
                           ' (but only a text box).
```

You can also declare an object variable that can refer to a control of any type:

```
Dim anyControl As Control   ' Generic control variable.
```

Notice that you can declare a form variable that refers to a specific form in the application, but you cannot declare a control variable that refers to a particular control. You can declare a control variable that can refer to a specific type of control (such as TextBox or ListBox), but not to one particular control of that type (such as `txtEntry` or `List1`). However, you can assign a particular control to a variable of that type. For example, for a form with a list box called lstSample, you could write:

```
Dim objDemo As ListBox
Set objDemo = lstSample
```

Assigning Object Variables

You assign an object to an object variable with the Set statement:

Set *variable* = *object*

Use the Set statement whenever you want an object variable to refer to an object.

Sometimes you may use object variables, and particularly control variables, simply to shorten the code you have to type. For example, you might write code like this:

```
If frmAccountDisplay!txtAccountBalance.Text < 0 Then
   frmAccountDisplay!txtAccountBalance.BackColor = 0
   frmAccountDisplay!txtAccountBalance.ForeColor = 255
End If
```

You can shorten this code significantly if you use a control variable:

```
Dim Bal As TextBox
Set Bal = frmAccountDisplay!txtAccountBalance
If Bal.Text < 0 Then
   Bal.BackColor = 0
   Bal.ForeColor = 255
End If
```

Specific and Generic Object Types

Specific object variables must refer to one specific type of object or class. A specific form variable can refer to only one form in the application (though it can refer to one of many instances of that form). Similarly, a specific control variable can refer to only one particular type of control in your application, such as TextBox or ListBox. To see an example, open a new project and place a text box on a form. Add the following code to the form:

```
Private Sub Form_Click()
   Dim anyText As TextBox
   Set anyText = Text1
   anyText.Text = "Hello"
End Sub
```

Run the application, and click the form. The Text property of the text box will be changed to "Hello."

Generic object variables can refer to one of many specific types of objects. A generic form variable, for example, can refer to any form in an application; a generic control variable can refer to any control on any form in an application. To see an example, open a new project and place several frame, label, and command button controls on a form, in any order. Add the following code to the form:

```
Private Sub Form_Click()
   Dim anyControl As Control
   Set anyControl = Form1.Controls(3)
   anyControl.Caption = "Hello"
End Sub
```

Run the application, and click the form. The caption of the control you placed third in sequence on the form will be changed to "Hello."

There are four generic object types in Visual Basic:

Generic Object Type	Object referenced
Form	Any form in the application (including MDI children and the MDI form).
Control	Any control in your application.
MDIForm	The MDI form in the application (if your application has one).
Object	Any object.

Generic object variables are useful when you don't know the specific type of object a variable will refer to at run time. For example, if you want to write code that can operate on any form in the application, you must use a generic form variable.

Note Because there can be only one MDI form in the application, there is no need to use the generic MDIForm type. Instead, you can use the specific MDIForm type (`MDIForm1`, or whatever you specified for the Name property of the MDI form) whenever you need to declare a form variable that refers to the MDI form. In fact, because Visual Basic can resolve references to properties and methods of specific form types before you run your application, you should always use the specific MDIForm type.

The generic MDIForm type is provided only for completeness; should a future version of Visual Basic allow multiple MDI forms in a single application, it might become useful.

Forms as Objects

Forms are most often used to make up the interface of an application, but they're also objects that can be called by other modules in your application. Forms are closely related to class modules. The major difference between the two is that forms can be visible objects, whereas class modules have no visible interface.

Adding Custom Methods and Properties

You can add custom methods and properties to forms and access them from other modules in your application. To create a new method for a form, add a procedure declared using Public.

```
' Custom method on Form1
Public Sub LateJobsCount()
    .
. ' <statements>
    .
End Sub
```

You can call the LateJobsCount procedure from another module using this statement:

```
Form1.LateJobsCount
```

Creating a new property for a form can be as simple as declaring a public variable in the form module:

```
Public IDNumber As Integer
```

You can set and return the value of IDNumber on Form1 from another module using these two statements:

```
Form1.IDNumber = 3
Text1.Text = Form1.IDNumber
```

You can also use Property procedures to add custom properties to a form.

For More Information Details on Property procedures are provided in Chapter 9, "Programming with Objects."

> **Note** You can call a variable, a custom method, or set a custom property on a form without loading the form. This allows you to run code on a form without loading it into memory. Also, referencing a control without referencing one of its properties or methods does not load the form.

Using the New Keyword

Use the New keyword to create a new object as defined by its class. New can be used to create instances of forms, classes defined in class modules, and collections.

Using the New Keyword with Forms

Each form you create at design time is a class. The New keyword can be used to create new instances of that class. To see how this works, draw a command button and several other controls on a form. Set the form's Name property to Sample in the Properties window. Add the following code to your command button's Click event procedure:

```
Dim x As New Sample
x.Show
```

Run the application, and click the command button several times. Move the front-most form aside. Because a form is a class with a visible interface, you can see the additional copies. Each form has the same controls, in the same positions as on the form at design time.

> **Note** To make a form variable and an instance of the loaded form persist, use a Static or Public variable instead of a local variable.

You can also use New with the Set statement. Try the following code in a command button's Click event procedure:

```
Dim f As Form1
Set f = New Form1
f.Caption = "hello"
f.Show
```

Using New with the Set statement is faster and is the recommended method.

Using the New Keyword with Other Objects

The New keyword can be used to create collections and objects from the classes you define in class modules. To see how this works, try the following example.

This example demonstrates how the New keyword creates instances of a class. Open a new project, and draw a command button on Form1. From the Project menu, choose Add Class Module to add a class module to the project. Set the class module's Name property to ShowMe.

The following code in the Form1 module creates a new instance of the class ShowMe, and calls the procedure contained in the class module.

```
Public clsNew As ShowMe
Private Sub Command1_Click()
   Set clsNew = New ShowMe
   clsNew.ShowFrm
End Sub
```

The ShowFrm procedure in the class module creates a new instance of the class Form1, shows the form, and then minimizes it.

```
Sub ShowFrm()
   Dim frmNew As Form1
   Set frmNew = New Form1
   frmNew.Show
   frmNew.WindowState = 1
End Sub
```

To use the example, run the application, and click the command button several times. You'll see a minimized form icon appear on your desktop as each new instance of the ShowMe class is created.

For More Information For information on using New to create objects, see Chapter 10, "Programming with Components."

New Keyword Restrictions

The following table describes what you cannot do with the New keyword.

You can't use New to create	Example of code not allowed
Variables of fundamental data types.	`Dim X As New Integer`
A variable of any generic object type.	`Dim X As New Control`
A variable of any specific control type.	`Dim X As New ListBox`
A variable of any specific control.	`Dim X As New lstNames`

Freeing References to Objects

Each object uses memory and system resources. It is good programming practice to release these resources when you are no longer using an object.

- Use Unload to unload a form or control from memory.
- Use Nothing to release resources used by an object variable. Assign Nothing to an object variable with the Set statement.

For More Information See "Unload Event" and "Nothing" in the *Microsoft Visual Basic 6.0 Language Reference*.

Passing Objects to Procedures

You can pass objects to procedures in Visual Basic. In the following code example, it's assumed that there is a command button on a form:

```
Private Sub Command1_Click()
   ' Calls the Demo sub, and passes the form to it.
   Demo Form1
End Sub

Private Sub Demo(x As Form1)
   ' Centers the form on the screen.
   x.Left = (Screen.Width - x.Width) / 2
End Sub
```

It's also possible to pass an object to an argument by reference and then, inside the procedure, set the argument to a new object. To see how this works, open a project, and insert a second form. Place a picture box control on each form. The following table shows the property settings that need changes:

Object	Property	Setting
Picture box on Form2	Name	Picture2
	Picture	c:\vb\icons\arrows\arw01dn.ico

The Form1_Click event procedure calls the GetPicture procedure in Form2, and passes the empty picture box to it.

```
Private Sub Form_Click()
Form2.GetPicture Picture1
End Sub
```

The GetPicture procedure in Form2 assigns the Picture property of the picture box on Form2 to the empty picture box on Form1.

```
Private objX As PictureBox
Public Sub GetPicture(x As PictureBox)
   ' Assign the passed-in picture box to an object
   ' variable.
   Set objX = x
   ' Assign the value of the Picture property to Form1
   ' picture box.
   objX.Picture = picture2.Picture
End Sub
```

To use the example, run the application, and click Form1. You'll see the icon from Form2 appear in the picture box on Form1.

For More Information The previous topics are intended to serve as an introduction to objects. To learn more, see Chapter 9, "Programming with Objects," and Chapter 10, "Programming with Components."

PART 2

What You Can Do with Visual Basic

Once you understand the basics of working with Visual Basic, you're ready to move on to new and bigger challenges. So, what can you do with Visual Basic? It might be more appropriate to ask what can't be done. The answer is: not much! From designing innovative user interfaces to taking advantage of other applications' objects, from manipulating text and graphics to working with databases, Visual Basic provides the tools that you'll need to get the job done right.

Part 1 of the *Microsoft Visual Basic 6.0 Programmer's Guide* provided the foundation; Part 2 provides the bricks and mortar to build upon that foundation to create increasingly complex applications with Visual Basic.

Chapter 6 Creating a User Interface

In-depth coverage of interface styles, forms, menus, toolbars, and more.

Chapter 7 Using Visual Basic's Standard Controls

Covers Visual Basic's intrinsic controls and how you can use them.

Chapter 8 More About Programming

A discussion of more programming concepts, techniques, and additional tools available in Visual Basic.

Chapter 9 Programming with Objects

In-depth coverage of objects, including creating classes and using ActiveX Designers.

Chapter 10 Programming with Components

Covers techniques for using ActiveX components in your own applications.

Chapter 11 Responding to Mouse and Keyboard Events

A discussion of processing user input, including drag and drop.

Chapter 12 Working with Text and Graphics

Explains how to use Visual Basic's text and graphics methods for display and printing.

Chapter 13 Debugging Your Code and Handling Errors

Explains what to do when something doesn't work as planned, either at design time or run time.

Chapter 14 Processing Drives, Folders, and Files

Techniques for working with the file system.

Chapter 15 Designing for Performance and Compatibility

Optimization techniques to make your applications faster or smaller.

Chapter 16 International Issues

A discussion of considerations for multilingual and multicultural applications.

Chapter 17 Distributing Your Applications

Explains how to use the Package and Deployment Wizard to create installation programs.

CHAPTER 6

Creating a User Interface

The user interface is perhaps the most important part of an application; it's certainly the most visible. To users, the interface is the application; they probably aren't aware of the code that is executing behind the scenes. No matter how much time and effort you put into writing and optimizing your code, the usability of your application depends on the interface.

When you design an application, a number of decisions need to be made regarding the interface. Should you use the single-document or multiple-document style? How many different forms will you need? What commands will your menus include, and will you use toolbars to duplicate menu functions? What about dialog boxes to interact with the user? How much assistance do you need to provide?

Before you begin designing the user interface, you need to think about the purpose of the application. The design for a primary application that will be in constant use should be different from one that is only used occasionally for short periods of time. An application with the primary purpose of displaying information has different requirements than one used to gather information.

The intended audience should also influence your design. An application aimed at a beginning user demands simplicity in its design, while one for experienced users may be more complex. Other applications used by your target audience may influence their expectations for an application's behavior. If you plan on distributing internationally, language and culture must be considered part of your design.

Designing a user interface is best approached as an iterative process — you will rarely come up with a perfect design on the first pass. This chapter introduces you to the process of designing an interface in Visual Basic, providing an introduction to the tools you need to create a great application for your users.

Contents

- Dialog Boxes
- Designing for Different Display Types
- Designing with the User in Mind

Sample Applications: Mdinote.vpb, Sdinote.vbp

Many of the code samples in this chapter are taken from the Mdinote.vbp and Sdinote.vbp sample applications which are listed in the Samples directory.

Interface Styles

If you've been using Windows-based applications for a while, you've probably noticed that not all user interfaces look or behave the same. There are two main styles of user interface: the *single-document interface* (*SDI*) and the *multiple-document interface* (*MDI*). An example of the SDI interface is the WordPad application included with Microsoft Windows (Figure 6.1). In WordPad, only a single document may be open; you must close one document in order to open another.

Figure 6.1 WordPad, a single-document interface (SDI) application

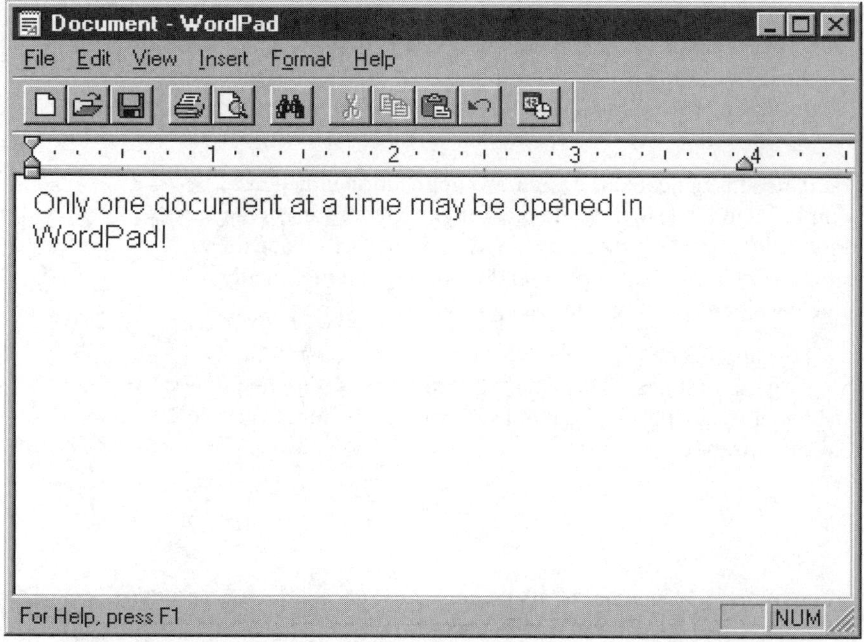

Applications such as Microsoft Excel and Microsoft Word for Windows are MDI interfaces; they allow you to display multiple documents at the same time, with each document displayed in its own window (Figure 6.2). You can recognize a MDI application by the inclusion of a Window menu item with submenus for switching between windows or documents.

Figure 6.2 Microsoft Excel, a multiple-document interface (MDI) application

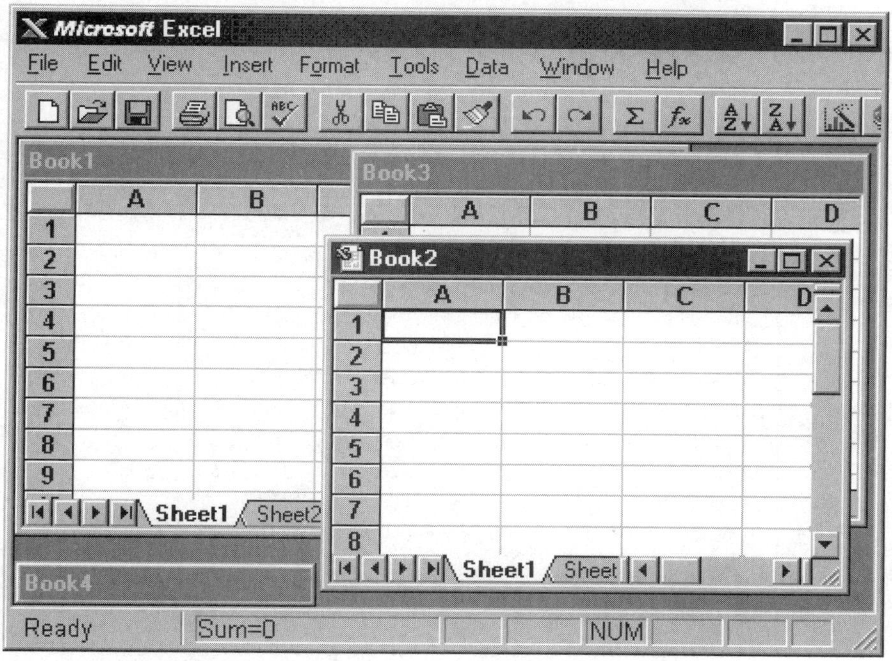

In determining which interface style is best, you need to look at the purpose of the application. An application for processing insurance claims might lend itself to the MDI style — a clerk is likely to be working on more than one claim at a time or might need to compare two claims. On the other hand, a calendar application would be best suited to the SDI style — it's not likely that you would need more than one calendar open at a time; in the rare event that you did, you could open a second instance of the SDI application.

The SDI style is the more common; most of the examples in the *Microsoft Visual Basic 6.0 Programmer's Guide* assume an SDI application. There are a number of considerations and techniques unique to creating MDI applications, which are addressed in "Multiple-Document Interface (MDI) Applications" later in this chapter.

In addition to the two most common interface styles, SDI and MDI, a third interface style is becoming more popular: the *explorer-style* interface (Figure 6.3). The explorer-style interface is a single window containing two *panes* or regions, usually consisting of a tree or hierarchical view on the left and a display area on the right, as in the Microsoft Windows Explorer. This type of interface lends itself to navigating or browsing large numbers of documents, pictures, or files.

Figure 6.3 The Windows Explorer, an explorer-style interface

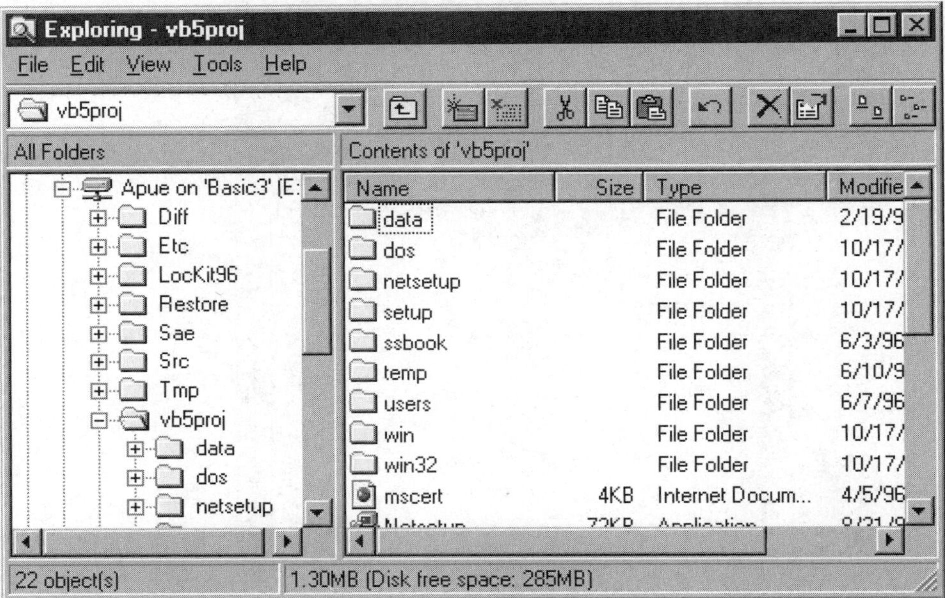

In addition to the MDI and SDI application examples that accompany this chapter, the Application Wizard provides a good way to compare the different interface styles. You can use the Wizard to generate a framework for each style and view the forms and code that it generates.

For More Information To learn more about MDI applications, see "Multiple-Document Interface (MDI) Applications." The basics of working with forms are covered in Chapter 3, "Forms, Controls, and Menus." For information on accessing the Application Wizard, see "Using Wizards and Add-Ins" in Chapter 4, "Managing Projects."

Multiple-Document Interface (MDI) Applications

The multiple-document interface (MDI) allows you to create an application that maintains multiple forms within a single container form. Applications such as Microsoft Excel and Microsoft Word for Windows have multiple-document interfaces.

An MDI application allows the user to display multiple documents at the same time, with each document displayed in its own window. Documents or *child windows* are contained in a *parent window*, which provides a workspace for all the child windows in the application. For example, Microsoft Excel allows you to create and display multiple-document windows of different types. Each individual window is confined to the area of the Excel parent window. When you minimize Excel, all of the document windows are minimized as well; only the parent window's icon appears in the task bar.

A child form is an ordinary form that has its MDIChild property set to True. Your application can include many MDI child forms of similar or different types.

At run time, child forms are displayed within the *workspace* of the MDI parent form (the area inside the form's borders and below the title and menu bars). When a child form is minimized, its icon appears within the workspace of the MDI form instead of on the taskbar, as shown in Figure 6.4.

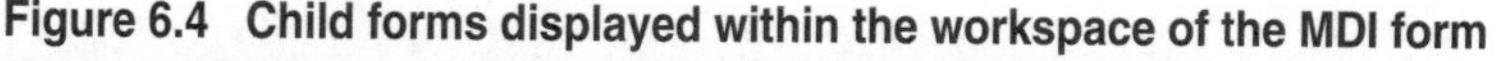

Figure 6.4 Child forms displayed within the workspace of the MDI form

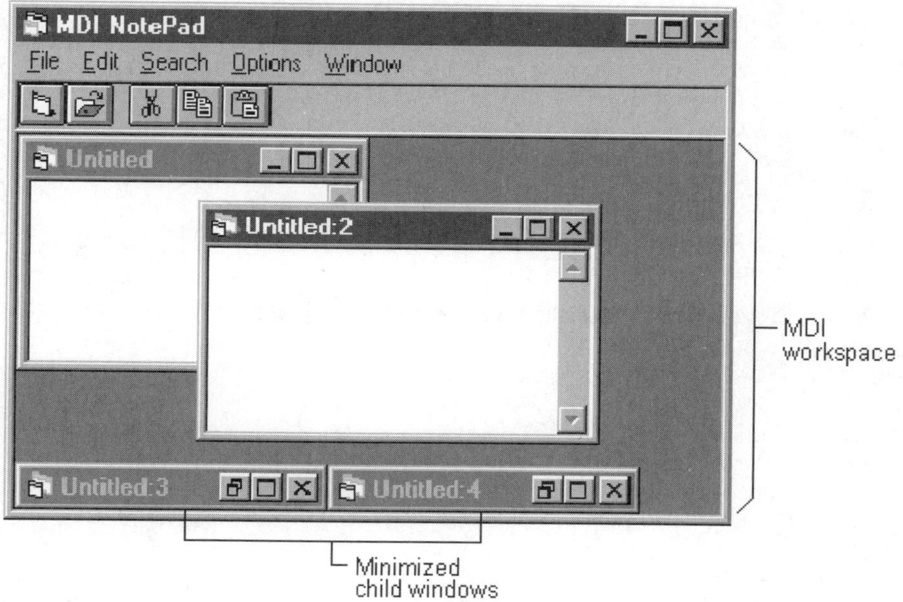

> **Note** Your application can also include standard, non-MDI forms that are not contained in the MDI form. A typical use of a standard form in an MDI application is to display a modal dialog box.

An MDI form is similar to an ordinary form with one restriction. You can't place a control directly on a MDI form unless that control has an Align property (such as a picture box control) or has no visible interface (such as a timer control).

Creating an MDI Application

Use the following procedure to create an MDI form and its child forms.

To create an MDI application

1. Create an MDI form.

   From the **Project** menu, choose **Add MDI Form**.

   > **Note** An application can have only one MDI form. If a project already has an MDI form, the Add MDI Form command on the Project menu is unavailable.

2. Create the application's child forms.

   To create an MDI child form, create a new form (or open an existing one) and set its MDIChild property to True.

Working with MDI Child Forms at Design Time

At design time, child forms are not restricted to the area inside the MDI form. You can add controls, set properties, write code, and design the features of child forms just as you would with any other Visual Basic form.

You can determine whether a form is an MDI child by looking at its MDIChild property, or by examining the Project Explorer. If the form's MDIChild property is set to True, it is a child form. Visual Basic displays special icons in the Project Explorer for the MDI and MDI child forms, as shown in Figure 6.5.

Figure 6.5 Icons in the Project Explorer identify MDI child, standard, and MDI forms

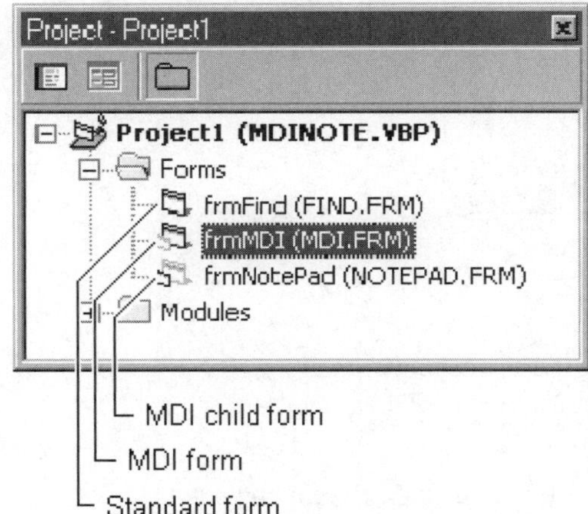

Run-Time Features of MDI Forms

At run time, an MDI form and all of its child forms take on special characteristics:

- All child forms are displayed within the MDI form's workspace. The user can move and size child forms like any other form; however, they are restricted to this workspace.
- When a child form is minimized, its icon appears on the MDI form instead of the taskbar. When the MDI form is minimized, the MDI form and all of its child forms are represented by a single icon. When the MDI form is restored, the MDI form and all the child forms are displayed in the same state they were in before being minimized.
- When a child form is maximized, its caption is combined with the caption of the MDI form and is displayed in the MDI form's title bar (see Figure 6.6).
- By setting the AutoShowChildren property, you can display child forms automatically when forms are loaded (True), or load child forms as hidden (False).
- The active child form's menus (if any) are displayed on the MDI form's menu bar, not on the child form.

Figure 6.6 A child form caption combined with the caption of an MDI form

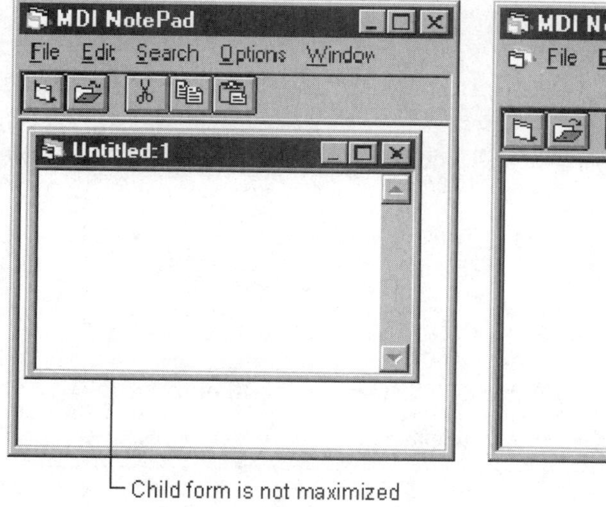

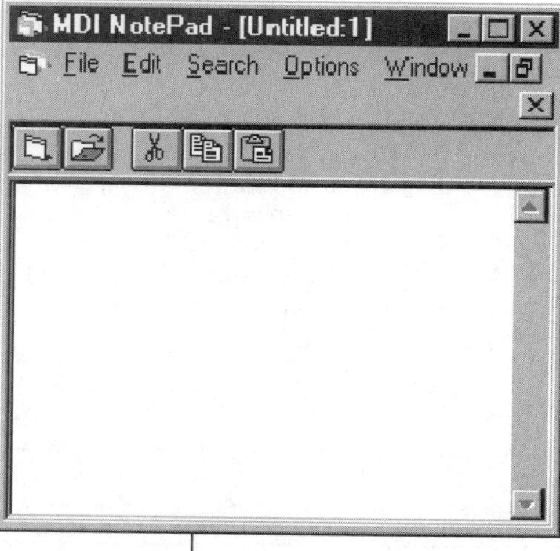

The MDI NotePad Application

The MDI NotePad sample application is a simple text editor similar to the NotePad application included with Microsoft Windows. The MDI NotePad application, however, uses a multiple-document interface (MDI). At run time, when the user requests a new document (implemented with the New command on the application's File menu), the application creates a new instance of the child form. This allows the user to create as many child forms, or documents, as necessary.

To create a document-centered application in Visual Basic, you need at least two forms — an MDI form and a child form. At design time, you create an MDI form to contain the application and a single child form to serve as a template for the application's document.

To create your own MDI NotePad application

1. From the **File** menu, choose **New Project**.
2. From the **Project** menu, choose **Add MDI Form** to create the container form.

   The project should now contain an MDI form (MDIForm1) and a standard form (Form1).
3. Create a text box (Text1) on Form1.
4. Set properties for the two forms and the text box as follows.

Object	Property	Setting
MDIForm1	Caption	MDI NotePad
Form1	Caption MDIChild	Untitled True
Text1	MultiLine Text Left Top	True (Empty) 0 0

5. Using the **Menu Editor** (from the **Tools** menu), create a File menu for MDIForm1.

Caption	Name	Indented
&File	mnuFile	No
&New	mnuFileNew	Yes

6. Add the following code to the mnuFileNew_Click procedure:

```
Private Sub mnuFileNew_Click ()
   ' Create a new instance of Form1, called NewDoc.
   Dim NewDoc As New Form1
   ' Display the new form.
   NewDoc.Show
End Sub
```

   This procedure creates and then displays a new instance (or copy) of Form1, called NewDoc. Each time the user chooses New from the File menu, an exact duplicate (instance) of Form1 is created, including all the controls and code that it contains.

7. Add the following code to the Form_Resize procedure for Form1:

```
Private Sub Form_Resize ()
   ' Expand text box to fill the current child form.
   Text1.Height = ScaleHeight
   Text1.Width = ScaleWidth
End Sub
```

   The code for the Form_Resize event procedure, like all the code in Form1, is shared by each instance of Form1. When several copies of a form are displayed, each form recognizes its own events. When an event occurs, the code for that event procedure is called. Because the same code is shared by each instance, you might wonder how to reference the form that has called the code — especially since each instance has the same name (Form1). This is discussed in "Working with MDI Forms and Child Forms," later in this chapter.

8. Press F5 to run the application.

   Tip The Mdinote.vbp sample application contains examples of many MDI techniques besides those mentioned in this chapter. Take some time to step through the example code to discover these techniques. The Sdinote.vbp sample application is an implementation of the same application converted to the SDI style; compare the two samples to learn the differences between MDI and SDI techniques.

Working with MDI Forms and Child Forms

When users of your MDI application open, save, and close several child forms in one session, they should be able to refer to the active form and maintain state information on child forms. This topic describes coding techniques you can use to specify the active child form or control, load and unload MDI and child forms, and maintain state information for a child form.

Specifying the Active Child Form or Control

Sometimes you want to provide a command that operates on the control with the focus on the currently active child form. For example, suppose you want to copy selected text from the child form's text box onto the Clipboard. In the Mdinote.vbp sample application, the Click event of the Copy item on the Edit menu calls EditCopyProc, a procedure that copies selected text onto the Clipboard.

Because the application can have many instances of the same child form, EditCopyProc needs to know which form to use. To specify this, use the MDI form's ActiveForm property, which returns the child form that has the focus or that was most recently active.

> **Note** At least one MDI child form must be loaded and visible when you access the ActiveForm property, or an error is returned.

When you have several controls on a form, you also need to specify which control is active. Like the ActiveForm property, the ActiveControl property returns the control with the focus on the active child form. Here's an example of a copy routine that can be called from a child form menu, a menu on the MDI form, or a toolbar button:

```
Private Sub EditCopyProc ()
   ' Copy selected text onto Clipboard.
   ClipBoard.SetText _
      frmMDI.ActiveForm.ActiveControl.SelText
End Sub
```

If you're writing code that will be called by multiple instances of a form, it's a good idea to *not* use a form identifier when accessing the form's controls or properties. For example, refer to the height of the text box on Form1 as `Text1.Height` instead of `Form1.Text1.Height`. This way, the code always affects the current form.

Another way to specify the current form in code is to use the Me keyword. You use Me to reference the form whose code is currently running. This keyword is useful when you need to pass a reference to the current form instance as an argument to a procedure.

For More Information For information on creating multiple instances of a form using the New keyword with the Dim statement, see "Introduction to Variables, Constants, and Data Types" in Chapter 5, "Programming Fundamentals," and "Dim Statement" in the *Microsoft Visual Basic 6.0 Language Reference* volume of the *Microsoft Visual Basic 6.0 Reference Library.*

Loading MDI Forms and Child Forms

When you load a child form, its parent form (the MDI form) is automatically loaded and displayed. When you load the MDI form, however, its children are not automatically loaded.

In the MDI NotePad example, the child form is the default startup form, so both the child and MDI forms are loaded when the application is run. If you change the startup form in the MDI NotePad application to frmMDI (on the General tab of Project Properties) and then run the application, only the MDI form is loaded. The first child form is loaded when you choose New from the File menu.

You can use the AutoShowChildren property to load MDI child windows as hidden, and leave them hidden until you display them using the Show method. This allows you to update various details such as captions, position, and menus before a child form becomes visible.

You can't show an MDI child form or the MDI form modally (using the Show method with an argument of vbModal). If you want to use a modal dialog box in an MDI application, use a form with its MDIChild property set to False.

Setting Child Form Size and Position

When an MDI child form has a sizable border (BorderStyle = 2), Microsoft Windows determines its initial height, width, and position when it is loaded. The initial size and position of a child form with a sizable border depends on the size of the MDI form, not on the size of the child form at design time. When an MDI child form's border is not sizable (BorderStyle = 0, 1, or 3), it is loaded using its design-time Height and Width properties.

If you set AutoShowChildren to False, you can change the position of the MDI child after you load it, but before you make it visible.

For More Information See "AutoShowChildren Property" and "Show Method" in the *Microsoft Visual Basic 6.0 Language Reference*.

Maintaining State Information for a Child Form

A user deciding to quit the MDI application must have the opportunity to save work. To make this possible, the application needs to be able to determine, at all times, whether the data in the child form has changed since the last time it was saved.

You can do this by declaring a public variable on each child form. For example, you can declare a variable in the Declarations section of a child form:

```
Public boolDirty As Boolean
```

Each time the text changes in Text1, the child form's text box Change event sets `boolDirty` to True. You can add this code to indicate that the contents of Text1 have changed since the last time it was saved:

```
Private Sub Text1_Change ()
   boolDirty = True
End Sub
```

Conversely, for each time the user saves the contents of the child form, the text box's Change event sets `boolDirty` to False to indicate that the contents of Text1 no longer need to be saved. In the following code, it is assumed that there is a menu command called Save (mnuFileSave) and a procedure called FileSave that saves the contents of the text box:

```
Sub mnuFileSave_Click ()
   ' Save the contents of Text1.
   FileSave
   ' Set the state variable.
   boolDirty = False
End Sub
```

Unloading MDI Forms with QueryUnload

The `boolDirty` flag becomes useful when the user decides to exit the application. This can occur when the user chooses Close from the MDI form's Control menu, or through a menu item you provide, such as Exit on the File menu. If the user closes the application using the MDI form's Control menu, Visual Basic will attempt to unload the MDI form.

When an MDI form is unloaded, the QueryUnload event is invoked first for the MDI form and then for every child form that is open. If none of the code in these QueryUnload event procedures cancels the Unload event, then each child is unloaded and finally, the MDI form is unloaded.

Because the QueryUnload event is invoked before a form is unloaded, you can give the user the opportunity to save a form before unloading it. The following code uses the `boolDirty` flag to determine if the user should be prompted to save the child before it is unloaded. Notice that you can access the value of a public form-level variable anywhere in the project. This code assumes that there is a procedure, FileSave, that saves the contents of Text1 in a file.

```
Private Sub mnuFExit_Click()
   ' When the user chooses File Exit in an MDI
   ' application, unload the MDI form, invoke
   ' the QueryUnload event for each open child.
   Unload frmMDI
   End
End Sub

Private Sub Form_QueryUnload(Cancel As Integer, _
   UnloadMode As Integer)
   If boolDirty Then
      ' Call routine to query the user and save
      ' file if necessary.
      FileSave
   End If
End Sub
```

For More Information See "QueryUnload Event" in the *Microsoft Visual Basic 6.0 Language Reference*.

More About Forms

In addition to the basics of form design, you need to think about the beginning and end of your application. There are several techniques available for determining what the user will see when your application starts. It's also important to be aware of the processes that occur when an application is unloaded.

Setting the Startup Form

By default, the first form in your application is designated as the *startup form*. When your application starts running, this form is displayed (so the first code to execute is the code in the Form_Initialize event for that form). If you want a different form to display when your application starts, you must change the startup form.

To change the startup form

1. From the **Project** menu, choose **Project Properties**.
2. Choose the **General** tab.
3. In the **Startup Object** list box, select the form you want as the new startup form.
4. Choose **OK**.

Starting Without a Startup Form

Sometimes you might want your application to start without any form initially loaded. For example, you might want to execute code that loads a data file and then displays one of several different forms depending on what is in the data file. You can do this by creating a Sub procedure called Main in a standard module, as in the following example:

```
Sub Main()
   Dim intStatus As Integer
   ' Call a function procedure to check user status.
   intStatus = GetUserStatus
   ' Show a startup form based on status.
   If intStatus = 1 Then
      frmMain.Show
   Else
      frmPassword.Show
   End If
```

This procedure must be a Sub procedure, and it cannot be in a form module. To set the Sub Main procedure as the startup object, from the Project menu, choose Project Properties, select the General tab, and select Sub Main from the Startup Object box.

Displaying a Splash Screen on Startup

If you need to execute a lengthy procedure on startup, such as loading a large amount of data from a database or loading several large bitmaps, you might want to display a splash screen on startup. A splash screen is a form, usually displaying information such as the name of the application, copyright information, and a simple bitmap. The screen that is displayed when you start Visual Basic is a splash screen.

To display a splash screen, use a Sub Main procedure as your startup object and use the Show method to display the form:

```
Private Sub Main()
   ' Show the splash screen.
   frmSplash.Show
   ' Add your startup procedures here.
   …
   ' Show the main form and unload the splash screen.
   frmMain.Show
   Unload frmSplash
End Sub
```

The splash screen occupies the user's attention while your startup routines are executing, giving the illusion that the application is loading faster. When the startup routines are completed, you can load your first form and unload the splash screen.

In designing a splash screen, it's a good idea to keep it simple. If you use large bitmaps or a lot of controls, the splash screen itself may be slow to load.

Ending an Application

An event-driven application stops running when all its forms are closed and no code is executing. If a hidden form still exists when the last visible form is closed, your application will appear to have ended (because no forms are visible), but will in fact continue to run until all the hidden forms are closed. This situation can arise because any access to an unloaded form's properties or controls implicitly loads that form without displaying it.

The best way to avoid this problem when closing your application is to make sure all your forms are unloaded. If you have more than one form, you can use the Forms collection and the Unload statement. For example, on your main form you could have a command button named cmdQuit that lets a user exit the program. If your application has only one form, the Click event procedure could be as simple as this:

```
Private Sub cmdQuit_Click ()
   Unload Me
End Sub
```

If your application uses multiple forms, you can unload the forms by putting code in the Unload event procedure of your main form. You can use the Forms collection to make sure you find and close all your forms. The following code uses the forms collection to unload all forms:

```
Private Sub Form_Unload (Cancel As Integer)
   Dim i as integer
   ' Loop through the forms collection and unload
   ' each form.
   For i = Forms.Count - 1 to 0 Step - 1
      Unload Forms(i)
   Next
End Sub
```

There may be cases where you need to end your application without regard for the state of any existing forms or objects. Visual Basic provides the End statement for this purpose.

The End statement ends an application immediately: no code after the End statement is executed, and no further events occur. In particular, Visual Basic will not execute the QueryUnload, Unload or Terminate event procedures for any forms. Object references will be freed, but if you have defined your own classes, Visual Basic will not execute the Terminate events of objects created from your classes.

In addition to the End statement, the Stop statement halts an application. However, you should use the Stop statement only while debugging, because it does not free references to objects.

For More Information For information on the Stop statement, see "Using Break Mode" in Chapter 13, "Debugging Your Code and Handling Errors," and "Stop Statement" in the *Microsoft Visual Basic 6.0 Language Reference*. For information on the forms collection or freeing references to objects, see Chapter 9, "Programming with Objects."

Using Menus in Your Application

Many simple applications consist of one form and several controls, but you can enhance your Visual Basic applications by adding menus. This section shows you how to create menus and use them in an application.

Creating Menus with the Menu Editor

You can use the Menu Editor to create new menus and menu bars, add new commands to existing menus, replace existing menu commands with your own commands, and change and delete existing menus and menu bars.

To display the Menu Editor

- From the **Tools** menu, choose **Menu Editor**.

  – or –

  Click the **Menu Editor** button on the toolbar.

This opens the Menu Editor, shown in Figure 6.7.

Figure 6.7 The Menu Editor

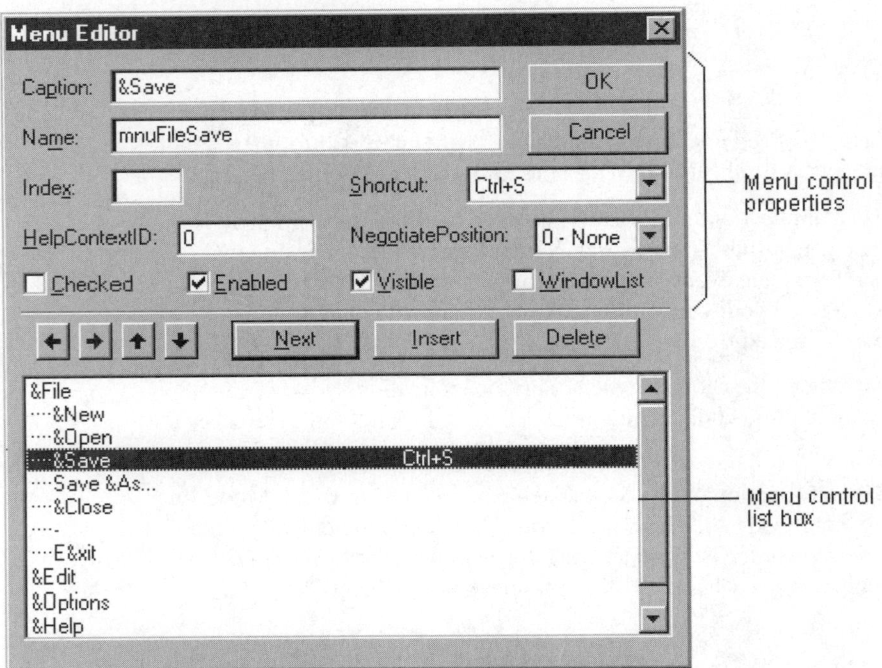

While most menu control properties can be set using the Menu Editor, all menu properties are available in the Properties window. The two most important properties for menu controls are:

- Name — This is the name you use to reference the menu control from code.
- Caption — This is the text that appears on the control.

Other properties in the Menu Editor, including Index, Checked, and NegotiatePosition, are described later in this chapter.

Using the List Box in the Menu Editor

The menu control list box (the lower portion of the Menu Editor) lists all the menu controls for the current form. When you type a menu item in the Caption text box, that item also appears in the menu control list box. Selecting an existing menu control from the list box allows you to edit the properties for that control.

For example, Figure 6.7 shows the menu controls for a File menu in a typical application. The position of the menu control in the menu control list box determines whether the control is a menu title, menu item, submenu title, or submenu item:

- A menu control that appears flush left in the list box is displayed on the menu bar as a menu title.
- A menu control that is indented once in the list box is displayed on the menu when the user clicks the preceding menu title.
- An indented menu control followed by menu controls that are further indented becomes a submenu title. Menu controls indented below the submenu title become items of that submenu.
- A menu control with a hyphen (-) as its Caption property setting appears as a separator bar. A *separator bar* divides menu items into logical groups.

  Note A menu control cannot be a separator bar if it is a menu title, has submenu items, is checked or disabled, or has a shortcut key.

To create menu controls in the Menu Editor

1. Select the form.
2. From the **Tools** menu, choose **Menu Editor**.

   – or –

   Click the **Menu Editor** button on the toolbar.
3. In the **Caption** text box, type the text for the first menu title that you want to appear on the menu bar. Also, place an ampersand (&) before the letter you want to be the access key for that menu item. This letter will automatically be underlined in the menu.

   The menu title text is displayed in the menu control list box.
4. In the **Name** text box, type the name that you will use to refer to the menu control in code. See "Menu Title and Naming Guidelines" later in this chapter.
5. Click the left arrow or right arrow buttons to change the indentation level of the control.
6. Set other properties for the control, if you choose. You can do this in the Menu Editor or later, in the Properties window.

7. Choose **Next** to create another menu control.

   – or –

   Click **Insert** to add a menu control between existing controls.

   You can also click the up arrow and down arrow buttons to move the control among the existing menu controls.

8. Choose **OK** to close the Menu Editor when you have created all the menu controls for that form.

   The menu titles you create are displayed on the form. At design time, click a menu title to drop down its corresponding menu items.

Separating Menu Items

A separator bar is displayed as a horizontal line between items on a menu. On a menu with many items, you can use a separator bar to divide items into logical groups. For example, the File menu in Visual Basic uses separator bars to divide its menu items into three groups, as shown in Figure 6.8.

Figure 6.8 Separator bars

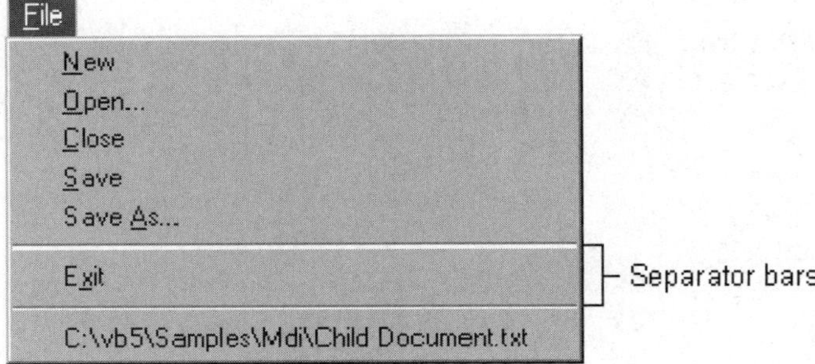

To create a separator bar in the Menu Editor

1. If you are adding a separator bar to an existing menu, choose **Insert** to insert a menu control between the menu items you want to separate.
2. If necessary, click the right arrow button to indent the new menu item to the same level as the menu items it will separate.
3. Type a hyphen (-) in the **Caption** text box.
4. Set the **Name** property.
5. Choose **OK** to close the Menu Editor.

   Note Although separator bars are created as menu controls, they do not respond to the Click event, and users cannot choose them.

Assigning Access Keys and Shortcut Keys

You can improve keyboard access to menu commands by defining access keys and shortcut keys.

Access Keys

Access keys allow the user to open a menu by pressing the ALT key and typing a designated letter. Once a menu is open, the user can choose a control by pressing the letter (the access key) assigned to it. For example, ALT+E might open the Edit menu, and P might select the Paste menu item. An access-key assignment appears as an underlined letter in the menu control's caption, as shown in Figure 6.9.

Figure 6.9 Access keys

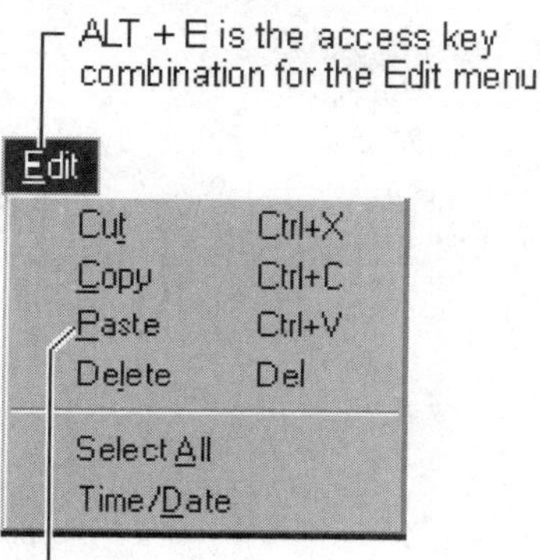

To assign an access key to a menu control in the Menu Editor

1. Select the menu item to which you want to assign an access key.
2. In the **Caption** box, type an ampersand (&) immediately in front of the letter you want to be the access key.

For example, if the Edit menu shown in Figure 6.9 is open, the following Caption property settings respond to the corresponding keys.

Menu control caption	Caption property	Access keys
Cut	Cu&t	t
Copy	C&opy	o
Paste	&Paste	p

Menu control caption	Caption property	Access keys
Delete	De&lete	l
Select All	Select &All	a
Time/Date	Time/&Date	d

Note Do not use duplicate access keys on menus. If you use the same access key for more than one menu item, the key will not work. For example, if C is the access key for both Cut and Copy, when you select the Edit menu and press C, the Copy command will be selected, but the application will not carry out the command until the user presses ENTER. The Cut command will not be selected at all.

Shortcut Keys

Shortcut keys run a menu item immediately when pressed. Frequently used menu items may be assigned a keyboard shortcut, which provides a single-step method of keyboard access, rather than a three-step method of pressing ALT, a menu title access character, and then a menu item access character. Shortcut key assignments include function key and control key combinations, such as CTRL+F1 or CTRL+A. They appear on the menu to the right of the corresponding menu item, as shown in Figure 6.10.

Figure 6.10 Shortcut keys

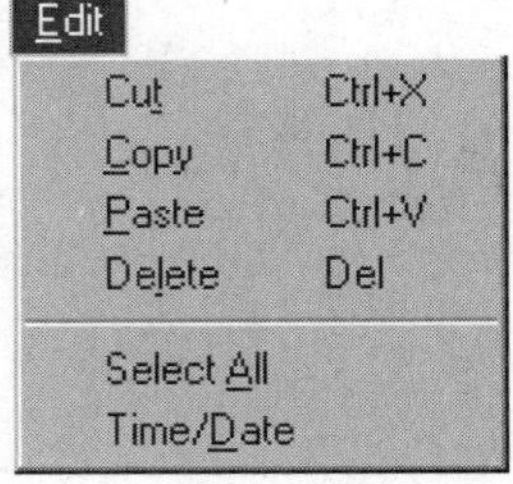

To assign a shortcut key to a menu item

1. Open the **Menu Editor**.
2. Select the menu item.
3. Select a function key or key combination in the **Shortcut** combo box.

   To remove a shortcut key assignment, choose "(none)" from the top of the list.

   Note Shortcut keys appear automatically on the menu; therefore, you do not have to enter CTRL+*key* in the Caption box of the Menu Editor.

Menu Title and Naming Guidelines

To maintain consistency with other applications, it's a good idea to follow established naming guidelines when creating menus.

Setting the Caption Property

When assigning captions for menu items, you should try to follow these guidelines:

- Item names should be unique within a menu, but may be repeated in different menus to represent similar actions.
- Item names may be single, compound, or multiple words.
- Each item name should have a unique mnemonic access character for users who choose commands with keyboards. The access character should be the first letter of the menu title, unless another letter offers a stronger mnemonic link; no two menu titles should use the same access character. For more information about assigning access and shortcut keys, see "Creating Menus with the Menu Editor" earlier in this chapter.
- An ellipsis (…) should follow names of commands that require more information before they can be completed, such as commands that display a dialog (Save As…, Preferences…).
- Keep the item names short. If you are localizing your application, the length of words tends to increase approximately thirty percent in foreign versions, and you may not have enough space to adequately list all of your menu items. For more details on localizing your application, see Chapter 16, "International Issues."

Menu Naming Conventions

To make your code more readable and easier to maintain, it's a good idea to follow established naming conventions when setting the Name property in the Menu Editor. Most naming convention guidelines suggest a prefix to identify the object (that is, mnu for a menu control) followed by the name of the top-level menu (for example, File). For submenus, this would be followed by the caption of the submenu (for example, mnuFileOpen).

For More Information For an example of suggested naming conventions, see Appendix B, "Visual Basic Coding Conventions."

Creating Submenus

Each menu you create can include up to five levels of submenus. A *submenu* branches off another menu to display its own menu items. You may want to use a submenu when:

- The menu bar is full.
- A particular menu control is seldom used.
- You want to emphasize one menu control's relationship to another.

If there is room on the menu bar, however, it's better to create an additional menu title instead of a submenu. That way, all the controls are visible to the user when the menu is dropped down. It's also good programming practice to restrict the use of submenus so users don't get lost trying to navigate your application's menu interface. (Most applications use only one level of submenus.)

In the Menu Editor, any menu control indented below a menu control that is *not* a menu title is a *submenu control*. In general, submenu controls can include submenu items, separator bars, and submenu titles.

To create a submenu

1. Create the menu item that you want to be the submenu title.
2. Create the items that will appear on the new submenu, and indent them by clicking the right arrow button.

   Each indent level is preceded by four dots (....) in the Menu Editor. To remove one level of indentation, click the left arrow button.

   Note If you're considering using more than a single level of submenus, think about using a dialog box instead. Dialog boxes allow users to specify several choices in one place. For information on using dialog boxes, see "Dialog Boxes" later in this chapter.

Creating a Menu Control Array

A *menu control array* is a set of menu items on the same menu that share the same name and event procedures. Use a menu control array to:

- Create a new menu item at run time when it must be a member of a control array. The MDI Notepad sample, for example, uses a menu control array to store a list of recently opened files.
- Simplify code, because common blocks of code can be used for all menu items.

Each menu control array element is identified by a unique index value, indicated in the Index property box on the Menu Editor. When a member of a control array recognizes an event, Visual Basic passes its Index property value to the event procedure as an additional argument. Your event procedure must include code to check the value of the Index property, so you can determine which control you're using.

For More Information For more information on control arrays, see "Working with Control Arrays" in Chapter 7, "Using Visual Basic's Standard Controls."

To create a menu control array in the Menu Editor

1. Select the form.
2. From the **Tools** menu, choose **Menu Editor**.

   – or –

   Click the **Menu Editor** button on the toolbar.
3. In the **Caption** text box, type the text for the first menu title that you want to appear on the menu bar.

   The menu title text is displayed in the menu control list box.
4. In the **Name** text box, type the name that you will use to refer to the menu control in code. Leave the **Index** box empty.
5. At the next indentation level, create the menu item that will become the first element in the array by setting its **Caption** and **Name**.
6. Set the **Index** for the first element in the array to 0.
7. Create a second menu item at the same level of indentation as the first.
8. Set the **Name** of the second element to the same as the first element and set its **Index** to 1.
9. Repeat steps 5–8 for subsequent elements of the array.

   Important Elements of a menu control array must be contiguous in the menu control list box and must be at the same level of indentation. When you're creating menu control arrays, be sure to include any separator bars that appear on the menu.

Creating and Modifying Menus at Run Time

The menus you create at design time can also respond dynamically to run-time conditions. For example, if a menu item action becomes inappropriate at some point, you can prevent users from selecting that menu item by *disabling* it. In the MDI NotePad application, for example, if the clipboard doesn't contain any text, the Paste menu item is dimmed on the Edit menu, and users cannot select it.

You can also dynamically add menu items, if you have a menu control array. This is described in "Adding Menu Controls at Run Time," later in this chapter.

You can also program your application to use a check mark to indicate which of several commands was last selected. For example, the Options, Toolbar menu item from the MDI NotePad application displays a check mark if the toolbar is displayed. Other menu control features described in this section include code that makes a menu item visible or invisible and that adds or deletes menu items.

Enabling and Disabling Menu Commands

All menu controls have an Enabled property, and when this property is set to False, the menu is disabled and does not respond to user actions. Shortcut key access is also disabled when Enabled is set to False. A disabled menu control appears dimmed, like the Paste menu item in Figure 6.11.

Figure 6.11 A disabled menu item

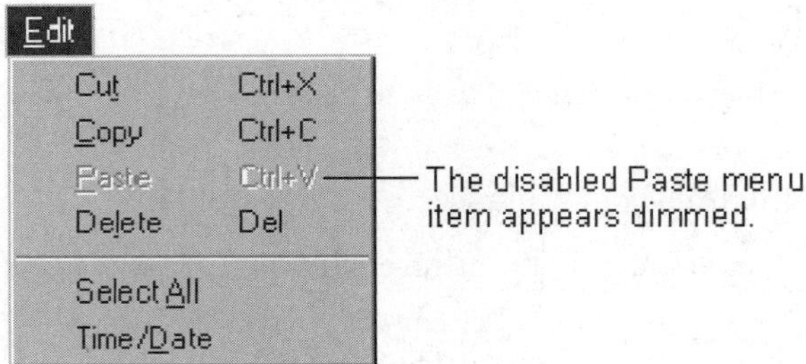

For example, this statement disables the Paste menu item on the Edit menu of the MDI NotePad application:

```
mnuEditPaste.Enabled = False
```

Disabling a menu title in effect disables the entire menu, because the user cannot access any menu item without first clicking the menu title. For example, the following code would disable the Edit menu of the MDI Notepad application:

```
mnuEdit.Enabled = False
```

Displaying a Check Mark on a Menu Control

Using the Checked property, you can place a check mark on a menu to:

- Tell the user the status of an on/off condition. Choosing the menu command alternately adds and removes the check mark.
- Indicate which of several modes is in effect. The Options menu of the MDI Notepad application uses a check mark to indicate the state of the toolbar, as shown in Figure 6.12.

Figure 6.12 A checked menu item

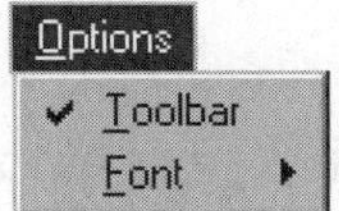

You create check marks in Visual Basic with the Checked property. Set the initial value of the Checked property in the Menu Editor by selecting the check box labeled Checked. To add or remove a check mark from a menu control at run time, set its Checked property from code. For example:

```
Private Sub mnuOptions_Click ()
    ' Set the state of the check mark based on
    ' the Visible property.
    mnuOptionsToolbar.Checked = picToolbar.Visible
End Sub
```

Making Menu Controls Invisible

In the Menu Editor, you set the initial value of the Visible property for a menu control by selecting the check box labeled Visible. To make a menu control visible or invisible at run time, set its Visible property from code. For example:

```
mnuFileArray(0).Visible = True ' Make the control
                               ' visible.

mnuFileArray(0).Visible = False' Make the control
                               ' invisible.
```

When a menu control is invisible, the rest of the controls in the menu move up to fill the empty space. If the control is on the menu bar, the rest of the controls on the menu bar move left to fill the space.

> **Note** Making a menu control invisible effectively disables it, because the control is inaccessible from the menu, access or shortcut keys. If the menu title is invisible, all the controls on that menu are unavailable.

Adding Menu Controls at Run Time

A menu can grow at run time. In Figure 6.13, for example, as files are opened in the SDI NotePad application, menu items are dynamically created to display the path names of the most recently opened files.

Figure 6.13 Menu control array elements created and displayed at run time

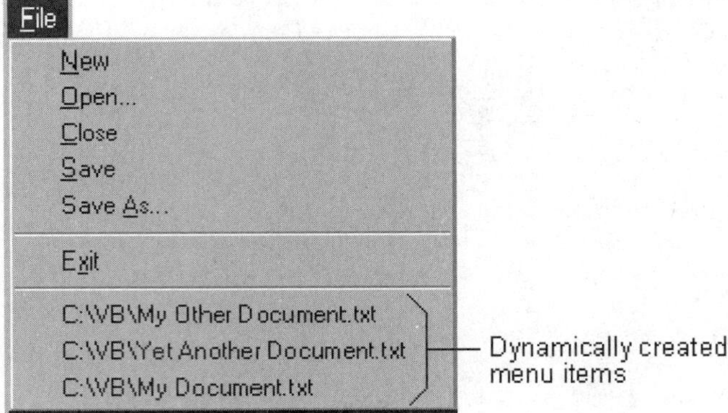

You must use a control array to create a control at run time. Because the mnuRecentFile menu control is assigned a value for the Index property at design time, it automatically becomes an element of a control array — even though no other elements have yet been created.

When you create mnuRecentFile(0), you actually create a separator bar that is invisible at run time. The first time a user saves a file at run time, the separator bar becomes visible, and the first file name is added to the menu. Each time you save a file at run time, additional menu controls are loaded into the array, making the menu grow.

Controls created at run time can be hidden by using the Hide method or by setting the control's Visible property to False. If you want to remove a control in a control array from memory, use the Unload statement.

Writing Code for Menu Controls

When the user chooses a menu control, a Click event occurs. You need to write a Click event procedure in code for each menu control. All menu controls except separator bars (and disabled or invisible menu controls) recognize the Click event.

The code that you write in a menu event procedure is no different than that which you would write in any other control's event procedure. For example, the code in a File, Close menu's Click event might look like this:

```
Sub mnuFileClose_Click()
   Unload Me
End Sub
```

Visual Basic displays a menu automatically when the menu title is chosen; therefore, it is not necessary to write code for a menu title's Click event procedure unless you want to perform another action, such as disabling certain menu items each time the menu is displayed.

Note At design time, the menus you create are displayed on the form when you close the Menu Editor. Choosing a menu item on the form displays the Click event procedure for that menu control.

Displaying Pop-up Menus

A *pop-up menu* is a floating menu that is displayed over a form, independent of the menu bar. The items displayed on the pop-up menu depend on where the pointer was located when the right mouse button was pressed; therefore, pop-up menus are also called *context menus*. In Microsoft Windows 95, you activate context menus by clicking the right mouse button.

Any menu that has at least one menu item can be displayed at run time as a pop-up menu. To display a pop-up menu, use the PopupMenu method. This method uses the following syntax:

[*object.*]**PopupMenu** *menuname* [, *flags* [,*x* [, *y* [, *boldcommand*]]]]

For example, the following code displays a menu named mnuFile when the user clicks a form with the right mouse button. You can use the MouseUp or MouseDown event to detect when the user clicks the right mouse button, although the standard is to use the MouseUp event:

```
Private Sub Form_MouseUp (Button As Integer, Shift As _
   Integer, X As Single, Y As Single)
   If Button = 2 Then' Check if right mouse button
                     ' was clicked.
      PopupMenu mnuFile ' Display the File menu as a
                     ' pop-up menu.
   End If
End Sub
```

Any code following a call to the PopupMenu method is not run until the user selects an item in the menu or cancels the menu.

Note Only one pop-up menu can be displayed at a time. While a pop-up menu is displayed, calls to the PopupMenu method are ignored. Calls to the PopupMenu method are also ignored whenever a menu control is active.

Often you want a pop-up menu to access options that are not usually available on the menu bar. To create a menu that will not display on the menu bar, make the top-level menu item invisible at design time (make sure the Visible check box in the Menu Editor is not checked). When Visual Basic displays a pop-up menu, the Visible property of the specified top-level menu is ignored.

The Flags Argument

You use the *flags* argument in the PopupMenu method to further define the location and behavior of a pop-up menu. The following table lists the flags available to describe a pop-up menu's location.

Location constants	Description
VbPopupMenuLeftAlign	Default. The specified *x* location defines the left edge of the pop-up menu.
vbPopupMenuCenterAlign	The pop-up menu is centered around the specified *x* location.
vbPopupMenuRightAlign	The specified *x* location defines the right edge of the pop-up menu.

The following table lists the flags available to describe a pop-up menu's behavior.

Behavior constants	Description
vbPopupMenuLeftButton	Default. The pop-up menu is displayed when the user clicks a menu item with the left mouse button only.
vbPopupMenuRightButton	The pop-up menu is displayed when the user clicks a menu item with either the right or left mouse button.

To specify a flag, you combine one constant from each group using the Or operator. The following code displays a pop-up menu with its top border centered on a form when the user clicks a command button. The pop-up menu triggers Click events for menu items that are clicked with either the right or left mouse button.

```
Private Sub Command1_Click ()
   ' Dimension X and Y variables.
   Dim xloc, yloc

   ' Set X and Y variables to center of form.
   xloc = ScaleWidth / 2
   yloc = ScaleHeight / 2

   ' Display the pop-up menu.
   PopupMenu mnuEdit, vbPopupMenuCenterAlign Or _
   vbPopupMenuRightButton, xloc, yloc
End Sub
```

The Boldcommand Argument

You use the *boldcommand* argument to specify the name of a menu control in the displayed pop-up menu that you want to appear in bold. Only one menu control in the pop-up menu can be bold.

Menus in MDI Applications

In an MDI application, the menus for each child are displayed on the MDI form, rather than on the child forms themselves. When a child form has the focus, that child's menu (if any) replaces the MDI form's menu on the menu bar. If there are no child forms visible, or if the child with the focus does not have a menu, the MDI form's menu is displayed (see Figures 6.14 and 6.15).

It is common for MDI applications to use several sets of menus. When the user opens a document, the application displays the menu associated with that type of document. Usually, a different menu is displayed when no child forms are visible. For example, when there are no files open, Microsoft Excel displays only the File and Help menus. When the user opens a file, other menus are displayed (File, Edit, View, Insert, Format, Tools, Data, Window, and so on).

Creating Menus for MDI Applications

You can create menus for your Visual Basic application by adding menu controls to the MDI form and to the child forms. One way to manage the menus in your MDI application is to place the menu controls you want displayed all of the time, even when no child forms are visible, on the MDI form. When you run the application, the MDI form's menu is automatically displayed when there are no child forms visible, as shown in Figure 6.14.

Figure 6.14 The MDI form menu is displayed when no child forms are loaded

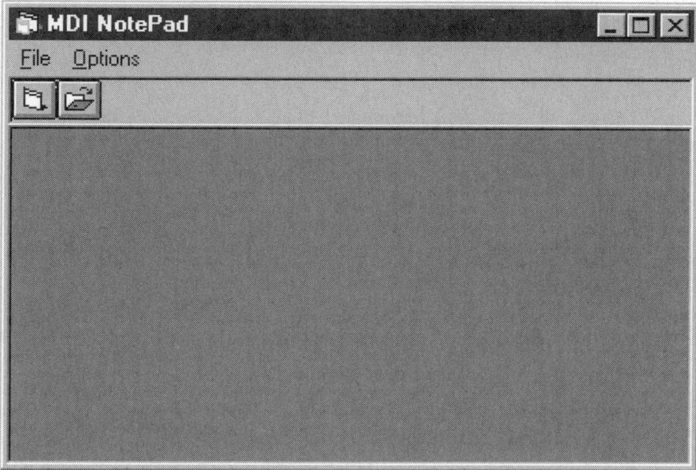

Place the menu controls that apply to a child form on the child form. At run time, as long as there is at least one child form visible, these menu titles are displayed in the menu bar of the MDI form.

Some applications support more than one type of document. For example, in Microsoft Access, you can open tables, queries, forms, and other document types. To create an application such as this in Visual Basic, use two child forms. Design one child with menus that perform spreadsheet tasks and the other with menus that perform charting tasks.

At run time, when an instance of a spreadsheet form has the focus, the spreadsheet menu is displayed, and when the user selects a chart, that form's menu is displayed. If all the spreadsheets and charts are closed, the MDI form's menu is displayed. For more information on creating menus, see "Using Menus in Your Application" earlier in this chapter.

Creating a Window Menu

Most MDI applications (for example, Microsoft Word for Windows and Microsoft Excel) incorporate a Window menu. This is a special menu that displays the captions of all open child forms, as shown in Figure 6.15. In addition, some applications place commands on this menu that manipulate the child windows, such as Cascade, Tile, and Arrange Icons.

Figure 6.15 The Window menu displays the name of each open child form

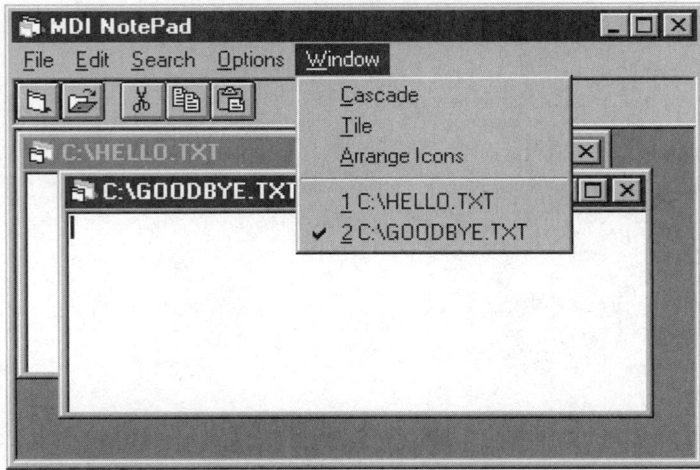

Any menu control on an MDI form or MDI child form can be used to display the list of open child forms by setting the WindowList property for that menu control to True. At run time, Visual Basic automatically manages and displays the list of captions and displays a check mark next to the one that had the focus most recently. In addition, a separator bar is automatically placed above the list of windows.

To set the WindowList property

1. Select the form where you want the menu to appear, and from the **Tools** menu, choose **Menu Editor**.

   Note The WindowList property applies only to MDI forms and MDI child forms. It has no effect on standard (non-MDI) forms.

2. In the **Menu Editor** list box, select the menu where you want the list of open child forms to display.
3. Select the **WindowList** check box.

At run time, this menu displays the list of open child forms. In addition, the WindowList property for this menu control returns as True.

For More Information See "WindowList Property" in the *Microsoft Visual Basic 6.0 Language Reference*.

Arranging Child Forms

As was mentioned earlier, some applications list actions such as Tile, Cascade, and Arrange Icons on a menu, along with the list of open child forms. Use the Arrange method to rearrange child forms in the MDI form. You can display child forms as cascading, as horizontally tiled, or as child form icons arranged along the lower portion of the MDI form. The following example shows the Click event procedures for the Cascade, Tile, and Arrange Icons menu controls.

```
Private Sub mnuWCascade_Click ()
   ' Cascade child forms.
   frmMDI.Arrange vbCascade
End Sub

Private Sub mnuWTile_Click ()
   ' Tile child forms (horizontal).
   frmMDI.Arrange vbTileHorizontal
End Sub

Private Sub mnuWArrange_Click ()
   ' Arrange all child form icons.
   frmMDI.Arrange vbArrangeIcons
End Sub
```

Note The intrinsic constants vbCascade, vbTileHorizontal, and vbArrangeIcons are listed in the Visual Basic (VB) object library of the Object Browser.

When you tile or cascade child forms that have a fixed border style, each child form is positioned as if it had a sizable border. This can cause child forms to overlap.

Toolbars

You can further enhance your application's menu interface with toolbars. Toolbars contain toolbar buttons, which provide quick access to the most frequently used commands in an application. For example, the Visual Basic toolbar contains toolbar buttons to perform commonly used commands, such as opening existing projects or saving the current project.

Creating a Toolbar

The *toolbar* (also called a ribbon or control bar) has become a standard feature in many Windows-based applications. A toolbar provides quick access to the most frequently used menu commands in an application. Creating a toolbar is easy and convenient using the toolbar control, which is available with the Professional and Enterprise editions of Visual Basic. If you are using the Learning Edition of Visual Basic, you can create toolbars manually as described in "Negotiating Menu and Toolbar Appearance" later in this chapter.

The following example demonstrates creating a toolbar for an MDI application; the procedure for creating a toolbar on a standard form is basically the same.

To manually create a toolbar

1. Place a picture box on the MDI form.

   The width of the picture box automatically stretches to fill the width of the MDI form's workspace. The workspace is the area inside a form's borders, not including the title bar, menu bar, or any toolbars, status bars, or scroll bars that may be on the form.

   > **Note** You can place only those controls that support the Align property directly on an MDI form (the picture box is the only standard control that supports this property).

2. Inside the picture box, place any controls you want to display on the toolbar.

   Typically, you create buttons for the toolbar using command buttons or image controls. Figure 6.16 shows a toolbar containing image controls.

   To add a control inside a picture box, click the control button in the toolbox, and then draw it inside the picture box.

   > **Note** When an MDI form contains a picture box, the internal area of the MDI form does not include the area of the picture box. For example, the ScaleHeight property of the MDI form returns the internal height of the MDI form, which does not include the height of the picture box.

Figure 6.16 You can create buttons for the toolbar using image controls

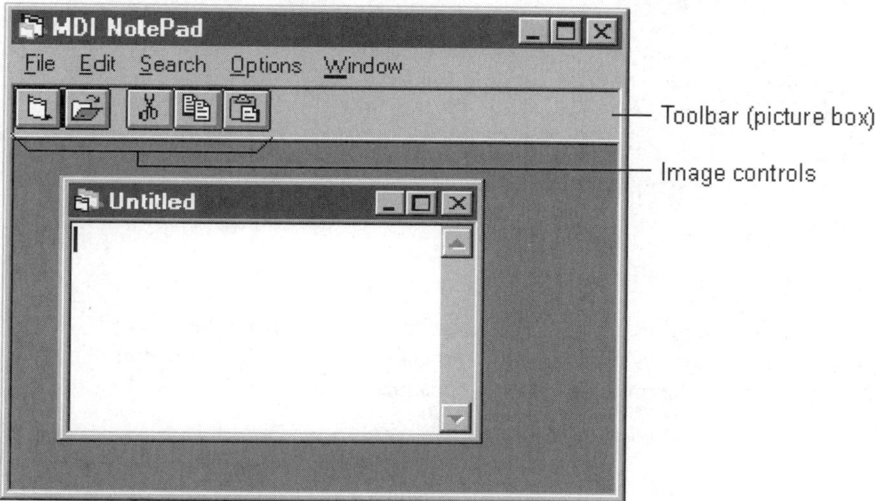

3. Set design-time properties.

   One advantage of using a toolbar is that you can present the user with a graphical representation of a command. The image control is a good choice as a toolbar button because you can use it to display a bitmap. Set its Picture property at design time to display a bitmap; this provides the user with a visual cue of the command performed when the button is clicked. You can also use *ToolTips*, which display the name of the toolbar button when a user rests the mouse pointer over a button, by setting the ToolTipText property for the button.

4. Write code.

   Because toolbar buttons are frequently used to provide easy access to other commands, most of the time you call other procedures, such as a corresponding menu command, from within each button's Click event.

   Tip You can use controls that are invisible at run time (such as the timer control) with an MDI form without displaying a toolbar. To do this, place a picture box on the MDI form, place the control in the picture box, and set the picture box's Visible property to False.

Writing Code for Toolbars

Toolbars are used to provide the user with a quick way to access some of the application's commands. For example, the first button on the toolbar in Figure 6.16 is a shortcut for the File New command. There are now three places in the MDI NotePad sample application where the user can request a new file:

- On the MDI form (New on the MDI form File menu)
- On the child form (New on the child form File menu)
- On the toolbar (File New button)

Rather than duplicate this code three times, you can take the original code from the child form's mnuFileNew_Click event and place it in a public procedure in the child form. You can call this procedure from any of the preceding event procedures. Here's an example:

```
' This routine is in a public procedure.
Public Sub FileNew ()
   Dim frmNewPad As New frmNotePad
   frmNewPad.Show
End Sub

' The user chooses New on the child form File menu.
Private Sub mnuchildFileNew_Click ()
   FileNew
End Sub

' The user chooses New on the MDI form File menu.
Private Sub mnumdiFileNew_Click ()
   frmNotePad.FileNew
End Sub

' The user clicks the File New button on the toolbar.
Private Sub btnFileNew_Click ()
   frmNotePad.FileNew
End Sub
```

Negotiating Menu and Toolbar Appearance

When an object supplied by another application is activated on a form, there are a number of ways that object's menus and toolbars may appear on the container form; therefore, you need to specify how they will be displayed. This process is called *user-interface negotiation* because Visual Basic and the object you have linked or embedded must negotiate for space in the container form.

Controlling Menu Appearance

You can determine whether a linked or embedded object's menu will appear in the container form by setting a form's NegotiateMenus property. If the child form's NegotiateMenus property is set to True (default) and the container has a menu bar defined, the object's menus are placed on the container's menu bar when the object is activated. If the container has no menu bar, or the NegotiateMenus property is set to False, the object's menus will not appear when it is activated.

Note The NegotiateMenus property does *not* apply to MDI Forms.

Controlling Toolbar Appearance

The MDI form's NegotiateToolbars property determines whether the linked or embedded object's toolbars will be floating palettes or placed on the parent form. This behavior does not require toolbars to be present on the MDI parent form. If the MDI form's NegotiateToolbars property is True, the object's toolbar appears on the MDI parent form. If NegotiateToolbars is False, the object's toolbar will be a floating palette.

Note The NegotiateToolbars property applies *only* to MDI forms.

If an MDI form includes a toolbar, it is usually contained in a picture box control on the parent form. The picture box's Negotiate property determines whether the container's toolbar is still displayed or is replaced by the object's toolbar when activated. If Negotiate is True, the object's toolbar is displayed in addition to the container's toolbar. If Negotiate is False, the object's toolbar replaces the container's toolbar.

Note Menu and toolbar negotiation will occur only for insertable objects that support in-place activation. For more information on in-place activation, see Chapter 10, "Programming with Components."

You can see how these three properties interact by using the following procedure.

To perform menu and toolbar negotiation

1. Add a toolbar to an MDI form. This is described in "Creating a Toolbar" earlier in this chapter.
2. Place an insertable object on a child form.
3. Set the **NegotiateMenus**, **NegotiateToolbars**, and **Negotiate** properties.
4. Run the application, and double-click the object.

Dialog Boxes

In Windows-based applications, dialog boxes are used to:

- Prompt the user for data needed by the application to continue.
- Display information to the user.

In Visual Basic, for example, you use the File Open dialog box to display existing projects. The About dialog box in Visual Basic is also an example of how you can use a dialog box to display information. When the user clicks the Help, About Visual Basic menu item on the menu bar, the About dialog box is displayed.

Modal and Modeless Dialog Boxes

Dialog boxes are either modal or modeless. A *modal* dialog box must be closed (hidden or unloaded) before you can continue working with the rest of the application. For example, a dialog box is modal if it requires you to click OK or Cancel before you can switch to another form or dialog box.

The About dialog box in Visual Basic is modal. Dialog boxes that display important messages should always be modal — that is, the user should always be required to close the dialog box or respond to its message before proceeding.

Modeless dialog boxes let you shift the focus between the dialog box and another form without having to close the dialog box. You can continue to work elsewhere in the current application while the dialog box is displayed. Modeless dialog boxes are rare. From the Edit menu, the Find dialog box in Visual Basic is an example of a modeless dialog box. Use modeless dialog boxes to display frequently used commands or information.

To display a form as a modal dialog box

- Use the Show method with a *style* argument of vbModal (a constant for the value 1).

  For example:

  ```
  ' Display frmAbout as a modal dialog.
  frmAbout.Show vbModal
  ```

To display a form as a modeless dialog box

- Use the Show method without a *style* argument.

  For example:

  ```
  ' Display frmAbout as a modeless dialog.
  frmAbout.Show
  ```

  Note If a form is displayed as modal, the code following the Show method is not executed until the dialog box is closed. However, when a form is shown as modeless, the code following the Show method is executed immediately after the form is displayed.

The Show method has another optional argument, *owner*, that can be used to specify a parent-child relationship for a form. You can pass the name of a form to this argument to make that form the owner of the new form.

To display a form as a child of another form

- Use the Show method with both *style* and *owner* arguments.

  For example:

```
' Display frmAbout as a modeless child of frmMain.
frmAbout.Show vbModeless, frmMain
```

Using the *owner* argument with the Show method ensures that the dialog box will be minimized when it's parent is minimized, or unloaded should the parent form be closed.

Using Predefined Dialog Boxes

The easiest way to add a dialog box to your application is to use a predefined dialog, because you don't have to worry about designing, loading, or showing the dialog box. However, your control over its appearance is limited. Predefined dialog boxes are always modal.

The following table lists the functions you can use to add predefined dialog boxes to your Visual Basic application.

Use this function	To do this
InputBox function	Display a command prompt in a dialog box, and return whatever is entered by the user.
MsgBox function	Display a message in a dialog box, and return a value indicating the command button was clicked by the user.

Prompting for Input with InputBox

Use the InputBox function to solicit data from the user. This function displays a modal dialog box that asks the user to enter some data. The text input box shown in Figure 6.17 prompts the user for the name of the file to open.

Figure 6.17 A dialog box using the InputBox function

The following code displays the input box shown in Figure 6.17:

```
FileName = InputBox("Enter file to open:", "File Open")
```

Note Remember that when you use the InputBox function, you have little control over the components of the dialog box. You can change only the text in the title bar, the command prompt displayed to the user, the position of the dialog box on the screen, and whether or not it displays a Help button.

For More Information See "InputBox Function" in the *Microsoft Visual Basic 6.0 Language Reference*.

Displaying Information with MsgBox

Use the MsgBox function to get yes or no responses from users, and to display brief messages, such as errors, warnings, or alerts in a dialog box. After reading the message, the user chooses a button to close the dialog box.

An application named Text Editor might display the message dialog box shown in Figure 6.18 if a file cannot be opened.

Figure 6.18 An error message dialog box created using the MsgBox function

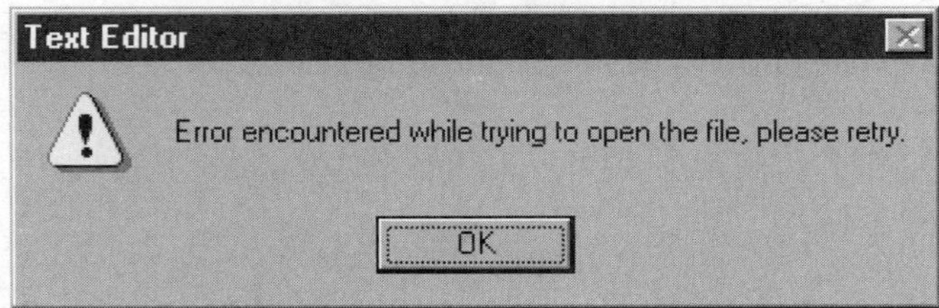

The following code displays the message box shown in Figure 6.18:

```
MsgBox "Error encountered while trying to open file, _
   please retry.", vbExclamation, "Text Editor"
```

Note Modality can either be limited to the application or the system. If a message box's modality is limited to the application (default), then users cannot switch to another part of the application until the dialog box is dismissed, but they can switch to another application. A system modal message box does not allow the user to switch to another application until the message box is dismissed.

For More Information See "MsgBox Function" in the *Microsoft Visual Basic 6.0 Language Reference*.

Using Forms as Custom Dialog Boxes

A *custom dialog box* is a form you create containing controls — including command buttons, option buttons, and text boxes — that lets the user supply information to the application. You customize the appearance of the form by setting property values. You also write code to display the dialog box at run time.

To create a custom dialog box, you can start with a new form or customize an existing dialog box. Over time, you can build up a collection of dialog boxes that can be used in many applications.

To customize an existing dialog box

1. From the **Project** menu, choose **Add Form** to add an existing form to your project.
2. From the **File** menu, choose **Save** *filename* **As** and enter a new file name. (This prevents you from making changes to the existing version of the form).
3. Customize the appearance of the form as needed.
4. Customize event procedures in the Code window.

To create a new dialog box

1. From the **Project** menu, choose **Add Form**.

   – or –

   Click the **Form** button on the toolbar to create a new form.
2. Customize the appearance of the form as needed.
3. Customize event procedures in the Code window.

You have considerable freedom to define the appearance of a custom dialog box. It can be fixed or movable, modal or modeless. It can contain different types of controls; however, dialog boxes do not usually include menu bars, window scroll bars, Minimize and Maximize buttons, status bars, or sizable borders. The remainder of this topic discusses ways to create typical dialog box styles.

Adding a Title

A dialog box should always have a title that identifies it. To create a title, set the form's Caption property to the text string that will appear in the title bar. Usually, this is done at design time using the Properties window, but you can also do this from code. For example:

```
frmAbout.Caption = "About"
```

> **Tip** If you want to remove the title bar completely, set the form's ControlBox, MinButton, and MaxButton properties to False; set the BorderStyle to a nonsizable setting (0, 1, or 3); and set the Caption equal to an empty string ("").

Setting Standard Dialog Box Properties

Generally, the user responds to a dialog box by providing information and then closing the dialog box with an OK or Cancel command button. Because a dialog box is temporary, users usually don't need to move, size, maximize, or minimize it. As a result, the sizable border style, Control menu box, Maximize button, and Minimize button that come with a new form are unnecessary on most dialog boxes.

You can remove these items by setting the BorderStyle, ControlBox, MaxButton, and MinButton properties. For example, an About dialog box might use the following property settings.

Property	Setting	Effect
BorderStyle	1	Changes the border style to fixed single, thus preventing the dialog box from being sized at run time.
ControlBox	False	Removes the Control menu box.
MaxButton	False	Removes the Maximize button, thus preventing the dialog box from being maximized at run time.
MinButton	False	Removes the Minimize button, thus preventing the dialog box from being minimized at run time.

Remember that if you remove the Control menu box (ControlBox = False), you must provide the user with another way to exit the dialog box. This is commonly done by adding an OK, Cancel, or Exit command button to the dialog box and adding code in the Click event for the button that hides or unloads the dialog.

Adding and Placing Command Buttons

Modal dialog boxes must contain at least one command button to exit the dialog box. Usually, two command buttons are used: one button to let the user start an action, and one button to close the dialog box without making any changes. Typically, the Caption property settings for these buttons are OK and Cancel. In this scenario, the OK command button has its Default property set to True, and the Cancel button has its Cancel property set to True. Although OK and Cancel are the most commonly used buttons, other button caption combinations work as well.

Dialog boxes that display messages usually use a label control to display the error message or command prompt, and one or two command buttons to perform an action. For example, you might assign the error message or command prompt to the Caption property of the label, and Yes and No to the Caption property of two command button controls. When users choose Yes, one action takes place; when they choose No, another action occurs.

Command buttons on this type of dialog are usually placed on the bottom or right side of the dialog box, with the top or left button being the default button, as shown in Figure 6.19.

Figure 6.19 Command button placement on dialog boxes

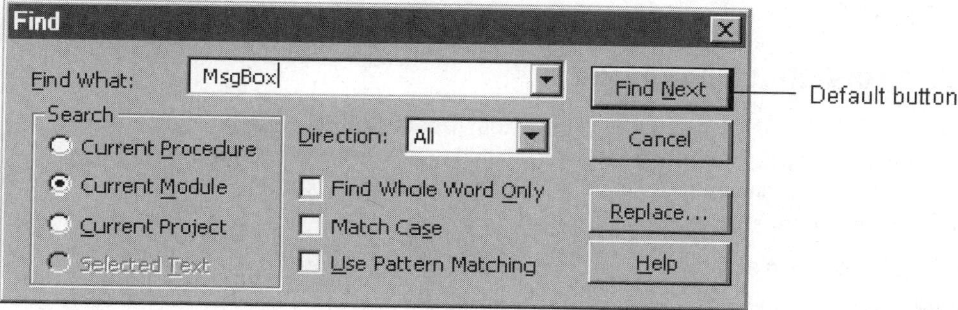

Setting Default, Cancel, and Focus

Command button controls provide the following properties:

- Default
- Cancel
- TabIndex
- TabStop

The Default button is selected when the user presses ENTER. Only one command button on a form can have its Default property set to True. Pressing the ENTER key invokes the Click event for the default command button. This feature works in conjunction with an edit control, such as a text box. For example, the user can type data in a text box and then press ENTER to generate a Click event instead of choosing an OK button.

The Cancel button is selected when the user presses ESC. Only one command button on a form can have its Cancel property set to True. Pressing the ESC key invokes the Click event for the Cancel command button. The Cancel button can also be the default command button. To specify the Cancel button for a dialog box, set the command button's Cancel property to True.

> **Tip** In general, the button that indicates the most likely or safest action should be the default action. For example, in a Text Replace dialog box, Cancel should be the default button, not Replace All.

You can also specify the button that will have the focus when the dialog is displayed. The control with the lowest TabIndex setting receives the focus when the form is displayed. Pressing the ENTER key invokes the Click event for the default command button or for the command button that has the focus. To give a command button the focus when the form is displayed, set the command button's TabIndex to 0 and its TabStop property to True. You can also use the SetFocus method to give a specific control the focus when a form is displayed.

For More Information See "TabIndex Property" and "TabStop Property" in the *Microsoft Visual Basic 6.0 Language Reference*.

Disabling Controls on a Dialog Box

Sometimes controls need to be disabled because their actions would be inappropriate in the current context. For example, when the Visual Basic Find dialog box is first displayed, the Find Next button is disabled, as shown in Figure 6.20. You can disable a control on a dialog by setting its Enabled property to False.

Figure 6.20 Disabled controls on a dialog box

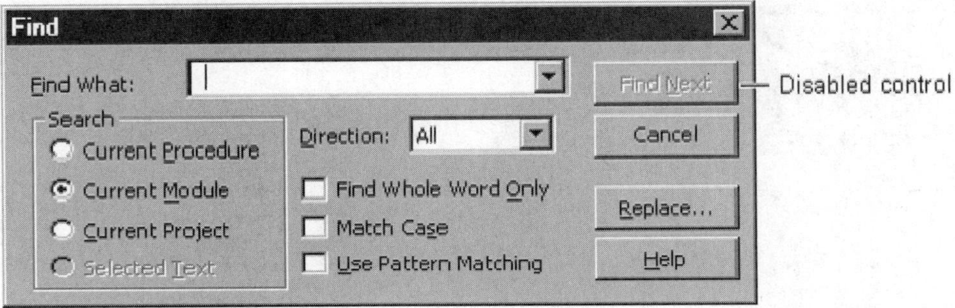

To disable a control on a dialog box

- Set each control's Enabled property to False. For example:

```
cmdFindNext.Enabled = False
cmdReplace.Enabled = False
```

Displaying a Custom Dialog Box

You display a dialog box in the same way you display any other form in an application. The startup form loads automatically when the application is run. When you want a second form or dialog box to appear in the application, you write code to load and display it. Similarly, when you want the form or dialog box to disappear, you write code to unload or hide it.

The following code displays the About dialog box when the user selects the Help, About menu item:

```
Private Sub mnuHelpAbout_Click ()
   ' The Show method with style = vbModal is used here
   ' to display the dialog as modal.
   frmAbout.Show vbModal
End Sub
```

Display Options

The code you write determines how a dialog box is loaded into memory and displayed. The following table describes various form displaying tasks and the keywords that are used to perform them.

Task	Keyword
Load a form into memory, but do not display it.	Use the Load statement, or reference a property or control on the form.
Load and display a modeless form.	Use the Show method.
Load and display a modal form.	Use the Show method with *style* = vbModal.
Display a loaded form.	Set its Visible property to True, or use the Show method.
Hide a form from view.	Set its Visible property to False, or use the Hide method.
Hide a form from view and unload from memory.	Use the Unload statement.

The Show method loads the form and sets its Visible property to True. The argument passed to the Show method indicates the style of the dialog box. If the *style* argument is omitted or set to vbModeless or 0 (default), the dialog box is modeless; if it is vbModal or 1, the dialog box is modal.

To exit the dialog box when the user chooses OK or Cancel, use either the Unload statement or the Hide method. For example:

```
Unload frmAbout
```

– or –

```
frmAbout.Hide
```

The Unload statement removes the dialog box from memory, while the Hide method merely removes the dialog box from view by setting its Visible property to False. When you unload a form, the form itself and its controls are unloaded from memory (including any controls that were loaded at run time). When you hide a form, the form and its controls remain in memory.

When you need to save space in memory, it's better to unload a form, because unloading a form frees memory. If you use the dialog box often, you can choose to hide the form. Hiding a form retains any data attached to it, including property values, print output, and dynamically created controls. By hiding a form, you can continue to refer to the properties and controls of a hidden form in code.

Designing for Different Display Types

Microsoft Windows is device-independent — a windows-based application can be run on many different computers with different display resolutions and color depths. The applications that you write in Visual Basic are likely to be run on different display types as well; you need to be aware of this when designing an application.

Designing Resolution-Independent Forms

By default, Microsoft Visual Basic doesn't change your form and control sizes as you change screen resolutions. What this means is that a form that you design at 1024 by 768 resolution may extend past the edges of the screen when run at 640 by 480 resolution. If you want to create forms and controls that have the same proportions no matter what screen resolution you use, you must either design your forms at the lowest resolution, or add code to your program that changes the forms.

The easiest way to avoid sizing problems is to design your forms at 640 by 480 resolution. If you prefer to work at a higher resolution, you still need to be aware of how your form will appear at a lower resolution. One way to do this is to use the Form Layout window to preview the size and location of your form. You can use Resolution Guides to see what portion of the screen will be visible at a lower resolution. To toggle the Resolution Guides, right click in the Form Layout window and select the Resolution Guides menu item from the pop-up menu.

Visual Basic also places your form at run time based on its location at design time. If you are running at 1024 by 768 resolution at design time and you place a form in the lower right-hand corner of the screen, it may not be visible when run at a lower resolution. To avoid this, set the startup position of your form at design time by selecting the Startup Position menu item from the Form Layout window pop-up menu.

Alternatively, you can set a form's position at runtime with code in the Form Load event:

```
Private Sub Form_Load()
   Me.Move 0, 0
End Sub
```

This has the same effect as setting both the Left and Top properties of the form to 0, but the Move method accomplishes it in a single step.

Visual Basic uses a device-independent unit of measurement, a *twip*, for calculating size and position. Two properties of the Screen object, TwipsPerPixelX and TwipsPerPixelY, can be used to determine the size of the display at run time. Using these properties, you can write code to adjust the size and position of your forms and controls:

```
Private Sub SetControls()
   Dim X As Integer
   Dim Y As Integer
```

```
    X = Screen.TwipsPerPixelX
    Y = Screen.TwipsPerPixelY
    Select Case X, Y
       Case 15, 15
          ' Resize and move controls.
          txtName.Height = 200
          txtName.Width = 500
          txtName.Move 200, 200
       ' Add code for other resolutions.
       …
End Sub
```

You also need to be aware of the position of Visual Basic's own windows at design time. If you position the Project window to the right side of the screen at high resolution, you may find that it is no longer accessible when you open your project at a lower resolution.

Designing for Different Color Depths

In designing an application, you also need to consider the color display capabilities of the computers that may be running your application. Some computers can display 256 or more colors, others are limited to 16. If you design a form using a 256-color palette, *dithering* (a process used to simulate colors that are not available) may cause some of the elements on the form to disappear when displayed at 16 colors.

To avoid this situation, it's best to limit the colors used in your application to the 16 standard Windows colors. These are represented by the Visual Basic color constants (vbBlack, vbBlue, vbCyan, and so on). If it's necessary to use more than 16 colors in your application, you should still stick with the standard colors for text, buttons, and other interface elements.

Designing with the User in Mind

Unless you're creating Visual Basic applications strictly for your own use, the value of your creations is going to be judged by others. The user interface of your application has the greatest impact on the user's opinion — no matter how technically brilliant or well optimized your code may be, if the user finds your application difficult to use, it won't be well received.

As a programmer, you are undoubtedly familiar with the technological aspects of computers. It's easy to forget that most users don't understand (and probably don't care) about the technology behind an application. They see an application as a means to an end: a way to accomplish a task, ideally more easily than they would without the aid of a computer. A well-designed user interface insulates the user from the underlying technology, making it easy to perform the intended task.

In designing the user interface for your application, you need to keep the user in mind. How easily can a user discover the various features of your application without instruction? How will your application respond when errors occur? What will you provide in terms of help or user assistance? Is the design aesthetically pleasing to the user? The answers to these and other questions relating to user-focused design are covered in this section.

The Basics of Interface Design

You don't need to be an artist to create a great user interface — most of the principles of user interface design are the same as the basic design principles taught in any elementary art class. The elementary design principles of composition, color, and so forth apply equally well to a computer screen as they do to a sheet of paper or a canvas.

Although Visual Basic makes it easy to create a user interface by simply dragging controls onto a form, a little planning up front can make a big difference in the usability of your application. You might consider drawing your form designs on paper first, determining which controls are needed, the relative importance of the different elements, and the relationships between controls.

Composition: The Look and Feel of an Application

The composition or layout of your form not only influences its aesthetic appeal, it also has a tremendous impact on the usability of your application. Composition includes such factors as positioning of controls, consistency of elements, affordances, use of white space, and simplicity of design.

Positioning of Controls

In most interface designs, not all elements are of equal importance. Careful design is necessary to ensure that the more important elements are readily apparent to the user. Important or frequently accessed elements should be given a position of prominence; less important elements should be relegated to less prominent locations.

In most languages, we are taught to read from left to right, top to bottom of a page. The same holds true for a computer screen — most user's eyes will be drawn to the upper left portion of the screen first, so the most important element should go there. For example, if the information on a form is related to a customer, the name field should be displayed where it will be seen first. Buttons, such as OK or Next, should be placed in the lower right portion of the screen; the user normally won't access these until they have finished working with the form.

Grouping of elements and controls is also important. Try to group information logically according to function or relationship. Because their functions are related, buttons for navigating a database should be grouped together visually rather than scattered throughout a form. The same applies to information; fields for name and address are generally grouped together, as they are closely related. In many cases, you can use frame controls to help reinforce the relationships between controls.

Consistency of Interface Elements

Consistency is a virtue in user interface design. A consistent look and feel creates harmony in an application — everything seems to fit together. A lack of consistency in your interface can be confusing, and can make an application seem chaotic, disorganized, and cheap, possibly even causing the user to doubt the reliability of an application.

For visual consistency, establish a design strategy and style conventions before you begin development. Design elements such as the types of controls, standards for size and grouping of controls, and font choices should be established in advance. You can create prototypes of possible designs to help you make design decisions.

The wide variety of controls available for use in Visual Basic make it tempting to use them all. Avoid this temptation; choose a subset of controls that best fit your particular application. While list box, combo box, grid, and tree controls can all be used to present lists of information, it's best to stick with a single style where possible.

Also, try to use controls appropriately; while a text box control can be set to read-only and used to display text, a label control is usually more appropriate for that purpose. Remain consistent in the setting of properties for your controls — if you use a white back color for editable text in one place, don't use grey in another unless there's a good reason.

Consistency between different forms in your application is important to usability. If you use a grey background and three-dimensional effects on one form and a white background on another, the forms will appear to be unrelated. Pick a style and stick with it throughout your application, even if it means redesigning some features.

Affordances: Form Follows Function

Affordances are visual clues to the function of an object. Although the term may be unfamiliar, examples of affordances are all around you. A handgrip on a bicycle has depressions where you place your fingers, an affordance that makes it obvious that it is meant to be gripped. Push buttons, knobs, and light switches are all affordances — just by looking at them you can discern their purpose.

A user interface also makes use of affordances. For instances, the three-dimensional effects used on command buttons make them look like they are meant to be pushed. If you were to design a command button with a flat border, you would lose this affordance and it wouldn't be clear to the user that it is a command button. There are cases where flat buttons might be appropriate, such as games or multimedia applications; this is okay as long as you remain consistent throughout your application.

Text boxes also provide a sort of affordance — users expect that a box with a border and a white background will contain editable text. While it's possible to display a text box with no border (BorderStyle = 0), this will make it look like a label and it won't be obvious to the user that it is editable.

Use of White Space

The use of *white space* in your user interface can help to emphasize elements and improve usability. White space doesn't necessarily have to be white — it refers to the use of blank space between and around controls a form. Too many controls on a form can lead to a cluttered interface, making it difficult to find an individual field or control. You need to incorporate white space in your design in order to emphasize your design elements.

Consistent spacing between controls and alignment of vertical and horizontal elements can make your design more usable as well. Just as text in a magazine is arranged in orderly columns with even spacing between lines, an orderly interface makes your interface easy to read.

Visual Basic provides several tools that make it easy to adjust the spacing, alignment, and size of controls. Align, Make Same Size, Horizontal Spacing, Vertical Spacing, and Center in Form commands can all be found under the Format menu.

Keep It Simple

Perhaps the most important principle of interface design is one of simplicity. When it comes to applications, if the interface looks difficult, it probably is. A little forethought can help you to create an interface that looks (and is) simple to use. Also, from an aesthetic standpoint, a clean, simple design is always preferable.

A common pitfall in interface design is to try and model your interface after real-world objects. Imagine, for instance, that you were asked to create an application for completing insurance forms. A natural reaction would be to design an interface that exactly duplicates the paper form on screen. This creates several problems: the shape and dimensions of a paper form are different than those of the screen, duplicating a form pretty much limits you to text boxes and check boxes, and there's no real benefit to the user.

It's far better to design your own interface, perhaps providing a printed duplicate (with print preview) of the original paper form. By creating logical groupings of fields from the original form and using a tabbed interface or several linked forms, you can present all of the information without requiring the user to scroll. You can also use additional controls, such as a list box preloaded with choices, which reduce the amount of typing required of the user.

You can also simplify many applications by taking infrequently used functions and moving them to their own forms. Providing defaults can sometimes simplify an application; if nine out of ten users select bold text, make the text bold by default rather than forcing the user to make a choice each time (don't forget to provide an option to override the default). Wizards can also help to simplify complex or infrequent tasks.

The best test of simplicity is to observe your application in use. If a typical user can't immediately accomplish a desired task without assistance, a redesign may be in order.

Using Color and Images

The use of color in your interface can add visual appeal, but it's easy to overuse it. With many displays capable of displaying millions of colors, it's tempting to use them all. Color, like the other basic design principles, can be problematic if not carefully considered in your initial design.

Preference for colors varies widely; the user's taste may not be the same as your own. Color can evoke strong emotions, and if you're designing for international audiences, certain colors may have cultural significance. It's usually best to stay conservative, using softer, more neutral colors.

Of course, your choice of colors may also be influenced by the intended audience and the tone or mood you are trying to convey. Bright reds, greens, and yellows may be appropriate for a children's application, but would hardly evoke an impression of fiscal responsibility in a banking application.

Small amounts of bright color can be used effectively to emphasize or draw attention to an important area. As a rule of thumb, you should try and limit the number of colors in an application, and your color scheme should remain consistent. It's best to stick to a standard 16-color palette if possible; dithering can cause some other colors to disappear when viewed on a 16-color display.

Another consideration in the use of color is that of colorblindness. Many people are unable to tell the difference between different combinations of primary colors such as red and green. To someone with this condition, red text on a green background would be invisible.

Images and Icons

The use of pictures and icons can also add visual interest to your application, but again, careful design is essential. Images can convey information compactly without the need for text, but images are often perceived differently by different people.

Toolbars with icons to represent various functions are a useful interface device, but if the user can't readily identify the function represented by the icon, they can be counterproductive. In designing toolbar icons, look at other applications to see what standards are already established. For example, many applications use a sheet of paper with a folded corner to represent a New File icon. There may be a better metaphor for this function, but representing it differently could confuse the user.

It's also important to consider the cultural significance of images. Many programs use a picture of a rural-style mailbox with a flag (Figure 6.21) to represent mail functions. This is primarily an American icon; users in other countries or cultures probably won't recognize it as a mailbox.

Figure 6.21 An icon representing a mailbox

In designing your own icons and images, try to keep them simple. Complex pictures with a lot of colors don't degrade well when displayed as a 16-by-16-pixel toolbar icon, or when displayed at high screen resolutions.

Choosing Fonts

Fonts are also an important part of your user interface, because they often communicate important information to the user. You need to select fonts that will be easily readable at different resolutions and on different types of displays. It's best to stick with simple sans serif or serif fonts where possible. Script and other decorative fonts generally look better in print than on screen, and can be difficult to read at smaller point sizes.

Unless you plan on distributing fonts along with your application, you should stick to standard Windows fonts such as Arial, New Times Roman, or System. If the user's system doesn't include a specified font, the system will make a substitution, resulting in a completely different appearance than what you intended. If you're designing for an international audience, you'll need to investigate what fonts are available in the intended languages. Also, you'll need to consider text expansion when designing for other languages — text strings can take up to 50% more space in some languages.

Again, design consistency is important in choosing fonts. In most cases, you shouldn't use more than two fonts at two or three different point sizes in a single application. Too many fonts can leave your application looking like a ransom note.

Designing for Usability

The usability of any application is ultimately determined by the user. Interface design is an iterative process; rarely is the first pass at designing an interface for your application going to yield a perfect interface. By getting users involved early in the design process, you can create a better, more usable interface with less effort.

What Is a Good Interface?

The best place to start when designing a user interface is to look at some of the best-selling applications from Microsoft or other companies; after all, they probably didn't get to be best-sellers because of poor interfaces. You'll find many things in common, such as toolbars, status bars, ToolTips, context-sensitive menus, and tabbed dialogs. It's no coincidence that Visual Basic provides the capabilities for adding all of these to your own applications.

You can also borrow from your own experience as a user of software. Think about some of the applications that you have used; what works, what doesn't, and how you would fix it. Remember, however, that your personal likes and dislikes may not match those of your users; you'll need to validate your ideas with them.

You may have also noticed that most successful applications provide choices to accommodate varying user preferences. For instance, the Microsoft Windows Explorer allows users to copy files with menus, keyboard commands, or by drag and drop. Providing options will broaden the appeal of your application; as a minimum you should make all functions accessible by both mouse and keyboard.

Windows Interface Guidelines

One of the main advantages of the Windows operating system is that it presents a common interface across all applications. A user that knows how to use one Windows-based application should be able to easily learn any other. Unfortunately, applications that stray too far from the established interface guidelines aren't as easily learned.

Menus are a good example of this — most Windows-based applications follow the standard of a File menu on the left, then optional menus such as Edit and Tools, followed by Help on the right. It could be argued that Documents would be a better name than File, or that the Help menu should come first. There's nothing to prevent you from doing this, but by doing so you will confuse your users and decrease the usability of your application. Users will have to stop and think every time they switch between your application and another.

The placement of submenus is also important. Users expect to find Copy, Cut and Paste beneath the Edit menu; moving them to the File menu would be confusing at best. Don't deviate from the established guidelines unless you have a good reason to do so.

Testing for Usability

The best way to test the usability of your interface is to involve users throughout the design phase. Whether you're designing a major shrink-wrap application or a small application for limited use, the design process should be pretty much the same. Using your established design guidelines, you'll want to start by designing the interface on paper.

The next step is to create one or more prototypes, designing your forms in Visual Basic. You'll need to add just enough code to make the prototype functional: displaying forms, filling list boxes with sample data, and so forth. Then you're ready to start usability testing.

Usability testing can be an informal process, reviewing your design with a few users, or a formal process in an established usability lab. Either way, the purpose is the same — learning first-hand from the users where your design works and where it needs improvement. Rather than questioning the user, it's more effective to simply turn the user loose with the application and observe them. Have the user verbalize their thought process as they attempt to perform a set of tasks: "I want to open a new document, so I will look under the File menu." Make note of where the interface design doesn't respond to their thought processes. Test with multiple users; if you see several users having difficulty with a particular task, that task probably needs more attention.

Next, you'll want to review your notes and consider how you can change the interface to make it more usable. Make the changes to your interface and test it again. Once you are satisfied that your application is usable, you're ready to start coding. You'll also want to test occasionally during the development process to make sure that the assumptions for the prototype were valid.

Discoverability of Features

One of the key concepts in usability testing is that of discoverability. If a user can't discover how to use a feature (or even that a feature exists), that feature is of little use. For example, the majority of Windows 3.1 users were never aware that the ALT, TAB key combination could be used to switch between open applications. There was no clue anywhere in the interface to help users discover this feature.

To test the discoverability of a feature, ask the user to perform a task without explaining how to do it (for example, "Create a new document using a Form Letter Template"). If they can't accomplish the task, or if it takes several attempts, the discoverability of that feature needs work.

When Things Go Wrong: Interacting with Users

In an ideal world, software and hardware would always work flawlessly, and users would never make mistakes. Reality dictates that mistakes can and will happen. A part of user interface design involves deciding how the application will respond when things go wrong.

A common response is to display a dialog box, asking for user input as to how the application should deal with the problem. A less common (but preferable) response would be to simply resolve the problem without bothering the user. After all, the user is primarily concerned with performing a task, not with technical details. In designing your user interface, think about the potential errors and determine which ones require user interaction and which ones can be resolved programmatically.

Creating Intelligent Dialog Boxes

Occasionally an error occurs in your application and it's necessary to make a decision in order to resolve the situation. This usually occurs as a branch in your code — an If…Then statement or a Case statement. If the decision requires user interaction, the question is usually posed to the user with a dialog box. Dialog boxes are a part of your user interface, and like the other parts of the interface, their design plays a role in the usability of your application.

Sometimes it seems as if many dialog boxes were designed by programmers who have never had an intelligent conversation with another human being. A message such as "A sector of fixed disk C: is corrupted or inaccessible. Abort, Retry, Ignore?" (see Figure 6.22) has little meaning to the average user. It's kind of like a waitress asking you "We're out of soup or the kitchen is on fire. Abort, Retry, Ignore?" How would you answer? It's important to phrase questions (and choices) in a manner that the user can understand. In the prior example, a better message might be "There is a problem saving your file on drive C. Save file on drive A, Don't save the file?"

Figure 6.22 Which dialog box presents the clearest message?

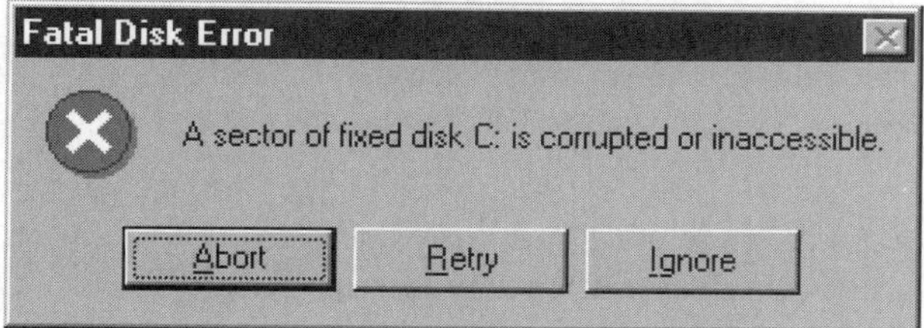

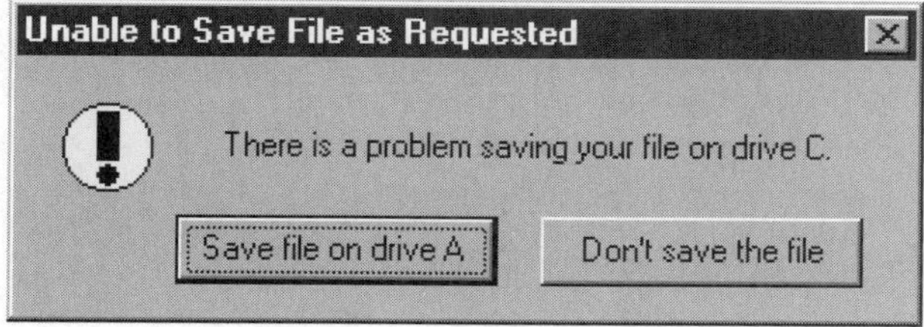

When creating dialog boxes for your application, keep the user in mind. Does the message convey useful information to the user? Is it easily understandable? Do the command buttons present clear choices? Are the choices appropriate for the given situation? Keep in mind that it only takes one annoying message box to give a user a bad impression of your application.

If you're designing your own custom dialog forms, try to stick to a standard style. If you vary too far from the standard message box layout, users may not recognize it as a dialog box.

For More Information To learn more about dialogs, see "Dialog Boxes" earlier in this chapter.

Handling Errors Without Dialog Boxes

It isn't always necessary to interrupt the user when an error occurs. Sometimes it's preferable to handle the error in code without notifying the user, or to warn the user in a way that doesn't stop their work flow. A good example of this technique is the AutoCorrect feature in Microsoft Word: if a common word is mistyped, Word fixes it automatically; if a less common word is misspelled, it is underlined in red so the user can correct it later.

There are a number of techniques that you can use; it's up to you to decide which techniques are appropriate for your own application. Here are a few suggestions:

- Add an Undo function to the Edit menu. Rather than interrupting the user with a confirmation dialog for deletions and so forth, trust that they are making the right decision and provide a Undo function in case they change their mind later.
- Display a message on a status bar or icon. If the error doesn't affect the user's current task, don't stop the application. Use a status bar or a brightly colored warning icon to warn the user — they can handle the problem when they are ready.
- Correct the problem. Sometimes the solution to an error is obvious. For instance, if a disk is full when the user tries to save a file, check the system for space on other drives. If space is available, save the file; put a message on the status bar to let the user know what you did.
- Save the message until later. Not all errors are critical or demand immediate attention; consider logging these to a file and displaying them to the user when they exit the application or at another convenient time. If the user makes a possible entry error (for example, Mian St. instead of Main St.), log it. Add a Review Entries button and a function to display the discrepancies so the user can correct them.
- Don't do anything. Sometimes an error isn't important enough to warrant a warning. For instance, the fact that a printer on LPT1 is out of paper doesn't mean much until you're ready to print. Wait until the message is appropriate to the current task.

For More Information To learn more about error handling techniques, see Chapter 13, "Debugging Your Code and Handling Errors."

Designing a User Assistance Model

No matter how great your user interface, there will be times that a user needs assistance. The user assistance model for your application includes such things as online Help and printed documentation; it may also contain user assistance devices such as ToolTips, Status Bars, What's This help, and Wizards.

The user assistance model should be designed just like any other part of your application: before you start developing. The contents of your model will vary depending on the complexity of the application and the intended audience.

Help and Documentation

Online Help is an important part of any application — it's usually the first place a user will look when they have a question. Even a simple application should provide Help; failing to provide it is like assuming that your users will never have questions.

In designing your Help system, keep in mind that its primary purpose is to answer questions. Try to think in terms of the user when creating topic names and index entries; for example, "How do I format a page?" rather than "Edit, Page Format menu" will make your topic easier to locate. Don't forget about context sensitivity; it's frustrating to most users if they press the F1 key for help on a specific field and find themselves at the Contents topic.

Conceptual documentation, whether printed and/or provided on compact disc, is helpful for all but the simplest applications. It can provide information that may be difficult to convey in the shorter Help topic. At the very least, you should provide documentation in the form of a ReadMe file that the user can print if desired.

User Assistance Devices

Within the user interface, there are several techniques for providing assistance to the user. Visual Basic makes it easy to add ToolTips, What's This help, Status displays, and Wizards to your applications. It's up to you to decide which of these devices are appropriate for your application.

ToolTips

ToolTips (Figure 6.23) are a great way to display information to the user as they navigate the user interface. A ToolTip is a small label that is displayed when the mouse pointer is held over a control for a set length of time, usually containing a description of the control's function. Normally used in conjunction with toolbars, ToolTips also work well in most any part of the interface.

Figure 6.23 A ToolTip for the Visual Basic toolbar

Most Visual Basic controls contain a single property for displaying ToolTips: ToolTipText. The following code would implement a ToolTip for a command button named cmdPrint:

```
cmdPrint.ToolTipText = "Prints the current document"
```

As with other parts of the interface, make sure that the text clearly conveys the intended message to the user.

For More Information To learn more about ToolTips, see "ToolTipText Property" in the *Microsoft Visual Basic 6.0 Language Reference*.

What's This Help

What's this Help provides a link to a pop-up Help topic (see Figure 6.24) when the user selects What's This Help and clicks the What's This cursor on a control. What's This Help can be initiated from a toolbar button, a menu item, or a button on the title bar of a dialog box.

Figure 6.24 A What's This Help pop-up window

Spelling button (Standard toolbar)

Checks spelling in the active document, including the text in headers, footers, footnotes, endnotes, and annotations.

To enable What's This Help from a menu or toolbar

1. Select the control for which you wish to provide help .
2. In the Properties window, select the **WhatsThisHelpID** property.
3. Enter a context ID number for the associated pop-up Help topic.
4. Repeat steps 1 through 3 for any additional controls.
5. Select the form.
6. In the Properties window, set the Form's **WhatsThisHelp** property to **True**.
7. In the Click event of the menu or toolbar button, enter the following:

   ```
   formname.WhatsThisHelp
   ```

   When the user clicks the button or menu, the mouse pointer will change to the What's This pointer.

To enable What's This Help on the title bar of a custom dialog form, set the form's WhatsThisButton and WhatsThisHelp properties to True.

For More Information To learn more about What's This Help, see "WhatsThisHelp Property" and "WhatsThisButton Property" in the *Microsoft Visual Basic 6.0 Language Reference*.

Status Displays

A status display can also be used to provide user assistance in much the same way as a ToolTip. Status displays are a good way to provide instructions or messages that may not fit easily into a ToolTip. The status bar control included in the Professional and Enterprise editions of Visual Basic works well for displaying messages; a label control can also be used as a status display.

The text displayed in a status display can be updated in one of two ways: in the GotFocus event of a control or form, or in the MouseMove event. If you want to use the display as a learning device, add an item to the Help menu to toggle its Visible property on and off.

To add a status display

1. Add a label control to your form.
2. Select the control for which you wish to display a message.
3. Add the following code to the control's MouseMove (or GotFocus) event:

   ```
   Labelname.Caption = "Enter the customer's ID number in this field"
   ```

   When the user moves the mouse over the control, the message will be displayed in the label control.
4. Repeat steps 2 and 3 for any additional controls.

Wizards

A wizard is a user assistance device that takes the user step by step through a procedure, working with the user's actual data. Wizards are usually used to provide task-specific assistance. They help a user accomplish a task that would otherwise require a considerable (and undesirable) learning curve; they provide expert information to a user that has not yet become an expert.

The Professional and Enterprise editions of Visual Basic include the Wizard Manager, a tool for creating wizards.

For More Information To learn more about wizards, see "Using Wizards and Add-Ins" in Chapter 4, "Managing Projects."

CHAPTER 7

Using Visual Basic's Standard Controls

You use controls to get user input and to display output. Some of the controls you can use in your applications include text boxes, command buttons, and list boxes. Other controls let you access other applications and process data as if the remote application was part of your code. Each control has its own set of properties, methods, and events. This chapter introduces you to the standard controls in Visual Basic.

For More Information See "Using ActiveX Controls" in the *Microsoft Visual Basic 6.0 Component Tools Guide* volume of the *Microsoft Visual Basic 6.0 Reference Library* for more information about the ActiveX controls available in the Professional and Enterprise versions of Visual Basic.

Contents

- Using the Horizontal and Vertical Scroll Bar Controls
- Using the Image Control
- Using the Label Control
- Using the Line Control
- Using the List Box Control
- Using the OLE Container Control
- Using the Option Button Control
- Using the Picture Box Control
- Using the RemoteData Control
- Using the Shape Control
- Using the Text Box Control
- Using the Timer Control

Sample Applications: Alarm.vbp, Calc.vbp, Controls.vbp, Flex.vbp, Winseek.vbp

Many of the code examples in this Chapter are taken from the Alarm.vbp, Calc.vbp, Controls.vbp, Flex.vbp, and Winseek.vbp sample applications. These sample applications are listed in the Samples directory.

Introduction to Visual Basic Controls

The Visual Basic toolbox contains the tools you use to draw controls on your forms.

Figure 7.1 The Visual Basic toolbox

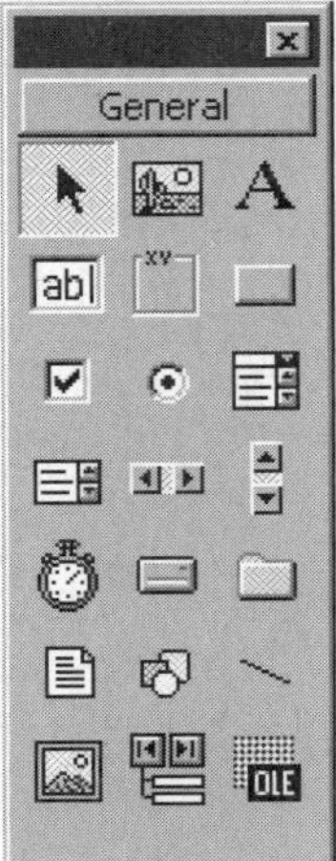

Control Categories

There are three broad categories of controls in Visual Basic:

- *Intrinsic controls*, such as the command button and frame controls. These controls are contained inside the Visual Basic .exe file. Intrinsic controls are always included in the toolbox, unlike ActiveX controls and insertable objects, which can be removed from or added to the toolbox.
- *ActiveX controls,* which exist as separate files with a .ocx file name extension. These include controls that are available in all editions of Visual Basic (DataCombo, DataList controls, and so on) and those that are available only in the Professional and Enterprise editions (such as Listview, Toolbar, Animation, and Tabbed Dialog). Many third-party ActiveX controls are also available.

  Note Controls with the .vbx file name extension use older technology and are found in applications written in earlier versions of Visual Basic. When Visual Basic opens a project containing a .vbx control, the default behavior is to replace the .vbx control with an .ocx control, but only if an .ocx version of the control is available. See "Updating Older Versions of Visual Basic Controls" later in this chapter for information on updating controls to the .ocx format.

- *Insertable Objects*, such as a Microsoft Excel Worksheet object containing a list of all your company's employees, or a Microsoft Project Calendar object containing the scheduling information for a project. Since these can be added to the toolbox, they can be considered controls. Some of these objects also support Automation (formerly called OLE Automation), which allows you to program another application's objects from within a Visual Basic application. See Chapter 9, "Programming with Objects," for more information on Automation.

For More Information See "Using ActiveX Controls" in the *Microsoft Visual Basic 6.0 Component Tools Guide* for more information about the ActiveX controls available in the Professional and Enterprise versions of Visual Basic.

Intrinsic Controls

The following table summarizes the intrinsic controls found in the Visual Basic toolbox.

Icon	Control name	Class name	Description
	Check box	CheckBox	Displays a True/False or Yes/No option. You can check any number of check boxes on a form at one time.
	Combo box	ComboBox	Combines a text box with a list box. Allows a user to type in a selection or select an item from a drop-down list.

Icon	Control name	Class name	Description
	Command button	CommandButton	Carries out a command or action when a user chooses it.
	Data	Data	Enables you to connect to an existing database and display information from it on your forms.
	Directory list box	DirListBox	Displays and allows a user to select directories and paths.
	Drive list box	DriveListBox	Displays and allows a user to select valid disk drives.
	File list box	FileListBox	Displays and allows a user to select from a list of files.
	Frame	Frame	Provides a visual and functional container for controls.
	Horizontal and vertical scroll bars	HScrollBar and VScrollBar	Allow a user to add scroll bars to controls that do not automatically provide them. (These are not the same as the built-in scroll bars found with many controls.)
	Image	Image	Displays bitmaps, icons, or Windows metafiles, JPEG, or GIF files; acts like a command button when clicked.
A	Label	Label	Displays text a user cannot interact with or modify.
	Line	Line	Adds a straight-line segment to a form.
	List box	ListBox	Displays a list of items that a user can choose from.
OLE	OLE container	OLE	Embeds data into a Visual Basic application.
	Option button	OptionButton	The Option Button control, as part of an option group with other option buttons, displays multiple choices, from which a user can choose only one.
	Picture box	PictureBox	Displays bitmaps, icons, or Windows metafiles, JPEG, or GIF files. It also displays text or acts as a visual container for other controls.

Icon	Control name	Class name	Description
	Shape	Shape	Adds a rectangle, square, ellipse, or circle to a form, frame, or picture box.
	Text box	TextBox	Provides an area to enter or display text.
	Timer	Timer	Executes timer events at specified time intervals.

Note The pointer tool (the first tool in the toolbox) provides a way to move and resize forms and controls. It is not a control.

Standard ActiveX Controls

The Learning edition of Visual Basic contains a number of ActiveX controls (referred to as standard ActiveX controls) that allow you to add advanced features to your applications. ActiveX controls have the file name extension .ocx and can be used in your project by manually adding them to the toolbox.

The following table summarizes the standard ActiveX controls available in the Learning edition of Visual Basic.

Icon	Control name	Class name	Description
	Common dialog	CommonDialog	Provides a standard set of dialog boxes for operations such as opening and saving files, setting print options, and selecting colors and fonts.
	DataCombo	DataCombo	Provides most of the features of the standard combo box control, plus increased data access capabilities.
	DataList	DataList	Provides most of the features of the standard list box control, plus increased data access capabilities.
	Microsoft FlexGrid	MSFlexGrid	Similar to the DataGrid control, but has additional formatting, grouping, and binding features, as well as customization options.

For More Information See "Using ActiveX Controls" in the *Microsoft Visual Basic 6.0 Component Tools Guide* for more information about the ActiveX controls available in the Professional and Enterprise versions of Visual Basic.

Adding and Removing ActiveX Controls

You move ActiveX controls to and from the toolbox using the following procedures.

To add an ActiveX control to the toolbox

1. From the **Project** menu, choose **Components**.
2. Select the check box next to the name of the .ocx control, and then choose **OK**. Once a control is placed in the toolbox, you can add it to a form just as you would an intrinsic control.

To remove an ActiveX control

1. Remove all instances of the control from the forms in your project. Delete any references to the control in the project's code. If references to a deleted control are left in your code, an error message will display when you compile the application.
2. From the **Project** menu, choose **Components**.

   Clear the check box next to the name of the .ocx control, and then choose **OK**. An error message will display if there are remaining instances of the control in your project.

For More Information See "Adding Controls to a Project" in Chapter 4, "Managing Projects," for more information about adding and removing controls and insertable objects to and from the Toolbox.

Updating Older Versions of Visual Basic Controls

Older 16-bit versions of Visual Basic controls with the file extension .vbx are incompatible with this version of Visual Basic. If you attempt to load an older project containing .vbx controls, Visual Basic will warn you that the controls are unavailable or incompatible. You have the option of continuing to load the project without the .vbx controls but, of course, the application will not function properly.

If you have older Visual Basic projects that contain third-party .vbx controls, contact the control's manufacturer to inquire about .ocx replacements.

Control Naming Conventions

When you first create an *object* (form or control), Visual Basic sets its Name property to a default value. For example, all command buttons have their Name property initially set to Command*n*, where *n* is 1, 2, 3, and so on. Visual Basic names the first command button drawn on a form Command1, the second Command2, and the third Command3.

You may choose to keep the default name; however, when you have several controls of the same type, it makes sense to change their Name properties to something more descriptive. Because it may be difficult to distinguish the Command1 button on MyForm from the Command1 button on YourForm, a naming convention can help. This is especially true when an application consists of several form, standard, and class modules.

You can use a prefix to describe the class, followed by a descriptive name for the control. Using this naming convention makes the code more self-descriptive and alphabetically groups similar objects in the Object list box. For example, you might name a Check Box control like this:

```
chkReadOnly
```

The names you give to forms and controls:

- must begin with a letter.
- must contain only letters, numbers, and the underscore character (_); punctuation characters and spaces are not allowed.
- must be no longer than 40 characters.

For More Information See Appendix B, "Visual Basic Coding Conventions," for more information on naming conventions.

Using the Value of a Control

All controls have a property that you can use to store or retrieve values just by referring to the control, without using the property name. This is called the *value* of the control and is usually the most important or most commonly used property of the control. The following table lists the property that is considered to be the value for each control.

Control	Value
Check box	Value
Combo box	Text
Command button	Value
Common dialog	Action
Data	Caption
DataCombo	Text
DataGrid	Text
DataList	Text
Directory list box	Path
Drive list box	Drive

Control	Value
File list box	FileName
FlexGrid	Text
Frame	Caption
Horizontal scroll bar	Value
Image	Picture
Label	Caption
Line	Visible
List box	Text
Option button	Value
Picture box	Picture
Shape	Shape
Text box	Text
Timer	Enabled
Vertical scroll bar	Value

Whenever you want to refer to a property on a control that happens to be the value of that control, you can do so without specifying the property name in your code. For example, this line sets the value of the Text property of a text box control:

```
Text1 = "This text is assigned to the Text property _
of Text1"
```

In this example, the Caption property of Label1 is set to the FileName property of File1 whenever the user clicks a file in the file list box:

```
Private Sub File1_Click ()
   Label1 = File1
End Sub
```

> **Note** Because using the value of a control makes your code somewhat less readable, the examples in this guide do not use it but instead refer explicitly to the properties on all controls. You may want to try writing your code both ways, and decide to use the value of controls in your code if you have no trouble reading it.

Validating Control Data by Restricting Focus

The Validate event and CausesValidation property are used in tandem to verify the input to a control before allowing the user to shift focus away from that control. For example, imagine an application with several text boxes and a Help button. When each text box receives the focus, you want to prevent the user from shifting the focus until the text box's particular validation criteria are met; however, you also want to allow users to click the Help button at any time. To do this, set the validation criteria in the Validate event and set the CausesValidation property of the Help button to False. If the property is set to True (the default setting), the Validate event will occur on the first control. If the property is set to False, the Validate event on the first control will be preempted from occurring.

The Validate event is more suited to validating data entry than the LostFocus event because the LostFocus event (by definition) occurs after the focus has shifted. In contrast, by using the Validate event you can prevent the focus from ever shifting to another control until all validation rules have been met.

Possible Uses

- A data entry application needs to perform more sophisticated data entry validation than can be provided by the Masked Edit control, or the validation occurs in a business rule.
- A form needs to prevent users from moving off a control using the TAB key or an accelerator until data has been entered in a field.
- An ActiveX document running inside Internet Explorer needs a way for the user to finish an operation on the form before the script moves the focus programmatically.

Control the Focus in the Validate Event

The Validate event includes a *keepfocus* argument. When the argument is set to True, the control will retain the focus. This effectively prevents the user from clicking any other control.

Working with Control Arrays

A *control array* is a group of controls that share the same name and type. They also share the same event procedures. A control array has at least one element and can grow to as many elements as your system resources and memory permit; its size also depends on how much memory and Windows resources each control requires. The maximum index you can use in a control array is 32767. Elements of the same control array have their own property settings. Common uses for control arrays include menu controls and option button groupings.

> **Note** Visual Basic includes the ability to dynamically add unreferenced controls to the Controls collection at run time. This topic refers only to referenced controls added at design time by cutting and pasting a control onto the form. For more information about adding controls at run time, see the reference topic "Add Method (Controls Collection)" and "Add Method (Licenses Collection)," online.

Why Use Control Arrays?

Adding controls with control arrays uses fewer resources than simply adding multiple controls of the same type to a form at design time. Control arrays are also useful if you want several controls to share code. For example, if three option buttons are created as a control array, the same code is executed regardless of which button was clicked.

If you want to create a new instance of a control at run time, that control must be a member of a control array. With a control array, each new element inherits the common event procedures of the array.

Using the control array mechanism, each new control inherits the common event procedures already written for the array. For example, if your form has several text boxes that each receive a date value, a control array can be set up so that all of the text boxes share the same validation code.

Sample Application: Calc.vbp

The Calculator sample application (which is listed in the Samples directory) shown in Figure 7.2 contains two control arrays — the number buttons and the operator buttons.

Figure 7.2 Control array example

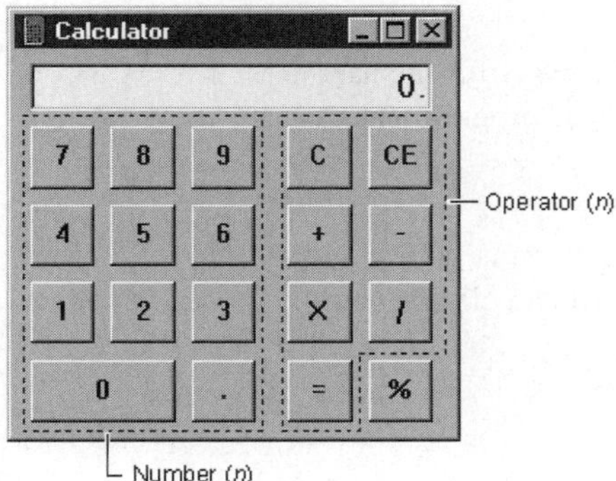

The Name and Index property values for the control arrays in the Calculator example are listed in the following table.

Number(*n*)	**Operator(*n*)**
0 = Number(0)	+ = Operator(1)
1 = Number(1)	– = Operator(2)
2 = Number(2)	X = Operator(3)
3 = Number(3)	/ = Operator(4)

Number(*n*)	Operator(*n*)
4 = Number(4)	= = Operator(5)
5 = Number(5)	
6 = Number(6)	
7 = Number(7)	
8 = Number(8)	
9 = Number(9)	

Notice how each control is referred to with the syntax *object(index)*. You specify the index of a control when you create it. In fact, specifying any index for a control at design time makes that control part of an array.

The Index property distinguishes one element of the control array from another. When one of the controls in the array recognizes an event, Visual Basic calls a common event procedure and passes an argument (the value of the Index property) to identify which control actually recognizes the event.

For example, the first line of the Number_Click event procedure is:

```
Private Sub Number_Click (Index As Integer)
```

If Number(0) recognizes the event, Visual Basic passes 0 as the *index* argument, and if Number(1) recognizes the event, Visual Basic passes 1 as the *index* argument. Other than the index value, the remainder of the Number_Click code that is executed is the same for both Number(0) through Number(9).

Creating a Control Array at Design Time

There are three ways to create a control array at design time:

- Assign the same name to more than one control.
- Copy an existing control and then paste it onto the form.
- Set the control's Index property to a value that is not Null.

> **Note** You must create menu control arrays in the Menu Editor. For details on how to do this, see "Creating and Modifying Menus at Run Time" in Chapter 6, "Creating a User Interface."

To add a control array element by changing its name

1. Draw the controls you want to be in the control array. (The controls must all be of the same type.) Decide which control will become the first element in the array.
2. Select one of the controls and change its Name setting to the Name setting for the first element in the array.

3. When you type an existing name for a control in the array, Visual Basic displays a dialog box asking you to confirm that you want to create a control array. Choose **Yes** to confirm the action.

For example, if the name of the first element in a control array is cmdCtlArr, you would choose a command button to add to the array and then set its name to cmdCtlArr. The message "You already have a control named 'cmdCtlArr.' Do you want to create a control array?" is displayed. Choose Yes to confirm the operation.

Controls added this way share only their Name property and control type; all other properties remain the same as when the control was originally drawn.

To add a control array element by copying an existing control

1. Draw a control in the control array.
2. While the control has the focus, choose **Copy** from the **Edit** menu.
3. From the **Edit** menu, choose **Paste**. Visual Basic displays a dialog box asking you to confirm that you want to create a control array. Choose **Yes** to confirm the action.

   This control is assigned an index value of 1. The first control you drew has a value of 0.

The index value of each new array element corresponds to the order in which the element was added to the control array. When controls are added this way, most of the visual properties, such as height, width, and color, are copied from the first control in the control array to the new controls.

Adding to a Control Array at Run Time

You can add and remove controls in a control array at run time using the Load and Unload statements. However, the control to be added must be an element of an existing control array. You must have created a control at design time with the Index property set, in most cases, to 0. Then, at run time, use this syntax:

Load *object*(*index%*)

Unload *object*(*index%*)

Argument	Description
object	Name of the control to add to or delete from the control array.
index%	The control's index value in the array.

When you load a new element of a control array, most of the property settings are copied from the lowest existing element in the array — in this example, the element with the 0 index value. The Visible, Index, and TabIndex property settings are not automatically copied to new elements of a control array, so to make the newly added control visible, you must set its Visible property to True.

Note Visual Basic generates an error if you attempt to use the Load statement with an index number already in use in the array.

Important You can use the Unload statement to remove any control created with Load. However, you cannot use Unload to remove controls created at design time, regardless of whether or not they are part of a control array.

Controls Scenario: Adding and Deleting Controls in a Control Array

The control array example demonstrates how controls — in this case, option buttons — are added and deleted at run time. The example allows the user to add option buttons that change the background color of a picture box.

Start with a form, and then draw a picture box, a label, two option buttons, and three command buttons, as shown in Figure 7.3.

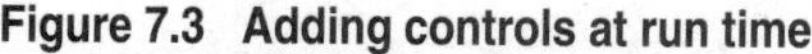

Figure 7.3 Adding controls at run time

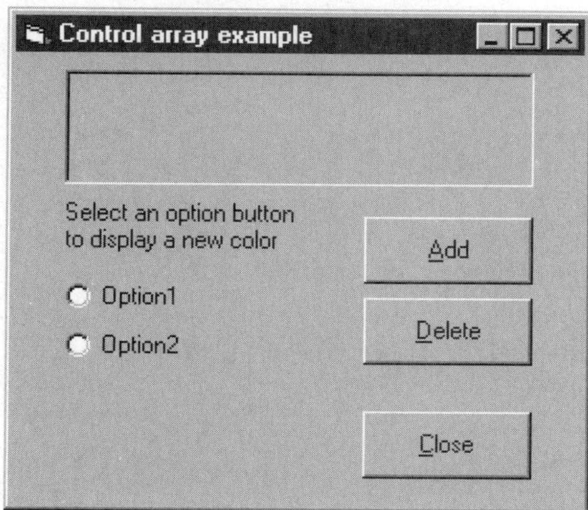

The following table lists the property settings for the objects in the application.

Object	Property	Setting
Form	Caption	Control Array Example
Picture box	Name	picDisplay
Label	Caption	Select an option button to display a new color
Option1	Name Index	optButton 0

Object	Property	Setting
Option2	Name Index	optButton 1
First command button	Name Caption	cmdAdd &Add
Second command button	Name Caption	cmdDelete &Delete
Third command button	Name Caption	cmdClose &Close

Events in the Control Array Application

Next, you need to add the event procedures for the option buttons and command buttons. Start by adding the form declaration:

```
Dim MaxId As Integer
```

The Click event procedure is shared by all the option buttons:

```
Private Sub optButton_Click (Index As Integer)
   picDisplay.BackColor = QBColor(Index + 1)
End Sub
```

New option buttons are added by the Click event procedure for the Add command button. In this example, the code checks that no more than ten option buttons are loaded before the Load statement is executed. Once a control is loaded, its Visible property must be set to True.

```
Private Sub cmdAdd_Click ()
   If MaxId = 0 Then MaxId = 1 ' Set total option
                               ' buttons.
   If MaxId > 8 Then Exit Sub  ' Only ten buttons
                               ' allowed.
   MaxId = MaxId + 1           ' Increment button count.
   Load optButton(MaxId)       ' Create new button.
   optButton(0).SetFocus       ' Reset button selection.
   ' Set new button under previous button.
   optButton(MaxId).Top = optButton(MaxId - 1)._
   Top + 400
   optButton(MaxId).Visible = True    ' Display new
                                      ' button.
   optButton(MaxId).Caption = "Option" & MaxId + 1
End Sub
```

Option buttons are removed by the Click event procedure for the Delete command button:

```
Private Sub cmdDelete_Click ()
   If MaxId <= 1 Then Exit Sub ' Keep first two buttons.
   Unload optButton(MaxId)     ' Delete last button.
   MaxId = MaxId - 1           ' Decrement button count.
   optButton(0).SetFocus       ' Reset button selection.
End Sub
```

The Close button Click event ends the application:

```
Private Sub cmdClose_Click ()
   Unload Me
End Sub
```

Using the ADO Data Control

The ADO Data control uses Microsoft ActiveX Data Objects (ADO) to quickly create connections between data-bound controls and data providers. Data-bound controls are any controls that feature a DataSource property. Data providers can be any source written to the OLE DB specification. You can also easily create your own data provider using Visual Basic's class module.

Although you can use the ActiveX Data Objects directly in your applications, the ADO Data control has the advantage of being a graphic control (with Back and Forward buttons) and an easy-to-use interface that allows you to create database applications with a minimum of code.

Figure 7.4 The ADO Data Control

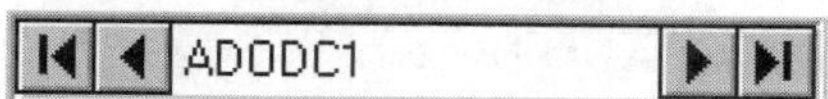

Several of the controls found in Visual Basic's Toolbox can be data-bound, including the CheckBox, ComboBox, Image, Label, ListBox, PictureBox, and TextBox controls. Additionally, Visual Basic includes several data-bound ActiveX controls such as the DataGrid, DataCombo, Chart, and DataList controls. You can also create your own data-bound ActiveX controls, or purchase controls from other vendors.

Previous versions of Visual Basic featured the intrinsic Data control and the Remote Data control (RDC) for data access. Both controls are still included with Visual Basic for backward compatibility. However, because of the flexibility of ADO, it's recommended that new database applications be created using the ADO Data Control.

For More Information A complete list of data-bound controls can be found in "Controls That Bind to the ADO Data Control" later in this chapter. To find out how to use the intrinsic Data control or the Remote Data control, see "Using the Data Control" or "Using the Remote Data Control" later in this chapter. For details about creating a data provider, see "Creating Data-Aware Classes" in Chapter 9, "Programming with Objects."

Possible Uses

- Connect to a local or remote database.
- Open a specified database table or define a set of records based on a Structured Query Language (SQL) query or stored procedure or view of the tables in that database.
- Pass data field values to data-bound controls, where you can display or change the values.
- Add new records or update a database based on any changes you make to data displayed in the bound controls.

To create a client, or front-end database application, add the ADO Data control to your forms just as you would any other Visual Basic control. You can have as many ADO Data controls on your form as you need. Be aware, however, that the control is a comparatively "expensive" method of creating connections, using at least two connections for the first control, and one more for each subsequent control.

Creating a Front-End Database Application with Minimal Code

It's possible to create a database application using a minimum of code by setting a few properties at design time. If you are using an OLE DB data source, the Microsoft Data Link Name (.MDL) must be created on your machine. See "Creating the Northwind OLE DB Data Link," online, for a step-by-step example.

To create a simple front-end database application

1. Draw an **ADO Data Control** on a form. (The icon's ToolTip is "ADODC.")

   If the control is not available in the Toolbox, press CTRL+T to display the **Components** dialog box. In the **Components** dialog, click **Microsoft ADO Data Control**.

2. On the Toolbox, click the **ADO Data Control** to select it. Then press F4 to display the Properties window.

3. In the **Properties** window, click **ConnectionString** to display the **ConnectionString** dialog box.

4. If you have created a Microsoft Data Link file (.MDL), select **Use OLE DB File** and click **Browse** to find the file on the computer. If you use a DSN, click **Use ODBC Data Source Name** and select a DSN from the box, or click **New** to create one. If you wish to use create a connection string, select **Use ConnectionString**, and then click **Build**, and use the **Data Link Properties** dialog box to create a connection string. After creating the connection string, click **OK**. The **ConnectionString** property will be filled with a string like:

   ```
   driver={SQL Server};server=bigsmile;uid=sa;pwd=pwd;database=pubs
   ```

5. In the Properties window, set the **RecordSource** property to a SQL statement. For example,

   ```
   SELECT * FROM Titles WHERE AuthorID = 72
   ```

   You should always include a WHERE clause when accessing a table. Failing to do so will lock the entire table, which would be a major hindrance to other users.

6. Draw a **TextBox** control on the form to display the database information.

7. In the Properties window, set the **DataSource** property for Text1 to the name of the ADO Data control (ADODC1). This binds the text box to the ADO Data control.

8. In the Properties window, click **DataField** and a list of available fields will drop down. Click the name of the field you want to display.

9. Repeat steps 6, 7, and 8 for each additional field you want to access.

10. Press F5 to run the application. You can use the four arrow buttons on the ADO Data control to move to the beginning of the data, to the end of the data, or from record to record through the data.

Setting the ConnectionString, Source, DataSource, and DataField Programmatically

The code below shows how to set these four properties programmatically. Note that setting the DataSource property requires the Set statement.

```
Private Sub Form_Load()
   With ADODC1
      .ConnectionString = "driver={SQL Server};" & _
      "server=bigsmile;uid=sa;pwd=pwd;database=pubs"
      .RecordSource = "Select * From Titles Where AuthorID = 7"
   End With
   Set Text1.DataSource = ADODC1
   Text1.DataField = "Title"
End Sub
```

ADO Data Control Events

The ADO Data control features several events that you can program. The table below shows the events and when they occur; however the table is not meant to be a complete list all of the conditions when the events occur. For complete information, see the reference topic for the individual event.

Event	Occurs
WillMove	On Recordset.Open, Recordset.MoveNext, Recordset.Move, Recordset.MoveLast, Recordset.MoveFirst, Recordset.MovePrevious, Recordset.Bookmark, Recordset.AddNew, Recordset.Delete, Recordset.Requery, Recordset.Resync
MoveComplete	After WillMove
WillChangeField	Before the Value property changes
FieldChangeComplete	After WillChangeField
WillChangeRecord	On Recordset.Update, Recordset.Delete, Recordset.CancelUpdate, Recordset.UpdateBatch, Recordset.CancelBatch
RecordChangeComplete	After WillChangeRecord
WillChangeRecordset	On Recordset.Requery, Recordset.Resync, Recordset.Close, Recordset.Open, Recordset.Filter
RecordsetChangeComplete	After WillChangeRecordset
InfoMessage	When the data provider returns a result

For More Information To try other step-by-step procedures using the ADO Data control, see "Creating a Simple Database Application with the DataGrid and ADO Data Control," "Creating a Simple DataCombo Application," and "Creating a DataGrid Linked to a DataList Control," online.

Setting Database-Related Properties of the ADO Data Control

When creating a connection, you can use one of three sources: a Connection String, an OLE DB file (.MDL), or an ODBC Data Source Name (DSN). When using a DSN, it's likely you will not have to alter any of the other properties of the control.

However, if you are familiar with database technology, you can alter some of the other properties exposed on the ADO Data Control. The following list describes database-related properties of the control. The list also suggests a logical order for setting the properties.

> **Note** Database technology is complex, and the suggestions below are not meant to be taken as rules.

1. **ConnectionString** — The ConnectionString property is a string that can contain all the settings necessary to make a connection. The parameters passed in the string are driver-dependent. For example, ODBC drivers allow the string to contain driver, provider, default database, server, username, and password.
2. **UserName** — The name of the user, necessary if the database is password-protected. Like the Provider property, this property can be specified in the ConnectionString. If you provide both a ConnectionString and a UserName, the ConnnectionString value will override the UserName property's value.
3. **Password** — Also needed when accessing a protected database. Like Provider and UserName, this property's value will be overridden if the value is specified in the ConnectionString.
4. **RecordSource** — This property generally contains a statement that determines what will be retrieved from the database.
5. **CommandType** — The CommandType property instructs the data provider if the Source is a SQL statement, a table name, a stored procedure, or an unknown type.
6. **CursorLocation** — This property specifies where the cursor is located, on the client or on the server. The consequences of this decision affect the next few properties you set.
7. **CursorType** — The CursorType property determines if the recordset is static, dynamic, or a keyset cursor type.
8. **LockType** — The LockType determines how the data is locked when others attempt to change data you are editing. How you set the LockType is a complex decision, dependent on many factors.
9. **Mode** — The Mode property determines what you intend to do with the recordset. For example, you can achieve some performance gains by setting it to read-only, if you are only interested in creating reports.
10. **MaxRecords** — This property determines how large the cursor will be. How you determine this depends on the size of the records you are retrieving and the resources available on your computer (memory). A large record (one with many columns and large strings) would take more resources than a smaller record. Consequently the MaxRecords property should be no larger than necessary.
11. **ConnectionTimeout** — Set the ConnectionTimeout to the number of seconds to wait while establishing the connection. An error is returned if the connection times out.
12. **CacheSize** — The CacheSize property specifies how many records can be retrieved from the cursor. If you've set the CursorLocation to client side, then this property can be set to a smaller number (as small as 1) with no adverse effects. If it's on the server side, you should optimize this figure to suit the number of rows you want to view at any one time. For example, if you use the DataGrid control to view 30 rows, set the CacheSize to 60, allowing you to scroll without retrieving more data.

13. **BOFAction, EOFAction** — These two properties determine what will happen when the control is at the beginning and end of the cursor. Choices include staying at the beginning or end, moving to the first or last record, or adding a new record (at the end only).

Controls that Bind to the ADO Data Control

Any control that has the DataSource property can be bound to an ADO Data Control. The following intrinsic controls can be bound to the ADO Data Control:

- CheckBox
- ComboBox
- Image
- Label
- ListBox
- PictureBox
- TextBox

The following data-bound ActiveX Controls are also supplied with all versions of Visual Basic:

- DataList
- DataCombo
- DataGrid
- Microsoft Hierarchical FlexGrid
- RichTextBox
- Microsoft Chart
- DateTimePicker
- ImageCombo
- MonthView

Finally, you can create your own ActiveX controls that are data-bound using the DataBinding object.

For More Information See "Binding a Control to Data Source" in Chapter 9 of the *Microsoft Visual Basic 6.0 Component Tools Guide* for details about creating your own data-bound controls.

Using the Check Box Control

The check box control displays a check mark when it is selected. It is commonly used to present a Yes/No or True/False selection to the user. You can use check box controls in groups to display multiple choices from which the user can select one or more.

Figure 7.5 The check box control

The check box control is similar to the option button control in that each is used to indicate a selection that is made by the user. They differ in that only one option button in a group can be selected at a time. With the check box control, however, any number of check boxes may be selected.

For More Information See "Selecting Individual Options with Check Boxes" in Chapter 3, "Forms, Controls, and Menus," for a simple demonstration of the check box control.

The Value Property

The Value property of the check box control indicates whether the check box is checked, unchecked, or unavailable (dimmed). When selected, the value is set to 1. For example:

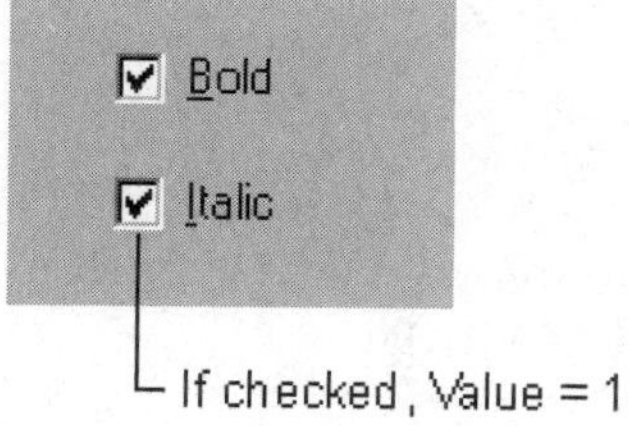

The following table lists the values and equivalent Visual Basic constants that are used to set the Value property.

Setting	Value	Constant
Unchecked	0	vbUnchecked
Checked	1	vbChecked
Unavailable	2	vbGrayed

The user clicks the check box control to indicate a checked or unchecked state. You can then test for the state of the control and program your application to perform some action based on this information.

By default, the check box control is set to vbUnchecked. If you want to preselect several check boxes in a series of check boxes, you can do so by setting the Value property to vbChecked in the Form_Load or Form_Initialize procedures.

You can also set the Value property to vbGrayed to disable the check box. For example, you may want to disable a check box until a certain condition is met.

The Click Event

Whenever the user clicks on the check box control, the Click event is triggered. You can then program your application to perform some action depending upon the state of the check box. In the following example, the check box control's Caption property changes each time the control is clicked, indicating a checked or unchecked state.

```
Private Sub Check1_Click()
   If Check1.Value = vbChecked Then
      Check1.Caption = "Checked"
   ElseIf Check1.Value = vbUnchecked Then
      Check1.Caption = "Unchecked"
   End If
End Sub
```

> **Note** If the user attempts to double-click the check box control, each click will be processed separately; that is, the check box control does not support the double-click event.

Responding to the Mouse and Keyboard

The Click event of the check box control is also triggered when the focus is shifted to the control with the keyboard by using the TAB key and then by pressing the SPACEBAR.

You can toggle selection of the check box control by adding an ampersand character before a letter in the Caption property to create a keyboard shortcut. For example:

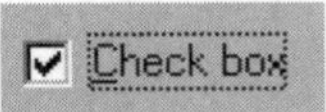

In this example, pressing the ALT+C key combination toggles between the checked and unchecked states.

Visually Enhancing the Check Box Control

The check box control, like the command button and option button controls, may be visually enhanced by altering the setting of the Style property and then using the Picture, DownPicture, and DisabledPicture properties. For example, you may want to add an icon or bitmap to a check box or display a different image when the control is clicked or disabled.

Using the Combo Box Control

A combo box control combines the features of a text box and a list box. This control allows the user to select an item either by typing text into the combo box, or by selecting it from the list.

Figure 7.6 The combo box control

Combo boxes present a list of choices to the user. If the number of items exceeds what can be displayed in the combo box, scroll bars will automatically appear on the control. The user can then scroll up and down or left to right through the list.

When to Use a Combo Box Instead of a List Box

Generally, a combo box is appropriate when there is a list of *suggested* choices, and a list box is appropriate when you want to limit input to what is on the list. A combo box contains an edit field, so choices not on the list can be typed in this field.

In addition, combo boxes save space on a form. Because the full list is not displayed until the user clicks the down arrow (except for Style 1, which is always dropped down), a combo box can easily fit in a small space where a list box would not fit.

For More Information See "Using List Boxes and Combo Boxes" in Chapter 3, "Forms, Controls, and Menus," for a simple demonstration of these controls. Also see "Using the List Box Control" later in this chapter for more information about the list box control.

Data-Bound Features

Visual Basic includes both standard and data-bound versions of the combo box control. While both versions allow you to display, edit, and update information from most standard types of databases, the data-bound combo box provides more advanced data access features. The Data-Bound combo box control also supports a different set of properties and methods than the standard combo box control.

For More Information See "Using the DataCombo and DataList Controls" in Chapter 7, "Using Visual Basic's Standard Controls," for more information.

Combo Box Styles

There are three combo box styles. Each style can be set at design time and uses values, or equivalent Visual Basic constants, to set the style of the combo box.

Style	Value	Constant
Drop-down combo box	0	vbComboDropDown
Simple combo box	1	vbComboSimple
Drop-down list box	2	vbComboDropDownList

Figure 7.7 Combo box styles

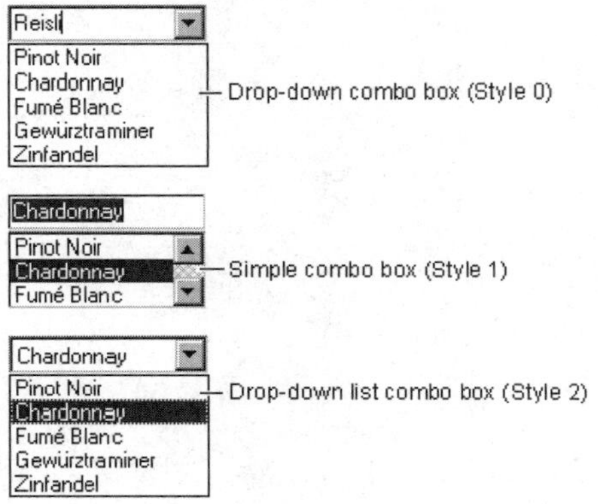

Drop-down Combo Box

With the default setting (Style = 0 – Dropdown Combo), a combo box is a drop-down combo box. The user can either enter text directly (as in a text box) or click the detached arrow at the right of the combo box to open a list of choices. Selecting one of the choices inserts it into the text portion at the top of the combo box. The user also can open the list by pressing ALT+ DOWN ARROW when the control has the focus.

Simple Combo Box

Setting the Style property of a combo box to 1 – Simple Combo specifies a simple combo box in which the list is displayed at all times. To display all entries in the list, you must draw the list box large enough to display the entries. A vertical scroll bar is automatically inserted when there are more entries than can be displayed. The user can still enter text directly or select from the list. As with a drop-down combo box, a simple combo box also allows users to enter choices not on the list.

Drop-down List Box

A drop-down list box (Style = 2 – Dropdown List) is like a regular list box — it displays a list of items from which a user must choose. Unlike list boxes, however, the list is not displayed until you click the arrow to the right of the box. The key difference between this and a drop-down combo box is that the user can't type into the box, he can only select an item from the list. Use this type of list box when space is at a premium.

Adding Items

To add items to a combo box, use the AddItem method, which has the following syntax:

box.**AddItem** *item*[, *index*]

Argument	Description
box	Name of the list or combo box.
item	String expression to add to the list. If *item* is a literal constant, enclose it in quotation marks.
index	Specifies where the new item is to be inserted in the list. An *index* of 0 represents the first position. If *index* is omitted, the item is inserted at the end (or in the proper sorted order).

While list items are commonly added in the Form_Load event procedure, you can use the AddItem method at any time. This gives you the ability to add items to the list dynamically (in response to user actions).

The following code places "Chardonnay," "Fumé Blanc," "Gewürztraminer," and "Zinfandel" into a combo box named Combo1 with its Style property set to 0 (vbComboDropDown):

```
Private Sub Form_Load ()
   Combo1.AddItem "Chardonnay"
   Combo1.AddItem "Fumé Blanc"
   Combo1.AddItem "Gewürztraminer"
   Combo1.AddItem "Zinfandel"
End Sub
```

Whenever the form is loaded at run time and the user clicks the down arrow, the list appears as shown in Figure 7.8.

Figure 7.8 "Wine list" combo box

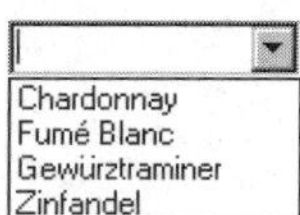

Adding Items at Design Time

You can also enter items into the list at design time by setting the List property in the Properties window of the combo box control. When you select the List property option and then click the down arrow, you can type list items and then press the CTRL+ENTER key combination to start a new line.

You can only add items to the end of the list. So, if you want to alphabetize the list, set the Sorted property to True. See "Sorting a List" below for more information.

Adding an Item at a Specified Position

To add an item to a list at a specific position, specify an index value after the new item. For example, the next line of code inserts "Pinot Noir" into the first position, adjusting the position of the other items downward:

```
Combo1.AddItem "Pinot Noir", 0
```

Notice that it is 0, not 1, that specifies the first item in a list (see Figure 7.9).

Figure 7.9 Adding an item to a list

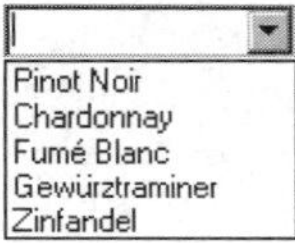

Sorting a List

You can specify that items be added to a list in alphabetical order by setting the Sorted property to True and omitting the index. The sort is not case-sensitive; thus, the words "chardonnay" and "Chardonnay" are treated the same.

When the Sorted property is set to True, using the AddItem method with the *index* argument can lead to unpredictable, unsorted results.

Removing Items

You can use the RemoveItem method to delete items from a combo box. RemoveItem has one argument, *index*, which specifies the item to remove:

box.**RemoveItem** *index*

The *box* and *index* arguments are the same as for AddItem.

For example, to remove the first entry in a list, you would add the following line of code:

```
Combo1.RemoveItem 0
```

To remove all list entries in a combo box, use the Clear method:

```
Combo1.Clear
```

Getting List Contents with the Text Property

Usually, the easiest way to get the value of the currently selected item is to use the Text property. The Text property corresponds to whatever is entered in the text box portion of the control at run time. This can be either a selected list item or a string that a user types in the text box.

For example, the following code displays information about Chardonnay if a user selects "Chardonnay" from a list box:

```
Private Sub Combo1_Click ()
   If Combo1.Text = "Chardonnay" Then
      Text1.Text = "Chardonnay is a medium-bodied _
      white wine."
   End If
End Sub
```

The Text property contains the currently selected item in the Combo1 list box. The code checks to see if "Chardonnay" has been selected and, if so, displays the information in the text box.

Accessing List Items with the List Property

The List property provides access to all items in the list. This property contains an array in which each item in the list is an element of the array. Each item is represented in string form. To refer to an item in the list, use this syntax:

box.**List**(*index*)

The *box* argument is a reference to a combo box, and *index* is the position of the item. The top item has an index of 0, the next has an index of 1, and so on. For example, the following statement displays the third item (*index* = 2) in a list in a text box:

```
Text1.Text = Combo1.List(2)
```

Determining Position with the ListIndex Property

If you want to know the position of the selected item in a list in a combo box, use the ListIndex property. This property sets or returns the index of the currently selected item in the control and is available only at run time. Setting the ListIndex property for a combo box also generates a Click event for the control.

The value of this property is 0 if the first (top) item is selected, 1 if the next item down is selected, and so on. ListIndex is –1 if no item is selected or if a user enters a choice in a combo box (Style 0 or 1) instead of selecting an existing item in the list.

> **Note** The NewIndex property allows you to keep track of the index of the last item added to the list. This can be useful when inserting an item into a sorted list.

Returning the Number of Items with the ListCount Property

To return the number of items in a combo box, use the ListCount property. For example, the following statement uses the ListCount property to determine the number of entries in a combo box:

```
Text1.Text = "You have " & Combo1.ListCount & " _
entries listed"
```

Using the Command Button Control

The command button control is used to begin, interrupt, or end a process. When clicked, it invokes a command that has been written into its Click event procedure.

Figure 7.10 The command button control

Most Visual Basic applications have command buttons that allow the user to simply click them to perform actions. When the user chooses the button, it not only carries out the appropriate action, it also looks as if it's being pushed in and released and is therefore sometimes referred to as a push button.

For More Information See "Clicking Buttons to Perform Actions" in Chapter 3, "Forms, Controls, and Menus," for a simple demonstration of the Command Button control.

Adding a Command Button to a Form

You will likely use one or more command buttons in your application. To add command buttons to a form, draw them on as you would any other control. Command buttons can be sized with the mouse or by setting their Height and Width properties.

Setting the Caption

To change the text displayed on the command button, use the Caption property. At design time, you can set this property by selecting it from the control's Properties window. When you set the Caption property at design time, the button text will be updated dynamically.

You can set the Caption property up to 255 total characters. If your caption exceeds the width of the command button, it will wrap to the next line. However, it will be clipped if the control cannot accommodate its overall height.

You can change the font displayed on the command button by setting its Font property.

Creating Keyboard Shortcuts

You can use the Caption property to create access key shortcuts for your command buttons by adding an ampersand (&) before the letter you want to use as the access key. For example, to create an access key for the caption "Print" you add an ampersand before the letter "P": "&Print". At run time, the letter "P" will be underlined and the user can select the command button by simultaneously pressing ALT+P.

> **Note** To include an ampersand in a caption without creating an access key, include two ampersands (&&). A single ampersand is displayed in the caption and no characters are underlined.

Specifying the Default and Cancel Properties

On each form, you can select a command button to be the default command button — that is, whenever the user presses the ENTER key the command button is clicked regardless of which other control on the form has the focus. To specify a command button as default set the Default property to True.

You can also specify a default cancel button. When the Cancel property of a command button is set to True, it will be clicked whenever the user presses the ESC key, regardless of which other control on the form has the focus.

Selecting the Command Button

A command button can be selected at run time by using the mouse or keyboard in the following ways:

- Use a mouse to click the button.
- Move the focus to the button by pressing the TAB key, and then choose the button by pressing the SPACEBAR or ENTER.
- Press an access key (ALT+ the underlined letter) for a command button.
- If the command button is the *default command button* for the form, pressing ENTER chooses the button, even if you change the focus to a different control.
- If the command button is the *default Cancel button* for the form, then pressing ESC chooses the button, even if you change the focus to another control.

The Value Property

Whenever the command button is selected, its Value property is set to True and the Click event is triggered. False (default) indicates the button isn't chosen. You can use the Value property in code to trigger the command button's Click event. For example:

```
cmdClose.Value = True
```

The Click Event

When clicked, the command button's Click event is triggered and the code you've written in the Click event procedure is invoked.

Clicking a command button control also generates the MouseDown and MouseUp events. If you intend to attach event procedures for these related events, be sure that their actions don't conflict. The order in which these three events occur varies from control to control. In the command button control, these events occur in this order: MouseDown, Click, MouseUp.

> **Note** If the user attempts to double-click the command button control, each click will be processed separately; that is, the command button control does not support the double-click event.

For More Information See Chapter 11, "Responding to Mouse and Keyboard Events," for more information on the MouseDown and MouseUp events.

Visually Enhancing the Command Button

The command button control, like the check box and option button controls, may be visually enhanced by altering the setting of the Style property and then using the Picture, DownPicture and DisabledPicture properties. For example, you may want to add an icon or bitmap to a command button or display a different image when the button is clicked or disabled.

Using the Common Dialog Control

The common dialog control provides a standard set of dialog boxes for operations such as opening and saving files, setting print options, and selecting colors and fonts. The control also has the ability to display Help by running the Windows Help engine.

Figure 7.11 The common dialog control

The common dialog control provides an interface between Visual Basic and the routines in the Microsoft Windows dynamic-link library Commdlg.dll. To create a dialog box using this control, Commdlg.dll must be in your Microsoft Windows \System directory.

You use the common dialog control in your application by adding it to a form and setting its properties. The dialog displayed by the control is determined by the methods of the control. At run time, a dialog box is displayed or the Help engine is executed when the appropriate method is invoked; at design time, the common dialog control is displayed as an icon on a form. This icon can't be sized.

The common dialog control allows you to display these commonly used dialog boxes:

- Open
- Save As
- Color
- Font
- Print

To use the common dialog control

1. If you haven't already done so, add the common dialog control to the toolbox by selecting **Components** from the **Project** menu. Locate and select the control in the **Controls** tabbed dialog, then click the **OK** button.
2. On the toolbox, click the **CommonDialog** control and draw it on a form.

   When you draw a common dialog control on a form, it automatically resizes itself. Like the timer control, the common dialog control is invisible at run time.
3. At run time, use the appropriate method, as listed in the following table, to display the desired dialog.

Method	Dialog displayed
ShowOpen	Open
ShowSave	Save As
ShowColor	Color
ShowFont	Font
ShowPrinter	Print
ShowHelp	Invokes Windows Help

Displaying Open and Save As Dialog Boxes

The Open dialog box allows the user to specify a drive, a directory, a file name extension, and a file name.

The Save As dialog box is identical to the Open dialog in appearance, except for the dialog's caption, and file names appearing dimmed out. At run time, when the user chooses a file and closes the dialog box, the FileName property is used to get the selected file name.

Figure 7.12 An Open dialog box

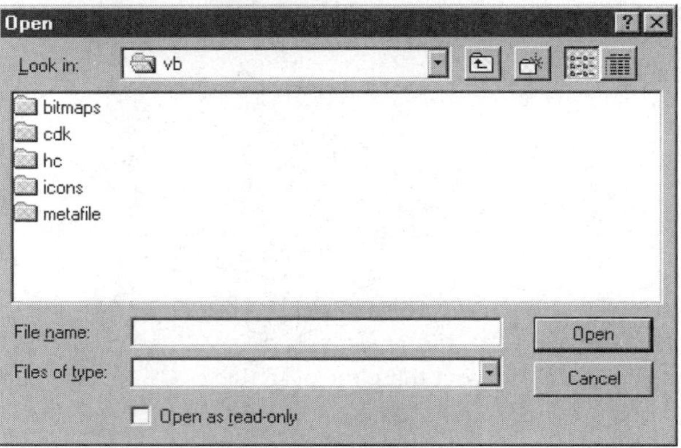

To display the Open dialog box

1. Specify the list of file filters that are displayed in the **Files of type** list box.

   You can do this by setting the Filter property using the following format:

   description1 | *filter1* | *description2* | *filter2*...

   Description is the string displayed in the list box — for example, "Text Files (*.txt)." *Filter* is the actual file filter — for example, "*.txt." Each *description* | *filter* set must be separated by a pipe symbol (|).

2. Use the ShowOpen method to display the dialog box.

After the user chooses a file, use the FileName property to get the name of the selected file.

With all the common dialog boxes, when the CancelError property is True, an error is generated when the user clicks the dialog box's Cancel button. You detect that the Cancel button was pressed by trapping the error when the dialog box is displayed.

The following code displays an Open dialog box and uses the selected file name as an argument to a procedure that opens a file:

```
Private Sub mnuFileOpen_Click ()
   ' CancelError is True.
   On Error GoTo ErrHandler
   ' Set filters.
   CommonDialog1.Filter = "All Files (*.*)|*.*|Text _
   Files (*.txt)|*.txt|Batch Files (*.bat)|*.bat"
   ' Specify default filter.
   CommonDialog1.FilterIndex = 2
```

```
    ' Display the Open dialog box.
    CommonDialog1.ShowOpen
    ' Call the open file procedure.
    OpenFile (CommonDialog1.FileName)
    Exit Sub

ErrHandler:
' User pressed Cancel button.
    Exit Sub
End Sub
```

Using the Color Dialog Box

The Color dialog box allows the user to select a color from a palette or to create and select a custom color. At run time, when the user chooses a color and closes the dialog box, you use the Color property to get the selected color.

Figure 7.13 The Color dialog box

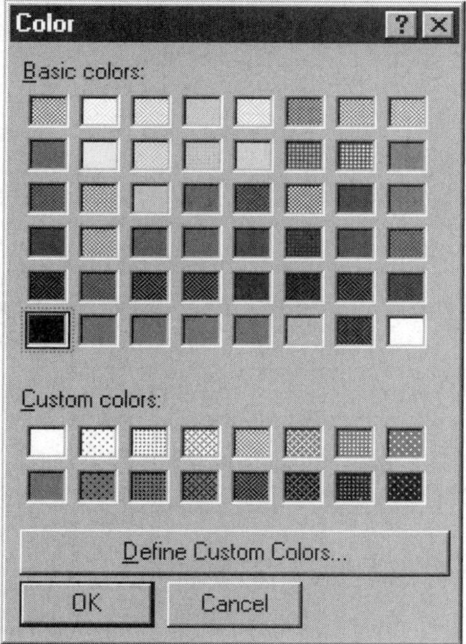

To display the Color dialog box

1. Set the Flags property for the common dialog control to the Visual Basic constant cdlCCRGBInit.
2. Use the ShowColor method to display the dialog box.

Use the Color property to get the RGB value of the color the user selects. The following code displays the Color dialog box when a user clicks the Command1 command button:

```
Private Sub Command1_Click ()
   ' Set Cancel to True.
   CommonDialog1.CancelError = True
   On Error GoTo ErrHandler
   ' Set the Flags property.
   CommonDialog1.Flags = cdlCCRGBInit
   ' Display the Color dialog box.
   CommonDialog1.ShowColor
   ' Set the form's background color to the selected
   ' color.
   Form1.BackColor = CommonDialog1.Color
   Exit Sub

ErrHandler:
   ' User pressed Cancel button.
   Exit Sub
End Sub
```

Using the Font Dialog Box

The Font dialog box allows the user to select a font by its size, color, and style. Once the user makes selections in the Font dialog box, the following properties contain information about the user's selection.

Property	Determines
Color	The selected color. To use this property, you must first set the Flags property to cdlCFEffects.
FontBold	Whether **bold** was selected.
FontItalic	Whether *italic* was selected.
FontStrikethru	Whether ~~strikethrough~~ was selected.
FontUnderline	Whether underline was selected.
FontName	The selected font name.
FontSize	The selected font size.

Figure 7.14 The Font dialog box

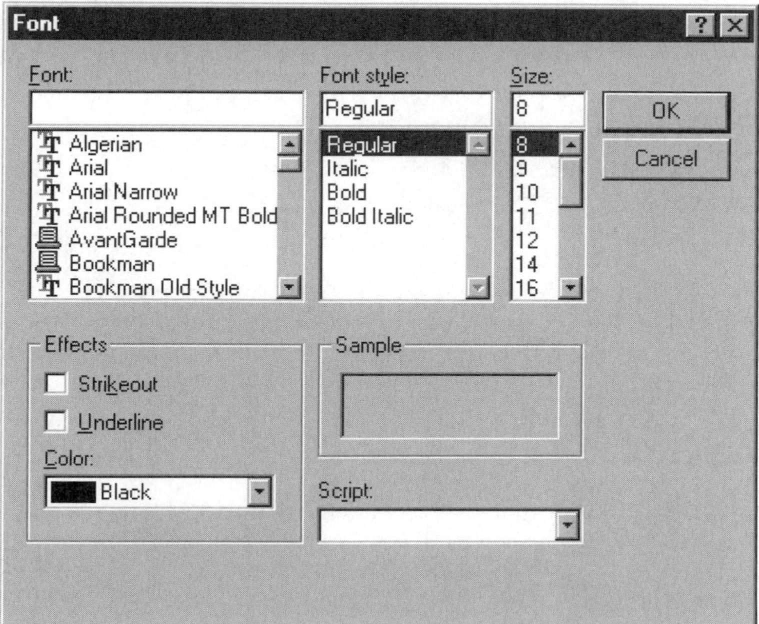

To display the Font dialog box

1. Set the Flags property to one of the following Visual Basic constant values:
   - cdlCFScreenFonts (screen fonts)
   - cdlCFPrinterFonts (printer fonts)
   - cdlCFBoth (for both screen and printer fonts)

     Caution You must set the Flags property to one of these values before displaying the Font dialog box. Otherwise, the error `No fonts exist` occurs.
2. Use the ShowFont method to display the dialog box.

The following code sets the font properties for a text box based on a user's selections in the Font dialog box:

```
Private Sub Command1_Click ()
   ' Set Cancel to True.
   CommonDialog1.CancelError = True
   On Error GoTo ErrHandler
   ' Set the Flags property.
   CommonDialog1.Flags = cdlCFBoth Or cdlCFEffects
   ' Display the Font dialog box.
```

```
    CommonDialog1.ShowFont
    ' Set text properties according to user's
    ' selections.
    Text1.Font.Name = CommonDialog1.FontName
    Text1.Font.Size = CommonDialog1.FontSize
    Text1.Font.Bold = CommonDialog1.FontBold
    Text1.Font.Italic = CommonDialog1.FontItalic
    Text1.Font.Underline = CommonDialog1.FontUnderline
    Text1.FontStrikethru = CommonDialog1.FontStrikethru
    Text1.ForeColor = CommonDialog1.Color
    Exit Sub
ErrHandler:
    ' User pressed Cancel button.
    Exit Sub
End Sub
```

Using the Print Dialog Box

The Print dialog box allows the user to specify how output should be printed. The user can specify a range of pages to be printed, a print quality, a number of copies, and so on. This dialog box also displays information about the currently installed printer and allows the user to configure or reinstall a new default printer.

> **Note** This dialog box does not actually send data to a printer. It allows users to specify how they want data printed. You must write code to print the data in the format they select.

For More Information See Chapter 12, "Working with Text and Graphics," for information on printing data.

At run time, when the user makes selections in the Print dialog box, the following properties contain information about the user's selection.

Property	Determines
Copies	The number of copies to print.
FromPage	The page to start printing.
ToPage	The page to stop printing.
hDC	The device context for the selected printer.
Orientation	The page's orientation (portrait or landscape).

Figure 7.15 The Print dialog box

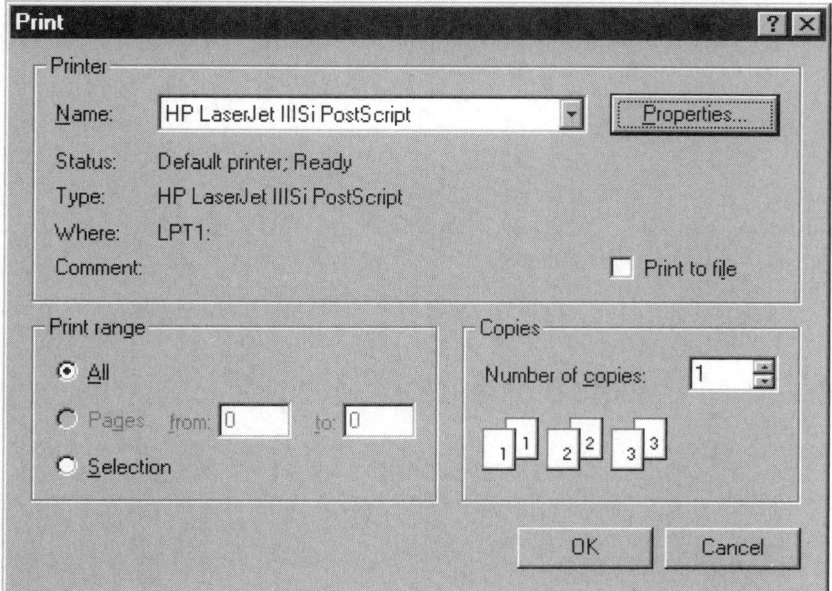

To display the Print dialog box

1. Set any desired default settings for the dialog by setting the appropriate Print dialog properties.

   For example, to display 2 in the Copies box when the dialog is displayed, set the Copies property to 2:

   ```
   CommonDialog1.Copies = 2
   ```

2. Use the ShowPrinter method to display the Print dialog box.

The following code displays the Print dialog box when the user clicks the Command1 command button:

```
Private Sub Command1_Click ()
   Dim BeginPage, EndPage, NumCopies, Orientation, i
   ' Set Cancel to True.
   CommonDialog1.CancelError = True
   On Error GoTo ErrHandler
   ' Display the Print dialog box.
   CommonDialog1.ShowPrinter
   ' Get user-selected values from the dialog box.
   BeginPage= CommonDialog1.FromPage
   EndPage     = CommonDialog1.ToPage
   NumCopies= CommonDialog1.Copies
   Orientation = CommonDialog1.Orientation
```

```
    For i = 1 to NumCopies
    ' Put code here to send data to your printer.
    Next
    Exit Sub
ErrHandler:
    ' User pressed Cancel button.
    Exit Sub
End Sub
```

Note If the PrinterDefault property is set to True, you can print to the Visual Basic Printer object. In addition, when the PrinterDefault property is True, any changes the user makes in the Setup portion of the Print dialog box are used to change the printer settings in the user's Printer setup.

Using the ShowHelp Method to Display a Help File

The ShowHelp method of the common dialog control allows you to display a Help file.

To display a Help file using the ShowHelp method

1. Set the HelpCommand and HelpFile properties.
2. Use the ShowHelp method to display the specified Help file.

The following code displays the specified Help file when the user clicks the Command1 command button:

```
Private Sub Command1_Click()
    ' Set Cancel to True.
    CommonDialog1.CancelError = True
    On Error GoTo ErrHandler
    ' Set the HelpCommand Property
    CommonDialog1.HelpCommand = cdlHelpForceFile
    ' Specify the Help file.
    CommonDialog1.HelpFile = "c:\Windows\Cardfile.hlp"
    ' Display the Windows Help engine.
    CommonDialog1.ShowHelp
    Exit Sub

ErrHandler:
    ' User pressed Cancel button.
    Exit Sub
End Sub
```

For More Information See "HelpCommand Property," "HelpFile Property," and "ShowHelp Method" in the *Microsoft Visual Basic 6.0 Language Reference* volume of the *Microsoft Visual Basic 6.0 Reference Library* for more information on displaying Help files with the common dialog control.

Using the Data Control

The intrinsic Data control implements data access by using the Microsoft Jet Database engine — the same database engine that powers Microsoft Access. This technology gives you seamless access to many standard database formats and allows you to create data-aware applications without writing any code. The intrinsic Data control is best suited to smaller (desktop) databases, such as Access and ISAM databases.

You can use the intrinsic Data control to create applications that display, edit, and update information from many types of existing databases, including Microsoft Access, Btrieve, dBASE, Microsoft FoxPro, and Paradox. You can also use it to access Microsoft Excel, Lotus 1-2-3, and standard ASCII text files as if they were true databases. In addition, the data control allows you to access and manipulate remote Open Database Connectivity (ODBC) databases such as Microsoft SQL Server and Oracle.

Note Both the Data control and Remote Data control are included with Visual Basic for backward compatibility. However, because of the flexibility of ActiveX Data Objects (ADO), it's recommended that you create new database applications using the ADO Data control. For more details, see "Using the ADO Data Control" earlier in this chapter.

The Data control, Remote Data control, and the ADO Data control are all conceptually similar: all three are "data controls" that connect a data source to a data-bound control. All three also share the same appearance — a set of four buttons that allow the user to go immediately to the beginning of the recordset, end of the recordset, and scroll backwards and forwards through the recordset.

Creating a Simple Database Application with the Data Control

To create a simple database application with the Data control

1. Draw a **Data** control on the form. The Data control is an intrinsic control and is always available.
2. Click the **Data** control to select it, and press F4 to display the Properties window.
3. In the Properties window, set the **Connect** property to the type of database you want to use.
4. In the Properties window, set the **DatabaseName** property to the file or directory name of the database you want to connect to.
5. On the Properties window, set the **RecordSource** property to the name of the database table you want to access.
6. Draw a **TextBox** control on the form.
7. Click the **TextBox** control to select it, and on the Properties window set the **DataSource** property to the Data control.

8. On the Properties window, set the **DataField** property to the name of the field in the database you want to view or modify.

9. Repeat steps 6, 7, and 8 for each additional field you want to access.

10. Press F5 to run the application.

Setting Data-Related Properties of the Data Control

The following data-related properties can be set at design time. The list suggests a logical order for setting the properties:

Note Database technology is a complex science, and the suggestions below are not meant to be taken as rules.

1. **RecordsetType** — The RecordsetType property determines if the recordset is a table, dynaset, or snapshot. The choice affects what recordset properties are available. For example, snapshot-type recordsets are more limited than dynaset recordsets.

2. **DefaultType** — The DefaultType property specifies whether JET or ODBCDirect workspaces are used.

3. **DefaultCursorType** — The DefaultCursorType property determines the location of the cursor. You can allow the ODBC driver to determine the cursor location, or specify server or ODBC cursors. The DefaultCursorType property is valid only when using ODBCDirect workspaces.

4. **Exclusive** — Determines if the data is for a single- or multi-user environment.

5. **Options** — The property determines the characteristics of the recordset. For example, in a multi-user environment, you can set the Options property to deny changes made by others.

6. **BOFAction, EOFAction** — These two properties determine what will happen when the control is at the beginning and end of the cursor. Choices include staying at the beginning or end, moving to the first or last record, or adding a new record (at the end only).

Using the DataCombo and DataList Controls

The DataCombo and DataList controls strongly resemble the standard list box and combo box controls described in "Types of Bound Controls," but there are some important differences that give them great flexibility and usefulness in database applications. Both controls can be automatically filled from a database field from the data control to which they are bound. In addition, they can optionally pass a selected field to a second data control, making them ideal for "lookup table" applications.

Possible Uses

- In a relational database, use the data from one table to supply values to be input into a second (related) table. For example, in an inventory database, the names of suppliers are stored in one table with each supplier having a unique ID. Another table showing products uses the unique ID to designate which company supplies the product. Use the DataList control to show the name of the supplier while (invisibly) supplying the ID of the supplier to the products table.
- Allow the user to narrow a search by selecting a criteria from a drop-down list. For example, a sales-reporting database application might use a DataList control to let the user pick a State or Sales Region. Once that selection is made, the choice is automatically passed to a second data control that positions itself on sales records from the selected region.

Like their built-in counterparts, the main difference between the DataList and the DataCombo controls is that the DataCombo box control provides a text box into whose contents may be edited.

For More Information For an explanation of the DataList and DataCombo controls' ability to link database tables, see "Linking Two Tables using the DataList and DataCombo Controls," online. To build a simple application using linked tables, see "Creating a Simple DataCombo Application," online.

Noteworthy Properties of the Controls

Some important properties of the DataList and DataCombo controls include:

Property	Description
BoundText	Contains the value of the field named in the BoundColumn property.
SelectedItem	Returns a bookmark for the row of a selected item.
MatchEntry	Enables extended search mode for locating items in a list generated by the DataCombo control.
IntegralHeight	Sizes the control to display an exact number of complete rows.
VisibleCount	Specifies the number of visible items in a list.

Note The DataFormat property of the DataCombo control is an Extender property. Therefore it's always visible on the property sheet and can be set in code. However the DataCombo control only formats the top item in its list. This can be disconcerting to the end user who sees a formatted top item, but is only given a list of unformatted items to select from. The formatted item may also mislead end users who assume the item will be entered in the database as formatted. For these reasons, it's advisable to not set the DataFormat property when using the DataCombo control.

For More Information To try a step-by-step tutorial that demonstrates the use of the BoundText property, see "Creating a DataGrid Linked to a DataList Control," later in this chapter. For a complete list of properties and methods of these controls, see "DataList Control" and "DataCombo Control," online.

Linking Two Tables Using the DataCombo and DataList Controls

The distinguishing characteristic of the DataCombo and DataList controls is the ability to access two different tables and link data from the first table to a field in the second. This is accomplished by using two data sources (such as the ADO Data control or the Data Environment).

Relational Tables and "Unfriendly" Values

In a relational database, information that is used repeatedly is not stored in its entirety in multiple places. Instead the bulk of the information is stored in a recordset comprised of many fields; among these fields is an ID field that uniquely identifies the recordset. For example, the Biblio database supplied with Visual Basic stores the names of several publishing companies in a table named "Publishers." The table contains many fields, such as address, city, zip code, and phone number. But for the sake of simplicity, consider the Name and PubID fields as the two essential fields in the table. The Name field stores the name of a publisher, while the PubID field stores a comparatively "unfriendly" value such as a number or code. But this unfriendly value is more important because it uniquely identifies the publisher, and serves as a link to the entire recordset. And it's that value that is stored in multiple recordsets in a second table.

The second table is named "Titles," and each recordset contains information such as Title, year of publication, and ISBN. Included among the fields is one named "PubID." This field is named exactly the same as the corresponding field in the Publishers table because it stores the value that links the title to a specific publisher.

This efficient scheme presents a small problem: Given a database application that allows users to insert new titles, the user must somehow input integers that identify the publisher. This is fine if the user has memorized each publisher's unique ID, but it would be easier for people to see the name of the publisher instead, and have the application store the associated value in the database. The DataList and DataCombo controls solve this problem easily.

Two Data Sources, Three Fields, No Coding

The DataList and DataCombo controls use two sources to surmount the problem. While displaying only the name of the publisher (from the Publishers table), the DataList or DataCombo control writes only the value of the PubID field to the Titles table. Through the Properties window, set the RowSource to the data source that will supply the data to be written (the Publishers table). Then set the DataSource property to the data source that will be written to (the Titles table). Finally, set the DataField, ListField, and BoundColumn properties. The figure below shows how the two data sources (in the form of two Data controls) and the three fields are assigned to a DataCombo control:

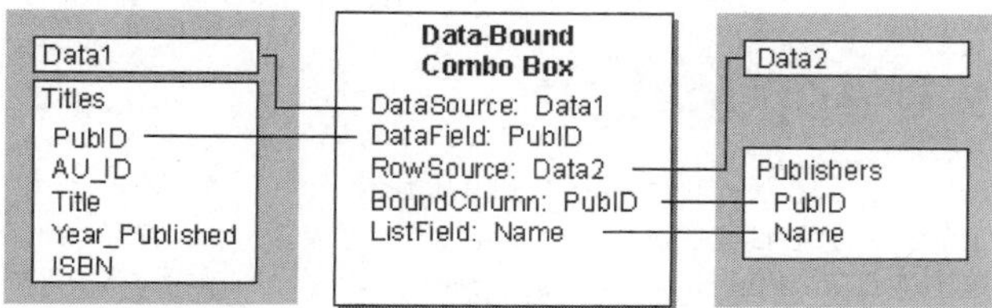

In brief, the ListField property determines which field is actually displayed by the control. In this case, it is the name of the publisher. The BoundColumn property, on the other hand, determines which field in the Publishers table supplies the actual value to the Titles table. Note that the PubID field in the Publishers table can't (and shouldn't) be edited. Instead, the value found in the PubID field is written to the field specified by the DataField property. In this case, it is the PubID of the Titles table.

The table below summarizes the properties and how to use them.

Property	Description
DataSource	The name of the data control to which the DataList or DataCombo control is bound.
DataField	The name of a field in the recordset specified by the DataSource property. This field will be used to determine which element in the list will be highlighted. If a new selection is made, it is this field that will be updated when you move to a new record.
RowSource	The name of the data control that will be used to fill the list.
BoundColumn	The name of a field in the recordset specified by the RowSource property. This field must be of the same type as the DataField that will be used to update the list.
ListField	The name of a field in the recordset specified by RowSource that will be used to fill the list.

Note You can also use the DataList and DataCombo controls with a single data control. To do this, set both the DataSource and RowSource properties to the same data control, and set the DataField and BoundColumn properties to the same field in the data control's recordset. In this case, the list will be filled with ListField values from the same recordset that is updated. If a ListField property is specified, but no BoundColumn property is set, BoundColumn will automatically be set to the ListField field.

For More Information To try a step-by-step procedure that builds a simple database application with the DataCombo control, see "Creating a Simple DataCombo Application," below.

Creating a Simple DataCombo Application

The following example uses the DataCombo box control to create a data entry screen for the Titles table of the Northwind.mdb sample database. It lets the user enter new products and assign them to existing suppliers by providing a lookup table of all the suppliers' names. When users get to the Supplier field in the entry form, they can choose a supplier from a list box. When they select a supplier, that supplier's SupplierID field is copied into the SupplierID field of the Products table.

To create a lookup table with the DataCombo control

1. Create an OLEDB Data Source for the Northwind database.

   If a Data Source has not been created, follow the steps in "Creating the Northwind OLE DB Data Source" later in this chapter.

2. Create a new Standard EXE project in Visual Basic.

   If the **DataGrid**, **DataCombo**, or **ADO Data Control** is not present in the Toolbox, right-click the **Toolbox**, and use the **Components** dialog box to add it.

3. Add a DataCombo, two ADO Data controls, and a DataGrid control to your form.

4. In the Properties window, set the properties of the first data control (Adodc1) as shown in the table below.

Property	Setting
Name	adoDataSource
ConnectionString	Northwind.mdl
RecordSource	Select * From Products;
Caption	Products

5. In the Properties window, set the properties of the second data control (Adodc2) as shown in the table below.

Property	Setting
Name	adoRowSource
ConnectionString	Northwind.mdl
RecordSource	Select CompanyName, SupplierID From Suppliers;
Caption	Suppliers
Visible	False

6. In the Properties window, set the properties of the DataGrid control as shown in the table below.

Property	Setting
Name	grdProducts
DataSource	AdoDataSource
Caption	Products

7. In the Properties window, set the properties of the DataCombo control as shown in the table below.

Property	Setting
Name	dcbSuppliers
DataSource	adoDataSource
DataField	SupplierID
RowSource	adoRowSource
ListField	CompanyName
BoundColumn	SupplierID

8. Finally, add the following code to the form's code module:

```
Private Sub Form_Load()
   ' Hide the SupplierID field in the DataGrid control, so the user is
   ' not confused on which value to change.
grdProducts.Columns("SupplierID").Visible = False
End Sub
```

9. Run the project.

You can navigate through the recordset by clicking the arrows on the visible ADO Data control. As you do so, the DataCombo control will update and display the name of the supplier for each product. To edit the SupplierID field, click the DataCombo control's arrow to display a drop-down list, then click again on a different supplier to change the value written to the SupplierID field.

Using the DataGrid Control

The DataGrid control is a spreadsheet-like bound control that displays a series of rows and columns representing records and fields from a Recordset object. You can use the DataGrid to create an application that allows the end user to read and write to most databases. The DataGrid control can be quickly configured at design time with little or no code. When you set the DataGrid control's DataSource property at design time, the control is automatically filled and its column headers are automatically set from the data source's recordset. You can then edit the grid's columns; delete, rearrange, add column headers to, or adjust any column's width.

At run time, the DataSource can be programmatically switched to view a different table, or you can modify the query of the current database to return a different set of records.

> **Note** The DataGrid control is code-compatible with the DBGrid control that shipped in Visual Basic 5.0 with one exception: the DataGrid control doesn't support the DBGrid notion of "unbound mode." The DBGrid control is included with Visual Basic in the Tools directory.

Possible Uses

- View and edit data on a remote or local database.
- Used in conjunction with another data-bound control, such as the DataList control, use the DataGrid control to display records from one table that are linked through a common field to another table displayed by the second data-bound control.

Using the Design-Time Features of the DataGrid Control

You can create a database application with the DataGrid control without writing a line of code by taking advantage of its design-time features. The following instructions outline the general steps needed to implement the DataGrid control in a typical use. For complete step-by-step instructions, see "DataGrid Scenario 1: Create a Simple Database Application with the DataGrid Control," online.

To implement a DataGrid control at design-time

1. Create a Microsoft Data Link (.MDL) file for the database you wish to access. See "Creating the Northwind OLE DB Data Link," later in this chapter, for an example.
2. Place an ADO Data control on a form, and set the **ConnectionString** property to the OLE DB data source created in step 1.
3. In the **RecordSource** field of the **Ado Data control**, type a SQL statement that returns a recordset. For example,

   ```
   Select * From MyTableName Where CustID = 12
   ```

4. Place a **DataGrid** control on a form, and set the **DataSource** property to the **ADO Data control**.
5. Right-click the **DataGrid** control and then click **Retrieve Fields**.
6. Right-click the **DataGrid** control and then click **Edit**.
7. Resize, delete, or add columns to the grid.
8. Right-click the **DataGrid** control and then click **Properties**.
9. Using the **Property Pages** dialog box, set the appropriate properties of the control to configure the grid as you wish it to appear and behave.

Changing Displayed Data at Run Time

Once you have created a grid using the design-time features, you may also wish to dynamically change the data source of the grid at run time. The general methods for accomplishing this are discussed below.

Changing the RecordSource of the DataSource

The most common method of changing displayed data is to alter the query of the DataSource. For example, if the DataGrid control uses an ADO Data control as its DataSource, rewriting the RecordSource and refreshing the ADO Data control will change the data displayed.

```
' The ADO Data control is connected to the Northwind database's
' Products table. The new query asks for all records which have
' the SupplierID = 12.
Dim strQuery As String
strQuery = "SELECT * FROM Suppliers WHERE SupplierID = 12"
Adodc1.RecordSource = strQuery
Adodc1.Refresh
```

Changing the DataSource

At run-time you can reset the DataSource property to a different data source. For example, you may have several ADO Data controls, each connected to different databases, or set to different RecordSource properties. Simply reset the DataSource from one ADO Data control to another:

```
' Reset the DataSource to an ADO Data control that is connected to
' the Pubs database, using the Authors table.
Set DataGrid1.DataSource = adoPubsAuthors
```

Rebind the DataSource

When using the DataGrid control with a remote database such as SQLServer, it's possible that the structure of the table may become altered. For example, a field may be added to the table. In that case, you can invoke the Rebind method to recreate the grid from the new structure. Note that if you have altered the columns' layout of the grid at design-time, the DataGrid control will attempt to recreate the current layout, including any empty columns. You can, however, force the grid to reset all columns by first invoking the ClearFields method.

Returning Values from the DataGrid

Once the DataGrid is connected to a database, you may want to monitor which cell the user has clicked. Use the RowColChange event — not the Click event — as shown below:

```
Private Sub DataGrid1_RowColChange(LastRow As Variant, ByVal LastCol As Integer)
   ' Print the Text, row, and column of the cell the user clicked.
   Debug.Print DataGrid1.Text; DataGrid1.Row; DataGrid1.Col
End Sub
```

Using the CellText and CellValue Methods

The CellText and CellValue properties are useful when a column has been formatted using the NumberFormat property. The NumberFormat property changes the format of any column that contains a number without changing the format of the actual data. For example, given a grid with a column named ProductID that contains integers, the code below will cause the DataGrid to display the values in the format "P-0000." In other words, although the actual value held in the ProductID field is "3," the value displayed by the grid will be "P-0003."

```
Private Sub Form_Load()
   DataGrid1.Columns("ProductID").NumberFormat = "P-0000"
End Sub
```

To return the actual value contained in the database, use the CellValue method, as shown below:

```
Private Sub DataGrid1_RowColChange(LastRow As Variant, ByVal LastCol As Integer)
   Debug.Print _
   DataGrid1.Columns("ProductID").CellValue(DataGrid1.Bookmark)
End Sub
```

> **Note** Both the CellValue used above, and the CellText value used below, require the bookmark property as an argument to function correctly.

Conversely, if you want to return the formatted value of the field, use the CellText method:

```
Private Sub DataGrid1_RowColChange(LastRow As Variant, ByVal LastCol As Integer)
   Debug.Print _
   DataGrid1.Columns("ProductID").CellText(DataGrid1.Bookmark)
End Sub
```

> **Note** The CellText method above is equivalent to using the Text property of the DataGrid control.

Where to Go From Here

To read a step-by-step procedure for building a simple application with the control, see "Creating a Simple Database Application with the DataGrid and ADO Data Control," or "Creating a DataGrid Linked to a DataList Control," later in this chapter.

To learn more about Split objects and how to program them, see "Manipulating DataGrid Views," later in this chapter.

Creating the Northwind OLE DB Data Link

An essential step in accessing data is creating an OLE DB data source for each database you want to access. The steps below create such an object for the Nwind.mdb (Northwind), supplied with Visual Basic. This data source is used in some of the example procedures supplied with the Visual Basic documentation. You need to create the OLE DB data source only once on a computer.

To create the Northwind OLE DB data source

1. Open Windows Explorer, or Windows NT Explorer.
2. Open a directory where you want to create the OLE DB data source. In this example, open Program Files, Microsoft Visual Studio, and VB98.
3. Right-click the right pane of Explorer, and then click **New** on the context menu. From the list of file types, click **Microsoft Data Link**.
4. Rename the new file **Northwind.MDL**.

5. Right-click the file and click **Properties** on the context menu to display the **Northwind.MDL Properties** dialog box.
6. Click the **Connection** tab.
7. Click the **Provider** box and select **Microsoft Jet 3.51 OLE DB Provider**.
8. In the **Data Source** box type the path to the nwind.mdb file.
9. Click **Test Connection** to check the connection.
10. If the connection passes, click **OK**.

   Note You can also create an OLE DB data source by going to the Control Panel and clicking the **Data Links** icon. On the **Organize Data Link Files** dialog box, click **New** to create a new data source.

Creating a Simple Database Application with the DataGrid and ADO Data Control

Using only a DataGrid and an ADO Data control you can create a database application that allows the end user to read and write to a recordset.

Create a simple database application using the ADO Data Control

1. Create an OLE DB data source for the Northwind database.

   If a Data Source has not been created, follow the steps in "Creating the Northwind OLE DB Data Link."

2. Create a new Standard EXE project in Visual Basic.

   If the **DataGrid** control is not present in the Toolbox, right-click the **Toolbox**, and use the **Components** dialog box to load it. Also load the ADO control.

3. Place an instance of each control on the blank form.
4. Set the ADO Control's **ConnectionString** property to the Northwind data source.

   Click the ADO Data control to select it, and press F4 to make the Properties window appear. Click **ConnectionString** and then click **OLE DB** File. Click the Northwind Data Source.

5. Set the ADO Control's **RecordSource** property.

   On the Properties window, click **RecordSource** and type a SQL statement to populate the DataGrid control. In this case, type in **Select * From Products**.

6. Set the DataGrid Control's **DataSource** property to the ADO Data control.

   Click the DataGrid control to select it. On the Properties window, click **DataSource** and a drop-down list of all data controls will be presented — in this case only the ADO Data control. Click the control.

7. Press F5 to run the project.

Creating a DataGrid Linked to a DataList Control

A common use of the DataGrid is to show "details" supplied by one table in a database. For example, the Northwind (Nwind.mdb) database includes two tables, one named "Suppliers," and the other named "Products." In this example, we'll use the DataList control to show the company names of suppliers from the "Suppliers" table. When the user clicks on any company name, the DataList control will furnish the SupplierID for the company. Using that ID, a query can be constructed to retrieve all records in the "Products" table which have a matching SupplierID. In other words, when the user clicks on a company (in the DataList control), all of the products produced by that company will appear in the DataGrid control.

To fill a DataGrid Control with products from a particular supplier

1. Ensure that an OLE DB data source for the Northwind database is present on the machine; if such a data source has not been created, follow the steps in "Creating the Northwind OLE DB Data Link."

2. Create a new standard EXE project in Visual Basic.

   If the **DataGrid** and **DataList** and **ADO Data** controls are not present in the Toolbox, right-click the **Toolbox**, and click **Components**. In the **Components** dialog box double-click **Microsoft DataGrid Control**, **Microsoft DataList Controls** and **Microsoft ADO Control**.

3. Place an instance of the **DataGrid** and **DataList** controls on the blank form.

   Place the **DataList** control in the top left corner of the form, and place the DataGrid control somewhat below it.

4. Place two instances of the **ADO Data control** on the form.

   Select the first **ADO Data control** and press F4 to display its Properties page. Set the **Name** property of the control to **adoSuppliers**. Select the second **ADO Data control** and set its **Name** property to **adoProducts**. Place the first control directly underneath the **DataList Control**, and the second directly below the **DataGrid** control.

5. Set the **ConnectionString** property of the two **ADO Data controls** to the Northwind OLE DB data source.

   Select the control named **adoSuppliers** and set the **ConnectionString** property to the Northwind OLE DB data source (Northwind.mdl). Select the control named **adoProducts** and repeat the operation.

6. Set the **RecordSource** property of the two **ADO Data controls**.

   Select **adoSuppliers** and click **RecordSource** on the **Properties** page. Type `Select * From Suppliers`. This query instructs the **ADO Data control** to return all records in the Suppliers table. Select **adoProducts**, click **RecordSource**, and type `Select * From Products`. This query returns all the records from the Products table.

7. Set the **RowSource** property of the **DataList** Control to **adoSuppliers.**

   The **RowSource** property determines which data source supplies the data for the **ListField** property.

8. Set the **ListField** property of the DataList control to **CompanyName**.

   The **ListField** property is set to the name of a field in the table named Suppliers. At run-time, the **DataList** control displays the value of the field specified in this property. In this example, the property will display the name of a company found in the Suppliers table.

9. Set the **BoundColumn** property of the DataList control to **SupplierID**.

   The BoundColumn property is set to a second field in the Suppliers table. In this case, the property is set to the SupplierID field. When the DataList control is clicked, the BoundText property returns the value of the SupplierID field associated with the company displayed in the DataList control. This value will be used in a query of the Products table, which provides data for the **DataGrid** control.

10. Set the **DataSource** property of the **DataGrid** control to **adoProducts**.

    The **DataSource** property specifies the data source for the control. In this case, the property is set to the ADO Data control named adoProducts, which returns all of the records in the Products table.

11. In the code module for the form, add the following:

```
Private Sub Datalist1_Click()
   ' Declare a string variable that will contain a new query. The
   ' new query uses the BoundText property of the DataList control
   ' to supply a SupplierID value. The new query simply asks for
   ' all products with the same SupplierID. This query is assigned
   ' to the RecordSource property of the ADO Data control named
   ' adoProducts. After refreshing the control, the DataGrid is
   ' updated with the new recordset of all products that are
   ' supplied by the same company.

   Dim strQuery As String
   strQuery = "Select * FROM Products WHERE SupplierID = " & _
   Datalist1.BoundText

   With adoProducts
      .RecordSource = strQuery
      .Refresh
   End With

   With DataGrid1
      .ClearFields
      .ReBind
   End With
End Sub
```

12. Run the project.

    Click any company name in the **DataList** control, and the **DataGrid** control is automatically updated with all products supplied by the company.

Working with Columns

You can dynamically change the data displayed in the DataGrid control by changing the DataSource property. For example, you can display a different table from the same database. If you do so, the DataGrid control will display the data with only default properties.

Adding, Deleting, or Hiding Columns

You can programmatically add, delete, or hide Columns by using the properties and methods of the Columns collection and the Column object.

Adding and Deleting a Column

To add a column at run time, use the Add method. If you first declare a variable and assign the new object to the variable, you can set various properties with concise code.

```
Private Sub AddColumn()
   ' Add a column in the rightmost position. Then set its Visible, Width,
   ' Caption, and Alignment properties. The DataField property specifies
   ' which field the column will be bound to.
   Dim c As Column
   Set c = DataGrid1.Columns.Add(DataGrid1.Columns.Count)
   With c
      .Visible = True
      .Width = 1000
      .Caption = "My New Column"
      .DataField = Adodc1.Recordset.Fields("ProductName").Name
      .Alignment = dbgRight
   End With
End Sub
```

You can delete any column by using the Remove method. Be sure to specify which column using the ColIndex argument. The following code will remove the clicked column.

```
Private Sub DataGrid1_HeadClick(ByVal ColIndex As Integer)
   DataGrid1.Columns.Remove ColIndex
End Sub
```

Hiding a Column

You can hide any column by setting its Visible property to False. This is especially useful when you want to limit columns that the user can view or edit. The example below simply iterates through the Columns collection, hiding all but a few columns.

```
Private Sub HideColumns()
   ' Use the DataField property to determine which column is being
   ' tested. Show only three columns: ProductName, UnitPrice, and
   ' UnitsInStock.

   Dim c As Column
   For Each c In DataGrid1.Columns
      Select Case c.DataField
      Case "ProductName"
         c.Visible = True
      Case "UnitPrice"
         c.Visible = True
      Case "UnitsInStock"
         c.Visible = True
         c.Caption = "In Stock" ' Change the column header.
      Case Else ' Hide all other columns.
         c.Visible = False
      End Select
   Next c
End Sub
```

Manipulating DataGrid Views

A grid that is "split" allows the end user to have more than one view on the same data. For example, imagine that you have a large table that consists of ten fields. In this case, the recordset viewed in the DataGrid control will be ten columns wide, and unless your form is very wide, the user will not be able to see more than a few columns. Further, imagine that the user is only interested in the first and last columns (for example, a name in the first column, and phone number in the last). In order to view both columns side-by-side (without having to rearrange the order of the columns), the grid can be split.

Creating a Split Object

At design time, you can create a split by right-clicking the grid, clicking Edit, right-clicking again, and then clicking Split. You can then edit the Split by right-clicking the control and clicking Properties to display the Property Pages dialog box. Use the Splits tab to customize the split. To remove a split, right-click the split and click Remove.

At run time, the end user can also split the grid manually (unless such an operation is disallowed) by clicking the tab located to the right of the grid control's lower left edge, as shown in the figure below:

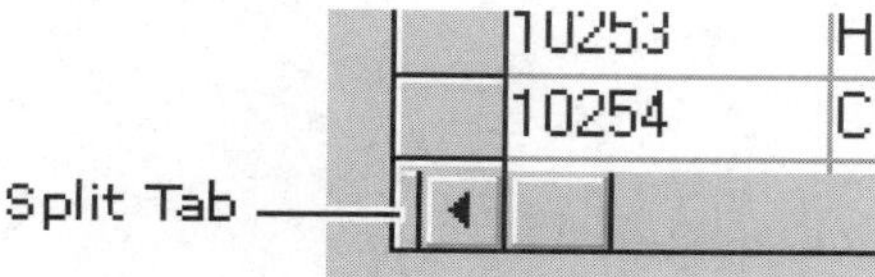

By default, the DataGrid control contains one Split object. The code to prevent the end user from adding splits is:

```
DataGrid1.Splits(0).AllowSizing = False
```

Programmatically Adding and Deleting Splits

The DataGrid control contains a collection of Split objects. In order to add splits programmatically, use the Add method, as shown below:

```
DataGrid1.Splits.Add 1
```

> **Note** The Add method requires the index of the new split as an argument. To append a split, set the index argument to the Count property of the Splits collection.

Using the Split collection's Add method, you can programmatically add splits as you require them. Since adding more than two splits can make the grid hard to use, you may wish to limit the number of splits using the Count property of the collection.

```
If DataGrid1.Splits.Count < 3 Then ' Append a split.
   DataGrid1.Splits.Add DataGrid1.Splits.Count
End If
```

Synchronizing Splits

When you have more than one split, you may wish to control how the splits scroll. For example, in a grid with three splits, you may decide to synchronize only the first and third splits, while allowing the middle split to scroll independently. To synchronize any two (or more) splits, set the ScrollGroup property of each Split object to the same value.

```
' Synchronize the first and third Split objects.
With DataGrid1
   .Splits(0).ScrollGroup = 1
.Splits(1).ScrollGroup = 2
.Splits(2).ScrollGroup = 1
End With
```

You can further customize the appearance of the split by setting the Scrollbars property to display only one scrollbar for the synchronized group.

Controlling Tab and Arrow Key Behavior

Using the WrapCellPointer, TabAcrossSplits, and TabAction properties you can determine how the grid will behave when the end user presses the tab or arrow keys.

Of these three properties, the TabAction property is at the highest level as it governs whether or not the WrapCellPointer and the TabAcrossSplits properties have any effect at all. The TabAction has three settings: Control Navigation, Column Navigation, and Grid Navigation. When the property is set to Control Navigation, pressing the tab key switches the focus to the next control in the TabIndex. This setting preempts WrapCellPointer and TabAcrossSplits.

The WrapCellPointer property determines how the tab and arrow keys behave within any single split. If the property is set to True, and the current cell is in the last column, when the end user presses the tab key the next row of the first column will become the current cell. However, if the current cell is in the last column of the last row, there will be nowhere to "wrap" to.

The TabAcrossSplits property determines how the tab and arrow keys behave when there are two or more splits on the grid. If the property is set to True, and the current cell is on the last column of any split but the last, pressing the tab or arrow key will cause the current cell to "jump" to the first column in next split. The current cell will remain in the same row.

> **Note** If both the WrapCellPointer and TabAcrossSplits properties are set to True, the current cell will not wrap until it is on the last column of the last split. It will then wrap to the next row in the first column of the first split.

Customizing the Columns Collection

Every Split object has a Columns property that allows you to manipulate a collection of Column objects. By doing so, you can change the appearance of every Split object. For example, one split may contain two columns showing first and last name fields, while a second split could show telephone and address fields. To accomplish this, hide the other columns by setting the Visible property of each to False, as shown below.

```
' Enumerate through the Columns collection to test each Column
' object's DataField property. If the test fails, hide the column.
Dim i As Integer

' Hide all but the ProductName column.
For i = 0 To DataGrid1.Splits(0).Columns.Count - 1
   If DataGrid1.Splits(0).Columns(i).DataField <> "ProductName" Then
      DataGrid1.Splits(0).Columns(i).Visible = False
   End If
Next i
```

```
' Hide all but the UnitPrice column.
For i = 0 To DataGrid1.Splits(0).Columns.Count - 1
   If DataGrid1.Splits(1).Columns(i).DataField <> "UnitPrice" Then
      DataGrid1.Splits(1).Columns(i).Visible = False
   End If
Next I
```

Tracking Records with Bookmarks and SelBookmarks

Bookmarks and SelBookmarks provide a means to track records. This is necessary when you program special functionality into an application, such as allowing the end user to manually select several discontiguous records, and performing a bulk update of the selected records. In that case, you will need to track which records have been selected, and you would therefore use the SelBookmarks collection and its properties.

Two functions, the CellText and CellValue methods, require bookmarks to perform properly.

Tracking User Selections

The SelBookmarks collection contains the bookmarks of all selected records. When the end user manually selects records (by holding down the CTRL key while clicking) the bookmark for each selected record is added to the collection. Using standard iteration methods, you can determine what has been selected, store the bookmarks (in case you need to restore a value), and perform the operation:

```
Dim i as Integer ' Counter
Dim intCount As Integer
intCount = DataGrid1.SelBookmarks.Count - 1
ReDim arrSelBK(intCount) ' Declare array to hold bookmarks.
For i = 0 To intCount
   ArrSelBK(i) = DataGrid1.SelBookmarks(i)
   ' Perform operations here. If the operations must be
   ' cancelled, exit the loop and use the array to
   ' rollback the changes.
Next i
```

Programmatically Select Records by Adding to the SelBookmarks Collection

You can also programmatically select records by adding them to the collection. For example, you may have a grid that shows all of the orders by a certain customer. To highlight all of the records where the customer spent more than $100, filter the records, and add the resulting bookmarks to the SelBookmarks collection.

```
Dim rs As Recordset
Set rs = Adodc1.Recordset

While Not rs.EOF
   If rs!SupplierID = 12 Then
      DataGrid1.SelBookmarks.Add rs.Bookmark
   End If
   rs.MoveNext
Wend
```

Displaying Calculated Fields

Suppose you have a field in a table named "Price," and you want to calculate the tax on every item in the table using the local tax rate. That is a calculated field, which you can create by modifying the query of the DataSource to calculate the value, and returning that value to the DataGrid control.

To create a calculated field in the DataGrid control

1. Ensure that an OLE DB data source for the Northwind database is present on the machine; if such a data source has not been created, follow the steps in "Creating the Northwind OLE DB Data Link," earlier in this chapter.
2. Place an ADO Data control and a DataGrid control on the form.
3. Set the ConnectionString property of the ADO Data control to the Northwind Data Source.
4. Set the RecordSource property of the ADO Data control.

   On the Properties window, click RecordSource and type **Select ProductName, UnitPrice, (UnitPrice * .082) As Tax From Products**.
5. Set the DataSource property of the DataGrid control to the ADO Data control.
6. Run the project.

Using the DataGrid Control with a Class Module

If the data you want to access exists in a custom format, or in a form not directly supported by an ODBC driver, you can create a class to encapsulate the data. You can then program the class with customized functions to retrieve the data. The class then becomes a data source that can be used by any data consumer, such as the DataGrid control.

In the class module's Initialize event, you first create an ADODB recordset object by declaring a variable as New ADODB.Recordset. After creating the recordset object, append fields to it, one for each field in your data source. Then fill the recordset with the appropriate data.

Note You can also create a data source using an OLEDB Simple Provider. See "Creating Data-Aware Classes" in Chapter 9 for more information about OLEDB Simple Providers.

The class module features a GetDataMember event that occurs whenever a data consumer (such as the DataGrid control) requests data. In the event, the Data argument is set to the recordset object created in the Initialize event.

To use the class module, create a form with a DataGrid control on it. In the form's Load event, place code that sets the control's DataSource property to the class.

Note The class module won't be available at design-time. For example, with the DataGrid control, all available data sources appear in a drop-down list when the user clicks DataSource on the Properties window. The class module will not appear among them, and can only be set through code.

Create a Data Source Using the Class Module

The example below uses a class module to create a simple data source. The DataGrid control is then bound to the module through the DataSource property.

To create a class for use with the DataGrid

1. Create a new **Standard Exe** project.
2. Add a **DataGrid** control to the form.

   If the DataGrid control is not available in the **Toolbox**, on the **Project** menu, click **Components**. Click **Microsoft DataGrid Control**, then click **OK**.
3. On the **Project** menu, click References. On the References dialog box, click **Microsoft ActiveX Data Objects 2.0 Library**.
4. On the **Project** menu, click **Add Class Module** to add a class module to the project.
5. In the Project Explorer window, click the Class icon to select it, and press F4 to display the Properties window.
6. On the Properties window, change the name of the class to **NamesData**.
7. On the Properties window, click **DataSourceBehavior** and change the property to **vbDataSource**.
8. In the Declarations section of the class module, create an ADODB Recordset variable, as shown below:

   ```
   Option Explicit
   Private WithEvents rsNames As ADODB.RecordSet
   ```

   Declaring the variables using the WithEvents keyword allows you to program the RecordSet object events.

9. In the class Initialize event, add the following code:

```
Private Sub Class_Initialize()
   ' Add the names of the new datamember to the DataMember collection
   ' This allows other objects to see the available DataMembers
   DataMembers.Add "Names"

   Set rsNames = New ADODB.RecordSet ' Set the object variable.

   ' Create a recordset with two fields and open the recordset. The
   ' first record has an integer data type and the second is a string,
   ' with a maximum of 256 characters. The CursorType is set to
   ' OpenStatic--an updatable snapshot of a set of records. The
   ' LockType is set to LockOptimistic to allow updates to the
   ' recordset
   With rsNames
      .Fields.Append "ID", adInteger
      .Fields.Append "Name", adBSTR, 255
      .CursorType = adOpenStatic
      .LockType = adLockOptimistic
      .Open
   End With

   Dim i As Integer
   For i = 1 to 10 ' Add ten records.
      rsNames.AddNew
      rsNames!ID = i
      rsNames!Name = "Name " & i
      rsNames.Update
   Next i
   rsNames.MoveFirst ' Move to the beginning of the recordset.
End Sub
```

The code first creates the recordset object, then appends two fields to the recordset. The code then adds ten records to the recordset.

10. In the class GetDataMember event, add the following code:

```
Private Sub Class_GetDataMember(ByVal DataMember As String, _
Data As Object)
   Set Data = rsNames
End Sub
```

The code returns the recordset object whenever the event occurs — whenever the class object is bound to a data consumer, such as the DataGrid control.

11. In the Form object's code module, declare an object variable for the class:

```
Option Explicit
Private datNames As NamesData ' Class variable
```

12. In the Form object's Load event, add the code to set the DataGrid control's DataSource to the class object.

```
Private Sub Form_Load()
   ' Create a new NamesData Object
   Set datNames = New NamesData

   ' Bind the DataGrid to the new DataSource datNames
    Set DataGrid1.DataSource = datNames
End Sub
```

13. Press F5 to run the project.

Programming the RecordSet Events

You can also program the events of the Recordset object. In the class module, click the Object Box (in the upper left corner), and then click **rsNames**. In the Procedures/Events box (upper right corner), the drop-down list will display all of the events of the Recordset object.

Add a Property to the Class

The class module can also be modified to respond to events or function calls. The code below shows how you can first add a property to the class. When invoked from another object, the property returns the RecordCount of the class.

```
Public Property Get RecordCount() As Long
   RecordCount = rsNames.RecordCount
End Sub
```

Using the DataMember Property

The GetDataMember event also includes the DataMember argument. Using this argument, you can include more than one recordset in the class module, and return the appropriate recordset by using a Select Case statement with the DataMember argument:

```
Private Sub Class_GetDataMember(ByVal DataMember As String, Data As _
Object)
   Select Case DataMember
   Case "Names"
      Set Data = rsNames
   Case "Dates"
      Set Data = rsDates
   Case Else
      ' Set a default data member.
      Set Data = rsYears
   End Select
End Sub
```

To specify which DataMember you want, set the DataMember property of the data consumer to the appropriate string, then set the DataSource as usual. For the DataGrid control, this would be:

```
Private Sub Form_Load()
   ' Create a new NamesData Object
   Set datNames = New NamesData

   ' Specify which DataMember you want, then set DataSource.
   DataGrid1.DataMember = "Names"
   Set DataGrid1.DataSource = datNames

End Sub
```

Using the File-System Controls (Directory List Box, Drive List Box, and File List Box)

Many applications must present information about disk drives, directories, and files. To allow users of your applications to explore the file system, Visual Basic provides two alternatives. You can use the standard dialog boxes provided by the common dialog control, or you can build custom dialogs using your own combinations of three specialized controls: the drive list box, the directory list box, and the file list box.

You can use the file-system controls to allow users to investigate and choose among available disk files in your applications. Consider using the common dialog control if you just need a standard File Open or Save dialog box.

For More Information See "Using the Common Dialog Control" earlier in this chapter for more information.

Sample Application: Winseek.vbp

Many of the code examples are taken from the Winseek sample application (Winseek.vbp) which is listed in the Samples directory.

Examining the File System

Each of the file-system controls has been carefully designed to combine flexible and sophisticated file-system inspection capabilities with easy programming. Each control performs its file-data retrieval tasks automatically, but you can write code both to customize their appearance and to specify which information they display.

Figure 7.16 The file-system controls

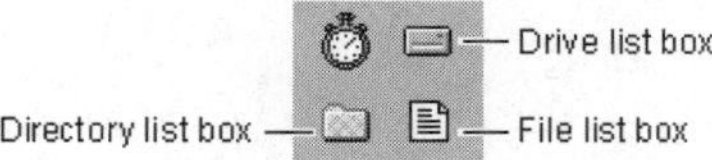

You can use file-system controls singly or in combination. With combinations, you can write code in each control's event procedures to determine how they interact. Or you can let them act independently. Figure 7.17 shows the three controls used together.

Figure 7.17 The file-system controls used together

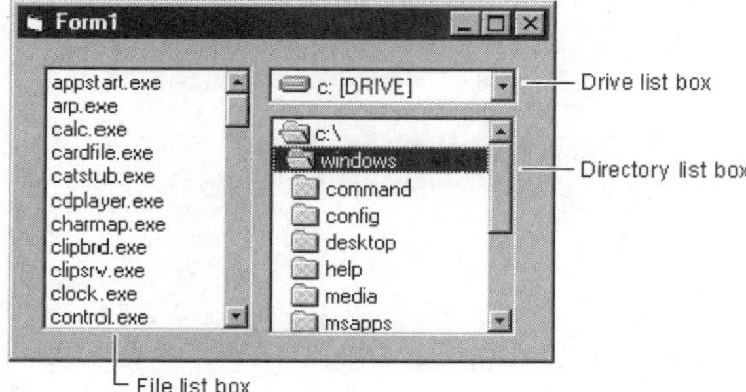

File-system controls obtain all their information from the operating system automatically; you can access this information or determine what is displayed by each control through its properties. For example, the contents of the current working directory is displayed by default (that is, the directory from which the application was launched, or what became the current directory as the result of a ChDir statement).

Your application can also display a list of the files with names matching a pattern, such as *.frm. Simply draw a file list box on the form and set its Pattern property to *.frm. You can specify the Pattern property at run time with the following code:

```
File1.Pattern = "*.FRM"
```

The file-system controls give you the flexibility that is not available with the common dialog control. You can mix and match them in a variety of ways, and you control their appearance and how they interact.

If your goal is simply to allow users to open and save files, a common dialog control provides a ready-to-run set of dialog boxes for these and other operations. These are the same dialog boxes used by many other Microsoft Windows–based applications, so they provide a standardized look-and-feel. They also recognize network drives when they're available.

For More Information See "Using the Common Dialog Control" earlier in this chapter for more information.

The Drive List Box

The drive list box is a drop-down list box. By default, the current drive is displayed on the user's system. When this control has the focus, the user can type in any valid drive designation or click the arrow at the right of the drive list box. When the user clicks the arrow, the list box drops down to list all valid drives. If the user selects a new drive from the list, that drive appears at the top of the list box.

You can use code to examine the Drive property of the drive list box to determine which drive is currently selected. Your application can also specify which drive appears at the top of the list box with this simple assignment:

```
Drive1.Drive = "c:\"
```

The drive list box displays valid available drives. Choosing a drive from the list box doesn't automatically change the current working drive; however, you can use the Drive property to change drives at the operating system level by specifying it as an argument to the ChDrive statement:

```
ChDrive Drive1.Drive
```

The Directory List Box

The directory list box displays the directory structure of the current drive on the user's system, beginning with the top-level directory. Initially, the name of the current directory appears highlighted and indented from directories above it in the hierarchy, back to the root. Subdirectories are indented beneath the current directory in the directory list box. As a user moves up or down the list, each of the items is highlighted in turn.

Identifying Individual Directories

Each directory in the box has an integer identifier associated with it that allows you to identify individual directories. This capability is not provided by the common dialog control. The directory specified by the Path property (`Dir1.Path`) always has the ListIndex value of –1. The directory immediately above it has the ListIndex value of –2, the one above that of –3, and so on up to the root. The first subdirectory of Dir1.Path has the ListIndex 0. If there are multiple directories at the first subdirectory level, the next has the ListIndex value of 1, then 2, and so on, as shown in Figure 7.18.

Figure 7.18 A directory structure displayed in the directory list box

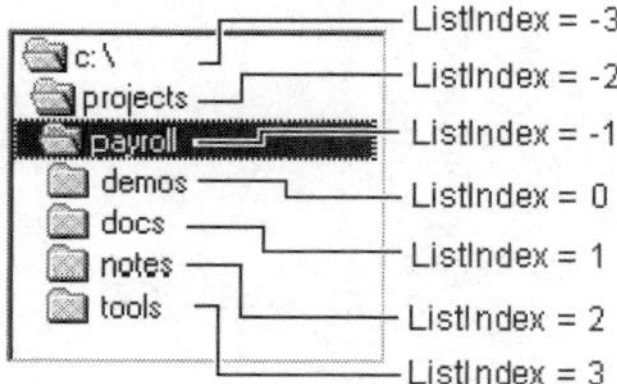

Setting the Current Directory

Use the Path property of the directory list box to set or return the current directory in the box (ListIndex = –1). For example, if you assign "c:\payroll" to `Drive1.Path` in Figure 7.18, the \Payroll directory becomes selected as the current working directory.

Similarly, you can assign the Drive property of the drive list box to the Path property of the directory list box:

```
Dir1.Path = Drive1.Drive
```

When this assignment is executed, the directory list box displays all the available directories and subdirectories on that drive. By default, the directory list box also displays all directories above, and any subdirectories immediately below, the current directory of a drive assigned to the `Dir1.Path` property. The directory list box doesn't *set* the current directory at the operating system level; it merely highlights the directory and gives it the ListIndex value of –1.

To set the current working directory, use the ChDir statement. For example, the following statement changes the current directory to the one displayed in the directory list box:

```
ChDir Dir1.Path
```

In an application that uses file controls, you can set the current directory to the directory where the application's executable (.exe) file is located with the Application object:

```
ChDrive App.Path    ' Set the drive.
ChDir App.Path      ' Set the directory.
```

Note The Path property is available only at run time, not at design time.

For More Information See "App Object" in the *Microsoft Visual Basic 6.0 Language Reference* for more information on the Application object.

Clicking a Directory Item

When a user clicks an item in a directory list box, that item is highlighted. When an item is double-clicked, it is assigned to the Path property, its ListIndex property gets the value –1, and the directory list box is redrawn to show its immediate subdirectories.

Finding a Directory's Relative Position

The ListCount property returns the number of directories below the currently expanded directory, not the total number of items in the directory list box. Because the ListIndex value of the currently expanded directory is always –1, you can write code to determine how far down from the root the currently expanded directory is in the hierarchy. For example:

```
' Initialize for currently expanded directory.

GoHigher = 0
' Dir1.List(x) returns empty string if the directory
' doesn't exist.
Do Until Dir1.List(GoHigher) = ""
   GoHigher = GoHigher - 1
Loop
' Convert to positive number, if desired.
LevelsAbove = Abs(GoHigher)
```

The File List Box

The file list box displays files contained in the directory specified by the Path property at run time. You can display all the files in the current directory on the current drive using the following statement:

```
File1.Path = Dir1.Path
```

You can then display a subset of these files by setting the Pattern property — for example, *.frm displays only files with that extension. The Pattern property can also accept a list delimited by semicolons. For example, a line with the following code displays all files with the extensions .frm and .bas:

```
File1.Pattern = "*.frm; *.bas"
```

Visual Basic supports the ? wildcard character. For instance, ???.txt displays files that have base names of only three characters with the extension .txt.

Working with File Attributes

The attributes of the currently selected file (Archive, Normal, System, Hidden, and ReadOnly) are also available through file list box properties. You use these properties to specify which kinds of files to display in a file list box. The default value for the System and Hidden attributes is False. The default value for the Normal, Archive, and ReadOnly attributes is True.

To display only read-only files in the list box, for example, simply set the ReadOnly property to True and the other attribute properties to False:

```
File1.ReadOnly = True
File1.Archive = False
File1.Normal = False
File1.System = False
File1.Hidden = False
```

When Normal = True, those files without the System or Hidden attribute are displayed. When Normal = False, you can still display files with ReadOnly and/or Archive attributes by setting these attributes to True.

> **Note** You cannot use the attribute properties to set file attributes. To set file attributes, use the SetAttr statement.

By default, you can highlight only a single selection in a file list box. To select multiple files, use the MultiSelect property.

For More Information For more information on SetAttr, see "SetAttr Statement," online. Also see "MultiSelect Property" in the *Microsoft Visual Basic 6.0 Language Reference.*

Using File-System Controls Together

If you use a combination of file-system controls, you can synchronize the information they display. For example, if you have a drive list box, a directory list box, and a file list box with the default names Drive1, Dir1, and File1, the sequence of events might work like this:

1. The user selects a drive in the Drive1 list box.
2. A Drive1_Change event is generated, and the display in Drive1 is updated to reflect the new drive.
3. Code in the Drive1_Change event procedure assigns the new selection (the `Drive1.Drive` property) to the Path property of the Dir1 list box with the following statements:

   ```
   Private Sub Drive1_Change ()
      Dir1.Path = Drive1.Drive
   End Sub
   ```

4. The assignment to the Path property generates a Dir1_Change event and updates the display in Dir1 to reflect the current directory of the new drive.
5. Code in the Dir1_Change event procedure assigns the new path (the `Dir1.Path` property) to the `File1.Path` property of the File1 list box:

   ```
   Private Sub Dir1_Change ()
      File1.Path = Dir1.Path
   End Sub
   ```

6. The assignment to the `File1.Path` property causes the display in the File1 list box to reflect the Dir1 path specification.

The event procedures you use and the properties you change depend on the way your application uses the combination of file-system controls. The code in "File-System Controls Scenario: A File Seeker Application" illustrates the synchronization of controls described here.

File-System Controls Scenario: A File Seeker Application

Because users often want to find a file or group of files available to an application quickly, many applications provide capabilities for investigating the file system. The Winseek.vbp sample application helps the user browse drives and directories, and displays any category of files.

Figure 7.19 File-system controls in the WinSeek application

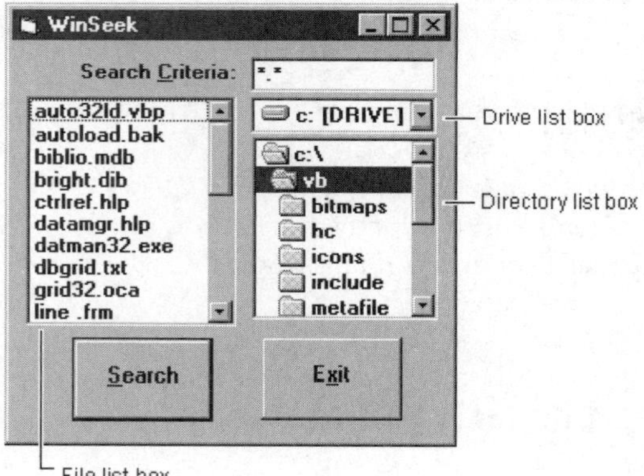

The following table summarizes the controls in Seek.frm from the WinSeek application.

Control	Property	Setting
Drive list box	Name	drvList
Directory list box	Name	dirList
File list box	Name Pattern	filList *.*
First command button	Name Caption Default	cmdSearch &Search True

Control	Property	Setting
Second command button	Name Caption	cmdExit E&xit
List box	Name	lstFoundFiles

Note The file-system controls do not have caption properties, although you can label them and give them access keys. For more information on using labels this way, see "Using the Label Control" later in this chapter.

Writing Code for the WinSeek Application

In the drive list box, a Change event is triggered by a single mouse click on an item. A Change event also occurs when the user selects an item and then changes the focus on the form. In the directory list box, a DblClick event is necessary to generate a Change event.

When users want to change directories without using a mouse, they typically use the arrow keys to select the desired directory and then press the ENTER key.

Because ENTER is commonly associated with the default command button control, WinSeek must recognize when the user simply wants to change directories rather than conduct a search for files.

The WinSeek application resolves this ambiguity by determining if the path of the dirList box differs from the currently highlighted directory. This situation can occur when the user single-clicks an item in the directory list box or navigates the directory list box using the arrow keys. The following code determines whether the `dirList.Path` is different from the path of the highlighted directory. If the paths are different, the `dirList.Path` is updated. If the paths are the same, the search is performed.

```
Private Sub cmdSearch_Click()
   .
   .
   .
' If the dirList.Path is different from the currently
' selected directory, update it; otherwise perform the
' search.
If dirList.Path <> dirList.List(dirList.ListIndex) Then
   dirList.Path = dirList.List(dirList.ListIndex)
   Exit Sub
End If
' Continue with search.
   .
   .
   .
End Sub
```

The WinSeek application uses the following procedures to handle significant events:

- The drvList_Change procedure
- The dirList_Change procedure
- The cmdSearch_Click procedure

The Drive List Box's Change Event

When the user clicks an item in the drive list box, its Change event is generated. The drvList_Change event procedure is invoked, and the following code is run:

```
Private Sub drvList_Change ()
   On Error GoTo DriveHandler
   ' If new drive was selected, the Dirl box
   ' updates its display.
   dirList.Path = drvList.Drive
   Exit Sub
' If there is an error, reset drvList.Drive with the
' drive from dirList.Path.
DriveHandler:
   drvList.Drive = dirList.Path
   Exit Sub
End Sub
```

Notice that the Change event in a drive list box occurs when a new drive is selected, either with a single mouse click or when the user moves the selection (for example, with an arrow key). The error handler is triggered by actions such as attempting to access a floppy disk drive while the drive door is open or selecting a network drive that has been inadvertently disconnected. Because the error prevents the original assignment, `dirList.Path` still contains the previous valid drive. Reassigning `dirList.Path` to `drvList.Drive` corrects this error.

For More Information See Chapter 13, "Debugging Your Code and Handling Errors," for more information.

The Directory List Box's Change Event

If the user double-clicks an item in the directory list box, or if the Path property of dirList is changed in code (as in the drvList_Change procedure), the dirList_Change event is initiated. The following code responds to that event:

```
Private Sub dirList_Change ()
   ' Update file list box to synchronize with the
   ' directory list box.
   filList.Path = dirList.Path
End Sub
```

This event procedure assigns the Path property of the dirList box to the Path property of the filList box. This causes a PathChange event in the filList list box, which is redrawn; you don't need to add code to the filList_PathChange procedure, because in this application, the event chain ends in the filList list box.

The Command Button's Click Event

This event procedure determines whether the highlighted item in the dirList list box is the same as the `dirList.Path`. If the items are different, then `dirList.Path` is updated. If the items are the same, then the search is performed.

```
Private Sub cmdSearch_Click ()
   .
   .
   .
   ' If the dirList.Path is different from the
   ' currently selected directory, update it;
   ' otherwise perform the search.
   If dirList.Path <> dirList.List _
   (dirList.ListIndex) Then
      dirList.Path = dirList.List(dirList.ListIndex)
      Exit Sub
   End If
   ' Continue with search.
   .
   .
   .
End Sub
```

Note You can enhance the WinSeek application with additional features. For example, you might want to use a file control's attribute properties. You could use check boxes to allow the user to set different combinations of file attributes so that the file list box displays files that are Hidden, System, and so on. This would restrict a search to conforming files.

Using the Frame Control

Frame controls are used to provide an identifiable grouping for other controls. For example, you can use frame controls to subdivide a form functionally — to separate groups of option button controls.

Figure 7.20 The frame control

In most cases, you will use the frame control passively — to group other controls — and will have no need to respond to its events. You will, however, most likely change its Name, Caption, or Font properties.

For More Information See "Grouping Options with Option Buttons" in Chapter 3, "Forms, Controls, and Menus," for a simple demonstration of using the frame control to group option buttons.

Adding a Frame Control to a Form

When using the frame control to group other controls, first draw the frame control, and then draw the controls inside it. This enables you to move the frame and the controls it contains together.

Drawing Controls Inside the Frame

To add other controls to the frame, draw them inside the frame. If you draw a control outside the frame, or use the double-click method to add a control to a form, and then try to move it inside the frame control, the control will be on top of the frame and you'll have to move the frame and controls separately.

Figure 7.21 Controls inside a frame

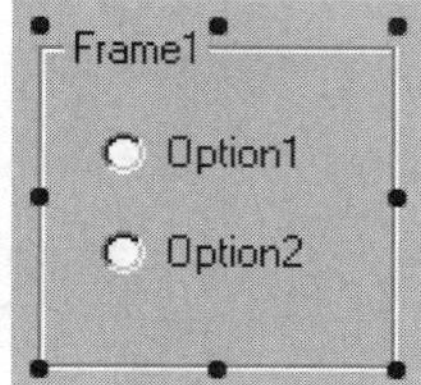

> **Note** If you have existing controls that you want to group in a frame, you can select all the controls, cut them to the clipboard, select the frame control, and then paste them into the frame control.

Selecting Multiple Controls in a Frame

To select multiple controls in a frame , hold down the CTRL key while using the mouse to draw a box around the controls. When you release the mouse, the controls inside the frame will be selected, as in Figure 7.22.

Figure 7.22 Selecting controls inside a frame

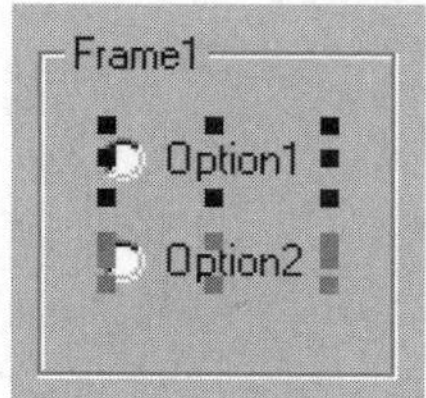

Using the Microsoft Hierarchical FlexGrid Control

The Microsoft Hierarchical FlexGrid (MSHFlexGrid) and Microsoft FlexGrid (MSFlexGrid) controls present Recordset data, from one or more tables, in a grid format.

The Hierarchical FlexGrid control provides you with advanced features for displaying data in a grid. It is similar to the Microsoft Data Bound grid (DataGrid) control, but with the distinct difference that the Hierarchical FlexGrid control does not allow the user to edit data bound to, or contained within, it. This control, therefore, allows you to display data to the user while ensuring that the original data remains secure and unchanged. It is also possible, however, to add cell-editing features to your Hierarchical FlexGrid control by combining it with a text box.

While the Hierarchical FlexGrid control is based on the FlexGrid control used in Visual Basic 5.0, the Hierarchical FlexGrid control is the more flexible of the two. The Hierarchical FlexGrid control also provides more display options with which you can define a custom format that best suits your needs.

These topics primarily focus on using the Hierarchical FlexGrid. For information on the former FlexGrid control, see your Visual Basic 5.0 documentation.

Visual Basic's FlexGrid controls

Icon	Abbreviation	Control Name
	MSHFlexGrid control	Microsoft Hierarchical FlexGrid control
	MSFlexGrid control	Microsoft FlexGrid control

The Hierarchical FlexGrid control supports the following features:

- Read-only data binding.
- Dynamic rearrangement of columns and rows.
- Automatic regrouping of data during column adjustment.
- Adaptation to existing Visual Basic code for the data-bound grid (DataGrid).
- Each cell may contain text, a picture, or both.
- Changing current cell text in code or at run time.
- Reading data automatically when the Hierarchical FlexGrid is assigned to a data control.
- Wordwrap for text within cells.

- ActiveX Data Binding when the **DataSource** and **DataMember** properties of the control are bound to a specific data provider. *
- Binding via the Data Binding Manager in Visual Basic. *
- Binding directly to grouped and related ADO Recordsets from a Command hierarchy. *
- Additional display options when the Hierarchical FlexGrid is bound to a hierarchy of Recordsets. These additional options enable a diverse display for grouped and related Recordsets, including bands. *

  Note To take advantage of the features marked with an asterisk (*) you must use the Hierarchical FlexGrid control. These features are not available in the FlexGrid control.

Due to limitations of the previous FlexGrid control, some features, such as bands, are not accessible using this control. To have access to all features, we recommend that you use the Hierarchical FlexGrid control when creating a new data-bound grid control. The FlexGrid control does not automatically update to the Hierarchical FlexGrid control.

Accessing the Hierarchical FlexGrid Control

Use the following procedure to install and access the Hierarchical FlexGrid control in Visual Basic.

To install and access the Hierarchical FlexGrid control

1. On the **Project** menu, select **Components**. The **Components** dialog box appears.
2. On the **Controls** tab, select **Microsoft Hierarchical FlexGrid Control 6.0**, and then click **OK**. The **MSHFlexGrid** control is added to the Visual Basic toolbox.
3. On the Visual Basic toolbox, click the **MSHFlexGrid** control, and then drop it on a Visual Basic form.

   – or –

   On the Visual Basic toolbox, double-click the **MSHFlexGrid** control to add it to a form.

Binding Data to the Hierarchical FlexGrid

Before you can use its features, you must bind data to the Hierarchical FlexGrid. You can bind data to this control either using Visual Basic's new Data Binding Manager or programmatically.

Once your Hierarchical FlexGrid is bound to a data source, the design-time display within the Hierarchical FlexGrid is a single blank column and single blank row. The field and band information is not automatically retrieved (to obtain this information, see Retrieving Structure). If the Hierarchical FlexGrid is run without field and band information, the data displays using the default property settings. That is, if the Hierarchical FlexGrid is bound to a hierarchical Command, the bands of data display horizontally with each band containing a column for each field in the Recordset.

Hierarchical FlexGrid bound to the Data Source

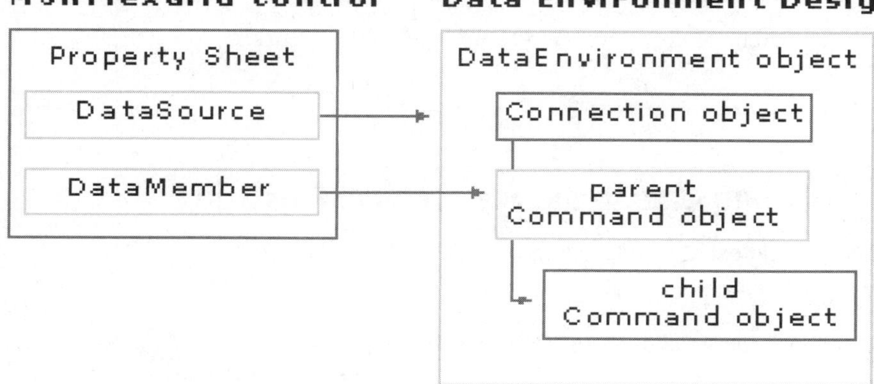

Using the Visual Basic Data Binding Manager to Bind Data to the Hierarchical FlexGrid

This section describes how to use the Visual Basic Data Binding Manager to bind data to your Hierarchical FlexGrid. This Data Binding Manager provides a user interface that promotes ease-of-use when binding data.

To set the DataSource using the Visual Basic Data Binding Manager

1. Create a source of data for your Hierarchical FlexGrid.

   The data source can be a DataEnvironment object or an ActiveX Data Object (ADO) Data Control, a new Visual Basic feature. For this procedure, create the data source as a DataEnvironment object.

2. On the Visual Basic toolbox, click the **MSHFlexGrid** control, and then drop it on a Visual Basic form.

   – or –

   On the Visual Basic toolbox, double-click the **MSHFlexGrid** control to drop it on a Visual Basic form.

3. On the Visual Basic Properties window, set the **DataSource** property to the DataEnvironment object that contains the Command object that you want to bind to the Hierarchical FlexGrid.

   Caution If the **DataSource** is reset, any user-defined modified data in the Hierarchical FlexGrid cells is lost.

4. On the Visual Basic Properties window, set the **DataMember** property to a Command object in the Data Environment. If you want to view hierarchical data in your Hierarchical FlexGrid, you must specify a top-most, parent Command object in a Command hierarchy as **DataMember**.

5. To view the data in the Hierarchical FlexGrid, on the **Run** menu, select **Start**.

   – or –

   Press F5.

Programmatically Binding Data to the Hierarchical FlexGrid

This section describes how to bind data to the Hierarchical FlexGrid programmatically.

To set the DataSource programmatically

1. On the Visual Basic toolbox, double-click the **MSHFlexGrid** control to place it on a Visual Basic form.

2. Right-click your Hierarchical FlexGrid and select **View Code** from the shortcut menu. The Code Editor window appears.

3. In the Form_Load event, add code to create an ADO Recordset and assign it to the Hierarchical FlexGrid. This code is provided in the following sub-steps.

   Note To set the data source programmatically, the project must have a reference to Microsoft ActiveX Data Objects: On the **Project** menu, choose **Select References**, and then select **Microsoft ActiveX Data Objects 2.0 Library**.

   - Create an ADO Connection and Recordset by inserting the following code, replacing the comments as appropriate (for example, replace `<myDataSource>` with the actual name of your data source):

     ```
     DIM Cn As New Connection, Rs As New Recordset

     ' You need to replace <myDataSource> with a valid
     ' DSN on your system.
     Cn.ConnectionString = "DSN=<myDataSource>"

     ' Use the following code for SHAPE Commands
     Cn.Provider = "MSDataShape"
     Cn.CursorLocation = adUseNone
     ```

```
' Alternatively, for SQL Commands, use the following code
Cn.CursorLocation = adUseNone

Cn.Open

' You need to specify a valid data source for
' your Recordset for the Connection created above
Rs.Source = "<valid SQL SELECT command>"

' Now associate the Command with the Connection
' and execute them.
Set Rs.ActiveConnection = Cn
Rs.Open
```

- Assign the open Recordset in Rs to the Hierarchical FlexGrid by inserting the following code:

```
Set MSHFlexGrid1.DataSource = Rs
```

4. To view the data in the Hierarchical FlexGrid, on the **Run** menu, select **Start**.

   – or –

   Press F5.

Using the Hierarchical FlexGrid with a Hierarchical Recordset

You can use the Hierarchical FlexGrid with a hierarchical Recordset to view relational information. You can display this information to the user while ensuring that the original data remains secure and unchanged, or you can add cell-editing features to your Hierarchical FlexGrid by adding a text box to the form. When the Hierarchical FlexGrid is bound to a hierarchy of Recordsets, you can display grouped and related Recordsets using bands.

> **Note** Data must be bound to your Hierarchical FlexGrid before performing this procedure. To do this, see Binding Data to the Hierarchical FlexGrid.

To use bands when displaying hierarchical Recordsets in a Hierarchical FlexGrid

1. Right-click your Hierarchical FlexGrid, and then select **Properties** from the shortcut menu. The Hierarchical FlexGrid's **Property Pages** dialog box appears.
2. On the **General** tab, set the **BandDisplay**. See "Formatting a Band" later in this chapter for a description of each band display.
3. On the **Bands** tab, select a band from the **Band** box. This list of available bands is based on the Recordsets in the Command hierarchy. For all bands, the name of the Command that generates the Recordset is shown in parentheses.

4. Modify the properties of each band as necessary. See “Formatting a Band” for more information.

5. Click **OK** to apply the band properties to your Hierarchical FlexGrid and close the **Property Pages** dialog box.

Formatting a Band

In your Hierarchical FlexGrid you can use band formatting to specify the display options for a particular Recordset. A band is created for each Recordset in an ADO hierarchical Recordset. For example, when binding a Hierarchical FlexGrid to an ADO hierarchical Recordset that contains Customers and Orders, the Hierarchical FlexGrid initially contains two bands.

You can customize the appearance of your Hierarchical FlexGrid by formatting a band. This enables you to highlight important information among multiple bands. Band elements you can format include column headers, gridlines, colors, and indentation.

When binding to a non-hierarchical Recordset there is only one band, and this band is referred to as Band 0. No other bands are available, because bands are based on the Recordsets in the Command hierarchy.

Changing Band Layout

You can change the way that fields display within a band by changing the band’s layout. By default, the fields display horizontally within bands, as in a standard grid.

Horizontal Band Display

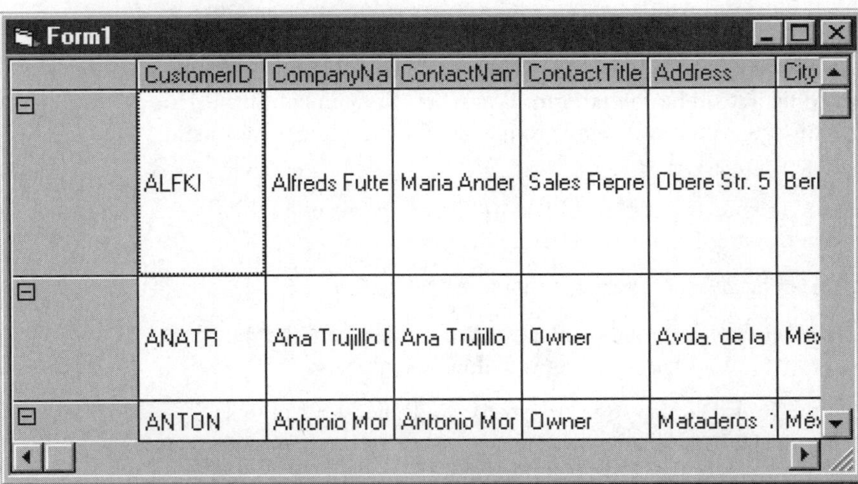

Vertical display may cause the band to expand its height to accommodate all fields in the band. Any other bands that display in the Hierarchical FlexGrid also expand, ensuring that all bands are of equal height.

Vertical Band Display

Form1

	CustomerID	CompanyNa	ContactNam	ContactTitle	Address
⊟	ALFKI	Alfreds Futte	Maria Ander	Sales Repre	Obere Str. 5
	10643	ALFKI	6	1995-09-25	1995-10-23
	10692	ALFKI	4	1995-11-03	1995-12-01
	10702	ALFKI	4	1995-11-13	1995-12-25
	10835	ALFKI	1	1996-02-15	1996-03-14
	10952	ALFKI	1	1996-04-15	1996-05-27
	11011	ALFKI	3	1996-05-09	1996-06-06
⊟	ANATR	Ana Trujillo E	Ana Trujillo	Owner	Avda. de la
	10308	ANATR	7	1994-10-19	1994-11-16
	10625	ANATR	3	1995-09-08	1995-10-06
	10759	ANATR	3	1995-12-29	1996-01-26

To set band layout

1. Right-click your Hierarchical FlexGrid, and then select **Properties** from the shortcut menu. The Hierarchical FlexGrid's **Property Pages** dialog box appears.
2. On the **General** tab, set the **BandDisplay**.
3. Click **OK** to apply the band's display properties to your Hierarchical FlexGrid and close the **Property Pages** dialog box.

Displaying Column Headers

When the band display is horizontal, you can set headers to display in your Hierarchical FlexGrid. The headers display directly above the band, repeating for each band in the Hierarchical FlexGrid. To display only one set of headers for each band, at the top or left of the Hierarchical FlexGrid, use fixed cells instead of headers. See "Customizing Fixed Appearance" (in the section "Customizing Areas of the Hierarchical FlexGrid"), later in this chapter for information on fixed cells.

Horizontal Column Headers

1. Right-click your Hierarchical FlexGrid, and then select **Properties** from the shortcut menu. The Hierarchical FlexGrid's **Property Pages** dialog box appears.
2. On the **Bands** tab, select **ColumnHeaders**, and then select a column header style from the **TextStyleHeader** list box.
3. Click **OK** to apply the column header properties to your Hierarchical FlexGrid and close the **Property Pages** dialog box.

Changing Column Order

You can change the order of columns within a band of your Hierarchical FlexGrid.

To change column order within a band

1. Select the column that you want to move.
2. Use the up and down arrows to move the column to a new position within the band.

Modifying Color and Gridlines

Band color and gridline information can be set globally or individually. You can modify color and gridlines to highlight important information within your Hierarchical FlexGrid and increase readability. In addition, you can specify whether to display gridlines between cells within a band. Use the following procedure to modify color and gridlines for all bands within your Hierarchical FlexGrid.

> **Note** To change color information for an individual band, you must programmatically perform the change using the BackColorBand property.

To globally modify color and gridlines

1. Right-click your Hierarchical FlexGrid, and then select **Properties** from the shortcut menu. The Hierarchical FlexGrid's **Property Pages** dialog box appears.
2. On the **Bands** tab, select a style from the **Gridlines** box, and then click **Apply**. This style determines the type of line drawn between the standard, text-filled, areas of your Hierarchical FlexGrid for the selected band.
3. On the **Style** tab, select a style from **GridLinesFixed**. Next, select a style from **GridLinesUnpopulated**, and then click **Apply**. These styles determine the type of lines drawn between fixed and unpopulated areas of your Hierarchical FlexGrid.
4. On the **Color** tab, assign each gridline property a color. To do this, first select a **Color Set**. Next, select the property to change (for example, **GridColor**), select a color from the **Color Palette**, and then click **Apply**. Repeat this for each of the Hierarchical FlexGrid gridlines that you wish to change.

   Note When using **Windows Default** colors, the Hierarchical FlexGrid appears in the colors specified in the your Display Control Panel. In addition to changing the Hierarchical FlexGrid property's colors to a standard or Windows default color, you can create your own color definitions by clicking **Edit Custom Color** and using the resulting **Color** dialog box.

5. Click **OK** to apply the gridline and color properties to your Hierarchical FlexGrid and close the **Property Pages** dialog box.

Indenting a Band

When displaying bands vertically, you can indent a band a specific number of columns. This enables you to clearly present bands of information to the user. The indented column before each band contains empty, non-working cells. Therefore, the user cannot place focus into these areas. The format characteristics of these cells are defined by the indent formatting properties, such as **GridLinesIndent**.

See the Vertical Band Display figure in Changing Band Layout, above.

To indent a band

1. Right-click your Hierarchical FlexGrid, and then select **Properties** from the shortcut menu. The Hierarchical FlexGrid's **Property Pages** dialog box appears.
2. On the **Bands** tab, select **BandIndent** and specify the number of columns by which to indent the band.
3. Click **OK** to apply the band properties to your Hierarchical FlexGrid and close the **Property Pages** dialog box.

Using the Band Functionality with a Non-Hierarchical Recordset

You can format the band of a non-hierarchical Recordset using any of the properties in the Hierarchical FlexGrid's Property Pages dialog box.

A non-hierarchical Recordset contains only one band, Band 0. There are no other bands available because bands are based on the Recordsets in the Command hierarchy.

Using Band Expand and Collapse Functionality

The expand and collapse functionality makes it easier to view the Recordset organization and to scroll through the Hierarchical FlexGrid. This functionality makes it possible for users to either view large amounts of data or condense the information. When a band is expandable, a default expand (+) or collapse (–) bitmap appears in the upper-left corner of the band. The expand and collapse functionality is available for both vertical and horizontal bands.

When bands are expanded the collapse (–) bitmap appears. In their expanded state, bands show their maximum amount of data. When collapsed, the expand (+) bitmap appears and bands shows a minimal amount of data.

When collapsed, bands may show unpopulated areas. These areas are formatted according to the unpopulated format specifications.

Collapsed Band

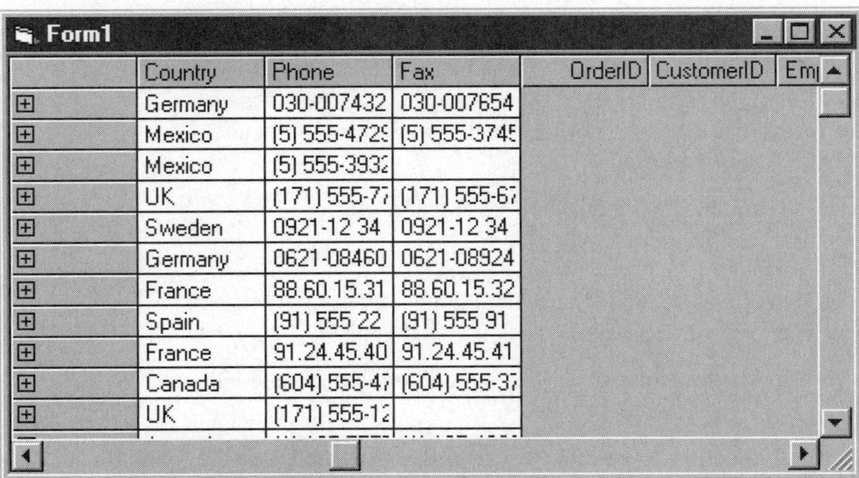

When a band is collapsed, so none of its records display, the columns from that band are not shown. As the user expands the band the columns display. As bands are expanded they maintain a uniform height. If necessary, smaller bands will enlarge to retain a height consistent with larger bands.

Expanded Band

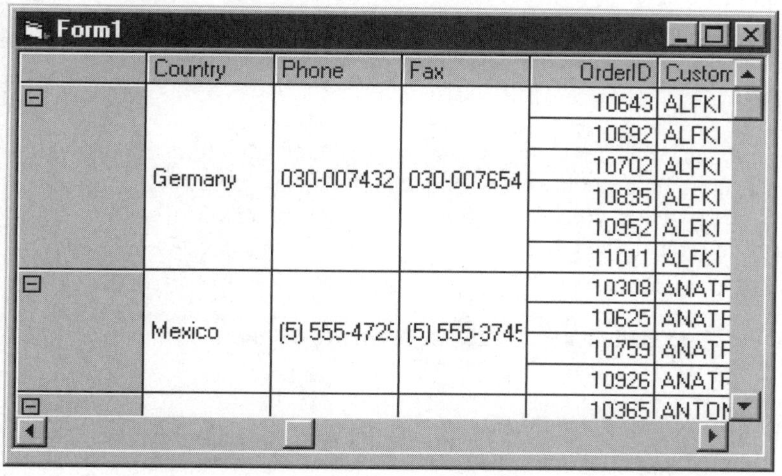

Expanding and Collapsing Bands

This section describes how to add expand and collapse functionality to a band in your Hierarchical FlexGrid. It also describes how to use the expand and collapse functionality.

To add expand and collapse functionality to a band

1. Right-click your Hierarchical FlexGrid, and then select **Properties** from the shortcut menu. The Hierarchical FlexGrid's **Property Pages** dialog box appears.
2. On the **Bands** tab, select **BandExpandable**. Next, select the band to expand from the **Band** list.

   Note For a band to be expandable, it must have at least one sub-band. Therefore, the **BandExpandable** check box is disabled if only Band 0 exists.
3. Click **OK** to apply the band properties to your Hierarchical FlexGrid and close the **Property Pages** dialog box.

To use the expand and collapse functionality

1. Once band functionality has been added to your Hierarchical FlexGrid through its **Property Pages** dialog box, on the **Run** menu, select **Start**.

   – or –

   Press F5.

2. Click the expand (+) graphic in the upper-left corner of the band to view maximum (expanded) Recordset information.
3. Click the collapse (–) graphic in the upper-left corner of the band to view minimal (collapsed) Recordset information.

   Note If you expand a band that contains a collapsed sub-band, the sub-band remains collapsed until you expand it.

Retrieving Structure

Your Hierarchical FlexGrid's structure information includes detailed band and column setup information. By default, the column order within each band is in the same order as the underlying ADO Recordset. Once retrieved, you can use the structure information to control how data appears in your Hierarchical FlexGrid.

To retrieve band and field information

- Right-click your Hierarchical FlexGrid, and then select **Retrieve Structure** from the shortcut menu.

  – or –

  Access the Hierarchical FlexGrid's **Property Pages** dialog box and select the **Bands** tab. This tab contains the structural information of your Hierarchical FlexGrid.

Following retrieval of the structure of the data, the information is stored with the Hierarchical FlexGrid. Once the structure information is retrieved, the design-time Hierarchical FlexGrid displays updated information for each band and field.

Note If the structure of the **DataSource** changes, you must re-retrieve the structure before the changes will appear in your Hierarchical FlexGrid.

Clearing Band and Column Information

When you clear band and column information, they are restored to their default settings.

To clear band and field information

- Right-click your Hierarchical FlexGrid, and select **Clear Structure** from the shortcut menu.

  Note If you have made any changes to the band or column properties of your Hierarchical FlexGrid, a warning message appears. At this point, you can click **OK** to reset the Hierarchical FlexGrid to its default state and discard all user-defined settings.

Customizing Areas of the Hierarchical FlexGrid

The Hierarchical FlexGrid contains different areas that you can customize. You can customize these areas using the Hierarchical FlexGrid's **Property Pages** dialog box or programmatically, using the **Code Editor** window. Customization of the areas can enhance readability and increase the usefulness of your Hierarchical FlexGrid.

The areas of the Hierarchical FlexGrid include:

- **Standard**

  The standard area of your Hierarchical FlexGrid is the cells that contain data-bound information.

- **Band**

  The band area contains display information for each Recordset within your Hierarchical FlexGrid. See "Formatting a Band" earlier in this chapter for more information.

- **Fixed**

  The fixed area consists of rows and columns that are fixed, or static.

- **Header**

  The column header area identifies information about the Recordset that is bound to your Hierarchical FlexGrid. When used, column headers repeat for each band in your Hierarchical FlexGrid. See "Formatting a Band" earlier in this chapter for more information.

- **Indent**

  When displaying bands vertically, the indent area of your Hierarchical FlexGrid is the area that indents a band of data by a specified number of columns. The indented column before each band contains empty, non-working cells. See "Formatting a Band" earlier in this chapter for more information.

- **Unpopulated**

  The unpopulated area of your Hierarchical FlexGrid contains the cells to the right and below the working areas of your Hierarchical FlexGrid. This area is empty and contains non-working cells.

Customizing Standard Appearance

You can customize the appearance of the standard area of your Hierarchical FlexGrid, making information more clear and accessible. The standard area contains the cells that are bound to data.

To customize the appearance of the standard area of a Hierarchical FlexGrid

1. Right-click your Hierarchical FlexGrid, and select **Properties** from the shortcut menu. The Hierarchical FlexGrid's **Property Pages** dialog box appears.
2. On the **General** tab, set the following standard properties:

Property	Description
Rows	Number of rows in the Hierarchical FlexGrid.
Columns	Number of columns in the Hierarchical FlexGrid.
AllowBigSelection	Enables the user to select an entire column or row within the Hierarchical FlexGrid by clicking on a column or row header.
MousePointer	Determines the type of mouse pointer. **Note** To use a custom mouse pointer, you must assign a custom icon to the **MouseIcon** property from the **Picture** tab.
FillStyle	Determines whether text and cell formatting should apply to a single cell or all selected cells.
SelectionMode	Determines how your Hierarchical FlexGrid will allow selection by the user.
AllowUserResizing	Determines whether the user is allowed to resize rows and columns using the mouse.
ScrollBars	Determines whether the Hierarchical FlexGrid has a scrollbar, and if so, whether this is horizontal or vertical, or both.
HighLight	Determines when cells should receive emphasis.
FocusRect	Defines the type of focus rectangle that your Hierarchical FlexGrid draws around the current cell.

3. On the **Style** tab, set the following standard properties:

Property	Description
MergeCells	Whether cells with identical contents are grouped into a single cell spanning multiple cells or rows.
RowHeightMin	A minimum row height for the entire control, in twips.
PictureType	Whether a picture displays in color or monochrome.
WordWrap	Whether your Hierarchical FlexGrid allows text within a cell to wrap or have multiple lines.

4. On the **Font** tab, set the following standard properties:

Property	Description
Font	The name of the font style.
Size	The size of the font, in points.
Effects	The text effect: underline or strikeout, or the text style: bold or italic. You can select up to four **Effects** check boxes.
Sample Text	A preview of the font selection.

5. Click **OK** to apply the standard properties to your Hierarchical FlexGrid and close the **Property Pages** dialog box.

Customizing Fixed Appearance

You can create fixed rows or columns to display in your Hierarchical FlexGrid. To increase readability, you should use a fixed area to display one heading set instead of using repeating column headers for each band. This area remains static, identifying the rows, below, or columns, to its right.

To customize the appearance of the fixed area of a Hierarchical FlexGrid

1. Right-click your Hierarchical FlexGrid, and select **Properties** from the shortcut menu. The Hierarchical FlexGrid's **Property Pages** dialog box appears.
2. On the **General** tab, specify the number of fixed rows and columns in the **Fixed Rows** and **Fixed Cols** text boxes, and then click **Apply**.
3. On the **Style** tab, select the style for the fixed text from the **TextStyleFixed** box, and then click **Apply**.
4. On the **Font** tab, set the following standard properties:

Property	Description
Font	The name of the font style.
Size	The size of the font, in points.
Effects	The text effect: underline or strikeout, or the text style: bold or italic. You can select up to four **Effects** check boxes.
Sample Text	A preview of the font selection.

5. From the **Color** tab, assign each fixed property a color. To do this, first select a **Color Set**. Next, click the property you wish to change (for example, **BackColorFixed**), click a color in the **Color Palette**, and then click **Apply**. Repeat this for each fixed area that you wish to change.

   Note When using **Windows Default** colors, the Hierarchical FlexGrid appears in the colors specified in the your system's Display Control Panel. In addition to changing Hierarchical FlexGrid color properties to a standard or Windows default color, you can create your own color definitions by clicking **Edit Custom Color** and using the resulting **Color** dialog box. For information on each property, see the Hierarchical FlexGrid's property topics.

6. Click **OK** to apply the fixed properties to your Hierarchical FlexGrid and close the **Property Pages** dialog box.

Customizing Header Appearance

You can change the formatting and display properties of the band header in your Hierarchical FlexGrid.

To customize the header appearance of a Hierarchical FlexGrid

1. Right-click your Hierarchical FlexGrid, and then select **Properties** from the shortcut menu. The Hierarchical FlexGrid's **Property Pages** dialog box appears.
2. On the **Bands** tab, select a heading style from the **TextStyleHeader** box, and then select **ColumnHeaders**.

   Note To prevent your Hierarchical FlexGrid from displaying duplicate headings, you must set the **Fixed Row** text box, from the **General** tab, to 0. In addition, if you want to display only one set of headers for a band at the top of the Hierarchical FlexGrid, fixed rows must be used instead of column headers.

3. In the **Column Caption** and **Column Name** list boxes, specify the columns to display. By default, this list includes all the fields in the Recordset with their field name. To remove a Field object from the display or to change its name, use the **Column Caption** list. To deselect a field, click the corresponding check mark. To change its name, click the name to select it, then click it again to access edit mode to rename it.
4. Click **OK** to apply the band properties to your Hierarchical FlexGrid and close the **Property Pages** dialog box.

Customizing Unpopulated Areas

You can change the formatting and display properties of the unpopulated area of your Hierarchical FlexGrid. This unpopulated area is empty and contains no data.

To customize the appearance of the unpopulated area of the Hierarchical FlexGrid

1. Right-click your Hierarchical FlexGrid, and then select **Properties** from the shortcut menu. The Hierarchical FlexGrid's **Property Pages** dialog box appears.
2. On the **Style** tab, change the **GridLinesUnpopulated** property.
3. On the **Color** tab, assign each fixed property a color. To do this, first select a **Color Set**. Next, click the property to change (for example, **BackColorUnpopulated**), click a color in the **Color Palette**, and then click **Apply**. Repeat this for each unpopulated area that you wish to change.

   Note When using **Windows Default** colors, the Hierarchical FlexGrid appears in the colors specified in the your Display Control Panel. In addition to changing Hierarchical FlexGrid colors properties to a standard or Windows default color, you can create your own color definitions by clicking **Edit Custom Color** and using the resulting **Color** dialog box.

4. Click **OK** to apply the fixed properties to your Hierarchical FlexGrid and close the **Property Pages** dialog box.

Binding Your Hierarchical FlexGrid to a Data Environment

Before you can use bands in your Hierarchical FlexGrid, you bind the FlexGrid to a Data Environment, which contains a top-level, parent Command object.

To bind your Hierarchical FlexGrid control to a Data Environment

1. Drag a **MSHFlexGrid** control onto a Visual Basic form.
2. From the Visual Basic Properties window, set the **DataSource** property to the DataEnvironment object that contains the Command object that you want to bind to the Hierarchical FlexGrid control. For example, DataEnvironment1.
3. From the Visual Basic Properties window, set the **DataMember** property to a top-level, parent Command object in your Data Environment. Your data is now bound to a Hierarchical FlexGrid control.
4. To view the data in the Hierarchical FlexGrid, select **Start** from the **Run** menu or press F5. The structure is retrieved and appears in the Hierarchical FlexGrid.

Sorting and Merging Data in the Hierarchical FlexGrid

In this scenario, you can sort and merge data in the Hierarchical FlexGrid. In most cases, you access data by downloading from a database into your Hierarchical FlexGrid. However, here you enter sample data using the Code Editor window to populate the columns and rows of your Hierarchical FlexGrid.

To create this data display

1. Set the properties of the Hierarchical FlexGrid.
2. Create the data.
3. Define the routines to calculate an index and do a sort.
4. Define the routine to enter the data (from step 2) into the Hierarchical FlexGrid.
5. Allow the control to switch data organization views.

To complete the scenario, follow the procedures in this section in the order shown.

Setting the Properties of the Control

Use the settings in the following table for the number of columns and rows, the font information, and to create the column headings of your Hierarchical FlexGrid.

MSHFlexGrid control

Property	Setting
Name	Fg1
Cols	4
Rows	20
MergeCells	2 – Restrict Rows
FormatString	<Region |<Product |<Employees |>Sales
FontName	Arial

Sorting and Merging the Data

Use the following procedures to complete the scenario of sorting and merging data in your Hierarchical FlexGrid.

To sort and merge the data

1. Create an array to store the sample data. To do this, insert the following routine in the Form_Load event of your Code Editor window:

```
Sub Form_Load ()
   Dim I As Integer
   ' Create array.
   For i = Fg1.FixedRows To Fg1.Rows - 1
      ' Region.
      Fg1.TextArray(fgi(i, 0)) = RandomString(0)
      ' Product.
      Fg1.TextArray(fgi(i, 1)) = RandomString(1)
      ' Employee.
      Fg1.TextArray(fgi(i, 2)) = RandomString(2)
      Fg1.TextArray(fgi(i, 3)) = _
      Format(Rnd * 10000, "#.00")
   Next

   ' Set up merging.
   Fg1.MergeCol(0) = True
   Fg1.MergeCol(1) = True
   Fg1.MergeCol(2) = True

   ' Sort to see the effects.
   DoSort

   ' Format Grid
   Fg1.ColWidth(0) = 1000
   Fg1.ColWidth(1) = 1000
   Fg1.ColWidth(2) = 1000
   Fg1.ColWidth(3) = 1000

End Sub
```

2. Calculate an index and complete a sort. To do this, define a routine to calculate an index and do a sort. The index is used with the **TextArray** property to sort the data. Insert the following routine to calculate an index:

```
Function Fgi (r As Integer, c As Integer) As Integer
   Fgi = c + Fg1.Cols * r
End Function
```

```
Sub DoSort ()
   Fg1.Col = 0
   Fg1.ColSel = Fg1.Cols - 1
   Fg1.Sort = 1' Generic ascending.
End Sub
```

3. Enter data into your Hierarchical FlexGrid. To do this, define a routine that populates the Hierarchical FlexGrid with the sample data:

```
Function RandomString (kind As Integer)
   Dim s As String
   Select Case kind

      Case 0' Region.
         Select Case (Rnd * 1000) Mod 5
            Case 0: s = "1. Northwest"
            Case 1: s = "2. Southwest"
            Case 2: s = "3. Midwest"
            Case 3: s = "4. East"
            Case Else: s = "5. Overseas"
         End Select

      Case 1' Product.
         Select Case (Rnd * 1000) Mod 5
            Case 0: s = "1. Chai"
            Case 1: s = "2. Peppermint"
            Case 2: s = "3. Chamomile"
            Case Else: s = "4. Oolong"
         End Select

      Case 2' Employee.
         Select Case (Rnd * 1000) Mod 4
            Case 0: s = "Clare"
            Case 1: s = "Tiffany"
            Case 2: s = "Sally"
            Case Else: s = "Lori"
         End Select
   End Select
   RandomString = s
End Function
```

If you run the project at this point, it should look something like this:

Region	Product	Employees	Sales
I. Northwest	1. Chai	Clare	5338.73
		Lori	7988.84
	3. Chamomile	Sally	5924.58
	4. Oolong	Tiffany	3262.06
		Sally	9193.77
:. Southwest	2. Peppermin	Sally	3640.19
	4. Oolong	Clare	157.04
		Sally	2613.68
		Clare	2895.63
			4013.74
3. Midwest	1. Chai	Sally	7607.24
4. East	1. Chai	Lori	6465.87

Next, you need to allow the user to reorganize the data. That is, you must allow the Hierarchical FlexGrid to switch data organization views.

4. Reorganize the data by adding the following routine, which will drag columns to new positions. This routine uses the **Tag** property to save the column number when the user presses the mouse button, triggering the MouseDown event.

```
Sub Fg1_MouseDown (Button As Integer, _
Shift As Integer, X As Single, Y As Single)
   Fg1.Tag = ""
   If Fg1.MouseRow <> 0 Then Exit Sub
   Fg1.Tag = Str(Fg1.MouseCol)
   MousePointer = vbSizeWE
End Sub
```

5. Add the following routine to readjust the columns and sort the data when the user releases the mouse button, triggering the MouseUp event.

```
Sub Fg1_MouseUp (Button As Integer, Shift As _
Integer, X As Single, Y As Single)
   MousePointer = vbDefault
   If Fg1.Tag = "" Then Exit Sub
   Fg1.Redraw = False
   Fg1.ColPosition(Val(Fg1.Tag)) = Fg1.MouseCol
   DoSort
   Fg1.Redraw = True
End Sub
```

Once the procedures in this scenario are complete, the data automatically reorganizes whenever you drag a column to a new position at run time. For example, if you drag the Employee column to the left, it would appear as follows:

Employees	Region	Product	Sales
Clare	1. Northwest	1. Chai	5338.73
	2. Southwes	4. Oolong	157.04
			2895.63
			4013.74
	5. Overseas	2. Peppermin	3820.11
Lori	4. East	1. Chai	6465.87
	5. Overseas	2. Peppermin	2268.66
	1. Northwest	1. Chai	7988.84
	5. Overseas	4. Oolong	6478.21
Sally	4. East	1. Chai	9619.53
		4. Oolong	5833.59
	2. Southwes	4. Oolong	2613.68
	[illegible]	[illegible]	[illegible]

Editing Cells in a Hierarchical FlexGrid Spreadsheet

In this scenario, you can edit cells in a Hierarchical FlexGrid spreadsheet. This scenario illustrates some of the capabilities of the Hierarchical FlexGrid's control events and containers, and shows how this control can be used to create a spreadsheet with in-cell editing using standard Visual Basic controls.

Note The sample application (Flex.vbp) demonstrates the functionality necessary for navigating around and selecting ranges of cells.

To create this data display

1. Create Hierarchical FlexGrid and TextBox controls.
2. Set the properties of these controls.
3. Add row and column headings to the Hierarchical FlexGrid.
4. Add in-cell editing to the Hierarchical FlexGrid.
5. Add functionality to the TextBox control (the "edit" box) for updating the data.
6. Copy the data from the text box to the Hierarchical FlexGrid.

To complete the scenario, follow the procedures in this section in the order shown.

Creating the Controls

Add a Hierarchical FlexGrid to your project, and then add a TextBox control to it to create a parent-child relationship, as shown:

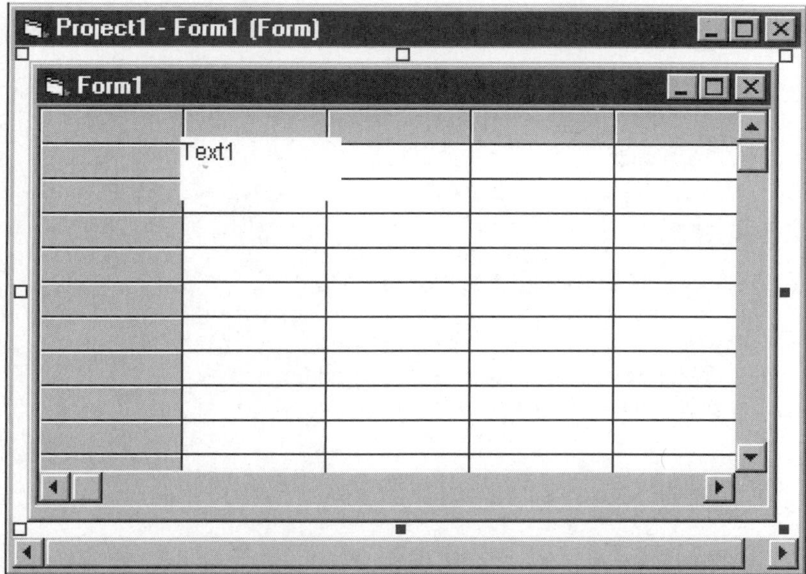

Setting the Properties of the Controls

Set the properties of the Hierarchical FlexGrid and TextBox controls as follows:

MSHFlexGrid control

Property	Setting
Name	Fg2
Cols	6
Rows	20
FillStyle	1 – Repeat
FocusRect	2 – Heavy
FontName	Arial
FontSize	9

TextBox control

Property	Setting
Name	TxtEdit
FontName	Arial
FontSize	9
BorderSize	0 – None
Visible	False

Editing Cells in a Spreadsheet

Use the following procedures to edit cells in your Hierarchical FlexGrid.

To edit cells in a spreadsheet

1. Modify your Hierarchical FlexGrid, so it resembles a spreadsheet, by adding the following code to the Form_Load procedure in the Code Editor window:

```
Sub Form_Load ()
   Dim i As Integer

   ' Make first column narrow.
   Fg2.ColWidth(0) = Fg2.ColWidth(0) / 2
   Fg2.ColAlignment(0) = 1 ' Center center.

   ' Label rows and columns.
   For i = Fg2.FixedRows To Fg2.Rows - 1
      Fg2.TextArray(fgi(i, 0)) = i
   Next
   For i = Fg2.FixedCols To Fg2.Cols - 1
      Fg2.TextArray(fgi(0, i)) = i
   Next

   ' Initialize edit box (so it loads now).
   txtEdit = ""
End Sub
```

2. Create a function to calculate an index for the **TextArray** property as follows:

```
Function Fgi (r As Integer, c As Integer) As Integer
   Fgi = c + Fg2.Cols * r
End Function
```

3. Add the following code to the Hierarchical FlexGrid's **KeyPress** and **DblClick** events:

```
Sub Fg2_KeyPress (KeyAscii As Integer)
   MSHFlexGridEdit Fg2, txtEdit, KeyAscii
End Sub

Sub Fg2_DblClick ()
   MSHFlexGridEdit Fg2, txtEdit, 32 ' Simulate a space.
End Sub
```

4. Add the following routine to initialize the text box and pass the focus from the Hierarchical FlexGrid to the TextBox control:

```
Sub MSHFlexGridEdit (MSHFlexGrid As Control, _
Edt As Control, KeyAscii As Integer)

   ' Use the character that was typed.
   Select Case keyascii

   ' A space means edit the current text.
   Case 0 To 32
      Edt = MSHFlexGrid
      Edt.SelStart = 1000

   ' Anything else means replace the current text.
   Case Else
      Edt = Chr(keyascii)
      Edt.SelStart = 1
   End Select

   ' Show Edt at the right place.
   Edt.Move MSHFlexGrid.Left + MSHFlexGrid.CellLeft, _
      MSHFlexGrid.Top + MSHFlexGrid.CellTop, _
      MSHFlexGrid.CellWidth - 8, _
      MSHFlexGrid.CellHeight - 8
   Edt.Visible = True

   ' And make it work.
   Edt.SetFocus
End Sub
```

5. Add updating data functionality to the text box by adding the following routines to its KeyPress and DblClick events:

```
Sub txtEdit_KeyPress (KeyAscii As Integer)
   ' Delete returns to get rid of beep.
   If KeyAscii = Asc(vbCr) Then KeyAscii = 0
End Sub

Sub txtEdit_KeyDown (KeyCode As Integer, _
Shift As Integer)
   EditKeyCode Fg2, txtEdit, KeyCode, Shift
End Sub

Sub EditKeyCode (MSHFlexGrid As Control, Edt As _
Control, KeyCode As Integer, Shift As Integer)

   ' Standard edit control processing.
   Select Case KeyCode

   Case 27   ' ESC: hide, return focus to MSHFlexGrid.
      Edt.Visible = False
      MSHFlexGrid.SetFocus

   Case 13   ' ENTER return focus to MSHFlexGrid.
      MSHFlexGrid.SetFocus

   Case 38      ' Up.
      MSHFlexGrid.SetFocus
      DoEvents
      If MSHFlexGrid.Row > MSHFlexGrid.FixedRows Then
         MSHFlexGrid.Row = MSHFlexGrid.Row - 1
      End If

   Case 40      ' Down.
      MSHFlexGrid.SetFocus
      DoEvents
      If MSHFlexGrid.Row < MSHFlexGrid.Rows - 1 Then
         MSHFlexGrid.Row = MSHFlexGrid.Row + 1
      End If
   End Select
End Sub
```

Next, you need to instruct the Hierarchical FlexGrid what to do with the data when it is entered into the text box. The focus returns to the control after the user enters the data and either presses ENTER or clicks a different cell in the Hierarchical FlexGrid. Therefore, you must copy the data from the text box into the active cell; to do this, continue with the following steps.

6. Copy the data from the text box to the Hierarchical FlexGrid by adding the following code to the GotFocus and LeaveCell event procedures:

```
Sub Fg2_GotFocus ()
   If txtEdit.Visible = False Then Exit Sub
   Fg2 = txtEdit
   txtEdit.Visible = False
End Sub

Sub Fg2_LeaveCell ()
   If txtEdit.Visible = False Then Exit Sub
   Fg2 = txtEdit
   txtEdit.Visible = False
End Sub
```

   Once the procedures in this scenario are complete, data can be entered into individual cells at run time, as shown here.

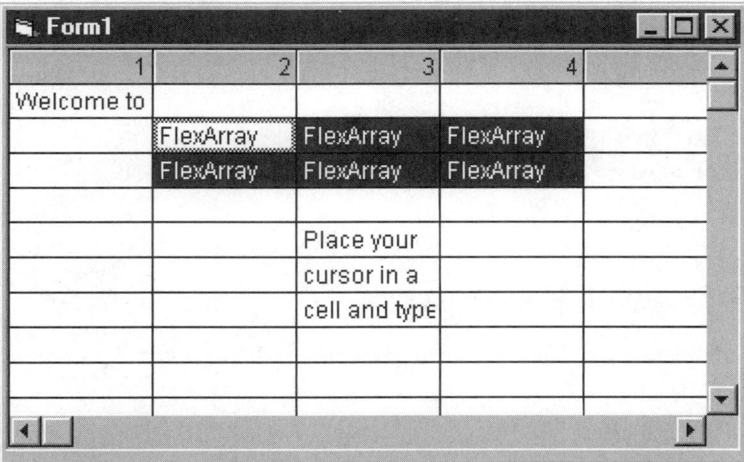

Displaying an Outline with Headings using the Hierarchical FlexGrid

In this scenario you can use the Hierarchical FlexGrid to create an outline-style display with heading items that you can collapse or expand.

To create this data display

1. Set the properties of the Hierarchical FlexGrid.
2. Create the data.
3. Add collapse and expand functionality.

To complete the scenario, follow the procedures in this section in the order shown.

Setting the Properties of the Control

Set four column headings using the **FormatString** property. Set the first column as narrow and empty (like a spreadsheet) and the other three to contain data (include the spacing between each heading). In addition, set the following:

MSHFlexGrid control

<table>
<tr><th>Property</th><th>Setting</th></tr>
<tr><td>Name</td><td>Fg3</td></tr>
<tr><td>Cols</td><td>4</td></tr>
<tr><td>Rows</td><td>2</td></tr>
<tr><td>Selection Mode</td><td>1 – By Row</td></tr>
<tr><td>FillStyle</td><td>1 – Repeat</td></tr>
<tr><td>FocusRect</td><td>0 – None</td></tr>
<tr><td>GridLines</td><td>0 – None</td></tr>
<tr><td>GridLinesFixed</td><td>2 – Inset</td></tr>
<tr><td>FormatString</td><td>^ |Description |>Date |>Amount</td></tr>
<tr><td>FontName</td><td>Arial</td></tr>
</table>

Creating an Outline Display with Headings

Use the following procedure to complete the scenario of creating an outline display with headings using the Hierarchical FlexGrid.

To create an outline display with headings

1. Create the sample data, and set the headings, column, and row properties. To do this, insert the following code into the Form_Load event of the Code Editor window. This creates sample data, sets up and calculates the headings at the top of the control, and sets the **Col** and **Row** properties to select the first cell at run time.

```
Sub Form_Load ()
   Dim i As Integer, tot As Integer
   Dim t As String, s As String

   ' Create sample data.
   t = Chr(9)
   Fg3.Rows = 1
```

```
    Fg3.AddItem "*" + t + "Airfare"
    s = "" +t+ "SFO-JFK" +t+ "9-Apr-95" +t+ "750.00"
    For i = 0 to 5
       Fg3.AddItem s
    Next

    Fg3.AddItem "*" + t + "Meals"
    s = "" +t+ "Flint's BBQ" +t+ "25-Apr-95" _
    +t+ "35.00"
    For i = 0 to 5
       Fg3.AddItem s
    Next

    Fg3.AddItem "*" +t+ "Hotel"
    s = "" +t+ "Center Plaza" +t+ "25-Apr-95" _
    +t+ "817.00"
    For i = 0 to 5
       Fg3.AddItem s
    Next

    ' Add up totals and format heading entries.
    For i = Fg3.Rows - 1 To 0 Step -1
       If Fg3.TextArray(i * Fg3.Cols) = "" Then
          tot = tot + Val(Fg3.TextArray _
          (i * Fg3.Cols + 3))
       Else
          Fg3.Row = i
          Fg3.Col = 0
          Fg3.ColSel = Fg3.Cols - 1
          Fg3.CellBackColor = &HC0C0C0
          Fg3.CellFontBold = True
          Fg3.CellFontWidth = 8
          Fg3.TextArray(i * Fg3.Cols + 3) = _
          Format(tot, "0")
          tot = 0
       End If
    Next
    Fg3.ColSel = Fg3.Cols - 1

    ' Format Grid
    Fg3.ColWidth(0) = 300
    Fg3.ColWidth(1) = 1500
    Fg3.ColWidth(2) = 1000
    Fg3.ColWidth(3) = 1000

End Sub
```

At run time, the rows are sorted into three divisions, grouped by their respective headings: Air Fare, Meals, and Hotels, as shown here:

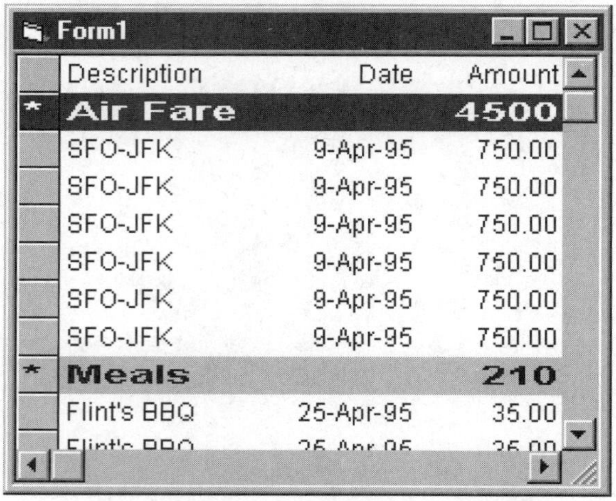

2. Add collapse and expand functionality to the row headings by inserting the following code in the DblClick event procedure of the Hierarchical FlexGrid:

```
Sub Fg3_DblClick ()
   Dim i As Integer, r As Integer

   ' Ignore top row.
   r = Fg3.MouseRow
   If r < 1 Then Exit Sub

   ' Find field to collapse or expand.
   While r > 0 And Fg3.TextArray(r * Fg3.Cols) = ""
      r = r - 1
   Wend

   ' Show collapsed/expanded symbol on first column.
   If Fg3.TextArray(r * Fg3.Cols) = "*" Then
      Fg3.TextArray(r * Fg3.Cols) = "+"
   Else
      Fg3.TextArray(r * Fg3.Cols) = "*"
   End If

   ' Expand items under current heading.
   r = r + 1
   If Fg3.RowHeight(r) = 0 Then
      Do While Fg3.TextArray(r * Fg3.Cols) = ""
         Fg3.RowHeight(r) = -1 ' Default row height.
         r = r + 1
         If r >= Fg3.Rows Then Exit Do
      Loop
```

```
      ' Collapse items under current heading.
   Else
      Do While Fg3.TextArray(r * Fg3.Cols) = ""
         Fg3.RowHeight(r) = 0  ' Hide row.
         r = r + 1
         If r >= Fg3.Rows Then Exit Do
      Loop
   End If
End Sub
```

Once all the steps in this scenario are complete, you can expand and collapse the row headings by double clicking on the "+" or "*" symbols in the first column at run time, as shown here:

	Description	Date	Amount
+	Air Fare		4500
+	Meals		210
*	Hotel		4902
	Center Plaza	25-Apr-95	817.00
	Center Plaza	25-Apr-95	817.00
	Center Plaza	25-Apr-95	817.00
	Center Plaza	25-Apr-95	817.00
	Center Plaza	25-Apr-95	817.00
	Center Plaza	25-Apr-95	817.00

Note You can modify this example to show images instead of the "+" and "*" characters, or to add additional levels to the outline.

Using the Horizontal and Vertical Scroll Bar Controls

Scroll bars provide easy navigation through a long list of items or a large amount of information by scrolling either horizontally or vertically within an application or control. Scroll bars are a common element of the Windows 95 and Windows NT interface.

Figure 7.23 The horizontal and vertical scroll bar controls

The horizontal and vertical scroll bar controls are not the same as the built-in scroll bars found in Windows or those that are attached to text boxes, list boxes, combo boxes, or MDI forms within Visual Basic. Those scroll bars appear automatically whenever the given application or control contains more information than can be displayed in the current window size (or, in the case of text boxes and MDI forms, when the ScrollBars property is also set to True).

In previous versions of Visual Basic, scroll bars were most often used as input devices. Windows interface guidelines now suggest, however, that slider controls be used as input devices instead of scroll bar controls. A Windows 95 slider control is included in the Professional and Enterprise versions of Visual Basic.

Scroll bar controls are still of value in Visual Basic because they provide scrolling to applications or controls that do not provide them automatically. See "Scroll Bar Controls Scenario: Creating a Scrollable Graphics Viewport," later in this chapter, for information on using scroll bars in this manner.

How the Scroll Bar Controls Work

The scroll bar controls use the Scroll and Change events to monitor the movement of the scroll box (sometimes referred to as the thumb) along the scroll bar.

Event	Description
Change	Occurs after the scroll box is moved.
Scroll	Occurs as the scroll box is moved. Does not occur if the scroll arrows or scroll bar is clicked.

Using the Scroll event provides access to the scroll bar value as it is being dragged. The Change event occurs after the scroll box is released or when the scroll bar or scroll arrows are clicked.

The Value Property

The Value property (which, by default, is 0) is an integer value corresponding to the position of the scroll box in the scroll bar. When the scroll box position is at the minimum value, it moves to the leftmost position (for horizontal scroll bars) or the top position (for vertical scroll bars). When the scroll box is at the maximum value, the scroll box moves to the rightmost or bottom position. Similarly, a value halfway between the bottom and top of the range places the scroll box in the middle of the scroll bar.

In addition to using mouse clicks to change the scroll bar value, a user can also drag the scroll box to any point along the bar. The resulting value depends on the position of the scroll box, but it is always within the range of the Min to Max properties set by the user.

> **Note** Min can be larger than Max if you want your scroll bar to display information changing from a larger to a smaller value.

The LargeChange and SmallChange Properties

To specify the amount of change to report in a scroll bar, use the LargeChange property for clicking in the scroll bar, and the SmallChange property for clicking the arrows at the ends of the scroll bar. The scroll bar's Value property increases or decreases by the values set for the LargeChange and SmallChange properties. You can position the scroll box at run time by setting Value between 0 and 32,767, inclusive.

Scroll Bar Controls Scenario: Creating a Scrollable Graphics Viewport

The horizontal and vertical scroll bar controls can be used, in addition to the picture box control, to create a scrollable graphics viewport application. The picture box control alone will not allow you to scroll a graphic if it exceeds its boundaries — the picture box control does not automatically add scroll bars.

This application uses two picture boxes. The first is referred to as the stationary *parent* picture box control. The second, which is contained within the parent, is referred to as the *child* picture box control. The child picture box contains the graphic image and is moved around within the parent picture box control when the scroll bar controls are used.

Figure 7.24 Adding scroll bar controls at design time

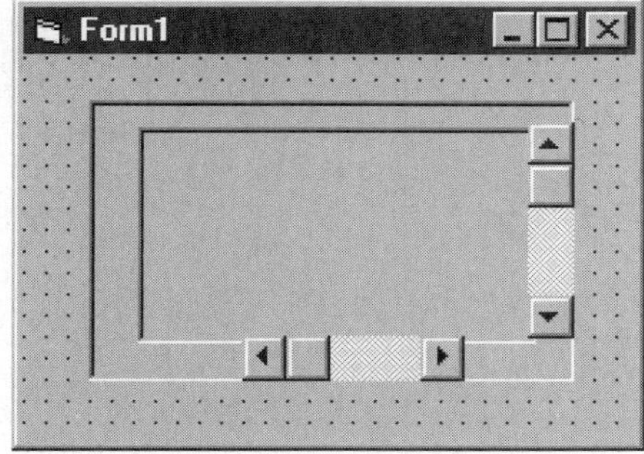

Start by creating a new project and then draw two picture boxes, a horizontal scroll bar, and a vertical scroll bar on the form, as shown in Figure 7.24.

The form's Form_Load event is used to set the scale mode, to size the child picture box within the parent picture box, to position and size the horizontal and vertical scroll bars, and then to load a bitmap graphic. Add the following code to the form's Form_Load event procedure:

```
Private Sub Form_Load()

   ' Set ScaleMode to pixels.
   Form1.ScaleMode = vbPixels
   Picture1.ScaleMode = vbPixels
```

```
    ' Autosize is set to True so that the boundaries of
    ' Picture2 are expanded to the size of the actual
    ' bitmap.
    Picture2.AutoSize = True

    ' Set the BorderStyle of each picture box to None.
    Picture1.BorderStyle = 0
    Picture2.BorderStyle = 0

    ' Load the bitmap.
    Picture2.Picture = _
    LoadPicture("c:\Windows\Winlogo.bmp")

    ' Initialize location of both pictures.
    Picture1.Move 0, 0, ScaleWidth - VScroll1.Width, _
    ScaleHeight - HScroll1.Height
    Picture2.Move 0, 0

    ' Position the horizontal scroll bar.
    HScroll1.Top = Picture1.Height
    HScroll1.Left = 0
    HScroll1.Width = Picture1.Width

    ' Position the vertical scroll bar.
    VScroll1.Top = 0
    VScroll1.Left = Picture1.Width
    VScroll1.Height = Picture1.Height

    ' Set the Max property for the scroll bars.
    HScroll1.Max = Picture2.Width - Picture1.Width
    VScroll1.Max = Picture2.Height - Picture1.Height

    ' Determine if the child picture will fill up the
    ' screen.
    ' If so, there is no need to use scroll bars.
    VScroll1.Visible = (Picture1.Height < _
    Picture2.Height)
    HScroll1.Visible = (Picture1.Width < _
    Picture2.Width)

End Sub
```

The horizontal and vertical scroll bars' Change event is used to move the child picture box up and down or left and right within the parent picture box. Add the following code to the Change event of both scroll bar controls:

```
Private Sub HScroll1_Change()
   Picture2.Left = -HScroll1.Value
End Sub

Private Sub VScroll1_Change()
   Picture2.Top = -VScroll1.Value
End Sub
```

The Left and Top properties of the child picture box are set to the negative value of the horizontal and vertical scroll bars so that as you scroll up or down or right or left, the display moves appropriately.

At run time, the graphic will be displayed as shown in Figure 7.25.

Figure 7.25 Scrolling the bitmap at run time

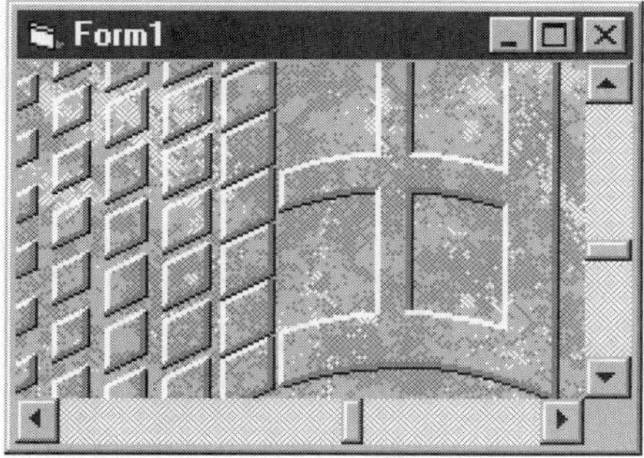

Resizing the Form at Run Time

In the example described above, the viewable size of the graphic is limited by the original size of the form. To resize the graphic viewport application when the user adjusts the size of the form at run time, add the following code to the form's Form_Resize event procedure:

```
Private Sub Form_Resize()
   ' When the form is resized, change the Picture1
   ' dimensions.
   Picture1.Height = Form1.Height
   Picture1.Width = Form1.Width
```

```
    ' Reinitialize the picture and scroll bar
    ' positions.
    Picture1.Move 0, 0, ScaleWidth - VScroll1.Width, _
    ScaleHeight - HScroll1.Height
    Picture2.Move 0, 0
    HScroll1.Top = Picture1.Height
    HScroll1.Left = 0
    HScroll1.Width = Picture1.Width
    VScroll1.Top = 0
    VScroll1.Left = Picture1.Width
    VScroll1.Height = Picture1.Height
    HScroll1.Max = Picture2.Width - Picture1.Width
    VScroll1.Max = Picture2.Height - Picture1.Width

    ' Check to see if scroll bars are needed.
    VScroll1.Visible = (Picture1.Height < _
    Picture2.Height)
    HScroll1.Visible = (Picture1.Width < _
    Picture2.Width)

End Sub
```

Using the Image Control

The image control is used to display graphics. Image controls can display graphics in the following formats: bitmap, icon, metafile, enhanced metafile, or as JPEG or GIF files.

Figure 7.26 The image control

In addition, image controls respond to the Click event and can be used as a substitute for command buttons, as items in a toolbar, or to create simple animations.

For More Information See "Lightweight Graphical Controls" in Chapter 3, "Forms, Controls, and Menus," for a simple demonstration of using the image control like a command button. See "Creating a Toolbar" in Chapter 6, "Creating a User Interface," for information on using image controls to create a toolbar. See "Creating Simple Animation" in Chapter 12, "Working with Text and Graphics," for more information on using the image control to create simple animations.

When to Use an Image Control Instead of a Picture Box Control

The image control uses fewer system resources and repaints faster than a picture box control, but it supports only a subset of the picture box control's properties, events, and methods. Both controls support the same picture formats. However, you can stretch pictures in an image control to fit the control's size. You cannot do this with the picture box control.

For More Information See "Cutting Back on Graphics" in Chapter 15, "Designing for Performance and Compatibility," for information on using image controls to conserve system resources.

Supported Graphic Formats

The image control can display picture files in any of the following standard formats.

Picture format	Description
Bitmap	A *bitmap* defines an image as a pattern of dots (pixels). A bitmap has the file name extensions .bmp or .dib. Bitmaps are also called "paint-type" graphics. You can use bitmaps of various color depths, including 2, 4, 8, 16, 24, and 32-bits, but a bitmap only displays correctly if the display device supports the color depth used by the bitmap. For example, an 8-bit-per-pixel (256 color) bitmap only displays in 16 colors when shown on a 4-bit-per-pixel (16 color) device.
Icon	An *icon* is a special kind of bitmap. Icons have a maximum size of 32 pixels by 32 pixels, but under Microsoft Windows 95, icons are also found in 16 by 16 pixel size. An icon has the file name extension .ico.
Cursor	Cursors, like icons, are essentially bitmaps. Cursors, however, also contain a hot spot, a pixel that tracks the location of the cursor by its x and y coordinates. Cursors have the file name extension .cur.
Metafile	A *metafile* defines an image as coded lines and shapes. Conventional metafiles have the file name extension .wmf. Enhanced metafiles have the file name extension .emf. Only files that are compatible with Microsoft Windows can be loaded. Metafiles are also called "draw-type" graphics.
JPEG	JPEG (Joint Photographic Experts Group) is a compressed bitmap format which supports 8- and 24-bit color. It is a popular file format on the Internet.
GIF	GIF (Graphic Interchange Format) is a compressed bitmap format originally developed by CompuServe. It supports up to 256 colors and is a popular file format on the Internet.

Loading a Graphic into the Image Control

Pictures can be loaded into the image control at design time by selecting the Picture property from the control's Properties window, or at run time by using the Picture property and the LoadPicture function.

```
Set Image1.Picture = LoadPicture("c:\Windows\Winlogo.cur", vbLPLarge, vbLPColor)
```

When a picture is loaded into the image control, the control automatically resizes to fit the picture — regardless of how small or large the image control was drawn on the form.

You may want to use icon (.ico) and cursor (.cur) files containing separate images at different sizes and color depths to support a range of display devices. The LoadPicture function's settings allow you to select images with specific color depths and sizes from an .ico or .cur file. In cases where an exact match to the requested settings isn't available, LoadPicture loads the image with the closest match available.

To clear the graphic from the image control, use the LoadPicture function without specifying a file name. For example:

```
Set Image1.Picture = LoadPicture
```

This will clear the image control even if a graphic was loaded into the Picture property at design time.

Using the Clipboard

You can also add a graphic to an image control at design time by pasting it from another application. For example, you may want to add a bitmap image that was created in Windows Paint. Simply copy the image to the Clipboard, select the image control, and either use the keyboard shortcut CTRL+V or the Paste command from the Edit menu.

The Stretch Property

The Stretch property determines whether the picture is stretched when the image control is resized at design time. If set to True, the picture loaded into the image control via the Picture property is stretched. Stretching a picture (especially a bitmap format) can produce a loss in image quality, as shown in Figure 7.27. Metafiles, which are "draw-type" graphics, are better suited for stretching.

Figure 7.27 Stretching a bitmap image

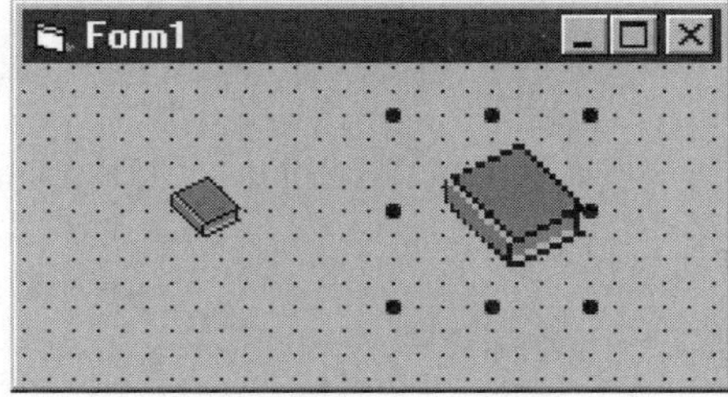

Using the Label Control

Label controls are used to display text and cannot be edited by the user. They are used to identify objects on a form — provide a description of what a certain control will do if clicked, for example — or at run time, they can display information in response to an event or process in your application.

Figure 7.28 The label control

Labels are used in many instances, for many different purposes. Most commonly, they are used to label controls that don't have their own Caption properties. For example, you can use the label control to add descriptive labels to text boxes, list boxes, combo boxes and so on. They can also be used to add descriptive text to a form, for example, to provide the user with Help information.

You can also write code that changes the text displayed by a label control in response to events at run time. For example, if your application takes a few minutes to process a change, you can display a processing-status message in a label.

Because the label control cannot receive the focus, it can also be used to create access keys for other controls.

Setting the Label's Caption

To change the text displayed in the label control, use the Caption property. At design time, you can set this property by selecting it from the control's Properties window.

You can set the length of the Caption property up to a maximum of 1024 bytes.

Aligning Text

The Alignment property allows you to set the alignment of the text within the label control to either Left Justify (0, the default), Center (1), or Right Justify (2).

The AutoSize and WordWrap Properties

By default, when text entered into the Caption property exceeds the width of the control, the text wraps to the next line and is clipped if it exceeds the control's height.

To allow the control to automatically adjust to the size of its contents, set the AutoSize property to True. The control will expand horizontally to fit the entire contents of the Caption property. To allow the contents to wrap down and expand vertically, set the WordWrap property to True.

For More Information See "Using Labels to Display Text" in Chapter 3, "Forms, Controls, and Menus," for a simple demonstration of the AutoSize and WordWrap properties.

Using Labels to Create Access Keys

Set the UseMnemonic property to True if you want to define a character in the Caption property of the label as an access key. When you define an access key in a label control, the user can press and hold down ALT+ the character you designate to move the focus to the next control in the tab order.

You can also create access keys for any other controls that have a Caption property by adding an ampersand (&) before the letter you want to use as the access key. To assign an access key to controls that don't have captions, use a label with the control. Because labels can't receive focus, focus automatically moves to the next control in the tab order. Use this technique to assign access keys to text boxes, picture boxes, combo boxes, list boxes, drive list boxes, directory list boxes, grids, and images.

To assign an access key to a control with a label

1. Draw the label first, and then draw the control.

   – or –

   Draw the controls in any order and set the TabIndex property of the label to one less than the control.

2. Use an ampersand in the label's Caption property to assign the access key for the label.

   Note You may want to display ampersands in a label control, rather than using them to create access keys. This may occur if you bind a label control to a field in a recordset where the data includes ampersands. To display ampersands in a label control, set the UseMnemonic property to False.

Using the Line Control

The line control is used to create simple line segments on a form, a frame, or in a picture box.

Figure 7.29 The line control

You can control the position, length, color, and style of line controls to customize the look of applications. Figure 7.30 shows a line control used to graphically separate the label containing the text "Company Name" from the rest of the form.

Figure 7.30 A line control on a form

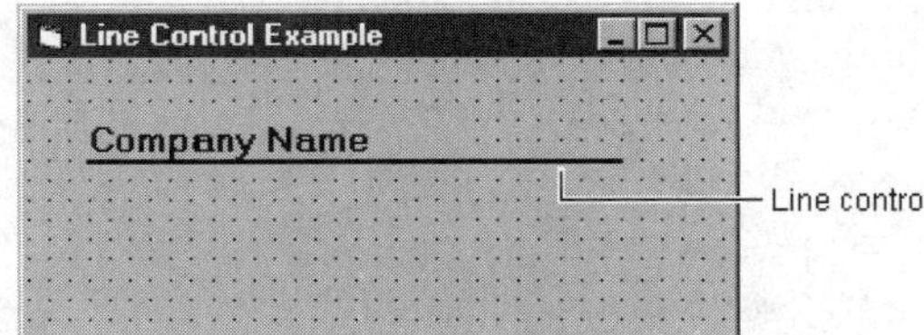

The line control has limited functionality and is intended for simple uses — display and printing. Line segments cannot be joined to form other shapes, for instance. For more advanced uses you need to use the line method.

For More Information See "Using Graphics Methods" in Chapter 12, "Working with Text and Graphics," for more information on drawing lines, rectangles, and filled-in boxes at run time using the line method or for more information on drawing circles, ellipses, and arcs at run time using the Circle method.

Setting Border Style and Color

You set the color and style of a line segment by using the BorderStyle and BorderColor properties.

The BorderStyle property provides you with six line styles:

- Transparent
- Solid
- Dash
- Dot
- Dash-Dot
- Dash-Dot-Dot
- Inside Solid

You can specify a line style at design time by choosing the BorderStyle property from the Properties window of the line control or, at run time, by specifying the style using its equivalent Visual Basic constant in code.

The BackColor property is used to specify the color of the line.

At design time, you can set the line color by choosing the BorderColor property from the Properties window of the line control and then selecting from the available palette or system colors.

To set colors at run time, use the Visual Basic color constants (vbGreen, for example) or the system color constants (vbWindowBackground, for example) or the RGB function to specify border colors.

> **Note** When BorderStyle is set to 0 (Transparent), the BorderColor property is ignored.

For More Information See "RGB Function" for information on specifying RGB colors. Also, refer to Chapter 12, "Working with Text and Graphics," for detailed information on creating graphics in Visual Basic.

Moving and Sizing a Line Segment

You can move or resize the line control at run time by altering its X1, X2, Y1, and Y2 properties. The X1 and Y1 properties set the horizontal and vertical positions of the left end of the line segment. The X2 and Y2 properties set the horizontal and vertical positions of the right end of the line segment. You can't move a line segment using the Move method.

Drawing Lines on a Form

You can use the line control to draw simple lines on forms.

To draw a line on a form

1. In the toolbox, select the line control.

   When the pointer moves onto the form, it changes to a cross hair.

2. Click the form where you want the line to begin and hold down the mouse button.
3. Drag the cross hair to where you want the line to end and release the mouse button.
4. From the Properties window, select the **BorderStyle** property if you want to change the appearance of the line.
5. In the **Settings** box, select the style you want.

Using the List Box Control

A list box control displays a list of items from which the user can select one or more.

Figure 7.31 The list box control

List boxes present a list of choices to the user. By default, the choices are displayed vertically in a single column, although you can set up multiple columns as well. If the number of items exceeds what can be displayed in the list box, scroll bars automatically appear on the control. The user can then scroll up and down, or left to right through the list. Figure 7.32 shows a single-column list box.

Figure 7.32 Single-column list box

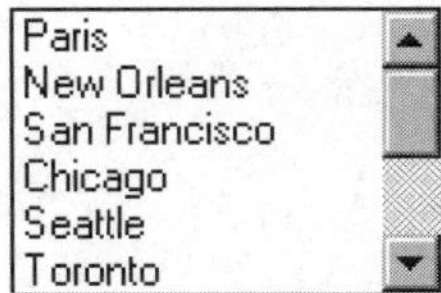

Data-Bound Features

Visual Basic includes both standard and data-bound versions of the list box control. While both versions of the list box control allow you to display, edit, and update information from most standard types of databases, the DataList provides more advanced data access features. The DataList control also supports a different set of properties and methods than the standard list box control.

For More Information See "Using the DataCombo and DataList Controls" for more information on the data-bound version of the list box control.

The Click and Double-Click Events

A recommended practice for list box events, especially when the list box appears as part of a dialog box, is to add a command button to use with the list box. The Click event procedure for this button should make use of the list-box selection, carrying out whatever action is appropriate for your application.

Double-clicking an item in the list should have the same effect as selecting the item and then clicking the command button. To do this, have the DblClick procedure for the list box call the Click procedure for the command button:

```
Private Sub List1_DblClick ()
   Command1_Click
End Sub
```

Or, set the value of the command button's Value property to True, which will automatically invoke the event procedure:

```
Private Sub List1_DblClick ()
   Command1.Value = True
End Sub
```

This provides mouse users with a shortcut, yet does not prevent keyboard users from performing the same action. Note that there is no keyboard equivalent for the DblClick event.

Adding Items to a List

To add items to a list box, use the AddItem method, which has the following syntax:

box.**AddItem** *item*[, *index*]

Argument	Description
box	Name of the list box.
item	String expression to add to the list. If *item* is a literal constant, enclose it in quotation marks.
index	Specifies where the new item is to be inserted in the list. An *index* of 0 represents the first position. If *index* is omitted, the item is inserted at the end (or in the proper sorted order).

While list items are commonly added in the Form_Load event procedure, you can use the AddItem method at any time. This gives you the ability to add items to the list dynamically (in response to user actions).

The following code places "Germany," "India," "France," and "USA" into a list box named List1:

```
Private Sub Form_Load ()
   List1.AddItem "Germany"
   List1.AddItem "India"
   List1.AddItem "France"
   List1.AddItem "USA"
End Sub
```

Whenever the form is loaded at run time, the list appears as shown in Figure 7.33.

Figure 7.33 "Countries" list box

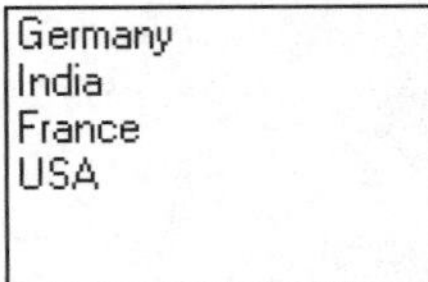

Adding an Item at a Specified Position

To add an item to a list at a specific position, specify an index value for the new item. For example, the next line of code inserts "Japan" into the first position, adjusting the position of the other items downward:

```
List1.AddItem "Japan", 0
```

Notice that it is 0, not 1, that specifies the first item in a list (see Figure 7.34).

Figure 7.34 Adding an item to a list

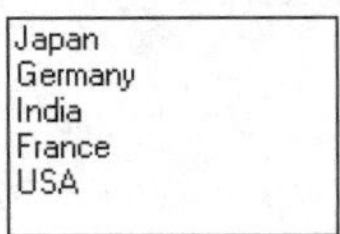

Adding Items at Design Time

You can also enter items into the list at design time by setting the List property in the Properties window of the list box control. When you select the List property option and then click the down arrow, you can type list items and then press the CTRL+ENTER key combination to start a new line.

You can only add items to the end of the list. So, if you want to alphabetize the list, set the Sorted property to True. See "Sorting a List" below for more information.

Sorting a List

You can specify that items be added to a list in alphabetical order by setting the Sorted property to True and omitting the index. The sort is not case-sensitive; thus, the words "japan" and "Japan" are treated the same.

When the Sorted property is set to True, using the AddItem method with the *index* argument can lead to unpredictable, unsorted results.

Removing Items from a List

You can use the RemoveItem method to delete items from a list box. RemoveItem has one argument, *index*, which specifies the item to remove:

box.**RemoveItem** *index*

The *box* and *index* arguments are the same as for AddItem.

For example, to remove the first entry in a list, you would add the following line of code:

```
List1.RemoveItem 0
```

To remove all list entries in bound or standard versions of the list and combo boxes, use the Clear method:

```
List1.Clear
```

Getting List Contents with the Text Property

Usually, the easiest way to get the value of the currently selected item is to use the Text property. The Text property always corresponds to a list item a user selects at run time.

For example, the following code displays information about the population of Canada if a user selects "Canada" from a list box:

```
Private Sub List1_Click ()
   If List1.Text = "Canada" Then
      Text1.Text = "Canada has 24 million people."
   End If
End Sub
```

The Text property contains the currently selected item in the List1 list box. The code checks to see if "Canada" has been selected and, if so, displays the information in the Text box.

Accessing List Items with the List Property

The List property provides access to all items in the list. This property contains an array in which each item in the list is an element of the array. Each item is represented in string form. To refer to an item in the list, use this syntax:

box.**List**(*index*)

The *box* argument is a reference to a list box, and *index* is the position of the item. The top item has an index of 0, the next has an index of 1, and so on. For example, the following statement displays the third item (*index* = 2) in a list in a text box:

```
Text1.Text = List1.List(2)
```

Determining Position with the ListIndex Property

If you want to know the position of the selected item in a list, use the ListIndex property. This property sets or returns the index of the currently selected item in the control and is available only at run time. Setting the ListIndex property for a list box also generates a Click event for the control.

The value of this property is 0 if the first (top) item is selected, 1 if the next item down is selected, and so on. ListIndex is –1 if no item is selected.

> **Note** The NewIndex property allows you to keep track of the index of the last item added to the list. This can be useful when inserting an item into a sorted list.

Returning the Number of Items with the ListCount Property

To return the number of items in a list box, use the ListCount property. For example, the following statement uses the ListCount property to determine the number of entries in a list box:

```
Text1.Text = "You have " & List1.ListCount & " _
entries listed"
```

Creating Multiple-Column and Multiple-Selection List Boxes

The Columns property allows you to specify the number of columns in a list box. This property can have the following values:

Value	Description
0	Single-column list box with vertical scrolling.
1	Single-column list box with horizontal scrolling.
>1	Multiple-column list box with horizontal scrolling.

Visual Basic takes care of wrapping list items to the next line and adding a horizontal scroll bar to the list if needed; if the list fills a single column, no scroll bar is added. Wrapping to the next column also occurs automatically as needed. Note that if a list box entry is wider than the width of a column, the text is truncated.

You can allow users to select multiple items from a list. Multiple selection in standard list boxes is handled by setting the MultiSelect property, which can have the following values.

Value	Type of selection	Description
0	None	Standard list box.
1	Simple multiple selection	A click or the SPACEBAR selects or deselects additional items in the list.
2	Extended multiple selection	The SHIFT+ click or SHIFT+ an arrow key extends the selection to include all the items between the current and previous selections. CTRL+ click selects or deselects an item in the list.

For More Information   See "List Box Control Scenario 2: Creating Multiple-Column List Boxes," later in this chapter, for more information on the Columns and MultiSelect properties.

List Box Control Scenario 1: Adding and Deleting Items

This example shows how you can use the AddItem, RemoveItem, and Clear methods with the ListIndex and ListCount properties to add and remove list entries at run time. The example in Figure 7.35 lets a user type a client's name in a text box, which can be added to the list box if the Add button is clicked. A user can remove a current list item by selecting the item and choosing the Remove button, or by choosing Clear to clear all list entries.

Figure 7.35   A list box using the AddItem, RemoveItem, and Clear methods

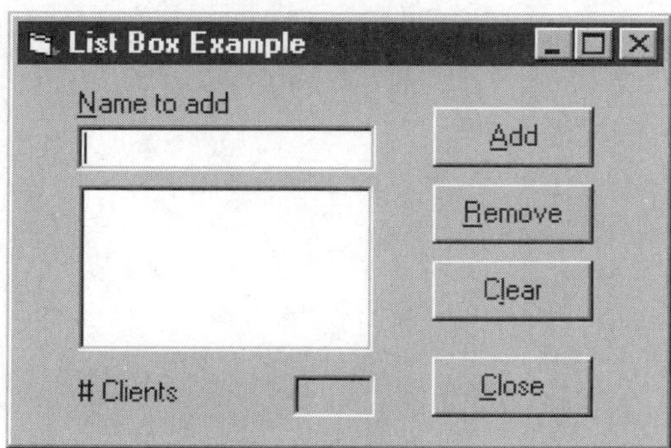

The number of clients in the list box is displayed in a label that looks like a text box (BorderStyle is set to 1-Fixed Single). This label is updated every time a client name is added or removed. Because the Sorted property for the list box is set to True, items are added to the list box in alphabetical order.

Create a form with a text box, a list box, three labels, and four command buttons. The following table lists the property settings for the objects in the application.

Object	Property	Setting
Top text box	Name Text	txtName (Empty)
Top label	Name Caption	lblName &Name to add
List box	Name Sorted	lstClient True
Bottom label	Name Caption	lblClients # Clients
Number of clients label (looks like a text box)	Name Caption BorderStyle	lblDisplay (Empty) 1-Fixed Single
First command button	Name Caption	cmdAdd &Add
Second command button	Name Caption	cmdRemove &Remove
Third command button	Name Caption	cmdClear &Clear
Fourth command button	Name Caption	cmdClose &Close

Events in the List Box Application

Add this code to the cmdAdd_Click event procedure:

```
Private Sub cmdAdd_Click ()
   lstClient.AddItem txtName.Text ' Add to list.
   txtName.Text = ""    ' Clear text box.
   txtName.SetFocus
   ' Display number.
   lblDisplay.Caption = lstClient.ListCount
End Sub
```

Add this code to the cmdRemove_Click event procedure:

```
Private Sub cmdRemove_Click ()
   Dim Ind As Integer

   Ind = lstClient.ListIndex   ' Get index.
   ' Make sure list item is selected.
   If Ind >= 0 Then
      ' Remove it from list box.
      lstClient.RemoveItem Ind
      ' Display number.
      lblDisplay.Caption = lstClient.ListCount
   Else
      Beep
   End If
   ' Disable button if no entries in list.
   cmdRemove.Enabled = (lstClient.ListIndex <> -1)
End Sub
```

Add this code to the cmdClear_Click event procedure:

```
Private Sub cmdClear_Click ()
   ' Empty list box.
   lstClient.Clear
   ' Disable Remove button.
   cmdRemove.Enabled = False
   ' Display number.
   lblDisplay.Caption = lstClient.ListCount
End Sub
```

Add this code to the cmdClose_Click event procedure:

```
Private Sub cmdClose_Click ()
   Unload Me
End Sub
```

Add this code to the lstClient_Click event procedure:

```
Private Sub lstClient_Click ()
   cmdRemove.Enabled = lstClient.ListIndex <> -1
End Sub
```

Add this code to the txtName_Change event procedure:

```
Private Sub txtName_Change ()
' Enable the Add button if at least one character
' in the name.
cmdAdd.Enabled = (Len(txtName.Text) > 0)
End Sub
```

List Box Control Scenario 2: Creating Multiple-Column List Boxes

To create a multiple-column, multiple-selection list box, you need to set both the Columns and the MultiSelect properties of a list box. In the following example, these properties are used to create such a list box.

You'll notice that when you run the application, the list box contains two columns, as shown in Figure 7.36.

Figure 7.36 Multiple-column list box

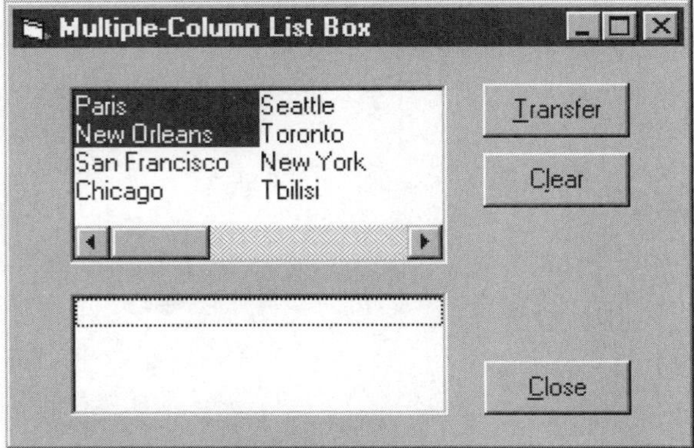

If you draw the list box large enough to hold all the items in one column, the second column will be empty; the other items will wrap, and horizontal scroll bars will appear automatically only if the list box is not long enough. Try resizing the top list box and adding additional list items to see how Visual Basic automatically handles multiple columns.

The example uses the Selected property — a Boolean array containing the selection status of a list box — to determine which items are selected. Each entry in the array corresponds to a list item and is set to True if the item is selected, or False if it is not selected. After the user selects items from the list, each array entry is checked to see if it is set (True). If so, the entry is added to the second list, a normal single-column list box, using the AddItem method.

Set the properties for the example as indicated in the following table.

Object	Property	Setting
Form	Caption	Multiple-Column List Box
Top list box	Name Columns MultiSelect	lstTop 2 2-Extended

Object	Property	Setting
Bottom list box	Name	lstBottom
First command button	Name Caption	cmdTransfer &Transfer
Second command button	Name Caption	cmdClear &Clear
Third command button	Name Caption	cmdClose &Close

The MultiSelect property allows you to select a range of values in a list box. If you click the first list item, and then press SHIFT and click the last item in the range (or use the SHIFT+ DOWN ARROW keys), all the items in the range are selected.

Events in the Multiple-Column List Box Application

Add code to the Form_Load procedure to initialize the top list, 1stTop:

```
Private Sub Form_Load ()
   lstTop.AddItem "Paris"
   lstTop.AddItem "New Orleans"
   lstTop.AddItem "San Francisco"
   lstTop.AddItem "Chicago"
   lstTop.AddItem "Seattle"
   lstTop.AddItem "Toronto"
   lstTop.AddItem "New York"
   lstTop.AddItem "Tbilisi"
   lstTop.AddItem "Moscow"
   lstTop.AddItem "Portland"
   ' Select a couple of items.
   lstTop.Selected(0) = True
   lstTop.Selected(1) = True
End Sub
```

> **Note** You can add items to list boxes without repeatedly using the AddItem method by typing items in the List property of the Properties window. After entering each item, press CTRL+ENTER to go to the next line. This allows you to type multiple entries in a multiple-column list box.

Add the following code to the 1stTop_DblClick event procedure:

```
Private Sub lstTop_DblClick ()
   cmdTransfer.Value = True' Press transfer button.
End Sub
```

Add the following code to the Click event procedure for the Transfer command button:

```
Private Sub cmdTransfer_Click ()
   For n = 0 To (lstTop.ListCount - 1)
' If selected, add to list.
      If lstTop.Selected(n) = True Then
         lstBottom.AddItem lstTop.List(n)
      End If
   Next
   cmdClear.Enabled = True
End Sub
```

Notice how the array index values start from 0 and go to `ListCount -1`.

Add the following code to the Click event procedure for the Clear command button:

```
Private Sub cmdClear_Click ()
   lstBottom.Clear
   cmdClear.Enabled = False
End Sub
```

Add the following code to the Click event procedure for the Close command button.

```
Private Sub cmdClose_Click ()
   Unload Me
End Sub
```

Using the OLE Container Control

You can link or embed any object that supports Automation (formerly called OLE Automation) into the OLE container control. Using this control, your Visual Basic application can display and manipulate data from other Windows-based applications, such as Microsoft Excel and Microsoft Word for Windows.

Figure 7.37 The OLE container control

The OLE container control is used to create a document-centered application. In such an application, the user combines data from different applications to create a single document. This type of application may be a word processor that allows the user to enter text and then embed a spreadsheet or chart.

The OLE container control allows you to add objects from other applications to your Visual Basic applications. With this control, you can:

- Create a placeholder in your application for an object. You can create the object that appears within the OLE container control at run time, or you can change an object you have placed in the OLE container control at design time.
- Create a linked object in your application.

- Bind the OLE container control to a database.
- Perform an action if the user moves, sizes, or updates the object in the OLE container control.
- Create objects from data that was copied onto the Clipboard.
- Display objects as icons.
- Provide backward compatibility with an application that includes many OLE container controls (called OLE client controls in previous versions of Visual Basic).

For More Information See "Using a Component's Visual Interface" in Chapter 10, "Programming with Components," for a detailed discussion and examples of how the OLE container control is used.

Using the Option Button Control

Option button controls are used to display options, usually in option button groups, from which the user can choose one.

Figure 7.38 The option button control

While option button controls and check box controls may appear to function similarly, there is an important difference: when a user selects an option button, the other option button controls in the same group are automatically unavailable. In contrast, any number of check box controls can be selected.

For More Information See "Grouping Options with Option Buttons" in Chapter 3, "Forms, Controls, and Menus," for a demonstration of the use of option buttons.

Creating Option Button Groups

You group option button controls by drawing them inside a container such as a frame control, a picture box control, or a form. At run time, the user may select a single option button from each distinct group of option buttons. For example, if you add option buttons to a form and option buttons to a frame control on the form, you have created two distinct groups of option buttons.

Figure 7.39 Creating option button groups

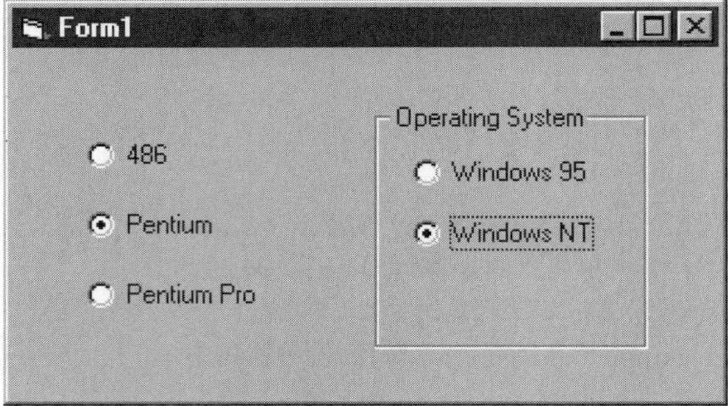

All option buttons that are added directly to the form become one group. To add additional groups, you need to place them inside frame or picture box controls.

To group option button controls in a frame or picture box, draw the frame or picture box first, and then draw the option button controls inside. At design time, option buttons contained within a frame or picture box control may be selected and moved as a single unit.

To select multiple controls contained inside a frame control, a picture box control, or a form, hold down the CTRL key while using the mouse to draw a box around the controls.

For More Information See "Using the Frame Control" earlier in this chapter for more information on drawing controls inside a frame.

Selecting an Option Button at Run Time

An option button may be selected at run time in several ways: clicking it with the mouse, using the TAB key to shift the focus to the control, using the TAB key to select a group of option button controls and then using the arrow keys to select one within the group, creating a shortcut key in the option button's caption, or, by setting its Value property to True in code.

The Click Event

When an option button is selected, its Click event is triggered. Depending upon the functionality of your application, you may or may not need to respond to this event. Responding to this event is useful when you want to update a label control's caption to provide the user with information about the option that has been selected, for example.

The Value Property

The Value property of the option button control indicates whether the option button is selected. When selected, the value is changed to True. You can select an option button in code by setting its Value property. For example:

```
optPentium.Value = True
```

To make an option button the default within an option button group, set the Value property at design time using the Properties window or at run time in code, as shown above.

When you present the user with a dialog box containing option buttons, you are asking them to select options that will determine what your application will do next. You can use the Value property of each of the option button controls to determine which option or options were selected and then respond accordingly.

Creating Keyboard Shortcuts

You can use the Caption property to create access key shortcuts for your option buttons by adding an ampersand (&) before the letter you want to use as the access key. For example, to create an access key for the option button caption "Pentium" you add an ampersand before the letter "P": "&Pentium". At run time, the letter "P" will be underlined and the user can select the command button by simultaneously pressing ALT+P.

> **Note** To include an ampersand in a caption without creating an access key, include two ampersands (&&). A single ampersand is displayed in the caption and no characters are underlined.

Disabling an Option Button

To disable an option button, set its Enabled property to False. At run time, the option button will appear dimmed, meaning that it is unavailable.

Visually Enhancing the Option Button Control

The look of the option button control may be enhanced by altering the setting of the Style property and then using the Picture, DownPicture and DisabledPicture properties.

Using the Picture Box Control

The picture box control is used to display graphics, to act as a container for other controls, and to display output from graphics methods or text using the Print method.

Figure 7.40 The picture box control

The picture box control is similar to the image control in that each can be used to display graphics in your application — each supports the same graphic formats. The picture box control, however, contains functionality which the image control does not, for example: the ability to act as a container for other controls and support for graphics methods.

For More Information See "Working with the Picture Box Control" in Chapter 3, "Forms, Controls, and Menus," for a demonstration of the use of picture boxes.

Supported Graphic Formats

The picture box control can display picture files in any of the following formats: bitmap, cursor, icon, metafile, enhanced metafile, or as JPEG or GIF files.

For More Information See "Using the Image Control," earlier in this chapter, for detailed descriptions of these graphic formats.

Loading a Graphic into the Picture Box Control

Pictures can be loaded into the picture box control at design time by selecting the Picture property from the control's Properties window, or at run time by using the Picture property and the LoadPicture function.

```
Set Picture1.Picture = _
LoadPicture("c:\Windows\Winlogo.cur", vbLPLarge, vbLPColor)
```

You may want to use icon (.ico) and cursor (.cur) files containing separate images at different sizes and color depths to support a range of display devices. The LoadPicture function's settings allow you to select images with specific color depths and sizes from an .ico or .cur file. In cases where an exact match to the requested settings isn't available, LoadPicture loads the image with the closest match available.

To clear the graphic from the picture box control, use the LoadPicture function without specifying a file name. For example:

```
Set Picture1.Picture = LoadPicture
```

This will clear the picture box control even if a graphic was loaded into the Picture property at design time.

Using the Clipboard

You can also add a graphic to a picture box control at design time by pasting it from another application. For example, you may want to add a bitmap image that was created in Windows Paint. Simply copy the image to the clipboard, select the picture box control, and either use the keyboard shortcut CTRL+V or the Paste command from the Edit menu.

Sizing a Picture

By default, graphics are loaded into a picture box at their original size, meaning that if the graphic is larger than the control, the image will be clipped — the picture box control does not provide scroll bars. To make a picture box control automatically resize to display an entire graphic, set its AutoSize property to True. The control will then size to the graphic — growing or shrinking.

Unlike the image control, the picture box control cannot stretch the image to fit the size of the control.

For More Information See "Scroll Bar Controls Scenario: Creating a Scrollable Graphics Viewport," earlier in this chapter, for information on using picture boxes to create a scrollable graphics viewport.

Using the Picture Box Control as a Container

You can use the picture box control as a container for other controls. For example, since the picture box can be placed inside the internal area of a MDI form, it is often used to manually create a toolbar or status bar.

For More Information See "Creating a Toolbar" in Chapter 6, "Creating a User Interface," for more information on using the picture box control as a container for other controls.

Graphics Methods

Picture boxes, like forms, can be used to receive the output of graphics methods such as Circle, Line, and Point. For example, you can use the Circle method to draw a circle in a picture box by setting the control's AutoRedraw property to True.

```
Picture1.AutoRedraw = True
Picture1.Circle (1200, 1000), 750
```

Setting AutoRedraw to True allows the output from these methods to be drawn to the control and automatically redrawn when the picture box control is resized or redisplayed after being hidden by another object.

For More Information See "Using Graphics Methods" in Chapter 12, "Working with Text and Graphics," for more information about using the picture box control with the graphics methods.

Using the Print Method

You can use the picture box control to output text by using the Print method and setting the AutoRedraw property to True. For example:

```
Picture1.Print "A text string"
```

When using the Print method you can also modify the font style and size or use the CurrentX, CurrentY, Height, and Width properties to align text within a picture box.

For More Information See Chapter 12, "Working with Text and Graphics."

Using the Remote Data Control

The Remote Data control implements data access by using the Microsoft Remote Data Objects. This technology gives you seamless access to many standard database formats and allows you to create data-aware applications without writing any code. The Remote Data control is suited to larger client-server databases, including Open Database Connectivity (ODBC) databases such as Microsoft SQL Server and Oracle.

It should be noted that the Remote Data control does not work with Image data types.

Note Both the Remote Data control and Data control are included with Visual Basic for backward compatibility. However, because of the flexibility of ActiveX Data Objects (ADO), it's recommended that you create new database applications using the ADO Data control. For more details, see "Using the ADO Data Control" earlier in this chapter.

The Data control, Remote Data control, and the ADO Data control are all conceptually similar: all three are "data controls" that connect a data source to a data-bound control. All three also share the same appearance — a set of four buttons that allow the user to go immediately to the beginning of the recordset, end of the recordset, or scroll backwards and forwards through the recordset.

Creating a Simple Database Application with the Remote Data Control

The following procedures create a simple database application using the Data control.

To create a simple database application with the Remote Data Control

1. Draw a **Remote Data control** on the form. (The icon's tooltip control is "MSRDC.")

   If the Remote Data control is not in the Toolbox, press CTRL+T to display the Components dialog box. In the **Components** dialog box, click **Microsoft Remote Data Control**. Click **OK** to add it to the Toolbox.

2. Click the **Remote Data control** to select it, and press F4 to display the Properties window.

3. In the Properties window, set the **DataSourceName** property to the DSN of the database you want to connect to.

4. On the Properties window, click the **SQL** property and type in a SQL statement, for example:

   ```
   SELECT * FROM Products WHERE AuthorID = 72
   ```

   You should always include a WHERE clause when accessing a table. Failing to do so will lock the entire table, which would be a major hindrance to other users.

5. Draw a **TextBox** control on the form.

6. Click the **TextBox** control to select it, and on the Properties window set the **DataSource** property to the **Remote Data control**.

7. On the Properties window, set the **DataField** property to the name of the field in the database you want to view or modify.
8. Repeat steps 5, 6, and 7 for each additional field you want to access.
9. Press F5 to run the application.

Setting Data-Related Properties of the RemoteData Control

The following data-related properties can be set at design time. The list suggests a logical order for setting the properties:

1. **Connect** — The Connect property is a string that can contain all the settings necessary to make a connection. The parameters passed in the string are driver-dependent. For example, ODBC drivers allow the string to contain driver, database, user name, and password.
2. **UserName** — Identifies a user to a protected database. The user must also supply a valid password that the database management system recognizes. The user name can also be contained in the Connect property value, making it redundant here.
3. **Password** — Along with UserName, the Password allows the user to access protected data. The password can also be contained in the Connect property value, making it redundant here.
4. **SQL** — The SQL property contains the SQL statement used to retrieve a resultset. The size of the resultset may determine whether you want to use a client-side or server-side cursor. For example, a small resultset can be managed on a client-side cursor.
5. **RowSetSize** — Sets the number of rows returned in a resultset, if the cursor is a keyset. You can fine-tune this number to the computer's resources (memory) for performance gains.
6. **ReadOnly** — Specifies if the data will be written to. If writing data is not needed, setting this property to True can give you a performance gain.
7. **CursorDriver** — Determines the location and type of driver. The setting of this property affects how you set other properties. For example, selecting ODBC client-side cursors may give you performance increases as long as the resultset is small.
8. **LockType** — The LockType determines how the data is locked when others attempt to change the data. If you do not expect others to change the data (while you are looking at it) you can set the LockType to "optimistic" — leaving the data free to be viewed and changed by others. If you set it to "pessimistic," others cannot access the data while you are accessing it.
9. **BOFAction, EOFAction** — These two properties determine what will happen when the control is at the beginning and end of the cursor. Choices include staying at the beginning or end, moving to the first or last record, or adding a new record (at the end only).

10. **ResultSetType** — Determines if the cursor is static or a keyset type.
11. **KeySetSize** — If the cursor is a keyset, you can optimize the size of the returned resultset with the KeySetSize property.
12. **LoginTimeout** — Sets the number of seconds to wait until an error is returned.
13. **MaxRows** — Specifies how large the cursor will be. How you determine this depends on the size of the records you are retrieving and the resources available on your computer (memory). A large record (one with many columns and large strings) would take more resources than a smaller record. The MaxRows property should be consequently decreased.
14. **Options** — Specifies whether or not the control executes queries asynchronously. Use asynchronous operation when you expect a query to take more than a few minutes to execute.
15. **Prompt** — When RDO opens a connection based on the parameters of the RemoteData control, the Connect property is expected to contain sufficient information to establish the connection. If information like the data source name, user name, or password is not provided, the ODBC driver manager exposes one or more dialog boxes to gather this information from the user. If you do not want these dialog boxes to appear, set the Prompt property accordingly to disable this feature.
16. **QueryTimeout** — Sets the number of seconds to wait for a query to complete before returning an error.
17. **BatchSize** — This property determines how many statements can be sent in a batch — if batch statements are allowed by the driver.

Using the Shape Control

The shape control is used to create the following predefined shapes on forms, frames, or picture boxes: rectangle, square, oval, circle, rounded rectangle, or rounded square.

Figure 7.41 The shape control

You can set the shape style, color, fill style, border color, and border style of any of the shapes you draw on a form.

For simple uses, the shape control allows you to create a variety of shapes without writing any code. For more advanced functionality you need to use the Line and Circle methods.

For More Information See "Using Graphics Methods" in Chapter 12, "Working with Text and Graphics," for more information on drawing lines, rectangles, and filled-in boxes at run time using the Line method or for more information on drawing circles, ellipses, and arcs at run time using the Circle method.

Predefined Shapes

The Shape property of the shape control provides you with six predefined shapes. The following table lists all the predefined shapes, their values and equivalent Visual Basic constants:

Shape	Style	Constant
Rectangle	0	vbShapeRectangle
Square	1	vbShapeSquare
Oval	2	vbShapeOval
Circle	3	vbShapeCircle
Rounded Rectangle	4	vbShapeRoundedRectangle
Rounded Square	5	vbShapeRoundedSquare

Figure 7.42 Predefined shapes

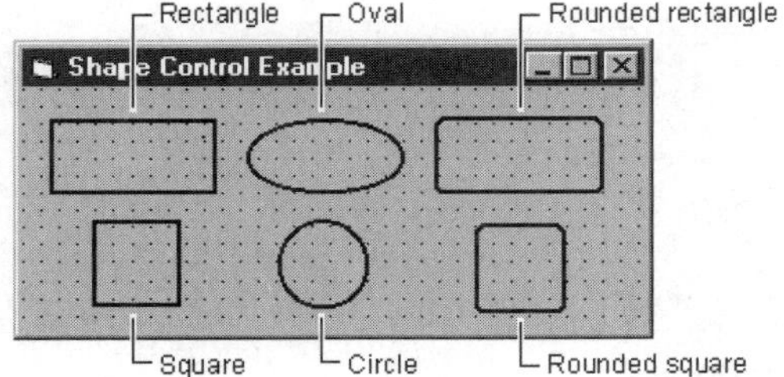

Fill and Line Styles

You can use the FillStyle and BorderStyle properties to set the fill style and border style of any of the shapes you draw on a form.

The FillStyle property, like the Style property, provides you with a number of predefined fill style patterns. These include: Solid, Transparent, Horizontal Line, Vertical Line, Upward Diagonal, Downward Diagonal, Cross, and Diagonal Cross.

The BorderStyle property provides you with a number of predefined border styles. These include: Transparent, Solid, Dash, Dot, Dash-Dot, Dash-Dot-Dot, and Inside Solid.

For More Information Both the FillStyle and BorderStyle properties provide you with constants that represent the styles listed above. See "FillStyle Property" and "BorderStyle Property" in the *Microsoft Visual Basic 6.0 Controls Reference* volume of the *Microsoft Visual Basic 6.0 Reference Library* for more information.

Setting Color Attributes

The BackColor and FillColor properties allow you to add color to the shape and its border.

At design time, you can set the fill or border colors by choosing either property from the Properties window of the shape control and then selecting from the available palette or system colors.

To set colors at run time, use the Visual Basic color constants (vbGreen, for example) or the system color constants (vbWindowBackground, for example) or the RGB function to specify fill colors.

> **Note** When the FillStyle or BackStyle properties are set to 1 (Transparent), the FillColor and BackColor properties are ignored.

For More Information See "RGB Function" in the *Microsoft Visual Basic 6.0 Language Reference* for information on specifying RGB colors. Also, refer to Chapter 12, "Working with Text and Graphics," for detailed information on creating graphics in Visual Basic.

Drawing Shapes on a Form

You can use the shape control to draw rectangles (regular or rounded corners), squares (regular or rounded corners), ovals, and circles on a form.

To draw a shape on a form

18. In the toolbox, select the **Shape** control.

    When the pointer moves onto the form, it changes to a cross hair.

19. Click and drag the cross hair to make the item the size you want.
20. From the Properties window, select the **Shape** property.
21. In the **Settings** box, select the style you want.

Shapes can be sized like any other controls, by selecting and dragging the control to the desired size, or by setting the Height and Width properties.

Using the Text Box Control

The text box control is used to display information entered by the user at run time, or assigned to the Text property of the control at design or run time.

Figure 7.43 The text box control

In general, the text box control should be used for editable text, although you can make it read-only by setting its Locked property to True. Text boxes also allow you to display multiple lines, to wrap text to the size of the control, and to add basic formatting.

The Text Property

Text entered into the text box control is contained in the Text property. By default, you can enter up to 2048 characters in a text box. If you set the MultiLine property of the control to True, you can enter up to 32K of text.

Formatting Text

When text exceeds the boundaries of the control, you can allow the control to automatically wrap text by setting the MultiLine property to True and add scroll bars by setting the ScrollBars property to add either a horizontal or vertical scroll bar, or both. Automatic text wrapping will be unavailable, however, if you add a horizontal scroll bar because the horizontal edit area is increased by the presence of the scroll bar.

When the MultiLine property is set to True, you can also adjust the alignment of the text to either Left Justify, Center, or Right Justify. The text is left-justified by default. If the MultiLine property is False, setting the Alignment property has no effect.

For More Information See "Working with Text Boxes," online, for a demonstration of the MultiLine, ScrollBar, and Alignment properties.

Selecting Text

You can control the insertion point and selection behavior in a text box with the SelStart, SelLength and SelText properties.

For More Information See "Working with Text Boxes" in Chapter 3, "Forms, Controls, and Menus," for a demonstration of the SelStart, SelText, and SelLength properties.

Creating a Password Text Box

A password box is a text box that allows a user to type in his or her password while displaying placeholder characters, such as asterisks. Visual Basic provides two text box properties, PasswordChar and MaxLength, which make it easy to create a password text box.

PasswordChar specifies the character displayed in the text box. For example, if you want asterisks displayed in the password box, you specify * for the PasswordChar property in the Properties window. Regardless of what character a user types in the text box, an asterisk is displayed, as shown in Figure 7.44.

Figure 7.44 Password example

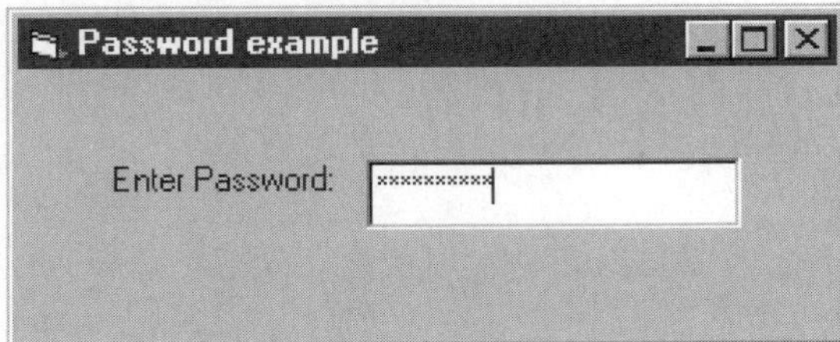

With MaxLength, you determine how many characters can be typed in the text box. After MaxLength is exceeded, the system emits a beep and the text box does not accept any further characters.

Canceling Keystrokes in a Text Box

You can use the KeyPress event to restrict or transform characters as they are typed. The KeyPress event uses one argument, *keyascii*. This argument is an integer that represents the numeric (ASCII) equivalent of the character typed in the text box.

The next example demonstrates how to cancel keystrokes as they are typed. If the character typed is not within the specified range, the procedure cancels it by setting `KeyAscii` to 0. The text box for this example is named txtEnterNums, and the procedure prevents the text box from receiving any characters other than digits. Compare `KeyAscii` directly to the numeric (Asc) values of various characters.

```
Private Sub txtEnterNums_KeyPress (KeyAscii As Integer)
   If KeyAscii < Asc("0") Or KeyAscii > Asc("9") Then
      KeyAscii = 0' Cancel the character.
      Beep           ' Sound error signal.
   End If
End Sub
```

For More Information See "Responding to Keyboard Events" in Chapter 11, "Responding to Mouse and Keyboard Events," for more information about the KeyPress event.

Creating a Read-Only Text Box

You can use the Locked property to prevent users from editing text box contents. Set the Locked property to True to allow users to scroll and highlight text in a text box without allowing changes. With the Locked property set to True, a Copy command will work in a text box, but Cut and Paste commands will not. The Locked property only affects *user interaction* at run time. You can still change text box contents *programmatically* at run time by changing the Text property of the text box.

Printing Quotation Marks in a String

Sometimes quotation marks (" ") appear in a string of text.

```
She said, "You deserve a treat!"
```

Because strings assigned to a variable or property are surrounded by quotation marks (" "), you must insert an additional set of quotation marks for each set to display in a string. Visual Basic interprets two quotation marks in a row as an embedded quotation mark.

For example, to create the preceding string, use the following code:

```
Text1.Text = "She said, ""You deserve a treat!"" "
```

To achieve the same effect, you can use the ASCII character (34) for a quotation mark:

```
Text1.Text = "She said, " & Chr(34) + "You deserve a treat!" & Chr(34)
```

Using the Timer Control

Timer controls respond to the passage of time. They are independent of the user, and you can program them to take actions at regular intervals. A typical response is checking the system clock to see if it is time to perform some task. Timers also are useful for other kinds of background processing.

Figure 7.45 The timer control

Each timer control has an Interval property that specifies the number of milliseconds that pass between one timer event to the next. Unless it is disabled, a timer continues to receive an event (appropriately named the Timer event) at roughly equal intervals of time.

The Interval property has a few limitations to consider when you're programming a timer control:

- If your application or another application is making heavy demands on the system — such as long loops, intensive calculations, or drive, network, or port access — your application may not get timer events as often as the Interval property specifies.
- The interval can be between 0 and 64,767, inclusive, which means that even the longest interval can't be much longer than one minute (about 64.8 seconds).
- The interval is not guaranteed to elapse exactly on time. To ensure accuracy, the timer should check the system clock when it needs to, rather than try to keep track of accumulated time internally.
- The system generates 18 clock ticks per second — so even though the Interval property is measured in milliseconds, the true precision of an interval is no more than one-eighteenth of a second.

Every timer control must be associated with a form. Therefore, to create a timer application, you must create at least one form (though you don't have to make the form visible if you don't need it for any other purpose).

> **Note** The word "timer" is used in several ways in Visual Basic, each closely related to the workings of the timer control. In addition to the control name and control type, "timer" is used in the Timer event and the Timer function.

Sample Application: Alarm.vbp

Techniques for working with the timer control are included in the Alarm sample application (Alarm.vbp) which is listed in the Samples directory.

Placing a Timer Control on a Form

Placing a timer control on a form is like drawing any other control: Click the timer button in the toolbox and drag it onto a form.

The timer appears on the form at design time only so you can select it, view its properties, and write an event procedure for it. At run time, a timer is invisible and its position and size are irrelevant.

Initializing a Timer Control

A timer control has two key properties.

Property	Setting
Enabled	If you want the timer to start working as soon as the form loads, set it to True. Otherwise, leave this property set to False. You might choose to have an outside event (such as a click of a command button) start operation of the timer.
Interval	Number of milliseconds between timer events.

Note that the Enabled property for the timer is different from the Enabled property for other objects. With most objects, the Enabled property determines whether the object can respond to an event caused by the user. With the Timer control, setting Enabled to False suspends timer operation.

Remember that the Timer event is *periodic*. The Interval property doesn't determine "how long" as much as it determines "how often." The length of the interval should depend on how much precision you want. Because there is some built-in potential for error, make the interval one-half the desired amount of precision.

> **Note** The more often a timer event is generated, the more processor time is used in responding to the event. This can slow down overall performance. Don't set a particularly small interval unless you need it.

Timer Control Scenario: Responding to the Timer Event

When a timer control's interval elapses, Visual Basic generates the Timer event. Typically, you respond to this event by checking some general condition, such as the system clock.

A digital clock is a very simple but very useful application involving a timer control. Once you understand how the application works, you can enhance it to work as an alarm clock, stopwatch, or other timing device.

The Digital Clock application includes a timer and a label with a border. At design time, the application looks like Figure 7.46.

Figure 7.46 The Digital Clock application

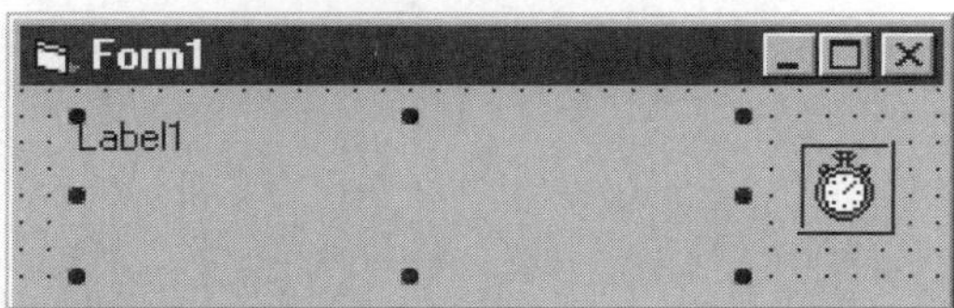

At run time, the timer is invisible. The following table lists the property settings for the Digital Clock application.

Control	Property	Setting
Label1	BorderStyle	Fixed Single
Timer1	Interval	500 (half a second)
Timer1	Enabled	True

The only procedure in this application is an event procedure for the timer:

```
Private Sub Timer1_Timer ()
   If lblTime.Caption <> CStr(Time) Then
      lblTime.Caption = Time
   End If
End Sub
```

The procedure displays the system time by calling the intrinsic Time function. This function returns a Variant containing the current time as a date/time value (VarType 7). When you assign it to a string variable or property, such as the Caption property in this case, Visual Basic converts it to a string using the time format specified in the Control Panel. If you want to display it using a different format, you can use the Format function.

For More Information See "Format Property" in the *Microsoft Visual Basic 6.0 Language Reference.*

The Interval property for the timer is set to 500, following the rule of setting the Interval to half of the shortest period you want to distinguish (one second in this case). This may cause the timer code to update the label with the same time twice in one second. This is wasteful and can cause some visible flicker, so the code tests to see if the time is different from what is displayed in the label before it changes the caption.

You can customize the look of the Digital Clock without having to write any additional statements. For example, you might want to select a different font for the label or change the BorderStyle property of the form.

CHAPTER 8

More About Programming

This chapter goes beyond the fundamentals of Visual Basic programming and introduces a variety of features that make it easier for you to create powerful, flexible applications.

For example, you can load multiple projects into a single session of the programming environment, work with Windows registry settings, or selectively compile certain parts of your program.

Beyond the fundamentals of writing code, Visual Basic provides a variety of language elements that enhance your code. The last four topics in this chapter discuss four of these language elements: user-defined types, enumerated constants, arrays, and collections.

Contents

Working with Multiple Projects

You can create many applications by working with a single project. However, as your applications become more complex, you may want to work with multiple projects in the same session of the programming environment. For example, you may want to use one project to build an application's executable file, and a second project to serve as a "scratch pad" for testing code before you add it to the application.

You can add a new or existing project to your current editing session by adding it to a *project group*. You can then save the project group and work with it in subsequent editing sessions. You can open either the project group or an individual project in the project group, or add the project group or its individual projects to another project group.

In a project group, one executable project serves as a startup project. When a project group is open and you choose Start from the Run menu, click the Start button on the toolbar, or press F5, Visual Basic runs the startup project.

In the Professional or Enterprise edition, you can use project groups to create and debug multiple-component applications. For example, you can create and debug project groups containing standard executable projects, ActiveX executable projects, ActiveX dynamic-link library projects, or ActiveX control projects. For more information, see "Creating ActiveX Components" in the *Microsoft Visual Basic 6.0 Component Tools Guide* volume of the *Microsoft Visual Basic 6.0 Reference Library*.

Adding or Removing a Project

When you create a new project either at startup or by selecting the New Project command on the File menu, Visual Basic automatically creates a project group for it. You can then add additional new or existing projects to the project group.

To add a new project to a project group

- Click the **Add Project** button on the Toolbar or choose **Add Project** from the **File** menu.

  In Visual Basic, Learning edition, Visual Basic automatically adds a new executable project to the project group. In the Professional and Enterprise editions, you can select the type of project you want to add from the popup menu of the **Add Project** button, or the icons displayed in the **New** tab of the **Add Project** dialog box.

To add an existing project to a project group

1. From the **File** menu, choose **Add Project**.

   Visual Basic displays the **Add Project** dialog box.

2. Click the **Existing** tab.

3. Select a project file, then choose **Open**.

   Visual Basic adds the selected project to the project group.

Visual Basic displays multiple projects in the Project window in a hierarchical view. Each project appears at the top level, with the project's forms, modules, controls, property pages, or document objects grouped under it in the hierarchical view.

Figure 8.1 The Project window with multiple projects

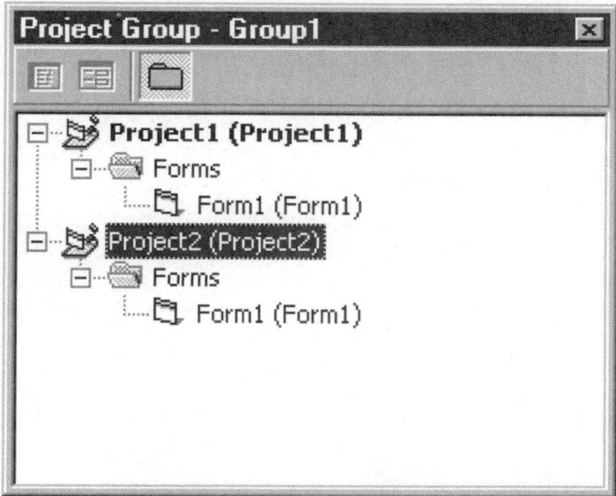

To remove a project from a project group

1. Select the name of the project in the Project window.
2. From the **File** menu, choose **Remove Project**.

   Visual Basic removes the selected project from the project group.

In the Professional and Enterprise editions of Visual Basic, you can change the type of a project by selecting the Project Properties command on the Project menu, then changing the Project Type option on the General tab in the Project Properties dialog box.

Figure 8.2 The General tab in the Project Properties dialog box

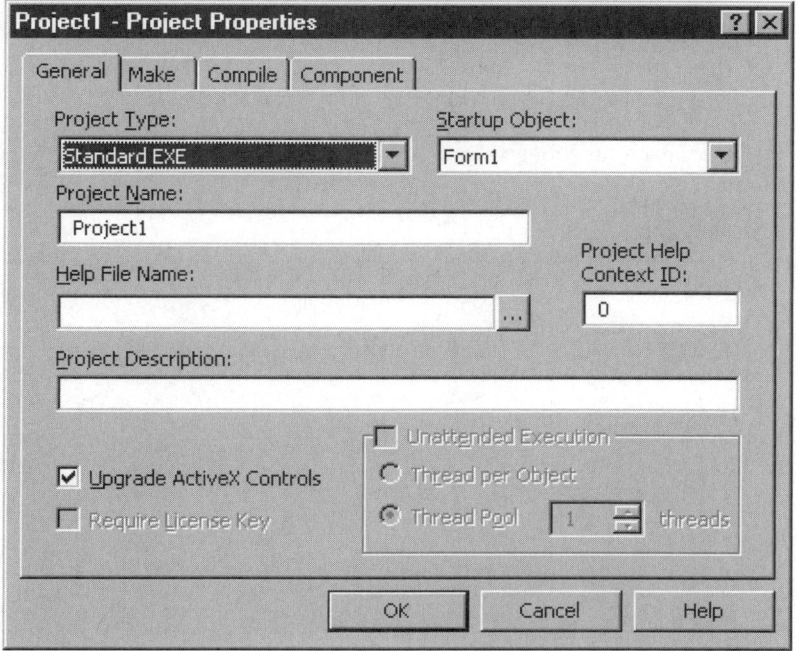

Specifying a Startup Project

Because a project group contains multiple projects, Visual Basic needs to know which project to run when you choose Start from the Run menu, click the Start button on the toolbar, or press F5. By default, Visual Basic runs the first executable (.exe) project that is added to a project group. However, you can specify a different startup component.

To specify a startup component

1. In the Project window, select a project.
2. Click the right mouse button and select **Set as Start Up** from the context menu.

Visual Basic displays the startup project's name in bold type in the Project window.

For More Information Debugging multiple projects is discussed in Chapter 7, "Debugging, Testing, and Deploying Components," in "Creating ActiveX Components" in the *Microsoft Visual Basic 6.0 Component Tools Guide* included with the Professional and Enterprise editions of Visual Basic.

Managing Application Settings

In Microsoft Windows 3.1 and earlier versions of Windows, program settings like window positions, files used, and other items were commonly stored in .ini files. In Windows NT, Windows 95, and later versions of Windows these program settings are stored in the system registry.

Visual Basic provides a standard registry location for storing program information for applications created in Visual Basic:

HKEY_CURRENT_USER\Software\VB and VBA Program Settings*appname**section**key*

Visual Basic also provides four statements and functions to manipulate the settings stored in your application's registry location.

Function or Statement	Description
GetSetting function	Retrieves registry settings.
SaveSetting statement	Saves or creates registry settings.
GetAllSettings function	Returns an array containing multiple registry settings.
DeleteSetting statement	Deletes registry settings.

Note To view registry entries, use the Regedit application, included with Windows 95 and Windows NT.

Creating or Saving Application Settings

You can use the SaveSetting statement to save a new value for a registry key stored in your application's registry location. For example, you could add code to the Form_Unload event in the application's main form in order to preserve settings at shutdown, or in the Form_Unload event on an Options dialog box to update user preferences.

Use the following syntax for the SaveSetting statement:

SaveSetting *appname*, *section*, *key*, *value*

The following code saves new values for the Backup and LastEntry keys in the Startup section of the registry for an application named "RegCust." This code assumes that the variables strDate and intLastEntry contain the new values.

```
Private Sub Form_Unload(Cancel As Integer)
   SaveSetting "RegCust", "Startup", "Backup", strDate
   SaveSetting "RegCust", "Startup", "LastEntry", _
   intLastEntry
End Sub
```

If an entry for the application "RegCust" or any of these sections or keys don't exist in the Software/Microsoft section in the registry, this code will create it.

For More Information See the "SaveSetting Statement" in the *Microsoft Visual Basic 6.0 Language Reference* volume of the *Microsoft Visual Basic 6.0 Reference Library.*

Retrieving Application Settings

You can use the GetSetting and GetAllSettings functions to retrieve registry values stored in your application's registry location. For example, your application can retrieve registry settings to recreate its condition at the time it was closed.

One Setting at a Time

To retrieve a single registry setting, use the following syntax for the GetSetting function:

GetSetting(*appname*, *section*, *key[, default]*)

The following code retrieves the value of the LastEntry key in the "RegCust" application's Startup section, and displays the value in the Immediate window.

```
Private Sub Form_Load()
   Dim intLastEntry As Integer
   intLastEntry = GetSetting("RegCust", "Startup", _
   "LastEntry", "0")
   Debug.Print intLastEntry
End Sub
```

Note that you can use the optional parameter, *default*, to set the value returned by Visual Basic when there is no value listed in the registry for the specified key.

Multiple Settings

To retrieve a list of registry keys and their values, use the following syntax for the GetAllSettings function:

GetAllSettings(*appname*, *section*)

The following code retrieves a two-column list of registry keys and their values in the "RegCust" application's Startup section, and displays the results in the Immediate window.

```
Private Sub Form_Load()
   Dim avntSettings As Variant
   Dim intX As Integer
   avntSettings = GetAllSettings("RegCust", "Startup")
   For intX = 0 To UBound(avntSettings, 1)
      Debug.Print avntSettings(intX, 0), _
      avntSettings(intX, 1)
   Next intX
End Sub
```

For More Information See "GetSetting Function" and "GetAllSettings Function" in the *Microsoft Visual Basic 6.0 Language Reference.*

Deleting Application Settings

You can use the DeleteSetting statement to delete a registry key, section, or an application's registry location. For example, you may want to delete all registry information for an application when the application is uninstalled.

Use the following syntax for the DeleteSetting statement:

DeleteSetting(*appname*, *section*, *key*)

The following code deletes the LastEntry key in the "RegCust" application's Startup section.

```
Private Sub cmdDelKey_Click()
   DeleteSetting "RegCust", "StartUp", "LastEntry"
End Sub
```

The following code deletes the "RegCust" application's entire Startup section of the registry.

```
Private Sub cmdDelSection_Click()
   DeleteSetting "RegCust", "StartUp"
End Sub
```

The following code deletes the entire registry location for the "RegCust" application.

```
Private Sub cmdUnInstall_Click()
   DeleteSetting "RegCust"
End Sub
```

For More Information See "DeleteSetting Statement" in the *Microsoft Visual Basic 6.0 Language Reference.*

Using Conditional Compilation

Conditional compilation lets you selectively compile certain parts of the program. You can include specific features of your program in different versions, such as designing an application to run on different platforms, or changing the date and currency display filters for an application distributed in several different languages.

Structuring Code for Conditional Compiling

To conditionally compile a part of your code, enclose it between #If...Then and #EndIf statements, using a Boolean constant as the branching test. To include this code segment in compiled code, set the value of the constant to –1 (True).

For example, to create French language and German language versions of the same application from the same source code, embed platform-specific code segments in #If...Then statements using the predefined constants conFrenchVersion and conGermanVersion.

```
#If conFrenchVersion Then
   ' <code specific to the French language version>.
#ElseIf conGermanVersion then
   ' <code specific to the German language version>.
#Else
   ' <code specific to other versions>.
#End If
```

If the value of the conFrenchVersion constant is set to True at compile time, the conditional code for the French language version will be compiled. If the value of the conGermanVersion constant is set to True, the compiler uses the German language version.

Declaring Conditional Compilation Constants

There are three ways to set conditional compilation constants: in the Conditional Compilation Arguments field of the Make tab on the Project Properties dialog box, on a command line, or in code.

Conditional compilation constants have a special scope and cannot be accessed from standard code. How you set a conditional compilation constant may depend on the scope you want the constant to have.

How Set	Scope
Project Properties dialog box	Public to all modules in the project
Command line	Public to all modules in the project
#Const statement in code	Private to the module in which they are declared

Setting Constants on the Project Properties Dialog Box

Before creating the executable file, from the Project menu, choose Project Properties, click the Make tab on the Project Properties dialog box, and enter an argument, such as conFrenchVersion = –1, in the Conditional Compilation Arguments field (if you are compiling your application for the French language version). When you compile the program, this argument will satisfy the #If...Then condition, and the code between the #If...Then and #EndIf statements will be included in the compiled program.

If you have a complex #If...Then statement, containing one or more #ElseIf statements, you will need to set additional constants. You can set multiple constants by separating them with colons, as in the following example:

```
conFrenchVersion=-1:conANSI=0
```

Setting Constants on the Command Line

If you want to start compilation from a command line, use the /d switch to enter conditional compilation constants, as shown here:

vb6.exe /make MyProj.vbp /d conFrenchVersion=–1:conANSI=0

No space is required between the /d switch and the first constant. Command-line declarations override declarations entered on the Project Properties dialog box, but do not erase them; arguments set on the Project Properties dialog box remain in effect for subsequent compilations.

For More Information See "#If...Then...#Else Directive" and "Const Statement" in the *Microsoft Visual Basic 6.0 Language Reference*.

Working with Resource Files

A resource file allows you to collect all of the version-specific text and bitmaps for an application in one place. This can include icons, screen text, and other material that may change between localized versions or between revisions or specific configurations.

Adding Resources to a Project

You can create a resource file using the Resource Editor add-in. The compiled resource file will have a .res file name extension. Each project can contain only one resource file.

The actual file consists of a series of individual strings, bitmaps, or other items, each of which has a unique identifier. The identifier is either a Long or a String, depending on the type of data represented by the resource. Strings, for example, have a Long identifier, while bitmaps have a Long or String identifier. To retrieve resources in your code, learn the identifier for each resource. The function parameters referring to the resources can use the Variant data type.

To add a new resource file to your project

1. Choose **Resource Editor** from the **Tools** menu. An empty resource file will be opened in the Resource Editor window.

   Note The Resource Editor add-in must be installed. For information on installing add-ins, see "Using Wizards and Add-Ins" in Chapter 4, "Managing Projects."

2. Select the **Save** button on the Resource Editor toolbar to save the resource file. The file will be added to the Project Explorer under the Related Documents section.

To add an existing resource file to your project

- Choose **Add New Resource File** from the **Project** menu. Any existing resource file in your project will be replaced.

  Caution If you make any modifications to an existing resource file it could affect other projects that use that resource file. Make sure that you save the file under a new filename.

  Note The Resource Editor add-in must be installed. For information on installing add-ins, see "Using Wizards and Add-Ins" in Chapter 4, "Managing Projects."

For More Information For more information on resource files, see "Using Resource Files for Localization" in Chapter 16, "International Issues."

Note Windows resource files are specific to 16-bit or 32-bit applications. Visual Basic will generate an error message if you try to add a 16-bit resource file to a project.

Using Resources in Code

Visual Basic provides three functions for retrieving data from the resource file for use in code.

Function	Description
LoadResString	Returns a text string.
LoadResPicture	Returns a Picture object, such as a bitmap, icon, or cursor.
LoadResData	Returns a Byte array. This is used for .wav files, for example.

For More Information See the appropriate function topic in the *Microsoft Visual Basic 6.0 Language Reference*.

Working with Templates

Visual Basic provides a variety of templates for creating common application components. Rather than creating all the pieces of your application from scratch, you can customize an existing template. You can also reuse custom components in multiple applications by creating your own templates.

You can open an existing template by selecting its icon in the Add Object dialog box when you create a new form, module, control, property page, or document. For example, Visual Basic provides built-in form templates for creating an About dialog box, Options dialog box, or splash screen.

Figure 8.3 The Add Form dialog box

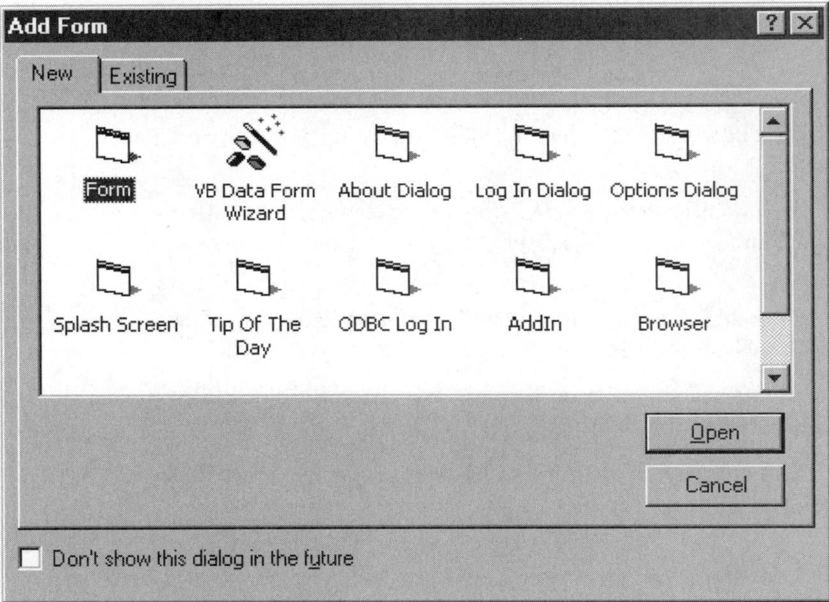

When you open a template, Visual Basic displays the object with placeholders that you can customize. For example, to create an About dialog box, open the About Dialog template and replace the Application Title, Version, and App Description placeholders with information specific to your application.

Figure 8.4 The About Dialog form template

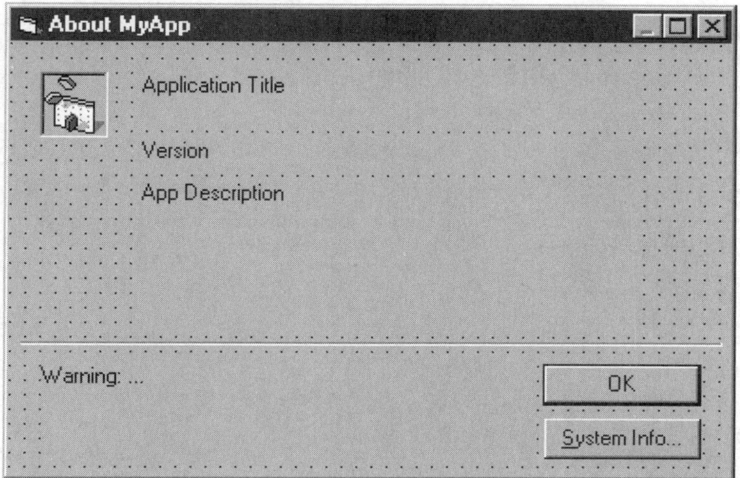

To create your own template, save the object that you want to use as a template, then copy it to the appropriate subdirectory of the Visual Basic Template directory. For example, to create a custom MyForm form template, save a form named MyForm, then copy the MyForm.frm file to the \VB\Template\Forms directory. When you select the Add Form command from the Project menu, Visual Basic displays the MyForm template in the Add Form dialog box, as shown in Figure 8.3.

You can disable display of templates in the Add object dialog box by selecting the Options command on the Tools menu and clearing the Show Templates options on the Environment tab of the Options dialog box. For example, to disable the display of form templates, clear the Forms option in the dialog box.

Figure 8.5 The Environment tab of the Options dialog box

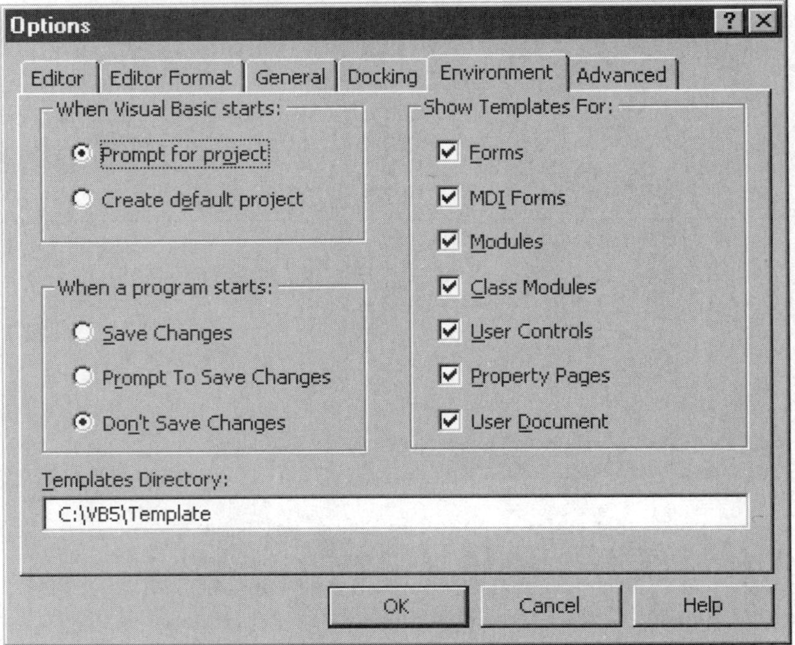

Working with Command Line Switches

Command line switches provide a way to control how Visual Basic executes. Using command line switches, you can start an instance of Visual Basic and run a specified project, make an executable file or dynamic-link library, or specify a string to be passed to the Command$ function.

For example, to run the project MyProj.vbp and then automatically exit, start Visual Basic with the following command line:

c:\Program Files\Microsoft Visual Studio\VB\vb6.exe /runexit MyProj.vbp

The following table summarizes the Visual Basic command line switches.

Switch	Description
/cmd *cmdstring*	Specifies a command string to be passed to the Command$ function. When used, it must be the last switch on the command line.
/d *compileconst*	Specifies one or more conditional compilation constants to use with the /make or /makedll switch.
/make *projectname*	Makes the specified project into an executable file.

Switch	Description
/makedll *projectname*	Makes the specified project into a dynamic-link library.
/mdi	Starts Visual Basic using the multiple document interface (MDI) programming environment.
/out *filename*	Outputs errors to a file when used with the /make or /makedll switch.
/run *projectname*	Runs the specified project.
/runexit *projectname*	Runs the specified project and then automatically exits.
/sdi	Starts Visual Basic using the single document interface (SDI) programming environment.
/?	Displays a list of valid command line switches.

Compiling Your Project to Native Code

If you have the Professional or Enterprise edition of Visual Basic, you can compile your code either in standard Visual Basic p-code format or in native code format. Native code compilation provides several options for optimizing and debugging that aren't available with p-code.

P-code, or *pseudo code*, is an intermediate step between the high-level instructions in your Basic program and the low-level *native code* your computer's processor executes. At run time, Visual Basic translates each p-code statement to native code. By compiling directly to native code format, you eliminate the intermediate p-code step.

You can debug compiled native code using standard native code debugging tools, such as the debugging environment provided by Visual C++. You can also use options available in languages such as Visual C++ for optimizing and debugging native code. For example, you can optimize code for speed or for size.

> **Note** All projects created with Visual Basic use the services of the run-time DLL (MSVBVM60.DLL). Among the services provided by this DLL are startup and shutdown code for your application, functionality for forms and intrinsic controls, and run-time functions like Format and CLng.
>
> Compiling a project with the Native Code option means that the code you write will be fully compiled to the native instructions of the processor chip, instead of being compiled to p-code. This will greatly speed up loops and mathematical calculations, and may somewhat speed up calls to the services provided by MSVBVM60.DLL. However, it does not eliminate the need for the DLL.

To compile a project to native code

1. In the Project window, select the project you want to compile.
2. From the **Project** menu, choose **Project Properties**.
3. In the **Project Properties** dialog box, click the **Compile** tab.

Figure 8.6 The Compile tab in the Project Properties dialog box

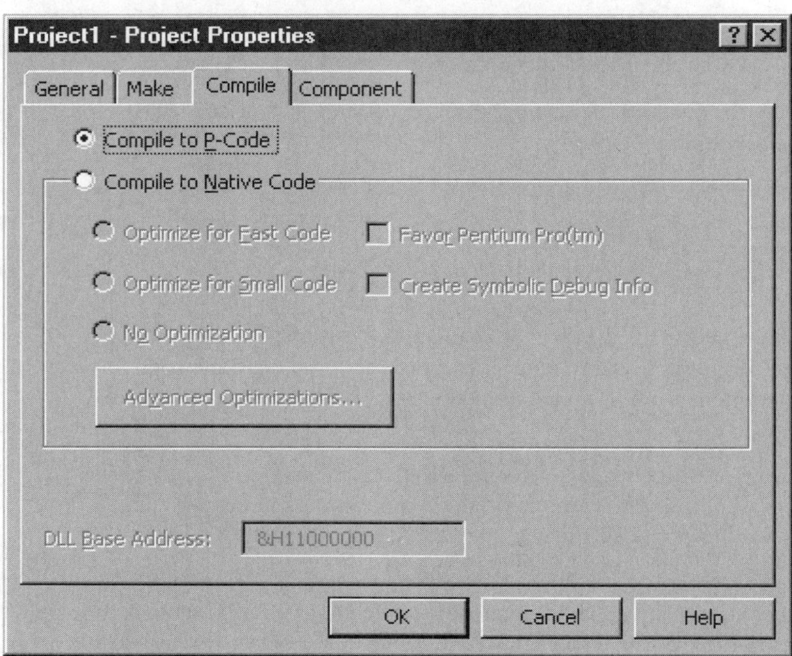

4. Select **Compile to Native Code**.

   Visual Basic enables several options for customizing and optimizing the executable file. For example, to create compiled code that will be optimized for size, select the **Optimize for Small Code** option.

   For additional advanced optimization options, click the **Advanced Optimizations** button.

5. Select the options you want, then click **OK**.
6. From the **File** menu, choose **Make Exe**, or **Make Project Group**.

The following table describes the native code options for optimization.

Option	Description
Assume No Aliasing (Advanced Optimization)	Tells the compiler that your program does not use aliasing. Checking this option allows the compiler to apply optimization such as storing variables in registers and performing loop optimizations.
Create Symbolic Debug Info	Produces a .pdb file and .exe or .dll file containing information to allow for debugging using Microsoft Visual C++ 5.0 or another compatible debugger.
Favor Pentium Pro	Optimizes code to favor the Pentium Pro processor.
No Optimization	Disables all optimizations.
Optimize for Fast Code	Maximizes the speed of .exe and .dll files by telling the compiler to favor speed over size.
Optimize for Small Code	Minimizes the size of .exe and .dll files by telling the compiler to favor size over speed.
Remove Array Bounds Checks (Advanced Optimization)	Disables Visual Basic array bounds checking.
Remove Floating Point Error Checks (Advanced Optimization)	Disables Visual Basic floating-point error checking.
Remove Integer Overflow Checks (Advanced Optimization)	Disables Visual Basic integer overflow checking.
Remove Safe Pentium FDIV Checks (Advanced Optimization)	Disables checking for safe Pentium processor floating-point division.

For More Information For more about native code options, see Appendix C, "Native Code Compiler Switches."

Creating Your Own Data Types

You can combine variables of several different types to create user-defined types (known as *structs* in the C programming language). User-defined types are useful when you want to create a single variable that records several related pieces of information.

You create a user-defined type with the Type statement, which must be placed in the Declarations section of a module. User-defined types can be declared as Private or Public with the appropriate keyword. For example:

```
Private Type MyDataType
```

– or –

```
Public Type MyDataType
```

For example, you could create a user-defined type that records information about a computer system:

```
' Declarations (of a standard module).
Private Type SystemInfo
   CPU As Variant
   Memory As Long
   VideoColors As Integer
   Cost As Currency
   PurchaseDate As Variant
End Type
```

Declaring Variables of a User-Defined Type

You can declare local, private module-level, or public module-level variables of the same user-defined type:

```
Dim MySystem As SystemInfo, YourSystem As SystemInfo
```

The following table illustrates where, and with what scope, you can declare user-defined types and their variables.

Procedure/Module	You can *create* a user-defined type as...	*Variables* of a user-defined type can be declared...
Procedures	Not applicable	Local only
Standard modules	Private or public	Private or public
Form modules	Private only	Private only
Class modules	Private or public	Private or public

Note If declared using the Dim keyword, user-defined types in Standard or Class modules will default to Public. If you intend a user-defined type to be private, make sure you declare it using the Private keyword.

Assigning and Retrieving Values

Assigning and retrieving values from the elements of this variable is similar to setting and getting properties:

```
MySystem.CPU = "486"
If MySystem.PurchaseDate > #1/1/92# Then
```

You can also assign one variable to another if they are both of the same user-defined type. This assigns all the elements of one variable to the same elements in the other variable.

```
YourSystem = MySystem
```

User-Defined Types That Contain Arrays

A user-defined type can contain an ordinary (fixed-size) array. For example:

```
Type SystemInfo
   CPU As Variant
   Memory As Long
   DiskDrives(25) As String' Fixed-size array.
   VideoColors As Integer
   Cost As Currency
   PurchaseDate As Variant
End Type
```

It can also contain a dynamic array.

```
Type SystemInfo
   CPU As Variant
   Memory As Long
   DiskDrives() As String   ' Dynamic array.
   VideoColors As Integer
   Cost As Currency
   PurchaseDate As Variant
End Type
```

You can access the values in an array within a user-defined type in the same way that you access the property of an object.

```
Dim MySystem As SystemInfo
ReDim MySystem.DiskDrives(3)
MySystem.DiskDrives(0) = "1.44 MB"
```

You can also declare an array of user-defined types:

```
Dim AllSystems(100) As SystemInfo
```

Follow the same rules to access the components of this data structure.

```
AllSystems(5).CPU = "386SX"
AllSystems(5).DiskDrives(2) = "100M SCSI"
```

Passing User-Defined Types to Procedures

You can pass procedure arguments using a user-defined type.

```
Sub FillSystem (SomeSystem As SystemInfo)
   SomeSystem.CPU = lstCPU.Text
   SomeSystem.Memory = txtMemory.Text
   SomeSystem.Cost = txtCost.Text
   SomeSystem.PurchaseDate = Now
End Sub
```

> **Note** If you want to pass a user-defined type in a form module, the procedure must be private.

You can return user-defined types from functions, and you can pass a user-defined type variable to a procedure as one of the arguments. User-defined types are always passed by reference, so the procedure can modify the argument and return it to the calling procedure, as illustrated in the previous example.

> **Note** Because user-defined types are always passed by reference, all of the data contained in the user-defined type will be passed to and returned from the procedure. For user-defined types that contain large arrays, this could result in poor performance, especially in client/server applications where a procedure may be running on a remote machine. In such a situation, it is better to extract and pass only the necessary data from the user-defined type.

For More Information To read more about passing by reference, see "Passing Arguments to Procedures" in Chapter 5, "Programming Fundamentals."

User-Defined Types that Contain Objects

User-defined types can also contain objects.

```
Private Type AccountPack
   frmInput as Form
   dbPayRollAccount as Database
End Type
```

> **Tip** Because the Variant data type can store many different types of data, a Variant array can be used in many situations where you might expect to use a user-defined type. A Variant array is actually more flexible than a user-defined type, because you can change the type of data you store in each element at any time, and you can make the array dynamic so that you can change its size as necessary. However, a Variant array always uses more memory than an equivalent user-defined type.

Nesting Data Structures

Nesting data structures can get as complex as you like. In fact, user-defined types can contain other user-defined types, as shown in the following example. To make your code more readable and easier to debug, try to keep all the code that defines user-defined data types in one module.

```
Type DriveInfo
   Type As String
   Size As Long
End Type
```

```
Type SystemInfo
   CPU As Variant
   Memory As Long
   DiskDrives(26) As DriveInfo
   Cost As Currency
   PurchaseDate As Variant
End Type

Dim AllSystems(100) As SystemInfo
AllSystems(1).DiskDrives(0).Type = "Floppy"
```

Using Enumerations to Work with Sets of Constants

Enumerations provide a convenient way to work with sets of related constants and to associate constant values with names. For example, you can declare an enumeration for a set of integer constants associated with the days of the week, then use the names of the days in code rather than their integer values.

You create an enumeration by declaring an enumeration type with the Enum statement in the Declarations section of a standard module or a public class module. Enumeration types can be declared as Private or Public with the appropriate keyword. For example:

```
Private Enum MyEnum
```

– or –

```
Public Enum MyEnum
```

By default, the first constant in an enumeration is initialized to the value 0, and subsequent constants are initialized to the value of one more that the previous constant. For example the following enumeration, Days, contains a constant named Sunday with the value 0, a constant named Monday with the value 1, a constant named Tuesday with the value of 2, and so on.

```
Public Enum Days
   Sunday
   Monday
   Tuesday
   Wednesday
   Thursday
   Friday
   Saturday
End Enum
```

> **Tip** Visual Basic provides a built-in enumeration, vbDayOfWeek, containing constants for the days of the week. To view the enumeration's predefined constants, type vbDayOfWeek in the code window, followed by a period. Visual Basic automatically displays a list of the enumeration's constants.

You can explicitly assign values to constants in an enumeration by using an assignment statement. You can assign any long integer value, including negative numbers. For example you may want constants with values less than 0 to represent error conditions.

In the following enumeration, the constant Invalid is explicitly assigned the value –1, and the constant Sunday is assigned the value 0. Because it is the first constant in the enumeration, Saturday is also initialized to the value 0. Monday's value is 1 (one more than the value of Sunday), Tuesday's value is 2, and so on.

```
Public Enum WorkDays
   Saturday
   Sunday = 0
   Monday
   Tuesday
   Wednesday
   Thursday
   Friday
   Invalid = -1
End Enum
```

> **Note** Visual Basic treats constant values in an enumeration as long integers. If you assign a floating-point value to a constant in an enumeration, Visual Basic rounds the value to the nearest long integer.

By organizing sets of related constants in enumerations, you can use the same constant names in different contexts. For example, you can use the same names for the weekday constants in the Days and WorkDays enumerations.

To avoid ambiguous references when you refer to an individual constant, qualify the constant name with its enumeration. The following code refers to the Saturday constants in the Days and WorkDays enumerations, displaying their different values in the Immediate window.

```
Debug.Print "Days.Saturday = " & Days.Saturday
Debug.Print "WorkDays.Saturday = " & WorkDays.Saturday
```

You can also use the value of a constant in one enumeration when you assign the value of a constant in a second enumeration. For example, the following declaration for the WorkDays enumeration is equivalent to the previous declaration.

```
Public Enum WorkDays
   Sunday = 0
   Monday
   Tuesday
   Wednesday
   Thursday
   Friday
   Saturday = Days.Saturday - 6
   Invalid = -1
End Enum
```

After you declare an enumeration type, you can declare a variable of that type, then use the variable to store the values of enumeration's constants. The following code uses a variable of the WorkDays type to store integer values associated with the constants in the WorkDays enumeration.

```
Dim MyDay As WorkDays
MyDay = Saturday          ' Saturday evaluates to 0.
If MyDay < Monday Then    ' Monday evaluates to 1,
                          ' so Visual Basic displays
                          ' a message box.
   MsgBox "It's the weekend. Invalid work day!"
End If
```

Note that when you type the second line of code in the example in the code window, Visual Basic automatically displays the WorkDays enumeration's constants in the Auto List Members list.

Figure 8.7 Visual Basic automatically displays an enumeration's constants

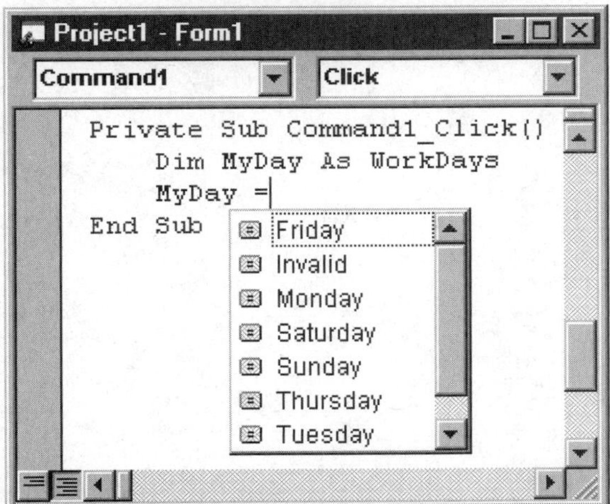

Because the constant Sunday also evaluates to 0, Visual Basic also displays the message box if you replace "Saturday" with "Sunday" in the second line of the example:

```
MyDay = Sunday        ' Sunday also evaluates to 0.
```

Note Although you normally assign only enumeration constant values to a variable declared as an enumeration type, you can assign any long integer value to the variable. Visual Basic will not generate an error if you assign a value to the variable that isn't associated with one of the enumeration's constants.

For More Information See "Enum Statement" in the *Microsoft Visual Basic 6.0 Language Reference.* Also see "Providing Named Constants for Your Component" in Chapter 6, "General Principals of Component Design" in Part 2, "Creating ActiveX Components" in the *Microsoft Visual Basic 6.0 Component Tools Guide*, available in the Professional and Enterprise editions.

Advanced Features of Arrays

Although arrays are most commonly used to store groups of variables, there are several other ways in which arrays are useful. You can assign the contents of one array to another, create functions that return arrays, and create properties that return arrays. In many cases these techniques can improve the performance of your application.

Assigning Arrays

Just as you can assign the contents of one variable to another, for example `strA = strB`, you can also assign the contents of one array to another. Imagine, for instance, that you wanted to copy an array of bytes from one location to another. You could do it by copying one byte at a time, like this:

```
Sub ByteCopy(oldCopy() As Byte, newCopy() As Byte)
   Dim i As Integer
   ReDim newCopy (Lbound(oldCopy) To UBound(oldCopy)

   For i - Lbound(oldCopy) To Ubound(oldCopy)
      newCopy(i) = oldCopy(i)
   Next
End Sub
```

A much more efficient way to do this is to assign one array to another:

```
Sub ByteCopy(oldCopy() As Byte, newCopy() As Byte)
   newCopy = oldCopy
End Sub
```

With variable assignment there are certain rules that you need to keep in mind. For example, although you can assign a variable declared as Integer to a variable declared as Long without any problem, assigning a Long to an Integer could easily lead to an overflow error. In addition to data typing rules, array assignments have additional rules involving the number of dimensions, the size of those dimensions, and whether an array is fixed or dynamic.

Attempting to assign arrays with different dimensions and/or data types may or may not succeed, depending on several factors:

- The type of array used on the left-hand side of the assignment: a fixed array (`Dim x(1 to 10) As Integer`) or a dynamic array (`Dim x() As Integer`).
- Whether or not the number of dimensions on the left-hand side match the number of dimensions of the array on the right-hand side of the assignment.
- Whether or not the number of elements for each dimension on each side of the assignment match. The dimensions may match even if the declarations are different, such as when one array is zero-based and another is one-based, as long as they have the same number of elements.
- The data types of all elements for each side of the assignment must be compatible. The rules are the same as for variable assignments.

The following table shows the effects of these factors:

Left-hand Side	Number of Dimensions Match?	Number of Elements Match?	Result of Assignment
Dynamic	No	Yes or No	Succeeds. Left side ReDim's to match right side if necessary.
Dynamic	Yes	No	Succeeds. Left side ReDim's to match right side if necessary.
Dynamic	Yes	Yes	Succeeds.
Fixed	Yes or No	Yes or No	Fails with a compilation error.

Errors can occur both at compile time and at run time (for example, if data types can't be coerced or if an assignment attempts to ReDim a fixed size array.) As the programmer, it's up to you to add error handling to make sure that the arrays are compatible before attempting an assignment.

Returning an Array from a Function

It's possible for a function to return an array of values. For example, you might want to return an array of bytes from a function without having to perform conversions to and from a string.

Returning an array from a function differs slightly from returning a single value: It requires an explicit type in the function declaration, and it requires that the return be passed in the Exit Function statement.

Here's a simple example of a function that returns an array of integers:

```
Private Sub Form_Load()
   Dim i As Integer
   Dim ReturnArray() As Integer

   i  = 1
   ReturnArray() = ArrayFunction(i)
End Sub

Public Function ArrayFunction(i As Integer) As Integer()
   Dim x(2) As Integer

   x(0) = i
   x(1) = i + 1

' Value is passed in the Exit Function statement.
   Exit Function x
End Function
```

After running the above example, ReturnArray() would be a two element array containing 1 and 2. Note that Exit Function statement passes an array as an argument; that array must be of the same data type as the function (in this case, Integer). Because this is a function call, you can pass the array without the parentheses.

> **Note** Although it's possible to return the array by assigning another array (`ArrayFunction = x()`), this isn't recommended for performance reasons.

You must specify a type for a function that returns an array; that type may be a Variant. Thus `Function X() As Variant()` would work whereas `Function X() As ()` would fail.

When calling a function that returns an array, the variable to hold the return values must be an array and must be of the same data type as the function, otherwise it will display a "Type Mismatch" error.

For More Information To learn more about using arrays, see "Arrays" in Chapter 5, "Programming Fundamentals." For information about returning arrays from properties, see "Putting Property Procedures to Work for You" in Chapter 9, "Programming with Objects."

Using Collections as an Alternative to Arrays

Although collections are most often used for working with objects, you can use a collection to work with any data type. In some circumstances, it may be more efficient to store items in a collection rather than an array.

You may want to use a collection if you're working with a small, dynamic set of items. The following code fragment shows how you might use a collection to save and display a list of URL addresses.

```
' Module-level collection.
Public colURLHistory As New Collection

' Code for adding a specified URL address
' to the collection.
Private Sub SaveURLHistory(URLAddress As String)
   colURLHistory.Add URLAddress
End Sub

' Code for displaying the list of URL addresses
' in the Immediate window.
Private Sub PrintURLHistory()
   Dim URLAddress As Variant
   For Each URLAddress in colURLHistory
      Debug.Print URLAddress
   Next URLAddress
End Sub
```

For More Information For more information on using collections, see "Programming with Your Own Objects" in Chapter 9, "Programming with Objects." To learn more about using arrays, see "Arrays" in Chapter 5, "Programming Fundamentals."

CHAPTER 9

Programming with Objects

Objects are central to Visual Basic programming. Forms and controls are objects. Databases are objects. There are objects everywhere you look.

If you've used Visual Basic for a while, or if you've worked through the examples in the first five chapters of this book, then you've already programmed with objects — but there's a lot more to objects than what you've seen so far.

In this chapter, user-defined types will take on personalities of their own, and become classes. You'll see how easy it is to create your own objects from the classes you define, and to use objects to simplify your coding and increase code reuse.

Contents

The following topics introduce the possibilities opened by programming with objects.

And it doesn't stop here. Chapter 10, "Programming with Components," takes the next step, showing how you can use Visual Basic to control objects provided by other applications.

Sample Applications: ProgWOb.vbp, Dataware.vbp

Some of the code examples in this chapter are taken from the Programming with Objects (ProgWOb.vbp) and Data-aware Classes (Dataware.vbp) samples. The sample applications are listed in the Samples directory.

What You Need to Know About Objects in Visual Basic

Visual Basic makes using objects easy, but more importantly it makes possible a gradual transition between procedural coding and programming with objects.

Of course, it helps that you've been using objects for as long as you've been using Visual Basic.

The One-Minute Terminologist

The following is a whirlwind tour of terms you'll meet in discussions of Visual Basic objects and their capabilities. If you're coming to Visual Basic from another programming language, or from having worked with ActiveX (formerly OLE) terminology, this topic will help you make the transition.

If you're new to objects, you may find it all a little bewildering. That's okay — by taking a quick tour of the terms you're going to meet, you'll start forming a picture of how they fit together. As you discover more about objects in the rest of this chapter, you can return to this topic to integrate each piece of information into the whole.

Here Goes

Objects are *encapsulated* — that is, they contain both their code and their data, making them more easier to maintain than traditional ways of writing code.

Visual Basic objects have *properties, methods,* and *events.* Properties are data that describe an object. Methods are things you can tell the object to do. Events are things the object does; you can write code to be executed when events occur.

Objects in Visual Basic are created from *classes;* thus an object is said to be *an instance of a class.* The class defines an object's interfaces, whether the object is public, and under what circumstances it can be created. Descriptions of classes are stored in *type libraries,* and can be viewed with *object browsers.*

To use an object, you must keep a *reference* to it in an *object variable.* The type of *binding* determines the speed with which an object's methods are accessed using the object variable. An object variable can be *late bound* (slowest), or *early bound.* Early-bound variables can be *DispID bound* or *vtable bound* (fastest).

A set of properties and methods is called an *interface.* The default interface of a Visual Basic object is a *dual interface* which supports all three forms of binding. If an object variable is *strongly typed* (that is, Dim … As *classname*), it will use the fastest form of binding.

In addition to their default interface, Visual Basic objects can implement extra interfaces to provide *polymorphism.* Polymorphism lets you manipulate many different kinds of objects without worrying about what kind each one is. *Multiple interfaces* are a feature of the Component Object Model (COM); they allow you to evolve your programs over time, adding new functionality without breaking old code.

Visual Basic classes can also be *data-aware.* A class can act as a *consumer* of data by binding directly to an external source of data, or it can act as a *source* of data for other objects by providing data from an external source.

On to Symphony Hall

Whew! If all of that seemed like old hat to you, you'll cruise through the rest of this chapter. If not, don't worry — there are strategically located explanations of all these terms sprinkled through the text (and presented at a much less frenetic pace).

Discovering the Class an Object Belongs To

Generic object variables (that is, variables you declare As Object) can hold objects of many different classes. Similarly, variables declared with Visual Basic's built-in Form and Control types can contain forms and controls of different classes.

When using variables of these types, you may need to take different actions based on the class of an object — for example, some objects may not support a particular property or method. Visual Basic provides two ways to do this: the TypeOf keyword and the TypeName function.

The TypeOf keyword can only be used in If ... Then ... Else statements. You must include the class name directly in your code. For example, `If TypeOf MyControl Is CheckBox Then`.

The TypeName function is more flexible. You can use it anywhere in your code, and because it returns the class name as a string, you can compare it to the value in a string variable.

Calling a Property or Method Using a String Name

Most of the time you can discover the properties and methods of an object at design time and write code to handle them. In a few cases, however, you may not know about an object's properties and methods in advance, or you may simply want the flexibility of allowing an end user to specify properties or execute methods at run time.

Consider, for example, a client application that evaluates expressions entered by the user by passing an operator to a server application. Now suppose that you are constantly adding new functions to the server that require new operators. Unfortunately, you would need to recompile and redistribute the client application before it would be able to use the new operators. In order to avoid this, you can use the CallByName function to pass the new operators as strings, without changing the application.

The CallByName function allows you to use a string to specify a property or method at run time. The signature for the CallByName function looks like this:

Result = CallByName(*Object*, *ProcedureName*, *CallType*, *Arguments()*)

The first argument to CallByName takes the name of the object that you want to act upon. The second argument, *ProcedureName,* takes a string containing the name of the method or property procedure to be invoked. The *CallType* argument takes a constant representing the type of procedure to invoke: a method (vbMethod), a property let (vbLet), a property get (vbGet), or a property set (vbSet). The final argument is optional, it takes a variant array containing any arguments to the procedure.

Suppose you had a server application, MathServer, with a new SquareRoot function. Your application has two TextBox controls: Text1 contains the expression to be evaluated upon; Text2 is used to enter the name of the function. You could use the following code in the Click event of a command button to invoke the SquareRoot function on the expression in Text1:

```
Private Sub Command1_Click()
   Text1.Text = CallByName(MathServer, Text2.Text, vbMethod, Text1.Text)
End Sub
```

If the user enters "64 / 4" in Text1 and "SquareRoot" in Text 2, the above code would invoke the SquareRoot function (which takes a string containing the expression to be evaluated as a required argument) and return "4" in Text1 (the square root of 16, or 64 divided by 4). Of course, if the user entered an invalid string in Text2, or if the string contained the name of a property instead of a method, or if the method had an additional required argument, a run-time error would occur. As you might guess, you'll need to add robust error handling code when you use CallByName to anticipate these or any other errors.

While the CallByName function may be useful in some situations, you need to weigh its usefulness against the performance implications — using CallByName to invoke a procedure is slightly slower than late-bound calls. If you're invoking a function that will be called repeatedly, such as inside a loop, CallByName could have a severe effect on performance.

Performing Multiple Actions on an Object

You often need to perform several different actions on the same object. For example, you might need to set several properties for the same object. One way to do this is to use several statements.

```
Private Sub Form_Load()
   Command1.Caption = "OK"
   Command1.Visible = True
   Command1.Top = 200
   Command1.Left = 5000
   Command1.Enabled = True
End Sub
```

Notice that all these statements use the same object variable, Command1. You can make this code easier to write, easier to read, and more efficient to run by using the With...End With statement.

```
Private Sub Form_Load()
   With Command1
      .Caption = "OK"
      .Visible = True
      .Top = 200
      .Left = 5000
      .Enabled = True
   End With
End Sub
```

You can also nest With statements by placing one With...End With statement inside another With...End With statement.

Using Default Properties

Many objects have *default properties*. You can use default properties to simplify your code, because you don't have to refer explicitly to the property when setting its value. For an object where Value is the default property, these two statements are equivalent:

```
object = 20
```

– and –

```
object.Value = 20
```

To see how this works, draw a command button and a text box on a form. Add the following statement to the command button's Click event:

```
Text1 = "hello"
```

Run the application and click the command button. Because Text is the default property of the text box, the text box will display the text, "hello."

Using Default Properties with Object Variables

When a reference to an object is stored in an object variable, you can still use the default property. The following code fragment demonstrates this.

```
Private Sub Command1_Click()
   Dim obj As Object
   ' Place a reference to Text1 in the object
   '  variable.
   Set obj = Text1
   ' Set the value of the default property (Text).
   obj = "hello"
End Sub
```

In the code above, `obj = "hello"` is exactly the same as typing `obj.Text = "hello"`.

Using Default Properties with Variants

Accessing default properties is different when an object reference is stored in a variable of type Variant, instead of in an object variable. This is because a Variant can contain data of many different types.

For example, you can read the default property of Text1 using a reference in a Variant, but trying to assign the string "goodbye" to the default property doesn't work. Instead, it replaces the object reference with the string, and changes the Variant type.

To see how this works, enter the following code in the Click event of the command button from the previous example:

```
Private Sub Command1_Click()
   Dim vnt As Variant
   ' Set the default property (Text) to "hello".
   Text1 = "hello"
   ' Place a reference to Text1 in the Variant.
   Set vnt = Text1
   ' Display the default property of Text1, and show
   '  that the Variant contains an object reference.
   MsgBox vnt, , "IsObject? " & IsObject(vnt)
   ' Attempt to set the default property of Text1.
   vnt = "goodbye"
   MsgBox vnt, , "IsObject? " & IsObject(vnt)
End Sub
```

When you run the application and click the command button, you first get a message box displaying the current value of the default property of Text1, "hello," which you can verify by looking at Text1. The caption of the message box confirms that the Variant contains an object reference — that is, a reference to Text1.

When you click the OK button on the message box, "goodbye" is assigned to the Variant, destroying the reference to Text1. Another message box is then displayed, showing the contents of the Variant — which as you can see doesn't match the current value of Text1.Text.

The caption of the message box confirms that the Variant no longer contains an object reference — it now contains the string "goodbye."

For More Information For details on Variants and other data types, see "Introduction to Variables, Constants, and Data Types" in Chapter 5, "Programming Fundamentals."

Other aspects of using objects with Variants are discussed in "The Visual Basic Collection Object," later in this chapter.

Creating Arrays of Objects

You can declare and use arrays of an object type just as you declare and use an array of any data type. These arrays can be fixed-size or dynamic.

Arrays of Form Variables

You can declare an array of forms with Private, Dim, ReDim, Static, or Public in the same way you declare an array of any other type. If you declare the array with the New keyword, Visual Basic automatically creates a new instance of the form for each element in the array as you use the elements in the array.

```
Private Sub Command1_Click ()
   Dim intX As Integer
   Dim frmNew(1 To 5) As New Form1
   For intX = 1 To 5
      frmNew(intX).Show
      frmNew(intX).WindowState = vbMinimized
      ' To create minimized forms without having them
      ' first appear briefly at normal size, reverse
      ' the order of the two lines above.
   Next
End Sub
```

Pressing the command button to execute the code above will create five minimized instances of Form1.

> **Note** If you look at the Taskbar, you'll see Form1 *six* times. The extra instance of Form1 isn't minimized — it's the one you started with.

Arrays of Control Variables

You can declare an array of controls with Private, Dim, ReDim, Static, or Public in the same way you declare an array of any other type. Unlike form arrays, however, control arrays cannot be declared with the New keyword. For example, you can declare an array to be a specific control type:

```
ReDim ActiveImages(10) As Image
```

When you declare an array to be a particular control type, you can assign only controls of that type to the array. In the case of the preceding declaration, for example, you can only assign image controls to the array — but those image controls can come from different forms.

Contrast this with the built-in Controls collection, which can contain many different types of controls — all which must be on the same form.

Alternatively, you can declare an array of generic control variables. For example, you might want to keep track of every control that was dropped onto a particular control, and not allow any control to be dropped more than once. You can do this by maintaining a dynamic array of control variables that contains references to each control that has been dropped:

```
Private Sub List1_DragDrop(Source As VB.Control, _
      X As Single, Y As Single)
   Dim intX As Integer
   Static intSize As Integer
   Static ctlDropped() As Control
   For intX = 1 To intSize
      ' If the dropped control is in the array, it's
      ' already been dropped here once.
      If ctlDropped(intX) Is Source Then
         Beep
         Exit Sub
      End If
   Next
   ' Enlarge the array.
   intSize = intSize + 1
   ReDim Preserve ctlDropped(intSize)
   ' Save a reference to the control that was dropped.
   Set ctlDropped(intSize) = Source
   ' Add the name of the control to the list box.
   List1.AddItem Source.Name
End Sub
```

This example uses the Is operator to compare the variables in the control array with the control argument. The Is operator can be used to test the identity of Visual Basic object references: If you compare two different references to the same object, the Is operator returns True.

The example also uses the Set statement to assign the object reference in the Source argument to an element in the array.

For More Information See "Is Operator" in Appendix C, "Operators" of the *Microsoft Visual Basic 6.0 Language Reference* volume of the *Microsoft Visual Basic 6.0 Reference Library*.

Arrays are introduced in "Arrays" and "Dynamic Arrays" in Chapter 5, "Programming Fundamentals."

Creating Collections of Objects

Collections provide a useful way to keep track of objects. Unlike arrays, Collection objects don't have to be re-dimensioned as you add and remove members.

For example, you might want to keep track of every control that was dropped onto a particular control, and not allow any control to be dropped more than once. You can do this by maintaining a Collection that contains references to each control that has been dropped:

```
Private Sub List1_DragDrop(Source As VB.Control, _
X As Single, Y As Single)
   Dim vnt As Variant
   Static colDroppedControls As New Collection
   For Each vnt In colDroppedControls
      ' If the dropped control is in the collection,
      ' it's already been dropped here once.
      If vnt Is Source Then
         Beep
         Exit Sub
      End If
   Next
   ' Save a reference to the control that was dropped.
   colDroppedControls.Add Source
   ' Add the name of the control to the list box.
   List1.AddItem Source.Name
End Sub
```

This example uses the Is operator to compare the object references in the `colDroppedControls` collection with the event argument containing the reference to the dropped control. The Is operator can be used to test the identity of Visual Basic object references: If you compare two different references to the same object, the Is operator returns True.

The example also uses the Add method of the Collection object to place a reference to the dropped control in the collection.

Unlike arrays, Collections are objects themselves. The variable `colDroppedControls` is declared As New, so that an instance of the Collection class will be created the first time the variable is referred to in code. The variable is also declared Static, so that the Collection object will not be destroyed when the event procedure ends.

For More Information See "Is Operator" in Appendix C, "Operators" of the *Microsoft Visual Basic 6.0 Language Reference*.

Properties and methods of the Collection object are discussed in "The Visual Basic Collection Object" later in this chapter.

To compare the code above with the code required to use arrays, see "Creating Arrays of Objects," earlier in this chapter.

To learn how to create more robust collections by wrapping the Collection object in your own collection class, see "Creating Your Own Collection Classes" later in this chapter.

"What You Need to Know About Objects in Visual Basic," earlier in this chapter, describes how objects are created and destroyed.

The Visual Basic Collection Object

A collection is a way of grouping a set of related items. Collections are used in Visual Basic to keep track of many things, such as the loaded forms in your program (the Forms collection), or all the controls on a form (the Controls collection).

Visual Basic provides the generic Collection class to give you the ability to define your own collections. You can create as many Collection objects — that is, instances of the Collection class — as you need. You can use Collection objects as the basis for your own collection classes and object models, as discussed in "Creating Your Own Collection Classes" and "Object Models" later in this chapter.

For example, collections are a good way to keep track of multiple forms. "Multiple Document Interface (MDI) Applications" in Chapter 6, "Creating a User Interface," discusses applications in which the user can open any number of document windows. The following code fragment shows how you might use the Add method of a collection object to keep a list of MDI child windows the user has created. This code assumes that you have a form named mdiDocument, whose MDIChild property is set to True.

```
' Module-level collection in the parent MDIForm.
Public colDocuments As New Collection

' Code for creating a new MDI child document form.
Private Sub mnuFileNew()
   Dim f As New mdiDocument
   Static intDocumentNumber As Integer
   intDocumentNumber = intDocumentNumber + 1
   ' The following line creates the form.
   f.Caption = "Document" & intDocumentNumber
   ' Add the object reference to the collection.
   colDocuments.Add f
   f.Show
End Sub
```

The `colDocuments` collection acts like a subset of the built-in Forms collection, containing only instances of the form mdiDocument. The size of the collection is adjusted automatically as each new form is added. You can use For Each ... Next to iterate through the collection. If you want to give the form a key by which it can be retrieved, you can supply a text string as the second parameter of the Add method, as described later in this section.

The New keyword in the declaration for the variable `colDocuments` causes a Collection object to be created the first time the variable is referred to in code. Because Collection is a class, rather than a data type, you must create an instance of it and keep a reference to that instance (object) in a variable.

Like any other object, a Collection object will be destroyed when the last variable that contains a reference to it is set to Nothing or goes out of scope. All the object references it contains will be released. For this reason, the variable `colDocuments` is declared in the parent MDIForm, so that it exists throughout the life of the program.

> **Note** If you use a collection to keep track of forms, use the collection's Remove method to delete the object reference from the collection after you unload the form. You cannot reclaim the memory the form was using as long as a reference to the form still exists, and the reference the Collection object is holding is just as good as a reference in an object variable.

What's a Collection Object Made Of?

A Collection object stores each item in a Variant. Thus the list of things you can add to a Collection object is the same as the list of things that can be stored in a Variant. This include standard data types, objects, and arrays — but not user-defined types.

Variants always take up 16 bytes, no matter what's stored in them, so using a Collection object is not as efficient as using arrays. However, you never have to ReDim a Collection object, which results in much cleaner, more maintainable code. In addition, Collection objects have extremely fast look-ups by key, which arrays do not.

> **Note** To be precise, a Variant always takes up 16 bytes *even if the data are actually stored elsewhere.* For example, if you assign a string or an array to a Variant, the Variant contains a pointer to a copy of the string or array data. Only 4 bytes of the Variant is used for the pointer on 32-bit systems, and none of the data is actually inside the Variant.
>
> If you store an object, the Variant contains the object reference, just as an object variable would. As with strings and arrays, only 4 bytes of the Variant are being used.
>
> Numeric data types are stored inside the Variant. Regardless of the data type, the Variant still takes up 16 bytes.
>
> Despite the size of Variants, there will be many cases where it makes sense to use a Collection object to store all of the data types listed above. Just be aware of the tradeoff you're making: Collection objects allow you to write very clean, maintainable code — at the cost of storing items in Variants.

Properties and Methods of the Collection Object

Each Collection object comes with properties and methods you can use to insert, delete, and retrieve the items in the collection.

Property or method	Description
Add method	Add items to the collection.
Count property	Return the number of items in the collection. Read-only.
Item method	Return an item, by index or by key.
Remove method	Delete an item from the collection, by index or by key.

These properties and methods provide only the most basic services for collections. For example, the Add method cannot check the type of object being added to a collection, to ensure that the collection contains only one kind of object. You can provide more robust functionality — and additional properties, methods, and events — by creating your own collection class, as described in "Creating Your Own Collection Classes" later in this chapter.

The basic services of adding, deleting, and retrieving from a collection depend on keys and indexes. A *key* is String value. It could be a name, a driver's license number, a social security number, or simply an Integer converted to a String. The Add method allows you to associate a key with an item, as described later in this section.

An *index* is a Long between one (1) and the number of items in the collection. You can control the initial value of an item's index, using the ***before*** and ***after*** named parameters, but its value may change as other items are added and deleted.

> **Note** A collection whose index begins at 1 is called *one-based*, as explained in "Collections in Visual Basic," online.

You can use the index to iterate over the items in a collection. For example, the following code shows two ways to give all the employees in a collection of Employee objects a 10 percent raise, assuming that the variable `mcolEmployees` contains a reference to a Collection object.

```
Dim lngCt As Long
For lngCt = 1 To mcolEmployees.Count
   mcolEmployees(lngCt).Rate = _
      mcolEmployees(lngCt).Rate * 1.1
Next

Dim emp As Employee
For Each emp In mcolEmployees
   emp.Rate = emp.Rate * 1.1
Next
```

Tip For better performance, use For Each to iterate over the items in a Collection object. For Each is significantly faster than iterating with the index. This is not true of all collection implementations — it's dependent on the way the collection stores data internally.

Adding Items to a Collection

Use the Add method to add an item to a collection. The syntax is:

Sub Add (*item* **As Variant [,** *key* **As Variant] [,** ***before*** **As Variant]**

[, ***after*** **As Variant])**

For example, to add a work order object to a collection of work orders using the work order's ID property as the key, you can write:

```
colWorkOrders.Add woNew, woNew.ID
```

This assumes that the ID property is a String. If the property is a number (for example, a Long), use the CStr function to convert it to the String value required for keys:

```
colWorkOrders.Add woNew, CStr(woNew.ID)
```

The Add method supports named arguments. To add an item as the third element, you can write:

```
colWorkOrders.Add woNew, woNew.ID, after:=2
```

You can use the ***before*** and ***after*** named arguments to maintain an ordered collection of objects. For example, `before:=1` inserts an item at the beginning of the collection, because Collection objects are one-based.

Deleting Items from a Collection

Use the Remove method to delete an item from a collection. The syntax is:

object.**Remove** *index*

The *index* argument can either be the position of the item you want to delete, or the item's key. If the key of the third element in a collection is "W017493," you can use either of these two statements to delete it:

```
colWorkOrders.Remove 3
```

– or –

```
colWorkOrders.Remove "W017493"
```

Retrieving Items from a Collection

Use the Item method to retrieve specific items from a collection. The syntax is:

[Set] *variable* = *object*.**Item(***index***)**

As with the Remove method, the index can be either the position in the collection, or the item's key. Using the same example as for the Remove method, either of these statements will retrieve the third element in the collection:

```
Set woCurrent = colWorkOrders.Item(3)
```

– or –

```
Set woCurrent = colWorkOrders.Item("W017493")
```

If you use whole numbers as keys, you must use the CStr function to convert them to strings before passing them to the Item or Remove methods. A Collection object always assumes that a whole number is an index.

> **Tip** Don't let Collection objects decide whether a value you're passing is an index or a key. If you want a value to be interpreted as a key, and the variable that contains the value is anything but String, use CStr to convert it. If you want a value to be interpreted as an index, and the variable that contains the value is not one of the integer data types, use CLng to convert it.

Item Is the Default Method

The Item method is the default method for a Collection object, so you can omit it when you access an item in a collection. Thus the previous code example could also be written:

```
Set woCurrent = colWorkOrders(3)
```

– or –

```
Set woCurrent = colWorkOrders("W017493")
```

> **Important** Collection objects maintain their numeric index numbers automatically as you add and delete elements. The numeric index of a given element will thus change over time. Do not save a numeric index value and expect it to retrieve the same element later in your program. Use keys for this purpose.

Using the Item Method to Invoke Properties and Methods

You don't have to retrieve an object reference from a collection and place it in an object variable in order to use it. You can use the reference while it's still in the collection.

For example, suppose the WorkOrder object in the code above has a Priority property. The following statements will both set the priority of a work order:

```
colWorkOrders.Item("W017493").Priority = 3
colWorkOrders("W017493").Priority = 3
```

The reason this works is that Visual Basic evaluates the expression from left to right. When it comes to the Item method — explicit or implied — Visual Basic gets a reference to the indicated item (in this case, the WorkOrder object whose key is `W017493`), and uses this reference to evaluate the rest of the line.

> **Tip** If you're going to invoke more than one property or method of an object in a collection, copy the object reference to a strongly typed object variable first. Using an object reference while it's still in a collection is slower than using it after placing it in a strongly typed object variable (for example, `Dim woCurrent As WorkOrder`), because the Collection object stores items in Variants. Object references in Variants are always late bound.

For More Information The Collection object is also a useful alternative to arrays for many ordinary programming tasks. See "Using Collections as an Alternative to Arrays" in Chapter 8, "More About Programming."

Collections in Visual Basic

What is a collection? In "The Visual Basic Collection Object," earlier in this chapter, a collection was defined as a way of grouping related objects. That leaves a lot of room for interpretation; it's more of a concept than a definition.

In fact, as you'll see when you begin comparing collections, there are a lot of differences even among the kinds of collections provided in Visual Basic. For example, the following code causes an error:

```
Dim col As Collection
Set col = Forms    ' Error!
```

What's happening here? The Forms collection is a collection; the variable `col` is declared As Collection; why can't you assign a reference to Forms to the variable `col`?

The reason for this is that the Collection class and the Forms collection are not *polymorphic*; that is, you can't exchange one for the other, because they were developed from separate code bases. They don't have the same methods, store object references in the same way, or use the same kinds of index values.

This makes the Collection class's name seem like an odd choice, because it really represents only one of many possible collection implementations. This topic explores some of the implementation differences you'll encounter.

Zero-Based and One-Based Collections

A collection is either *zero-based* or *one-based*, depending on what its starting index is. As you might guess, the former means that the index of the first item in the collection is zero, and the latter means it's one. Examples of zero-based collections are the Forms and Controls collections. The Collection object is an example of a one-based collection.

Older collections in Visual Basic are more likely to be zero-based, while more recent additions are more likely to be one-based. One-based collections are somewhat more intuitive to use, because the index ranges from one to Count, where Count is the property that returns the number of items in a collection.

The index of a zero-based collection, by contrast, ranges from zero to one less than the Count property.

Index and Key Values

Many collections in Visual Basic allow you to access an item using either a numeric index or a string key, as the Visual Basic Collection object does. (Visual Basic's Collection object allows you to add items without specifying a key, however.)

The Forms collection, by contrast, allows only a numeric index. This is because there's no unique string value associated with a form. For example, you can have multiple forms with the same caption, or multiple loaded forms with the same Name property.

Adding and Removing Items

Collections also differ in whether or not you can add items to them, and if so, how those items are added. You can't add a printer to the Printers collection using Visual Basic code, for example.

Because the Collection object is a general-purpose programming tool, it's more flexible than other collections. It has an Add method you can use to put items into the collection, and a Remove method for taking items out.

By contrast, the only way to get a form into the Forms collection is to load the form. If you create a form with the New operator, or by referring to a variable declared As New, it will not be added to the Forms collection until you use the Load statement to load it.

The Forms and Controls collections don't have Remove methods. You add and remove forms and controls from these collections indirectly, by using the Load and Unload statements.

What Has It Got in Its Pocketses?

As noted above, a form is not added to the Forms collection until it's loaded. Thus the most accurate specification of the Forms collection is that it contains *all of the currently loaded forms in the program.*

Even that's not completely accurate. If your project uses Microsoft Forms (included for compatibility with Microsoft Office), you'll find those forms in a separate collection named UserForms. So the Forms collection contains *all of the currently loaded Visual Basic forms in the program.*

The contents of the Collection class are very precisely specified: *anything that can be stored in a* Variant. Thus the Collection object can contain an object or an integer, but not a user-defined type.

Unfortunately, this specification covers a lot of territory — a given instance of the Collection class could store any mongrel assortment of data types, arrays, and objects.

> **Tip** One of the most important reasons for creating your own collection classes, as discussed in "Creating Your Own Collection Classes," later in this chapter, is so you can control the contents of your collections — a concept called *type safety*.

Enumerating a Collection

You can use For Each … Next to enumerate the items in a collection, without worrying about whether the collection is zero-based or one-based. Of course, this is hardly a defining characteristic of collections, because Visual Basic allows you to use For Each … Next to enumerate the items in an array.

What makes For Each … Next work is a tiny object called an *enumerator*. An enumerator keeps track of where you are in a collection, and returns the next item when it's needed.

When you enumerate an array, Visual Basic creates an array enumerator object on the fly. Collections have their own enumerator objects, which are also created as needed.

Enumerators Don't Skip Items

The enumerators of collections in Visual Basic don't skip items. For example, suppose you enumerate a collection containing "A," "B," and "C," and that while doing so you remove "B." Visual Basic collections will not skip over "C" when you do this.

Enumerators May Not Catch Added Items

If you add items to a collection while enumerating it, some enumerators will include the added items, while some will not. The Forms collection, for example, will not enumerate any forms you load while enumerating.

The Collection object will enumerate items you add while enumerating, if you allow them to be added at the end of the collection. Thus the following loop never ends (until you hit CTRL+BREAK, that is):

```
Dim col As New Collection
Dim vnt As Variant
col.Add "Endless"
col.Add "Endless"
For Each vnt In col
   MsgBox vnt
   col.Add "Endless"
Next
```

On the other hand, items you add at the beginning of the collection will not be included in the enumeration:

```
Dim col As New Collection
Dim vnt As Variant
col.Add "Will be enumerated"
For Each vnt In col
   MsgBox vnt
   ' Add the item at the beginning.
   col.Add "Won't be enumerated", Before:=1
Next
```

Why Enumerators?

By emitting a new enumerator each time a For Each … Next begins, a collection allows nested enumerations. For example, suppose you have a reference to a Collection object in the variable `mcolStrings`, and that the collection contains only strings. The following code prints all the combinations of two different strings:

```
Dim vnt1 As Variant
Dim vnt2 As Variant
For Each vnt1 In mcolStrings
   For Each vnt2 In mcolStrings
      If vnt1 <> vnt2 Then
         Debug.Print vnt1 & " " & vnt2
      End If
   Next
Next
```

For More Information See "Creating Your Own Collection Classes" later in this chapter.

Finding Out About Objects

The Object Browser is based on *type libraries*, resources that contain detailed descriptions of classes, including properties, methods, events, named constants, and more.

Visual Basic creates type library information for the classes you create, provides type libraries for the objects it includes, and lets you access the type libraries provided by other applications.

You can use the Object Browser to display the classes available in projects and libraries, including the classes you've defined. The objects you create from those classes will have the same members — properties, methods, and events — that you see in the Object Browser.

Figure 9.1 The Object Browser

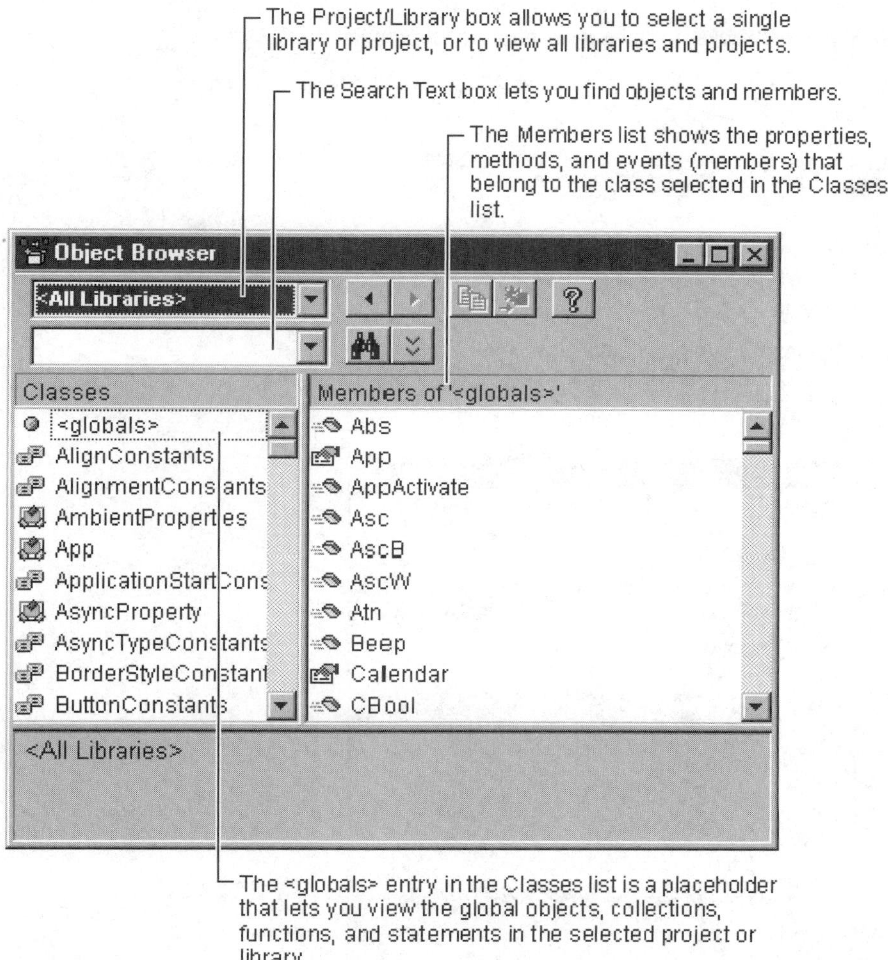
The Project/Library box allows you to select a single library or project, or to view all libraries and projects.
The Search Text box lets you find objects and members.
The Members list shows the properties, methods, and events (members) that belong to the class selected in the Classes list.
Object Browser
<All Libraries>
Classes
<globals>
AlignConstants
AlignmentConstants
AmbientProperties
App
ApplicationStartCons
AsyncProperty
AsyncTypeConstants
BorderStyleConstant
ButtonConstants
Members of '<globals>'
Abs
App
AppActivate
Asc
AscB
AscW
Atn
Beep
Calendar
CBool
<All Libraries>
The <globals> entry in the Classes list is a placeholder that lets you view the global objects, collections, functions, and statements in the selected project or library.

To display the Object Browser

- From the **View** menu, choose **Object Browser**.

  – or –

  Press F2.

  – or –

  Click the **Object Browser** button on the toolbar.

By default, the Object Browser cannot be docked to other windows. This allows you to move between the Object Browser and code windows using CTRL+TAB. You can change this by right-clicking the Object Browser to open its context menu, and clicking Dockable.

Note When the Object Browser is dockable, you cannot use CTRL+TAB to move to it from your code windows.

Contents of the Object Browser

The Object Browser displays information in a three-level hierarchy, as shown in Figure 9.2. Beginning from the top, you can select from available projects and libraries, including your own Visual Basic projects, using the Project/Library box.

Figure 9.2 Viewing a class's members in the Object Browser

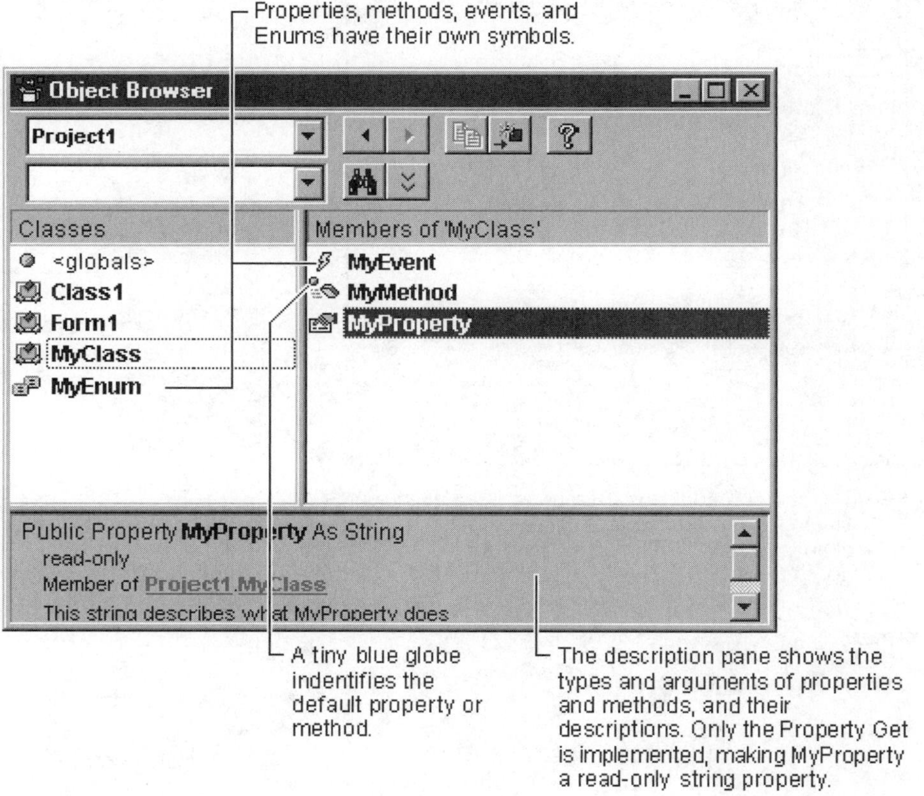

- Click on a class in the Classes list to view its description in the description pane at the bottom. The class's properties, methods, events, and constants will appear in the Members list on the right. The classes available are drawn from the project or library selected in the Project/Library box, or from all projects and libraries if <All Libraries> is selected.
- You can view the arguments and return values of a member of the selected class, by clicking on the member in the Members list. The description pane at the bottom of the Object Browser shows this information.
- You can jump to the library or object that includes a member by clicking the library or object name in the description pane. You can return by clicking the Go Back button at the top of the Object Browser.

  Tip When you're in either the Classes list or the Members list, typing the first character of a name will move to the next name that begins with that character.

Controlling the Contents of the Object Browser

The context menu, shown in Figure 9.3, provides an alternative to the Copy and View Definition buttons on the Object Browser. It also allows you to open the References dialog box, and — if a class or member is selected — to view the properties of the selected item. You can set descriptions for your own objects using this menu item, as described in "Adding Descriptions for Your Objects" later in this chapter.

Figure 9.3 The Object Browser's context menu

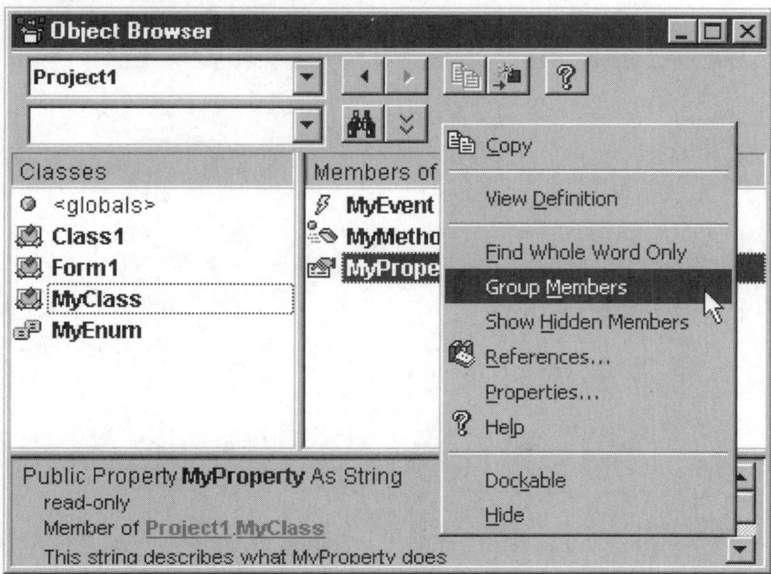

Right-clicking on the Object Browser brings up the context menu. In addition to the functions mentioned above, the context menu controls the contents of the Classes list and the Members list.

- When Group Members is checked, all the properties of an object are grouped together, all the methods are grouped together, and so on. When Group Members is not checked, the Members list is alphabetical.
- When Show Hidden Members is checked, the Class list and Members list display information marked as hidden in the type library. Normally you don't need to see this information. Hidden members are shown in light gray type.

  Tip When Group Members is selected, typing the first letter of a name will jump to the next name that begins with that character, even if the name is in another group.

Finding and Browsing Objects

You can use the Object Browser to find objects and their members, and to identify the projects or libraries they come from.

Enter text in the Search Text box and then click the Search button (or press ENTER). The classes and members whose names include the text you specified will appear in the Search Results list.

For example, Figure 9.4 shows the results of typing "printer" in the Search Text box and clicking the Search button.

Figure 9.4 Using the Search button

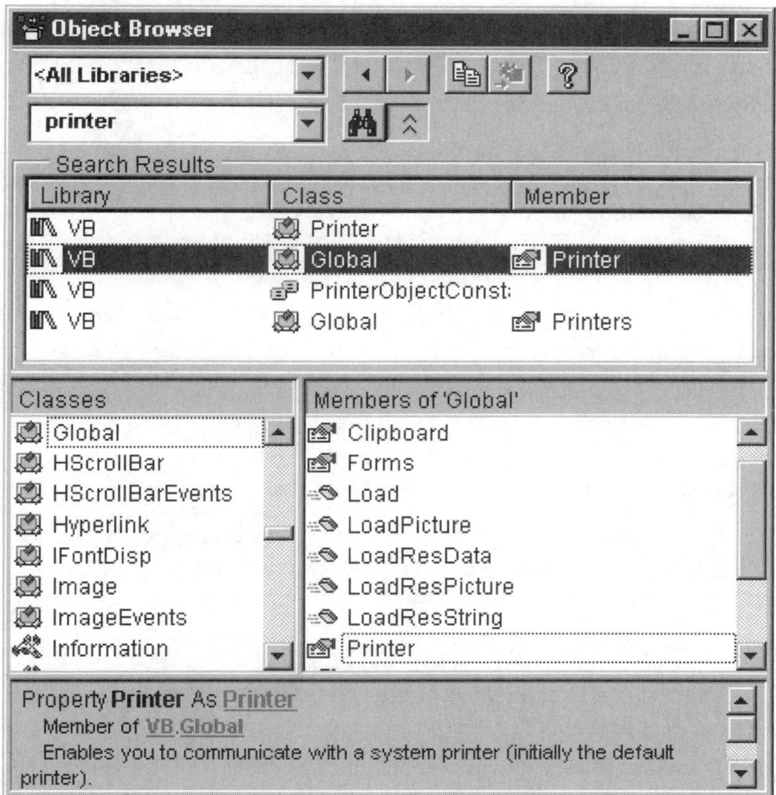

You can select an item in the Search Results list, and view its description in the description pane at the bottom of the Object Browser. Clicking on the underlined jumps in the description pane selects the indicated library or navigates to the object or member.

You can restrict the search to items that exactly match the string in the Search box by checking Find Whole Word Only on the context menu.

Adding Descriptions for Your Objects

You can use the Object Browser to add descriptions and HelpContextIDs to your own procedures, modules, classes, properties, and methods. You may find these descriptions useful while working with your classes.

> **Note** You can also enter descriptions for properties, methods, and events using the Procedure Attributes dialog box, accessed from the Tools menu.

To enter description strings and link your classes and their members to Help topics

1. Press F2 to open the **Object Browser**. In the **Project/Library** box, select your project.
2. In the **Classes** list, right click the name of a class to bring up the context menu, and click **Properties** to open the **Member Options** dialog box.

   Alternatively, in the **Members** list you can right click the name of a property, method, or event you added to the class. On the context menu, click **Properties**. If the member is Private or Friend, this will open the **Member Options** dialog box. If the member is Public — that is, part of the class's interface — it will open the **Procedure Attributes** dialog box instead.

   Note The difference between these two dialog boxes is that the **Procedure Attributes** dialog box has an **Advanced** button that can be used to make a member the default for the class, as described in "Making a Property or Method the Default" later in this chapter.

3. In the **Help Context ID** box, type the context ID of the Help topic to be shown if you click the "?" button when this class or member is selected in the **Object Browser**.

   Note You can create a Help file for your own use, and link topics to your classes and their members. To specify a Help file for your project, use the **General** tab of the **Project Properties** dialog box, accessed from the **Project** menu.

4. In the **Description** box, type a brief description of the class or member.
5. Click **OK** to return to the **Object Browser**. The description string you entered should appear in the description pane at the bottom of the browser.
6. Repeat steps 2 through 5 for each class and for each member of each class.

   Note You cannot supply browser strings or Help topics for enumerations.

For More Information Enumerations are introduced in "Using Enumerations to Work with Sets of Constants" in Chapter 8, "More About Programming."

Moving Between Procedures

You can use the Object Browser to move quickly to the code for a class, module, or procedure in your project.

To move to a class, module, or procedure

1. (Optional) Select your project from the **Project/Library** box.

   Step 1 is optional if you have **<All Libraries>** selected in the **Project/Library** box, because all of your projects are included.

2. Names of classes, modules, and members that belong to your projects are shown in bold type. Double-click any name shown in bold type to move to that class, module, or member. (Or right-click a name and then select **View Definition** from the context window.)

   The selected item is displayed in the Code window.

Browsing Objects from Other Applications

From within Visual Basic, you can access and control objects supplied by other applications. For example, if you have Microsoft Project and Microsoft Excel on your system, you could use a Graph object from Microsoft Excel and a Calendar object from Microsoft Project as part of your application.

You can use the Object Browser to explore the type libraries of other applications. A *type library* provides information about the objects provided by other applications.

> **Note** In the Project/Library list, there are separate entries for Visual Basic (VB) and Visual Basic for Applications (VBA). Although we speak of "objects provided by Visual Basic," you'll notice that the Collection object is provided by VBA.

You can add libraries to your project by selecting References from the Object Browser's context menu, to open the References dialog box.

For More Information For more details on using Automation to combine and manipulate objects from other applications, see Chapter 10, "Programming with Components."

Creating Your Own Classes

If you're an experienced programmer, you already have a library of useful functions you've written over the years. Objects don't replace functions — you'll still write and use utility functions — but they provide a convenient, logical way to organize procedures and data.

In particular, the classes from which you create objects combine data and procedures into a unit.

Classes: Putting User-Defined Types and Procedures Together

User-defined types are a powerful tool for grouping related items of data. Consider, for example, the user-defined type named `udtAccount` defined here:

```
Public Type udtAccount
   Number As Long
   Type As Byte
   CustomerName As String
   Balance As Double
End Type
```

You can declare a variable of type `udtAccount`, set the values of its fields individually, and then pass the whole record to procedures that print it, save it to a database, perform computations on it, validate its fields, and so on.

Powerful as they are, user-defined types present the programmer with some problems. You may create a Withdrawal procedure that raises an error if a withdrawal exceeds the balance in the account, but there's nothing to prevent the Balance field from being reduced by other code in your program.

In other words, the connection between procedures and user-defined types depends on the discipline, memory, and knowledge of the programmer maintaining the code.

Objects: User-Defined Types with an Attitude

Object-oriented programming solves this problem by combining data and procedures in a single entity, as shown in Figure 9.5.

Figure 9.5 Objects combine data and procedures

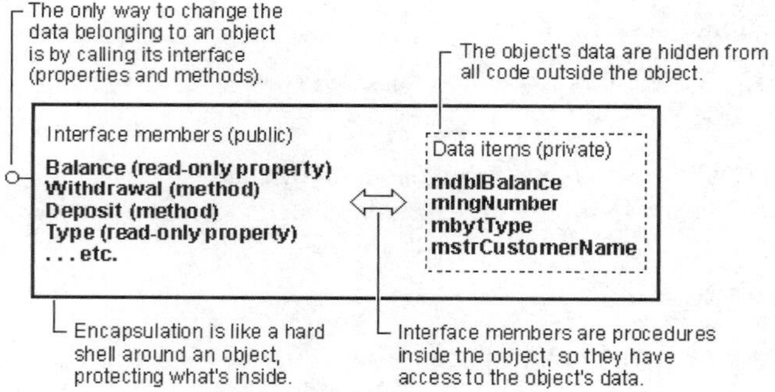

When the user-defined type `udtAccount` becomes the Account class, its data become private, and the procedures that access them move inside the class and become properties and methods. This is what's meant by the term *encapsulation* — that is, an object is a unit (a *capsule*, if you will) containing both code and data.

When you create an Account object from the class, the only way you can access its data is through the properties and methods that make up its interface. The following code fragment shows how the procedures inside the Account class support encapsulation:

```
' The account balance is hidden from outside code.
Private mdblBalance As Double

' The read-only Balance property allows outside code
' to find out the account balance.
Public Property Get Balance() As Double
   Balance = mdblBalance
End Property
```

```
' The Withdrawal method changes the account balance,
' but only if an overdraft error doesn't occur.
Public Sub Withdrawal(ByVal Amount As Double)
   If Amount > Balance Then
      Err.Raise Number:=vbObjectError + 2081, _
      Description:="Overdraft"
   End If
   mdblBalance = mdblBalance - Amount
End Sub
```

For the moment, don't worry about how you get the procedures inside the class, or about understanding the syntax of property procedures and private variables. The important thing to remember is that you can define an object that encapsulates and validates its own data.

With the Account object, you never have be concerned about whether you've called the right procedures to update the account, because the only procedures you can call are built into the object.

For More Information "Customizing Form Classes," below, puts property and method creation into a framework you're already familiar with. Later in this chapter, "Adding Properties and Methods to a Class" will explain the syntax.

You can read about user-defined types in "Creating Your Own Data Types" in Chapter 8, "More About Programming."

For details about Sub and Function procedures, see "Introduction to Procedures" in Chapter 5, "Programming Fundamentals."

Customizing Form Classes

It may surprise you to learn that you've been creating classes for as long as you've been programming in Visual Basic. It's true: Form1, that familiar denizen of every project you've ever started, is really — a class.

To see this, open a new Standard Exe project. Add a button to Form1, and place the following code in its Click event:

```
Private Sub Command1.Click()
   Dim f As New Form1
   f.Show
End Sub
```

Press F5 to run the project, and click the button. Holy smokes, there's another instance of Form1! Click its button. There's another! Every instance you create looks the same, and has the same behavior, because they're all instances of the Form1 class.

What's Going On Here?

If you've read "Working with Objects" in Chapter 5, "Programming Fundamentals," you know that an object variable declared As New contains Nothing until the first time you refer to it in code. When you use the variable for the first time, Visual Basic notices that it contains the special value Nothing, and creates an instance of the class. (And a good thing it does, too, or `f.Show` would cause an error.)

Me and My Hidden Global Variable

You may be wondering how it is that you can refer to Form1 in code, as if it were an object variable. There's no magic involved. Visual Basic creates a hidden global object variable for every form class. It's as if Visual Basic had added the following declaration to your project:

```
Public Form1 As New Form1
```

When you select Form1 as your startup object, or type `Form1.Show` in code, you're referring to this hidden global object variable. Because it's declared As New, an instance of the Form1 class is created the first time you use this predeclared variable in code.

The reason this declaration is hidden is that Visual Basic changes it every time you change the Name property of a form. In this way, the hidden variable always has the same name as the form class.

A Very Short Quiz

Which of the instances of Form1 you created in the exercise above was associated with the hidden global variable? If you guessed the first one, you're right. Form1 is the default startup object for the project, and to Visual Basic that's just like using the predeclared global variable `Form1` in code.

> **Tip** After you unload a form, you should always set any references to the form to Nothing in order to free the memory and resources the form was using. The reference most often overlooked is the hidden global form variable.

What About All Those Other Instances of Form1?

In Chapter 5, "Programming Fundamentals," you learned that to refer to an object, you need an object variable, and that an object exists only as long as there's at least one object variable containing a reference to it. So what was keeping all those other instances alive?

The second instance of Form1, and all the ones that followed, had an object variable for just as long as it took to call their Show methods. Then that variable went out of scope, and was set to Nothing. But Visual Basic keeps a special collection named Forms, which you can read about in "More About Forms" in Chapter 6, "Creating a User Interface." The Forms collection contains a reference to each of the loaded forms in your project, so that you can always find and control them.

Note As you'll learn, this is not true of all classes. For example, the classes you design won't have hidden global variables or global collections to keep track of them — those are special features of form classes. However, you can declare your own global variables, and you can create your own collections — as described in "Creating Your Own Collection Classes," later in this chapter.

Properties, Methods, and Events of Form Classes

The first time you added a property to a form class, you probably did it visually, by dropping a command button (or some other control) on Form1. In doing so, you added a read-only Command1 property to the form class. Thereafter, you invoked this property of Form1 whenever you needed to call a method or property of the command button:

```
Command1.Caption = "Click Me"
```

When you changed the Name property of any control on a form, Visual Basic quietly changed the name of the read-only property, so they always matched.

If you still have the project open from the earlier exercise, you can see this Command1 property by pressing F2 to open the Object Browser. In the Project/Library box, select Project1. You'll see Form1 in the Classes pane. In the Members pane, scroll down until you find Command1, and select it.

Command1 has a property symbol beside it, and if you look in the description pane, you'll see that it's a WithEvents property. As you'll learn in "Adding Events to a Class," later in this chapter, this means that the property (or object variable) has event procedures associated with it. One of those event procedures, Command1_Click(), may have been the first place you ever wrote Visual Basic code.

But Wait, There's More

Dropping controls on a form is not the only way to add new members to the form class. You can add your own custom properties, methods, and events, as easily as you create new variables and procedures.

To see this, add the following code to the Declarations section of Form1:

```
' The Comment property of the Form1 class.
Public Comment As String
```

Add the following code to the Click event of Form1:

```
Private Sub Form_Click()
   MsgBox Comment, , "My comment is:"
End Sub
```

Finally, change the code in the Command1_Click() event procedure by adding a line, as follows:

```
Private Sub Command1.Click()
   Dim f As New Form1
   f.Comment = InputBox("What's my comment?")
   f.Show
End Sub
```

Press F5 to run the project. Click Command1, and when the input box appears, type in some racy comment and click OK. When the new instance of Form1 appears, click on it to play back its Comment property.

Click on the first instance of Form1, and notice that its Comment property is blank. Because Visual Basic created this instance as the Startup Object, you never got a chance to set its Comment property.

Forms Can Call Each Other's Methods

If you were watching closely, you may have noticed that the code you added to the Form1 class didn't set the object's own Comment property — it set the Comment property of the *new* instance of Form1 it was creating.

This ability of forms to set each other's properties and call each other's methods is a very useful technique. For example, when an MDIForm is opening a new child window, it can initialize the new window by setting its properties and calling its methods.

You can also use this technique to pass information between forms.

> **Tip** You can create custom events for forms. "Adding an Event to a Form" later in this chapter, provides a step by step procedure.

Other Kinds of Modules

You add properties, methods, and events to form classes by putting code in their code modules. In the same way, you can add properties, methods, and events to class modules and — if you have the Professional or Enterprise Edition of Visual Basic — to UserControl and UserDocument code modules.

As you read "Adding Properties and Methods to a Class" and "Adding Events to a Class," later in this chapter, remember that everything you read applies to form classes as well as to class modules.

For More Information What the heck is a class module? "Class Module Step by Step," on the next page, shows how to define a class and illustrates the life cycle of the objects you create from that class.

Class Module Step by Step

This example shows how you can use class modules to define classes, from which you can then create objects. It will also show you how to create properties and methods for the new class, and demonstrate how objects are created and destroyed.

Open a new Standard Exe project, and insert a class module by selecting Add Class Module from the Project menu. Draw four command buttons on the form. The following table lists the property values you need to set for the objects in this example.

Object	Property	Setting
Class module	Name	Thing
Command1	Caption	Show the Thing
Command2	Caption	Reverse the Thing's Name
Command3	Caption	Create New Thing
Command4	Caption	Temporary Thing

> **Note** Class modules are saved in files with the extension .cls.

In the class module Declarations section, add the following:

```
Option Explicit
Public Name As String
Private mdtmCreated As Date
```

The variable `Name` will be a property of the Thing object, because it's declared Public.

> **Note** Don't confuse this Name property with the Name property of the class module, which the table above instructed you to set. (The Name property of the class module gives the Thing class its name.) Why would you give the Thing class a Name property? A better question might be, why not? You may want to give the Thing class a Name property because Things should have names! Remember that there's nothing special about the property and method names Visual Basic uses. You can use those same property and method names for your classes.

The variable `mdtmCreated` is a private data member that is used to store the value of the read-only Created property. The Created property returns the date and time a Thing object was created. To implement the Created property, add the following Property Get to the Declarations section of the class module:

```
Property Get Created() As Date
   Created = mdtmCreated
End Property
```

Note If you added the property procedure using the Add Procedure dialog box, on the Tools menu, be sure to delete the Property Let declaration that is automatically added by this dialog. Property Let is only required for read-write properties, as explained in "Putting Property Procedures to Work for You," later in this chapter.

The Thing object has one method, ReverseName, which simply reverses the order of the letters in the Name property. It doesn't return a value, so it's implemented as a Sub procedure. Add the following Sub procedure to the class module.

```
Public Sub ReverseName()
   Dim intCt As Integer
   Dim strNew As String
   For intCt = 1 To Len(Name)
      strNew = Mid$(Name, intCt, 1) & strNew
   Next
   Name = strNew
End Sub
```

Class modules have two events, Initialize and Terminate. In the Object drop down of the class module, select Class. The Procedure drop down will show the events. Place the following code in the event procedures:

```
Private Sub Class_Initialize()
   ' Set date/time of object creation, to be returned
   '  by the read-only Created property.
   mdtmCreated = Now
   ' Display object properties.
   MsgBox "Name: " & Name & vbCrLf & "Created: " _
   & Created, , "Thing Initialize"
End Sub

Private Sub Class_Terminate()
   ' Display object properties.
   MsgBox "Name: " & Name & vbCrLf & "Created: " _
   & Created, , "Thing Terminate"
End Sub
```

Usually, the Initialize event procedure contains any code that needs to be executed at the moment the object is created, such as providing the time stamp for the Created property. The Terminate event contains any code you need to execute in order to clean up after the object when it is being destroyed.

In this example, the two events are being used primarily to give you a visual indication that a Thing object is being created or destroyed.

Using the Thing Object

Add this declaration to the Declarations section of the form module:

```
Option Explicit
Private mth As Thing
```

The variable `mth` will hold a reference to a Thing object, which will be created in the form's Load event. Put the following code in the Form_Load event procedure, and in the Click event procedures for the four buttons.

```
Private Sub Form_Load()
   Set mth = New Thing
   mth.Name = InputBox("Enter a name for the Thing")
End Sub

' Button "Show the Thing"
Private Sub Command1_Click()
   MsgBox "Name: " & mth.Name & vbCrLf _
   & "Created: " & mth.Created, , "Form Thing"
End Sub

' Button "Reverse the Thing's Name"
Private Sub Command2_Click()
   mth.ReverseName
   ' Click "Show the Thing"
   Command1.Value = True
End Sub

' Button "Create New Thing"
Private Sub Command3_Click()
   Set mth = New Thing
   mth.Name = InputBox( _
   "Enter a name for the new Thing")
End Sub

' Button "Temporary Thing".
Private Sub Command4_Click()
   Dim thTemp As New Thing
   thTemp.Name = InputBox( _
   "Enter a name for the Temporary Thing")
End Sub
```

Running the Project

Press F5 to run the project. Looking at the code in the Form_Load event procedure, you can see that the New operator is used to create a Thing object. A reference to this Thing is assigned to the variable `mth`.

You will see the InputBox asking you for a name for the Thing. When you type a name and press ENTER, the return value is assigned to the Name property of the Thing object.

Show the Form Thing

You can verify that the Name property has been assigned by pressing the first button, "Show the Thing," which displays a message box with all the properties of the Thing object.

Reverse the Thing's Name

Press the second button, "Reverse the Thing's Name." This button calls the ReverseName method to turn the Thing object's name around, and then clicks the first button to display the updated property values.

Create New Thing

Click the "Create New Thing" button to destroy the existing Thing object and create a new one. (Or, as it turns out, to create a new Thing and then destroy the old one.)

The New operator causes a new Thing to be created, so you'll see the MsgBox displayed by the new Thing's Initialize event. When you click OK, a reference to the new Thing is placed in the form-level variable `mth`.

This wipes out the reference to the old Thing. Because there are no more references to it, it's destroyed, and you'll see its Terminate event message box. When you click OK, the InputBox statement requests a name for the new Thing.

> **Note** If you want to destroy the old Thing before creating the new one, you can add the line of code `Set mth = Nothing` at the beginning of the event procedure.

Temporary Thing

The fourth button demonstrates another aspect of object lifetime. When you press it, you'll be prompted for a name for the temporary Thing.

But wait — there isn't a temporary Thing object yet. You haven't seen its Initialize message box. How can you assign it a name?

Because the variable `thTemp` was declared As New, a Thing object will be created the moment one of its properties or methods is invoked. This will happen when the return value of the InputBox is assigned to the Name property. Type a name and click OK on the InputBox.

You'll now see the Thing Initialize message box, which shows you that the Name property is still blank. When you click OK to dismiss the message box, the value from the InputBox statement is finally assigned to the Name property. That's a lot of activity for one line of code.

Of course, as soon as you've done that, the Click event procedure ends, and the variable `thTemp` goes out of scope. The object reference for the temporary Thing is released, so you'll see the Thing Terminate message box. Notice that it contains the name you supplied.

Each time you click this button, another temporary Thing will be created, named, and destroyed.

Closing the Program

Close the program by clicking the form's close button. *Do not use the End button on the toolbar.* When the program closes, Form1 is destroyed. The variable `mth` goes out of scope, and Visual Basic cleans up the reference to the Thing. There are no remaining references to the Thing, so it's destroyed, and its Terminate event message box is displayed.

Run the program again, and this time end it using the End button on the toolbar. Notice that the Terminate message box for the Thing object is *not* displayed.

It's important to remember that ending your program with the End button, or with an End statement in your code, halts the program *immediately,* without executing the Terminate events of any objects. It's always better to shut down your program by unloading all the forms.

You may find it useful to run the example by pressing F8 to step through the code one line at a time. This is a good way to understand the order of events for object creation and destruction.

> **Important** In an actual application, the Initialize and Terminate events should not contain message boxes, or any other code that allows Windows messages to be processed. In general, it's better to use Debug.Print statements when debugging object lifetimes.

For More Information Forms and controls are a bit different from other objects, as discussed later in this chapter in "Life Cycle of Visual Basic Forms."

You can read more about what you can do with classes and class modules earlier in this chapter in "Adding Properties and Methods to a Class" and "Adding Events to a Class."

Debugging Class Modules

Debugging class modules differs slightly from debugging ordinary programs. This is because an error in a property or method of a class module always acts like a handled error. (That is, there's always a procedure on the call stack that can handle the error — namely the procedure that called the class module's property or method.)

Visual Basic compensates for this difference by providing the error-trapping option Break in Class Module, in addition to the older options Break on Unhandled Errors and Break on All Errors.

Note You can set the Default Error Trapping State on the General tab of the Options dialog box, available from the Tools menu. The option you select affects the current session, and becomes the default for all subsequent instances of Visual Basic. To change the setting only for the current session, without affecting the default, select Toggle from the Code window context menu (which is available by right-clicking on the Code window).

For example, suppose the class module Class1 contains the following code:

```
Public Sub Oops()
   Dim intOops As Integer
   intOops = intOops / 0
End Sub
```

Now suppose a procedure in another class module, form, or standard module calls the member Oops:

```
Private Sub Command1_Click()
   Dim c1 As New Class1
   c1.Oops
End Sub
```

If the error trapping option is set to Break on Unhandled Errors, execution will not stop on the zero divide. Instead, the error will be raised in the calling procedure, Command1_Click. Execution will stop on the call to the Oops method.

You could use Break on All Errors to stop in the zero divide, but Break on All Errors is a very inconvenient option for most purposes. It stops on every error, even errors for which you've written error handling code.

Break in Class Module is a compromise setting:

- Execution will not stop on class module code for which you've written an error handler.
- Execution only stops on an error that's unhandled in the class module, and therefore would be returned to the caller of the method.
- When the Visual Basic development environment is started, it defaults to Break in Class Module.
- If there are no class modules involved, Break in Class Module is exactly the same as Break on Unhandled Errors.

Tip When you hit a break point using Break in Class Module or Break on All Errors, you can step or run past the error — into your error handling code or into the code that called procedure in which the error occurred — by pressing ALT+F8 or ALT+F5.

For More Information Debugging is discussed in detail in Chapter 13, "Debugging Your Code and Handling Errors."

Life Cycle of Visual Basic Forms

Because they're visible to the user, forms and controls have a different life cycle than other objects. For example, a form will not close just because you've released all your references to it. Visual Basic maintains a global collection of all forms in your project, and only removes a form from that collection when you unload the form.

In similar fashion, Visual Basic maintains a collection of controls on each form. You can load and unload controls from control arrays, but simply releasing all references to a control is not sufficient to destroy it.

For More Information The Forms and Controls collections are discussed in "Collections in Visual Basic" earlier in this chapter.

States a Visual Basic Form Passes Through

A Visual Basic form normally passes through four states in its lifetime:

1. Created, but not loaded.
2. Loaded, but not shown.
3. Shown.
4. Memory and resources completely reclaimed.

There's a fifth state a form can get into under certain circumstances: Unloaded and unreferenced while a control is still referenced.

This topic describes these states, and the transitions between them.

Created, but Not Loaded

The beginning of this state is marked by the Initialize event. Code you place in the Form_Initialize event procedure is therefore the first code that gets executed when a form is created.

In this state, the form exists as an object, but it has no window. None of its controls exist yet. *A form always passes through this state*, although its stay there may be brief.

For example, if you execute `Form1.Show`, the form will be created, and Form_Initialize will execute; as soon as Form_Initialize is complete, the form will be loaded, which is the next state.

The same thing happens if you specify a form as your Startup Object, on the General tab of the Project Properties dialog box (which is available from the Project menu). A form specified as the Startup Object is created as soon as the project starts, and is then immediately loaded and shown.

> **Note** You can cause your form to load from within Form_Initialize, by calling its Show method or by invoking its built-in properties and methods, as described below.

Remaining Created, but Not Loaded

By contrast, the following code creates an instance of Form1 without advancing the form to the loaded state:

```
Dim frm As Form1
Set frm = New Form1
```

Once Form_Initialize has ended, the only procedures you can execute without forcing the form to load are Sub, Function, and Property procedures you've added to the form's code window. For example, you might add the following method to Form1:

```
Public Sub ANewMethod()
   Debug.Print "Executing ANewMethod"
End Sub
```

You could call this method using the variable `frm` (that is, `frm.ANewMethod`) without forcing the form on to the next state. In similar fashion, you could call ANewMethod in order to create the form:

```
Dim frm As New Form1
frm.ANewMethod
```

Because `frm` is declared As New, the form is not created until the first time the variable is used in code — in this case, when ANewMethod is invoked. After the code above is executed, the form remains created, but not loaded.

> **Note** Executing `Form1.ANewMethod`, without declaring a form variable, has the same effect as the example above. As explained in "Customizing Form Classes," Visual Basic creates a hidden global variable for each form class. This variable has the same name as the class; it's as though Visual Basic had declared `Public Form1 As New Form1`.

You can execute as many custom properties and methods as you like without forcing the form to load. However, the moment you access one of the form's built-in properties, or any control on the form, the form enters the next state.

> **Note** You may find it helpful to think of a form as having two parts, a code part and a visual part. Before the form is loaded, only the code part is in memory. You can call as many procedures as you like in the code part without loading the visual part of the form.

The Only State All Forms Pass Through

Created, But Not Loaded is the only state *all* forms pass through. If the variable `frm` in the examples above is set to Nothing, as shown here, the form will be destroyed before entering the next state:

```
Dim frm As New Form1
frm.ANewMethod
Set frm = Nothing    ' Form is destroyed.
```

A form used in this fashion is no better than a class module, so the vast majority of forms pass on to the next state.

Loaded, but Not Shown

The event that marks the beginning of this state is the familiar Load event. Code you place in the Form_Load event procedure is executed as soon as the form enters the loaded state.

When the Form_Load event procedure begins, the controls on the form have all been created and loaded, and the form has a window — complete with window handle (hWnd) and device context (hDC) — although that window has not yet been shown.

Any form that becomes visible must first be loaded.

Many forms pass automatically from the Created, But Not Loaded state into the Loaded, but Not Shown state. A form will be loaded automatically if:

- The form has been specified as the Startup Object, on the General tab of the Project Properties dialog box.
- The Show method is the first property or method of the form to be invoked, as for example `Form1.Show`.
- The first property or method of the form to be invoked is one of the form's built-in members, as for example the Move method.

  Note This case includes any controls on the form, because each control defines a property of the form; that is, in order to access the Caption property of Command1, you must go through the form's Command1 property: `Command1.Caption`.

- The Load statement is used to load the form, without first using New or As New to create the form, as described earlier.

Forms That Are Never Shown

In the first two cases listed above, the form will continue directly on to the visible state, as soon as Form_Load completes. In the last two cases, the form will remain loaded, but not shown.

It has long been common coding practice in Visual Basic to load a form but never show it. This might be done for several reasons:

- To use the Timer control to generate timed events.
- To use controls for their functionality, rather than their user interface — for example, for serial communications or access to the file system.
- To execute DDE transactions.

  Note With the Professional or Enterprise edition, you can create ActiveX components (formerly called OLE servers), which are often better at providing code-only functionality than controls are. See "Creating ActiveX Components" in the *Microsoft Visual Basic 6.0 Component Tools Guide* volume in the *Microsoft Visual Basic 6.0 Reference Guide.*

Always Coming Home

Forms return from the visible state to the loaded state whenever they're hidden. Returning to the loaded state does not re-execute the Load event, however. Form_Load is executed only once in a form's life.

Shown

Once a form becomes visible, the user can interact with it. Thereafter, the form may be hidden and shown as many times as you like before finally being unloaded.

Interlude: Preparing to Unload

A form may be either hidden or visible when it's unloaded. If not explicitly hidden, it remains visible until unloaded.

The last event the form gets before unloading is the Unload event. Before this event occurs, however, you get a very important event called QueryUnload. QueryUnload is your chance to stop the form from unloading. If there's data the user might like to save, this is the time to prompt the user to save or discard changes.

> **Important** Setting the Cancel argument of the QueryUnload to True will stop the form from unloading, negating an Unload statement.

One of most powerful features of this event is that it tells you *how* the impending unload was caused: By the user clicking the Close button; by your program executing the Unload statement; by the application closing; or by Windows closing. Thus QueryUnload allows you to offer the user a chance to cancel closing the form, while still letting you close the form from code when you need to.

> **Important** Under certain circumstances, a form will not receive a QueryUnload event: If you use the End statement to terminate your program, or if you click the End button (or select End from the Run menu) in the development environment.

For More Information See "QueryUnload Event" in the *Microsoft Visual Basic 6.0 Language Reference* volume of the *Microsoft Visual Basic 6.0 Language Reference Library*.

Returning to the Created, but Not Loaded State

When the form is unloaded, Visual Basic removes it from the Forms collection. Unless you've kept a variable around with a reference to the form in it, the form will be destroyed, and its memory and resources will be reclaimed by Visual Basic.

If you kept a reference to the form in a variable somewhere, such as the hidden global variable described in "Customizing Form Classes" earlier in this chapter, then the form returns to the Created, But Not Loaded state. The form no longer has a window, and its controls no longer exist.

The object is still holding on to resources and memory. All of the data in the module-level variables in the form's code part are still there. (Static variables in event procedures, however, are gone.)

You can use that reference you've been keeping to call the methods and properties that you added to the form, but if you invoke the form's built-in members, or access its controls, the form will load again, and Form_Load will execute.

Memory and Resources Completely Reclaimed

The only way to release all memory and resources is to unload the form and then set all references to Nothing. The reference most commonly overlooked when doing this is the hidden global variable mentioned earlier. If at any time you have referred to the form by its class name (as shown in the Properties Window by the Name property), you've used the hidden global variable. To free the form's memory, you must set this variable to Nothing. For example:

```
Set Form1 = Nothing
```

Your form will receive its Terminate event just before it is destroyed.

> **Tip** Many professional programmers avoid the use of the hidden global variable, preferring to declare their own form variables (for example, `Dim dlgAbout As New frmAboutBox`) to manage form lifetime.

> **Note** Executing the End statement unloads all forms and sets all object variables in your program to Nothing. However, this is a very abrupt way to terminate your program. None of your forms will get their QueryUnload, Unload, or Terminate events, and objects you've created will not get their Terminate events.

Unloaded and Unreferenced, but a Control Is Still Referenced

To get into this odd state, you have to unload and free the form while keeping a reference to one of its controls. If this sounds like a silly thing to do, rest assured that it is.

```
Dim frm As New Form1
Dim obj As Object
frm.Show vbModal
' When the modal form is dismissed, save a
' reference to one of its controls.
Set obj = frm.Command1
Unload frm
Set frm = Nothing
```

The form has been unloaded, and all references to it released. However, you still have a reference to one of its controls, and this will keep the code part of the form from releasing the memory it's using. If you invoke any of the properties or methods of this control, the form will be reloaded:

```
obj.Caption = "Back to life"
```

The values in module-level variables will still be preserved, but the property values of all the controls will be set back to their defaults, as if the form were being loaded for the first time. Form_Load will execute.

Note In some previous versions of Visual Basic, the form did not completely re-initialize, and Form_Load did not execute again.

Note Not all forms behave as Visual Basic forms do. For example, the Microsoft Forms provided in Microsoft Office don't have Load and Unload events; when these forms receive their Initialize events, all their controls exist and are ready to use.

For More Information Forms are discussed in "Designing a Form" in Chapter 3, "Forms, Controls, and Menus," and in "More About Forms" in Chapter 6, "Creating a User Interface."

Class Modules vs. Standard Modules

Classes differ from standard modules in the way their data is stored. There's never more than one copy of a standard module's data. This means that when one part of your program changes a public variable in a standard module, and another part of your program subsequently reads that variable, it will get the same value.

Class module data, on the other hand, exists separately for each instance of the class (that is, for each object created from the class).

By the same token, data in a standard module has program scope — that is, it exists for the life of your program — while class module data for each instance of a class exists only for the lifetime of the object; it's created when the object is created, and destroyed when the object is destroyed.

Finally, variables declared Public in a standard module are visible from anywhere in your project, whereas Public variables in a class module can only be accessed if you have an object variable containing a reference to a particular instance of a class.

All of the above are also true for public procedures in standard modules and class modules. This is illustrated by the following example. You can run this code by opening a new Standard Exe project and using the Project menu to add a module and a class module.

Place the following code in Class1:

```
' The following is a property of Class1 objects.
Public Comment As String

' The following is a method of Class1 objects.
Public Sub ShowComment()
   MsgBox Comment, , gstrVisibleEverywhere
End Sub
```

Place the following code in Module1:

```
' Code in the standard module is global.
Public gstrVisibleEverywhere As String

Public Sub CallableAnywhere(ByVal c1 As Class1)
   ' The following line changes a global variable
   ' (property) of an instance of Class1. Only the
   ' particular object passed to this procedure is
   ' affected.
   c1.Comment = "Touched by a global function."
End Sub
```

Put two command buttons on Form1, and add the following code to Form1:

```
Private mc1First As Class1
Private mc1Second As Class1

Private Sub Form_Load()
   ' Create two instances of Class1.
   Set mc1First = New Class1
   Set mc1Second = New Class1
   gstrVisibleEverywhere = "Global string data"
End Sub

Private Sub Command1_Click()
   Call CallableAnywhere(mc1First)
   mc1First.ShowComment
End Sub

Private Sub Command2_Click()
   mc1Second.ShowComment
End Sub
```

Press F5 to run the project. When Form1 is loaded, it creates two instances of Class1, each having its own data. Form1 also sets the value of the global variable `gstrVisibleEverywhere`.

Press Command1, which calls the global procedure and passes a reference to the first Class1 object. The global procedure sets the Comment property, and Command1 then calls the ShowComment method to display the object's data.

As Figure 9.6 shows, the resulting message box demonstrates that the global procedure CallableAnywhere set the Comment property of the object that was passed to it, and that the global string is visible from within Class1.

Figure 9.6 Message box from the first Class1 object

Press Command2, which simply calls the ShowComment method of the second instance of Class1.

As Figure 9.7 shows, both objects have access to the global string variable; but the Comment property of the second object is blank, because calling the global procedure CallableAnywhere only changed the Comment property for the first object.

Figure 9.7 Message box from the second Class1 object

> **Important** Avoid making the code in your classes dependent on global data — that is, public variables in standard modules. Many instances of a class can exist simultaneously, and all of these objects share the global data in your program.
>
> Using global variables in class module code also violates the object-oriented programming concept of encapsulation, because objects created from such a class do not contain all their data.

Static Class Data

There may be occasions when you want a single data item to be shared among all objects created from a class module. This is sometimes referred to as *static class data*.

You cannot implement true static class data in a Visual Basic class module. However, you can simulate it by using Property procedures to set and return the value of a Public data member in a standard module, as in the following code fragment:

```
' Read-only property returning the application name.
Property Get CommonString() As String
   ' The variable gstrVisibleEverywhere is stored in a
   ' standard module, and declared Public.
   CommonString = gstrVisibleEverywhere
End Property
```

> **Note** You cannot use the Static keyword for module-level variables in a class module. The Static keyword can only be used within procedures.

It's possible to simulate static class data that's not read-only by providing a corresponding Property Let procedure — or Property Set for a property that contains an object reference — to assign a new value to the standard module data member. Using global variables in this fashion violates the concept of encapsulation, however, and is not recommended.

For example, the variable `gstrVisibleEverywhere` can be set from anywhere in your project, even from code that doesn't belong to the class that has the CommonString property. This can lead to subtle errors in your program.

For More Information Global data in ActiveX components requires different handling than in ordinary programs. If you have the Professional or Enterprise Edition of Visual Basic, see "Standard Modules vs. Class Modules" in Chapter 6, "General Principles of Component Design," of "Creating ActiveX Components" in the *Microsoft Visual Basic 6.0 Component Tools Guide* volume of the *Microsoft Visual Basic 6.0 Reference Library*.

Adding Properties and Methods to a Class

The properties and methods of a class make up its default interface. The default interface is the most common way of manipulating an object.

In general, properties represent *data about an object*, while methods represent *actions an object can take*. To put it another way, properties provide the description of an object, while methods are its behavior.

> **Important** The following names cannot be used as property or method names, because they belong to the underlying IUnknown and IDispatch interfaces: QueryInterface, AddRef, Release, GetTypeInfoCount, GetTypeInfo, GetIDsOfNames, and Invoke. These names will cause a compilation error.

For More Information Events are discussed in "Adding Events to a Class" later in this chapter.

Adding Properties to a Class

The easiest way to define properties for a class is by adding public variables to the class module. For example, you could very easily create an Account class by declaring two public variables in a class module named Account:

```
Public Balance As Double
Public Name As String
```

This is pretty easy. It's just as easy to create private data for a class; simply declare a variable Private, and it will be accessible only from code within the class module:

```
Private mstrMothersMaidenName As String
Private mintWithdrawalsMonthToDate As Integer
```

Data Hiding

The ability to protect part of an object's data, while exposing the rest as properties, is called *data hiding*. This is one aspect of the object-oriented principle of encapsulation, as explained in "Classes: Putting User-Defined Types and Procedures Together."

Data hiding means that you can make changes in the implementation of a class — for example, increasing the Account class's private variable `mintWithdrawalsMonthToDate` from an Integer to a Long — without affecting existing code that uses the Account object.

Data hiding also allows you to define properties that are read-only. For example, you could use a Property Get procedure to return the value of the private variable containing the number of withdrawals in a month, while only incrementing the variable from within the Account object's code. Which brings us to property procedures.

Property Procedures

Data hiding wouldn't be much use if the only way you could create properties was by declaring public variables. How much good would it do you to give the Account class a Type property, if any code that had a reference to an Account object could blithely set the account type to any value at all?

Property procedures allow you to execute code when a property value is set or retrieved. For example, you might want to implement the Type property of the Account object as a pair of Property procedures:

```
Public Enum AccountTypes
   atSavings = 1
   atChecking
   atLineOfCredit
End Enum

' Private data storage for the Type property.
Private mbytType As AccountTypes

Public Property Get Type() As AccountTypes
   Type = mbytType
End Property

Public Property Let Type(ByVal NewType As AccountTypes)
   Select Case NewType
      Case atChecking, atSavings, atLineOfCredit
         ' No need to do anything if NewType is valid.
      Case Else
         Err.Raise Number:=vbObjectError + 32112, _
         Description:="Invalid account type"
   End Select
```

```
   If mbytType > NewType Then
      Err.Raise Number:=vbObjectError + 32113, _
      Description:="Cannot downgrade account type"
   Else
      mbytType = NewType
   End If
End Property
```

Now suppose you have a variable named `acct` that contains a reference to an Account object. When the code `x = acct.Type` is executed, the Property Get procedure is invoked to return the value stored in the class module's private data member `mbytType`.

When the code `acct.Type = atChecking` is executed, the Property Let is invoked. If the Account object is brand new, `mbytType` will be zero, and any valid account type can be assigned. If the current account type is atSavings, the account will be upgraded.

However, if the current account type is atLineOfCredit, the Property Let will raise an error, preventing the downgrade. Likewise, if the code `acct.Type = 0` is executed, the Select statement in the Property Let will detect the invalid account type and raise an error.

In short, *property procedures allow an object to protect and validate its own data.*

For More Information Are public variables good for anything, then? "Property Procedures vs. Public Variables" outlines the appropriate uses of both.

The capabilities of property procedures are explored further in "Putting Property Procedures to Work for You."

Property Procedures vs. Public Variables

Property procedures are clearly such a powerful means for enabling encapsulation that you may be wondering if you should even bother with public variables. The answer, as always in programming, is "Of course — sometimes." Here are some ground rules:

Use property procedures when:

- The property is read-only, or cannot be changed once it has been set.
- The property has a well-defined set of values that need to be validated.
- Values outside a certain range — for example, negative numbers — are valid for the property's data type, but cause program errors if the property is allowed to assume such values.
- Setting the property causes some perceptible change in the object's state, as for example a Visible property.
- Setting the property causes changes to other internal variables or to the values of other properties.

Use public variables for read-write properties where:

- The property is of a self-validating type. For example, an error or automatic data conversion will occur if a value other than True or False is assigned to a Boolean variable.
- Any value in the range supported by the data type is valid. This will be true of many properties of type Single or Double.
- The property is a String data type, and there's no constraint on the size or value of the string.

Note Don't implement a property as a public variable just to avoid the overhead of a function call. Behind the scenes, Visual Basic will implement the public variables in your class modules as pairs of property procedures anyway, because this is required by the type library.

Putting Property Procedures to Work for You

Visual Basic provides three kinds of property procedures, as described in the following table.

Procedure	Purpose
Property Get	Returns the value of a property.
Property Let	Sets the value of a property.
Property Set	Sets the value of an object property (that is, a property that contains a reference to an object).

As you can see from the table, each of these property procedures has a particular role to play in defining a property. The typical property will be made up of a pair of property procedures: A Property Get to retrieve the property value, and a Property Let or Property Set to assign a new value.

These roles can overlap in some cases. The reason there are two kinds of property procedures for assigning a value is that Visual Basic has a special syntax for assigning object references to object variables:

```
Dim wdg As Widget
Set wdg = New Widget
```

The rule is simple: Visual Basic calls Property Set if the Set statement is used, and Property Let if it is not.

Tip To keep Property Let and Property Set straight, hearken back to the Basics of yore, when instead of `x = 4` you had to type `Let x = 4` (syntax supported by Visual Basic to this very day). Visual Basic always calls the property procedure that corresponds to the type of assignment — Property Let for `Let x = 4`, and Property Set for `Set c1 = New Class1` (that is, object properties).

For More Information "Working with Objects" in Chapter 5, "Programming Fundamentals," explains the use of the Set statement with object variables.

Read-Write Properties

The following code fragment shows a typical read-write property:

```
' Private storage for property value.
Private mintNumberOfTeeth As Integer

Public Property Get NumberOfTeeth() As Integer
   NumberOfTeeth = mintNumberOfTeeth
End Property

Public Property Let NumberOfTeeth(ByVal NewValue _
   As Integer)
   ' (Code to validate property value omitted.)
   mintNumberOfTeeth = NewValue
End Property
```

The name of the private variable that stores the property value is made up of a scope prefix (`m`) that identifies it as a module-level variable; a type prefix (`int`); and a name (`NumberOfTeeth`). Using the same name as the property serves as a reminder that the variable and the property are related.

As you've no doubt noticed, here and in earlier examples, the names of the property procedures that make up a read-write property must be the same.

> **Note** Property procedures are public by default, so if you omit the Public keyword, they will still be public. If for some reason you want a property to be private (that is, accessible only from within the object), you must declare it with the Private keyword. It's good practice to use the Public keyword, even though it isn't required, because it makes your intentions clear.

Property Procedures at Work and Play

It's instructive to step through some property procedure code. Open a new Standard Exe project and add a class module, using the Project menu. Copy the code for the NumberOfTeeth property, shown above, into Class1.

Switch to Form1, and add the following code to the Load event:

```
Private Sub Form_Load()
   Dim c1 As Class1
   Set c1 = New Class1
   ' Assign a new property value.
   c1.NumberOfTeeth = 42
   ' Display the property value.
   MsgBox c1.NumberOfTeeth
End Sub
```

Press F8 to step through the code one line at a time. Notice that when the property value is assigned, you step into the Property Let, and when it's retrieved, you step into the Property Get. You may find it useful to duplicate this exercise with other combinations of property procedures.

Arguments of Paired Property Procedures Must Match

The property procedure examples you've seen so far have been simple, as they will be for most properties. However, property procedures can have multiple arguments — and even optional arguments. Multiple arguments are useful for properties that act like arrays, as discussed below.

When you use multiple arguments, the arguments of a pair of property procedures must match. The following table demonstrates the requirements for arguments in property procedure declarations.

Procedure	Declaration syntax
Property Get	Property Get *propertyname*(1,..., *n*) As *type*
Property Let	Property Let *propertyname*(1,..., *n*, *n*+1)
Property Set	Property Set *propertyname*(1,..., *n*, *n*+1)

The first argument through the second-to-last argument (1,..., *n*) must share the same names and data types in all Property procedures with the same name. As with other procedure types, all of the required parameters in this list must precede the first optional parameter.

You've probably noticed that a Property Get procedure declaration takes one less argument than the related Property Let or Property Set. The data type of the Property Get procedure must be the same as the data type of the last argument (*n*+1) in the related Property Let or Property Set.

For example, consider this Property Let declaration, for a property that acts like a two-dimensional array:

```
Public Property Let Things(ByVal X As Integer, _
ByVal Y As Integer, ByVal Thing As Variant)
   ' (Code to assign array element omitted.)
End Property
```

The Property Get declaration must use arguments with the same name and data type as the arguments in the Property Let procedure:

```
Public Property Get Things(ByVal X As Integer, _
ByVal Y As Integer) As Variant
   ' (Code for retrieval from array omitted.)
End Property
```

The data type of the final argument in a Property Set declaration must be either an object type or a Variant.

Matching Up the Arguments

The reason for these argument matching rules is illustrated in Figure 9.8, which shows how Visual Basic matches up the parts of the assignment statement with the arguments of a Property Let.

Figure 9.8 Calling a Property Let procedure

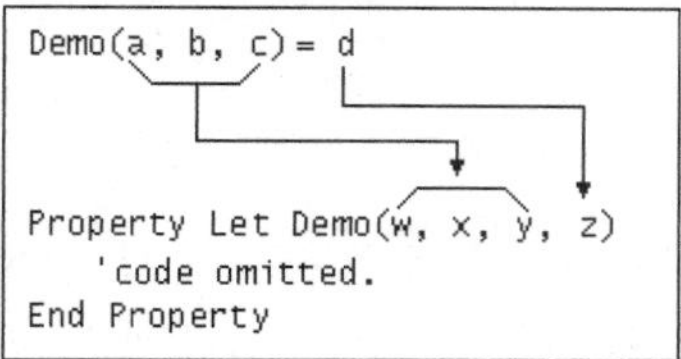

The most common use for property procedures with multiple arguments is to create property arrays.

Read-Only Properties

To create a read-only property, simply omit the Property Let or (for object properties) the Property Set.

Object Properties

If you're creating a read-write object property, you use a Property Get and a Property Set, as here:

```
Private mwdgWidget As Widget

Public Property Get Widget() As Widget
   ' The Set statement must be used to return an
   ' object reference.
   Set Widget = mwdgWidget
End Property

Public Property Set Widget(ByVal NewWidget As Widget)
   Set mwdgWidget = NewWidget
End Property
```

Variant Properties

Read-write properties of the Variant data type are the most complicated. They use all three property procedure types, as shown here:

```
Private mvntAnything As Variant

Public Property Get Anything() As Variant
   ' The Set statement is used only when the Anything
   ' property contains an object reference.
   If IsObject(mvntAnything) Then
      Set Anything = mvntAnything
   Else
      Anything = mvntAnything
   End If
End Property

Public Property Let Anything(ByVal NewValue As Variant)
   ' (Validation code omitted.)
   mvntAnything = NewWidget
End Property

Public Property Set Anything(ByVal NewValue As Variant)
   ' (Validation code omitted.)
   Set mvntAnything = NewWidget
End Property
```

The Property Set and Property Let are straightforward, as they're always called in the correct circumstances. However, the Property Get must handle both of the following cases:

```
strSomeString = objvar1.Anything
Set objvar2 = objvar1.Anything
```

In the first case, the Anything property contains a string, which is being assigned to a String variable. In the second, Anything contains an object reference, which is being assigned to an object variable.

The Property Get can be coded to handle these cases, by using the IsObject function to test the private Variant before returning the value.

Of course, if the first line of code is called when Anything contains an object reference, an error will occur, but that's not Property Get's problem — that's a problem with using Variant properties.

Write-Once Properties

There are many possible combinations of property procedures. All of them are valid, but some are relatively uncommon, like write-only properties (only a Property Let, no Property Get). And some depend on factors other than the kinds of property procedures you combine.

For example, when you organize the objects in your program by creating an object model, as described in "Object Models" later in this chapter, you may want an object to be able to refer back to the object that contains it. You can do this by implementing a Parent property.

You need to set this Parent property when the object is created, but thereafter you may want to prevent it from being changed — accidentally or on purpose. The following example shows how the Account object might implement a Parent property that points to the Department object that contains the account.

```
' Private data storage for Parent property.
Private mdeptParent As Department

Property Get Parent() As Department
   ' Use the Set statement for object references.
   Set Parent = mdeptParent
End Property

' The property value can only be set once.
Public Property Set Parent(ByVal NewParent _
As Department)
   If deptParent Is Nothing Then
      ' Assign the initial value.
      Set mdeptParent = NewParent
   Else
      Err.Raise Number:=vbObjectError + 32144, _
      Description:="Parent property is read-only"
   End If
End Property
```

When you access the parent of an Account object, for example by coding `strX = acctNew.Parent.Name` to get the department name, the Property Get is invoked to return the reference to the parent object.

The Property Set in this example is coded so that the Parent property can be set only once. For example, when the Department object creates a new account, it might execute the code `Set acctNew.Parent = Me` to set the property. Thereafter the property is read-only.

For More Information Because forms in Visual Basic are classes, you can add custom properties to forms. See "Customizing Form Classes" earlier in this chapter.

Adding Methods to a Class

The methods of a class are just the public Sub or Function procedures you've declared. Since Sub and Function procedures are public by default, you don't even have to explicitly specify the Public keyword to create a method.

For example, to create a Withdrawal method for the Account class, you could add this Public Function procedure to the class module:

```
Public Function WithDrawal(ByVal Amount As Currency, _
ByVal TransactionCode As Byte) As Double
   ' (Code to perform the withdrawal and return the
   ' new balance, or to raise an Overdraft error.)
End Function
```

Tip Although you don't have to type the Public keyword, doing so is good programming practice, because it makes your intent clear to people maintaining your code later.

Declaring Methods as Public Subs

Returning the new balance is optional, since you could easily call the Balance property of the Account object after calling the Withdrawal method. You could thus code Withdrawal as a Public Sub procedure.

Tip If you find yourself calling Balance almost every time you call Withdrawal, returning the new balance will be slightly more efficient. This is because any property access, even reading a public variable, means a function call — an explicit or implicit Property Get.

Important The following names cannot be used as property or method names, because they belong to the underlying IUnknown and IDispatch interfaces: QueryInterface, AddRef, Release, GetTypeInfoCount, GetTypeInfo, GetIDsOfNames, and Invoke. These names will cause a compilation error.

For More Information For more information on Sub and Function procedures, see "Introduction to Procedures" in Chapter 5, "Programming Fundamentals."

Protecting Implementation Details

The public interface of a class is defined by the property and method declarations in the class module. As with data hiding, procedures you declare as Private are not part of the interface. This means that you can make changes to utility procedures that are used internally by a class module, without affecting code that uses the objects.

Even more important, you can also change the code inside the public Sub or Function procedure that implements a method, without affecting code that uses the method. As long as you don't change the data types of the procedure's arguments, or the type of data returned by a Function procedure, the interface is unchanged.

Hiding the details of an object's implementation behind the interface is another facet of encapsulation. Encapsulation allows you to enhance the performance of methods, or completely change the way a method is implemented, without having to change code that uses the method.

Note The guidelines for naming interface elements — discussed in "Naming Properties, Methods, and Events" later in this chapter — apply not only to property and method names, but to the names of parameters in the Sub and Function procedures that define your methods. These parameter names are visible when you view the methods in the Object Browser, and can be used as named parameters (that is, *parametername:=value*) when the methods are invoked.

For More Information Named arguments are introduced in "Passing Arguments to Procedures" in Chapter 5, "Programming Fundamentals."

Adding methods to form classes is a powerful programming technique, discussed in "Customizing Form Classes" earlier in this chapter.

Sometimes it's not clear whether a member should be a property or a method. "Is it a Property or a Method?" offers some guidelines.

Is It a Property or a Method?

In general, a property is data about an object, while a method is an action the object can be asked to perform. Some things are obviously properties, like Color and Name, and some are obviously methods, like Move and Show.

As with any facet of human endeavor, however, there's a gray area in which an argument can be made either way.

For example, why is the Item method of the Visual Basic Collection class a method and not an indexed property? Aren't the items in the collection just data? The Item method of a hypothetical Widgets collection class could be implemented either way, as shown here:

```
' Private storage for the objects in the Widgets
' collection (same for both implementations).
Private mcol As New Collection

Public Property Get Item(Index As Variant) As Widget
   Set Item = mcol.Item(Index)
End Function
```

– or –

```
Public Function Item(Index As Variant) As Widget
   Set Item = mcol.Item(Index)
End Function
```

There's not a whole lot of difference between these two implementations. Both are read-only, so both depend on the Add method of the Widgets class to get Widget objects into the collection. Both delegate everything to a Collection object — even their errors are generated by the Collection!

For More Information Delegation is explained in "The Many (Inter)Faces of Code Reuse" and "Creating Your Own Collection Classes" later in this chapter.

You can get really nit-picky trying to decide whether a member is data about the object or object behavior. For example, you could argue that Item is a method because the collection is doing something for you — looking up the Widget you want. This kind of argument can usually be made with equal validity on either side, however.

You may find it more useful to turn the argument on its head, and ask yourself how you *want* to think of the member. If you want people to think of it as data about the object, make it a property. If you want them to think of it as something the object does, make it a method.

The Syntax Argument

A strong reason for implementing a member using property procedures depends on the way you want to use the member in code. That is, will the user of a Widgets collection be allowed to code the following?

```
Set Widgets.Item(4) = wdgMyNewWidget
```

If so, implement the member as a read-write property, using Property Get and Property Set, because methods don't support this syntax.

> **Note** In most collection implementations you encounter, this syntax is not allowed. Implementing a Property Set for a collection is not as easy as it looks.

The Property Window Argument

You can also suppose for a moment that your object is like a control. Can you imagine the member showing up in the Property window, or on a property page? If that doesn't make sense, don't implement the member as a property.

The Sensible Error Argument

If you forget that you made Item a read-only property and try to assign a value to it, you'll most likely find it easier to understand the error message Visual Basic raises for a Property Get — "Can't assign to read-only property" — than the error message it raises for a Function procedure — "Function call on left side of assignment must return Variant or Object."

The Argument of Last Resort

As a last resort, flip a coin. If none of the other arguments in this topic seem compelling, it probably doesn't make much difference.

For More Information Property procedures are introduced in "Adding Properties to a Class" earlier in this chapter. Methods are discussed in "Adding Methods to Classes," online.

Making a Property or Method the Default

You can give objects created from your classes default properties, like the default properties of objects provided by Visual Basic. The best candidate for default member is the one you use most often.

To set a property or method as the default

1. On the **Tools** menu, select **Procedure Attributes** to open the **Procedure Attributes** dialog box.
2. Click **Advanced** to expand the **Procedure Attributes** dialog box.
3. In the **Name** box, select the property or method that is currently the default for the class. If the class does not currently have a default member, skip to step 5.

   Note You can use the Object Browser to find out what the current default member of a class is. When you select the class in the Classes list, you can scroll through the members in the Members list; the default member will be marked with a small blue globe beside its icon.
4. In the **Procedure ID** box, select **None** to remove the default status of the property or method.
5. In the **Name** box, select the property or method you want to be the new default.
6. In the **Procedure ID** box, select **(Default)**, then click **OK**.

   Important A class can have only one default member. If a property or method is already marked as the default, you must reset its procedure ID to None before making another property or method the default. No compile errors will occur if two members are marked as default, but there is no way to predict which one Visual Basic will pick as the default.

You can also open the Procedure Attributes dialog box from the Object Browser. This is convenient when you're changing the default member of a class, because it allows you to locate the existing default member quickly.

To change a default property using the Object Browser

1. Press F2 to open the **Object Browser**.
2. In the **Classes** list, select the class whose default you want to change.
3. In the **Members** list, right-click the member with the small blue globe beside its icon to open the context menu. Click **Properties** to show the **Property Attributes** dialog box.
4. Click **Advanced** to expand the **Procedure Attributes** dialog box.
5. In the **Procedure ID** box, select **None** to remove the default status of the property or method, then click **OK**.

6. In the **Members** list, right-click the member you want to be the new default to open the context menu. Click **Properties** to show the **Property Attributes** dialog box.
7. Click **Advanced** to expand the **Procedure Attributes** dialog box.
8. In the **Procedure ID** box, select **(Default)**, then click **OK**.

   Note You cannot use the Procedure Attributes dialog box to change the default member of a class provided by Visual Basic.

Fixing Defaults You Have Accidentally Made Private or Friend

The Procedure Attributes dialog box only allows you to select public properties and methods as the default for a class. If you make a public property or method the default for a class, and later change the declaration to Private or Friend, the property or method may continue to behave as if it were still declared Public.

To correct this problem, you must make the property or method Public again, because the Procedure Attributes dialog box will not show procedures declared Private and Friend. Once you have changed the declaration to Public, you can use the Procedure Attributes dialog to remove the Default attribute. You can then change the declaration back to Friend or Private.

Friend Properties and Methods

In addition to declaring properties and methods Public and Private, you can declare them Friend. Friend members look just like Public members to other objects in your project. That is, they appear to be part of a class's interface. They are not.

In the ActiveX components you can create with the Professional and Enterprise editions of Visual Basic, Friend members play an important role. Because they're not part of an object's interface, they can't be accessed by programs that use the component's objects. They're visible to all the other objects within the component, however, so they allow safe internal communication within the component.

Important Because Friend members aren't part of an object's public interface, they can't be accessed late bound — that is, through variables declared As Object. To use Friend members, you must declare variables with early binding — that is, As *classname*.

Standard Exe projects can't be ActiveX components, because their class modules can't be Public, and thus can't be used by other applications. All communication between objects in a Standard Exe project is therefore private, and there's no need for Friend members.

However, Friend members have one particularly useful feature. Because they're not part of an ActiveX interface, they can be used to pass user-defined types between objects without exposing them publicly. For example, suppose you have the following user-defined type in a standard module:

```
Public Type udtDemo
   intA As Integer
   lngB As Long
   strC As String
End Type
```

You can define the following private variable and Friend members in Class1:

```
Private mDemo As udtDemo

Friend Property Get Demo() As udtDemo
   Demo = mDemo
End Property

' Note that udtDemo must be passed by reference.
Friend Property Let Demo(NewDemo As udtDemo)
   mDemo = NewDemo
End Property

Friend Sub SetDemoParts(ByVal A As Integer, _
      ByVal B As Long, ByVal C As String)
   mDemo.intA = A
   mDemo.lngB = B
   mDemo.strC = C
End Sub

Public Sub ShowDemo()
   MsgBox mDemo.intA & vbCrLf _
   & mDemo.lngB & vbCrLf & mDemo.strC
End Sub
```

Note When you pass user-defined types as Sub, Function, or property procedure arguments, you must pass them by reference. (ByRef is the default for procedure arguments.)

You can then write the following code to use Class1:

```
Private Sub Command1_Click()
   Dim c1A As New Class1
   Dim c1B As New Class1
   c1A.SetDemoParts 42, 1138, "Howdy"
   c1B.Demo = c1A.Demo
   c1B.ShowDemo
End Sub
```

The message box will display 42, 1138, and "Howdy."

> **Note** Because Friend procedures are not part of a class's interface, they are not included when you use the Implements statement to implement multiple interfaces, as described in "Polymorphism."

For More Information The use of Friend members in components is discussed in "Private Communications Between Your Objects" in Chapter 6, "General Principles of Component Design," in the *Microsoft Visual Basic 6.0 Component Tools Guide*.

Adding Events to a Class

Okay, let's say you've created a dinosaur simulation, complete with Stegosaur, Triceratops, and Tyrannosaur classes. As the final touch, you want the Tyrannosaur to roar, and when it does you want every other dinosaur in your simulation to sit up and take notice.

If the Tyrannosaur class had a Roar event, you could handle that event in all your other dinosaur classes. This topic discusses the declaration and handling of events in your class modules.

> **Note** Kids, don't try this at home, at least with more than a few dinosaurs. Connecting every dinosaur with every other dinosaur using events could make your dinosaurs so slow that mammal objects would take over the simulation.

Properties and methods are said to belong to *incoming interfaces*, because they're invoked from outside the object. By contrast, events are called *outgoing interfaces*, because they're initiated within the object, and handled elsewhere.

For More Information Part 2, "Creating ActiveX Components," of the *Microsoft Visual Basic 6.0 Component Tools Guide* provided with the Professional and Enterprise editions, discusses the use of events in designing your own software components.

For a discussion of a better way to handle dinosaurs, see "Polymorphism," later in this chapter.

Declaring and Raising Events

Assume for the moment that you have a Widget class. Your Widget class has a method that can take a long time to execute, and you'd like your application to be able to put up some kind of completion indicator.

Of course, you could make the Widget object show a percent-complete dialog box, but then you'd be stuck with that dialog box in every project in which you used the Widget class. A good principle of object design is to let the application that uses an object handle the user interface — unless the whole purpose of the object is to manage a form or dialog box.

The Widget's purpose is to perform other tasks, so it's reasonable to give it a PercentDone event, and to let the procedure that calls the Widget's methods handle that event. The PercentDone event can also provide a mechanism for canceling the task.

You can start building the code example for this topic by opening a Standard Exe project, and adding two buttons and a label to Form1. On the Project menu, select Add Class Module to add a class module to the project. Name the objects as shown in the following table.

Object	Property	Setting
Class module	Name	Widget
First Button	Caption	Start Task
Second Button	Caption	Cancel
Label	Name Caption	lblPercentDone "0"

The Widget Class

You declare an event in the Declarations section of a class module, using the Event keyword. An event can have ByVal and ByRef arguments, as the Widget's PercentDone event demonstrates:

```
Option Explicit
Public Event PercentDone(ByVal Percent As Single, _
ByRef Cancel As Boolean)
```

When the calling object receives a PercentDone event, the Percent argument contains the percentage of the task that's complete. The ByRef Cancel argument can be set to True to cancel the method that raised the event.

> **Note** You can declare event arguments just as you do arguments of procedures, with the following exceptions: Events cannot have named arguments, optional arguments, or ParamArray arguments. Events do not have return values.

Raising the PercentDone Event

The PercentDone event is raised by the LongTask method of the Widget class. The LongTask method takes two arguments: the length of time the method will pretend to be doing work, and the minimum time interval before LongTask pauses to raise the PercentDone event.

```
Public Sub LongTask(ByVal Duration As Single, _
ByVal MinimumInterval As Single)
   Dim sngThreshold As Single
   Dim sngStart As Single
   Dim blnCancel As Boolean

   ' The Timer function returns the fractional number
   ' of seconds since Midnight, as a Single.
   sngStart = Timer
   sngThreshold = MinimumInterval
```

```
      Do While Timer < (sngStart + Duration)
         ' In a real application, some unit of work would
         ' be done here each time through the loop.

         If Timer > (sngStart + sngThreshold) Then
            RaiseEvent PercentDone( _
            sngThreshold / Duration, blnCancel)
            ' Check to see if the operation was canceled.
            If blnCancel Then Exit Sub
            sngThreshold = sngThreshold + MinimumInterval
         End If
      Loop
   End Sub
```

Every `MinimumInterval` seconds, the PercentDone event is raised. When the event returns, LongTask checks to see if the Cancel argument was set to True.

> **Note** For simplicity, LongTask assumes you know in advance how long the task will take. This is almost never the case. Dividing tasks into chunks of even size can be difficult, and often what matters most to users is simply the amount of time that passes before they get an indication that something is happening.

Handling an Object's Events

An object that raises events is called an *event source.* To handle the events raised by an event source, you can declare a variable of the object's class using the WithEvents keyword.

To handle the PercentDone event of a Widget, place the following code in the Declarations section of Form1:

```
Option Explicit
Private WithEvents mWidget As Widget
Private mblnCancel As Boolean
```

The WithEvents keyword specifies that the variable `mWidget` will be used to handle an object's events. You specify the kind of object by supplying the name of the class from which the object will be created.

The variable `mWidget` is declared in the Declarations section of Form1 because WithEvents variables must be module-level variables. This is true regardless of the type of module you place them in.

The variable `mblnCancel` will be used to cancel the LongTask method.

Limitations on WithEvents Variables

You should be aware of the following limitations on the use of WithEvents variables:

- A WithEvents variable cannot be a generic object variable. That is, you cannot declare it As Object — you must specify the class name when you declare the variable.
- You cannot declare a WithEvents variable As New. The event source object must be explicitly created and assigned to the WithEvents variable.
- You cannot declare WithEvents variables in a standard module. You can declare them only in class modules, form modules, and other modules that define classes.
- You cannot create arrays of WithEvents variables.

Writing Code to Handle an Event

As soon as you declare a variable WithEvents, the variable name appears in the left drop down of the module's code window. When you select `mWidget`, the Widget class's events will appear in the right drop down, as shown in Figure 9.9.

Figure 9.9 An event associated with a WithEvents variable

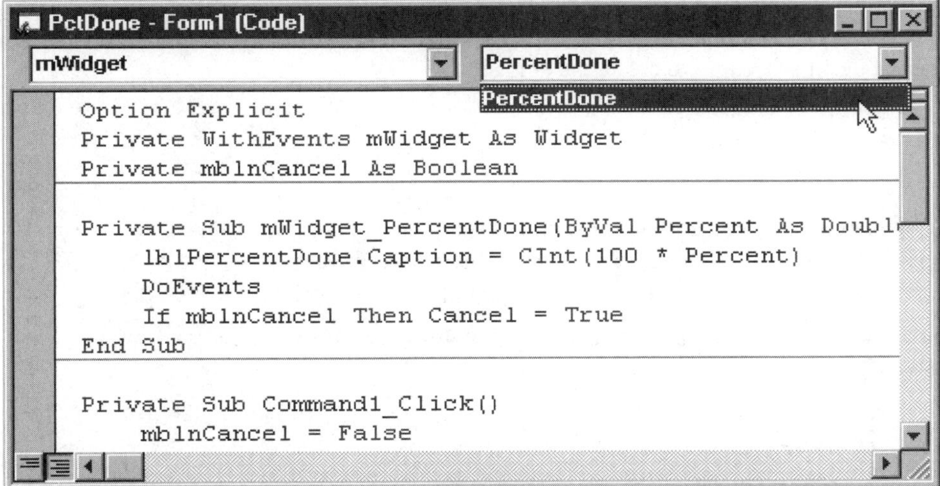

Selecting an event will display the corresponding event procedure, with the prefix `mWidget_`. All the event procedures associated with a WithEvents variable will have the variable name as a prefix. Add the following code to the mWidget_PercentDone event procedure.

```
Private Sub mWidget_PercentDone(ByVal Percent As _
Single, Cancel As Boolean)
   lblPercentDone.Caption = CInt(100 * Percent) & "%"
   DoEvents
   If mblnCancel Then Cancel = True
End Sub
```

Whenever the PercentDone event is raised, the event procedure displays the percent complete in a Label control. The DoEvents statement allows the label to repaint, and also gives the user the opportunity to click the Cancel button. Add the following code for the Click event of the button whose caption is Cancel.

```
Private Sub Command2_Click()
   mblnCancel = True
End Sub
```

If the user clicks the Cancel button while LongTask is running, the Command2_Click event will be executed as soon as the DoEvents statement allows event processing to occur. The module-level variable `mblnCancel` is set to True, and the mWidget_PercentDone event then tests it and sets the ByRef Cancel argument to True.

Connecting a WithEvents Variable to an Object

Form1 is all set up to handle a Widget object's events. All that remains is to find a Widget somewhere.

When you declare a variable WithEvents at design time, there is no object associated with it. A WithEvents variable is just like any other object variable. You have to create an object and assign a reference to the object to the WithEvents variable. Add the following code to the Form_Load event procedure to create the Widget.

```
Private Sub Form_Load()
   Set mWidget = New Widget
End Sub
```

When the code above is executed, Visual Basic creates a Widget and connects its events to the event procedures associated with `mWidget`. From that point on, whenever the Widget raises its PercentDone event, the mWidget_PercentDone event procedure will be executed.

To call the LongTask method, add the following code to the Click event of the button whose caption is Start Task.

```
' Start Task button.
Private Sub Command1_Click()
   mblnCancel = False
   lblPercentDone.Caption = "0%"
   lblPercentDone.Refresh

   Call mWidget.LongTask(14.4, 0.66)

   If Not mblnCancel Then lblPercentDone.Caption = 100
End Sub
```

Before the LongTask method is called, the label that displays the percent complete must be initialized, and the module-level Boolean flag for canceling the method must be set to False.

LongTask is called with a task duration of 14.4 seconds. The PercentDone event is to be raised once every two-thirds of a second. Each time the event is raised, the mWidget_PercentDone event procedure will be executed.

When LongTask is done, `mblnCancel` is tested to see if LongTask ended normally, or if it stopped because `mblnCancel` was set to True. The percent complete is updated only for the former case.

Running the Program

Press F5 to put the project in Run mode. Click the Start Task button. Each time the PercentDone event is raised, the label is updated with the percentage of the task that's complete. Click the Cancel button to stop the task. Notice that the appearance of the Cancel button doesn't change immediately when you click it. The Click event can't happen until the DoEvents statement allows event processing.

You may find it instructive to run the program with F8, and step through the code a line at a time. You can clearly see how execution enters LongTask, and then re-enters Form1 briefly each time the PercentDone event is raised.

What would happen if, while execution was back in Form1's code, the LongTask method was called again? Confusion, chaos, and eventually (if it happened every time the event was raised) a stack overflow.

Handling Events for a Different Widget

You can cause the variable `mWidget` to handle events for a different Widget object by assigning a reference to the new Widget to `mWidget`. In fact, you can make the code in Command1 do this every time you click the button, by adding two lines of code:

```
Set mWidget = New Widget    '<- New line.
Call mWidget.LongTask(14.4, 0.66)
Set mWidget = Nothing       '<- New line.
```

The code above creates a new Widget each time the button is pressed. As soon as the LongTask method completes, the reference to the Widget is released by setting `mWidget` to Nothing, and the Widget is destroyed.

A WithEvents variable can only contain one object reference at a time, so if you assign a different Widget object to `mWidget`, the previous Widget object's events will no longer be handled. If `mWidget` is the only object variable containing a reference to the old Widget, the object will be destroyed.

> **Note** You can declare as many WithEvents variables as you need, but arrays of WithEvents variables are not supported.

Terminating Event Handling for a WithEvents Variable

As long as there is a Widget object assigned to the variable `mWidget`, the event procedures associated with `mWidget` will be called whenever the Widget raises an event. To terminate event handling, you can set `mWidget` to Nothing, as shown in the following code fragment.

```
' Terminate event handling for mWidget.
Set mWidget = Nothing
```

When a WithEvents variable is set to Nothing, Visual Basic disconnects the object's events from the event procedures associated with the variable.

> **Important** A WithEvents variable contains an object reference, just like any other object variable. This object reference counts toward keeping the object alive. When you are setting all references to an object to Nothing in order to destroy it, don't forget the variables you declared WithEvents.

Comparing WithEvents to Control Events on Forms

You've probably noticed some similarities between the way you use WithEvents variables and the way you handle the events raised by controls on a form. In both cases, when you select the event in the right drop down of a code window, you get an event procedure containing the correct arguments for the event.

In fact, the mechanism is exactly the same. A control is treated as a *property* of the form class, and the name of that property is the value you assigned to the control's Name property in the Properties window.

It's as if there's a Public module-level variable with the same name as the control, and all of the control's event procedure names begin with that variable name, just as they would with a WithEvents variable.

You can easily see this by declaring the variable `mWidget` Public instead of Private. The moment you do this, `mWidget` will show up in the Object Browser as a property of Form1, just like the controls on the form.

The difference between the two cases is that Visual Basic automatically creates instances of all the controls on a form when the form is created, whereas you have to create your own instances of classes whose events you want to handle, and assign references to those objects to WithEvents variables.

Adding an Event to a Form

The following step by step procedure shows how you can create custom events for forms. To try this exercise, open a new Standard Exe project and do the following:

To add an event to Form1

1. On the **Project** menu, select **Add Class Module** to add a class module to the project. Place the following code in the **Declarations** section of Class1:

   ```
   Public Property Get Form1() As Form1
      Set Form1 = mForm1
   End Property

   Public Property Set Form1(ByVal NewForm1 As Form1)
      Set mForm1 = NewForm1
   End Property
   ```

   If you're using Procedure View, the property procedures can't be viewed at the same time. Click the **Full Module View** button at the bottom left corner of the code window to switch to Full Module View. You can return to Procedure View by clicking the **Procedure View** button next to it. (Hover the mouse over the buttons to see which is which.)

2. Add the following code to the **Declarations** section of Form1:

   ```
   Event Gong
   Private mc1 As Class1
   ```

   Now that Class1 has been created, it's possible to create a variable of type Class1. This procedure switches between Form1 and Class1 several times, because a step in one module requires first adding code to the other.

3. Go back to Class1 and add the following code to the **Declarations** section.

   ```
   Private WithEvents mForm1 As Form1
   ```

   As discussed in "Adding Events to a Class," the WithEvents keyword means this instance of Form1 is associated *with events*. Note that this step wasn't possible until the Gong event had been created.

4. In the left (**Object**) drop down on Class1's **Code** window, select **mForm1** to get the event procedure for the Gong event. Add the following code to the event procedure:

   ```
   Private Sub mForm1_Gong()
      MsgBox "Gong!"
   End Sub
   ```

5. Go back to Form1. In the **Object** drop down, select **Form**. In the right (**Procedure**) drop down, select **Load**. Add the following code to the event procedure:

   ```
   Private Sub Form_Load()
      Set mc1 = New Class1
      Set mc1.Form1 = Me
   End Sub
   ```

   The first line creates a Class1 object, and the second assigns to its **Form1** property (created in step 1) a reference to Form1 (that is, Me — when you're in Form1's Code window, Me refers to Form1; when you're in Class1's Code window, Me refers to Class1).

6. Put three text boxes on Form1. Use the **Object** and **Procedure** drop downs to select the Change event procedure for each control in turn, and place the same line of code in each:

   ```
   Private Sub Text1_Change()
      RaiseEvent Gong
   End Sub
   ```

   Each time the contents of a text box change, the form's Gong event will be raised.

7. Press F5 to run the project. Each time you type a character in one of the text boxes, the message box rings a bell. It's very annoying, but it shows how you can add an event to a form, and thus get notifications from several controls.

As shown in "Declaring and Raising Events," you can add arguments to events. For example, you might pass the name of the control — or better still, a reference to the control — to the receiver of the event.

Summary of Declaring, Raising, and Handling Events

To add an event to a class and then use the event, you must:

- In the Declarations section of the class module that defines the class, use the Event statement to declare the event with whatever arguments you want it to have. Events are always Public.

  Note Events cannot have named arguments, optional arguments, or ParamArray arguments. Events do not have return values.

- At appropriate places in the class module's code, use the RaiseEvent statement to raise the event, supplying the necessary arguments.

- In the Declarations section of the module that will handle the event, add a variable of the class type, using the WithEvents keyword. This must be a module-level variable.

- In the left drop down of the code window, select the variable you declared WithEvents.
- In the right drop down, select the event you wish to handle. (You can declare multiple events for a class.)
- Add code to the event procedure, using the supplied arguments.

Creating Data-Aware Classes

If you've read the preceding material on creating classes, you know by now that a class is an object that encapsulates data and code, and that the properties of a class are the data that describe an object. You also know that you can use property procedures or public properties to expose the data represented by those properties.

So far, so good — all of the examples thus far have dealt with transient data, that is, data that is created and consumed at run time. For many programs, this may be all that you need, but what if you need to store data between sessions, or utilize data that already exists outside of your program? In order to work with external sources of data, you need to make your class data-aware.

Data-aware classes can be divided into two categories — data consumers and data sources. Class modules have two design-time properties, DataBindingBehavior and DataSourceBehavior, that determine how a class will interact with external data. The BindingCollection object is used to bind data-aware classes to controls or to each other.

Data Sources

A data source is a class that provides data from an external source to be consumed by other objects. A Data control is in reality an instance of a class that is a data source, but classes that have been set up to act as data sources can be much more powerful than a Data control. Unlike the Data control, a data-aware class doesn't have to have a visual representation, and it isn't limited to a particular data interface such as Data Access Objects (DAO) or Remote Data Objects (RDO). In fact, a data-aware class can act as a data source for any type of data, including traditional ODBC sources, ActiveX Data Objects (ADO), or any OLE DB provider.

The DataSourceBehavior property determines whether or not a class can act as a data source. By setting the DataSourceBehavior to 1 (vbDataSource), your class can act as a source of data for other objects.

Data Consumers

Simply put, a data consumer is a class that can be bound to an external source of data, much as a TextBox control can be bound to a Data control. In earlier versions of Visual Basic, controls were the only objects that could be bound to a data source. Data-aware classes set up as data consumers allow you to bind any object to any object created from a class that has been set up as a data source.

The DataBindingBehavior property allows a class to bind to external data. By setting this property to 1 (vbSimpleBound), an object created from your class will be bound to a single data field in an external data source. By setting the DataBindingBehavior to 2 (vbComplexBound), your class will be bound to a row of data in an external data source. Think of it this way — if your objects were controls, a TextBox control would be simple bound, whereas a grid control would be complex bound.

The BindingCollection Object

Just as you would bind a control to a database through a Data control, data-aware classes need a central object to bind them together. That object is the BindingCollection object. Just as it sounds, the BindingCollection is a collection of bindings between a data source and one or more data consumers.

In order to use the BindingCollection object you must first add a reference to the Microsoft Data Binding Collection by selecting it in the References dialog, available from the Project menu. As with any object, you'll need to create an instance of the BindingCollection object at run time.

The DataSource property of the BindingCollection object is used to specify the object that will provide the data. This object must be a class or UserControl with its DataSourceBehavior property set to vbDataSource.

Once the BindingCollection has been instantiated and its DataSource set, you can use the Add method to define the binding relationships. The Add method takes three required arguments: the name of the consumer object, the property of that object to be bound to the source, and the field from the source that will be bound to the property. You can add multiple bindings to the BindingCollection by repeating the Add method; you can use the Remove method to delete a binding.

For More Information For step-by-step examples of creating data-aware classes, see the next section, "Creating a Data Source," and "Creating a Data Consumer," later in this chapter.

Creating a Data Source

In this section, we'll walk step-by-step through the process of creating a data-aware class that acts as a data source. This example will bind a TextBox control to our data source class in order to display the data. The next section, "Creating a Data Consumer," demonstrates how to bind our data source class to a data consumer class.

The code examples in this section are taken from the Data-aware Classes (Dataware.vbp) sample. You'll find this application in the Samples directory.

Creating a data source is a two-step process. In the first step we'll create the data source class; in the second step we'll hook it up to a TextBox control in order to display the output.

Creating the Source Class

The first step in creating a source class is to define a new class and give it the properties and methods necessary to provide data:

1. Open a new Standard EXE project, and insert a class module by selecting **Add Class Module** from the **Project** menu.
2. In the Properties window, set the properties of the class as follows:

Property	Setting
Name	MySource
DataSourceBehavior	vbDataSource

   When DataSourceBehavior is set to vbDataSource, a new Sub procedure GetDataMember is added to the class module. You can see this by selecting **Class** from the Object list in the code editor, then selecting the **Event** list.

3. Select **References** from the **Project** menu, and add a reference to the Microsoft ActiveX Data Objects 2.0 Library.
4. Add the following to the **Declarations** section of the class module:

```
Option Explicit
Private rs As ADODB.Recordset
```

   This declares an object variable for the ADO Recordset object.

5. Add the following code to the class module's Initialize event procedure:

```
Private Sub Class_Initialize()
   Dim strPath As String, strName As String
   Dim i As Integer

   ' Create an instance of the Recordset.
   Set rs = New ADODB.Recordset

   ' Set the properties of the Recordset.
   With rs
      .Fields.Append "DirID", adInteger
      .Fields.Append "Directory", adBSTR, 255
      .CursorType = adOpenStatic
      .LockType = adLockOptimistic
      .Open
   End With

   ' Loop through the directories and populate
   ' the Recordset.
   strPath = "C:\"
```

```
    strName = Dir(strPath, vbDirectory)
    i = 0
    Do While strName <> ""
       If strName <> "." And strName <> ".." Then
          If (GetAttr(strPath & strName) And _
             vbDirectory) = vbDirectory Then
             i = i + 1
             With rs
                .AddNew
                .Fields.Item("DirID") = i
                .Fields.Item("Directory") = strName
                .Update
             End With
          End If
       End If
       strName = Dir
    Loop

    ' Return to the first record.
    rs.MoveFirst
End Sub
```

In this example we're creating a ADO Recordset object on the fly and populating it with a list of directories. Alternatively, you could use an existing recordset by assigning to the Connect property of the ADO Recordset in the Initialize event.

6. Select **Class** from the **Object** list in the **Code Editor**, then select GetDataMember from the **Event** list. Add the following code to the GetDataMember Sub procedure:

```
Private Sub Class_GetDataMember(DataMember As String, Data As Object)
    ' Assign the Recordset to the Data object.
    Set Data = rs
End Sub
```

The GetDataMember procedure sets the source of the data for the class. Your data source class can provide multiple data sources by adding a Select Case statement to the GetDataMember procedure and passing in a source name in the DataMember argument.

7. Add a new Sub procedure to provide a public method to loop through the Recordset:

```
Public Sub Cycle()
    ' Cycle through the Recordset.
    rs.MoveNext
    If rs.EOF = True Then
       rs.MoveFirst
    End If
End Sub
```

In order to move through the recordset, we need to expose the navigation methods for our class. For simplicity, this example can only loop forward through the recordset. To make the class more useful, you might want to expose methods such as MoveFirst, MoveNext, Add, and Delete.

Using the Source Class

Now that the source class is defined, we can do something useful with it. In this example we'll bind it to a TextBox control so that we can see its output; we'll also use a CommandButton to execute our Cycle method.

1. Select **Form1** and add a TextBox control and a CommandButton control to the form.
2. In the Properties window, set the properties of the TextBox as follows:

Property	Setting
Name	txtConsumer
Text	(blank)

3. In the Properties window, set the properties of the CommandButton as follows:

Property	Setting
Name	cmdCycle
Caption	Cycle

4. Select **References** from the **Project** menu, and add a reference to the Microsoft Data Binding Collection.

   The DataBinding object provided by the Data Binding Collection is the "glue" that binds a data source to a data consumer.

5. Add the following to the **Declarations** section of the class module:

```
Option Explicit
Private objSource As MySource
Private objBindingCollection As BindingCollection
```

   We need to declare our source class (MySource) and the BindingCollection object using early binding.

6. Add the following code to the Form_Load event procedure:

```
Private Sub Form_Load()
   Set objSource = New MySource
   Set objBindingCollection = New BindingCollection
```

```
    ' Assign the source class to the Binding
    ' Collection's DataSource property.
    Set objBindingCollection.DataSource = objSource
    ' Add a binding.
    ObjBindingCollection.Add txtConsumer, "Text", "Directory"
```

In the Load event we create instances of the source class and the BindingCollection object, then we assign the source object to the DataSource property of the BindingCollection. Finally, we add a binding by specifying the name of the consumer (txtConsumer), the Property of the consumer to be bound (the Text property), and the Field property of the source object that we are binding to (Directory).

7. Add the following code to the cmdCycle Click event procedure:

```
Private cmdCycle_Click()
    ' Call the Cycle method of the data source.
    ObjSource.Cycle
End Sub
```

   This will execute the Cycle method of our source class.

8. Press F5 to run the project.

   As you click the Cycle button, directory names from the recordset created in our source class will appear in the TextBox. Congratulations — you've just bound a control to a data source class without using a Data control!

9. Save the project. When prompted for filenames, use the following names.

   Save the source class as "MySource.cls."

   Save the form as "Dataform.frm."

   Save the project as "Dataware.vbp."

   These files will be used later in "Creating a Data Consumer."

In the next section, "Creating a Data Consumer," we'll look at the process of creating a data-aware class that acts a consumer of data.

Creating a Data Consumer

In this section, we'll walk step-by-step through the process of creating a data-aware class that acts as a data consumer. The previous section, "Creating a Data Source," demonstrates how to create a data source to which a data consumer can be bound. This example shows how to create a data consumer class and bind it to the data source created in the previous section.

The code examples in this section are taken from the Data-aware Classes (Dataware.vbp) sample. You'll find this application in the Samples directory.

Binding a Data Consumer to a Data Source Object

This example demonstrates how to create a data consumer class and bind it to a data source class. The example uses the MySource class created in the "Creating a Data Source" topic.

1. Open the Dataware.vbp project. (Select **Open Project** from the **File** menu.)

   Note If you haven't previously completed the "Creating a Data Source" example this project won't exist. You can also find a completed version of the Dataware.vbp project in the Samples directory.

2. Insert a new class module by selecting **Add Class Module** from the **Project** menu.

3. In the Properties window, set the properties of the new class as follows:

Property	Setting
Name	MyConsumer
DataBindingBehavior	vbSimpleBound

4. Add the following to the **Declarations** section of the class module:

```
Option Explicit
Private mDirectory As String
```

5. Add a pair of Property Get / Property Let procedures for a public **DirName** property:

```
Public Property Get DirName() As String
   DirName = mDirectory
End Property

Public Property Let DirName(mNewDir As String)
   mDirectory = mNewDir
   ' Display the new value in the Immediate window.
   Debug.Print mDirectory
End Property
```

   Since MySource is a nonvisual class, we need to use a Debug.Print statement in the Property Let procedure to prove that it's retrieving new values from the data source.

6. Select **Form1** and add the following code to the **Declarations** section:

```
Option Explicit
Private objSource As MySource
Private objBindingCollection As BindingCollection
Private objConsumer As MyConsumer
```

   The new line of code adds a reference to our consumer class.

7. Add the following code to the Form Load event procedure:

```
Private Sub Form_Load()
   Set objSource = New MySource
   Set objBindingCollection = New BindingCollection
   Set objConsumer = New MyConsumer

   ' Assign the source class to the Binding
   ' Collection's DataSource property.
   Set objBindingCollection.DataSource = objSource
   ' Add a binding.
   objBindingCollection.Add txtConsumer, "Text", "Directory"
   objBindingCollection.Add objConsumer, "DirName", "Directory"
```

   The new code creates an instance of the consumer class and adds it to the Binding Collection, binding the DirName property of the consumer to the Directory field of the data source.

8. Press F5 to run the project. Make sure that the Immediate window is visible.

   As you click the Cycle button, the directory names provided by MySource will appear in both the TextBox and the Immediate window, proving that MyConsumer is bound to MySource.

Naming Properties, Methods, and Events

The properties, methods, and events you add to a class module define the interface that will be used to manipulate objects created from the class. When naming these elements, and their arguments, you may find it helpful to follow a few simple rules.

- Use entire words whenever possible, as for example SpellCheck. Abbreviations can take many forms, and hence can be confusing. If whole words are too long, use complete first syllables.
- Use mixed case for your identifiers, capitalizing each word or syllable, as for example ShortcutMenus or AsyncReadComplete.
- Use the correct plural for collection class names, as for example Worksheets, Forms, or Widgets. If the collection holds objects with a name that ends in "s," append the word "Collection," as for example SeriesCollection.
- Use either verb/object or object/verb order consistently for your method names. That is, use InsertWidget, InsertSprocket, and so on, or always place the object first, as in WidgetInsert and SprocketInsert.

  Note While it's possible to use an underscore character in a property name, an underscore in an event name will cause an error. The underscore character is used in Event procedures to separate the event name from the object name. For this reason, it's best to avoid the underscore character altogether when naming properties, methods, and events.

One of the chief benefits of programming with objects is code reuse. Following the rules above, which are part of the ActiveX guidelines for interfaces, makes it easier to remember the names and purposes of properties, methods, and events.

For More Information If you have the Professional or Enterprise Edition of the Visual Basic 6.0 Language Reference Library, see the expanded list in "What's In a Name?" in Chapter 6, "General Principles of Component Design," in Part 2, "Creating ActiveX Components," in the *Microsoft Visual Basic 6.0 Component Tools Guide.*

Polymorphism

Polymorphism means that many classes can provide the same property or method, and a caller doesn't have to know what class an object belongs to before calling the property or method.

For example, a Flea class and a Tyrannosaur class might each have a Bite method. Polymorphism means that you can invoke Bite without knowing whether an object is a Flea or a Tyrannosaur — although you'll certainly know afterward.

For More Information With the Professional and Enterprise editions of Visual Basic, Polymorphism becomes a powerful mechanism for evolving systems of software components. This is discussed in Chapter 6, "General Principles of Component Design," in Part 2, "Creating ActiveX Components," in the *Microsoft Visual Basic 6.0 Component Tools Guide*.

How Visual Basic Provides Polymorphism

Most object-oriented programming systems provide polymorphism through *inheritance*. That is, the hypothetical Flea and Tyrannosaur classes might both inherit from an Animal class. Each class would override the Animal class's Bite method, in order to provide its own bite characteristics.

The polymorphism comes from the fact that you could call the Bite method of an object belonging to any class that derived from Animal, without knowing which class the object belonged to.

Providing Polymorphism with Interfaces

Visual Basic doesn't use inheritance to provide polymorphism. Visual Basic provides polymorphism through multiple ActiveX *interfaces*. In the Component Object Model (COM) that forms the infrastructure of the ActiveX specification, multiple interfaces allow systems of software components to evolve without breaking existing code.

An *interface* is a set of related properties and methods. Much of the ActiveX specification is concerned with implementing standard interfaces to obtain system services or to provide functionality to other programs.

In Visual Basic, you would create an Animal interface and implement it in your Flea and Tyrannosaur classes. You could then invoke the Bite method of either kind of object, without knowing which kind it was.

Polymorphism and Performance

Polymorphism is important for performance reasons. To see this, consider the following function:

```
Public Sub GetFood(ByVal Critter As Object, _
ByVal Food As Object)
   Dim dblDistance As Double
   ' Code to calculate distance to food (omitted).
   Critter.Move dblDistance ' Late bound
   Critter.Bite Food        ' Late bound
End Sub
```

The Move and Bite methods are *late bound* to `Critter`. Late binding happens when Visual Basic can't determine at compile time what kind of object a variable will contain. In this example, the Critter argument is declared As Object, so at run time it could contain a reference to any kind of object — like a Car or a Rock.

Because it can't tell what the object will be, Visual Basic compiles some extra code to ask the object if it supports the method you've called. If the object supports the method, this extra code invokes it; if not, the extra code raises an error. Every method or property call incurs this additional overhead.

By contrast, interfaces allow *early binding*. When Visual Basic knows at compile time what interface is being called, it can check the type library to see if that interface supports the method. Visual Basic can then compile in a direct jump to the method, using a virtual function table (vtable). This is many times faster than late binding.

Now suppose the Move and Bite methods belong to an Animal interface, and that all animal classes implement this interface. The Critter argument can now be declared As Animal, and the Move and Bite methods will be early bound:

```
Public Sub GetFood(ByVal Critter As Animal, _
ByVal Food As Object)
   Dim dblDistance As Double
   ' Code to calculate distance to food (omitted).
   Critter.Move dblDistance' Early bound (vtable).
   Critter.Bite Food        ' Early bound (vtable).
End Sub
```

Creating and Implementing an Interface

As explained in "How Visual Basic Provides Polymorphism," earlier in this chapter, an interface is a set of properties and methods. In the following code example, you'll create an Animal interface and implement it in two classes, Flea and Tyrannosaur.

You can create the Animal interface by adding a class module to your project, naming it Animal, and inserting the following code:

```
Public Sub Move(ByVal Distance As Double)

End Sub

Public Sub Bite(ByVal What As Object)

End Sub
```

Notice that there's no code in these methods. Animal is an *abstract class,* containing no implementation code. An abstract class isn't meant for creating objects — its purpose is to provide the template for an interface you add to other classes. (Although, as it turns out, sometimes it's useful to implement the interface of a class that isn't abstract; this is discussed later in this topic.)

> **Note** Properly speaking, an abstract class is one from which you can't create objects. You can always create objects from Visual Basic classes, even if they contain no code; thus they are not truly abstract.

Now you can add two more class modules, naming one of them Flea and the other Tyrannosaur. To implement the Animal interface in the Flea class, you use the Implements statement:

```
Option Explicit
Implements Animal
```

As soon as you've added this line of code, you can click the left (Object) drop down in the code window. One of the entries will be Animal. When you select it, the right (Procedure) drop down will show the methods of the Animal interface.

Select each method in turn, to create empty procedure templates for all the methods. The templates will have the correct arguments and data types, as defined in the Animal class. Each procedure name will have the prefix `Animal_` to identify the interface.

> **Important** An interface is like a contract. By implementing the interface, a class agrees to respond when any property or method of the interface is invoked. Therefore, you must implement *all* the properties and methods of an interface.

You can now add the following code to the Flea class:

```
Private Sub Animal_Move(ByVal Distance As Double)
   ' (Code to jump some number of inches omitted.)
   Debug.Print "Flea moved"
End Sub

Private Sub Animal_Bite(ByVal What As Object)
   ' (Code to suck blood omitted.)
   Debug.Print "Flea bit a " & TypeName(What)
End Sub
```

You may be wondering why the procedures are declared Private. If they were Public, the procedures Animal_Jump and Animal_Bite would be part of the Flea interface, and we'd be stuck in the same bind we were in originally, declaring the Critter argument As Object so it could contain either a Flea or a Tyrannosaur.

Multiple Interfaces

The Flea class now has two interfaces: The Animal interface you've just implemented, which has two members, and the default Flea interface, which has no members. Later in this example you'll add a member to one of the default interfaces.

You can implement the Animal interface similarly for the Tyrannosaur class:

```
Option Explicit
Implements Animal

Private Sub Animal_Move(ByVal Distance As Double)
   ' (Code to pounce some number of yards omitted.)
   Debug.Print "Tyrannosaur moved"
End Sub

Private Sub Animal_Bite(ByVal What As Object)
   ' (Code to take a pound of flesh omitted.)
   Debug.Print "Tyrannosaur bit a " & TypeName(What)
End Sub
```

Exercising the Tyrannosaur and the Flea

Add the following code to the Load event of Form1:

```
Private Sub Form_Load()
   Dim fl As Flea
   Dim ty As Tyrannosaur
   Dim anim As Animal
```

```
    Set fl = New Flea
    Set ty = New Tyrannosaur
    ' First give the Flea a shot.
    Set anim = fl
    Call anim.Bite(ty)'Flea bites dinosaur.
    ' Now the Tyrannosaur gets a turn.
    Set anim = ty
    Call anim.Bite(fl)'Dinosaur bites flea.
End Sub
```

Press F8 to step through the code. Notice the messages in the Immediate window. When the variable `anim` contains a reference to the Flea, the Flea's implementation of Bite is invoked, and likewise for the Tyrannosaur.

The variable `anim` can contain a reference to any object that implements the Animal interface. In fact, it can *only* contain references to such objects. If you attempt to assign a Form or PictureBox object to `anim`, an error will occur.

The Bite method is early bound when you call it through `anim`, because Visual Basic knows at compile time that whatever object is assigned to `anim` will have a Bite method.

Passing Tyrannosaurs and Fleas to Procedures

Remember the GetFood procedure from "How Visual Basic Provides Polymorphism?" You can add the *second* version of the GetFood procedure — the one that illustrates polymorphism — to Form1, and replace the code in the Load event with the following:

```
Private Sub Form_Load()
    Dim fl As Flea
    Dim ty As Tyrannosaur

    Set fl = New Flea
    Set ty = New Tyrannosaur
    'Flea dines on dinosaur.
    Call GetFood(fl, ty)
    ' And vice versa.
    Call GetFood(ty, fl)
End Sub
```

Stepping through this code shows how an object reference that you pass to an argument of another interface type is converted into a reference to the second interface (in this case, Animal). What happens is that Visual Basic queries the object to find out whether it supports the second interface. If the object does, it returns a reference to the interface, and Visual Basic places that reference in the argument variable. If the object does not support the second interface, an error occurs.

Implementing Methods That Return Values

Suppose the Move method returned a value. After all, you know how far you want an Animal to move, but an individual specimen might not be able to move that far. It might be old and decrepit, or there might be a wall in the way. The return value of the Move method could be used to tell you how far the Animal actually moved.

```
Public Function Move(ByVal Distance As Double) _
As Double

End Function
```

When you implement this method in the Tyrannosaur class, you assign the return value to the procedure name, just as you would for any other Function procedure:

```
Private Function Animal_Move(ByVal Distance _
As Double) As Double
   Dim dblDistanceMoved As Double
   ' Code to calculate how far to pounce (based on
   ' age, state of health, and obstacles) is omitted.
   ' This example assumes that the result has been
   ' placed in the variable dblDistanceMoved.
   Debug.Print "Tyrannosaur moved"; dblDistanceMoved
   Animal_Move = dblDistanceMoved
End Function
```

To assign the return value, use the full procedure name, including the interface prefix.

Implementing Properties

Suppose we give the Animal class an Age property, by adding a Public variable to the Declarations section:

```
Option Explicit
Public Age As Double
```

The Procedure drop downs in the code modules for the Tyrannosaur and Flea classes now contain property procedures for implementing the Age property, as shown in Figure 9.10.

Figure 9.10 Implementing property procedures

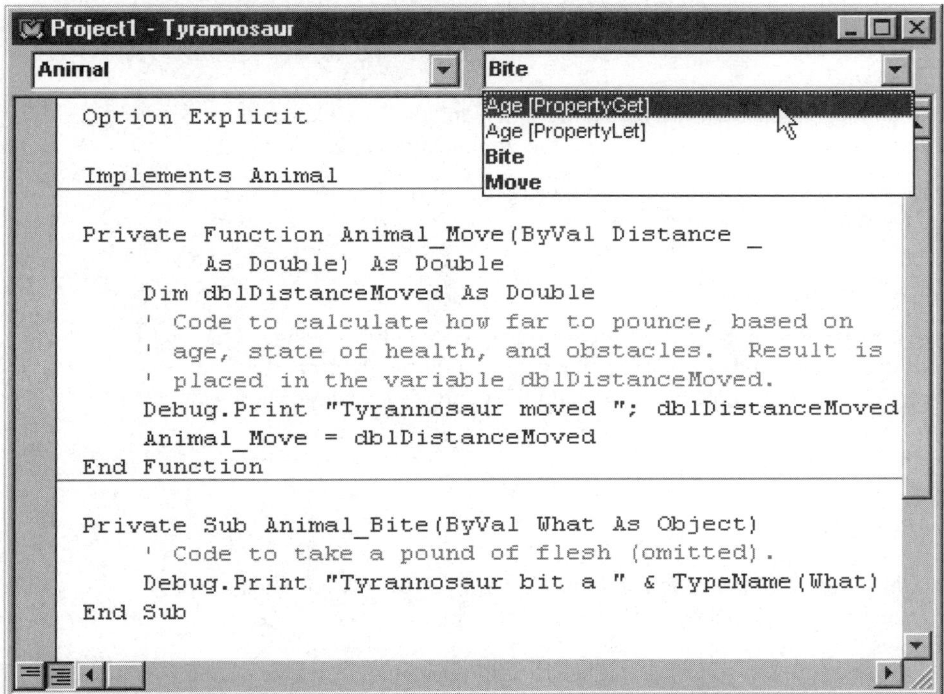

This illustrates a point made in "Adding Properties to a Class," earlier in this chapter. Using a public variable to implement a property is strictly a convenience for the programmer. Behind the scenes, Visual Basic implements the property as a pair of property procedures.

You must implement both procedures. The property procedures are easily implemented by storing the value in a private data member, as shown here:

```
Private mdblAge As Double

Private Property Get Animal_Age() As Double
   Animal_Age = mdblAge
End Property

Private Property Let Animal_Age(ByVal RHS As Double)
   mdblAge = RHS
End Property
```

The private data member is an implementation detail, so you have to add it yourself.

> **Note** When Implements provides the template for a Property Set or Property Let, it has no way of determining the name of the last argument, so it substitutes the name `RHS`, as shown in the code example above.

There's no data validation on a property implemented as a public data member, but that doesn't mean you can't add validation code to the Property Let for Animal_Age. For example, you might want to restrict the values to ages appropriate for a Tyrannosaur or a Flea, respectively.

In fact, this shows the independence of interface and implementation. As long as the interface matches the description in the type library, the implementation can be anything.

Before you go on to the next step, remove the implementation of the read-write Age property from both class modules.

Implementing a Read-Only Property

Of course, allowing the age of an animal to be set arbitrarily is bad object design. The object should know its own age, and provide it to the user as a read-only property. Remove the public variable `Age` from the Animal class, and add the template for a read-only age property, like this:

```
Public Property Get Age() As Double

End Property
```

Now the Procedure drop downs in the code windows for the Tyrannosaur and Flea classes contain only a single entry, Age [PropertyGet]. You might implement this for the Tyrannosaur as follows:

```
Private mdblBirth As Double

Private Property Get Animal_Age() As Double
   Animal_Age = Now - mdblBirth
End Property
```

The code above returns the age of the Tyrannosaur in days. You could set `mdblBirth` in the Initialize event of the Tyrannosaur class, as here:

```
Private Sub Class_Initialize()
   mdblBirth = Now
End Sub
```

And of course you could return the property value in more commonly used units, such as dog years.

Time Out for a Brief Discussion of Objects and Interfaces

The Tyrannosaur and Flea code example seems to play fast and loose with interfaces and objects. References to objects are assigned to one object variable, and references to interfaces to another.

In fact, *all of the references are object references.* A reference to an interface is also a reference to the object that implements the interface. Furthermore, an object may have multiple interfaces, but it's still the same object underneath.

In Visual Basic, each class has a default interface that has the same name as the class. Well, almost the same. By convention, an underscore is prefixed to the class name. The underscore indicates that this interface is hidden in the type library.

Thus the Tyrannosaur class has a default interface called _Tyrannosaur. Because Tyrannosaur also implements Animal, the class has a second interface named Animal.

However, underneath it all, the object is still a Tyrannosaur. Place a command button on Form1, and add the following code:

```
Private Sub Command1_Click()
   Dim ty As Tyrannosaur
   Dim anim As Animal

   Set ty = New Tyrannosaur
   Set anim = ty
   MsgBox TypeName(anim)
End Sub
```

You might expect the message box to display "Animal," but in fact it displays "Tyrannosaur."

Querying for Interfaces

When you assign a Tyrannosaur object to variable of type `Animal`, Visual Basic asks the Tyrannosaur object if it supports the Animal interface. (The method used for this is called QueryInterface, or QI for short; you may sometimes hear QI used as a verb.) If the answer is no, an error occurs.

If the answer is yes, the object is assigned to the variable. Only the methods and properties of the Animal interface can be accessed through this variable.

Generic Object Variables and Interfaces

What happens if you assign the object reference to a generic object variable, as in the following code?

```
Private Sub Command1_Click()
   Dim ty As Tyrannosaur
   Dim anim As Animal
   Dim obj As Object

   Set ty = New Tyrannosaur
   Set anim = ty
   Set obj = anim
   MsgBox TypeName(obj)
End Sub
```

The result is again Tyrannosaur. Now, what interface do you get when you call properties and methods through the variable `obj`? Add the following method to the Tyrannosaur class:

```
Public Sub Growl()
   Debug.Print "Rrrrrr"
End Sub
```

The Growl method belongs to the Tyrannosaur object's default interface. In the code for the command button's Click event, replace the MsgBox statement with the following two lines of code:

```
obj.Move 42
obj.Growl
```

When you run the project and click the button, execution stops on the Growl method, with the error "Object does not support this property or method." Clearly, the interface is still Animal.

This is something to bear in mind when using variables of type Object with objects that have multiple interfaces. The interface the variable will access is the *last interface assigned.* For example:

```
Private Sub Command1_Click()
   Dim ty As Tyrannosaur
   Dim anim As Animal
   Dim obj As Object

   Set ty = New Tyrannosaur
   Set anim = ty
   Set obj = anim
   obj.Move 42      ' Succeeds
   obj.Growl    ' Fails

   Set obj = ty
   obj.Move 42      ' Fails
   obj.Growl    ' Succeeds
End Sub
```

Fortunately, there's very little reason to use the slower, late-bound Object data type with objects that have multiple interfaces. One of the main reasons for using multiple interfaces is to gain the advantage of early binding through polymorphism.

Other Sources of Interfaces

Visual Basic class modules are not your only source of interfaces to implement. You can implement any interface contained in a type library, as long as that interface supports Automation.

If you have the Professional or Enterprise Edition of Visual Basic, you can create your own type libraries of abstract classes. These type libraries can be used in many projects, as described in Chapter 6, "General Principles of Component Design," in Part 2, "Creating ActiveX Components," in the *Microsoft Visual Basic 6.0 Component Tools Guide*.

The Professional and Enterprise editions also include the MkTypLib (Make Type Library) utility in the Tools directory. If you've used this utility with Microsoft Visual C++, you may find it a more congenial way to create interfaces.

Using Interfaces in Your Project

To use an interface in your project, click References on the Project menu to open the References dialog box. If the type library is registered, it will appear in the list of references, and you can check it. If the type library is not in the list, you can use the Browse button to locate it.

Once you have a reference to a type library, you can use Implements to implement any Automation interfaces the type library contains.

The Many (Inter)Faces of Code Reuse

There are two main forms of code reuse — binary and source. Binary code reuse is accomplished by creating and using an object, while source code reuse is achieved by inheritance, which isn't supported by Visual Basic. (Source code reuse can also be achieved by copying and modifying the source code, but this technique is nothing new, and has many well-known problems.)

Visual Basic has been a pioneer of binary code reuse — controls being the classic example. You reuse the code in a control by placing an instance of the control on your form. This is known as a *containment* relationship or a *has-a* relationship; that is, the form *contains* or *has a* CommandButton.

For More Information Containment relationships are discussed in "Object Models" later in this chapter.

Delegating to an Implemented Object

Implements provides a powerful new means of code reuse. You can implement an abstract class (as discussed in "Creating and Implementing an Interface"), or you can implement the interface of a fully functional class. You can create the *inner object* (that is, the implemented object) in the Initialize event of the *outer object* (that is, the one that implements the inner object's interface).

As noted in "Creating and Implementing an Interface," earlier in this chapter, an interface is like a contract — you must implement all the members of the inner object's interface in the outer object's class module. However, you can be very selective in the way you delegate to the properties and methods of the inner object. In one method you might delegate directly to the inner object, passing the arguments unchanged, while in another method you might execute some code of your own before calling the inner object — and in a third method you might execute only your own code, ignoring the inner object altogether!

For example, suppose you have a OneManBand class and a Cacophony class, both of which generate sounds. You'd like to add the functionality of the Cacophony class to the OneManBand class, and reuse some of the implementation of the Cacophony class's methods.

```
' OneManBand implements the Cacophony interface.
Implements Cacophony

' Object variable to keep the reference in.
Private mcac As Cacophony

Private Sub Class_Initialize()
   ' Create the object.
   Set mcac = New Cacophony
End Sub
```

You can now go to the Object drop down and select Cacophony, and then get procedure templates for the methods of the Cacophony interface. To implement these methods, you can delegate to the Cacophony object. For example, the Beep method might look like this:

```
Private Sub Cacophony_Beep(ByVal Frequency As Double, _
ByVal Duration As Double)
   ' Delegate to the inner Cacophony object.
   Call mcac.Beep(Frequency, Duration)
End Sub
```

The implementation above is very simple. The outer object (OneManBand) delegates directly to the inner (Cacophony), reusing the Cacophony object's Beep method without any changes. This is a good thing, but it's only the beginning.

The Implements statement is a very powerful tool for code reuse, because it gives you enormous flexibility. You might decide to alter the effects of the OneManBand class's Beep method, by inserting your own code before (or after) the call to the inner Cacophony object:

```
Private Sub Cacophony_Beep(ByVal Frequency As Double, _
ByVal Duration As Double)
   ' Bump everything up an octave.
   Frequency = Frequency * 2
   ' Based on another property of the OneManBand
   ' class, Staccato, cut the duration of each beep.
```

```
    If Staccato Then Duration = Duration * 7 / 8
    Call mcac.Beep(Frequency, Duration)
    ' You can even call other methods of OneManBand.
    If Staccato Then Pause(Duration * 1 / 8)
End Sub
```

For some of the methods, your implementation may delegate directly to the inner Cacophony object, while for others you may interpose your own code before and after delegating — or even omit delegation altogether, using entirely your own code to implement a method.

Because the OneManBand class implements the Cacophony interface, you can use it with any musical application that calls that interface. Your implementation details are hidden from the calling application, but the resulting sounds are all your own.

> **Note** COM provides another mechanism for binary code reuse, called *aggregation*. In aggregation, an entire interface is reused, without any changes, and the implementation is provided by an instance of the class being aggregated. Visual Basic does not support this form of code reuse.

Doesn't This Get Tedious?

Writing delegation code can indeed become tedious, especially if most of the outer object's properties and methods simply delegate directly to the corresponding properties and methods of the inner object.

If you have the Professional or Enterprise Edition of Visual Basic, you can use the Visual Basic Extensibility model to create your own delegation wizard to automate the task, similar to the Class Wizard that's included in the Professional and Enterprise editions.

For More Information The use of polymorphism and multiple interfaces in component software is discussed in Chapter 6, "General Principles of Component Design," in Part 2, "Creating ActiveX Components," in the *Microsoft Visual Basic 6.0 Component Tools Guide*.

Using the Extensibility Model is documented in Part 3, "Extending the Visual Basic Environment with Add-Ins," in the *Microsoft Visual Basic 6.0 Component Tools Guide*.

Programming with Your Own Objects

You can start using objects gradually, finding useful tasks for which combining code and data is an advantage. You can use the functionality of these objects by declaring object variables, assigning new objects to them, and calling the objects' properties and methods.

As you add more and more objects to your programs, you'll start to see relationships between them. You can begin making program design more dependent on objects and their relationships, and you can begin using more robust techniques — like creating custom collection classes — for expressing those relationships in code.

At some point, you'll suddenly see how linking objects together changes the very nature of your program, and you'll be ready to start designing object-based programs from the ground up.

The following topics provide an overview of these evolutionary changes in your coding style. Read them now, to give yourself a rough picture of where you're headed, and read them again when your ideas of object-based programming begin to gel.

For More Information ActiveX components open up yet another dimension of code reuse and object-based programming. If you have the Professional or Enterprise Edition of Visual Basic, you can begin to explore that dimension through Part 2, "Creating ActiveX Components," in the *Microsoft Visual Basic 6.0 Component Tools Guide*.

Object References and Reference Counting

The primary rule for object lifetime is very simple: An object is destroyed when the last reference to it is released. However, as with so much of life, simple doesn't always mean easy.

As you use more objects, and keep more variables containing references to those objects, you may go through periods when it seems impossible to get your objects to go away when you want them to.

At some point, it will occur to you that Visual Basic must be keeping track of object references — otherwise how could it know when the last reference to an object is released? You may start thinking that if only you could get access to Visual Basic's reference counts, debugging would be much easier.

Unfortunately, that's not true. To make using objects more efficient, the Component Object Model (COM) specifies a number of complex shortcuts to its reference counting rules. The net result is that you couldn't trust the value of the reference count even if you had access to it.

According to COM rules, the only information you can depend on is *whether or not the reference count is zero*. You know when the reference count reaches zero, because your object's Terminate event occurs. Beyond that, there's no reliable information to be gleaned from reference counts.

> **Note** The fact that you don't have to remember the COM reference counting rules is no small thing. Managing reference counts yourself is a lot more difficult than keeping track of which object variables in your program contain references to objects.

> **Tip** Declare your object variables as class types, instead of As Object. That way, if you have a Widget object that isn't terminating, the only variables you need to worry about are those declared As Widget.

For collections of object references, don't use the Visual Basic Collection object by itself. Object references in a Visual Basic Collection object are stored in Variants — which, like variables declared As Object, can hold references to objects of any class. Instead create collection classes of your own that accept objects of only one class, as described in "Creating Your Own Collection Classes," later in this chapter. That way, the only collections you need to search for your Widget object are those of type Widget.

Organize your object into a hierarchy, as described ins the next section, "Object Models." If all of your objects are connected, It's easy to write a procedure that walks through the whole model and reports on all the existing objects.

Don't declare variables As New. They're like those birthday candles that re-ignite after you blow them out: If you use one after you've set it to Nothing, Visual Basic obligingly creates another object.

For More Information Circular references are the most difficult kind to shut down cleanly. See "Object Models."

Object Models

Once you've defined a class by creating a class module and giving it properties and methods, you can create any number of objects from that class. How do you keep track of the objects you create?

The simplest way to keep track of objects is to declare an object variable for each object you plan to create. Of course, this places a limit on the number of objects you can create.

You can keep multiple object references in an array or a collection, as discussed in "Creating Arrays of Objects" and "Creating Collections of Objects," earlier in this chapter.

In the beginning, you'll probably locate object variables, arrays, and collections in forms or standard modules, as you do with ordinary variables. As you add more classes, though, you'll probably discover that the objects you're using have clear relationships to each other.

Object Models Express Containment Relationships

Object models give structure to an object-based program. By defining the relationships between the objects you use in your program, an object model organizes your objects in a way that makes programming easier.

Typically, an object model expresses the fact that some objects are "bigger," or more important than others — these objects can be thought of as containing other objects, or as being made up of other objects.

For example, you might create a SmallBusiness object as the core of your program. You might want the SmallBusiness object to have other types of objects associated with it, such as Employee objects and Customer objects. You would probably also want it to contain a Product object. An object model for this program is shown in Figure 9.11.

Figure 9.11 An object model

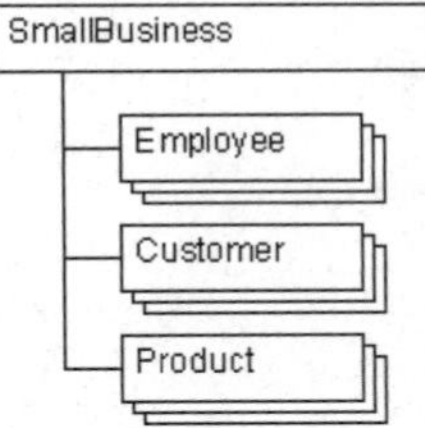

You can define four class modules, named SmallBusiness, Employee, Customer, and Product, and give them each appropriate properties and methods, but how do you make the connections between objects? You have two tools for this purpose: Object properties and the Collection object. The following code fragment shows one way to implement the hierarchy in Figure 9.11.

```
' Code for the Declarations section of the
' SmallBusiness class module.
Public Name As String
Public Product As New Product
Public Employees As New Collection
Public Customers As New Collection
```

The first time you refer to the Product property, the object will be created, because it was declared As New. For example, the following code might create and set the name and price of the SmallBusiness object's Product object.

```
' Code for a standard module.
Public sbMain As New SmallBusiness
Sub Main
   sbMain.Name = "Velociraptor Enterprises, Inc."
   ' The first time the Product variable is used in
   ' code, the Product object is created.
   sbMain.Product.Name = "Inflatable Velociraptor"
   sbMain.Product.Price = 1.98
   .
   .  ' Code to initialize and show main form.
   .
End Sub
```

> **Note** Implementing an object property with public variables is sloppy. You could inadvertently destroy the Product object by setting the property to Nothing somewhere in your code. It's better to create object properties as read-only properties, as shown in the following code fragment.

```
' Code for a more robust object property. Storage for
' the property is private, so it can't be set to
' Nothing from outside the object.
Private mProduct As New Product
```

```
Property Get Product() As Product
   ' The first time this property is called, mProduct
   ' contains Nothing, so Visual Basic will create a
   ' Product object.
   Set Product = mProduct
End If
```

One-to-Many Object Relationships

Object properties work well when the relationship between objects is one-to-one. It frequently happens, however, that an object of one type contains a number of objects of another type. In the SmallBusiness object model, the Employees property is implemented as a Collection object, so that the SmallBusiness object can contain multiple Employee objects. The following code fragment shows how new Employee objects might be added to this collection.

```
Public Function NewEmployee(Name, Salary, HireDate, _
ID) As Employee
   Dim empNew As New Employee
   empNew.Name = Name   ' Implicit object creation.
   empNew.Salary = Salary
   empNew.HireDate = HireDate
   ' Add to the collection, using the ID as a key.
   sbMain.Employees.Add empNew, CStr(ID)
   ' Return a reference to the new Employee.
   Set NewEmployee = empNew
End Function
```

The NewEmployee function can be called as many times as necessary to create employees for the business represented by the SmallBusiness object. The existing employees can be listed at any time by iterating over the Employees collection.

> **Note** Once again, this is not a very robust implementation. Better practice is to create your own collection classes, and expose them as read-only properties. This is discussed in "Creating Your Own Collection Classes," later in this chapter.

> **Tip** The Class Builder utility, included in the Professional and Enterprise editions of Visual Basic, can generate much of the code you need to implement an object model. Class Builder creates robust object properties and collection classes, and allows you to rearrange your model easily.

Parent Properties

When you have a reference to an object, you can get to the objects it contains by using its object properties and collections. It's also very useful to be able to navigate up the hierarchy, to get to the object that contains the object you have a reference to.

Navigating upward is usually done with Parent properties. The Parent property returns a reference to the object's container. For a discussion of object model navigation, see "Navigating Object Models" in Chapter 10, "Programming with Components."

You can find an example of a Parent property in "Adding Properties to a Class" earlier in this chapter.

> **Tip** When you assign a Parent property to an object in a collection, don't use a reference to the Collection object. The real parent of the object is the object that contains the collection. If the Parent property points to the collection, you'll have to use two levels of indirection to get to the real parent — that is, `obj.Parent.Parent` instead of `obj.Parent`.

Parent Properties, Circular References, and Object Teardown

One of the biggest problems with Parent properties is that they create circular references. The "larger" object has a reference to the object it contains, and the contained object has a reference through its Parent property, creating a loop as shown in Figure 9.12.

Figure 9.12 A case of circular references

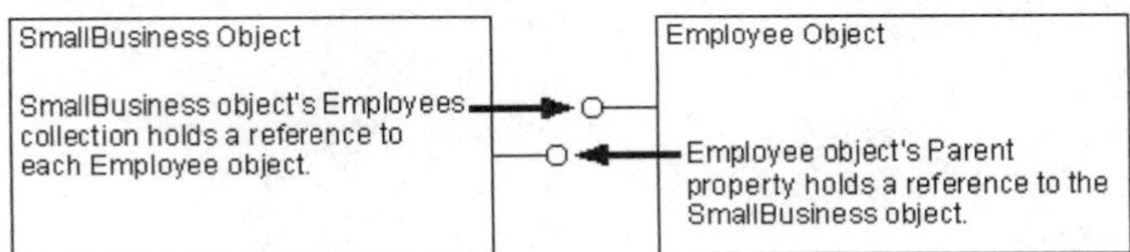

What's wrong with this picture? The way you get rid of objects when you're done with them is to release all references to them. Assuming the reference to the SmallBusiness object is in a variable named `sbMain`, as earlier in this topic, you might write the following code:

```
Set sbMain = Nothing
```

Unfortunately, there's still a reference to the SmallBusiness object — in fact, there may be many references, because each Employee object's Parent property will hold a reference to the SmallBusiness object.

Since the SmallBusiness object's Employees collection holds a reference to each Employee object, none of the objects ever get destroyed.

TearDown Methods

One solution is to give the SmallBusiness object a TearDown method. This could set all of the SmallBusiness object's object properties to Nothing, and also set all the Collection objects (Employees, Customers) to Nothing.

When a Collection object is destroyed, Visual Basic sets all the object references it was holding to Nothing. If there are no other references to the Employee and Customer objects that were contained in the Employees and Customers collections, they'll be destroyed.

Of course, if the Employee object is made up of finer objects, it will have the same circular reference problem its parent does. In that case, you'll have to give the Employee class a TearDown method. Instead of just setting the Employees Collection object to Nothing, the SmallBusiness object will first have to iterate through the collection, calling the TearDown method of each Employee object.

It's Not Over Yet

Even then, not all the objects may be destroyed. If there are variables anywhere in your program that still contain references to the SmallBusiness object, or to any of the objects it contains, those objects won't be destroyed. Part of the cleanup for your program must be to ensure that all object variables everywhere are set to Nothing.

To test whether this is happening, you may want to add some debugging code to your objects. For example, you can add the following code to a standard module:

```
' Global debug collection
Public gcolDebug As New Collection

' Global function to give each object a unique ID.
Public Function DebugSerial() As Long
   Static lngSerial As Long
   lngSerial = lngSerial + 1
   DebugSerial = lngSerial
End Function
```

In each class module, you can put code similar to the following. Each class provides its own name where "Product" appears.

```
' Storage for the debug ID.
Private mlngDebugID As Long

Property Get DebugID() As Long
   DebugID = mlngDebugID
End Property

Private Sub Class_Initialize()
   mlngDebugID = DebugSerial
   ' Add a string entry to the global collection.
   gcolDebug.Add "Product Initialize; DebugID=" _
   & DebugID, CStr(DebugID)
End Sub

Private Sub Class_Terminate()
   ' Remove the string entry, so you know the object
   ' isn't around any more.
   gcolDebug.Remove CStr(DebugID)
End Sub
```

As each object is created, it places a string in the global collection; as it's destroyed it removes the string. At any time, you iterate over the global collection to see what objects haven't been destroyed.

For More Information Object models assume new importance, and a different set of problems, when you use the Professional or Enterprise Edition of Visual Basic to create ActiveX components. See Chapter 6, "General Principles of Component Design," in Part 2, "Creating ActiveX Components," of the *Microsoft Visual Basic 6.0 Component Tools Guide*.

Creating Your Own Collection Classes

There are three general approaches you can take to implementing object containment using collections. Consider the Employees collection of the SmallBusiness object discussed in "Object Models." To implement this collection you might:

- In the SmallBusiness class module, declare an `Employees` variable As Collection, and make it Public. This is the cheap solution.
- In the SmallBusiness class module, declare an `mcolEmployees` variable As Collection, and make it Private. Give the SmallBusiness object a set of methods for adding and deleting objects. This is the least object-oriented of the three designs.
- Implement your own collection class, by creating a collection class module named Employees, as described later in this chapter. Give the SmallBusiness object a read-only property of the Employees class.

The strategies are listed in order of increasing robustness. They could be characterized as the house of straw, house of sticks, and house of bricks approaches.

Public Collection Example: The House of Straw

To create the example, open a new project and insert two class modules. Draw five command buttons, a list box, two text boxes, and two labels on the form, as shown in Figure 9.13.

Figure 9.13 Employees collection example

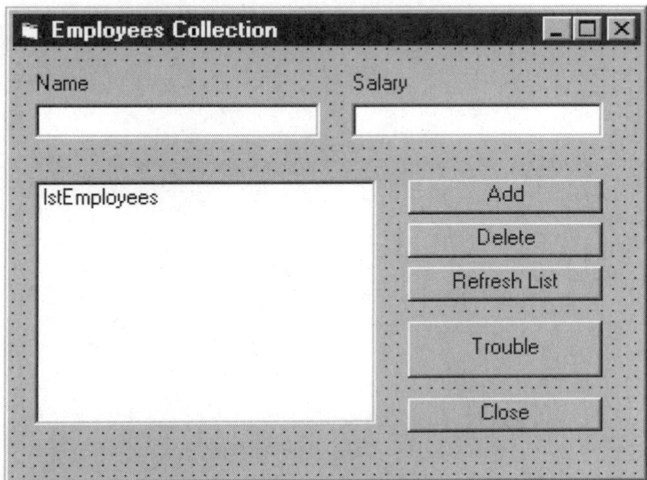

The following table lists the property values you need to set for this example.

Object	Property	Setting
Class module	Name	Employee
Class module	Name	SmallBusiness
Form	Caption	Employees Collection
First command button	Caption Name	Add cmdAddEmployee
Second command button	Caption Name	Delete cmdDeleteEmployee
Third command button	Caption Name	Refresh List cmdListEmployees
Fourth command button	Caption Name	Trouble cmdTrouble
Fifth command button	Caption Name	Close cmdClose
First label control	Caption	Name
Second label control	Caption	Salary
First text box	Name Text	TxtName (blank)

Object	Property	Setting
Second text box	Name Text	TxtSalary (blank)
List Box	Name	LstEmployees

In the Employee class module, add the following declarations and property procedures:

```
Option Explicit
' Properties of the Employee class.
Public Name As String
Public Salary As Long

' Private data for the write-once ID property.
Private mstrID As String

Property Get ID() As String
   ID = mstrID
End Property

' The first time the ID property is set, the static
' Boolean is also set.  Subsequent calls do nothing.
' (It would be better to raise an error, instead.)
Property Let ID(strNew As String)
   Static blnAlreadySet As Boolean
   If Not blnAlreadySet Then
      blnAlreadySet = True
      mstrID = strNew
   End If
End Property
```

The ID property is the key for retrieving or deleting an Employee object from the collection, so it must be set once and never changed. This is accomplished with a Static Boolean variable that is set to True the first time the property is set. The property can always be read, because there is a Property Get.

In the SmallBusiness class module, add the following declaration. The collection object will be created the first time the `Employees` variable is referred to in code.

```
Option Explicit
Public Employees As New Collection
```

The Form Does All the Work

All of the remaining code goes into the form module. Add the following declaration in the Declarations section.

```
Option Explicit
Public sbMain As New SmallBusiness
```

The code in the cmdEmployeeAdd_Click event adds a member to the collection.

```
Private Sub cmdEmployeeAdd_Click()
   Dim empNew As New Employee
   Static intEmpNum As Integer
   ' Using With makes your code faster and more
   ' concise (.ID vs. empNew.ID).
   With empNew
      ' Generate a unique ID for the new employee.
      intEmpNum = intEmpNum + 1
      .ID = "E" & Format$(intEmpNum, "00000")
      .Name = txtName.Text
      .Salary = CDbl(txtSalary.Text)
      ' Add the Employee object reference to the
      ' collection, using the ID property as the key.
      sbMain.Employees.Add empNew, .ID
   End With
   txtName.Text = ""
   txtSalary.Text = ""
   ' Click the Refresh List button.
   cmdListEmployees.Value = True
End Sub
```

The code in the cmdListEmployees_Click event procedure uses a For Each ... Next statement to add all the employee information to the ListBox control.

```
Private Sub cmdListEmployees_Click()
   Dim emp As Employee
   lstEmployees.Clear
   For Each emp In sbMain.Employees
      lstEmployees.AddItem emp.ID & ", " & emp.Name _
      & ", " & emp.Salary
   Next
End Sub
```

The cmdEmployeeDelete_Click event uses the Collection object's Remove method to delete the collection member currently selected in the ListBox control.

```
Private Sub cmdEmployeeDelete_Click()
   ' Check to make sure there's an employee selected.
   If lstEmployees.ListIndex > -1 Then
      ' The first six characters are the ID.
      sbMain.Employees.Remove _
      Left(lstEmployees.Text, 6)
   End If
   ' Click the Refresh List button.
   cmdListEmployees.Value = True
End Sub
```

Add the following code to the Trouble button.

```
Private Sub cmdTrouble_Click()
   ' Say what!?
   sbMain.Employees.Add Me
End Sub
```

The cmdClose_Click event closes the application. When you close projects that use objects, do so by unloading all the forms, to ensure that any Terminate event procedures in your class modules will get executed. By contrast, using the End statement stops a program abruptly, without executing Terminate events.

```
Private Sub cmdClose_Click()
   Unload Me
End Sub
```

To add employees in the example, run the application, enter values in the two text boxes, and then choose the Add button. Add a few employees, and then experiment with the delete and list buttons.

Robust as a Straw House

This simple implementation is not very robust. Because the Employees property is just a public Collection object, you could inadvertently access it from anywhere in your program. Furthermore, the Add method of the Collection object doesn't do any type checking. For example, the code in the Trouble button's Click event blithely inserts an object reference to the form into the collection of employees.

Click the Trouble button, and notice that no error occurs. Now click the Refresh List button. When the For Each ... Next loop encounters the unexpected object type, it causes error 13, Type mismatch.

This is an example of the kind of error you're exposed to when you build an object model with public Collection objects. Objects can be added from anywhere in your project, and there's no guarantee that they'll be properly initialized. If a programmer clones the code to add an employee, and the original code is later changed, the resulting errors can be very difficult to track down.

Private Collection Example: The House of Sticks

A somewhat more robust way to link Employee objects with the SmallBusiness object is to make the Collection object private. For this example, you'll reuse the form and most of the code from the "Public Collection" example.

The Employee class module is unchanged. The SmallBusiness class module, however, gets a complete facelift. Replace the declaration of the public Collection object with the following declaration, and add the Sub and Function procedures described in the following paragraphs.

```
Option Explicit
Private mcolEmployees As New Collection
```

As before, the code that adds an employee does most of the work. (You can take the block of code between the dotted lines out of the cmdEmployeeAdd_Click event procedure in the previous example.)

The important change is that the Add method of the Collection object can no longer be called from any module in your program, because `mcolEmployees` is Private. You can only add an Employee object using the EmployeeAdd method, which correctly initializes the new object:

```
' Method of the SmallBusiness class.
Public Function EmployeeAdd(ByVal Name As String, _
ByVal Salary As Double) As Employee
   ' - - - - - - - - - - - - - - - - -
   Dim empNew As New Employee
   Static intEmpNum As Integer
   ' Using With makes your code faster and more
   ' concise (.ID vs. empNew.ID).
   With empNew
      ' Generate a unique ID for the new employee.
      intEmpNum = intEmpNum + 1
      .ID = "E" & Format$(intEmpNum, "00000")
      .Name = Name
      .Salary = Salary
      ' Add the Employee object reference to the
      ' collection, using the ID property as the key.
      ' - - - - - - - - - - - - - - - - -
      mcolEmployees.Add empNew, .ID
   End With
   ' Return a reference to the new Employee.
   Set EmployeeAdd = empNew
End Function
```

The EmployeeAdd method returns a reference to the newly added Employee object. This is a good practice, because as soon as you create an object you will most likely want to do something with it.

The EmployeeCount, EmployeeDelete, and Employees methods *delegate* to the corresponding methods of the Collection object. Delegation means that the Collection object does all the work.

```
' Methods of the SmallBusiness class.
Public Function EmployeeCount() As Long
   EmployeeCount = mcolEmployees.Count
End Function
```

```
Public Sub EmployeeDelete(ByVal Index As Variant)
   mcolEmployees.Remove Index
End Sub

Public Function Employees(ByVal Index As Variant) _
As Employee
   Set Employees = mcolEmployees.Item(Index)
End Function
```

> **Note** You can add extra functionality to these methods. For example, you can raise your own errors if an index is invalid.

The last method is Trouble. This method attempts to add an uninitialized Employee object to the collection. Any guesses what will happen?

```
' Method of the SmallBusiness class.
Public Sub Trouble()
   Dim x As New Employee
   mcolEmployees.Add x
End Sub
```

Changes to the Form

You'll have to make a few changes to the form module. You can use the same module-level declarations used for the previous example, and the Click event for the Close button is the same, but the other event procedures have changed — the Add button code is much shorter, while the code for the Delete and List Employees buttons have changed in small but significant ways:

```
Private Sub cmdEmployeeAdd_Click()
   sbMain.EmployeeAdd txtName.Text, txtSalary.Text
   txtName.Text = ""
   txtSalary.Text = ""
   cmdListEmployees.Value = True
End Sub

Private Sub cmdEmployeeDelete_Click()
   ' Check to make sure there's an employee selected.
   If lstEmployees.ListIndex > -1 Then
      ' The first six characters are the ID.
      sbMain.EmployeeDelete Left(lstEmployees.Text, 6)
   End If
   cmdListEmployees.Value = True
End Sub
```

```
Private Sub cmdListEmployees_Click()
   Dim lngCt As Long
   lstEmployees.Clear
   For lngCt = 1 To sbMain.EmployeeCount
      With sbMain.Employees(lngCt)
         lstEmployees.AddItem .ID & ", " & .Name _
         & ", " & .Salary
      End With
   Next
End Sub
```

But what's all this extra code in cmdListEmployees_Click? Unfortunately, in pursuit of robustness you've given up the ability to use For Each ... Next to iterate through the items in the collection, because the Collection object is now declared Private. If you try to code the following, you'll just get an error:

```
' Won't work, because Employees isn't really a
' collection.
For Each emp In sbMain.Employees
```

Fortunately, the EmployeeCount method can be used to delimit the iteration range.

The Trouble button changes a little, too, but it's still, well, Trouble.

```
Private Sub cmdTrouble_Click()
   sbMain.Trouble
End Sub
```

Run the project and experiment with the Add, Delete, and Refresh List buttons. Everything works just like before.

When you click the Trouble button, once again no error is generated. However, if you now click the Refresh List button, you can see that the uninitialized Employee object has somehow been added to the collection.

How can this be? By making the Collection object private, you protect it from all the code in your program that's *outside* the SmallBusiness object, but not from the code *inside*. The SmallBusiness object may be large and complex, with a great deal of code in it. For example, it will very likely have methods like CustomerAdd, ProductAdd, and so on.

A coding error, or the creation of a duplicate of the EmployeeAdd method, can still result in erroneous data — even invalid objects — being inserted into the collection, because the private variable is visible throughout the class module.

Creating Your Own Collection Class: The House of Bricks

The most robust way to implement a collection is by making it a class module. In contrast to the preceding examples, moving all the code for object creation into the collection class follows good object design principles.

This example uses the same form and the same Employee class module as the previous examples. Insert a new class module, and set its Name property to "Employees." Insert the following declarations and code into the new class module.

```
Option Explicit
Private mcolEmployees As New Collection
```

The Add, Count, and Delete methods of the Employees class are essentially the same as those of the old SmallBusiness class. You can simply remove them from the SmallBusiness class module, paste them into the Employees class module, and change their names.

The names can change because it's no longer necessary to distinguish EmployeeAdd from, say, CustomerAdd. Each collection class you implement has its own Add method.

```
' Methods of the Employees collection class.
Public Function Add(ByVal Name As String, _
ByVal Salary As Double) As Employee
   Dim empNew As New Employee
   Static intEmpNum As Integer
   ' Using With makes your code faster and more
   ' concise (.ID vs. empNew.ID).
   With empNew
      ' Generate a unique ID for the new employee.
      intEmpNum = intEmpNum + 1
      .ID = "E" & Format$(intEmpNum, "00000")
      .Name = Name
      .Salary = Salary
      ' Add the Employee object reference to the
      ' collection, using the ID property as the key.
      mcolEmployees.Add empNew, .ID
   End With
   ' Return a reference to the new Employee.
   Set Add = empNew
End Function

Public Function Count() As Long
   Count = mcolEmployees.Count
End Function
```

```
Public Sub Delete(ByVal Index As Variant)
   mcolEmployees.Remove Index
End Sub
```

The Employees method of the SmallBusiness object becomes the Item method of the collection class. It still delegates to the Collection object, in order to retrieve members by index or by key.

```
' Method of the Employees collection class.
Public Function Item(ByVal Index As Variant) _
As Employee
   Set Item = mcolEmployees.Item(Index)
End Function
```

There's a nice touch you can add here. By making Item the default method of the Employees class, you gain the ability to code `Employees("E00001")`, just as you could with the Collection object.

To make Item the default property

1. On the **Tools** menu, click **Procedure Attributes** to open the **Procedure Attributes** dialog box. In **Name** box, select the Item method.
2. Click **Advanced** to show the advanced features. In the **Procedure ID** box, select **(Default)** to make the Item method the default. Click **OK**.

   Note A class can have only one default member (property or method).

Enabling for Each ... Next

Along with robustness, you get For Each … Next back. Once again you can delegate all the work to the Collection object, by adding the following method:

```
' NewEnum must return the IUnknown interface of a
' collection's enumerator.
Public Function NewEnum() As IUnknown
   Set NewEnum = mcolEmployees.[_NewEnum]
End Function
```

The important thing you're delegating to the Collection object is its *enumerator*. An enumerator is a small object that knows how to iterate through the items in a collection. You can't write an enumerator object with Visual Basic, but because the Employees class is based on a Collection object, you can return the Collection object's enumerator — which naturally enough knows how to enumerate the items the Collection object is holding.

The square brackets around the Collection object's _NewEnum method are necessary because of the leading underscore in the method name. This leading underscore is a convention indicating that the method is hidden in the type library. You can't name your method _NewEnum, but you can hide it in the type library and give it the procedure ID that For Each … Next requires.

To hide the NewEnum method and give it the necessary procedure ID

1. On the **Tools** menu, click **Procedure Attributes** to open the **Procedure Attributes** dialog box. In **Name** box, select the NewEnum method.
2. Click **Advanced** to show the advanced features. Check **Hide this member** to make NewEnum hidden in the type library.
3. In the **Procedure ID** box, type **–4** (minus four) to give NewEnum the procedure ID required by For Each … Next. Click **OK**.

   Important In order for your collection classes to work with For Each … Next, you must provide a hidden NewEnum method with the correct procedure ID.

Not Much Left of the SmallBusiness Class

The SmallBusiness class will have considerably less code in it now. To replace the Collection object and all the methods you removed, there's a new declaration and a read-only property:

```
Option Explicit
Private mEmployees As New Employees

Public Property Get Employees() As Employees
   Set Employees = mEmployees
End If
```

This deserves a word of explanation. Suppose for a moment that you left out the Property Get, and simply declared `Public Employees As New Employees`.

Everything would work fine as long as nobody made any mistakes, but what if you accidentally coded `Set sbMain.Employees = Nothing`? That's right, the Employees collection would be destroyed. By making Employees a read-only property, you avert that possibility.

Changes to the Form

The code for the form module is very similar to the preceding example. You can use the same module-level declarations, and the Click event for the Close button is the same.

The only change in most of the event procedures is replacing the old methods of the SmallBusiness class with the new methods of the Employees collection object:

```
Private Sub cmdEmployeeAdd_Click()
   sbMain.Employees.Add txtName.Text, txtSalary.Text
   txtName.Text = ""
   txtSalary.Text = ""
   cmdListEmployees.Value = True
End Sub
```

```
Private Sub cmdEmployeeDelete_Click()
   ' Check to make sure there's an employee selected.
   If lstEmployees.ListIndex > -1 Then
      ' The first six characters are the ID.
      sbMain.Employees.Delete _
      Left(lstEmployees.Text, 6)
   End If
   cmdListEmployees.Value = True
End Sub

Private Sub cmdListEmployees_Click()
   Dim emp As Employee
   lstEmployees.Clear
   For Each emp In sbMain.Employees
      lstEmployees.AddItem emp.ID & ", " & emp.Name _
      & ", " & emp.Salary
   Next
End Sub
```

Notice that you can use For Each … Next again to list the employees.

Run the project and verify that everything works. There's no code for the Trouble button this time, because encapsulation has banished trouble.

For More Information Read "The Visual Basic Collection Object" and "Collections in Visual Basic," online, for background on collections.

The Class Builder utility included in the Professional and Enterprise editions will create collection classes for you.

The Benefits of Good Object-Oriented Design

Creating the Employees collection class results in a very clean, modular coding style. All the code for the collection is in the collection class (encapsulation), reducing the size of the SmallBusiness class module. If collections of Employee objects appear in more than one place in your object hierarchy, reusing the collection class requires no duplication of code.

Enhancing Collection Classes

You can implement additional methods and properties for your collection classes. For example, you could implement Copy and Move methods, or a read-only Parent property that contains a reference to the SmallBusiness object.

You could also add an event. For example, every time the Add or Remove method changed the number of items in your collection, you could raise a CountChanged event.

Robustness, Robustness, Robustness

You don't always have to implement collections in the most robust way possible. However, one of the benefits of programming with objects is code reuse; it's much easier to reuse objects than to copy source code, and it's much safer to use robust, encapsulated code.

A wise man once said, "If you want to write really robust code, you have to assume that really bad things will happen."

Collection Classes and Component Software

If you're using the Professional or Enterprise Edition of Visual Basic, you can turn your project into an ActiveX component, so that other programmers in your organization can use the objects you've created.

Steps to Implement a Collection Class

The following list summarizes the steps required to create a collection class.

1. Add a class module to your project, and give it a name — usually the plural of the name of the object the collection class will contain. (See "Naming Properties, Methods, and Events," earlier in this chapter.)
2. Add a private variable to contain a reference to the Collection object your properties and methods will delegate to.
3. In the Class_Initialize event procedure, create the Collection object. (If you want to defer creation of this object until it's needed, you can declare the private variable in step 2 As New Collection. This adds a small amount of overhead each time the Collection is accessed.)
4. Add a Count property and Add, Item, and Remove methods to your class module; in each case, delegate to the private Collection by calling its corresponding member.
5. When you implement the Add method, you can override the behavior of the Collection object's undiscriminating Add method by accepting only objects of one type. You can even make it impossible to add externally created objects to your collection, so that your Add method completely controls the creation *and initialization* of objects.
6. Use the **Procedure Attributes** dialog box to make the Item method the default for your collection class.
7. Add a NewEnum method, as shown below. Use the **Procedure Attributes** dialog box to mark it as hidden, and to give it a Procedure ID of –4 so that it will work with For Each … Next.

   ```
   Public Function NewEnum() As IUnknown
      Set NewEnum = mcol.[_NewEnum]
   End Function
   ```

   Note The code above assumes that the private variable in step 2 is named `mcol`.

8. Add custom properties, methods, and events to the collection class.

   Note The Class Builder utility, included in the Professional and Enterprise editions of Visual Basic, will create collection classes for you. You can customize the resulting source code.

For More Information You can read more about software components in Part 2, "Creating ActiveX Components," of the *Microsoft Visual Basic 6.0 Component Tools Guide*.

ActiveX Designers

A *designer* provides a visual design window in the Visual Basic development environment. You can use this window to design new classes visually. Visual Basic has built-in designers for forms and — in the Professional and Enterprise editions — ActiveX controls and documents.

Objects created from the classes you design in this fashion have separate design-time and run-time behavior and appearance, although many objects — such as forms and controls — look very similar in the two modes.

In addition to its built-in designers, Visual Basic allows third parties to develop designers for use in the Visual Basic development environment. These *ActiveX designers* work just like the built-in designers in Visual Basic, making them easy to learn and use.

What Are ActiveX Designers?

ActiveX designers can provide visual interfaces for tasks that otherwise might require a great deal of code. For example, the UserConnection designer included in the Enterprise Edition of Visual Basic provides visual tools for defining complex database queries. At run time, these queries can be invoked with very little code.

Similarities Between ActiveX Designers and Built-in Designers

ActiveX designers are like form designers in the following ways:

- ActiveX designers produce classes from which you can create objects. These classes appear in the Project window, just like form classes.
- Each class you create with an ActiveX designer has its own code module, in which you can write code for the event procedures provided by the designer.
- You can customize a class, by adding your own properties, methods, and events to the ones provided by the ActiveX designer.
- The objects created from classes you design can have different characteristics at design time and run time.

- An ActiveX designer's design window is fully integrated into the development environment. It can be sized and arranged just like built-in design windows.
- You can add as many instances of an ActiveX designer to your project as you need, just as you can add as many form designers as you need.

Figure 9.14 compares the built-in Visual Basic form designer with the UserConnection Designer, an ActiveX designer included in the Enterprise Edition of Visual Basic.

Figure 9.14 An ActiveX designer and a built-in Visual Basic designer

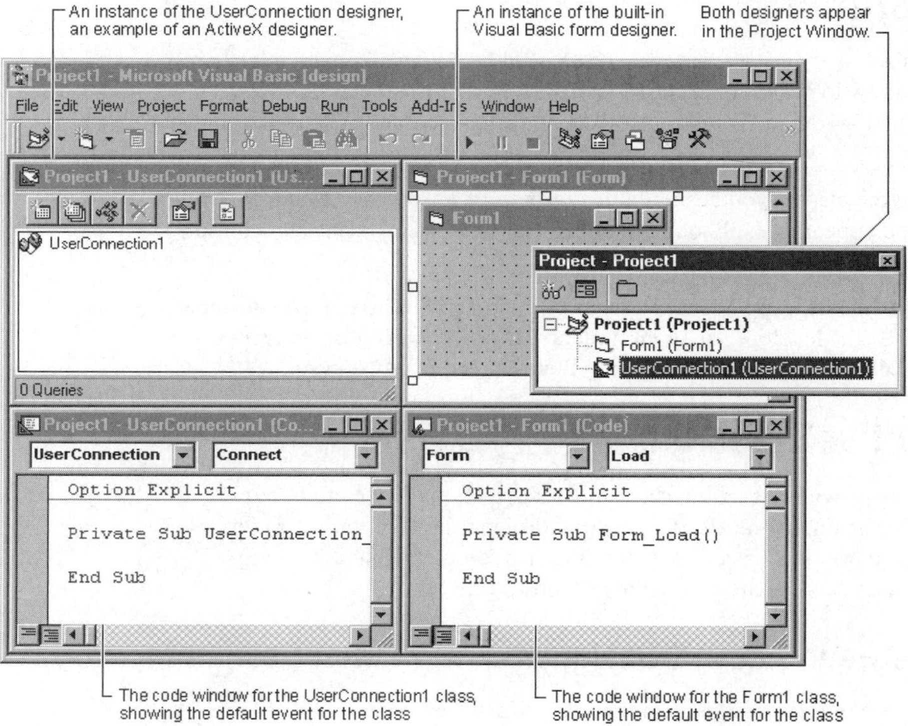

Comparing ActiveX Designer Classes to Other Visually Designed Classes

ActiveX designers are extremely flexible. Some, like the UserConnection designer, create classes whose run-time instances are programmable, but not visible. Others, like the Microsoft Forms designer used by Microsoft Office, produce visible objects similar to Visual Basic forms.

ActiveX designers that have visible run-time components may be able to host ActiveX controls. In effect, they become alternate forms packages, which can be used in addition to Visual Basic's native forms.

The following list compares classes produced with ActiveX designers to those produced with built-in Visual Basic designers.

- If an object created from an ActiveX designer class is visible at run time, it has its own window. It is not contained within another form, as ActiveX controls are.
- Like form classes, but unlike ActiveX controls, the classes produced by ActiveX designers are private classes. If you're using the Professional or Enterprise Edition of Visual Basic to create ActiveX components, you cannot declare public methods that use these classes as argument types or return types.

  For example, the following method declarations produce compile-time errors if they appear in a public class:

```
Public Function A() As UseConnection1       'Error
Public Sub B(CallBack As UseConnection1)    'Error
```

> **Caution** Although it is possible to pass references to private objects outside your project, by declaring return values As Object, this is very bad practice, and may destabilize your program. For more information, see Part 2, "Creating ActiveX Components," in the *Microsoft Visual Basic 6.0 Component Tools Guide.*

Using ActiveX Designer Objects at Run Time

Like the built-in form designer, ActiveX designers are available only in the development environment. Once you make your project into an executable, it only uses the ActiveX designer's run-time .dll. This may be much smaller than the design-time .dll, because it doesn't include the visual design tool. Figure 9.15 illustrates this concept.

Figure 9.15 Designer components in memory

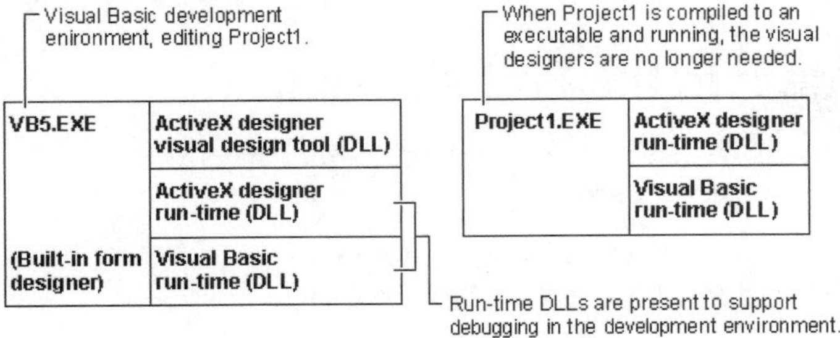

As noted earlier, ActiveX designers may produce classes whose objects are not visible at run time. The UserConnection designer shown in Figure 9.14 is an example. The UserConnection designer produces classes whose objects manage connections to SQL databases at run time. There is no reason for these objects to be visible at run time.

To use a class created with the UserConnection designer, declare a variable of the class type and create an instance of the class. For example, if you added a UserConnection designer and set its Name property to GeneralLedger, you could create a GeneralLedger object as shown in the following code fragment:

```
' Global variable in a standard module, to keep a
' reference to the GeneralLedger object.
Public gGeneralLedger As GeneralLedger

' Code in a Form module to create the GeneralLedger
' object and establish a database connection.
Private Sub Command1_Click()
   Set gGeneralLedger = New gGeneralLedger
   gGeneralLedger.EstablishConnection
   ' (Code that uses the object.)
End Sub
```

Creating ActiveX Designers

You can use the ActiveX Designer Software Development Kit to create new ActiveX designers for use with Visual Basic. The SDK includes full instructions and sample code. You can find it on the Microsoft Development Network under the heading "SDK Documentation."

> **Note** The ActiveX Designer SDK requires a C++ compiler, such as Microsoft Visual C++. ActiveX designers cannot be written using Visual Basic.

For More Information Procedures for incorporating ActiveX designers in your project are provided in the next two sections, "Adding an ActiveX Designer to the Project Menu" and "Inserting a New Instance of an ActiveX Designer."

Adding an ActiveX Designer to the Project Menu

After you install a new ActiveX designer, using the Setup program supplied by the vendor, you must make the designer available to your projects by adding it to the project menu.

Installing the ActiveX designer will register it in the Windows Registry, under the appropriate component category. It will then be available from the Designers tab of the Components dialog box.

To add an ActiveX designer to the Project menu

1. On the **Project** menu, click **Components** to open the **Components** dialog box.
2. Click the **Designers** tab and select the designer you want to use, as shown in the following figure. Click **OK**.

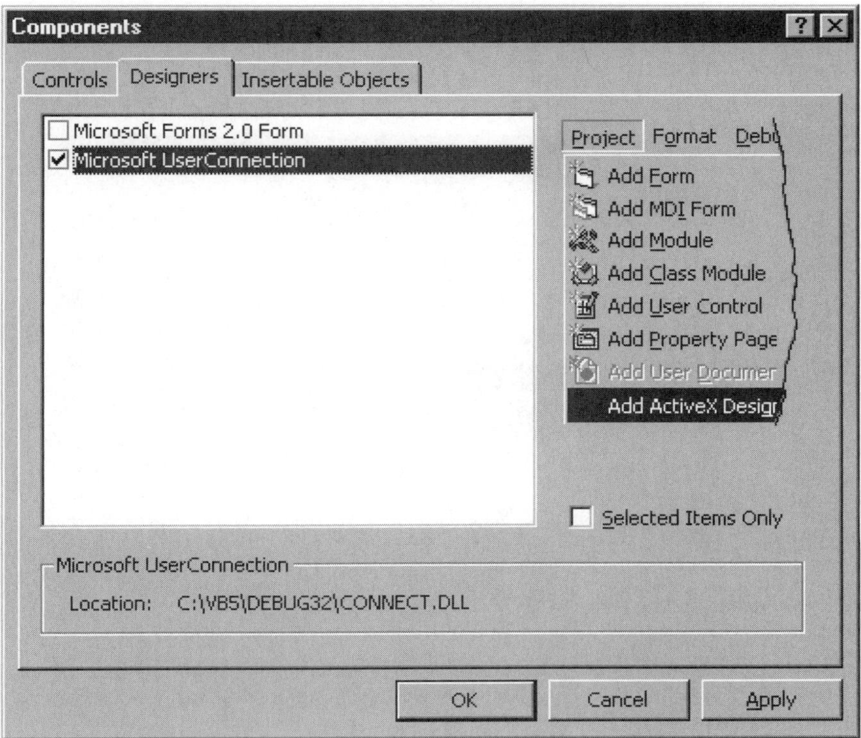

Note The Microsoft Forms designer is included in all versions of Visual Basic, to allow forms created in Microsoft Office applications to be ported easily. Like all designers, the Microsoft Forms designer has its own run-time .dll. Using this designer in a Visual Basic project will therefore increase the memory requirements of the resulting executable.

Inserting a New Instance of an ActiveX Designer

Once you've used the Components dialog box to add a designer to the Project menu, as shown in "Adding an ActiveX Designer to the Project Menu," you can insert as many instances of the designer as you need.

To insert an instance of an OLE Designer

- On the **Project** menu, click **Add ActiveX Designer** to display a list of installed designers. Pick the designer you want from the list, as shown in the following figure:

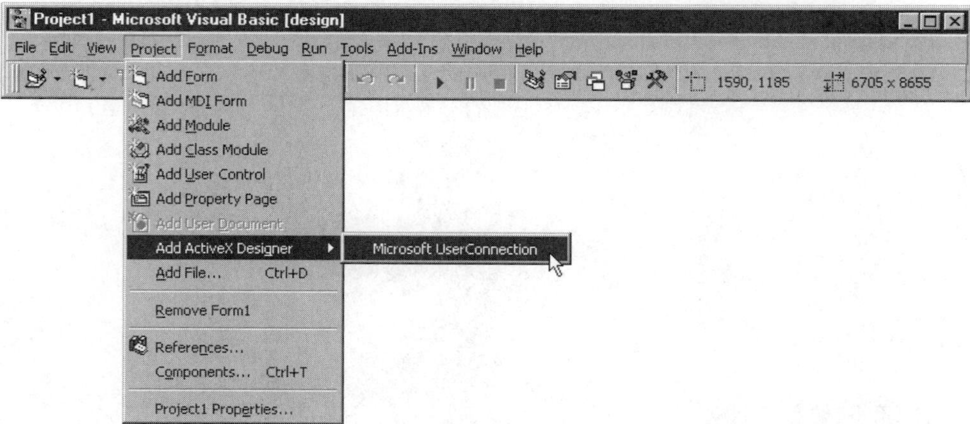

Once you've added an instance of an ActiveX designer to your project, you can use its visual interface to design a class. You can click the Code button on the Project window to open the code module for the designer, and add code to event procedures. You can further customize the class by adding by adding your own properties, methods, and events, just as you would in a Visual Basic class module.

For More Information Designers are introduced in "ActiveX Designers," earlier in this chapter. To add a designer to the Project menu, see "Adding an ActiveX Designer to the Project Menu," earlier in this chapter.

CHAPTER 10

Programming with Components

Do you sometimes need to provide the same analysis and calculation capabilities as Microsoft Excel in your Visual Basic application? Or, perhaps you'd like to format a document using Microsoft Word formatting tools, or store and manage data using the Microsoft Jet database engine. Even better, would you like to be able to create or buy standard components, then use them in multiple applications without having to modify them?

All this and more can be accomplished by building your applications using ActiveX components. An *ActiveX component* is a reusable piece of programming code and data made up of one or more objects created using ActiveX technology. Your applications can use existing components, such as those included in Microsoft Office applications, code components, ActiveX documents, or ActiveX controls (formerly called OLE controls) provided by a variety of vendors. Or, if you have the Visual Basic, Professional or Enterprise Edition, you can create your own ActiveX controls.

For components that support object linking and embedding, you can insert objects into your application without writing any code by using the component's visual interface. You can insert an OLE-enabled object into your application by using the OLE container control or by adding the object's class to the Toolbox.

To fully understand ActiveX components, you should first be familiar with how to work with classes, objects, properties, and methods, which are explained in Chapter 9, "Programming with Objects." To fully understand ActiveX components, you should first be familiar with how to work with classes, objects, properties, and methods, which are explained in "Programming with Objects."

Contents

- Handling Run-Time Errors in ActiveX Components
- Handling Requests Pending to an ActiveX Component
- Using a Component's Visual Interface

Interfaces: Geofacts.vbp and Olecont.vbp

Many of the concepts in this chapter are demonstrated in the sample applications Geofacts.vbp and Olecont.vbp. The sample applications are listed in the Samples directory.

Types of ActiveX Components

ActiveX components give you the power to put together sophisticated applications from pieces that already exist. Your Visual Basic applications can include several types of ActiveX components:

- Applications that support ActiveX technology, such as Microsoft Excel, Microsoft Word, and Microsoft Access, provide objects that you can manipulate programmatically from within your Visual Basic application. For example, you can use the properties, methods, and events of a Microsoft Excel spreadsheet, Microsoft Word document, or Microsoft Access database in your application.
- Code components provide libraries of programmable objects. For example, a code component could include a library of specialized financial functions for spreadsheet users, or user-interface elements, such as dialog boxes, that are common to multiple applications. Unlike an object in an ActiveX-enabled application, an object in a code component can run in the same process as your application, allowing faster access to the object.
- You can add features without having to create them yourself by using ActiveX controls as components. ActiveX controls are available from a variety of vendors to provide many specialized features, such as displaying a calendar on a form or reading data in a particular format.
- ActiveX documents let you create interactive Internet applications. You can create forms that can be contained within Internet Explorer. ActiveX documents can show message boxes and secondary forms and contain ActiveX controls. ActiveX documents can also function as code components. For a step-by-step introduction to ActiveX documents, see Part 2, "Creating an ActiveX Document" in the *Microsoft Visual Basic 6.0 Component Tools Guide* volume of the *Microsoft Visual Basic 6.0 Reference Library,* available in the Professional and Enterprise editions.

  Note In addition to Internet applications using ActiveX documents, you can create both client-based and server-based Internet applications using a combination of Visual Basic code and HTML pages. See "Introduction to Internet Applications" in Part 5, "Building Internet Applications" in the *Microsoft Visual Basic Component Tools Guide* for more information on your options for creating Internet and intranet applications.

Some ActiveX components run in the same process as your application, while others run in a separate process. For more information, see "In-Process and Out-of-Process Servers," online.

In addition to components in existing ActiveX-enabled applications, code component libraries, ActiveX controls, and ActiveX documents, you can create your own components. For more information on creating your own ActiveX components, see "Creating ActiveX Components" in the *Microsoft Visual Basic 6.0 Component Tools Guide* volume of the *Microsoft Visual Basic 6.0 Reference Library,* available in the Professional and Enterprise editions.

In-Process and Out-of-Process Servers

ActiveX components interact with your application — and with each other — through a *client/server* relationship. The *client* is the application code or component that uses the features of a component. The *server* is the component and its associated objects. For example, suppose your application uses an ActiveX control to provide a standard Employee form for multiple applications in your company. The ActiveX control that provides the Employee form is the server; the applications that use the control are its clients.

Depending on how an ActiveX component has been implemented, it may run in the same process as its client applications, or in a different process. For example, if your application uses a component that is part of an ActiveX-enabled application, it runs in a separate process. If the component has been implemented as a programmable object in a dynamic-link library (.dll file), it runs in the same process as your application.

In general, if an ActiveX component has been implemented as part of an executable file (.exe file), it is an *out-of-process* server and runs in its own process. If it has been implemented as a dynamic-link library, it is an *in-process* server and runs in the same process as the client application. Applications that use in-process servers usually run faster than those that use out-of-process servers because the application doesn't have to cross process boundaries to use an object's properties, methods, and events.

The following table shows how you can implement the different types of components:

Component	Server Type
ActiveX-enabled application	Out-of-process
Code component	Either in-process or out-of-process
ActiveX control	In-process
ActiveX document	Either in-process or out-of-process

Using in-process components is one way to optimize the performance of your application. Another way to optimize performance is to use early binding. For more information, see "Speeding Object References" later in this chapter.

Working with ActiveX Components

You work with object provided by ActiveX components in much the same way that you work with other objects. You assign an object reference to a variable, then write code that uses the object's methods, properties, and events. However, there are some things you need to be aware of when you work with objects provided by components.

This topic provides an overview of the top-level tasks for working with objects provided by components and an example of using objects in an ActiveX-enabled application. For details on each task, see the appropriate topic described under each task item.

To use most objects provided by ActiveX components

1. Create a reference to the object you want to use. How you do this depends on the type of object and whether the ActiveX component supplies a type library.

   For more information See "Creating a Reference to an Object," later in this chapter.

2. Write code using the object's methods, properties, and events.

   For more information See "Using an Object's Properties, Methods, and Events," later in this chapter.

3. Release the object when you are finished using it.

   For more information See "Releasing an ActiveX Component," later in this chapter.

4. Create error-handlers.

   For more information See "Handling Run-Time Errors in ActiveX Components," later in this chapter.

For example, suppose you have created a form with three text boxes (Text1, Text2, and Text3) and a command button (Command1), and added a reference in your project to the Microsoft Excel 8.0 Object Library. You can then add code to the command button's Command1_Click event procedure that uses the Microsoft Excel Formula method to add two numbers entered in Text1 and Text2, displaying the result in Text3. (To avoid a type mismatch error, you may want to remove the default text value of each text box by setting its Text property to an empty string):

```
Private Sub Command1_Click()
   ' Declare object variables for Microsoft Excel,
   ' application workbook, and worksheet objects.
   Dim xlApp As Excel.Application
   Dim xlBook As Excel.Workbook
   Dim xlSheet As Excel.Worksheet

   ' Assign object references to the variables. Use
   ' Add methods to create new workbook and worksheet
   ' objects.
   Set xlApp = New Excel.Application
   Set xlBook = xlApp.Workbooks.Add
   Set xlSheet = xlBook.Worksheets.Add
```

```
    ' Assign the values entered in the text boxes to
    ' Microsoft Excel cells.
    xlSheet.Cells(1, 1).Value = Text1.Text
    xlSheet.Cells(2, 1).Value = Text2.Text

    ' Use the Formula method to add the values in
    ' Microsoft Excel.
    xlSheet.Cells(3, 1).Formula = "=R1C1 + R2C1"
    Text3.Text = xlSheet.Cells(3, 1)

    ' Save the Worksheet.
    xlSheet.SaveAs "c:\Temp.xls"

    ' Close the Workbook
    xlBook.Close

    ' Close Microsoft Excel with the Quit method.
    xlApp.Quit

    ' Release the objects.
    Set xlApp = Nothing
    Set xlBook = Nothing
    Set xlSheet = Nothing
End Sub
```

For simplicity, this example doesn't include error handling. However, it is highly recommended that you include error handling in applications that use objects provided by ActiveX components.

Creating a Reference to an Object

Before you can use an object's properties, methods, and events in your application, you must declare an object variable, then assign an object reference to the variable. How you assign an object reference depends on two factors:

- Whether the ActiveX component supplies a type library. An ActiveX component's type library contains definitions of all the objects the component provides, including definitions for all available methods, properties, and events. If an ActiveX component provides a type library, you need to add a reference to the type library in your Visual Basic project before you can use the library's objects.
- Whether the object is a top-level, *externally creatable object*, or a *dependent object.* You can assign a reference to an externally created object directly, while references to dependent objects are assigned indirectly.

If an object is externally creatable, you can assign an object reference to a variable by using the New keyword, CreateObject, or GetObject in a Set statement from outside the component. If the object is a dependent object, you assign an object reference by using a method of a higher-level object in a Set statement.

In Microsoft Excel, for example, an Application object is an externally creatable object — you can assign a reference to it directly from your Visual Basic application by using the New keyword, CreateObject, or GetObject in a Set statement. A Range object, by contrast, is a dependent object — you assign a reference to it by using the Cells method of a Worksheet object in a Set statement. For more information on externally creatable and dependent objects, see "Navigating Object Models," later in this chapter.

If the object's class is included in a type library, you can make your application run faster by creating an object reference using a variable of that specific class. Otherwise, you must use a variable of the generic Object class, which results in late binding. For more information, see "Speeding Object References," later in this chapter.

To create a reference to an object defined in a type library

1. From the **Project** menu, choose **References**.
2. In the **References** dialog box, select the name of the ActiveX component containing the objects you want to use in your application.
3. You can use the **Browse** button to search for the type library file containing the object you need. Type libraries can have a .tlb or .olb file-name extension. Executable (.exe) files and dynamic link libraries (dlls) can also supply type libraries, so you can also search for files with these file-name extensions.

   If you are not sure if an application is ActiveX-enabled and supplies a type library, try adding a reference to it using the **Browse** button. If the reference fails, Visual Basic displays the error message, "Can't add a reference to the specified file," indicating that the type library doesn't exist. For more information about working with objects that aren't associated with a type library, see "Creating a Reference to an Object," earlier.
4. From the **View** menu, choose **Object Browser** to view the referenced type library. Select the appropriate type library from the **Project/Library** list. You can use all the objects, methods, and properties listed in the **Object Browser** in your application.

   For more information See "Browsing ActiveX Component Type Libraries," later in this chapter.
5. Declare an object variable of the object's class. For example, you could declare a variable of the class Excel.Chart to refer to a Microsoft Excel Chart object.

   ```
   Dim xlChart As Excel.Chart
   ```

   For more information See "Declaring an Object Variable," later in this chapter.
6. Assign an object reference to the variable by using the New keyword, CreateObject, or GetObject in a Set statement. For more information, see "Assigning an Object Reference to a Variable," later in this chapter.

   If the object is a dependent object, assign an object reference by using a method of a higher-level object in a Set statement.

To create a reference to an object not defined in a type library

1. Declare an object variable of the Object data type.

   Because the object isn't associated with a type library, you won't be able to use the **Object Browser** to view the properties, methods, and events of the object. You need to know what properties, methods, and events the object provides, including any methods for creating a reference to a dependent object.

   For more information See "Declaring an Object Variable," later in this chapter.

2. Assign an object reference to the variable by using CreateObject or GetObject in a Set statement. For more information, see "Assigning an Object Reference to a Variable," later in this chapter.

   If the object is a dependent object, assign an object reference by using a method of a higher-level object in a Set statement.

Ambiguous References and Reference Priority

When you refer to a constant or object in code, Visual Basic searches for the constant or object class in each type library selected in the References dialog box in the order the type libraries are displayed. If two type libraries contain constants or classes with identical names, Visual Basic uses the definition provided by the type library listed higher in the Available References box.

Figure 10.1 The References dialog box

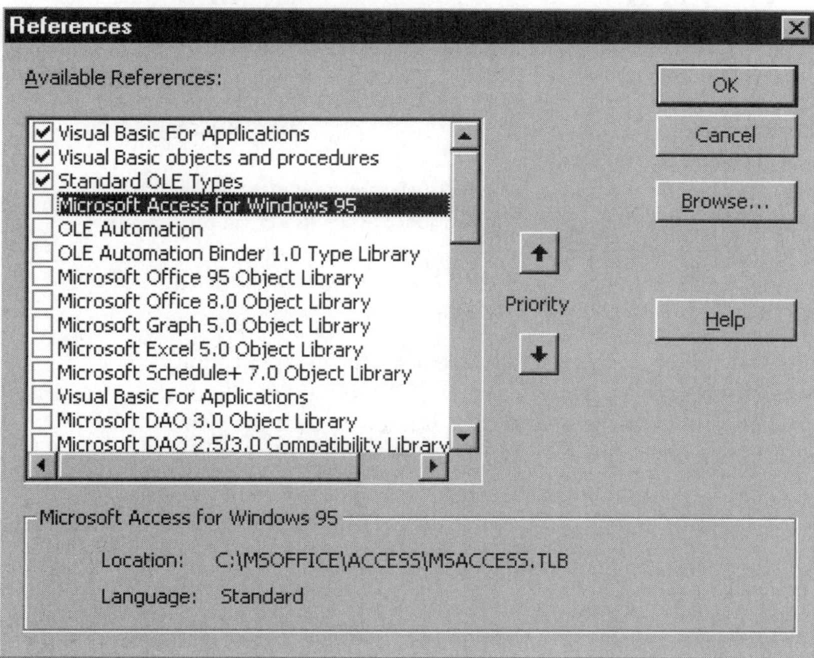

The best way to handle potentially ambiguous references is to explicitly specify the type library that supplies the constant or class when you use it. For example, the constant vbCancel evaluates to different values in the Visual Basic and Visual Basic for Applications type libraries. The following code shows fully qualified and ambiguous references to the constant vbCancel:

```
' Print the Visual Basic vbCancel.
Debug.Print "VB.vbCancel = "; VB.vbCancel
' Print the Visual Basic for Applications vbCancel.
Debug.Print "VBA.vbCancel = "; VBA.vbCancel
' Ambiguous reference prints the value of vbCancel
' that appears highest in the type library highest
' in the Available References list.
Debug.Print "vbCancel = "; vbCancel
```

The following code example shows fully qualified and ambiguous declarations for an Application object variable. If Microsoft Word appears higher in the Available References box than Microsoft Excel, xlApp2 is declared using the Microsoft Word Application class rather than the Microsoft Excel Application class.

```
' Fully qualified object variable declaration.
Dim xlApp1 As Excel.Application
' Ambiguous object variable declaration.
Dim xlApp2 As Application

' Assign an object reference.
Set xlApp1 = New Excel.Application
' The following generates a type mismatch error.
Set xlApp2 = xlApp1
```

You may be tempted to handle potentially ambiguous references by changing the order in which Visual Basic searches for references. The References dialog box includes two Priority buttons that let you move a type library higher in the list, so that its constants and classes will be found sooner than constants or classes with identical names lower on the list. However, changing the priority order can cause unexpected problems in your applications if there are other ambiguous references. In general, it's better to explicitly specify the type library in any references.

> **Note** The Excel.Application syntax for referring to the Microsoft Excel Application class is not supported in versions prior to Microsoft Excel 97. To refer to the Microsoft Excel Application class in Microsoft Excel 5.0 and Microsoft Excel 95, use the syntax [_ExcelApplication] instead. For example:
>
> ```
> Set xlApp = New [_ExcelApplication]
> ```

Browsing ActiveX Component Type Libraries

If an ActiveX component provides a type library, you can use the Object Browser to view the component's classes, as well as the properties, methods, events, and constants associated with the objects of each class.

To view the classes available in an ActiveX Component's type library

1. If you haven't already done so, add a reference to the type library to your Visual Basic project.

   For more information See "Creating a Reference to an Object," earlier in this chapter.

2. Open the **Object Browser** and select the name of the type library from the **Project/Library** list.

   The **Object Browser** displays the available classes in the **Classes** list.

Figure 10.2 The Object Browser

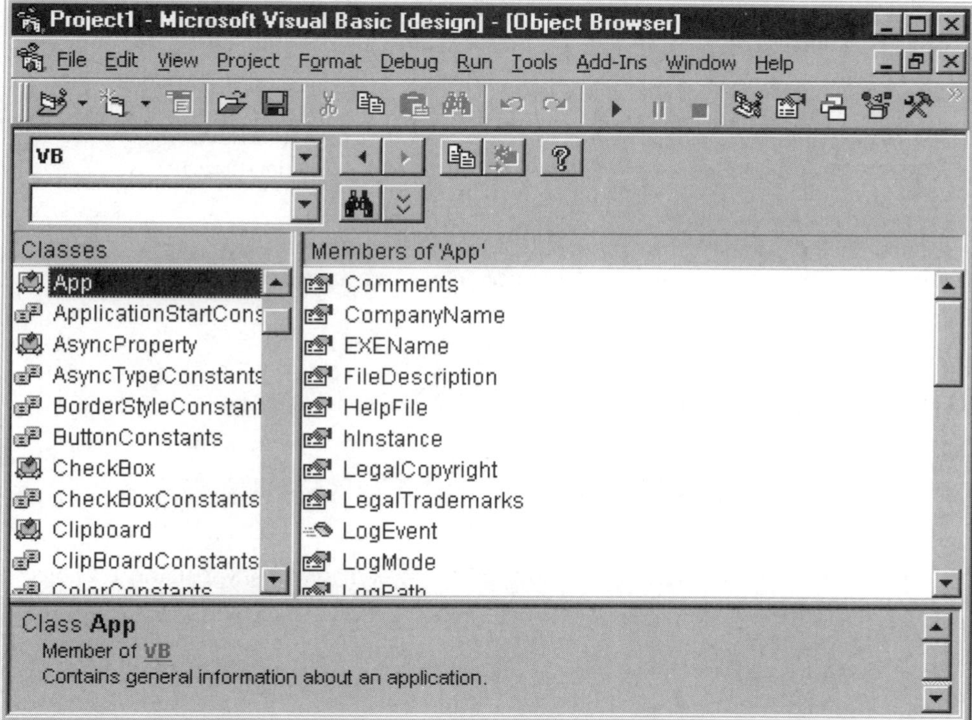

For example, to view the classes available in the Data Access Object (DAO) type library, add a reference to the library in the References dialog box, then select DAO in the Project/Library list in the Object Browser.

To view the members of a class

- Select the name of the class from the **Classes** list in the **Object Browser**.

  The **Object Browser** displays the members of the class in the **Members of** list.

If you're looking for information about a particular class or member in a type library, use the Object Browser's Search feature.

To use the Search feature

- Type what you're looking for in the **Search Text** box, and then click the **Search** button.

  The **Object Browser** displays a **Search Results** box showing the libraries, classes, and members returned by the search.

Declaring an Object Variable

Before you can use the properties, methods, and events of an object provided by an ActiveX component, you must first declare an object variable. The way you declare an object variable depends on whether or not the ActiveX component supplies a type library.

To declare a variable for an object defined in a type library

1. Add a reference to the type library to your Visual Basic project. For more information on adding a reference to a type library, see "Creating a Reference to an Object," earlier in this chapter.
2. Specify the name of a class supplied by that type library in your variable declaration. Declaring an object variable of a specific class can speed object references. Use the following syntax:

   Dim *variable* **As** [**New**] *class*

   The *class* argument can be composed of two parts, in the form *component.class*.

Part	Description
component	The name of the component that supplies the object. Choices are displayed in the Project/Library list of the Object Browser.
class	The object's class name (provided by the component's type library). Choices are shown in the Classes/Modules box of the Object Browser.

For example, you can declare a variable for a Microsoft Excel Chart object in either of the following ways:

```
Dim xlChart As Chart
Dim xlChart As Excel.Chart
```

If you declare an object variable using the New keyword, Visual Basic will automatically create an object and assign an object reference the first time you use the variable. For example, the following statements assign a reference to a new DAO table object to the variable tdfOrders, setting the table's Name property to "Orders":

```
Dim tdfOrders As New TableDef
tdfOrders.Name = "Orders"
```

Note Using variables declared using the New keyword can slow your application. Every time Visual Basic encounters a variable declared using New, it must test whether or not an object reference has already been assigned to the variable.

To declare an object variable for an object not defined in a type library

- Declare an object variable of the generic Object class, as follows:

  Dim *variable* **As Object**

For example, the variable `objAny` in the following declaration can be used for a Microsoft Excel Chart object or any other object provided by an ActiveX component:

```
Dim objAny As Object
```

The main difference between declaring a variable of a specific class and declaring a variable of the generic Object class is in how ActiveX binds the variable to the object. When you declare a variable of the generic Object class, ActiveX must use late binding. When you declare an object variable of a specific class, ActiveX uses early binding, which can speed object references. For more information, see "Speeding Object References" later in this chapter.

For More Information For more information on declaring object variables, see "Dim Statement" in the *Microsoft Visual Basic 6.0 Language Reference* volume of the *Microsoft Visual Basic 6.0 Reference Library*. For more information on assigning an object reference to a variable, see the next section, "Assigning an Object Reference to a Variable."

Assigning an Object Reference to a Variable

After you declare an object variable, you must assign an object reference to the variable before you can use the object's properties, methods, and events. You can assign a new object reference in several ways:

- If you declared the variable using the New keyword, Visual Basic will automatically assign a new object reference the first time you use the variable.
- You can assign a reference to a new object in a Set statement by using the New keyword or CreateObject function.
- You can assign a reference to a new or existing object in a Set statement by using the GetObject function.

Assigning an Object Reference Using the New Keyword

If the ActiveX component supplies a type library, you can use the New keyword in a variable declaration or Set statement to create a new object and assign an object reference to an object variable.

If you declare an object variable with the New keyword, Visual Basic will automatically create a new object the first time you use the variable. For more information, see "Declaring an Object Variable," online.

You can also use the New keyword in a Set statement to assign a reference to a new object of the specified class. For example, the following statements assign a reference to a new DAO table object to the variable tdfOrders, setting the table's Name property to "Orders":

```
Dim tdfOrders As DAO.TableDef
Set tdfOrders = New DAO.TableDef
tdfOrders.Name = "Orders"
```

For More Information See "Dim Statement" or "Set Statement" in the *Microsoft Visual Basic 6.0 Language Reference*.

Assigning an Object Reference Using CreateObject

Regardless of whether or not an ActiveX component supplies a type library, you can use the CreateObject function in a Set statement to create a new object and assign an object reference to an object variable. You must specify the object's programmatic identifier as an argument to the function, and the object you want to access must be externally creatable.

To assign an object reference using CreateObject

- Use the following syntax for CreateObject.

  Set *objectvariable* **= CreateObject(**"*progID*"", *["servername"]*)

The *progID* argument is usually the fully qualified class name of the object being created; for example, Word.Document. However, progID can be different from the class name. For example, the progID for a Microsoft Excel object is "Sheet" rather than "Worksheet." The optional *servername* argument can be specified to create an object on a remote machine across a network. It takes the Machine Name portion of a share name. For example, with a network share named \\MyServer\Public, the *servername* argument would be "MyServer."

The following code example starts Microsoft Excel (if Microsoft Excel is not already running) and establishes the variable `xlApp` to refer to an object of the Application class. The argument "`Excel.Application`" fully qualifies Application as a class defined by Microsoft Excel:

```
Dim xlApp As Excel.Application
Set xlApp = CreateObject("Excel.Application")
```

For More Information See "CreateObject Function" in the *Microsoft Visual Basic 6.0 Language Reference*.

Assigning an Object Reference Using GetObject

The GetObject function is most often used to assign a reference to an existing object, although you can also use it to assign a reference to a new object.

To assign a reference to an existing object, use the following syntax.

Set *objectvariable* **= GetObject(**[*pathname*] [**,** *progID*]**)**

The *pathname* argument can be the path to an existing file, an empty string, or omitted entirely. If it is omitted, then *progID* is required. Specifying the path to an existing file causes GetObject to create an object using the information stored in the file. Using an empty string for the first argument causes GetObject to act like CreateObject — it will create a new object of the class whose programmatic identifier is progID. The following table describes the results of using GetObject.

If the ActiveX component is running	Result
`Set X = GetObject(, "MySrvr.Application")`	X references an existing Application object.
`Set X = GetObject("", "MySrvr.Object")`	X references a new, externally creatable object.

If the ActiveX component is not running	Result
`Set X = GetObject(, "MySrvr.Object")`	An error is returned.
`Set X = GetObject("", "MySrvr.Object")`	The ActiveX component (MySrvr) is started, and X references a new object.

For example, the variable `wrdApp` refers to a running Microsoft Word Application:

```
Dim wdApp As Word.Application
Set wdApp = GetObject("", "Word.Application")
```

Just as with CreateObject, the argument `"Word.Application"` is the programmatic identifier for the Application class defined by Microsoft Word. If multiple instances of Microsoft Word are running, you cannot predict to which instance `wdApp` will refer.

> **Important** You can also use GetObject to assign a reference to an object in a compound document file. A *compound document file* contains references to multiple types of objects. For example, a compound document file could contain a spreadsheet, text, and bitmaps.

The following example starts the spreadsheet application, if it is not already running, and opens the file Revenue.xls:

```
Dim xlBook As Excel.Workbook
Set xlBook = GetObject("C:\Accounts\Revenue.xls")
```

For More Information See "GetObject Function" in the *Microsoft Visual Basic 6.0 Language Reference*.

Speeding Object References

You can make your Visual Basic applications run faster by optimizing the way Visual Basic resolves object references. The speed with which Visual Basic handles object references can be affected by:

- Whether or not the ActiveX component has been implemented as an in-process server or an out-of-process server.
- Whether an object reference is early-bound or late-bound.

In general, if a component has been implemented as part of an executable file (.exe file), it is an *out-of-process* server and runs in its own process. If it has been implemented as a dynamic-link library, it is an *in-process* server and runs in the same process as the client application.

Applications that use in-process servers usually run faster than those that use out-of-process servers because the application doesn't have to cross process boundaries to use an object's properties, methods, and events. For more information about in-process and out-of-process servers, see "In-Process and Out-of-Process Servers" earlier in this chapter.

Object references are *early-bound* if they use object variables declared as variables of a specific class. Object references are *late-bound* if they use object variables declared as variables of the generic Object class. Object references that use early-bound variables usually run faster than those that use late-bound variables.

For example, you could assign a reference to an Excel object to either of the following variables:

```
Dim xlApp1 As Excel.Application
Set xlApp1 = New Excel.Application

Dim xlApp2 As Object
Set xlApp2 = CreateObject("Excel.Application")
```

Code that uses variable xlApp1 is early-bound and will execute faster than code that uses variable xlApp2, which is late-bound.

Late Binding

When you declare a variable As Object, Visual Basic cannot determine at compile time what sort of object reference the variable will contain. In this situation, Visual Basic must use *late binding* — that is, Visual Basic must determine at run time whether or not that object will actually have the properties and methods you used in your code.

For example, Visual Basic will compile the following code without generating errors, even though it refers to a method that doesn't exist, because it uses a late-bound object variable. It doesn't check for the existence of the method until run time, so it will produce a run-time error:

```
Dim xlApp As Object
Set xlApp = CreateObject("Excel.Application")
xlApp.TheImpossibleMethod  ' Method doesn't exist.
```

This code runs slower than code that uses an early-bound object variable because Visual Basic must include code in the compiled executable that will determine at run time whether or not the Microsoft Excel Application object has a TheImpossibleMethod method.

Although late binding is the slowest way to invoke the properties and methods of an object, there are times when it is necessary. For example, you may write a function that uses an object variable to act on any of several different classes of objects. Because you don't know in advance what class of object will be assigned to the variable, declare it as a late-bound variable using As Object.

Early Binding

If Visual Basic can detect at compile time what object a property or method belongs to, it can resolve the reference to the object at compile time. The compiled executable contains only the code to invoke the object's properties, methods, and events. This is called *early binding*.

When you declare an object variable using the class that defines the object, the variable can only contain a reference to an object of that class. Visual Basic can use early binding for any code that uses the variable.

Early binding dramatically reduces the time required to set or retrieve a property value, because the call overhead can be a significant part of the total time. For method calls, the improvement depends on the amount of work the method does. Short methods, where the call overhead is comparable to the time required to complete the task, will benefit the most.

Using an Object's Properties, Methods, and Events

After you assign an object reference to an object variable, you can use the variable to manipulate the object's properties and methods. You can also declare an object variable using the WithEvents keyword and use it to make your application respond to the object's events.

Using an Object's Properties and Methods

You can use the *object.property* syntax to set and return an object's property values or the *object.method* syntax to use methods on the object. For example, you could set the Caption property of the Application object as follows:

```
Dim xlApp As Excel.Application
Set xlApp = New Excel.Application
xlApp.Caption = "MyFirstObject"
```

Note The Excel.Application syntax for referring to the Microsoft Excel Application class is not supported in versions prior to Microsoft Excel 97. To refer to the Microsoft Excel Application class in Microsoft Excel 5.0 and Microsoft Excel 95, use the syntax [_ExcelApplication] instead. For example:

```
Set xlApp = New [_ExcelApplication]
```

You could call the Quit method of the Microsoft Excel Application object like this:

```
xlApp.Quit
```

In general, it is a good idea to be as specific as possible when referring to methods or properties of objects defined by other applications or projects. For example:

```
' Fully qualified property name sets
' the Microsoft Project window caption.
Dim pjWindow As Project.Window
' Get a reference to the first Window object.
Set pjWindow = ActiveProject.Windows(1)
pjWindow.Caption = "Project Caption"

' Unqualified name causes Visual Basic to use
' the first object it finds with a property
' named Caption - in this case, Form1.
Caption = "Microsoft Form1 Caption"
```

Note If you need to import binary data into your Visual Basic application and you plan to share the data between applications using ActiveX, use a Byte array to store the data. If you assign binary data to a string and then try to pass this data to an Automation object that takes a string, the data may not be converted correctly. For more information on data types, see Chapter 5, "Programming Fundamentals."

For More Information For more information on working with an object's properties and methods, see Chapter 9, "Programming with Objects."

Responding to an Object's Events

In addition to responding to events that occur to Visual Basic objects, your application can respond to events in an object provided by an ActiveX component. For example, your Visual Basic application can display a message box if an event occurs in a Microsoft Excel workbook.

You make your application respond to an object's events by adding code to an event procedure for the object. However, event procedures for objects provided by components are not automatically available in Visual Basic. You must first declare an object variable using the WithEvents keyword.

After you declare an object variable using WithEvents, the Visual Basic code window uses the variable to display event procedures for the object. You can then add code to these event procedures to respond to the object's events. When you assign an object reference to the variable, you establish a connection between the variable and the object at run time.

To create an event procedure for an object provided by a component

1. Add a reference to the component's type library to your Visual Basic project. For more information on adding a reference to a type library, see "Creating a Reference to an Object," earlier in this chapter.
2. In the Declarations section of a form or class module, declare an object variable using the WithEvents keyword. For example:

   ```
   Dim WithEvents xlBook As Excel.Workbook
   ```

   Visual Basic adds the name of the object variable to the Object box in the code window. When you select the variable name, Visual Basic displays the object's event procedures in the Procedure list box.
3. Select an event procedure, then add code to the procedure that you want your application to run when the event occurs.

   For example, suppose your Visual Basic application relies on data displayed in a Microsoft Excel workbook and that you've already declared a WithEvents variable `xlBook` for the workbook. When a user tries to close the workbook, you can display a message and keep the workbook from closing by adding the following code to the xlBook_BeforeClose event procedure in your application:

   ```
   Private Sub xlBook_BeforeClose(Cancel As Boolean)
      ' Hide the Microsoft Excel window so the message
      ' will be visible.
      xlBook.Application.Visible = False
      ' Display the message.
      MsgBox "This workbook must remain open."
      ' Unhide the Microsoft Excel window.
      xlBook.Application.Visible=True
      ' Set the event procedure's Cancel argument
      ' to True, cancelling the event.
      Cancel = True
   End Sub
   ```

4. Assign an object reference to the WithEvents object variable.

   For example, you could add the following to the Visual Basic form's Form_Load event procedure to assign the variable `xlBook` a reference to a Microsoft Excel workbook, Sales.xls:

   ```
   Private Sub Form_Load()
      Set xlBook = GetObject("Sales.xls")
      ' Display Microsoft Excel and the Worksheet
      ' window.
      xlBook.Application.Visible = True
      xlBook.Windows(1).Visible = True
   End Sub
   ```

For More Information See "Dim Statement" in the *Microsoft Visual Basic 6.0 Language Reference*.

Releasing an ActiveX Component

When you are finished using an object, clear any variables that reference the object so the object can be released from memory. To clear an object variable, set it to Nothing. For example:

```
Dim acApp As Access.Application
Set acApp = New Access.Application
MsgBox acApp.SysCmd(acSysCmdAccessVer)
Set acApp = Nothing
```

All object variables are automatically cleared when they go out of scope. If you want the variable to retain its value across procedures, use a public or form-level variable, or create procedures that return the object. The following code shows how you would use a public variable:

```
Public wdApp as Word.Application
.
.
.
' Create a Word object and start Microsoft Word.
Set wdApp = New Word.Application
.
.
.
' Microsoft Word will not close until the
' application ends or the reference is set to Nothing:
Set wdApp = Nothing
```

Also, be careful to set all object references to Nothing when finished, even for dependent objects. For example:

```
Dim xlApp As Excel.Application
Dim xlBook As Excel.Workbook
Set xlApp = New Excel.Application
Set xlBook = xlApp.Workbooks.Add
Set xlApp = Nothing   ' Careful! xlBook may still
                      ' contain an object reference.
Set xlBook = Nothing  ' Now all the references
                      ' are cleared.
```

Navigating Object Models

Once you understand how to use objects provided by components, you can use any object that is a component exposes to you. Components can range from a simple code component or ActiveX control to large components, such as Microsoft Excel and the Microsoft Data Access Object (DAO) programming interface, which expose many objects.

Each object exists somewhere in the component's object hierarchy, and you can access the objects in two ways:

- Directly, if the object is externally creatable.
- Indirectly, if the object is a dependent object. You can get a reference to it from another object higher in the component's hierarchy.

The best way to navigate an object hierarchy is to use the Object Browser (if the component provides an object library).

Navigating the Object Hierarchy

As you've seen, you navigate down an object hierarchy by setting references to dependent objects through externally creatable objects. You can also use a method on a collection object to return an individual object. For more information see "Working with Externally Creatable and Dependent Objects," later in this chapter.

Figure 10.3 shows the object navigation path in a Microsoft Excel application.

Figure 10.3 Navigating down a Microsoft Excel object hierarchy using collections

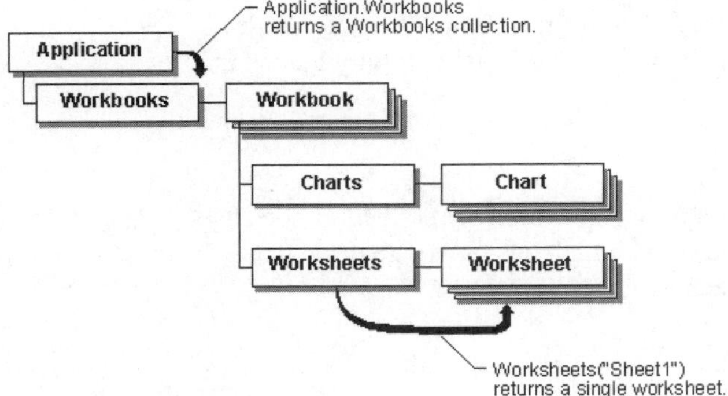

To navigate back up, most applications use the Parent and Application, as shown in Figure 10.4.

Figure 10.4 Navigating back up a Microsoft Excel object hierarchy using the Parent and Application properties

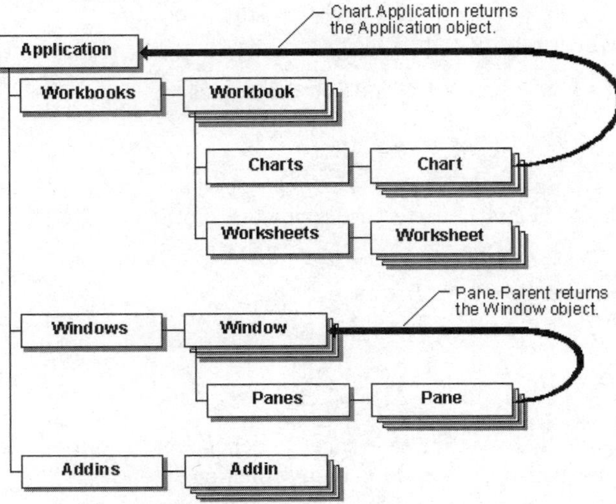

Collection Objects

Collection objects are containers for groups of other objects. These objects provide an easy way to keep track of a set of objects that are of the same type. For example, a collection of all the Menu objects in an application can be accessed using the Menus collection object. You can use the following code to refer to *all* the workbooks that are currently loaded in Microsoft Excel:

```
Application.Workbooks
```

Notice that Workbooks is plural. The standard naming convention for collection objects is the plural of the type of object that makes up the collection. You can iterate through the objects in a collection by using the For Each statement, as follows:

```
Dim xlBook As Excel.Workbook
.
.
.
For Each xlBook In Application.Workbooks
   ' Display the name of each workbook.
   MsgBox xlBook.FullName
Next xlBook
```

Individual objects in many collections can also be referenced by name or by their index order in the collection. The following example shows how you would refer to Style objects named "Normal," "Example," and "Heading":

```
xlBook.Styles("Normal")
xlBook.Styles("Example")
xlBook.Styles("Heading")
```

Assuming these objects are the first three objects in the Styles, and that the collection is zero-based, you could also refer to them as follows:

```
xlBook.Styles(1)      ' Refers the Normal Style object.
xlBook.Styles(2)      ' Refers the Example Style
                      ' object.
xlBook.Styles(3)      ' Refers the Heading Style
                      ' object.
```

For More Information For more information on working with collection objects, see Chapter 9, "Programming with Objects."

Working with Externally Creatable and Dependent Objects

How you create a reference to an object provided by a component depends on whether the object is an externally creatable or dependent object. You can directly create a reference to an externally creatable object; you create a reference to a dependent object indirectly by using a method of a higher-level object in the component's object hierarchy.

Externally Creatable Objects

Most large ActiveX-enabled applications and other ActiveX components provide a top-level externally creatable object in their object hierarchy that:

- Provides access to other objects in the hierarchy.
- Provides methods and properties that affect the entire application.

For example, the Microsoft Office applications each provide a top-level Application object. The following example shows how you can assign references to the Application objects of Microsoft Excel, Microsoft Word, and Microsoft Access:

```
Dim xlApp As Excel.Application
Dim wdApp As Word.Application
Dim acApp As Access.Application

Set xlApp = New Excel.Application
Set wdApp = New Word.Application
Set acApp = New Access.Application
```

You can then using these variables to access the dependent objects in each application and the properties and methods of these objects. For more information see "Creating a Reference to an Object," earlier in this chapter.

> **Note** The Excel.Application syntax for referring to the Microsoft Excel Application class is not supported in versions prior to Microsoft Excel 97. To refer to the Microsoft Excel Application class in Microsoft Excel 5.0 and Microsoft Excel 95, use the syntax [_ExcelApplication] instead. For example:
>
> ```
> Set xlApp = New [_ExcelApplication]
> ```

In addition to these top-level externally creatable objects, ActiveX components can also provide externally creatable objects that are lower on the component's object hierarchy. You can access these objects either directly as an externally creatable object or indirectly as a dependent object of a higher-level externally creatable object. For example, you can create a reference to a DAO TableDef object either directly or indirectly:

```
' Create a reference to daoTable1 directly.
Dim daoTable1 As DAO.TableDef
Set daoTable1 = New DAO.TableDef
daoTable1.Name = "Table1"

' Create a reference to daoTable2 indirectly,
' as a dependent object of the DAO DBEngine object.
Dim daoDBE As DAO.DBEngine
Dim daoWs As DAO.Workspace
Dim daoDb As DAO.Database
Dim daoTable2 As DAO.TableDef

Set daoDBE = DAO.DBEngine
Set daoWs = daoDBE.Workspaces(0)
Set daoDb = daoWs.CreateDatabase("db1.mdb", _
dbLangGeneral)
Set daoTable2 = daoDb.CreateTableDef("Table2")
```

Some objects provide an Application object, but give it a different name. For example, the Microsoft Jet database engine in Microsoft Access calls its top-level object the DBEngine object.

Dependent Objects

You can get a reference to a dependent object in only one way — by using a property or method of an externally creatable object to return a reference to the dependent object. Dependent objects are lower in an object hierarchy, and they can be accessed only by using a method of an externally creatable object. For example, suppose you want a reference to a Button object from Microsoft Excel. You can't get a reference to this object using the following code (an error will result):

```
Dim xlButton As Excel.Button
Set xlButton = New Excel.Button
```

Instead, use the following code to get a reference to a Button object:

```
Dim xlApp As Excel.Application
Dim xlBook As Excel.Workbook
Dim xlSheet As Excel.Worksheet
Dim xlButton As Excel.Button

Set xlApp = New Excel.Application
Set xlBook = xlApp.Workbooks.Add
Set xlSheet = xlBook.Worksheets.Add
Set xlButton = xlSheet.Buttons.Add(44, 100, 100, 44)

' Now you can use a Button object property.
xlButton.Caption = "FirstButton"
```

Figure 10.5 illustrates how a Visual Basic application gets a reference to the Button object.

Figure 10.5 Accessing dependent objects

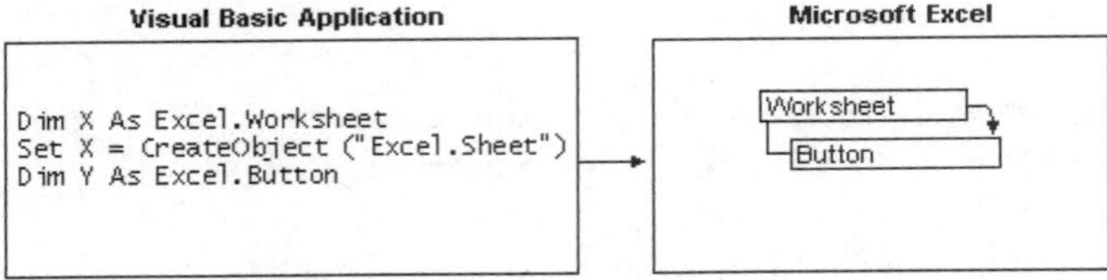

Handling Run-Time Errors in ActiveX Components

Error-handling code is especially important when you're working with ActiveX components, because code from the component is used from within your Visual Basic application. Where possible, you should include code to handle errors that the component may generate. For example, it is good practice to check for the error that occurs if a user unexpectedly closes a component application:

```
Function StartWord()
' Starts Microsoft Word.
On Error Goto ErrorTrap

   ' Declare a Microsoft Word Application variable
   ' and an integer variable for error trap.
   Dim wdApp As Word.Application
   Dim iTries As Integer

   ' Assign an object reference.
   Set wdApp = New Word.Application

   ' Release object variable.
   Set wdApp = Nothing

   Exit Function
```

```
ErrorTrap:
   ' Trap for the error that occurs if Microsoft Word
   ' can't be started.
   Select Case Err.Number
      Case 440             ' Automation error.
         iTries = iTries + 1
         ' Make up to 5 attempts to restart Word.
         If iTries < 5 Then
            Set wdApp = New Word.Application
            Resume
         Else
            Err.Raise Number:=VBObjectError + 28765, _
            Description:= "Couldn't restart Word"
         End If
      Case Else
         Err.Raise Number:= Err.Number
   End Select
End Function
```

If any error other than error 440 occurs in the preceding example, the procedure displays the error and raises an error. The application that provides the object might pass back its own error. In some cases, an application might use the same error code that Visual Basic uses for a different error. In these cases, you should use On Error Resume Next and check for errors immediately after each line that might cause an error. This type of error checking is called *inline error-handling*.

Testing for Object References

Before using an object variable in your code, you may want to make sure the variable holds a valid object reference. You can determine whether or not an object reference has been assigned to the variable by using Is Nothing. For example, the following code checks whether or not an object reference has been assigned to the variable `wdDoc`:

```
If wdDoc Is Nothing Then MsgBox "No object reference."
```

However, Is Nothing won't detect whether or not a valid object reference has become unavailable. For example, if you assign a Microsoft Word object reference to an object variable and Microsoft Word becomes unavailable, the variable will still hold a valid object reference. In this situation, use your error handler to trap the error that results when your code tries to use the variable.

For More Information For information about the errors that a particular application might pass back, see that application's documentation. For more information about trapping errors, see Chapter 13, "Debugging Your Code and Handling Errors."

Handling Requests Pending to an ActiveX Component

It usually takes only a fraction of a second to set a property or call a method of an object. At times, however, your request may not be finished immediately.

- If you call the Close method of a Workbook in Microsoft Excel while the user has a dialog box open, Microsoft Excel signals that it is busy and cannot execute your request. This can lead to a *component busy* condition.
- If you call a method that performs a lengthy operation, such as a large amount of database work when the database is very active, you may try to perform another operation while the first operation is still pending. This can lead to a *request pending* condition.
- If you have two or more programs making calls to a shared component, one call must be completed before another can begin. Components handle such conflicts by *serializing* the requests, that is, making them wait in line. This can also lead to a request pending condition.

Component busy is like getting a busy signal when you make a telephone call. You know you're not going to get through, so you may as well hang up and try again later.

Request pending is like having your call go through, and then having the person you're calling keep you talking much longer than you intended. If your request is serialized, then request pending is like having the other party pick up the telephone and say immediately, "Can you hold, please?"

The Component Busy Condition

A component may reject your request because it has a modal dialog box open, or because a user edit operation is in progress. For example, Microsoft Excel rejects requests from a client application while a spreadsheet cell is being edited.

Visual Basic assumes that the busy condition is temporary and keeps trying the request for a specified timeout interval. When that time is up, Visual Basic displays the Component Busy dialog box, as shown in Figure 10.6.

Figure 10.6 The Component Busy dialog box

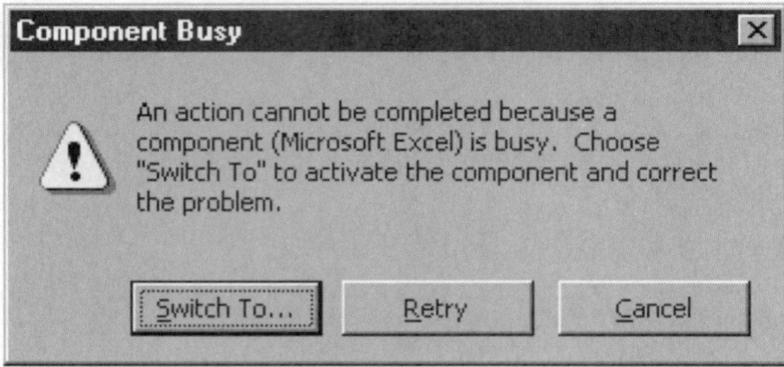

The user can retry the request, cancel the request, or switch to the component and fix the problem (for example, by dismissing the dialog box). If the user chooses Cancel, the error &h80010001 (RPC_E_CALL_REJECTED) is raised in the procedure that made the request.

The Request Pending Condition

Once a component has accepted your application's request, your application must wait until the request has been completed. If the request takes a long time, the user may attempt to minimize your program or resize it to get it out of the way.

After a short timeout interval, Visual Basic responds to such attempts by displaying the Component Request Pending dialog.

The appearance of the Component Request Pending dialog box is slightly different from the Component Busy dialog. The Cancel button is disabled, as shown in Figure 10.7, because the request in progress cannot be canceled.

Figure 10.7 The Component Request Pending dialog box

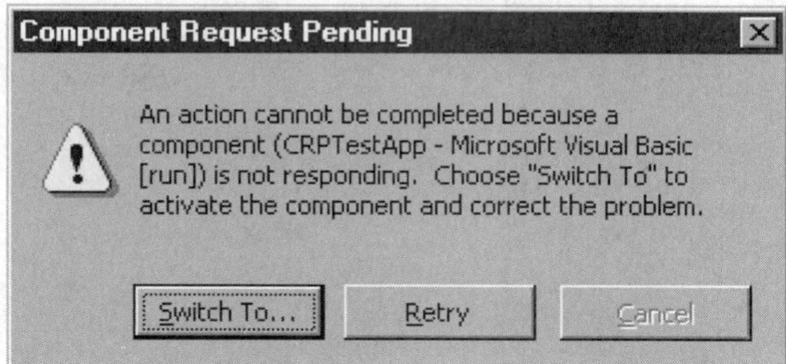

Switching to the component is useful only if it has halted to display an error message as a result of your request. This should not be a common occurrence, because the proper behavior for a component is to return an error condition to the program that called it.

For More Information For more information, see "Changing the Component Busy or Request Pending Messages," "Controlling Timeout Intervals," and "Raising an Error on Component Busy Timeout," later in this chapter.

Changing the Component Busy or Request Pending Messages

The Component Busy and Component Request Pending dialog boxes are provided by Visual Basic as simple default messages. There are many situations where these dialog boxes may not meet your needs.

- Your program may call a method of an object provided by a component that has no user interface. Components created using Visual Basic, Professional or Enterprise Editions, for example, may run in the background without any visible forms.
- The component you call may have been created using the Remote Automation features of Visual Basic, Enterprise Edition, and may be running on another computer located at some distance from the user.
- If your program has loaded a Microsoft Excel workbook using the GetObject function, the workbook will not be visible when the user switches to Microsoft Excel. In fact, Microsoft Excel itself may not be visible, in which case the Switch To button does nothing.

In these situations, the Switch To button is inappropriate and may confuse the user of your program. You can specify a substitute message for either or both of the timeouts. Your messages will be displayed in a simple message box, without a Switch To button.

For the request pending condition, the message box has only an OK button. For the component busy condition, an OK button and a Cancel button are provided. If the user presses Cancel, error -2147418111 (&h80010001) will be raised in the procedure in which you made the request.

The following properties of the App object determine whether the Component Busy or Component Request Pending dialog box will be replaced by a message box and allow you to specify the text and caption of the message box.

OLEServerBusyMsgText Property

Specifies the message text to be displayed when the component busy condition occurs. Setting this property causes the alternate message box to be used in place of the usual Component Busy dialog box.

OLEServerBusyMsgTitle Property

Specifies the caption to be used if an alternate message is supplied for the component busy condition. (Only setting this property will not cause the alternate message box to be used.)

OLERequestPendingMsgText Property

Specifies the message text to be displayed when the request pending condition occurs. Setting this property causes the alternate message box to be used in place of the usual Component Request Pending dialog box.

OLERequestPendingMsgTitle Property

Specifies the caption to be used if an alternate message is supplied for the request pending condition. (Only setting this property will not cause the alternate message box to be used.)

The following example sets titles and message texts for both the component busy and pending request conditions, completely overriding the Component Busy and Component Request Pending dialog boxes.

```
Public Const APP_TITLE = "Demo Application"

Private Sub cmdLongTransaction_Click()
   On Error Goto LongTransaction_Error
   ' You may wish to set the titles once, in Sub Main.
   App.OLEServerBusyMsgTitle = APP_TITLE

   App.OLERequestPendingMsgTitle = APP_TITLE
   ' Message texts specific to this request.
   App.OLEServerBusyMsgText = "The component for _
      the " & "Long Transaction has not responded. _
      If " & "you have been waiting more than five " _
      & "minutes, you may wish to cancel this " _
      & "request and try it later." & vbCrLf _
      & "Call Network Services to verify that the " _
      & "component is running, or to report problems."
   App.OLERequestPendingMsgText = "Your request " _
      & "is still executing. " & vbCrLf _
      & "Call Network Services to verify that the " _
      & " component is running, or to report _
      problems."
   ' Code to make a request and use results...
   ' ...
LongTransaction_Cleanup:
   ' Code to perform any necessary cleanup...
   ' ...
   Exit Sub
```

```
LongTransaction_Error:
   If Err.Number = &h80010001 Then
      MsgBox "Transaction cancelled"
   Else
      ' Code to handle other errors.
   End If
   Resume LongTransaction_Cleanup
End Sub
```

Important The length of your messages may be limited by the operating system. Messages more than a thousand characters in length can be used when the target operating system is Windows NT or Windows 95.

Controlling Timeout Intervals

You can set the timeout intervals that determine when Visual Basic displays the Component Busy and Component Request Pending dialog boxes, using two properties of the App object.

OLEServerBusyTimeout Property

Determines how long Visual Basic will go on retrying your Automation requests before displaying the Component Busy dialog. The default value is 10000 milliseconds (10 seconds).

OLERequestPendingTimeout Property

Determines how long Visual Basic waits before responding to mouse clicks, keypress events, and other events by displaying the Component Request Pending dialog. The default value is 5000 milliseconds (5 seconds).

The following example shows how the timeout values might be adjusted and reset for a call to the StockAnalysis method of a hypothetical BusinessRules object.

```
Public Sub SetTimeouts(ByVal lngComponentBusy As _
Long, ByVal lngRequestPending As Long)
   App.OLEServerBusyTimeout = lngComponentBusy
   App.OLERequestPendingTimeout = lngRequestPending
End Sub

Public Sub ResetTimeouts()
   App.OLEServerBusyTimeout = 10000

   App.OLERequestPendingTimeout = 5000
End Sub
```

```
Private Sub cmdFullAnalysis_Click()
   On Error Goto FullAnalysis_Error
   ' Set very short timeouts. After 2 seconds,
   ' the user will be notified and keypresses or
   ' clicks will display the Component Busy
   ' and Component Request Pending dialogs.
   SetTimeouts 2, 2
   Me.MousePointer = vbHourglass
   gobjBusinessRules.StockAnalysis txtNYSECode.Text, _
   ATYPE_FULL
FullAnalysis_Cleanup:
   Me.MousePointer = vbDefault
   ResetTimeouts
   Exit Sub

FullAnalysis_Error:
   If Err.Number = &h80010001 Then
      MsgBox "Analysis cancelled"
   Else
      ' Code to handle other errors...
   End If
   Resume FullAnalysis_Cleanup
End Sub
```

You can set either of these timeouts to very large values, because they are stored as Longs. For example, 86,400,000 milliseconds is a day, which is equivalent to an infinite timeout. When you do this, however, you risk having your program lock up until the component is no longer busy, or until a pending request has completed.

Important Because these timeout values are properties of the App object, they also affect documents you link or embed using the OLE container control or the Toolbox. If you are using linked or embedded documents and you change these properties for an Automation request, it is a good idea to reset the values afterward.

Raising an Error on Component Busy Timeout

For the component busy condition, you can bypass both the Component Busy dialog box and the replacement message by setting the Boolean OLEServerBusyRaiseError property of the App object to True. Visual Basic will retry your request for the length of time specified by the OLEServerBusyTimeout property, and then raise an error in the procedure that made the Automation request, just as if the user had pressed the Cancel button on the Component Busy dialog box.

The error returned is –2147418111 (&h80010001). In the error handler for the procedure, you can then take whatever action is most appropriate. For example, you could display a complex dialog box that offered the user several retry options or alternatives.

This property will be particularly useful for components designed to run on remote network computers, using the Remote Automation feature of Visual Basic, Enterprise Edition. Such a component may call on other components, and it must handle errors in those calls without displaying any forms.

There is no corresponding property for the request pending condition. Once an Automation request has been accepted by the component, the client program must wait until the request is complete.

Using a Component's Visual Interface

If a component supports object linking and embedding (OLE), you can link or embed an object into your application without writing any code by using the component's visual interface. You can use a component's visual interface in one of two ways:

- By adding an OLE container control to your application, then inserting an object into the control.
- By adding the object's class to the Toolbox, then adding an object of that class to your application just as you would add a control to a form.

Inserting an Object with the OLE Container Control

The OLE container control gives you the most flexibility in using an object's visual interface. With the OLE container control, you can:

- Create a placeholder in your application for an object. You can create the object that appears within the OLE container control at run time, or you can change an object you have placed in the OLE container control at design time.
- Create a linked object in your application.
- Bind the OLE container control to a database.
- Perform an action if the user moves, sizes, or updates the object in the OLE container control.
- Create objects from data that was copied onto the Clipboard.
- Display objects as icons.

An OLE container control can contain only one object at a time. There are several ways to create a linked or embedded object in the OLE container control — the one you choose depends on whether you are creating the linked or embedded object at design time or run time. Once you have an OLE container control drawn on your form, you can insert an object into the container control by:

- Using the Insert Object or Paste Special dialog box. See "Inserting Objects at Design Time with the OLE Container Control" and "Creating Objects at Run Time with the OLE Container Control," later in this chapter.

- Setting the Class, SourceDoc, and SourceItem properties in the Properties window. See "Creating Objects at Run Time with the OLE Container Control," later in this chapter.
- Calling the CreateEmbed or CreateLink method. See "Creating Objects at Run Time with the OLE Container Control," later in this chapter.

For More Information For more information on using the OLE container control, see "Using the OLE Container Control" in Chapter 7, "Using Visual Basic's Standard Controls."

Inserting an Object by Adding Its Class to the Toolbox

In the same way that you use the Toolbox to add one of Visual Basic's built-in controls to an application, you can use the Toolbox to add an object. First, add the object's class to the Toolbox, then add the object to a form.

To add an object's class to the Toolbox

1. From the **Project** menu, choose **Components**.
2. In the **Components** dialog box, click the **Insertable Objects** tab.
3. Select the class you want to add to the Toolbox, then click **OK**. Visual Basic adds a button of that class to the toolbox.

   For example, to add a Microsoft Excel Worksheet button to the Toolbox, select Microsoft Excel Worksheet.

Once you've added the object's class to the Toolbox, you can draw it on a form to create an object of that class. For example, after you add a Microsoft Excel Worksheet button to the Toolbox, you can draw it on a form to create a worksheet object on the form.

Contrasting Linked and Embedded Objects

You use a component's visual interface to contain data from another application by linking or embedding that data into your Visual Basic application. The primary difference between a linked and embedded object is where their data is stored. For example, data associated with a *linked object* is managed by the application that created it and stored outside an OLE container control. Data associated with an *embedded object* is contained in an OLE container control and can be saved with your Visual Basic application.

When a linked or embedded object is created, it contains the *name* of the application that supplied the object, its data (or, in the case of a linked object, a *reference* to the data), and an *image* of the data.

> **Note** To place an object in an OLE container control, the component that provides the object must be registered in your system registry. When you install an application that supplies the objects you want to use in your project, that application should register its object library on your system so that application's objects appear in the Insert Object dialog box. You can use Regedit.exe to search the system registry for an object, but take care not to alter the contents of the registry.

Linked Objects

When you link an object, you are inserting a *placeholder* (not the actual data itself) for the *linked object* into your application. For example, when you link a range of spreadsheet cells to a Visual Basic application, the data associated with the cells is stored in another file; only a link to the data and an image of the data are stored in the OLE container control. While working with your Visual Basic application, a user can activate the linked object (by double-clicking the object, for example), and the spreadsheet application will start automatically. The user can then edit those spreadsheet cells using the spreadsheet application. When editing a linked object, the editing is done in a separate window outside the OLE container control.

When an object is linked to a Visual Basic application, the object's current data can be viewed from any other applications that contain links to that data. The data exists in only one place — the ActiveX component — which is the source application that provides the object. For example, in Figure 10.8, Visual Basic contains a link to the Graph application. Microsoft Word also contains a link to the graph. If the graph's data is changed by either application, the modified graph will appear in *both* the Visual Basic application and the Microsoft Word document.

Figure 10.8 An object's data can be accessed from many different applications that contain links to that data

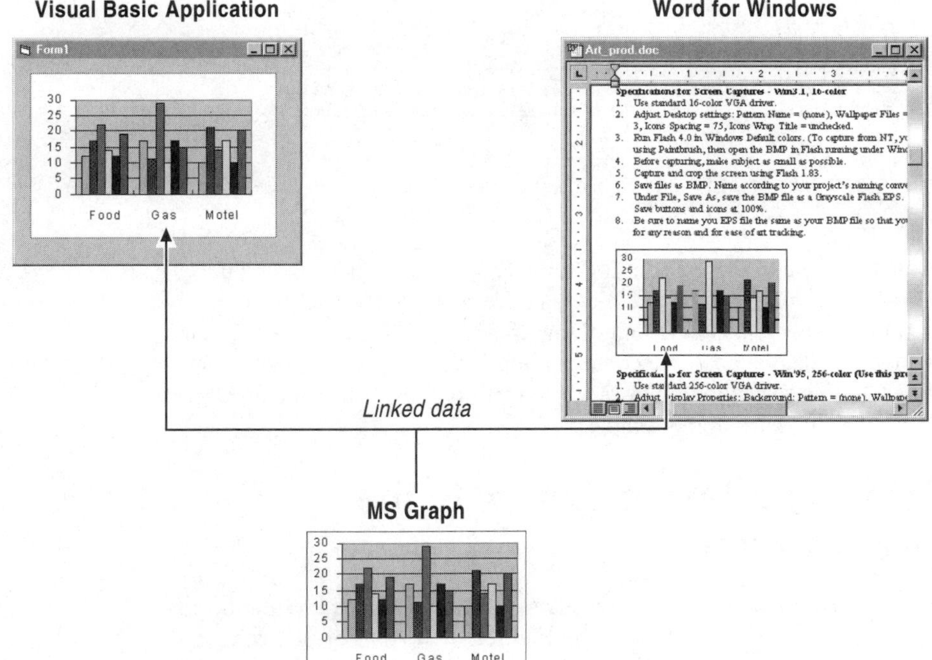

As you can see, linking makes it easy to track identical information that appears in more than one application. Linking is useful when you want to maintain one set of data that is accessed from several applications.

Embedded Objects

To create an embedded object, you can either use an OLE container control or add an object's class to the Toolbox. With an *embedded object*, all the data associated with the object is copied to and contained in the OLE container control. When you save the contents of the control to a file, the file contains the name of the application that produced the object, the object's data, and a metafile image of the object. For this reason, embedded objects can greatly increase file size.

Unlike linked objects, no other application has access to the data in an embedded object. Embedding is useful when you want your application to maintain data that is produced and edited in another application, as shown in Figure 10.9.

Figure 10.9 Your application maintains data for an embedded object

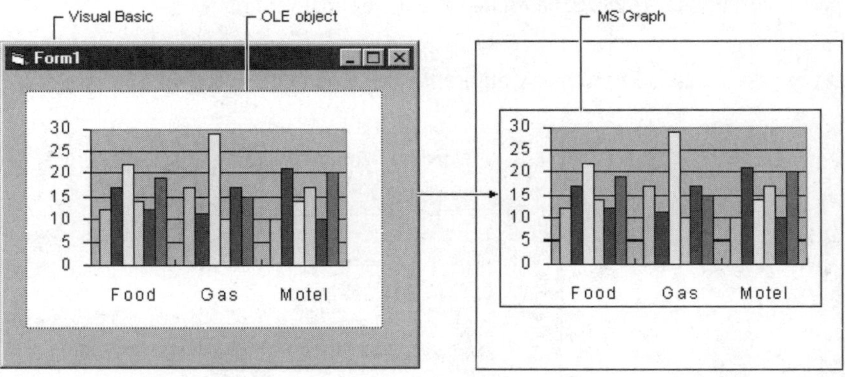

When the user activates the object (the graph), the ActiveX component that created the object (Microsoft Graph) is invoked by the container application (your Visual Basic application), and the object's data is opened for editing. In addition, the user interface and menu system of the object is displayed in the container application so the user can control the object in place. For more information on in-place activation, see "Activating an Object in the OLE Container Control," later in this chapter.

Inserting Objects at Design Time with the OLE Container Control

Each time you draw an OLE container control on a form, Visual Basic displays the Insert Object dialog box. You use this dialog box, shown in Figure 10.10, to insert linked or embedded objects at design time. The Insert Object dialog box presents a list of the available objects you can link or embed into your application.

Figure 10.10 The Insert Object dialog box

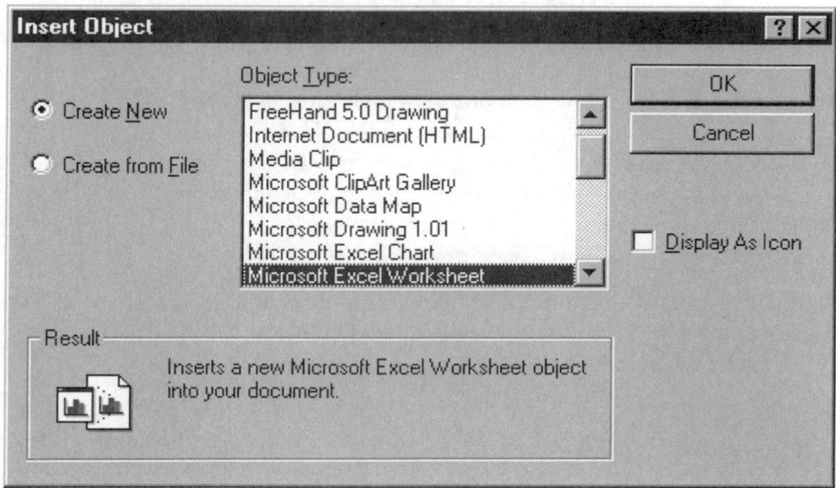

When you insert an object into the OLE container control at design time, the Class, SourceDoc, and SourceItem properties are automatically set for you. These properties identify the application that supplies the object, the source file name, and any specific data that is linked from within that file.

Inserting Linked Objects at Design Time

When you insert a linked object, the data displayed in the OLE container control exists in one place — the source file. The object's current data can be viewed from any other applications that contain links to that data. The OLE container control maintains the object's link information, such as the name of the application that supplied the object, the name of the linked file, and an image of the linked data.

To insert a linked object using the Insert Object dialog box

1. Draw an **OLE container control** on a form.

   The **Insert Object** dialog box is displayed. You can also display this dialog box at any time by clicking the **OLE container control** with the right mouse button and then choosing the **Insert Object** command.

2. Select the **Create from File** option button.

3. Choose the **Browse** button.

   A **Browse** dialog box is displayed.

4. Select the file you want to link.

5. Click **Insert** to return to the **Insert Object** dialog box.
6. Select the **Link** check box in the **Insert Object** dialog box, and choose **OK** to create the linked object.

When you use a linked object, every user who runs your application must have access (a valid path) to the linked file and a copy of the application that created the file. Otherwise, when your application is run, an image of the original data is displayed, but the user will not be able to modify the data, nor will the user see changes others may have made to the linked data. This may be a concern if your application is running on a network.

If your application contains a linked object, it is possible for that object's data to be changed by another application when your application is not running. The next time your application is run, changes to the source file do not automatically appear in the OLE container control. To display the current data in the OLE container control, use the control's Update method:

```
oleObj.Update
```

For More Information See "Update Method (OLE Container)" in the *Microsoft Visual Basic 6.0 Language Reference*.

If a user wants to save changes to a linked object, the user must save it from the ActiveX component's menu. The OLE container control's SaveToFile method applies only to embedded objects.

Creating Embedded Objects at Design Time

When you create an embedded object, you can either embed data from a file or create a new, empty object that can be filled with data later. When you embed data from a file, a copy of the specified file's data is displayed in the OLE container control. When you create a new object, the application that created the object is invoked and you can enter data into the object.

Typically, you create embedded objects that display existing data at design time. This allows you to view the object's data as it will appear to the user. You can then move and size the OLE container control and the other controls on the form to create your application's user interface.

To display existing data in an embedded object, create the object using an existing file as a template. The OLE container control then contains an image of the data in the file. An application that displays data using an embedded object will be larger than an application that displays the same data using a linked object, because the application with the embedded object actually contains the source file's data.

To create an embedded object using an existing file

1. Draw an **OLE container control** on your form.

   The **Insert Object** dialog box is automatically displayed.

2. Select the **Create from File** option button.
3. Choose the **Browse** button.

   A **Browse** dialog box is displayed.

4. Select the file you want to embed.
5. Choose **Insert** to return to the **Insert Object** dialog box.
6. In the **Insert Object** dialog box, choose **OK** to create the embedded object.

Unlike the data in a linked object, data in an embedded object is not persistent. In other words, if you want changes entered by the user to appear the next time your application is run, you must use the SaveToFile method to save the data. For more information on saving embedded data to a file, see "Saving and Retrieving Embedded Data," later in this chapter.

Creating Objects Using the Paste Special Dialog Box

Another way to create an object at design time is to use the Paste Special dialog box (shown in Figure 10.11). This dialog box is helpful if you only want to use a portion of a file—for instance, a range of cells from a spreadsheet, or a paragraph from a Word document.

Figure 10.11 The Paste Special dialog box

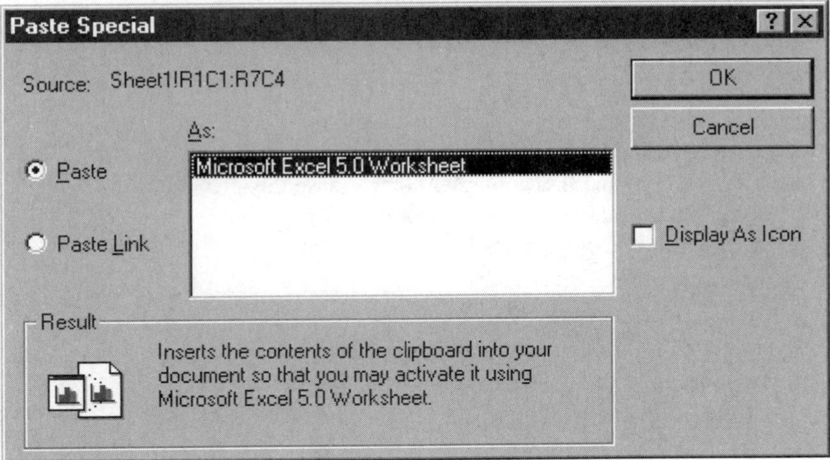

To create an object using the Paste Special dialog box

1. Run the application containing the data you want to link or embed.
2. Select the data you want to link or embed.
3. From the ActiveX component's **Edit** menu, choose **Copy**.

   The data is copied onto the Clipboard.
4. In Visual Basic, click the **OLE container control** with the right mouse button, and choose the **Paste Special** command from the pop-up menu.
5. Select the **Paste** option button if you want to create an embedded object.

   – or –

   Select the **Paste Link** option button if you want to create a linked object.

   If there is already an object embedded or linked in the control, a message asks whether you'd like to delete that existing object and create a new one in its place.
6. Choose **OK** to create the object.

Creating Objects at Run Time with the OLE Container Control

To create a linked or embedded object at run time, you use methods and properties in code. The OLE container control has a variety of properties and methods that you can use for manipulating linked or embedded objects. For a complete list of the properties and methods that apply to the OLE container control, see "OLE Container Control."

Using the Object Property

By using the OLE container control's Object property, you can also use the properties and methods of the linked or embedded object. The Object property is a run-time, read-only property that holds a reference to the object in an OLE container control. Use this property to perform Automation tasks with the OLE container control, including programmatically manipulating the properties and methods an object supports:

```
strObjName = oleObj1.Object.Name
```

To use this property, the OLE container control must contain an object that is programmable. For more information on programmable objects, see "Types of ActiveX Components," online.

Creating Linked Objects at Run Time

You can create a linked object from a file at run time with the OLE container control's CreateLink method. This method takes one argument, *sourcedoc*, which is the file from which the object is created, and an optional argument, *sourceitem*, which specifies the data you want to link from within the source file. The following code fragment creates a linked object at run time:

```
oleObj1.CreateLink "C:\Excel\Test.xls"
```

> **Note** If you use CreateLink to create a linked object, you do not have to set the Class, SourceDoc, and SourceItem properties in the Properties window.

For More Information See "CreateLink Method" in the *Microsoft Visual Basic 6.0 Language Reference*.

Creating Embedded Objects at Run Time

To create an embedded object from a file at run time, you can use the CreateEmbed method. This method has two arguments, *sourcedoc* and *class* (which is optional if SourceDoc is specified). *Sourcedoc* determines the template for the object, and *class* determines the object type. When you use CreateEmbed, you do not need to set the SourceDoc and Class properties.

The following code fragment creates an embedded object using an existing file as a template for the object.

```
oleObj1.CreateEmbed "Q1profit.xls"
```

For More Information See "CreateEmbed Method," in the *Microsoft Visual Basic 6.0 Language Reference*.

When you create an empty embedded object, it is a good idea to activate the ActiveX component that will provide data for the object. You can do this with the DoVerb method. This allows the user to enter any data into the application at run time. The user can then show this newly entered data in the OLE container control by choosing the ActiveX component's Update command (this menu command should appear on the component's File menu).

To create an empty embedded object at run time

1. Use the CreateEmbed method without specifying a source document to create an empty embedded object. For example, this code fragment inserts a file template for a Microsoft Excel Worksheet in the OLE container control:

   ```
   oleObj1.CreateEmbed "","Excel.Sheet"
   ```

2. Use the DoVerb method. The default verb for the DoVerb method depends on the application. With Microsoft Excel, the default verb is Edit.

For example, the following code fragment creates an empty embedded object and then activates the application that created it using the default DoVerb action.

```
oleObj1.CreateEmbed "", "Excel.Sheet"
oleObj1.DoVerb -5   ' Activate
```

Providing empty embedded objects is useful when creating a document-centered application that uses a variety of information from different applications. For more information, see "Letting the User Specify Objects at Run Time," below.

Binding a Database to the OLE Container Control

You can bind the OLE container control to data stored in the Microsoft Jet database engine or Microsoft Access database. You may want to do this, for example, if you have a database with a table of employee pictures. If the pictures are stored as objects, you can bind them to the OLE container control and display them on a form as each record is accessed with the data control. To bind data to one of these databases, specify the source of data (recordset name) in the DataSource property and the field name from that data source in the DataField property of the OLE container control. When displaying an object from a database, the OLE container control allows the user to activate, edit, and update the object. As with any bound control, the updated object is automatically written back to the database when the record position is changed.

Letting the User Specify Objects at Run Time

By displaying the Paste Special and Insert Object dialog boxes at run time, you can allow the user to create a variety of objects. You may do this when creating a document-centered application. In such an application, the user combines data from different applications to create a single document. For instance, this application might be a word processor in which the user might enter some text and then embed a spreadsheet and a chart using the Insert Object or Paste Special dialog box.

You use the OLE container control's InsertObjDlg method to display the Insert Object dialog box, or you can use the PasteSpecialDlg method to display the Paste Special dialog. These two dialogs let the user make decisions about what goes into the OLE container control.

- The Insert Object dialog box presents a list of available objects and creates an object based on the user's selection.
- The Paste Special dialog box allows the user to paste an object from the system Clipboard into an OLE container control.

You can display these dialog boxes at run time by calling the appropriate method on an event — for instance, a menu's Click event:

```
Private Sub cmdInsert_Click ()
   ' Display Insert Object dialog box.
   oleObj1.InsertObjDlg
   ' Check to make sure object was created with the
   ' OLEType property.
   If oleObj1.OLEType = vbOLENone Then
      MsgBox "Object Not Created."
   End If
End Sub

Private Sub oleObj1_Click ()
   ' Determine if the data contained on the Clipboard
   ' can be pasted into the OLE container control.
   If oleObj1.PasteOK Then
      ' Display Paste Special dialog box.
      oleObj1.PasteSpecialDlg
      ' Check to make sure object was created.
      If oleObj1.OLEType = vbOLENone Then
         MsgBox "Object Not Created."
      End If
   End If
End Sub
```

Once the dialog box is displayed, you do not need to write more code to create the object. The user makes choices in the dialog box and chooses OK to create an object. If the user cancels a dialog, an object is not created.

Note Before displaying the Insert Object or Paste Special dialog box, you may want to determine the value of the OLEType property to see if the OLE container control contains a linked object, embedded object, or no object, as demonstrated in the preceding code example.

The constant vbOLENone and other intrinsic constants are listed in the Visual Basic (VB) object library of the Object Browser.

Determining How an Object is Displayed in the OLE Container Control

You can use the OLE container control's DisplayType property to indicate if the object will appear as an icon (set DisplayType = 1), or if the object's data will be displayed in the control (set DisplayType = 0). This property also determines the default setting of the Display As Icon check box when the Insert Object and Paste Special dialog boxes are displayed at both run time and design time.

Note Once the OLE container control contains an object, you cannot change its display type. You can, however, delete the linked or embedded object, set the DisplayType property, and then insert a new object.

You use the SizeMode property to determine how an object's icon or data image is displayed in the OLE container control when the control is not UI (user-interface) active. A setting of 0-Clip or 3-Zoom clips the image to fit the control, but it doesn't change the actual size of the image (you might not see all of the image when editing it). An object that is smaller than the control is edited in an area smaller than the control. An object larger than the control fills the entire container area and may be clipped if it is larger than the control area. Alternately, setting SizeMode to 2-AutoSize resizes the control to fit the image.

Activating an Object in the OLE Container Control

While the OLE container control's DoVerb method activates an object at run time, you can use the AppIsRunning property to determine whether the application supplying the object is activated and running. You can set AppIsRunning to True to start the ActiveX component, which causes objects to activate more quickly. You can also set this property to False to close the application or take another appropriate action when the object loses focus.

In-Place Activation

Some embedded objects can be edited (activated) from within the OLE container control. This is called *in-place activation*, because users can double-click an object in your application and interact with application supplying the object, without switching to a different application or window.

For objects that support in-place activation, you can set the AutoActivate property so that users can activate an object at any time. That is, when the OLE container control's AutoActivate property is set to Double-Click, users can double-click the control to activate it. It is important to note that activating an object launches that object's application if it is not already running.

> **Note** If you want to display the ActiveX component's menus at run time when the user clicks the OLE container control, you must define at least one menu item for the form and set its Visible property to False. This can be an invisible menu if you don't want any menus displayed. See Chapter 6, "Creating a User Interface," for more information on displaying an ActiveX component's menus and toolbars in a container application when an object is activated at run time.

Responding to Moving or Sizing the Container

The OLE container control has the ObjectMove event, which is triggered when the object associated with the OLE container control is moved or resized. The arguments to ObjectMove represent the coordinates of the object (excluding its border) within the object's container. If the object is moved off the form, the arguments have values representing the position relative to the upper-left corner of the form. These can be positive or negative. If the Width or Height of the ActiveX component is changed, the OLE container control is notified.

The ObjectMove event is the only way the OLE container control can determine if the object has been moved or resized. An ObjectMove event occurs when the user moves or resizes the object contained in the OLE container control. For example:

```
Private Sub oleObj1_ObjectMove(Left As Single, Top As _
   Single, Width As Single, Height As Single)
   ' This method resizes the OLE container control to
   ' the new object size.
   oleObj1.Move oleObj1.Left, oleObj1.Top, _
      Width, Height
   ' This method moves the OLE container control
   ' to the new object position.
   oleObj1.Move Left, Top, _
      oleObj1.Width, oleObj1.Height
' Repaints the form.
   Me.Refresh
End Sub
```

Saving and Retrieving Embedded Data

Data associated with an embedded object is not persistent; that is, when a form containing an OLE container control is closed, any changes to the data associated with that control are lost. To save updated data from an object to a file, you use the OLE container control's SaveToFile method. Once the data has been saved to a file, you can open the file and restore the object.

If the object is linked (OLEType = 0-Linked), then only the link information and an image of the data is saved to the specified file. The object's data is maintained by the application that created the object. If a user wants to save changes to a linked file, the user must choose the Save command from the ActiveX component's File menu because the SaveToFile method applies only to embedded objects.

If the object is embedded (OLEType = 1-Embedded), the object's data is maintained by the OLE container control and can be saved by your Visual Basic application.

Objects in the OLE container control can be saved only to open, binary files.

To save the data from an object to a file

1. Open a file in binary mode.
2. Use the SaveToFile method.

The cmdSaveObject_Click event procedure illustrates these steps:

```
Private Sub cmdSaveObject_Click ()
   Dim FileNum as Integer
   ' Get file number.
   FileNum = FreeFile
   ' Open file to be saved.
```

```
    Open "TEST.OLE" For Binary As #FileNum
    ' Save the file.
    oleObj1.SaveToFile FileNum
    ' Close the file.
    Close #FileNum
End Sub
```

Once an object has been saved to a file, it can be opened and displayed in an OLE container control.

> **Note** When you use the SaveToFile or ReadFromFile methods, the file position is located immediately following the object. Therefore, if you save multiple objects to a file, you should read them in the same order you write them.

To read data from a file into an OLE container control

1. Open the file in binary mode.
2. Use the ReadFromFile method on the object.

The cmdOpenObject_Click event procedure illustrates these steps:

```
Private Sub cmdOpenObject_Click ()
    Dim FileNum as Integer
    ' Get file number.
    FileNum = FreeFile
    ' Open the file.
    Open "TEST.OLE" For Binary As #FileNum
    ' Read the file.
    oleObj1.ReadFromFile FileNum
    ' Close the binary file.
    Close #FileNum
End Sub
```

The Updated event is invoked each time the contents of an object is changed. This event is useful for determining if an object's data has been changed because it was last saved. To do this, set a global variable in the Updated event indicating the object needs to be saved. When you save the object, reset the variable.

CHAPTER 11

Responding to Mouse and Keyboard Events

Your Visual Basic applications can respond to a variety of mouse events and keyboard events. For example, forms, picture boxes, and image controls can detect the position of the mouse pointer, can determine whether a left or right mouse button is being pressed, and can respond to different combinations of mouse buttons and SHIFT, CTRL, or ALT keys. Using the key events, you can program controls and forms to respond to various key actions or interpret and process ASCII characters.

In addition, Visual Basic applications can support both event-driven drag-and-drop and OLE drag-and-drop features. You can use the Drag method with certain properties and events to enable operations such as dragging and dropping controls. OLE drag and drop gives your applications all the power you need to exchange data throughout the Windows environment — and much of this technology is available to your application without writing code.

You can also use the mouse or keyboard to manage the processing of long background tasks, which allows your users to switch to other applications or interrupt background processing.

Other actions and events that involve the mouse or keyboard (the Click and DblClick events, the Focus events, and the Scroll event) are not covered in this chapter. For more information on the Click and DblClick events, see "Clicking Buttons to Perform Actions" and "Understanding Focus" in Chapter 3, "Forms, Controls, and Menus," and see "Click Event" and "DblClick Event" in the *Microsoft Visual Basic 6.0 Language Reference* volume in the *Microsoft Visual Basic 6.0 Reference Library.* Also see "Scroll Event," online.

Contents

Sample Application: Mouse.vbp

Many of the code examples in this chapter are taken from the Mouse.vbp sample application. You'll find this application listed in the Samplesdirectory.

Responding to Mouse Events

You can use the MouseDown, MouseUp, and MouseMove events to enable your applications to respond to both the location and the state of the mouse. (This list excludes drag events, which are introduced in "Dragging and Dropping" later in this chapter.) These mouse events are recognized by most controls.

Event	Description
MouseDown	Occurs when the user presses any mouse button.
MouseUp	Occurs when the user releases any mouse button.
MouseMove	Occurs each time the mouse pointer is moved to a new point on the screen.

A form can recognize a mouse event when the pointer is over a part of the form where there are no controls. A control can recognize a mouse event when the pointer is over the control.

When the user holds down a mouse button, the object continues to recognize all mouse events until the user releases the button. This is true even when the pointer is moved off the object.

The three mouse events use the following arguments.

Argument	Description
Button	A bit-field argument in which the three least-significant bits give the status of the mouse buttons.
Shift	A bit-field argument in which the three least-significant bits give the status of the SHIFT, CTRL, and ALT keys.
x, y	Location of the mouse pointer, using the coordinate system of the object that receives the mouse event.

A *bit-field argument* returns information in individual bits, each indicating whether a certain condition is on or off. Using binary notation, the three leftmost bits are referred to as *most-significant* and the three rightmost bits as *least-significant.* Techniques for programming with these arguments are described in "Detecting Mouse Buttons" and "Detecting SHIFT, CTRL, and ALT States" later in this chapter.

The MouseDown Event

MouseDown is the most frequently used of the three mouse events. It can be used to reposition controls on a form at run time or to create graphical effects, for instance. The MouseDown event is triggered when a mouse button is pressed.

> **Note** The mouse events are used to recognize and respond to the various mouse states as separate events and should not be confused with the Click and DblClick events. The Click event recognizes when a mouse button has been pressed and released, but only as a single action — a click. The mouse events also differ from the Click and DblClick events in that they enable you to distinguish between the left, right, and middle mouse buttons and the SHIFT, CTRL, and ALT keys.

Using MouseDown with the Move Method

The MouseDown event is combined with the Move method to move a command button to a different location on a form. The new location is determined by the position of the mouse pointer: When the user clicks anywhere on the form (except on the control), the control moves to the cursor location.

A single procedure, Form_MouseDown, performs this action:

```
Private Sub Form_MouseDown (Button As Integer, _
      Shift As Integer, X As Single, Y As Single)
   Command1.Move X, Y
End Sub
```

The Move method places the command button control's upper-left corner at the location of the mouse pointer, indicated by the *x* and *y* arguments. You can revise this procedure to place the *center* of the control at the mouse location:

```
Private Sub Form_MouseDown (Button As Integer, _
      Shift As Integer, X As Single, Y As Single)
   Command1.Move (X - Command1.Width / 2), _
   (Y - Command1.Height / 2)
End Sub
```

Using MouseDown with the Line Method

The Click-A-Line sample application responds to a mouse click by drawing a line from the previous drawing location to the new position of the mouse pointer. This application uses the MouseDown event and the Line method. Using the following syntax, the Line method will draw a line from the last point drawn to the point (*x2*, *y2*):

Line – (*x2*, *y2*)

Click-A-Line uses a blank form with one procedure, Form_MouseDown:

```
Private Sub Form_MouseDown (Button As Integer, _
      Shift As Integer, X As Single, Y As Single)
   Line -(X, Y)
End Sub
```

The first line starts at the upper-left corner, which is the default origin. Thereafter, whenever the mouse button is pressed, the application draws a straight line extending from the previous line to the present location of the mouse pointer. The result is a series of connected lines, as shown in Figure 11.1.

Figure 11.1 Connecting lines are drawn whenever MouseDown is invoked

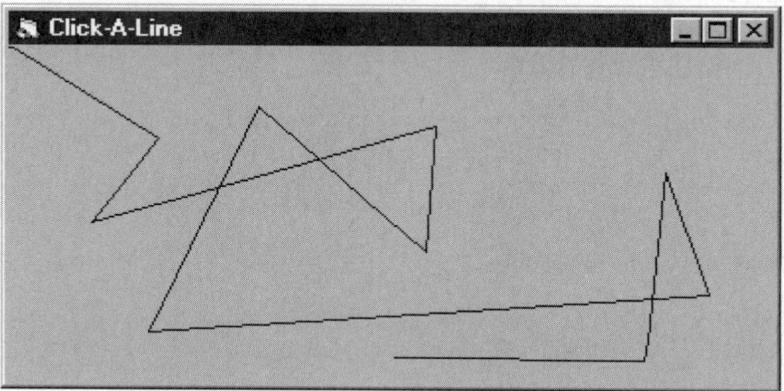

For More Information See "MouseDown Event" in the *Microsoft Visual Basic 6.0 Language Reference*.

The MouseMove Event

The MouseMove event occurs when the mouse pointer is moved across the screen. Both forms and controls recognize the MouseMove event while the mouse pointer is within their borders.

Using MouseMove with the Line Method

Graphics methods can produce very different effects when used in a MouseMove procedure instead of in a MouseDown procedure. For example, in the topic "The MouseDown Event" earlier in this chapter, the Line method drew connected line segments. In the Scribble application described below, the same method is used in a Form_MouseMove procedure to produce a continuous curved line instead of connected segments.

In the Scribble application, the MouseMove event is recognized whenever the mouse pointer changes position. The following code draws a line between the current and previous location.

```
Private Sub Form_MouseMove (Button As Integer, _
      Shift As Integer, X As Single, Y As Single)
   Line -(X, Y)
End Sub
```

Like the MouseDown procedure, the line created by the MouseMove procedure starts at the upper-left corner, as shown in Figure 11.2.

Figure 11.2 The MouseMove event and the Line method create a simple sketch program

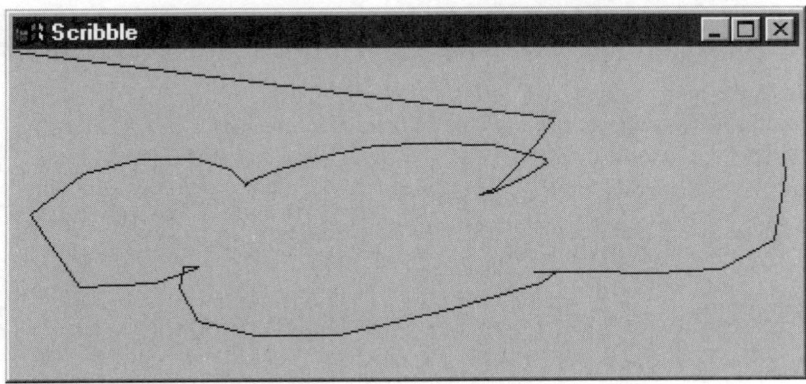

How MouseMove Works

How many times does the MouseMove event get called as the user moves the pointer across the screen? Or, to put it another way, when you move the pointer from the top of the screen to the bottom, how many locations are involved?

Visual Basic doesn't necessarily generate a MouseMove event for every pixel the mouse moves over. The operating environment generates a limited number of mouse messages per second. To see how often MouseMove events are actually recognized, you can enhance the Scribble application with the following code so that it draws a small circle at each location where a MouseMove event is recognized. The results are shown in Figure 11.3.

```
Private Sub Form_MouseMove (Button As Integer,_
      Shift As Integer, X As Single, Y As Single)
   Line -(X, Y)
   Circle (X, Y), 50
End Sub
```

Figure 11.3 A demonstration of where MouseMove events occur

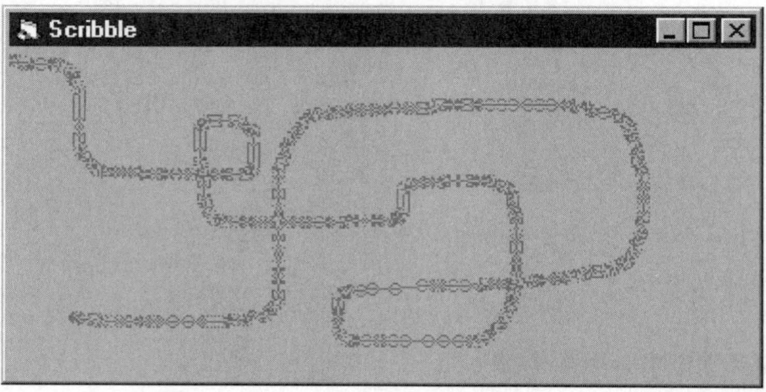

Note that the faster the user moves the pointer, the fewer MouseMove events are recognized between any two points. Many circles close together indicate that the user moved the mouse slowly.

Your application can recognize many MouseMove events in quick succession. Therefore, a MouseMove event procedure shouldn't do anything that requires large amounts of computing time.

For More Information See "MouseMove Event" in the *Microsoft Visual Basic 6.0 Language Reference*.

The MouseUp Event

The MouseUp event occurs when the user releases the mouse button. MouseUp is a useful companion to the MouseDown and MouseMove events. The example below illustrates how all three events can be used together.

The Scribble application is more useful if it allows drawing only while the mouse button is held down and stops drawing when the button is released. To do this, the application would have to respond to three actions:

- The user presses the mouse button (MouseDown).
- The user moves the mouse pointer (MouseMove).
- The user releases the mouse button (MouseUp).

MouseDown and MouseUp will tell the application to turn drawing on and off. You specify this by creating a form-level variable that represents the drawing state. Type the following statement in the Declarations section of the form code module:

```
Dim DrawNow As Boolean
```

`DrawNow` will represent two values: True will mean "draw a line," and False will mean "do not draw a line."

Because variables are initialized to 0 (False) by default, the application starts with drawing off. Then the first line in the MouseDown and MouseUp procedures turns drawing on or off by setting the value of the form-level variable `DrawNow`:

```
Private Sub Form_MouseDown (Button As Integer, _
      Shift As Integer, X As Single, Y As Single)
   DrawNow = True
   CurrentX = X
   CurrentY = Y
End Sub

Private Sub Form_MouseUp (Button As Integer, _
      Shift As Integer, X As Single, Y As Single)
   DrawNow = False
End Sub
```

The MouseMove procedure draws a line only if `DrawNow` is True. Otherwise, it takes no action:

```
Private Sub Form_MouseMove (Button As Integer, _
      Shift As Integer, X As Single, Y As Single)
   If DrawNow Then Line -(X, Y)
End Sub
```

Each time the user presses a mouse button, the MouseDown event procedure is executed and turns drawing on. Then as the user holds the Mouse button down, the MouseMove event procedure is executed repeatedly as the pointer is dragged across the screen.

Note that the Line method omits the first endpoint, causing Visual Basic to start drawing at the mouse pointer's current coordinates. By default, the drawing coordinates correspond to the last point drawn; the form's `CurrentX` and `CurrentY` properties were reset in the Form_MouseDown procedure.

For More Information See "MouseUp Event" in the *Microsoft Visual Basic 6.0 Language Reference*.

Detecting Mouse Buttons

You can make your applications more powerful by writing code that responds differently to mouse events, depending on which mouse button is used or whether the SHIFT, CTRL, or ALT key is pressed. To provide these options, you use the arguments button and shift with the MouseDown, MouseUp, and MouseMove event procedures. Techniques for using the *shift* argument are described in "Detecting SHIFT, CTRL , and ALT States" later in this chapter.

The MouseDown, MouseUp, and MouseMove events use the *button* argument to determine which mouse button or buttons are pressed. The *button* argument is a bit-field argument — a value in which each bit represents a state or condition. These values are expressed as integers. The three least-significant (lowest) bits represent the left, right, and middle mouse buttons, as shown in Figure 11.4.

Figure 11.4 How bits represent the state of the mouse

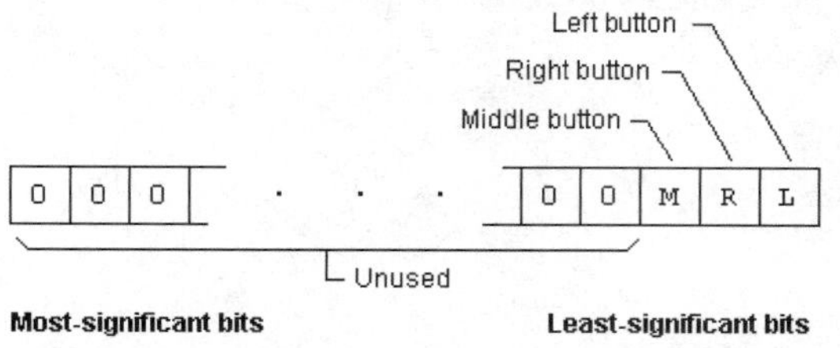

The default value of each bit is 0 (False). If no buttons are pressed, the binary value of the three bits is 000. If you press the left button, the binary value, or pattern, changes to 001. The left-button bit-value changes from 0 (False) to 1 (True).

The *button* argument uses either a decimal value or an constant to represent these binary patterns. The following table lists the binary value of the bits, the decimal equivalent, and the Visual Basic constant:

Binary Value	Decimal Value	Constant	Meaning
001	1	vbLeftButton	The left button is pressed.
010	2	vbRightButton	The right button is pressed.
100	4	vbMiddleButton	The middle button is pressed.

Note Visual Basic provides constants that represent the binary values of the *button* and *shift* arguments. These constants can be used interchangeably with their equivalent decimal values. Not all values have corresponding constants, however. The values for some button and/or shift combinations are derived by simply adding decimal values.

The middle button is assigned to decimal value 4. Pressing the left and right buttons simultaneously produces a single digit value of 3 (1+2). On a three-button mouse, pressing all three buttons simultaneously produces the decimal value of 7 (4+2+1). The following table lists the remaining button values derived from the possible button combinations:

Binary Value	Decimal Value	Constant	Meaning
000	0		No buttons are pressed.
011	3	vbLeftButton + vbRightButton	The left and right buttons are pressed.
101	5	vbLeftButton + vbMiddleButton	The left and middle buttons are pressed.
110	6	vbRightButton + vbMiddleButton	The right and middle buttons are pressed.
111	7	vbRightButton + vbMiddleButton + vbLeftButton	All three buttons are pressed.

Using Button with MouseDown and MouseUp

You use the *button* argument with MouseDown to determine which button is being pressed and with MouseUp to determine which button has been released. Because only one bit is set for each event, you can't test for whether two or more buttons are being used at the same time. In other words, MouseDown and MouseUp only recognize one button press at a time.

> **Note** In contrast, you can use the MouseMove event to test for whether two or more buttons are being pressed simultaneously. You can also use MouseMove to test for whether a particular button is being pressed, regardless of whether or not another button is being pressed at the same time. For more information, see "Using Button with MouseMove," later in this chapter.

You can specify which button causes a MouseDown or MouseUp event with simple code. The following procedure tests whether *button* equals 1, 2, or 4:

```
Private Sub Form_MouseDown (Button As Integer, _
      Shift As Integer, X As Single, Y As Single)
   If Button = 1 Then Print "You pressed _
      the left button."
   If Button = 2 Then Print "You pressed _
      the right button."
   If Button = 4 Then Print "You pressed _
      the middle button."
End Sub
```

If the user presses more than one button, Visual Basic interprets that action as two or more separate MouseDown events. It sets the bit for the first button pressed, prints the message for that button, and then does the same for the next button. Similarly, Visual Basic interprets the release of two or more buttons as separate MouseUp events.

The following procedure prints a message when a pressed button is released:

```
Private Sub Form_MouseUp(Button As Integer, _
      Shift As Integer, X As Single, Y As Single)
   If Button = 1 Then Print "You released _
      the left button."
   If Button = 2 Then Print "You released _
      the right button."
   If Button = 4 Then Print "You released _
      the middle button."
End Sub
```

Using Button with MouseMove

For the MouseMove event, *button* indicates the complete state of the mouse buttons — not just which button caused the event, as with MouseDown and MouseUp. This additional information is provided because all, some, or none of the bits might be set. This compares with just one bit per event in the MouseDown and MouseUp procedures.

Testing for a Single Button

If you test MouseMove for equality to 001 (decimal 1), you're testing to see if *only* the left mouse button is being held down while the mouse is moved. If another button is held down with the left button, the following code doesn't print anything:

```
Private Sub Form_MouseMove (Button As Integer, _
      Shift As Integer, X As Single, Y As Single)
   If Button = 1 Then Print "You're pressing _
      only the left button."
End Sub
```

To test for whether a particular button is down, use the And operator. The following code prints the message for each button pressed, regardless of whether another button is pressed:

```
Private Sub Form_MouseMove (Button As Integer, _
      Shift As Integer, X As Single, Y As Single)
   If Button And 1 Then Print "You're pressing _
      the left button."
   If Button And 2 Then Print "You're pressing _
      the right button."
End Sub
```

Pressing both buttons simultaneously prints both messages to the form. The MouseMove event recognizes multiple button states.

Testing for Multiple Buttons

In most cases, to isolate which button or buttons are being pressed, you use the MouseMove event.

Building on the previous examples, you can use the If...Then...Else statement to determine whether the left, right, or both buttons are being pressed. The following example tests for the three button states (left button pressed, right button pressed, and both buttons pressed) and prints the corresponding message.

Add the following code to the form's MouseMove event:

```
Private Sub Form_MouseMove(Button As Integer, _
      Shift As Integer, X As Single, Y As Single)
   If Button = 1 Then
      Print "You're pressing the left button."
   ElseIf Button = 2 Then
      Print "You're pressing the right button."
   ElseIf Button = 3 Then
      Print "You're pressing both buttons."
   End If
End Sub
```

You could also use the And operator with the Select Case statement to determine *button* and *shift* states. The And operator combined with the Select Case statement isolates the possible button states of a three-button mouse and then prints the corresponding message.

Create a variable called `ButtonTest` in the Declarations section of the form:

```
Dim ButtonTest as Integer
```

Add the following code to the form's MouseMove event:

```
Private Sub Form_MouseMove(Button As Integer, _
      Shift As Integer, X As Single, Y As Single)
ButtonTest = Button And 7
   Select Case ButtonTest
      Case 1 ' or vbLeftButton
         Print "You're pressing the left button."
      Case 2 ' or vbRightButton
         Print "You're pressing the right button."
      Case 4 ' or vbMiddleButton
         Print "You're pressing the middle button."
      Case 7
         Print "You're pressing all three buttons."
   End Select
End Sub
```

Using Button to Enhance Graphical Mouse Applications

You can use the *button* argument to enhance the Scribble application described in "The MouseMove Event" earlier in this chapter. In addition to drawing a continuous line when the left mouse button is pressed and stopping when the button is released, the application can draw a straight line from the last point drawn when the user presses the right button.

When writing code, it is often helpful to note each relevant event and the desired response. The three relevant events here are the mouse events:

- Form_MouseDown:This event takes a different action depending on the state of the mouse buttons: If the left button is down, set `DrawNow` to True and reset drawing coordinates; If the right button is down, draw a line.
- Form_MouseUp: If the left button is up, set `DrawNow` to False.
- Form_MouseMove:If `DrawNow` is True, draw a line.

The variable `DrawNow` is declared in the Declarations section of the form:

```
Dim DrawNow As Boolean
```

The MouseDown procedure has to take a different action, depending on whether the left or right mouse button caused the event:

```
Private Sub Form_MouseDown (Button As Integer, _
      Shift As Integer, X As Single, Y As Single)
   If Button = vbLeftButton Then
      DrawNow = True
      CurrentX = X
      CurrentY = Y
   ElseIf Button = vbRightButton Then
      Line -(X, Y)
   End If
End Sub
```

The following MouseUp procedure turns off drawing only when the left button is released:

```
Private Sub Form_MouseUp (Button As Integer, _
      Shift As Integer, X As Single, Y As Single)
   If Button = vbLeftButton Then DrawNow = False
End Sub
```

Note that within the MouseUp procedure, a bit set to 1 (vbLeftButton) indicates that the corresponding mouse button is released and drawing is turned off.

The following MouseMove procedure is identical to the one in the version of the Scribble application found in “The MouseMove Event” earlier in this chapter.

```
Private Sub Form_MouseMove (Button As Integer, _
      Shift As Integer, X As Single, Y As Single)
   If DrawNow Then Line -(X, Y)
End Sub
```

Detecting SHIFT, CTRL, and ALT States

The mouse and keyboard events use the shift argument to determine whether the SHIFT, CTRL, and ALT keys are pressed and in what, if any, combination. If the SHIFT key is pressed, shift is 1; if the CTRL key is pressed, shift is 2; and if the ALT key is pressed, shift is 4. To determine combinations of these keys, use the total of their values. For example, if SHIFT and ALT are pressed, shift equals 5 (1 + 4).

The three least-significant bits in shift correspond to the state of the SHIFT, CTRL, and ALT keys, as shown in Figure 11.5.

Figure 11.5 How bits represent the state of the SHIFT, CTRL, and ALT keys

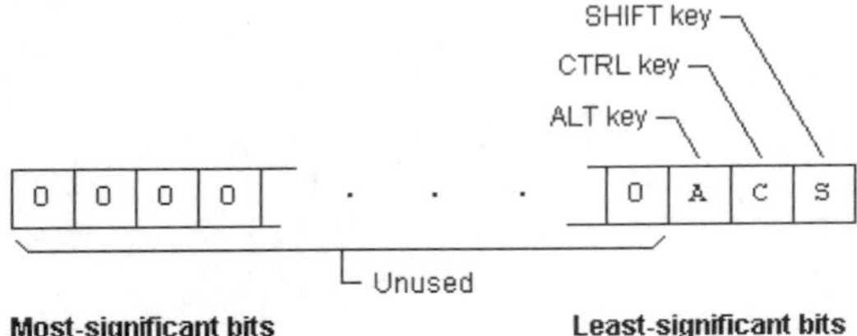

Any or all of the bits in *shift* can be set, depending on the state of the SHIFT, CTRL, and ALT keys. These values and constants are listed in the following table:

Binary Value	Decimal Value	Constant	Meaning
001	1	vbShiftMask	The SHIFT key is pressed.
010	2	vbCtrlMask	The CTRL key is pressed.
100	4	vbAltMask	The ALT key is pressed.
011	3	vbShiftMask + vbCtrlMask	The SHIFT and CTRL keys are pressed.
101	5	vbShiftMask + vbAltMask	The SHIFT and ALT keys are pressed.
110	6	vbCtrlMask + vbAltMask	The CTRL and ALT keys are pressed.
111	7	vbCtrlMask + vbAltMask + vbShiftMask	The SHIFT, CTRL, and ALT keys are pressed.

As with the mouse events' *button* argument, you can use the If…Then…Else statement or the And operator combined with the Select Case statement to determine whether the SHIFT, CTRL, or ALT keys are being pressed and in what, if any, combination.

Open a new project and add the variable `ShiftTest` to the Declarations section of the form:

```
Dim ShiftTest as Integer
```

Add the following code to the form's MouseDown event:

```
Private Sub Form_MouseDown(Button As Integer, _
      Shift As Integer, X As Single, Y As Single)
   ShiftTest = Shift And 7
   Select Case ShiftTest
      Case 1 ' or vbShiftMask
         Print "You pressed the SHIFT key."
      Case 2 ' or vbCtrlMask
         Print "You pressed the CTRL key."
      Case 4 ' or vbAltMask
         Print "You pressed the ALT key."
      Case 3
         Print "You pressed both SHIFT and CTRL."
      Case 5
         Print "You pressed both SHIFT and ALT."
      Case 6
         Print "You pressed both CTRL and ALT."
      Case 7
         Print "You pressed SHIFT, CTRL, and ALT."
      End Select
End Sub
```

Dragging and Dropping

When you design Visual Basic applications, you often drag controls around on the form. The drag-and-drop features in Visual Basic allow you to extend this ability to the user at run time. The action of holding a mouse button down and moving a control is called *dragging,* and the action of releasing the button is called *dropping*.

Note Dragging a control at run time doesn't automatically change its location — you must program the relocation yourself, as described in "Changing the Position of a Control." Often, dragging is used only to indicate that some action should be performed; the control retains its original position after the user releases the mouse button.

Using the following drag-and-drop properties, events, and method, you can specify both the meaning of a drag operation and how dragging can be initiated (if at all) for a given control.

Category	Item	Description
Properties	DragMode	Enables automatic or manual dragging of a control.
	DragIcon	Specifies what icon is displayed when the control is dragged.
Events	DragDrop	Recognizes when a control is dropped onto the object.
	DragOver	Recognizes when a control is dragged over the object.
Methods	Drag	Starts or stops manual dragging.

All controls except menus, timers, lines, and shapes support the DragMode and DragIcon properties and the Drag method. Forms recognize the DragDrop and DragOver events, but they don't support the DragMode and DragIcon properties or the Drag method.

Note Controls can only be dragged when they do not have the focus. To prevent a control from getting the focus, set its TabStop property to False.

Enabling Automatic Drag Mode

To allow the user to drag a control, set its DragMode property to 1-Automatic.

When you set dragging to Automatic, dragging is always "on." For more control over dragging operations, use the 0-Manual setting described in "Controlling When Dragging Starts or Stops" later in this chapter.

Note While an automatic drag operation is taking place, the control being dragged doesn't recognize other mouse events.

Changing the Drag Icon

When dragging a control, Visual Basic uses a gray outline of the control as the default drag icon. You can substitute other images for the outline by setting the DragIcon property. This property contains a Picture object that corresponds to a graphic image.

The easiest way to set the DragIcon property is to use the Properties window. Select the DragIcon property, and then click the Properties button to select a file containing a graphic image from the Load Icon dialog box.

You can assign icons to the DragIcon property from the Icon Library included with Visual Basic. (The icons are located in the \Program files\Microsoft Visual Basic\Icons directory.) You can also create your own drag icons with a graphics program.

At run time, you can select a drag icon image by assigning the DragIcon property of one control to the same property of another:

```
Set Image1.DragIcon = Image2.DragIcon
```

You can also set the DragIcon property at run time by assigning the Picture property of one control to the DragIcon property of another:

```
Set Image1.DragIcon = Image3.Picture
```

Or, you can use the LoadPicture function:

```
Set Image1.DragIcon = LoadPicture("c:\Program _
files\Microsoft Visual Basic\Icons _
\Computer\Disk04.ico")
```

For More Information For information on the Picture property and the LoadPicture function, see Chapter 12, "Working with Text and Graphics." Also see "Picture Property" and "LoadPicture Function" in the *Microsoft Visual Basic 6.0 Language Reference*.

Responding When the User Drops the Object

When the user releases the mouse button after dragging a control, Visual Basic generates a DragDrop event. You can respond to this event in many ways. Remember that the control doesn't automatically move to the new location, but you can write code to relocate the control to the new location (indicated by the last position of the gray outline). See "Changing the Position of a Control," later in this chapter for more information.

Two terms are important when discussing drag-and-drop operations:*source* and *target.*

Term	Meaning
Source	The control being dragged. This control can be any object except a menu, timer, line, or shape.
Target	The object onto which the user drops the control. This object, which can be a form or control, recognizes the DragDrop event.

A control becomes the target if the mouse position is within its borders when the button is released. A form is the target if the pointer is in a blank portion of the form.

The DragDrop event provides three arguments: *source*, *x*, and *y*. The *source* argument is a reference to the control that was dropped onto the target.

Because *source* is declared As Control, you use it just as you would a control — you can refer to its properties or call one of its methods.

The following example illustrates how the source and target interact. The source is an Image control with its Picture property set to load a sample icon file representing a few file folders. Its DragMode property has been set to 1-Automatic and its DragIcon property to a sample drag-and-drop icon file. The target, also an image control, contains a picture of an open file cabinet.

Add the following procedure to the second image control's DragDrop event:

```
Private Sub Image2_DragDrop(Source As Control, _
      X As Single, Y As Single)
   Source.Visible = False
   Image2.Picture = LoadPicture("c:\Program _
      Files\Microsoft Visual _
      Basic\Icons\Office\Files03a.ico")
End Sub
```

Dragging and dropping Image1 onto Image2 causes Image1 to vanish and Image2 to change its picture to that of a closed file cabinet. Using the *source* argument, the Visible property of Image1 was changed to False.

> **Note** You should use the *source* argument carefully. Although you know that it always refers to a control, you don't necessarily know which type of control. For example, if the control is a text box and you attempt to refer to `Source.Value`, the result is a run-time error because text boxes have no Value property.

You can use the If...Then...Else statement with the TypeOf keyword to determine what kind of control was dropped.

For More Information See "If…Then…Else" in the *Microsoft Visual Basic 6.0 Language Reference* and see Chapter 9, "Programming with Objects."

Controlling When Dragging Starts or Stops

Visual Basic has a Manual setting for the DragMode property that gives you more control than the Automatic setting. The Manual setting allows you to specify when a control can and cannot be dragged. (When DragMode is set to Automatic, you can always drag the control as long as the setting isn't changed.)

For instance, you may want to enable dragging in response to MouseDown and MouseUp events, or in response to a keyboard or menu command. The Manual setting also allows you to recognize a MouseDown event before dragging starts, so that you can record the mouse position.

To enable dragging from code, leave DragMode in its default setting (0-Manual). Then use the Drag method whenever you want to begin or stop dragging an object. Use the following Visual Basic constants to specify the *action* of the Drag argument.

Constant	Value	Meaning
vbCancel	0	Cancel drag operation
vbBeginDrag	1	Begin drag operation
vbEndDrag	2	End drag operation

The syntax for the Drag method is as follows:

[*object*.]**Drag** *action*

If *action* is set to vbBeginDrag, the Drag method initiates dragging of the control. If *action* is set to vbEndDrag, the control is dropped, causing a DragDrop event. If *action* is set to vbCancel, the drag is canceled. The effect is similar to giving the value vbEndDrag, except that no DragDrop event occurs.

Building on the example given in "Responding When the User Drops the Object," earlier in this chapter, you can add a MouseDown event for Image1 that illustrates the Drag method. Set the Image1 DragMode property to 0-Manual, then add the following procedure:

```
Private Sub Image1_MouseDown(Button As Integer, _
      Shift As Integer, X As Single, Y As Single)
   Image1.Drag vbBeginDrag
   Set Image1.DragIcon = LoadPicture("c:\Program _
      files\ Microsoft Visual _
      Basic\Icons\Dragdrop\Dragfldr.ico")
End Sub
```

Adding a DragOver event procedure to Image2 allows you to terminate dragging when the source enters the target. This example closes the file cabinet when Image1 is passed over Image2.

```
Private Sub Image2_DragOver(Source As Control, _
      X As Single, Y As Single, State As Integer)
   Source.Drag vbEndDrag
   Source.Visible = False
   Image2.Picture = LoadPicture("c:\Program _
      files\Microsoft Visual _
      Basic\Icons\Office\Files03a.ico")
End Sub
```

Adding a third Image control to the form demonstrates canceling a drag operation. In this example the Image3 Picture property contains an icon of a trash can. Using the DragOver event and the *source* argument, dragging the files over Image3 cancels the drag operation.

```
Private Sub Image3_DragOver(Source As Control, _
      X As Single, Y As Single, State As Integer)
   Source.Drag vbCancel
End Sub
```

Changing the Position of a Control

You may want the source control to change position after the user releases the mouse button. To move a control to the new mouse location, use the Move method with any control that has been drag-enabled.

You can reposition a control when it is dragged and dropped to any location on the form not occupied by another control. To illustrate this, start a new Visual Basic project, add an Image control to the form and assign it any icon or bitmap by setting the Picture property, and then change the Image control's DragMode property to 1-Automatic.

Add the following procedure to the form's DragDrop event:

```
Private Sub Form_DragDrop (Source As Control, _
      X As Single, Y As Single)
   Source.Move X, Y
End Sub
```

This code may not produce precisely the effects you want, because the upper-left corner of the control is positioned at the mouse location. This code positions the center of the control at the mouse location:

```
Private Sub Form_DragDrop (Source As Control, _
      X As Single, Y As Single)
   Source.Move (X - Source.Width / 2), _
      (Y - Source.Height / 2)
End Sub
```

The code works best when the DragIcon property is set to a value other than the default (the gray rectangle). When the gray rectangle is being used, the user usually wants the control to move precisely into the final position of the gray rectangle. To do this, record the initial mouse position within the source control. Then use this position as an offset when the control is moved.

To record the initial mouse position

1. Specify manual dragging of the control.
2. Declare two form-level variables, `DragX` and `DragY`.
3. Turn on dragging when a MouseDown event occurs.
4. Store the value of *x* and *y* in the form-level variables in this event.

The following example illustrates how to cause drag movement for an image control named Image1. The control's DragMode property should be set to 0-Manual at design time. The Declarations section contains the form-level variables `DragX` and `DragY`, which record the initial mouse position within the Image control:

```
Dim DragX As Single, DragY As Single
```

The MouseDown and MouseUp procedures for the control turn dragging on and drop the control, respectively. In addition, the MouseDown procedure records the mouse position inside the control at the time dragging begins:

```
Private Sub Image1_MouseDown (Button As Integer, _
      Shift As Integer, X As Single, Y As Single)
   Image1.Drag 1
   DragX = X
   DragY = Y
End Sub
```

The Form_DragDrop procedure actually moves the control. To simplify this example, assume that Image1 is the only control on the form. The target can therefore only be the form itself. The Form_DragDrop procedure repositions the control, using `DragX` and `DragY` as offsets:

```
Private Sub Form_DragDrop (Source As Control, _
      X As Single, Y As Single)
   Source.Move (X - DragX), (Y - DragY)
End Sub
```

Note that this example assumes that Image1 and the form use the same units in their respective coordinate systems. If they don't, then you'll have to convert between units.

For More Information For information on coordinate systems, see Chapter 12, "Working with Text and Graphics," and "ScaleMode Property" in the *Microsoft Visual Basic 6.0 Language Reference*.

OLE Drag and Drop

One of the most powerful and useful features you can add to your Visual Basic applications is the ability to drag text or graphics from one control to another, or from a control to another Windows application, and vice versa. OLE drag-and-drop allows you to add this functionality to your applications.

With OLE drag and drop, you're not dragging one control to another control to invoke some code (as with the drag and drop discussed earlier in this chapter); you're moving *data* from one control or application to another control or application. For example, the user selects and drags a range of cells in Excel, then drops the range of cells into the Data-Bound Grid control in your application.

Almost all Visual Basic controls support OLE drag-and-drop to some degree. Some standard and ActiveX controls (those provided in the Professional and Enterprise editions of Visual Basic) provide automatic support for OLE drag-and-drop, which means that no code needs to be written to either drag from or drop to the control, including:

DataGrid	PictureBox	Rich Text Box
Image	Textbox	Masked Edit box

To enable automatic OLE dragging and dropping for these controls, you set the OLEDragMode and OLEDropMode properties to Automatic.

Some controls only provide automatic support for the OLE drag operation. To enable automatic dragging from these controls, set the OLEDragMode property to Automatic.

ComboBox	DBList	FileListBox
DBCombo box	DirectoryListBox	ListBox
TreeView	ListView	

Some controls support only the OLE drag-and-drop events, meaning that you can program them to act either as the source or target of the OLE drag-and-drop operations.

CheckBox	Frame	OptionButton
CommandButton	Label	DriveListBox
Data		

> **Note** To determine if other ActiveX controls support OLE drag and drop, load the control into Visual Basic and check for the existence of the OLEDragMode and OLEDropMode properties, or for the OLEDrag method. (A control that does not have automatic support for OLE drag will not have the OLEDragMode property, but it will have an OLEDrag method if it supports OLE drag through code.)

Note Forms, MDI forms, Document Objects, User Controls, and Property Pages contain the OLEDropMode property and provide support for manual dragging and dropping only.

Using the following OLE drag-and-drop properties, events, and method, you can specify how a given control responds to dragging and dropping.

Category	Item	Description
Properties	OLEDragMode	Enables automatic or manual dragging of a control (if the control supports manual but not automatic OLE drag, it will not have this property but it will support the OLEDrag method and the OLE drag-and-drop events).
	OLEDropMode	Specifies how the control will respond to a drop.
Events	OLEDragDrop	Recognizes when a source object is dropped onto a control.
	OLEDragOver	Recognizes when a source object is dragged over a control.
	OLEGiveFeedback	Provides customized drag icon feedback to the user, based on the source object.
	OLEStartDrag	Specifies which data formats and drop effects (copy, move, or refuse data) the source supports when dragging is initiated.
	OLESetData	Provides data when the source object is dropped.
	OLECompleteDrag	Informs the source of the action that was performed when the object was dropped into the target.
Method	OLEDrag	Starts manual dragging.

Automatic vs. Manual Dragging and Dropping

It is helpful to think of OLE drag-and-drop implementation as either *automatic* or *manual*.

Automatic dragging and dropping means that, for example, you can drag text from one text box control to another by simply setting the OLEDragMode and OLEDropMode properties of these controls to Automatic: You don't need to write any code to respond to any of the OLE drag-and-drop events. When you drag a range of cells from Excel into a Word document, you've performed an automatic drag-and-drop operation. Depending upon how a given control or application supports OLE drag and drop and what type of data is being dragged, automatically dragging and dropping data may be the best and simplest method.

Manual dragging and dropping means that you have chosen (or have been forced to) manually handle one or more of the OLE drag-and-drop events. Manual implementation of OLE drag and drop may be the better method when you want to gain greater control over each step in the process, to provide the user with customized visual feedback, to create your own data format. Manual implementation is the only option when a control does not support automatic dragging and dropping.

It is also helpful to define the overall model of the OLE drag-and-drop operation. In a drag and drop operation, the object from which data is dragged is referred to as the *source*. The object into which the data is dropped is referred to as the *target*. Visual Basic provides the properties, events, and method to control and respond to actions affecting both the source and the target. It is also helpful to recognize that the source and the target may be in different applications, in the same application, or even in the same control. Depending upon the scenario, you may need to write code for either the source or target, or both.

Enabling Automatic OLE Drag and Drop

If your controls support automatic dragging and dropping, you can drag data from and/or drop data into a Visual Basic control by setting the control's OLEDragMode and/or OLEDropMode properties to Automatic. For instance, you may want to drag text from a text box control into a Word for Windows document, or allow the text box control to accept data dragged from the Word for Windows document.

To allow dragging from the text box control, set the OLEDragMode property to Automatic. At run time, you can select text typed into the text box control and drag it into the open Word for Windows document.

When you drag text from the text box control into a Word for Windows document, it is, by default, moved rather than copied into the document. If you hold the CTRL key down while dropping text, it will be copied rather than moved. This is the default behavior for all objects or applications that support OLE drag-and-drop. To restrict this operation by allowing data to only be moved or only be copied, you need to modify the automatic behavior by using the manual dragging and dropping techniques. For more information, see "Using the Mouse and Keyboard to Modify Drop Effects and User Feedback," later in this chapter.

To allow the text box control to automatically retrieve data in a OLE drag-and-drop operation, set its OLEDropMode property to Automatic. At run time, data dragged from an OLE-enabled application into the text box control will be moved rather than copied unless you hold down the CTRL key during the drop, or alter the default behavior through code.

Automatic support for dragging and dropping data has its limitations; some of these limitations are derived from the functionality of the controls themselves. For instance, if you move text from a Word for Windows document into a text box control, all the rich text formatting in the Word document will be stripped out because the text box control doesn't support this formatting. Similar limitations exist for most controls. Another limitation of automatic operations is that you don't have complete control over what kind of data is dragged and/or dropped.

> **Note** When dragging data, you may notice that the mouse pointer indicates if the object that it is passing over supports OLE drag and drop for the type of data that you are dragging. If the object supports OLE drag and drop for the type of data, the "drop" pointer is displayed. If the object does not, a "no drop" pointer is displayed.

The OLE Drag and Drop DataObject Object

OLE drag and drop uses the same *source* and *target* model as the simple event-driven drag-and-drop techniques discussed in "Dragging and Dropping." In this case, however, you're not dragging one control to another control to invoke some code; you're moving *data* from one control or application to another control or application. For example, the user selects and drags a range of cells in Excel (*source*) then drops the range of cells into the DataGrid control (*target*) in your application.

In Visual Basic, the vehicle, or repository, of this data is the DataObject object — it is the means by which data is moved from the source to the target. It does this by providing the methods needed to store, retrieve, and analyze the data. The following table lists the property and methods used by the DataObject object:

Category	Item	Description
Property	Files	Holds the names of files dragged to or from the Windows Explorer.
Methods	Clear	Clears the content of the DataObject object.
	GetData	Retrieves data from the DataObject object.
	GetFormat	Determines if a specified data format is available in the DataObject object.
	SetData	Places data into the DataObject object, or indicates that a specified format is available upon request.

Used with the OLE drag-and-drop events, these methods allow you to manage data in the DataObject object on both the source and target sides (if both are within your Visual Basic application). For instance, you can place data into the DataObject object on the source side using the SetData method, and then use the GetData method to accept the data on the target side.

The Clear method is used to clear the content of the DataObject object on the source side when the OLEStartDrag event is triggered. When data from a control is dragged in an automatic drag operation, its data formats are placed into the DataObject object before the OLEStartDrag event is triggered. If you don't want to use the default formats, you use the Clear method. If you want to add to the default data formats, you do not use the Clear method.

The Files property allows you to store the names of a range of files that can be then dragged into a drop target. See "Dragging Files from the Windows Explorer," online, for more information on this property.

You can also specify the format of the data being transferred. The SetData and GetData methods use the following arguments to place or retrieve data in the DataObject object:

Argument	Description
Data	Allows you to specify the type of data that is placed into the DataObject object (optional argument if the *format* argument has been set; otherwise, it's required).
Format	Allows you to set several different formats that the source can support, without having to load the data for each (optional argument if the *data* argument has been set or if Visual Basic understands the format; otherwise, it's required).

> **Note** When data is dropped onto the target and no format has been specified, Visual Basic is able to detect if it is a bitmap, metafile, enhanced metafile, or text. All other formats must be specified explicitly or an error will be generated.

The *format* argument uses the following constants or values to specify the format of the data:

Constant	Value	Meaning
vbCFText	1	Text
vbCFBitmap	2	Bitmap (.bmp)
vbCFMetafile	3	Metafile (.wmf)
vbCFEMetafile	14	Enhanced metafile (.emf)
vbCFDIB	8	Device-independent bitmap (.dib or .bmp)
vbCFPalette	9	Color palette
vbCFFiles	15	List of files
vbCFRTF	–16639	Rich text format (.rtf)

The SetData, GetData, and GetFormat methods use the *data* and *format* arguments to return either the type of data in the DataObject object or to retrieve the data itself if the format is compatible with the *target*. For example:

```
Private Sub txtSource_OLEStartDrag(Data As _
      VB.DataObject, AllowedEffects As Long)
   Data.SetData txtSource.SelText, vbCFText
End Sub
```

In this example, *data* is the text selected in a textbox and *format* has been specified as text (vbCFText).

Note You should use the vbCFDIB data format instead of vbCFBitmap and vbCFPalette, in most cases. The vbCFDIB format contains both the bitmap and palette and is therefore the preferred method of transferring a bitmap image. You can, however, also specify the vbCFBitmap and vbCFPalette for completeness. If you chose not to use the vbCFDIB format, you must specify both the vbCFBitmap and vbCFPalette formats so that the bitmap and the palette are correctly placed into the DataObject object.

For More Information See "Creating a Custom Data Format," later in this chapter, for information on defining your own data format.

How OLE Drag and Drop Works

When an OLE drag-and-drop operation is performed, certain events are generated on the source and target sides. The events associated with the source object are always generated, whether the drag-and-drop operation is automatic or manual. The target-side events, however, are only generated in a manual drop operation. The following illustration shows which events occur and can be responded to on the drag source, and which occur and can be responded to on the drop target.

Figure 11.6 Source-side and target-side events

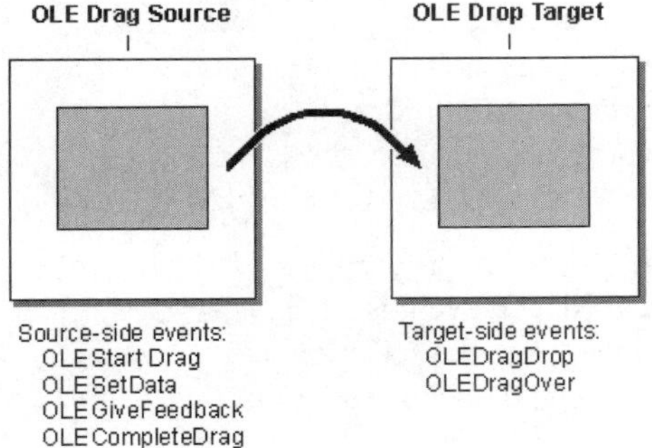

Which events you'll need to respond to depends upon how you've chosen to implement the drag-and-drop functionality. For example, you may have created an application with a text box that you want to allow to automatically accept dragged data from another application. In this case, you simply set the control's OLEDropMode property to Automatic. If you want to allow data to be automatically dragged from the text box control as well, you set its OLEDragMode property to Automatic.

If, however, you want to change the default mouse cursors or enhance the functionality for button states and shift keys, you need to manually respond to the source- and target-side events. Likewise, if you want to analyze the data before it is dropped into a control (to verify that the data is compatible, for instance), or delay when the data is loaded into the DataObject object (so that multiple formats don't need to be loaded at the beginning), you'll need to use manual OLE drag-and-drop operations.

Because you can drag and drop data into numerous Visual Basic controls and Windows applications — with varying limitations and requirements — implementing OLE drag and drop can range from straightforward to fairly complex. The simplest implementation, of course, would be dragging and dropping between two automatic objects, whether the object is a Word document, an Excel spreadsheet, or a control in your application that has been set to Automatic. Specifying multiple data formats that would be acceptable to your drop target would be more complicated.

Starting the Drag

What happens in a basic manual OLE drag-and-drop operation within your Visual Basic application? When the user drags data from an OLE drag source (a text box control, for example) by selecting and then holding down the left mouse button, the OLEStartDrag event is triggered and you can then either store the data or simply specify the formats that the source supports. You also need to specify whether copying or moving the data, or both, is allowed by the source.

For More Information See "Starting the OLE Drag Operation," later in this chapter, for more information on the OLEDrag method, the OLEstartDrag event, using the SetData method to specify the supported data formats, and placing data into the DataObject.

Dragging over the Target

As the user drags over the target, the target's OLEDragOver event is triggered, indicating that the source is within its boundaries. You then specify what the target would do if the data were dropped there — either copy, move, or refuse the data. By convention, the default is usually move, but it may be copy.

When the target specifies which drop effect will be performed if the source is dropped there, the OLEGiveFeedback event is triggered. The OLEGiveFeedback event is used to provide visual feedback to the user on what action will be taken when the selection is dropped — i.e., the mouse pointer will be changed to indicate a copy, move, or "no drop" action.

As the source is moved around within the boundaries of the target — or if the user presses the SHIFT, CTRL, or ALT keys while holding down the mouse button — the drop effect may be changed. For example, instead of allowing a copy or a move, the data may be refused.

If the user passes beyond the target or presses the ESC key, for example, then the drag operation may be canceled or modified (the mouse pointer may be changed to indicate that the object it is currently passing over will not accept the data).

For More Information See "Dragging the OLE Drag Source over the OLE Drop Target," later in this chapter, for more information on the OLEDragOver and OLEGiveFeedback events.

Completing the Drag

When the user drops the source onto the target, the target's OLEDragDrop event is triggered. The target queries the source for the format of the data it contains (or supports, if the data wasn't placed into the source when the drag was started) and then either retrieves or rejects the data.

If the data was stored when the drag started, the target retrieves the data by using the GetData method. If the data wasn't stored when the drag started, the data is retrieved by triggering the source's OLESetData event and then using the SetData method.

When the data is accepted or rejected, the OLECompleteDrag event is triggered and the source can then take the appropriate action: if the data is accepted and a move is specified, the source deletes the data, for example.

For More Information See "Dropping the OLE Drag Source onto the OLE Drop Target," later in this chapter, for more information on the OLEDragDrop event, the OLECompleteDrag event, and using the GetFormat and GetData methods to retrieve data from the DataObject object.

Starting the OLE Drag Operation

If you want to be able to specify which data formats or drop effects (copy, move, or no drop) are supported, or if the control you want to drag from doesn't support automatic dragging, you need to make your OLE drag operation manual.

The first phase of a manual drag-and-drop operation is calling the OLEDrag method, setting the allowed drop effects, specifying the supported data formats, and, optionally, placing data into the DataObject object.

You use the OLEDrag method to manually start the drag operation and the OLEStartDrag event to specify the allowed drop-action effects and the supported data formats.

The OLEDrag Method

Generally, the OLEDrag method is called from an object's MouseMove event when data has been selected, the left mouse button is pressed and held, and the mouse is moved.

The OLEDrag method does not provide any arguments. Its primary purpose is to initiate a manual drag and then allow the OLEStartDrag event to set the conditions of the drag operation (for example, specifying what will happen when the data is dragged into another control).

If the source control supports the OLEDragMode property, to have manual control over the drag operation you must set the property to Manual and then use the OLEDrag method on the control. If the control supports manual but not automatic OLE drag, it will not have the OLEDragMode property, but it will support the OLEDrag method and the OLE drag-and-drop events.

> **Note** The OLEDrag method will also work if the source control's OLEDragMode property is set to Automatic.

Specifying Drop Effects and Data Formats

In a manual OLE drag operation, when the user begins dragging the source and the OLEDrag method is called, the control's OLEStartDrag event fires. Use this event to specify what drop effects and data formats the source supports.

The OLEStartDrag event uses two arguments to specify supported data formats and whether the data can be copied or moved when the data is dropped (drop effects).

> **Note** If no drop effects or data formats are specified in the OLEStartDrag event, the manual drag will not be started.

The AllowedEffects Argument

The *allowedeffects* argument specifies which drop effects the drag source supports. For example:

```
Private Sub txtSource_OLEStartDrag(Data As _
      VB.DataObject, AllowedEffects As Long)
   AllowedEffects = vbDropEffectMove Or _
      vbDropEffectCopy
End Sub
```

The target can then query the drag source for this information and respond accordingly.

The *allowedeffects* argument uses the following values to specify drop effects:

Constant	Value	Description
vbDropEffectNone	0	Drop target cannot accept the data.
vbDropEffectCopy	1	Drop results in a copy. The original data is untouched by the drag source.
vbDropEffectMove	2	Drag source removes the data.

The Format Argument

You specify which data formats the object supports by setting the *format* argument of the OLEStartDrag event. To do this, you use the SetData method. For example, in a scenario using a rich text box control as a source and a text box control as a target, you might specify the following supported formats:

```
Private Sub rtbSource_OLEStartDrag(Data As _
      VB.DataObject, AllowedEffects As Long)
   AllowedEffects = vbDropEffectMove Or _
      vbDropEffectCopy

   Data.SetData , vbCFText
   Data.SetData , vbCFRTF
End Sub
```

The target can query the source to determine which data formats are supported and then respond accordingly — e.g., if the format of the dropped data is not supported by the target, reject the dropped data. In this case, the only data formats that are supported by the source are the text and rich-text formats.

For More Information See "The OLE Drag and Drop DataObject Object," earlier in this chapter, for more information on format values for the SetData method.

Placing Data into the DataObject object

In many cases, especially if the source supports more than one format, or if it is time-consuming to create the data, you may want to place data into the DataObject object only when it is requested by the target. You can, however, place the data into the DataObject object when you begin a drag operation by using the SetData method in the OLEStartDrag event. For example:

```
Private Sub txtSource_OLEStartDrag(Data As _
      VB.DataObject, AllowedEffects As Long)
   Data.Clear
   Data.SetData txtSource.SelText, vbCFText
End Sub
```

This example clears the default data formats from the DataObject object using the Clear method, specifies the data format (text) of the selected data, and then places the data into the DataObject object with the SetData method.

Dragging the OLE Drag Source over the OLE Drop Target

With a manual target, you can determine and respond to the position of the source data within the target and respond to the state of the mouse buttons and the SHIFT, CTRL, and ALT keys. Where both the source and the target are manual, you can modify the default visual behavior of the mouse.

To	Use the
Determine and respond to the position of the source object	*state* argument of the OLEDragOver event
Respond to the state of the mouse buttons	*button* argument of the OLEDragDrop and OLEDragOver events
Respond to the state of the SHIFT, CTRL, and ALT keys	*shift* arguments of the OLEDragDrop and OLEDragOver events
Modify the default visual behavior of the mouse	*effect* argument of the OLEDragOver event and the *effect* argument of the OLEGiveFeedback

For More Information For more information about changing the mouse cursor, see "Dragging the OLE Drag Source over the OLE Drop Target," above. For more information about using the *button* and *shift* arguments, see "Using the Mouse and Keyboard to Modify Drop Effects and User Feedback," later in this chapter.

The OLEDragOver Event State Argument

Depending upon its position, the *effect* argument may be changed to indicate the currently acceptable drop effect.

The *state* argument of the OLEDragOver event allows you to respond to the source data entering, passing over, and leaving the target control. For example, when the source data enters the target control, the *state* argument is set to vbEnter.

When the drag source is moved around within the boundaries of the drop target, the *state* argument is set to vbOver. Depending upon the position (the *x* and *y* arguments) of the mouse pointer, you may want to change the drag effect. Notice that the OLEDragOver event is generated several times a second, even when the mouse is stationary.

The *state* argument of the OLEDragOver event specifies when the data enters, passes over, and leaves the target control by using the following constants:

Constant	Value	Meaning
vbEnter	0	Data has been dragged within the range of a target.
vbLeave	1	Data has been dragged out of the range of a target.
vbOver	2	Data is still within the range of a target, and either the mouse has moved, a mouse or keyboard button has changed, or a certain system-determined amount of time has elapsed.

Providing the User with Customized Visual Feedback

If you want to modify the default visual behavior of the mouse in an OLE drag-and-drop operation, you can manipulate the OLEDragOver event on the target side and the OLEGiveFeedback event on the source side.

OLE drag and drop provides automatic visual feedback during a drag-and-drop operation. For example, when you start a drag, the mouse pointer is changed to indicate that a drag has been initiated. When you pass over objects that do not support OLE drop, the mouse pointer is changed to the "no drop" cursor.

Modifying the mouse pointer to indicate how a control will respond if the data is dropped onto it involves two steps: determining what type of data is in the DataObject object using the GetFormat method, and then setting the *effect* argument of the OLEDragOver event to inform the source what drop effects are allowed for this control.

The OLEDragOver Event

When a target control's OLEDropMode property is set to Manual, the OLEDragOver event is triggered whenever dragged data passes over the control.

The *effect* argument of the OLEDragOver event is used to specify what action would be taken if the object were dropped. When this value is set, the source's OLEGiveFeedback event is triggered. The OLEGiveFeedback event contains its own *effect* argument, which is used to provide visual feedback to the user on what action will be taken when the selection is dragged — i.e., the mouse pointer is changed to indicate a copy, move, or "no drop" action.

The *effect* argument of the OLEDragOver event uses the following constants to indicate the drop action:

Constant	Value	Description
vbDropEffectNone	0	Drop target cannot accept the data.
vbDropEffectCopy	1	Drop results in a copy. The original data is untouched by the drag source.
vbDropEffectMove	2	Drag source removes the data.

> **Note** The *effect* argument of the OLEDragOver and OLEGiveFeedback events express the same drop effects (copy, move, no drop) as the *allowedeffects* argument of the OLEStartDrag event. They differ only in that the OLEStartDrag event specifies which effects are allowed, and the OLEDragOver and OLEGiveFeedback use the *effect* argument to indicate to the source which of these actions will be taken.

The following code example queries the DataObject object for a compatible data format for the target control. If the data is compatible, the *effect* argument informs the source that a move will be performed if the data is dropped. If the data is not compatible, the source will be informed and a "'no drop" mouse pointer will be displayed.

```
Private Sub txtTarget_OLEDragOver(Data As _
      VB.DataObject, Effect As Long, Button As _
      Integer, Shift As Integer, X As Single, _
      Y As Single, State As Integer)
   If Data.GetFormat(vbCFText) Then
      Effect = vbDropEffectMove And Effect
   Else
      Effect = vbDropEffectNone
   End If
End Sub
```

When the source data is dragged over the target, and the OLEDragOver event is triggered, the source tells the target which effects it allows (move, copy, no drop). You must then chose which single effect will occur if the data is dropped. The *effect* argument of the OLEDragOver event informs the source which drop action it supports, and the source then informs the user by using the OLEGiveFeedback event to modify the mouse pointer.

The OLEGiveFeedback Event

To change the default behavior of the mouse pointer based on the *effect* argument of the OLEDragOver event, you need to manually specify new mouse pointer values using the OLEGiveFeedback event. The source's OLEGiveFeedback event is triggered automatically when the *effect* argument of the OLEDragOver event is set.

The OLEGiveFeedback event contains two arguments (*effect* and *defaultcursors) that allow you to modify the default mouse pointers in an OLE drag-and-drop operation.*

The *effect* argument, like the other OLE drag-and-drop events, specifies whether data is to be copied, moved, or rejected. The purpose of this argument in the OLEGiveFeedback event, however, is to allow you to provide customized visual feedback to the user by changing the mouse pointer to indicate these actions.

Constant	Value	Description
vbDropEffectNone	0	Drop target cannot accept the data.
vbDropEffectCopy	1	Drop results in a copy. The original data is untouched by the drag source.
vbDropEffectMove	2	Drag source removes the data.
vbDropEffectScroll	&H80000000&	Scrolling is about to start or is currently occurring in the target. The value is used in addition to the other values.

Note The vbDropEffectScroll value can be used by some applications or controls to indicate that the user is causing scrolling by moving the mouse pointer near the edge of an application's window. Scrolling is automatically supported by some but not all of the Visual Basic standard controls. You may need to program for the scroll effect if you drag data into a program that contains scroll bars — Word for Windows, for example.

The *defaultcursors* argument specifies whether the default OLE cursor set is used. Setting this argument to False allows you to specify your own cursors using the Screen.MousePointer property of the Screen object.

In most cases, specifying custom mouse pointers is unnecessary because the default behavior of the mouse is handled by OLE. If you decide to specify custom mouse pointers using the OLEGiveFeedback event, you need to account for every possible effect, including scrolling. It is also a good idea to program for effects that may be added later by creating an option that gives the control of the mouse pointer back to OLE if an unknown effect is encountered.

The following code example sets the *effect* and *defaultcursors* arguments and specifies custom cursors (.ico or .cur files) for the copy, move, and scroll effects by setting the MousePointer and MouseIcon properties of the Screen object. It also returns control of the mouse pointer back to OLE if an unknown effect is encountered.

```
Private Sub TxtSource_OLEGiveFeedback(Effect As Long, _
      DefaultCursors As Boolean)
   DefaultCursors = False
   If Effect = vbDropEffectNone Then
      Screen.MousePointer = vbNoDrop
   ElseIf Effect = vbDropEffectCopy Then
      Screen.MousePointer = vbCustom
      Screen.MouseIcon = LoadPicture("c:\copy.ico")
   ElseIf Effect = (vbDropEffectCopy Or _
         vbDropEffectScroll) Then
      Screen.MousePointer = vbCustom
      Screen.MouseIcon = _
         LoadPicture("c:\copyscrl.ico")
   ElseIf Effect = vbDropEffectMove Then
      Screen.MousePointer = vbCustom
      Screen.MouseIcon = LoadPicture("c:\move.ico")
   ElseIf Effect = (vbDropEffectMove Or _
         vbDropEffectScroll) Then
      Screen.MousePointer = vbCustom
      Screen.MouseIcon = _
         LoadPicture("c:\movescrl.ico")
   Else
      ' If some new format is added that we do not
      '  understand, allow OLE to handle it with
      '  correct defaults.
      DefaultCursors = True
   End If
End Sub
```

Note You should always reset the mouse pointer in the OLECompleteDrag event if you specify a custom mouse pointer in the OLEGiveFeedback event. For more information about informing the source when data is dropped, see "Dropping the OLE Drag Source onto the OLE Drop Target."

For More Information See "Customizing the Mouse Pointer," later in this chapter, for information on setting the MousePointer and MouseIcon properties.

Dropping the OLE Drag Source onto the OLE Drop Target

If your target supports manual OLE drag-and-drop operations, you can control what happens when the cursor is moved within the target and can specify what kind of data the target will accept. When the user drops the source object onto the target control, the OLEDragDrop event is used to query the DataObject object for a compatible data format, and then retrieve the data.

The OLEDragDrop event also informs the source of the drop action, allowing it to delete the original data if a move has been specified, for example.

Retrieving the Data

The OLEDragDrop event is triggered when the user drops the source onto the target. If data was placed into the DataObject object when the drag operation was initiated, it can be retrieved when the OLEDragDrop event is triggered, by using the GetData method. If, however, only the supported source formats were declared when the drag operation was initiated, then the GetData method will automatically trigger the OLESetData event on the source to place the data into, and then retrieve the data from, the DataObject object.

The following example retrieves data that was placed into the DataObject object when the drag operation was initiated. The drag operation may have been initiated manually (using the OLEDrag method on the source) or automatically (by setting the OLEDragMode property of the source to Automatic). The dragged data is retrieved using the DataObject object's GetData method. The GetData method provides you with constants that represent the data types that the DataObject object supports. In this case, we are retrieving the data as text.

```
Private Sub txtTarget_OLEDragDrop(Data As _
      VB.DataObject, Effect As Long, Button As _
      Integer, Shift As Integer, X As Single, _
      Y As Single)
   txtTarget.Text = Data.GetData(vbCFText)
End Sub
```

For More Information For a complete list of GetData format constants, see "The OLE Drag and Drop DataObject Object," earlier in this chapter.

Querying the DataObject Object

You may need to query the DataObject object for the types of data that are being dropped onto the target. You use the GetFormat method in an If…Then statement to specify which types of data the target control can accept. If the data within the DataObject object is compatible, the drop action will be completed.

```
Private Sub txtTarget_OLEDragDrop(Data As _
      VB.DataObject, Effect As Long, Button As _
      Integer, Shift As Integer, X As Single, _
      Y As Single)
   If Data.GetFormat(vbCFText) Then
      txtTarget.Text = Data.GetData(vbCFText)
   End If
End Sub
```

Placing Data into the DataObject Object

When the target uses the GetData method to retrieve data from the source, the OLESetData event is only triggered if the data was not placed into the source when the drag operation was initiated.

In many cases, especially if the source supports more than one format, or if it is time-consuming to create the data, you may want to place data into the DataObject object only when it is requested by the target. The OLESetData event allows the source to respond to only one request for a given format of data.

For example, if the supported data formats were specified using the OLEStartDrag event when the drag operation was initiated, but data was not placed into the DataObject object, the OLESetData event is used to place a specific format of data into the DataObject object.

```
Private Sub txtSource_OLESetData(Data As _
      VB.DataObject, DataFormat As Integer)
   If DataFormat = vbCFText Then
      Data.SetData txtSource.SelText, vbCfText
   End If
End Sub
```

Informing the Source When Data is Dropped

The *effect* argument of the OLEDragDrop event specifies how the data was incorporated into the target when the data was dropped. When this argument is set, the OLECompleteDrag event is triggered on the source with its *effect* argument set to this value. The source can then take the appropriate action: If a move is specified, the source deletes the data, for example.

The *effect* argument of the OLEDragDrop event uses the same constants as the *effect* argument of the OLEDragOver event to indicate the drop action. The following table lists these constants:

Constant	Value	Description
vbDropEffectNone	0	Drop target cannot accept the data.
vbDropEffectCopy	1	Drop results in a copy. The original data is untouched by the drag source.
vbDropEffectMove	2	Drag source removes the data.

The following example sets the *effect* argument to indicate the drop action.

```
Private Sub txtTarget_OLEDragDrop(Data As _
      VB.DataObject, Effect As Long, Button As _
      Integer, Shift As Integer, X As Single, _
      Y As Single)
   If Data.GetFormat(vbCFText) Then
      txtTarget.Text = Data.GetData(vbCFText)
   End If
   Effect = vbDropEffectMove
End Sub
```

On the source side, the OLECompleteDrag event is triggered when the source is dropped onto the target, or when the OLE drag-and-drop operation is canceled. OLECompleteDrag is the last event in the drag-and-drop operation.

The OLECompleteDrag event contains only one argument (*effect*), which is used to inform the source of the action that was taken when the data is dropped onto the target.

The *effect* argument returns the same values that are used by the *effect* argument of the other OLE drag-and-drop events: vbDropEffectNone, vbDropEffectCopy, and vbDropEffectMove.

By setting this argument after a move has been specified by the target and the source has been dropped into the target, for example, the source will delete the original data in the control. You should also use the OLECompleteDrag event to reset the mouse pointer if you specified a custom mouse pointer in the OLEGiveFeedback event. For example:

```
Private Sub txtSource_OLECompleteDrag(Effect As Long)
   If Effect = vbDropEffectMove Then
      txtSource.SelText = ""
   End If
   Screen.MousePointer = vbDefault
End Sub
```

Using the Mouse and Keyboard to Modify Drop Effects and User Feedback

You can enhance the OLEDragDrop and OLEDragOver events by using the *button* and *shift* arguments to respond to the state of the mouse buttons and the SHIFT, CTRL, and ALT keys. For instance, when dragging data into a control, you can allow the user to perform a copy operation by pressing the CTRL key, or a move operation by pressing the SHIFT key.

In the following example, the *shift* argument of the OLEDragDrop event is used to determine if the SHIFT key is pressed when the data is dropped. If it is, a move is performed. If it is not, a copy is performed.

```
Private Sub txtTarget_OLEDragDrop(Data As _
      VB.DataObject, Effect As Long, Button As _
```

```
      Integer, Shift As Integer, X As Single, _
      Y As Single)
   If Shift And vbCtrlMask Then
      txtTarget.Text = Data.GetData(vbCFText)
      Effect = vbDropEffectCopy
   Else
      txtTarget.Text = Data.GetData(vbCFText)
      Effect = vbDropEffectMove
   End If
End Sub
```

The *button* argument can be used to isolate and respond to the various mouse button states. For instance, you may want to allow the user to move the data by pressing both the right and left mouse buttons simultaneously.

To indicate to the user what action will be taken when the source object is dragged over the target when a mouse button or the SHIFT, CTRL, and ALT keys are pressed, you can set the *shift* and *button* arguments of the OLEDragOver event. For example, to inform the user what action will be taken when the SHIFT button is pressed during a drag operation, you can add the following code to the OLEDragOver event:

```
Private Sub txtTarget_OLEDragOver(Data As _
      VB.DataObject, Effect As Long, Button As _
      Integer, Shift As Integer, X As Single, _
      Y As Single, State As Integer)
   If Shift And vbCtrlMask Then
      Effect = vbDropEffectCopy
   Else
      Effect = vbDropEffectMove
   End If
End Sub
```

For More Information See "Detecting Mouse Buttons" and "Detecting SHIFT, CTRL, and ALT States," earlier in this chapter for more information on responding to mouse and keyboard states.

Creating a Custom Data Format

If the formats supplied in Visual Basic are insufficient for some specific purpose, you can create a custom data format for use in an OLE drag-and-drop operation. For example, a custom data format is useful if your application defines a unique data format that you need to drag between two instances of your application, or just within the application itself.

To create a custom data format, you have to call the Windows API RegisterClipboardFormat function. For example:

```
Private Declare Function RegisterClipboardFormat Lib _
      "user32.dll" Alias "RegisterClipboardFormatA" _
      (ByVal lpszFormat$) As Integer
Dim MyFormat As Integer
```

Once defined, you can use your custom format as you would any other DataObject object data format. For example:

```
Dim a() As Byte
a = Data.GetData(MyFormat)
```

To use this functionality, you have to place data into and retrieve data from the DataObject object as a Byte array. You can then assign your custom data format to a string variable because it is automatically converted.

> **Caution** Retrieving your custom data format with the GetData method may yield unpredictable results.

Because Visual Basic doesn't understand your custom data format (because you defined it), it doesn't have a way to determine the size of the data. Visual Basic can determine the memory size of the Byte array because it has been allocated by Windows, but the operating system usually assigns more memory than is needed.

Therefore, when you retrieve a custom data format, you get back a Byte array containing at least, and possibly more than, the number of bytes that the source actually placed into the DataObject object. You must then correctly interpret your custom data format when it is retrieved from the DataObject object. For example, in a simple string, you have to search for the NULL character and then truncate the string to that length.

Dragging Files from the Windows Explorer

You can use OLE drag-and-drop to drag files from the Windows Explorer into an appropriate Visual Basic control, or vice versa. For example, you can select a range of text files in the Windows Explorer and then open them all in a single text box control by dragging and dropping them onto the control.

To illustrate this, the following procedure uses a text box control and the OLEDragOver and OLEDragDrop events to open a range of text files using the Files property and the vbCFFiles data format of the DataObject object.

To drag text files into a text box control from the Windows Explorer

1. Start a new project in Visual Basic.
2. Add a text box control to the form. Set its OLEDropMode property to Manual. Set its **MultiLine** property to **True** and clear the **Text** property.
3. Add a function to select and index a range of files. For example:

```
Sub DropFile(ByVal txt As TextBox, ByVal strFN$)
   Dim iFile As Integer
   iFile = FreeFile

   Open strFN For Input Access Read Lock Read _
   Write As #iFile
```

```
   Dim Str$, strLine$
   While Not EOF(iFile) And Len(Str) <= 32000
      Line Input #iFile, strLine$
      If Str <> "" Then Str = Str & vbCrLf
      Str = Str & strLine
   Wend
   Close #iFile

   txt.SelStart = Len(txt)
   txt.SelLength = 0
   txt.SelText = Str

End Sub
```

4. Add the following procedure to the OLEDragOver event. The GetFormat method is used to test for a compatible data format (vbCFFiles).

```
Private Sub Text1_OLEDragOver(Data As _
VB.DataObject, Effect As Long, Button As Integer, _
Shift As Integer, X As Single, Y As Single, State _
As Integer)
   If Data.GetFormat(vbCFFiles) Then
      'If the data is in the proper format, _
inform the source of the action to be taken
   Effect = vbDropEffectCopy And Effect
      Exit Sub
   End If
   'If the data is not desired format, no drop
   Effect = vbDropEffectNone

End Sub
```

5. Finally, add the following procedure to the OLEDragDrop event.

```
Private Sub Text1_OLEDragDrop(Data As _
VB.DataObject, Effect As Long, Button As Integer, _
Shift As Integer, X As Single, Y As Single)
   If Data.GetFormat(vbCFFiles) Then
      Dim vFN

      For Each vFN In Data.Files
         DropFile Text1, vFN
      Next vFN
   End If
End Sub
```

6. Run the application, open the Windows Explorer, highlight several text files, and drag them into the text box control. Each of the text files will be opened in the text box.

Customizing the Mouse Pointer

You can use the MousePointer and MouseIcon properties to display a custom icon, cursor, or any one of a variety of predefined mouse pointers. Changing the mouse pointer gives you a way to inform the user that long background tasks are processing, that a control or window can be resized, or that a given control doesn't support drag and drop, for instance. Using custom icons or mouse pointers, you can express an endless range of visual information about the state and functionality of your application.

With the MousePointer property you can select any one of sixteen predefined pointers. These pointers represent various system events and procedures. The following table describes several of these pointers and their possible uses in your application.

Mouse pointer	Constant	Description
	vbHourglass	Alerts the user to changes in the state of the program. For example, displaying an hourglass tells the user to wait.
	vbSizePointer	Notifies the user of changes in function. For example, the double arrow sizing pointers tell users they can resize a window.
	vbNoDrop	Warns the user an action can't be performed. For example, the no drop pointer tells users they can't drop a file at this location.

Each pointer option is represented by an integer value setting. The default setting is 0–Default and is usually displayed as the standard Windows arrow pointer. However, this setting is controlled by the operating system and can change if the system mouse settings have been changed by the user. To control the mouse pointer in your application, you set the MousePointer property to an appropriate value.

A complete list of mouse pointers is available by selecting the MousePointer property of a control or form and scanning the pull-down settings list or by using the Object Browser and searching for MousePointerConstants.

When you set the MousePointer property for a control, the pointer appears when the mouse is over the corresponding control. When you set the MousePointer property for a form, the selected pointer appears both when the mouse is over blank areas of the form and when the mouse is over controls with the MousePointer property set to 0–Default.

At run time you can set the value of the mouse pointer either by using the integer values or the Visual Basic mouse pointer constants. For example:

```
Form1.MousePointer = 11 'or vbHourglass
```

For More Information For a complete list of mouse pointer constants, see "MousePointer Constants" in the *Microsoft Visual Basic 6.0 Language Reference*.

Icons and Cursors

You can set the mouse pointer to display a custom icon or cursor. Using custom icons or cursors allows you to further modify the look or functionality of your application. Icons are simply .ico files, like those shipped with Visual Basic. Cursors are .cur files and, like icons, are essentially bitmaps. Cursors, however, are created specifically to show the user where actions initiated by the mouse will take place — they can represent the state of the mouse and the current input location.

Cursors also contain *hot spot* information. The hot spot is a pixel which tracks the location of the cursor — the *x* and *y* coordinates. Typically, the hot spot is located at the center of the cursor. Icons, when loaded into Visual Basic through the MouseIcon property, are converted to the cursor format and the hot spot is set to the center pixel. The two differ in that the hot spot location of a .cur file can be changed, whereas that of an .ico file cannot. Cursor files can be edited in Image Editor, which is available in the Windows SDK, online.

To use a custom icon or cursor, you set both the MousePointer and MouseIcon properties.

To use an .ico file as a mouse pointer

1. Select a form or control and set the MousePointer property to 99-Custom.
2. Load an .ico file into the MouseIcon property. For example, for a form:

```
Form1.MouseIcon = LoadPicture("c:\Program _
Files\Microsoft Visual _
Basic\Icons\Computer\Disk04.ico")
```

Both properties must be set appropriately for an icon to appear as a mouse pointer. If no icon is loaded into MouseIcon when the MousePointer property is set to 99-Custom, the default mouse pointer is used. Likewise, if the MousePointer property is not set to 99-Custom, the setting of MouseIcon is ignored.

Note Visual Basic does not support animated cursor (.ani) files.

For More Information See "MouseIcon Property" and "MousePointer Property" in the *Microsoft Visual Basic 6.0 Language Reference*.

Responding to Keyboard Events

Keyboard events, along with mouse events, are the primary elements of a user's interaction with your program. Clicks and key presses trigger events and provide the means of data input and the basic forms of window and menu navigation.

Although the operating system provides the seamless back-end for all these actions, it's sometimes useful or necessary to modify or enhance them. The KeyPress, KeyUp, and KeyDown events allow you to make these modifications and enhancements.

Programming your application to respond to key events is referred to as writing a *keyboard handler.* A keyboard handler can work on two levels: at the control level and at the form level. The control level (*low-level*) handler allows you to program a specific control. For instance, you might want to convert all the typed text in a Textbox control to uppercase. A *form-level* handler allows the form to react to the key events first. The focus can then be shifted to a control or controls on the form, and the events can either be repeated or initiated.

With these key events you can write code to handle most of the keys on a standard keyboard. For information on dealing with international character sets and keyboards, see Chapter 16, "International Issues."

Writing Low-Level Keyboard Handlers

Visual Basic provides three events that are recognized by forms and by any control that accepts keyboard input. They are described in the following table.

Keyboard event	Occurs
KeyPress	When a key corresponding to an ASCII character is pressed
KeyDown	As any key on the keyboard is pressed
KeyUp	As any key on the keyboard is released

Only the object that has the focus can receive a keyboard event. For keyboard events, a form has the focus only if it is active and no control on that form has the focus. This happens only on blank forms and forms on which all controls have been disabled. However, if you set the KeyPreview property on a form to True, the form receives all keyboard events for every control on the form before the control recognizes them. This is extremely useful when you want to perform the same action whenever a certain key is pressed, regardless of which control has the focus at the time.

The KeyDown and KeyUp events provide the lowest level of keyboard response. Use these events to detect a condition that the KeyPress event is unable to detect, for instance:

- Special combinations of SHIFT, CTRL, and ALT keys.
- Arrow keys. Note that some controls (command buttons, option buttons, and check boxes) do not receive arrow-key events: Instead, arrow keys cause movement to another control.
- PAGEUP and PAGEDOWN.
- Distinguishing the numeric keypad from numbers on the typewriter keys.
- Responding to a key being released as well as pressed (KeyPress responds only to a key being pressed).
- Function keys not attached to menu commands.

The keyboard events are not mutually exclusive. When the user presses a key, both the KeyDown and KeyPress events are generated, followed by a KeyUp event when the user releases the key. When the user presses one of the keys that KeyPress does not detect, only a KeyDown event occurs, followed by a KeyUp event.

Before using the KeyUp and KeyDown events, make sure that the KeyPress event isn't sufficient. This event detects keys that correspond to all the standard ASCII characters: letters, digits, and punctuation on a standard keyboard, as well as the ENTER, TAB, and BACKSPACE keys. It's generally easier to write code for the KeyPress event.

You also should consider using shortcut and access keys, which are described in "Menu Basics" in Chapter 3, "Forms, Controls, and Menus." Shortcut keys must be attached to menu commands, but they can include function keys (including some function-key–shift-key combinations). You can assign shortcut keys without writing additional code.

> **Note** The Windows ANSI (American National Standards Institute) character set corresponds to the 256 characters that include the standard Latin alphabet, publishing marks (such as copyright symbol, em dash, ellipsis), as well as many alternate and accented letters. These characters are represented by a unique 1-byte numeric value (0–255). ASCII (American Standard Code for Information Interchange) is essentially a subset (0–127) of the ANSI character set and represents the standard letters, digits, and punctuation on a standard keyboard. The two character sets are often referred to interchangeably.

The KeyPress Event

The KeyPress event occurs when any key that corresponds to an ASCII character is pressed. The ASCII character set represents not only the letters, digits, and punctuation on a standard keyboard but also most of the control keys. The KeyPress event only recognizes the ENTER, TAB, and BACKSPACE keys, however. The other function, editing, and navigation keys can be detected by the KeyDown and KeyUp events.

Use the KeyPress event whenever you want to process the standard ASCII characters. For example, if you want to force all the characters in a text box to be uppercase, you can use this event to change the case of the keys as they are typed:

```
Private Sub Text1_KeyPress (KeyAscii As Integer)
   KeyAscii = Asc(UCase(Chr(KeyAscii)))
End Sub
```

The *keyascii* argument returns an integer value corresponding to an ASCII character code. The procedure above uses Chr to convert the ASCII character code into the corresponding character, UCase to make the character uppercase, and Asc to turn the result back into a character code.

Using the same ASCII character codes, you can test whether a key recognized by the KeyPress event is pressed. For instance, the following event procedure uses KeyPress to detect if the user is pressing the BACKSPACE key:

```
Private Sub Text1_KeyPress (KeyAscii As Integer)
   If KeyAscii = 8 Then MsgBox "You pressed the _
      BACKSPACE key."
End Sub
```

You can also use the Visual Basic key-code constants in place of the character codes. The BACKSPACE key in the example above has an ASCII value of 8. The constant value for the BACKSPACE key is vbKeyBack.

For More Information For a complete list of character codes, see "Character Set (0–127)" and "Character Set (128–255)" in the *Microsoft Visual Basic 6.0 Language Reference*. A complete list of key code constants with corresponding ASCII values is available in "Key Code Constants" or by using the Object Browser and searching for KeyCodeConstants.

You can also use the KeyPress event to alter the default behavior of certain keys. For example, pressing ENTER when there is no Default button on the form causes a beep. You can avoid this beep by intercepting the ENTER key (character code 13) in the KeyPress event.

```
Private Sub Text1_KeyPress (KeyAscii As Integer)
   If KeyAscii = 13 Then KeyAscii = 0
End Sub
```

The KeyDown and KeyUp Events

The KeyUp and KeyDown events report the exact physical state of the keyboard itself: A key is pressed down (KeyDown) and a key is released (KeyUp). In contrast, the KeyPress event does not report the state of the keyboard directly — it doesn't recognize the up or down state of the key, it simply supplies the character that the key represents.

A further example helps to illustrate the difference. When the user types uppercase "A," the KeyDown event gets the ASCII code for "A." The KeyDown event gets the same code when the user types lowercase "a." To determine whether the character pressed is uppercase or lowercase, these events use the *shift* argument. In contrast, the KeyPress event treats the uppercase and lowercase forms of a letter as two separate ASCII characters.

The KeyDown and KeyUp events return information on the character typed by providing the following two arguments.

Argument	Description
Keycode	Indicates the physical key pressed. In this case, "A" and "a" are returned as the same key. They have the identical *keycode* value. But note that "1" on the typewriter keys and "1" on the numeric keypad are returned as different keys, even though they generate the same character.
Shift	Indicates the state of the SHIFT, CTRL, and ALT keys. Only by examining this argument can you determine whether an uppercase or lowercase letter was typed.

The Keycode Argument

The *keycode* argument identifies a key by the ASCII value or by the key-code constant. Key codes for letter keys are the same as the ASCII codes of the uppercase character of the letter. So the *keycode* for both "A" and "a" is the value returned by Asc("A"). The following example uses the KeyDown event to determine if the "A" key has been pressed:

```
Private Sub Text1_KeyDown(KeyCode As Integer, _
      Shift As Integer)
   If KeyCode = vbKeyA Then MsgBox "You pressed _
      the A key."
End Sub
```

Pressing SHIFT + "A" or "A" without the SHIFT key displays the message box — that is, the argument is true in each case. To determine if the uppercase or lowercase form of the letter has been pressed you need to use the *shift* argument. See the topic, "The Shift Argument" later in this chapter.

Key codes for the number and punctuation keys are the same as the ASCII code of the number on the key. So the *keycode* for both "1" and "!" is the value returned by Asc("1"). Again, to test for the "!" character you need to use the *shift* argument.

The KeyDown and KeyUp events can recognize most of the control keys on a standard keyboard. This includes the function keys (F1–F16), the editing keys (HOME, PAGE UP, DELETE, etc.), the navigation keys (RIGHT, LEFT, UP, and DOWN ARROW), and the keypad. These keys can be tested for by using either the key-code constant or the equivalent ASCII value. For example:

```
Private Sub Text1_KeyDown(KeyCode As Integer, _
      Shift As Integer)
   If KeyCode = vbKeyHome Then MsgBox "You _
      pressed the HOME key."
End Sub
```

For More Information For a complete list of character codes, see "Character Set (0–127)" and "Character Set (128–255)" in the *Microsoft Visual Basic 6.0 Language Reference*. A complete list of key code constants with corresponding ASCII values is available by using the Object Browser and searching for KeyCodeConstants.

The Shift Argument

The key events use the *shift* argument in the same way that the mouse events do — as integer and constant values that represent the SHIFT, CTRL, and ALT keys. You can use the shift argument with KeyDown and KeyUp events to distinguish between uppercase and lowercase characters, or to test for the various mouse states.

Building on the previous example, you can use the *shift* argument to determine whether the uppercase form of a letter is pressed.

```
Private Sub Text1_KeyDown(KeyCode As Integer, _
      Shift As Integer)
   If KeyCode = vbKeyA And Shift = 1 _
   Then MsgBox "You pressed the uppercase A key."
End Sub
```

Like the mouse events, the KeyUp and KeyDown events can detect the SHIFT, CTRL, and ALT individually or as combinations. The following example tests for specific shift-key states.

Open a new project and add the variable `ShiftKey` to the Declarations section of the form:

```
Dim ShiftKey as Integer
```

Add a Textbox control to the form and this procedure in the KeyDown event:

```
Private Sub Text1_KeyDown(KeyCode As Integer, _
      Shift As Integer)
   ShiftKey = Shift And 7
   Select Case ShiftKey
      Case 1 ' or vbShiftMask
         Print "You pressed the SHIFT key."
      Case 2 ' or vbCtrlMask
         Print "You pressed the CTRL key."
      Case 4 ' or vbAltMask
         Print "You pressed the ALT key."
      Case 3
         Print "You pressed both SHIFT and CTRL."
      Case 5
         Print "You pressed both SHIFT and ALT."
      Case 6
         Print "You pressed both CTRL and ALT."
      Case 7
         Print "You pressed SHIFT, CTRL, and ALT."
      End Select
End Sub
```

As long as the Textbox control has the focus, each key or combination of keys prints a corresponding message to the form when pressed.

For More Information See "Detecting SHIFT, CTRL, and ALT States" earlier in this chapter.

Writing Form-Level Keyboard Handlers

Each KeyDown and KeyUp event is attached to a specific object. To write a keyboard handler that applies to all objects on the form, set the KeyPreview property of the form to True. When the KeyPreview property is set to True, the form recognizes the KeyPress, KeyUp, and KeyDown events for all controls on the form before the controls themselves recognize the events. This makes it very easy to provide a common response to a particular keystroke.

You can set the KeyPreview property of the form to True in the Properties window or through code in the Form_Load procedure:

```
Private Sub Form_Load
   Form1.KeyPreview = True
End Sub
```

You can test for the various key states on a form by declaring a `ShiftKey` variable and using the Select Case statement. The following procedure will print the message to the form regardless of which control has the focus.

Open a new project and add the variable `ShiftKey` to the Declarations section of the form:

```
Dim ShiftKey as Integer
```

Add a Textbox and a CommandButton control to the form. Add the following procedure to the form's KeyDown event:

```
Private Sub Form_KeyDown(KeyCode As Integer, _
      Shift As Integer)
   ShiftKey = Shift And 7
   Select Case ShiftKey
      Case 1 ' or vbShiftMask
         Print "You pressed the SHIFT key."
      Case 2 ' or vbCtrlMask
         Print "You pressed the CTRL key."
      Case 4 ' or vbAltMask
         Print "You pressed the ALT key."
   End Select
End Sub
```

If you have defined a shortcut key for a menu control, the Click event for that menu control occurs automatically when the user types that key, and no key event occurs.

Similarly, if there is a command button on the form with the Default property set to True, the ENTER key causes the Click event for that command button to occur instead of a key event. If there is a command button with the Cancel property set to True, the ESC key causes the Click event for that command button to occur instead of a key event.

For example, if you add a Click event procedure to the CommandButton and then set either the Default or Cancel properties to True, pressing the RETURN or ESC keys will override the KeyDown event. This procedure closes the application:

```
Private Sub Command1_Click()
   End
End Sub
```

Notice that the TAB key moves the focus from control to control and does not cause a key event unless every control on the form is disabled or has TabStop set to False.

When the KeyPreview property of the form is set to True, the form recognizes the keyboard events before the controls, but the events still occur for the controls. To prevent this, you can set the *keyascii* or *keycode* arguments in the form key-event procedures to 0. For example, if there is no default button on the form, you can use the ENTER key to move the focus from control to control:

```
Private Sub Form_KeyPress (KeyAscii As Integer)
Dim NextTabIndex As Integer, i As Integer
   If KeyAscii = 13 Then
      If Screen.ActiveControl.TabIndex = _
      Count - 1 Then
         NextTabIndex = 0
      Else
         NextTabIndex = Screen.ActiveControl._
         TabIndex + 1
      End If
      For i = 0 To Count - 1
         If Me.Controls(i).TabIndex = _
         NextTabIndex Then
            Me.Controls(i).SetFocus
            Exit For
         End If
      Next i
      KeyAscii = 0
   End If
End Sub
```

Because this code sets *keyascii* to 0 when it is 13, the controls never recognize the ENTER key being pressed, and their key-event procedures are never called.

Interrupting Background Processing

Your application may utilize long background processing to accomplish certain tasks. If this is the case, it is helpful to provide the user with a way to either switch to another application or interrupt or cancel the background task. The Windows operating environment gives users the first option: switching to another application by using the ALT+TAB key combination, for instance. You can provide the other options by writing code that responds when a user either clicks a cancel button or presses the ESC key.

In considering how to implement this in your application, it's important to understand how tasks from various applications are handled by the operating system. Windows is a preemptively multitasking operating system, which means that idle processor time is efficiently shared among background tasks. These background tasks can originate from the application the user is working with, from another application, or perhaps from some system-controlled events. Priority is always given to the application that the user is working with, however. This ensures that the mouse and keyboard always respond immediately.

Background processing can be placed into two categories: constant and intermittent. An example of a constant task would be copying a file from a server. Periodically updating a value would be an example of an intermittent task. Both types of tasks can be interrupted or canceled by the user. However, because background processing is usually a complex matter, it is important to consider how these tasks are initiated in the first place. The next section, "Allowing Users to Interrupt Tasks," later in this chapter describes these considerations and techniques.

Allowing Users to Interrupt Tasks

During long background tasks, your application cannot respond to user input. Therefore, you should provide the user with a way to interrupt or cancel the background processing by writing code for either the mouse or keyboard events. For example, when a long background task is running, you can display a dialog box that contains a Cancel button that the user can initiate by clicking the ENTER key (if the focus is on the Cancel button) or by clicking on it with the mouse.

> **Note** You may also want to give the user a visual cue when a long task is processing. For example, you might show the user how the task is progressing (using a Label or Gauge control, for instance), or by changing the mouse pointer to an hourglass.

There are several techniques, but no one way, to write code to handle background processing. One way to allow users to interrupt a task is to display a Cancel button and allow its Click event to be processed. You can do this by placing the code for your background task in a timer event, using the following guidelines.

- Use static variables for information that must persist between occurrences of the Timer event procedure.
- When the Timer event gets control, allow it to run slightly longer than the time you specified for the Interval property. This ensures that your background task will use every bit of processor time the system can give it. The next Timer event will simply wait in the message queue until the last one is done.
- Use a fairly large value — five to ten seconds — for the timer's Interval property, as this makes for more efficient processing. Preemptive multitasking prevents other applications from being blocked, and users are generally tolerant of a slight delay in canceling a long task.
- Use the Enabled property of the Timer as a flag to prevent the background task from being initiated when it is already running.

For More Information See "Using the Timer Control" in Chapter 7, "Using Visual Basic's Standard Controls."

Using DoEvents

Although Timer events are the best tool for background processing, particularly for very long tasks, the DoEvents function provides a convenient way to allow a task to be canceled. For example, the following code shows a "Process" button that changes to a "Cancel" button when it is clicked. Clicking it again interrupts the task it is performing.

```
' The original caption for this button is "Process".
Private Sub Command1_Click()
   ' Static variables are shared by all instances
   ' of a procedure.
   Static blnProcessing As Boolean
   Dim lngCt As Long
   Dim intYieldCt As Integer
   Dim dblDummy As Double
   ' When the button is clicked, test whether it's
    'already processing.
   If blnProcessing Then
      ' If processing is in progress, cancel it.
      blnProcessing = False
   Else
      Command1.Caption = "Cancel"
      blnProcessing = True
      lngCt = 0
      ' Perform a million floating-point
      ' multiplications. After every
      ' thousand, check for cancellation.
      Do While blnProcessing And (lngCt < 1000000)
```

```
            For intYieldCt = 1 To 1000
                lngCt = lngCt + 1
                dblDummy = lngCt * 3.14159
            Next intYieldCt
            ' The DoEvents statement allows other
            ' events to occur, including pressing this
            ' button a second time.
            DoEvents
        Loop
        blnProcessing = False
        Command1.Caption = "Process"
        MsgBox lngCt & " multiplications were performed"
    End If
End Sub
```

DoEvents switches control to the operating-environment kernel. Control returns to your application as soon as all other applications in the environment have had a chance to respond to pending events. This doesn't cause the current application to give up the focus, but it does enable background events to be processed.

The results of this yielding may not always be what you expect. For example, the following Click-event code waits until ten seconds after the button was clicked and then displays a message. If the button is clicked while it is already waiting, the clicks will be finished in reverse order.

```
Private Sub Command2_Click()
    Static intClick As Integer
    Dim intClickNumber As Integer
    Dim dblEndTime As Double
        ' Each time the button is clicked,
        ' give it a unique number.
    intClick = intClick + 1
    intClickNumber = intClick
        ' Wait for ten seconds.
    dblEndTime = Timer + 10#
    Do While dblEndTime > Timer
        ' Do nothing but allow other
        ' applications to process
        ' their events.
        DoEvents
    Loop
    MsgBox "Click " & intClickNumber & " is finished"
End Sub
```

You may want to prevent an event procedure that gives up control with DoEvents from being called again before DoEvents returns. Otherwise, the procedure might end up being called endlessly, until system resources are exhausted. You can prevent this from happening either by temporarily disabling the control or by setting a static "flag" variable, as in the earlier example.

Avoiding DoEvents When Using Global Data

It may be perfectly safe for a function to be called again while it has yielded control with DoEvents. For example, this procedure tests for prime numbers and uses DoEvents to periodically enable other applications to process events:

```
Function PrimeStatus (TestVal As Long) As Integer
   Dim Lim As Integer
   PrimeStatus = True
   Lim = Sqr(TestVal)
   For I = 2 To Lim
      If TestVal Mod I = 0 Then
         PrimeStatus = False
         Exit For
      End If
      If I Mod 200 = 0 Then DoEvents
   Next I
End Function
```

This code calls the DoEvents statement once every 200 iterations. This allows the PrimeStatus procedure to continue calculations as long as needed while the rest of the environment responds to events.

Consider what happens during a DoEvents call. Execution of application code is suspended while other forms and applications process events. One of these events might be a button click that launches the PrimeStatus procedure again.

This causes PrimeStatus to be re-entered, but since each occurrence of the function has space on the stack for its parameters and local variables, there is no conflict. Of course, if PrimeStatus gets called too many times, an Out of Stack Space error could occur.

The situation would be very different if PrimeStatus used or changed module-level variables or global data. In that case, executing another instance of PrimeStatus before DoEvents could return might result in the values of the module data or global data being different than they were before DoEvents was called. The results of PrimeStatus would then be unpredictable.

For More Information See "DoEvents Function" and "Refresh Method" in the *Microsoft Visual Basic 6.0 Language Reference*.

CHAPTER 12

Working with Text and Graphics

Visual Basic includes sophisticated text and graphics capabilities for use in your applications. If you think of text as a visual element, you can see that size, shape and color can be used to enhance the information presented. Just as a newspaper uses headlines, columns and bullets to break the words into bite-sized chunks, text properties can help you emphasize important concepts and interesting details.

Visual Basic also provides graphics capabilities allowing you great flexibility in design, including the addition of animation by displaying a sequence of images.

This chapter describes ways of placing and manipulating text and graphics. Details on formatting, fonts, color palettes, and printing are included. By combining these capabilities with good design concepts, you can optimize the attractiveness and ease of use of your applications.

Contents

Sample Applications: Blanker.vbp, Palettes.vbp

Some of the code examples in this chapter are taken from the Blanker (Blanker.vbp) and Palettes (Palettes.vbp) samples. You'll find these applications listed in the Samples directory.

Working with Fonts

Text is displayed using a *font* — a set of characters of the same typeface, available in a particular size, style, and weight.

The Windows 95 and Windows NT operating systems provide you and your users with a complete set of standard fonts. TrueType fonts are scaleable, which means they can reproduce a character at any size. When you select a TrueType font, it is rendered into the selected point size and displayed as a bitmap on the screen.

When printing, the selected TrueType font or fonts are rendered into the appropriate size and then sent to the printer. Therefore, there is no need for separate screen and printer fonts. Printer fonts will be substituted for TrueType fonts, however, if an equivalent font is available, which increases print speed.

Choosing Fonts for Your Application

Remember that a user of your application may not have the fonts you used to create the application. If you select a TrueType font that a user doesn't have, Windows selects the closest matching font on the user's system. Depending on the design of your application, this may cause problems for the user. For example, the font Windows selects may enlarge text so that labels overlap on the screen.

One way to avoid font problems is to distribute the necessary fonts with your application. (You will probably need to obtain permission from the copyright holder of the font to distribute it with your application.)

You can also program your application to check among the fonts available in the operating system for the fonts you use. If the font doesn't reside in the operating system, you can program the application to choose a different font from the list.

Another way to avoid font problems is to use fonts users are most likely to have on their systems. If you use fonts from a specific version of Windows, you may have to specify that version as a system requirement of your application.

Checking Available Fonts

Your program can easily determine whether matching fonts are available on both the user's system and printer. The Fonts property applies to the Printer and Screen objects. An array returned by the Fonts property is a list of all of the fonts available to a printer or screen. You can iterate through the property array, and then search for matching name strings. This code example determines whether the system has a printer font that matches the font of the selected form:

```
Private Sub Form_Click ()
Dim I As Integer, Flag As Boolean
   For I = 0 To Printer.FontCount - 1
      Flag = StrComp (Font.Name,Printer.Fonts(I), 1)
      If Flag = True Then
         Debug.Print "There is a matching font."
         Exit For
      End If
   Next I
End Sub
```

For More Information For information about fonts in East Asian systems, see "Font, Display, and Print Considerations in a DBCS Environment" in Chapter 16, "International Issues." For information about setting font properties, see "Setting Font Characteristics," later in this chapter.

Creating Your Own Font Types

If you set a reference to Standard OLE Types using the References dialog box, you can use the StdFont class to create your own font types. If you view the Object Browser, you will notice that there are StdFont and Font classes. The Font class is derived from the StdFont base class and is supported by all controls.

You can use the following syntax:

```
Dim MyFont As Font
```

But, you cannot use:

```
Dim MyFont As New Font
```

Instead, to create your own font or picture types, use code like the following:

```
Dim MyFont As New StdFont
With MyFont
   .Bold = True
   .Name = "Arial"
End With
Set Text1.Font = MyFont
```

Setting Font Characteristics

Forms, controls that display text (as text or captions), and the Printer object support a Font property, which determines the visual characteristics of text, including:

- Font name (typeface)
- Font size (in points)
- Special characteristics (bold, italic, underline, or strikethrough)

For details on the Printer object, see "Printing from an Application" later in this chapter.

Setting Font Properties

You can set any of the font properties at design time by double-clicking Font in the Properties window and setting the properties in the Font dialog box.

At run time, you set font characteristics by setting the Font object's properties for each form and control. The following table describes the properties for the Font object.

Property	Type	Description
Name	String	Specifies name of font, such as Arial or Courier.
Size	Single	Specifies font size in points (72 points to an inch when printed).
Bold	Boolean	If True, the text is bold.
Italic	Boolean	If True, the text is italic.
StrikeThrough	Boolean	If True, Visual Basic strikes through the text.
Underline	Boolean	If True, the text is underlined.
Weight	Integer	Returns or sets the weight of the font. Above a certain weight, the Bold property is forced to True.

For example, the following statements set various font properties for a label named lblYearToDate:

```
With lblYearToDate.Font
    .Name = "Arial"        ' Change the font to Arial.
    .Bold = True           ' Make the font bold.
End With
```

The order in which you select font properties is important, because not all fonts support all font variations. Set the Name property first. Then you can set any of the Boolean properties, such as Bold and Italic, to True or False.

You can also store a set of font properties in a Font object. You can declare a Font object just as you would any other object, using the StdFont class:

```
Dim MyFont As New StdFont
With MyFont
    .Name = "Arial"
    .Size = 10
    .Bold = True
End With
```

> **Note** Before you can create a new Font object, you must use the References dialog box (available from the Project menu) to create a reference to Standard OLE Types.

You can then easily switch from one set of font properties to another, by setting the form or control's Font object to the new object:

```
Set lblYearToDate.Font = MyFont
```

For More Information See "Font Object" in the *Microsoft Visual Basic 6.0 Language Reference* volume of the *Microsoft Visual Basic 6.0 Language Reference Library*.

Working with Small Fonts

Some fonts do not support the sizes smaller than 8 points. When you set the Size property for one of these fonts to a size smaller than 8 points, either the Name property or the Size property will automatically change to a different font or a different size. To avoid unpredictable results, each time you set the Size property to a font size smaller than 8 points, examine the values of the Name property and the Size property again after setting it.

Applying Font Properties to Specific Objects

The effect of setting font properties varies depending on the technique used to display text. If the text is specified by a property (such as Text or Caption), then changing a font property applies to all the text in that control. Labels, text boxes, frames, buttons, check boxes, and all the file-system controls use a property to specify text.

If the application shows text with the Print method, then changing a font property affects all uses of Print after the property change. Text printed before the property change is not affected. Only forms, picture boxes, and the Debug and Printer objects support the Print method.

Because changes in font properties apply to all the text in text boxes and labels, you cannot mix fonts in these controls. If you need to mix fonts (for example, making some words bold but leaving others in normal font), then create a picture box and use the Print method to display text. "Displaying Text on Forms and Picture Boxes," later in this chapter, explains how to use the Print method.

The FontTransparent Property

Forms and picture boxes have an additional font property, FontTransparent. When FontTransparent is True, the background shows through any text displayed on the form or picture box. Figure 12.1 shows the effects of the FontTransparent property.

Figure 12.1 The effects of the FontTransparent property

Font Transparent set to True

Font Transparent set to False

Displaying Text on Forms and Picture Boxes

To display text on a form or picture box, use the Print method, preceded by the name of the form or picture box. To send output text to a printer, use the Print method on the Printer object.

Using the Print Method

The Print method syntax is:

[*object*.]**Print** [*outputlist*] [{ ; | , }]

The *object* argument is optional; if omitted, the Print method applies to the current form.

For example, the following statements print messages to:

- A form named MyForm:

  ```
  MyForm.Print "This is a form."
  ```

- A picture box named picMiniMsg:

  ```
  picMiniMsg.Print "This is a picture box."
  ```

- The current form:

  ```
  Print "This is the current form."
  ```

- The Printer object:

  ```
  Printer.Print "This text is going to the printer."
  ```

The *outputlist* argument is the text that appears on the form or picture box. Multiple items in the *outputlist* argument must be separated by commas or semicolons or both, as explained in "Displaying Different Items on a Single Line," later in this chapter.

Truncated Text

If the form or picture box is too small to display all the text, the text is cut off. Where the form or picture box cuts off the text depends on the coordinates of the location at which you began printing the text. You cannot scroll through a form or picture box.

Layering

When you print text to a form, the text appears in a layer *behind* any controls that have been placed on the form. So printing to a form usually works best on a form specifically created to hold the text. For more information about how text and graphics appear in layers on a form, see "Layering Graphics with AutoRedraw and ClipControls," later in this chapter.

Displaying Different Items on a Single Line

The items you display or print can include property values, constants, and variables (either string or numeric). The Print method, discussed in "Displaying Text on Forms and Picture Boxes," prints the value of numeric items. Positive number values have a leading and a trailing space. Negative numeric values display their sign instead of a leading space.

Use a semicolon (;) or a comma (,) to separate one item from the next. If you use a semicolon, Visual Basic prints one item after another, without intervening spaces. If you use a comma, Visual Basic skips to the next tab column.

For example, the following statement prints to the current form:

```
Print "The value of X is "; X; "and the value of Y _
   is "; Y
```

If X contains the value 2 and Y contains the value 7, the statement produces this output:

```
The value of X is 2 and the value of Y is 7
```

By default, each Print method prints the text and moves to the next line. If there are no items, Print simply skips a line. A series of Print statements (in the following example, for a picture box named picLineCount) automatically uses separate lines:

```
picLineCount.Print "This is line 1."
picLineCount.Print "This is line 2."
```

By placing a semicolon (or comma) at the end of the first statement, however, you cause the output of the next Print statement to appear on the same line:

```
picLineCount.Print "This all appears ";
picLineCount.Print "on the same line."
```

Displaying Print Output at a Specific Location

You can control placement of Print output by specifying the drawing coordinates, using either or both of these techniques:

- Use the Cls (clear) method to erase a form or picture box and reset the drawing coordinates to the origin (0,0).
- Set drawing coordinates with the CurrentX and CurrentY properties.

The Cls Method

All the text and graphics on the object that were created with Print and graphics methods can be deleted with the Cls method. The Cls method also resets the drawing coordinates to the origin (0,0), which is the upper-left corner by default. For example, these statements clear:

- A picture box named Picture1:

```
Picture1.Cls
```

- The current form:

```
Cls
```

Setting Drawing Coordinates

You can set the drawing coordinates of forms and picture boxes directly with the CurrentX and CurrentY properties. For example, these statements reset the drawing coordinates to the upper-left corner for Picture1 and for the current form:

- A picture box named Picture1:

```
Picture1.CurrentX = 0
Picture1.CurrentY = 0
```

- The current form:

```
CurrentX = 0
CurrentY = 0
```

Any new text you print appears on top of any text and graphics already at that location. To erase text selectively, draw a box with the Line method and fill it with the background color. Keep in mind that the drawing coordinates specified by CurrentX and CurrentY usually change location when you use a graphics method.

By default, forms and picture boxes use a coordinate system where each unit corresponds to a twip (1,440 twips equal an inch, and approximately 567 twips equal a centimeter). You may want to change the ScaleMode property of the form, picture box, or Printer object from twips to points, because text height is measured in points. Using the same unit of measure for the text and for the object where you will print the text makes it easier to calculate the position of the text.

For More Information For more information about twips and drawing coordinates, see "Understanding the Coordinate System," later in this chapter.

The TextHeight and TextWidth Methods

Before using the Print method, you can use the TextHeight and TextWidth methods to determine where to position the CurrentX and CurrentY properties. TextHeight returns the height of a line of text, taking into account the object's font size and style. The syntax is:

[*object.*]**TextHeight**(*string*)

If the *string* argument contains embedded carriage-return characters (Chr(13)), then the text corresponds to multiple lines, and TextHeight returns the height of the number of lines of text contained in the string. If there are no embedded carriage returns, TextHeight always returns the height of one line of text.

One way to use the TextHeight method is to set the CurrentY property to a particular line. For example, the following statements set the drawing coordinates to the beginning of the fifth line:

```
CurrentY = TextHeight("sample") * 4
CurrentX = 0
```

Assuming there are no carriage returns in the sample text, you would use this syntax to set CurrentY to the *nth* line:

CurrentY = [*object.*]**TextHeight**(*string*) * (n – 1)

If *object* is omitted, the method applies to the current form. The *object* argument can be a form, a picture box, or the Printer object.

The TextWidth method returns the width of a string, taking into account the object's font size and style. This method is useful because many fonts have proportional-width characters. The TextWidth method helps you determine whether the width of the string is larger than the width of the form, picture box, or Printer object.

For example, the following statements use TextWidth and TextHeight to center the text in a box by positioning CurrentX and CurrentY. The name of the box in this example is MealCard.

```
CurrentX = (BoxWidth - TextWidth("MealCard")) / 2
CurrentY = (Boxheight - TextHeight("MealCard")) / 2
```

For More Information See "TextHeight Method" and "TextWidth Method" in the *Microsoft Visual Basic 6.0 Language Reference*.

Formatting Numbers, Dates, and Times

Visual Basic provides great flexibility in displaying number formats, as well as date and time formats. You can easily display international formats for numbers, dates, and times.

The Format function converts the numeric value to a text string and gives you control over the string's appearance. For example, you can specify the number of decimal places, leading or trailing zeros, and currency formats. The syntax is:

Format(*expression*[, *format*[, *firstdayofweek*[, *firstweekofyear*]]])

The *expression* argument specifies a number to convert, and the *format* argument is a string made up of symbols that shows how to format the number. The most commonly used symbols are listed in the table below.

Symbol	Description
0	Digit placeholder; prints a trailing or a leading zero in this position, if appropriate.
#	Digit placeholder; never prints trailing or leading zeros.
.	Decimal placeholder.
,	Thousands separator.
– + $ ( ) space	Literal character; characters are displayed exactly as typed into the format string.

The *firstdayofweek* argument is a constant that specifies the first day of the week; the *firstweekofyear* argument is a constant that specifies the first week of the year. Both arguments are optional. For more information about these constants, see "Format Function" in the *Microsoft Visual Basic 6.0 Language Reference.*

Named Formats

Visual Basic provides several standard formats to use with the Format function. Instead of designating symbols in the *format* argument, you specify these formats by name in the *format* argument of the Format function. Always enclose the format name in double quotation marks ("").

The following table lists the format names you can use.

Named format	Description
General Number	Displays number with no thousand separator.
Currency	Displays number with thousand separator, if appropriate; display two digits to the right of the decimal separator. Output is based on user's system settings.
Fixed	Displays at least one digit to the left and two digits to the right of the decimal separator.

Named format	Description
Standard	Displays number with thousand separator, at least one digit to the left and two digits to the righseparator.
Percent	Multiplies the value by 100 with a percent sign at the end.
Scientific	Uses standard scientific notation.
General Date	Shows date and time if *expression* contains both. If *expression* is only a date or a time, the missing information is not displayed. Date display is determined by user's system settings.
Long Date	Uses the Long Date format specified.
	by user's system settings.
Medium Date	Uses the *dd-mmm-yy* format (for example, 03-Apr-93). Date display is determined by user's system settings.
Short Date	Uses the Short Date format specified by user's system settings.
Long Time	Displays a time using user's system's long-time format; includes hours, minutes, seconds.
Medium Time	Shows the hour, minute, and "AM" or "PM" using the "*hh:mm* AM/PM" format.
Short Time	Shows the hour and minute using the *hh:mm* format.
Yes/No	Any nonzero numeric value (usually –1) is Yes. Zero is No.
True/False	Any nonzero numeric value (usually –1) is True. Zero is False.
On/Off	Any nonzero numeric value (usually –1) is On. Zero is Off.

The Format function supports many other special characters, such as the percentage placeholder and exponents.

For More Information See "Format Function" in the *Microsoft Visual Basic 6.0 Language Reference.*

Number Formats

The following number conversions assume that the country in the Windows Control Panel is set to "English(United States)."

Format syntax	Result
Format(8315.4, "00000.00")	08315.40
Format(8315.4, "#####.##")	8315.4
Format(8315.4, "##,##0.00")	8,315.40
Format(315.4,"$##0.00")	$315.40

The symbol for the decimal separator is a period (.), and the symbol for the thousands separator is a comma (,). However, the separator character that is actually displayed depends on the country specified in the Windows Control Panel.

Printing Formatted Dates and Times

To print formatted dates and times, use the Format function with symbols representing date and time. These examples use the Now and Format functions to identify and format the current date and time. The following examples assume that the Regional Settings dialog box of the Windows Control Panel is set to "English(United States)."

Format syntax	Result
Format(Now, "*m/d/yy*")	1/27/93
Format(Now, "*dddd, mmmm dd, yyyy*")	Wednesday, January 27, 1993
Format(Now, "*d-mmm*")	27-Jan
Format(Now, "*mmmm-yy*")	January-93
Format(Now, "*hh:mm* AM/PM")	07:18 AM
Format(Now, "*h:mm:ss* a/p")	7:18:00 a
Format(Now, "*d-mmmm h:mm*")	3-January 7:18

By using the Now function with the format "*ddddd*" and "*ttttt*," you can print the current date and time in a format appropriate for the selection in the Regional Settings dialog box of the Windows Control Panel.

Country	Format syntax	Result
Sweden	Format(Now, "*ddddd ttttt*")	1992-12-31 18.22.38
United Kingdom	Format(Now, "*ddddd ttttt*")	31/12/92 18:22:38
Canada (French)	Format(Now, "*ddddd ttttt*")	92-12-31 18:22:38
United States	Format(Now, "*ddddd ttttt*")	12/31/92 6:22:38 PM

For More Information For more information about international considerations when using the Format function, see "Locale-Aware Functions" in Chapter 16, "International Issues." For more information about dates based on system locale, see "Writing International Code in Visual Basic" in Chapter 16, "International Issues."

Working with Selected Text

Text boxes and combo boxes have a series of properties for selected text that are especially useful when working with the Clipboard. These properties, which refer to the block of text selected (highlighted) inside the control, allow you to create cut-and-paste functions for the user. The following properties can all be changed at run time.

Property	Description
SelStart	A Long integer that specifies the starting position of the selected block of text. If no text is selected, this property specifies the position of the insertion point. A setting of 0 indicates the position just before the first character in the text box or combo box. A setting equal to the length of the text in the text box or combo box indicates the position just after the last character in the control.
SelLength	A Long integer that specifies the number of characters selected.
SelText	The String containing the selected characters (or an empty string, if no characters are selected).

You can control what text is selected by setting the SelStart and SelLength properties. For example, these statements highlight all the text in a text box:

```
Text1.SetFocus
' Start highlight before first character.
Text1.SelStart = 0
' Highlight to end of text.
Text1.SelLength = Len(Text1.Text)
```

If you assign a new string to SelText, that string replaces the selected text, and the insertion point is placed just after the end of the newly inserted text. For example, the following statement replaces the selected text with the string "I've just been inserted!":

```
Text1.SelText = "I've just been inserted!"
```

If no text was selected, the string is simply pasted into the text box at the insertion point.

For More Information See "SelStart Property," "SelLength Property," and "SelText Property" in the *Microsoft Visual Basic 6.0 Controls Reference* volume of the *Microsoft Visual Basic 6.0 Reference Library*.

Transferring Text and Graphics with the Clipboard Object

The Clipboard object has no properties or events, but it has several methods that allow you to transfer data to and from the environment's Clipboard. The Clipboard methods fall into three categories. The GetText and SetText methods are used to transfer text. The GetData and SetData methods transfer graphics. The GetFormat and Clear methods work with both text and graphic formats.

For More Information For information about transferring data within your application or between applications, see "OLE Drag and Drop" in Chapter 11, "Responding to Mouse and Keyboard Events."

Cutting, Copying, and Pasting Text with the Clipboard

Two of the most useful Clipboard methods are SetText and GetText. These two methods transfer string data to and from the Clipboard, as shown in Figure 12.2.

Figure 12.2 Moving data to and from the Clipboard with SetText and GetText

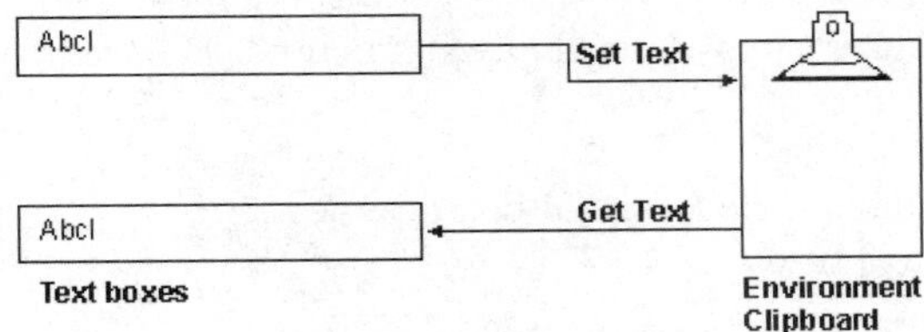

SetText copies text onto the Clipboard, replacing whatever text was stored there before. You use SetText like a statement. Its syntax is:

Clipboard.SetText *data*[, *format*]

GetText returns text stored on the Clipboard. You use it like a function:

destination = **Clipboard.GetText**()

By combining the SetText and GetText methods with the selection properties introduced in "Working with Selected Text," you can easily write Copy, Cut, and Paste commands for a text box. The following event procedures implement these commands for controls named mnuCopy, mnuCut, and mnuPaste:

```
Private Sub mnuCopy_Click ()
   Clipboard.Clear
   Clipboard.SetText Text1.SelText
End Sub

Private Sub mnuCut_Click ()
   Clipboard.Clear
   Clipboard.SetText Text1.SelText
   Text1.SelText = ""
End Sub

Private Sub mnuPaste_Click ()
   Text1.SelText = Clipboard.GetText()
End Sub
```

> **Note** The example works best if these are menu controls, because you can use menus while Text1 has the focus.

Notice that both the Copy and Cut procedures first empty the Clipboard with the Clear method. (The Clipboard is not cleared automatically because you may want to place data on the Clipboard in several different formats, as described in "Working with Multiple Formats on the Clipboard" later in this chapter.) Both the Copy and Cut procedures then copy the selected text in Text1 onto the Clipboard with the following statement:

```
Clipboard.SetText Text1.SelText
```

In the Paste command, the GetText method returns the string of text currently on the Clipboard. An assignment statement then copies this string into the selected portion of the text box (Text1.SelText). If no text is currently selected, Visual Basic places this text at the insertion point in the text box:

```
Text1.SelText = Clipboard.GetText()
```

This code assumes that all text is transferred to and from the text box Text1, but the user can copy, cut, and paste between Text1 and controls on other forms.

Because the Clipboard is shared by the entire environment, the user can also transfer text between Text1 and any application using the Clipboard.

Working with the ActiveControl Property

If you want the Copy, Cut, and Paste commands to work with any text box that has the focus, use the ActiveControl property of the Screen object. The following code provides a reference to whichever control has the focus:

```
Screen.ActiveControl
```

You can use this fragment just like any other reference to a control. If you know that the control is a text box, you can refer to any of the properties supported for text boxes, including Text, SelText, and SelLength. The following code assumes that the active control is a text box, and uses the SelText property:

```
Private Sub mnuCopy_Click ()
   Clipboard.Clear
   Clipboard.SetText Screen.ActiveControl.SelText
End Sub

Private Sub mnuCut_Click ()
   Clipboard.Clear
   Clipboard.SetText Screen.ActiveControl.SelText
   Screen.ActiveControl.SelText = ""
End Sub

Private Sub mnuPaste_Click ()
   Screen.ActiveControl.SelText = Clipboard.GetText()
End Sub
```

Working with Multiple Formats on the Clipboard

You can actually place several pieces of data on the Clipboard at the same time, as long as each piece is in a different format. This is useful because you don't know what application will be pasting the data, so supplying the data in several different formats enhances the chance that you will provide it in a format that the other application can use. The other Clipboard methods — GetData, SetData, and GetFormat — allow you to deal with data formats other than text by supplying a number that specifies the format. These formats are described in the following table, along with the corresponding number.

Constant	Description
vbCFLink	Dynamic data exchange link.
vbCFText	Text. Examples earlier in this chapter all use this format.
vbCFBitmap	Bitmap.
vbCFMetafile	Metafile.
vbCFDIB	Device-independent bitmap.
vbCFPalette	Color palette.

You can use the last four formats when cutting and pasting data from picture box controls. The following code provides generalized Cut, Copy, and Paste commands that work with any of the standard controls.

```
Private Sub mnuCopy_Click ()
   Clipboard.Clear
   If TypeOf Screen.ActiveControl Is TextBox Then
      Clipboard.SetText Screen.ActiveControl.SelText
   ElseIf TypeOf Screen.ActiveControl Is ComboBox Then
      Clipboard.SetText Screen.ActiveControl.Text
   ElseIf TypeOf Screen.ActiveControl Is PictureBox _
         Then
      Clipboard.SetData Screen.ActiveControl.Picture
   ElseIf TypeOf Screen.ActiveControl Is ListBox Then
      Clipboard.SetText Screen.ActiveControl.Text
   Else
      ' No action makes sense for the other controls.
   End If
End Sub

Private Sub mnuCut_Click ()
   ' First do the same as a copy.
   mnuCopy_Click
   ' Now clear contents of active control.
   If TypeOf Screen.ActiveControl Is TextBox Then
      Screen.ActiveControl.SelText = ""
```

```
    ElseIf TypeOf Screen.ActiveControl Is ComboBox Then
       Screen.ActiveControl.Text = ""
    ElseIf TypeOf Screen.ActiveControl Is PictureBox _
          Then
       Screen.ActiveControl.Picture = LoadPicture()
    ElseIf TypeOf Screen.ActiveControl Is ListBox Then
       Screen.ActiveControl.RemoveItem Screen.ActiveControl.ListIndex
    Else
       ' No action makes sense for the other controls.
    End If
End Sub

Private Sub mnuPaste_Click ()
    If TypeOf Screen.ActiveControl Is TextBox Then
       Screen.ActiveControl.SelText = Clipboard.GetText()
    ElseIf TypeOf Screen.ActiveControl Is ComboBox Then
       Screen.ActiveControl.Text = Clipboard.GetText()
    ElseIf TypeOf Screen.ActiveControl Is PictureBox _
          Then
       Screen.ActiveControl.Picture = _
          Clipboard.GetData()
    ElseIf TypeOf Screen.ActiveControl Is ListBox Then
       Screen.ActiveControl.AddItem Clipboard.GetText()
    Else
       ' No action makes sense for the other controls.
    End If
End Sub
```

Checking the Data Formats on the Clipboard

You can use the GetFormat method to determine whether the data on the Clipboard is in a particular format. For example, you can disable the Paste command depending on whether the data on the Clipboard is compatible with the currently active control.

```
Private Sub mnuEdit_Click ()
' Click event for the Edit menu.
   mnuCut.Enabled = True
   mnuCopy.Enabled = True
   mnuPaste.Enabled = False
   If TypeOf Screen.ActiveControl Is TextBox Then
      If Clipboard.GetFormat(vbCFText) Then mnuPaste.Enabled = True
   ElseIf TypeOf Screen.ActiveControl Is ComboBox Then
      If Clipboard.GetFormat(vbCFText) Then mnuPaste.Enabled = True
   ElseIf TypeOf Screen.ActiveControl Is ListBox Then
      If Clipboard.GetFormat(vbCFText) Then mnuPaste.Enabled = True
   ElseIf TypeOf Screen.ActiveControl Is PictureBox _
         Then
      If Clipboard.GetFormat(vbCFBitmap) Then mnuPaste.Enabled = True
```

```
    Else
        ' Can't cut or copy from the other types
        '  of controls.
        mnuCut.Enabled = False
        mnuCopy.Enabled = False
    End If
End Sub
```

Note You might also want to check for other data formats with the constants vbCFPalette, vbCFDIB, and vbCFMetafile. If you want to replace a picture's palette using Clipboard operations, you should request vbCFBitmap rather than vbCFDIB from the Clipboard. See "Working with 256 Colors," later in this chapter, for more information on working with the color palette.

For More Information See "Clipboard Object" in the *Microsoft Visual Basic 6.0 Language Reference*.

Understanding the Coordinate System

Every graphical operation described in this chapter (including resizing, moving, and drawing) uses the coordinate system of the drawing area or container. Although you can use the coordinate system to achieve graphical effects, it is also important to know how to use the coordinate system to define the location of forms and controls in your application.

The coordinate system is a two-dimensional grid that defines locations on the screen, in a form, or other container (such as a picture box or Printer object). You define locations on this grid using coordinates in the form:

(*x*, *y*)

The value of x is the location of the point along the x-axis, with the default location of 0 at the extreme left. The value of y is the location of the point along the y-axis, with the default location of 0 at the extreme top. This coordinate system is illustrated in Figure 12.3.

Figure 12.3 The coordinate system of a form

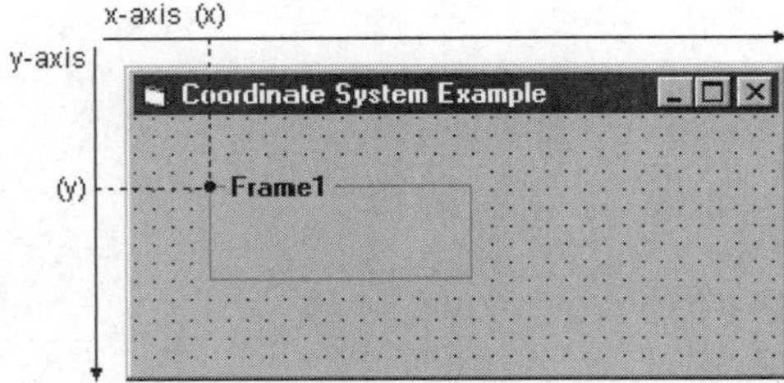

The following rules apply to the Visual Basic coordinate system:

- When you move or resize a control, you use the coordinate system of the control's container. If you draw the object directly on the form, the form is the container. If you draw the control inside a frame or picture box, the frame or the control is the container.
- All graphics and Print methods use the coordinate system of the container. For example, statements that draw inside a picture box use the coordinate system of that control.
- Statements that resize or move a form always express the form's position and size in twips.

  When you create code to resize or move a form, you should first check the Height and Width properties of the Screen object to make sure the form will fit on the screen.
- The upper-left corner of the screen is always (0, 0). The default coordinate system for any container starts with the (0, 0) coordinate in the upper-left corner of the container.

The units of measure used to define locations along these axes are collectively called the *scale*. In Visual Basic, each axis in the coordinate system can have its own scale.

You can change the direction of the axis, the starting point, and the scale of the coordinate system, but use the default system for now. "Changing an Object's Coordinate System," later in this chapter, discusses how to make these changes.

Twips Explained

By default, all Visual Basic movement, sizing, and graphical-drawing statements use a unit of one twip. A *twip* is 1/20 of a printer's point (1,440 twips equal one inch, and 567 twips equal one centimeter). These measurements designate the size an object will be when printed. Actual physical distances on the screen vary according to the monitor size.

Changing an Object's Coordinate System

You set the coordinate system for a particular object (form or control) using the object's scale properties and the Scale method. You can use the coordinate system in one of three different ways:

- Use the default scale.
- Select one of several standard scales.
- Create a custom scale.

Changing the scale of the coordinate system can make it easier to size and position graphics on a form. For example, an application that creates bar charts in a picture box can change the coordinate system to divide the control into four columns, each representing a bar in the chart. The following sections explain how to set default, standard, and custom scales to change the coordinate system.

Using the Default Scale

Every form and picture box has several scale properties (ScaleLeft, ScaleTop, ScaleWidth, ScaleHeight, and ScaleMode) and one method (Scale) you can use to define the coordinate system. The default scale for objects in Visual Basic places the coordinate (0,0) at the upper-left corner of the object. The default scale uses twips.

If you want to return to the default scale, use the Scale method with no arguments.

Selecting a Standard Scale

Instead of defining units directly, you can define them in terms of a standard scale by setting the ScaleMode property to one of the settings shown in the following table.

ScaleMode setting	Description
0	User-defined. If you set ScaleWidth, ScaleHeight, ScaleTop, or ScaleLeft directly, the ScaleMode property is automatically set to 0.
1	Twips. This is the default scale. There are 1,440 twips to one inch.
2	Points. There are 72 points to one inch.
3	Pixels. A pixel is the smallest unit of resolution on the monitor or printer. The number of pixels per inch depends on the resolution of the device.
4	Characters. When printed, a character is 1/6 of an inch high and 1/12 of an inch wide.
5	Inches.
6	Millimeters.
7	Centimeters.

All of the modes in the table, except for 0 and 3, refer to printed lengths. For example, an item that is two units long when ScaleMode is set to 7 is two centimeters long when printed.

```
' Set scale to inches for this form.
ScaleMode = 5
' Set scale to pixels for picPicture1.
picPicture1.ScaleMode = 3
```

Setting a value for ScaleMode causes Visual Basic to redefine ScaleWidth and ScaleHeight so that they are consistent with the new scale. ScaleTop and ScaleLeft are then set to 0. Directly setting ScaleWidth, ScaleHeight, ScaleTop, or ScaleLeft automatically sets ScaleMode to 0.

Creating a Custom Scale

You can use an object's ScaleLeft, ScaleTop, ScaleWidth, and ScaleHeight properties to create a custom scale. Unlike the Scale method, these properties can be used either to set the scale or to get information about the current scale of the coordinate system.

Using ScaleLeft and ScaleTop

The ScaleLeft and ScaleTop properties assign numeric values to the upper-left corner of an object. For example, these statements set the value of the upper-left corner for the current form and upper-left corner for a picture box named picArena.

```
ScaleLeft = 100
ScaleTop = 100
picArena.ScaleLeft = 100
picArena.ScaleTop = 100
```

These scale values are shown in Figure 12.4.

Figure 12.4 The ScaleLeft and ScaleTop properties for a form and a control

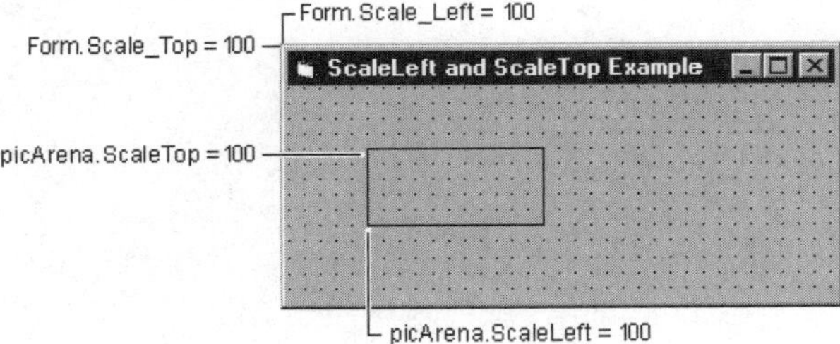

These statements define the upper-left corner as (100, 100). Although the statements don't directly change the size or position of these objects, they alter the effect of subsequent statements. For example, a subsequent statement that sets a control's Top property to 100 places the object at the very top of its container.

Using ScaleWidth and ScaleHeight

The ScaleWidth and ScaleHeight properties define units in terms of the current width and height of the drawing area. For example:

```
ScaleWidth = 1000
ScaleHeight = 500
```

These statements define a horizontal unit as 1/1,000 of the current internal width of the form and a vertical unit as 1/500 of the current internal height of the form. If the form is later resized, the units remain the same.

Note ScaleWidth and ScaleHeight define units in terms of the internal dimensions of the object; these dimensions do not include the border thickness or the height of the menu or caption. Thus, ScaleWidth and ScaleHeight always refer to the amount of room available *inside* the object. The distinction between internal and external dimensions (specified by Width and Height) is particularly important with forms, which can have a thick border. The units can also differ: Width and Height are always expressed in terms of the *container's* coordinate system; ScaleWidth and ScaleHeight determine the coordinate system of the object itself.

Setting Properties to Change the Coordinate System

All four of these scale properties can include fractions and they can also be negative numbers. Negative settings for the ScaleWidth and ScaleHeight properties change the orientation of the coordinate system.

The scale shown in Figure 12.5 has ScaleLeft, ScaleTop, ScaleWidth, and Scale Height all set to 100.

Figure 12.5 Scale running from (100, 100) to (200, 200)

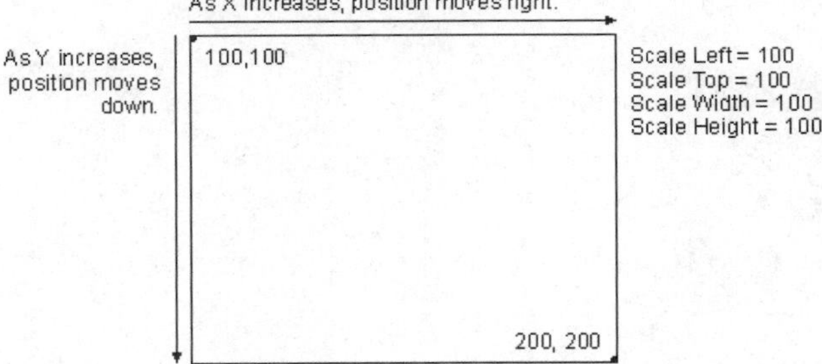

Using the Scale Method to Change the Coordinate System

A more efficient way to change the coordinate system, other than setting individual properties, is to use the Scale method. You specify a custom scale using this syntax:

[*object.*]**Scale** (*x1, y1*) – (*x2, y2*)

The values of x1 and y1 determine the settings of the ScaleLeft and ScaleTop properties. The differences between the two x-coordinates and the two y-coordinates determine the settings of ScaleWidth and ScaleHeight, respectively. For example, suppose you set the coordinate system for a form by setting end points (100, 100) and (200, 200):

```
Scale (100, 100)-(200, 200)
```

This statement defines the form as 100 units wide and 100 units high. With this scale in place, the following statement moves a shape control one-fifth of the way across the form:

```
shpMover.Left = shpMover.Left + 20
```

Specifying a value of *x1* > *x2* or *y1* > *y2* has the same effect as setting ScaleWidth or ScaleHeight to a negative value.

Converting Scales

Use the ScaleX and ScaleY methods to convert from one scale mode to another scale mode. Those methods have the following syntax:

[*object*.]**ScaleX** (*value* [, *fromScale* [, *toScale*]]

[*object*.]**ScaleY** (*value* [, *fromScale* [, *toScale*]]

The destination *object* is a form, picture box, or Printer object. The *value* is expressed in the coordinate system specified by the scale mode *fromScale*. The value returned is expressed in the scale mode specified by *toScale*, or the scale mode of *object* if *toScale* is omitted. If *fromScale* is omitted, the scale mode for *value* is HIMETRIC.

HIMETRIC is the scale mode that specifies physical sizes. For example, the number of HIMETRIC units in a line of 10 centimeters is 10,000. The resulting line drawn on the screen is ten centimeters long, regardless of the size of the video display area. For information on the HIMETRIC scale mode and physical sizes, see the Microsoft Windows SDK.

The following statement stretches the content of the picture box control MyPic to twice its width. MyPic.Picture.Width returns the width of the picture contained in the picture control, which is a HIMETRIC value that needs to be converted into the scale mode of Form1.

```
Form1.PaintPicture MyPic.Picture, X, Y, _
   Form1.ScaleX(MyPic.Picture.Width) * 2
```

The following example illustrates two equivalent ways to specify a form's Width to *np* pixels wide.

```
' The ScaleMode of the form is set to pixels.
ScaleMode = vbPixels

' Option 1:
' Temporarily set the form's ScaleMode to twips.
ScaleMode = vbTwips
' ScaleX() returns the value in twips.
Width = Width - ScaleWidth + ScaleX(np, vbPixels)
' Set back the ScaleMode of the form to pixels.
ScaleMode = vbPixels
' Option 2:
' Conversion from pixels to twips without changing
'  the ScaleMode of the form.
Width = Width + ScaleX(np - ScaleWidth, vbPixels, _
   vbTwips)
```

For More Information See "ScaleX, ScaleY Methods" in the *Microsoft Visual Basic 6.0 Language Reference.*

Using Graphical Controls

Visual Basic provides three controls designed to create graphical effects in an application:

- The image control
- The line control
- The shape control

Advantages of Graphical Controls

The image, line, and shape controls are very useful for creating graphics at design time. One advantage of graphical controls is that they require fewer system resources than other Visual Basic controls, which improves the performance of your Visual Basic application.

Another advantage of graphical controls is that you can create graphics with less code than with graphics methods. For example, you can use either the Circle method or the shape control to place a circle on a form. The Circle method requires that you create the circle with code at run time, while you can simply draw the shape control on the form and set the appropriate properties at design time.

Limitations of Graphical Controls

While graphical controls are designed to maximize performance with minimal demands on the application, they accomplish this goal by limiting other features common to controls in Visual Basic. Graphical controls:

- Cannot appear on top of other controls, unless they are inside a container that can appear on top of other controls (such as a picture box).
- Cannot receive focus at run time.
- Cannot serve as containers for other controls.
- Do not have an hWnd property.

For More Information For information about the graphics methods, see "Using Graphics Methods" later in this chapter. For information about the graphical controls, see "Using the Image Control," "Using the Line Control," and "Using the Shape Control" in Chapter 7, "Using Visual Basic's Standard Controls." For information about the effect of graphics on your application's performance, see especially "Cutting Back on Graphics" in Chapter 15, "Designing for Performance and Compatibility."

Adding Pictures to Your Application

Pictures can be displayed in three places in Visual Basic applications:

- On a form
- In a picture box
- In an image control

Pictures can come from paint programs, such as those that ship with the various versions of Microsoft Windows, other graphics applications, or clip-art libraries. Visual Basic provides a large collection of icons you can use as graphics in applications. Visual Basic allows you to add .jpg and .gif files, as well as .bmp, .dib, .ico, .cur, .wmf, and .emf files to your applications. For more information about the graphics formats supported by Visual Basic, see "Using the Image Control" and "Using the Picture Box Control" in Chapter 7, "Using Visual Basic's Standard Controls."

You use different techniques to add a picture to a form, a picture box, or an image control depending on whether you add the picture at design time or run time.

Adding a Picture at Design Time

There are two ways to add a picture at design time:

- Load a picture onto a form, or into a picture box or image control from a picture file:

  In the Properties window, select Picture from the Properties list and click the Properties button. Visual Basic displays a dialog box, from which you select a picture file.

  If you set the Picture property for a form, the picture you select is displayed on the form, behind any controls you've placed on it. Likewise, if you set the Picture property for a picture box, the picture is displayed in the box, behind any controls you've placed on it.

- Paste a picture onto a form or into a picture box or image control:

  Copy a picture from another application (such as Microsoft Paint) onto the Clipboard. Return to Visual Basic, select the form, picture box, or image control, and from the Edit menu, choose Paste.

Once you've set the Picture property for a form, picture box, or image control — either by loading or pasting a picture — the word displayed in the Settings box is "(Bitmap)," "(Icon)," or "(Metafile)." To change the setting, load or paste another picture. To set the Picture property to "(None)" again, double-click the word displayed in the Settings box and press the DEL key.

Adding a Picture at Run Time

There are four ways to add a picture at run time:

- Use the LoadPicture function to specify a file name and assign the picture to the Picture property.

  The following statement loads the file Cars.bmp into a picture box named picDisplay (you name a control by setting its Name property):

  ```
  picDisplay.Picture = LoadPicture("C:\Picts\Cars.bmp")
  ```

  You can load a new picture file onto a form or into a picture box or image control whenever you want. Loading a new picture completely replaces the existing picture, although the source files of the pictures are never affected.

- Use the LoadResPicture function to assign a picture from the project's .res file into the Picture property.

  The following statement loads the bitmap resource ID, 10, from the resource file into a picture box named picResource:

  ```
  Set picResource.Picture = LoadResPicture(10, _
     vbResBitmap)
  ```

- Copy a picture from one object to another.

  Once a picture is loaded or pasted onto a form or into a picture box or image control, you can assign it to other forms, picture boxes, or image controls at run time. For example, this statement copies a picture from a picture box named picDisplay to an image control named imgDisplay:

  ```
  Set imgDisplay.Picture = picDisplay.Picture
  ```

- Copy a picture from the Clipboard object.

For More Information For more information about copying a picture from the Clipboard, see "Working with Multiple Formats on the Clipboard," earlier in this chapter.

For information on resource files, see "Working with Resource Files" in Chapter 8, "More About Programming."

> **Note** If you load or paste pictures from files at design time, the pictures are saved and loaded with the form, and the application copies pictures from one object to another. Then, when you create an .exe file, you don't need to give your users copies of the picture files; the .exe file itself contains the images. Also, consider supplying a .res file and using LoadResPicture. The .res file gets built into the .exe, and the bitmaps are saved in a standard format that any resource editor can read. If you load pictures at run time with the LoadPicture function, you must supply the picture files to your users along with your application.

Removing a Picture at Run Time

You can also use the LoadPicture function to remove a picture at run time without replacing it with another picture. The following statement removes a picture from an image control named imgDisplay:

```
Set imgDisplay.Picture = LoadPicture("")
```

Moving and Sizing Pictures

If a form, picture box, or image control is moved (at design time or run time), its picture automatically moves with it. If a form, picture box, or image control is resized so that it is too small to display a picture, the picture gets clipped at the right and bottom. A picture also gets clipped if you load or copy it onto a form or into a picture box or image control that is too small to display all of it.

AutoSize Property

If you want a picture box to automatically expand to accommodate a new picture, set the AutoSize property for the picture box to True. Then when a picture is loaded or copied into the picture box at run time, Visual Basic automatically expands the control down and to the right enough to display all of the picture. If the image you load is larger than the edges of the form, it appears clipped because the form size doesn't change.

You can also use the AutoSize property to automatically shrink a picture box to reflect the size of a new picture.

> **Note** Image controls do not have an AutoSize property, but automatically size themselves to fit the picture loaded into them. Forms don't have an AutoSize property, and they do not automatically enlarge to display all of a picture.

Stretch Property of Image Controls

If you want a picture in an image control to automatically expand to fit a particular size, use the Stretch property. When the Stretch property is False, the image control automatically adjusts its size to fit the picture loaded into it. To resize the picture to fit the image control, set the Stretch property for the image control to True.

Selecting Art for the Picture Control

Where do you get picture files? If you want icons, you can use the Icon Library included with Visual Basic. You can find the icon files within the subdirectories of the main Visual Basic directory (\Vb\Graphics\Icons). You can create .bmp files with Microsoft Paint, or you can buy a clip-art collection that includes bitmap or icon files, or metafiles. You can also create a resource (.res) file containing pictures.

For More Information See "Working with Resource Files" in Chapter 8, "More About Programming," for more information on creating a resource file.

Introduction to Graphics Properties for Forms and Controls

Forms and various controls have graphics properties. The following table lists these properties.

Category	Properties
Display processing	AutoRedraw, ClipControls
Current drawing location	CurrentX, CurrentY
Drawing techniques	DrawMode, DrawStyle, DrawWidth, BorderStyle, BorderWidth
Filling techniques	FillColor, FillStyle
Colors	BackColor, ForeColor, BorderColor, FillColor

Forms and picture boxes have additional properties:

- Scale properties, as described in "Changing an Object's Coordinate System," earlier in this chapter.
- Font properties, as described in "Setting Font Characteristics," earlier in this chapter.

There are two properties of forms and picture boxes you'll probably want to use right away: BackColor and ForeColor. BackColor paints the background of the drawing area. If BackColor is light blue, then the entire area is light blue when you clear it. ForeColor (foreground) determines the color of text and graphics drawn on an object, although some graphics methods give you the option of using a different color. For more information about color, see "Working with Color," later in this chapter.

Creating Persistent Graphics with AutoRedraw

Each form and picture box has an AutoRedraw property. AutoRedraw is a Boolean property that, when set to True, causes graphics output to be saved in memory. You can use the AutoRedraw property to create persistent graphics.

Persistent Graphics

Microsoft Windows manipulates the screen image to create an illusion of overlapping windows. When one window is moved over another, temporarily hiding it, and is then moved away again, the window and its contents need to be redisplayed. Windows takes care of redisplaying the window and controls. But your Visual Basic application must handle redisplaying graphics in a form or picture box.

If you create graphics on the form using graphics methods, you usually want them to reappear exactly as you placed them (*persistent graphics*). You can use the AutoRedraw property to create persistent graphics.

AutoRedraw and Forms

The default setting of AutoRedraw is False. When AutoRedraw is set to False, any graphics created by graphics methods that appear on the form are lost if another window temporarily hides them. Also, graphics that extend beyond the edges of the form are lost if you enlarge the form. The effects of setting AutoRedraw to False are shown in Figure 12.6.

Figure 12.6 The effects of setting AutoRedraw to False

When the AutoRedraw property of a form is set to True, Visual Basic applies graphics methods to a "canvas" in memory. The application copies the contents of this memory canvas to redisplay graphics temporarily hidden by another window. In most cases, the size of this canvas for forms is the size of the screen. If the form's MaxButton property is False and the border of the form is not sizable, the size of the canvas is the size of the form.

This canvas also lets the application save graphics that extend beyond the edges of the form when the form is resizable. The effects of setting AutoRedraw to True are shown in Figure 12.7.

Figure 12.7 The effects of setting AutoRedraw to True

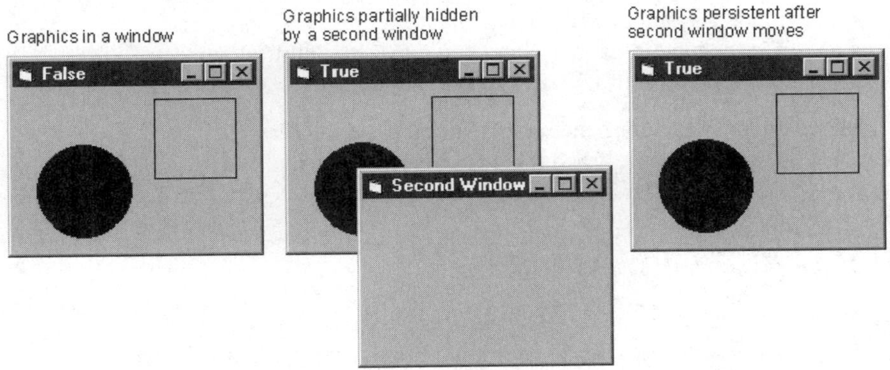

AutoRedraw and Picture Boxes

When the AutoRedraw property of a picture box is set to True, Visual Basic saves only the visible contents of the picture box in memory. This is because the memory canvas used to save the contents of the picture box is the same size as the picture box. Graphics that extend outside the picture box are cropped and never appear later, even if the size of the picture box changes.

Using Nonpersistent Graphics

You can leave AutoRedraw set to False for the form and all its picture boxes to conserve memory. But then the graphics are not automatically persistent: You have to manage redrawing all graphics in code as needed.

You can include code in the Paint event for a form or picture box that redraws all lines, circles, and points as appropriate. This approach usually works best when you have a limited amount of graphics that you can reconstruct easily.

A Paint event procedure is called whenever part of a form or picture box needs to be redrawn — for example, when a window that covered the object moves away, or when resizing causes graphics to come back into view. If AutoRedraw is set to True, the object's Paint procedure is never called unless your application calls it explicitly. The visible contents of the object are stored in the memory canvas, so the Paint event isn't needed.

Keep in mind that the decision to use nonpersistent graphics can affect the way graphics paint on the form or container. The next section, "Clipping Regions with ClipControls," and "Layering Graphics with AutoRedraw and ClipControls," later in this chapter, discuss other factors that may determine whether or not you should use nonpersistent graphics.

Changing AutoRedraw at Run Time

You can change the setting of AutoRedraw at run time. If AutoRedraw is False, graphics and output from the Print method are written only to the screen, not to memory. If you clear the object with the Cls method, any output written when AutoRedraw was set to True does not get cleared. This output is retained in memory, and you must set AutoRedraw to True again and then use the Cls method to clear it.

For More Information To learn about the performance implications of AutoRedraw, see "Optimizing Display Speed" in Chapter 15, "Designing for Performance and Compatibility."

Clipping Regions with ClipControls

Each form, picture box, and frame control has a ClipControls property. ClipControls is a Boolean property that, when set to True, causes the container to define a clipping region when painting the container around all controls except:

- The shape control
- The line control
- The image control
- Labels
- Any ActiveX graphical controls

By setting the ClipControls property to False, you can improve the speed with which a form paints to the screen. The speed improvement is greatest on forms with many controls that do not overlap, like dialog boxes.

Clipping Regions

Clipping is the process of determining which parts of a form or container are painted when the form or container is displayed. The outline used to determine what parts of the form or container are painted or "clipped" defines the *clipping region* for that form or container. Clipping regions are useful when a Windows-based application needs to save one part of the display and simultaneously repaint the rest.

Clipping Forms and Containers

The default setting of ClipControls is True. When the ClipControls property is True, Windows defines a clipping region for the background of the form or container before a Paint event. This clipping region surrounds all nongraphical controls. When using ClipControls, labels act like graphical controls.

During a Paint event, Windows repaints only the background inside the clipping region, avoiding the nongraphical controls. Figure 12.8 shows a form with four controls, a box painted with the Line method, and the clipping region created for that form by setting ClipControls to True. Notice that the clipping region did not clip around the label or shape controls on the form. The box drawn in the background with the Line method paints only in the clipping region.

Figure 12.8 The clipping region created when ClipControls is True

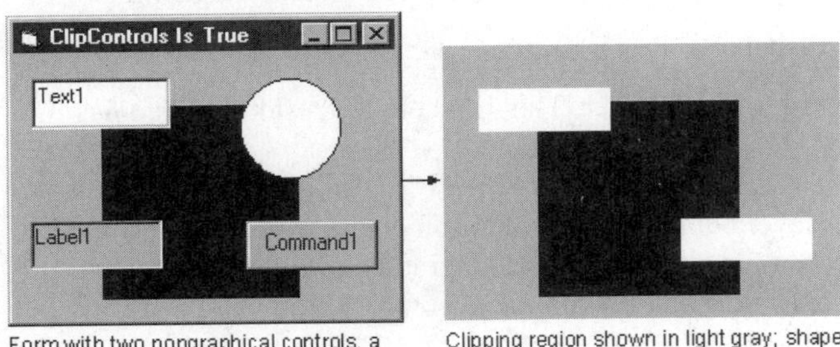

Form with two nongraphical controls, a shape control, a label, and a box created with the Line method.

Clipping region shown in light gray; shape control and label not clipped.The box paints only in the clipping region.

When ClipControls is False, Windows does not define a clipping region for the background of the form or container before a Paint event. Also, output from graphics methods within the Paint event appears only in the parts of the form or container that need to be repainted. Since calculating and managing a clipping region takes time, setting ClipControls to False may cause forms with many nonoverlapping controls (such as complex dialog boxes) to display faster.

> **Note** Avoid nesting controls with ClipControls set to True inside controls with ClipControls set to False. Doing so may result in the nested controls not repainting correctly. To fix this, set ClipControls to True for both the containers and the controls.

For More Information See "Optimizing Display Speed" in Chapter 15, "Designing for Performance and Compatibility."

Layering Graphics with AutoRedraw and ClipControls

Different combinations of AutoRedraw and ClipControls have different effects on the way graphical controls and graphics methods paint to the screen.

As you create graphics, keep in mind that graphical controls and labels, nongraphical controls, and graphics methods appear on different layers in a container. The behavior of these layers depends on three factors:

- The AutoRedraw setting.
- The ClipControls setting.
- Whether graphics methods appear inside or outside the Paint event.

Normal Layering

Usually, the layers of a form or other container are, from front to back, as follows:

Layer	Contents
Front	Nongraphical controls like command buttons, check boxes, and file controls.
Middle	Graphical controls and labels.
Back	Drawing space for the form or container. This is where the results of graphics methods appear.

Anything in one layer covers anything in the layer behind, so graphics you create with the graphical controls appear behind the other controls on the form, and all graphics you create with the graphics methods appear below all graphical and nongraphical controls. The normal arrangement of layers is shown in Figure 12.9.

Figure 12.9 Normal layering of graphics on a form

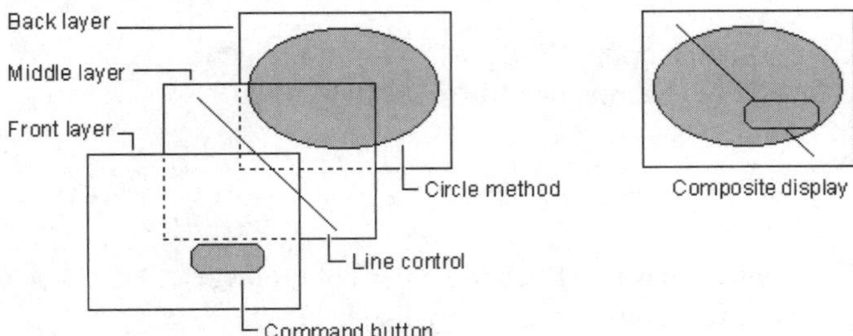

Effects on Layering

You can produce normal layering using any of several approaches. Combining settings for AutoRedraw and ClipControls and placing graphics methods inside or outside the Paint event affects layering and the performance of the application.

The following table lists the effects created by different combinations of AutoRedraw and ClipControls and placement of graphics methods.

AutoRedraw	ClipControls	Graphics methods in/out of Paint event	Layering behavior
True	True (default)	Paint event ignored	Normal layering.
True	False	Paint event ignored	Normal layering. Forms with many controls that do not overlap may paint faster because no clipping region is calculated or created.
False (default)	True (default)	In	Normal layering.
False	True	Out	Nongraphical controls in front. Graphics methods and graphical controls appear mixed in the middle and back layers. Not recommended.
False	False	In	Normal layering, affecting only pixels that were previously covered or that appear when resizing a form.
False	False	Out	Graphics methods and all controls appear mixed in the three layers. Not recommended.

The Effects of AutoRedraw

Setting AutoRedraw to True always produces normal layering. While using AutoRedraw is the easiest way to layer graphics, applications with large forms may suffer from reduced performance due to the memory demands of AutoRedraw.

The Effects of ClipControls

When AutoRedraw is True, the setting of ClipControls has no effect on how graphics layer on a form or in a container. But ClipControls can affect how fast the form displays. When ClipControls is False, the application doesn't create a clipping region. Not having to calculate or paint to avoid holes in a clipping region may cause the form to display faster.

Also, when AutoRedraw and ClipControls are both False, the application repaints only the pixels of a form or container that are exposed by:

- Covering the form or container with another window and then moving the window away.
- Resizing the form or container.

The Effects of the Paint Event

When AutoRedraw is False, the best place to use graphics methods is within the Paint event of the form or container. Confining graphics methods to the Paint event causes those methods to paint in a predictable sequence.

Using graphics methods outside a Paint event when AutoRedraw is False can produce unstable graphics. Each time the output of a graphics method appears on the form or container, it may cover any controls or graphics methods already there (if ClipControls is False). When an application uses more than a few graphics methods to create visual effects, managing the resulting output can be extremely difficult unless the methods are all confined to the Paint event.

Moving Controls Dynamically

With Visual Basic, one of the easiest effects to achieve is moving a control at run time. You can either directly change the properties that define the position of a control or use the Move method.

Using the Left and Top Properties

The Left property is the distance between the upper-left corner of the control and the left side of the form. The Top property is the distance between the upper-left corner of the control and the top of the form. Figure 12.10 shows the Left and Top properties of a control.

Figure 12.10 The Left and Top properties

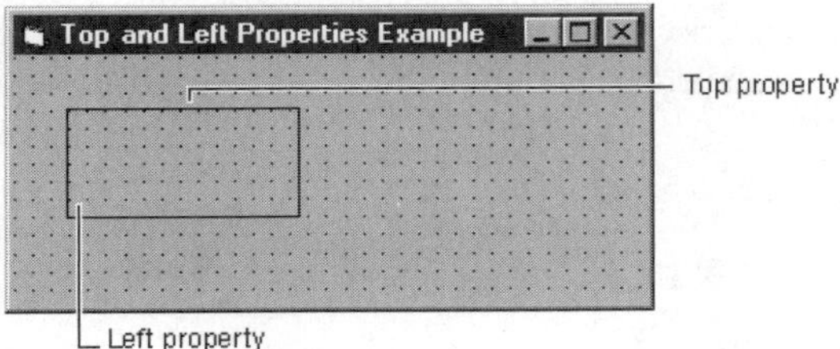

You can move a control by changing the settings of its Left and Top properties with statements such as these:

```
txtField1.Left = txtField1.Left + 200
txtField1.Top = txtField1.Top - 300
```

Moving a Line Control

As mentioned previously, line controls don't have Left or Top properties. Instead, you use special properties to control the position of line controls on a form. The following table lists these properties and how they determine the position of a line control.

Property	Description
X1	The x-coordinate of the start of the line. The coordinate is given in current scale units. The start of the line is the end created when you start drawing.
Y1	The y-coordinate of the start of the line.
X2	The x-coordinate of the end of the line. The end of the line is the end created when you stop drawing.
Y2	The y-coordinate of the end of the line.

The Jumpy Line demo of the Blanker application randomly changes the position of a line control on the DemoForm using these statements:

```
' Set random X position for 1st line end.
linLineCtl.X1 = Int(DemoForm.Width * Rnd)
' Set random Y position for 1st line end.
linLineCtl.Y1 = Int(DemoForm.Height * Rnd)
' Set random X position for 2nd line end.
linLineCtl.X2 = Int(DemoForm.Width * Rnd)
' Set random Y position for 2nd line end.
linLineCtl.Y2 = Int(DemoForm.Height * Rnd)
' Clear stray pixels from moving line.
Cls
' Pause display briefly before next move.
Delay
```

Using the Move Method

Changing the Left and Top or X and Y properties produces a jerky effect as the control first moves horizontally and then vertically. The Move method produces a smoother diagonal movement.

The syntax for the Move method is:

[*object*.]**Move** *left* [, *top*[, *width*[, *height*]]]

The *object* is the form or control to be moved. If *object* is omitted, the current form moves. The *left* and *top* arguments are the new settings for the Left and Top properties of *object*, while *width* and *height* are new settings for its Width and Height properties. Only *left* is required, but to specify other arguments, you must include all arguments that appear in the argument list before the argument you want to specify.

Absolute Movement

Absolute movement occurs when you move an object to specific coordinates in its container. The following statement uses absolute movement to move a control named txtField1 to the coordinates (100, 200):

```
txtField1.Move 100, 200
```

Relative Movement

Relative movement occurs when you move an object by specifying the distance it should move from its current position. The following statement uses relative movement to move txtField1 to a position 100 twips down and to the right of its current position:

```
txtField1.Move txtField1.Left + 100, txtField1.Top _
   + 100
```

This section shows control movement in the Blanker sample application. The Rebound demo moves a picture box diagonally around the form, so the picture box appears to "bounce" off the sides of the form. This demo uses a picture box instead of an image control because the image control flickers as the movement causes it to repaint.

Figure 12.11 shows the main form of the Blanker application (DemoForm) and the picture box used in this example.

Figure 12.11 Picture box (picBall) in the Blanker application

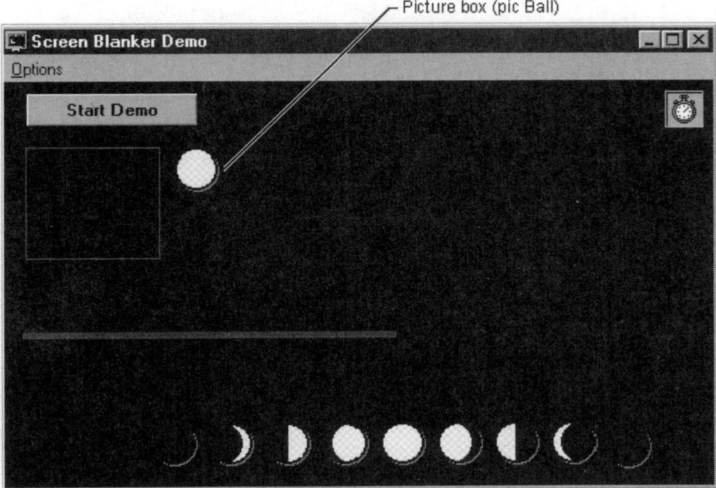

The name of the picture box is picBall. This control begins moving around the form after you choose the Rebound command from the Options menu and then click the Start Demo button. The event procedure for this command button then calls the CtlMoveDemo procedure.

The CtlMoveDemo procedure randomly selects a starting direction from one of these four possibilities:

- Left and up
- Right and up
- Left and down
- Right and down

The picBall picture box moves along the chosen direction until the control reaches one of the four edges of the form. Then the picture box changes direction away from the edge it has reached; the variable Motion controls the direction. For example, when the picture box is moving left and up, this portion of the procedure changes the value of Motion and directs the code to move picBall in another direction.

The following statements come from the CtlMoveDemo procedure in the Blanker application:

```
Select Case Motion
Case 1
   ' If motion is left and up, move the control
   '  20 twips.
   picBall.Move picBall.Left - 20, picBall.Top - 20
```

```
' If control touches left edge, change motion
'  to right and up.
If picBall.Left <= 0 Then
   Motion = 2
' If control touches top edge, change motion to
'  left and down.
ElseIf picBall.Top <= 0 Then
   Motion = 4
End If
```

Notice that the line of code that moves picBall subtracts 20 twips from the current values of its Left and Top properties to establish the new location of the control. This ensures that the control always moves relative to its current position.

The speed and smoothness of the control's movement depend on the number of twips (or other units) used in the Move method. Increasing the number of twips increases the speed but decreases the smoothness of motion. Decreasing the number of twips decreases the speed but improves the smoothness of the control's motion.

For More Information For additional information on the Move method, see "Move Method" in the *Microsoft Visual Basic 6.0 Language Reference.*

Resizing Controls Dynamically

In a Visual Basic application, you can change the size and shape of a picture box, image control, or form at run time, just as you can change its position.

The following properties affect size.

Property	Applies to	Description
Align	Picture boxes and Data controls	If set to align a picture box to the top (1) or bottom (2) of a form, the width of the picture box always equals the width of the inside of the form. If set to align a picture box to the left (3) or the right (4) of a form, the height of the picture box is the height of the inside of the form.
Height	All forms and all controls except timers, menus, and lines	Height of the object expressed in the scale mode of the form (twips by default).
Width	All forms and all controls except timers, menus, and lines	Width of the object expressed in the scale mode of the form (twips by default).
AutoSize	Labels and picture boxes	If True, always causes Visual Basic to adjust the picture box dimensions to the size of the contents.
Stretch	Image controls	If True, the bitmap or metafile stretches to fit the size of the image control. If False, the size of the image control changes to match the size of the bitmap or metafile it contains.

In this example, a command button named cmdGrow grows larger each time the user clicks it:

```
Private Sub cmdGrow_Click ()
   cmdGrow.Height = cmdGrow.Height + 300
   cmdGrow.Width = cmdGrow.Width + 300
End Sub
```

Creating Simple Animation

You can create simple animation by changing pictures at run time. The easiest way to do this is to toggle between two images. You can also use a series of pictures to create animation with several frames. Also, by moving the picture dynamically, you can create more elaborate effects.

Toggling Between Two Pictures

Some icons can be used in pairs. For instance, there are two matching envelope icons in the \Vb\Graphics\Icons subdirectory, one with the envelope unopened and one with the envelope torn open, as shown in Figure 12.12. By switching, or *toggling*, between the two, you can create an animation that shows your user the status of mail.

Figure 12.12 Mail icons

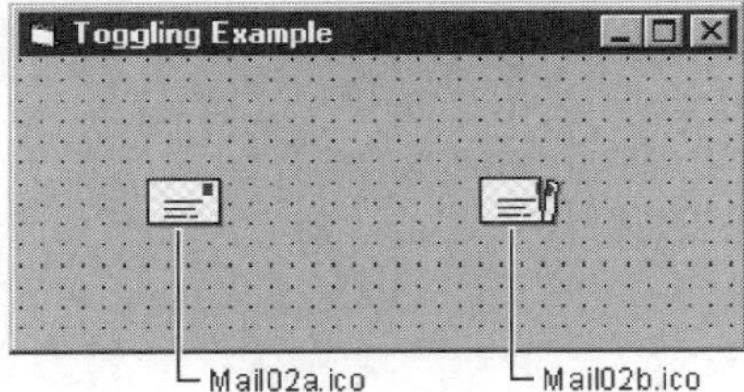

The following statement changes the Picture property of an image control named imgMailStatus to toggle its picture from an unopened envelope to an open envelope.

```
imgMailStatus.Picture = imgMailOpen.Picture
```

Rotating Through Several Pictures

You can also rotate through several pictures to make longer animations. This technique is basically the same as toggling between two pictures, but requires the application to select which bitmap acts as the current image. One way to control the individual pictures in an animation is with a control array.

For More Information See "Creating Arrays of Objects" in Chapter 9, "Programming with Objects," for more information about control arrays.

The Blanker sample application includes an animation that shows a rotating moon. The Spinning Moon demo uses an array of nine image controls to create the animation. To view how the images in a control array work with each other at run time, choose Spinning Moon from the Options menu, and then choose the Start Demo button, which calls the ImageDemo procedure.

Using Graphics Methods

In addition to the graphical controls, Visual Basic provides several methods for creating graphics. The graphics methods, summarized in the following table, apply to forms and picture boxes.

Method	Description
Cls	Clears all graphics and Print output.
Pset	Sets the color of an individual pixel.
Point	Returns the color value of a specified point.
Line	Draws a line, rectangle, or filled-in box.
Circle	Draws a circle, ellipse, or arc.
PaintPicture	Paints graphics at arbitrary locations.

Note The Print method can also be considered a graphics method, because its output is written to the object and is saved in the memory image (if AutoRedraw is on) just like the PSet, Line, and Circle methods. For more information about the Print method, see "Displaying Text on Forms and Picture Boxes," earlier in this chapter.

Advantages of Graphics Methods

The graphics methods work well in situations where using graphical controls require too much work. For example, creating gridlines on a graph would need an array of line controls but only a small amount of code using the Line method. Tracking the position of line controls in an array as the form changes size is more work than simply redrawing lines with the Line method.

When you want a visual effect to appear briefly on a form, such as a streak of color when you display an About dialog, you can write a couple of lines of code for this temporary effect instead of using another control.

Graphics methods offer some visual effects that are not available in the graphical controls. For example, you can only create arcs or paint individual pixels using the graphics methods. Graphics you create with these graphics methods appear on the form in a layer of their own. This layer is below all other controls on a form, so using the graphics methods can work well when you want to create graphics that appear behind everything else in your application.

For More Information See "Layering Graphics with AutoRedraw and ClipControls," earlier in this chapter.

Limitations of Graphics Methods

Creating graphics with the graphics methods takes place in code, which means you have to run the application to see the effect of a graphics method. Graphics methods therefore don't work as well as graphical controls for creating simple design elements of an interface. Changing the appearance of graphical controls at design time is easier than modifying and testing the code for a graphics method.

For More Information For information about creating graphical applications with the mouse events and the Line or Move methods, see "The MouseDown Event," "The MouseMove Event," and "Using Button to Enhance Graphical Mouse Applications" in Chapter 11, "Responding to Mouse and Keyboard Events."

The Fundamentals of Drawing with Graphics Methods

Every graphics method draws output on a form, in a picture box, or to the Printer object. To indicate where you want to draw, precede a graphics method with the name of a form or picture box control. If you omit the object, Visual Basic assumes you want to draw on the form to which the code is attached. For example, the following statements draw a point on:

- A form named MyForm

  ```
  MyForm.PSet (500, 500)
  ```

- A picture box named picPicture1

  ```
  picPicture1.PSet (500, 500)
  ```

- The current form

  ```
  PSet (500, 500)
  ```

Each drawing area has its own coordinate system that determines what units apply to the coordinates. In addition, every drawing area has its own complete set of graphics properties.

For More Information See "Printing from an Application," later in this chapter, for more information about the Printer object. See "Understanding the Coordinate System," earlier in this chapter, for more information about coordinates.

Clearing the Drawing Area

Any time you want to clear a drawing area and start over, use the Cls method. The specified drawing area is repainted in the background color (BackColor):

[*object.*]**Cls**

Using the Cls method without a specified *object* clears the form to which the code is attached.

Plotting Points

Controlling an individual pixel is a simple graphics operation. The PSet method sets the color of a pixel at a specified point:

[*object.*]**PSet** (*x, y*)[, *color*]

The x and y arguments are single precision, so they can take either integer or fractional input. The input can be any numeric expression, including variables.

If you don't include the *color* argument, PSet sets a pixel to the foreground color (ForeColor). For example, the following statements set various points on the current form (the form to which the code is attached), MyForm, and picPicture1:

```
PSet (300, 100)
PSet (10.75, 50.33)
MyForm.PSet (230, 1000)
picPicture1.PSet (1.5, 3.2)
```

Adding a *color* argument gives you more control:

```
' Set 50, 75 to bright blue.
PSet (50, 75), RGB(0, 0, 255)
```

The Blanker application plots points with randomly selected colors to create the Confetti demo. The PSetDemo procedure creates the confetti:

```
Sub PSetDemo ()
   ' Set Red to random value.
   R = 255 * Rnd
   ' Set Green to random value.
   G = 255 * Rnd
   ' Set Blue to random value.
   B = 255 * Rnd
   ' Set horizontal position.
   XPos = Rnd * ScaleWidth
   ' Set vertical position.
   YPos = Rnd * ScaleHeight
   ' Plot point with random color.
   PSet (XPos, YPos), RGB(R, G, B)
End Sub
```

The resulting confetti display is shown in Figure 12.13.

Figure 12.13 Confetti display in the Blanker application

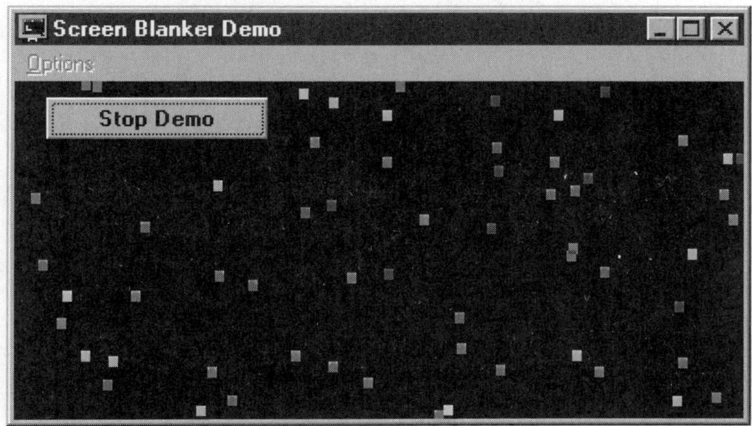

To "erase" a point, set it to the background color:

```
PSet (50, 75), BackColor
```

As described in the next section, "Drawing Lines and Shapes," you can precede the (*x, y*) coordinates by Step, which makes the point relative to the last location drawn.

The Point method is closely related to the PSet method, but it returns the color value at a particular location:

```
PointColor = Point (500, 500)
```

For More Information For more information, see "PSet Method" and "Point Method" in the *Microsoft Visual Basic 6.0 Language Reference.*

Drawing Lines and Shapes

Although clearing the drawing area and plotting individual points can be useful, the most interesting graphics methods draw complete lines and shapes.

Drawing Lines

To draw a line between two coordinates, use the simple form of the Line method, which has this syntax:

[*object.*]**Line** [(*x1*, *y1*)]–(*x2*, *y2*)[, *color*]

Object is optional; if omitted, the method draws on the form to which the code is attached (the current form). The first pair of coordinates is also optional. As with all coordinate values, the *x* and *y* arguments can be either integer or fractional numbers. For example, this statement draws a slanted line on a form.

```
Line (500, 500)-(2000, 2000)
```

Visual Basic draws a line that includes the first end point, but not the last end point. This behavior is useful when drawing a closed figure from point to point. To draw the last point, use this syntax:

PSet [Step] (0, 0)[, *color*]

The first pair of coordinates (*x1, y1*) is optional. If you omit these coordinates, Visual Basic uses the object's current x, y location (drawing coordinates) as the end point. The current location can be specified with the CurrentX and CurrentY properties, but otherwise it is equal to the last point drawn by a previous graphics or Print method. If you haven't previously used a graphics or Print method or set CurrentX and CurrentY, the default location is the object's upper-left corner.

For example, the following statements draw a triangle by connecting three points.

```
' Set x-coordinate of starting point.
CurrentX = 1500
' Set y-coordinate of starting point.
CurrentY = 500
' Draw line down and right of starting point.
Line -(3000, 2000)
' Draw line to the left of current point.
Line -(1500, 2000)
' Draw line up and right to starting point.
Line -(1500, 500)
```

The results are shown in Figure 12.14.

Figure 12.14 A triangle drawn with the Line method

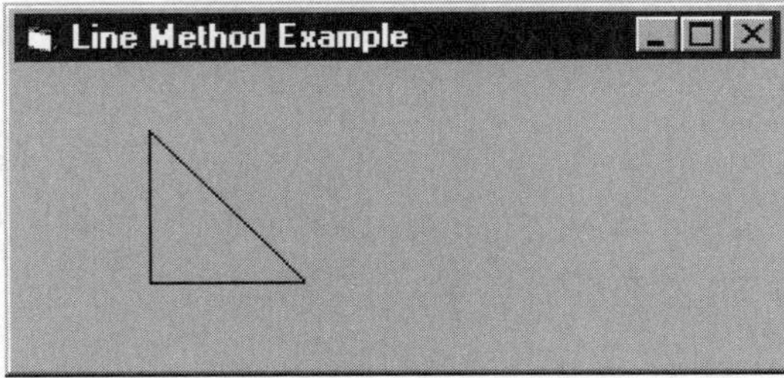

The Blanker application uses the Line method to create interesting patterns. To view this, from the Options menu, choose Crossfire, and then choose the Start Demo button.

The Step Keyword

The PSet, Line, and Circle methods specify one or more points using this syntax:

(*x*, *y*)

You can precede each of these points with the Step keyword, specifying that the location of the point is relative to the last point drawn. Visual Basic adds the x and y values to the values of the last point drawn. For example, the statement:

```
Line (100, 200)-(150, 250)
```

is equivalent to:

```
Line (100, 200)-Step(50, 50)
```

In many situations, the Step keyword saves you from having to constantly keep track of the last point drawn. Often you may be more interested in the relative position of two points than their absolute position.

Using the Color Argument

To vary the color of the line, use the optional *color* argument with graphics methods. For example, this statement draws a dark blue line:

```
Line (500, 500)-(2000, 2000), RGB(0, 0, 255)
```

If you omit the *color* argument, the ForeColor property for the object where the line is being drawn determines its color.

Drawing Boxes

You can draw and fill boxes using the Line method. The following example draws a box with an upper-left corner at (500, 500) and measuring 1,000 twips on each side:

```
Line (500, 500)-Step(1000, 0)
Line -Step(0, 1000)
Line -Step(-1000, 0)
Line -Step(0, -1000)
```

However, Visual Basic provides a much simpler way to draw a box. When you use the B option with the Line method, Visual Basic draws a rectangle, treating the specified points as opposite corners of the rectangle. Thus, you could replace the four statements of the previous example with the following:

```
Line (500, 500)-Step(1000, 1000), , B
```

Note that two commas are required before B, to indicate the color argument was skipped. The syntax of the Line method is covered in "Drawing Lines and Shapes," earlier in this chapter.

FillStyle and FillColor

As long as you do not change the setting of the FillStyle property, the box appears empty. (The box does get filled with the default FillStyle and settings, but FillStyle defaults to 1-Transparent.) You can change the FillStyle property to any of the settings listed in the following table.

Setting	Description
0	Solid. Fills in box with the color set for the FillColor property.
1	Transparent (the default). Graphical object appears empty, no matter what color is used.
2	Horizontal lines.
3	Vertical lines.
4	Upward diagonal lines.
5	Downward diagonal lines.
6	Crosshatch.
7	Diagonal crosshatch.

Thus, setting FillStyle to 0 fills the box solidly with the color set for the FillColor property.

Another way to fill the box is to specify **F** after the **B**. (Note that **F** cannot be used without **B**.) When you use the **F** option, the Line method ignores FillColor and FillStyle. The box is always filled solid when you use the **F** option. The following statement fills the box with a solid pattern, using the ForeColor property:

```
Line (500, 500)-Step(1000, 1000), , BF
```

The result is shown in Figure 12.15.

Figure 12.15 A box filled with a solid pattern

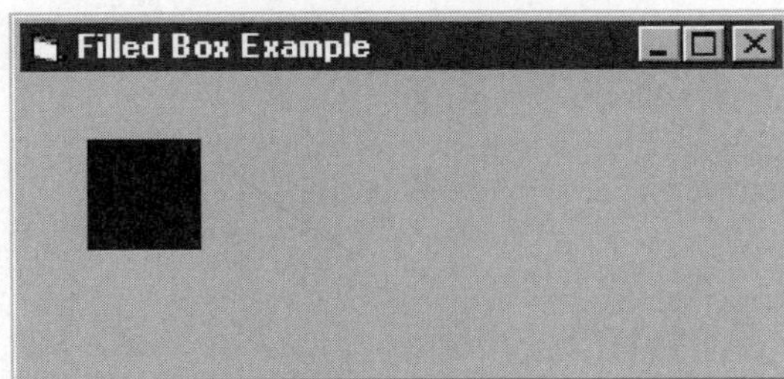

Drawing Circles

The Circle method draws a variety of circular and elliptical (oval) shapes. In addition, Circle draws arcs (segments of circles) and pie-shaped wedges. You can produce many kinds of curved lines using variations of the Circle method.

To draw a circle, Visual Basic needs the location of a circle's center and the length of its radius. The syntax for a perfect circle is:

[*object.*]**Circle** [**Step**](*x, y*), *radius*[, *color*]

The brackets indicate that both *object* and the Step keyword are optional. If you don't specify *object*, the current form is assumed. The x and y arguments are the coordinates of the center, and *radius* is the radius of the circle. For example, this statement draws a circle with a center at (1200, 1000) and radius of 750:

```
Circle (1200, 1000), 750
```

The exact effect of this statement depends on the size and coordinate system of the form. Because the size of the form is unknown, you don't know if the circle will be visible. Using the drawing area's scale properties puts the center of the circle at the center of the form:

```
Circle ((ScaleWidth + ScaleLeft) / 2, (ScaleHeight + _
   ScaleTop) / 2), ScaleWidth / 4
```

For now, all you need to know about ScaleWidth and ScaleHeight is that they help position graphics in the center of a form.

For More Information "Changing an Object's Coordinate System," earlier in this chapter, discusses the ScaleWidth and ScaleHeight properties in detail.

> **Note** The radius of the circle is always specified in terms of horizontal units. If your coordinate system uses the same horizontal and vertical units (which it does by default), you can ignore this fact. However, if you use a custom scale, horizontal and vertical units may correspond to different distances. In the preceding examples, the radius is specified in horizontal units, and the actual height of the circle is guaranteed to be equal to its actual width.

The Blanker application creates circles as part of the Rainbow Rug demo. This demo draws a series of dashed line circles around the center of the form. In time the circles resemble a woven circular rug. The CircleDemo procedure creates the circles in the Rainbow Rug demo with the following statements:

```
Sub CircleDemo ()
   Dim Radius
' Set Red to a random value.
   R = 255 * Rnd
' Set Green to a random value.
   G = 255 * Rnd
```

```
' Set Blue to a random value.
   B = 255 * Rnd
' Set x-coordinate in middle of form.
   XPos = ScaleWidth / 2
' Set y-coordinate in middle of form.
   YPos = ScaleHeight / 2
   ' Set radius between 0 & 50% of form height.
   Radius = ((YPos * 0.9) + 1) * Rnd
   ' Draw the circle using a random color.
   Circle (XPos, YPos), Radius, RGB(R, G, B)
End Sub
```

The results of the Rainbow Rug demo are shown in Figure 12.16.

Figure 12.16 The Rainbow Rug demo in the Blanker application

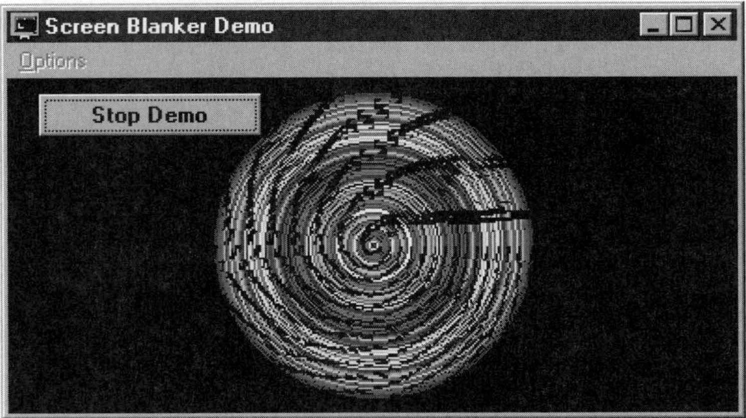

Drawing Arcs

To draw arcs with the Circle method, you need to give angle arguments in radians to define the *start* and the *end* of the arc. The syntax for drawing an arc is:

[*object.*]**Circle** [**Step**](*x*, *y*), *radius*, [*color*], *start*, *end*[, *aspect*]

If the *start* or *end* argument is negative, Visual Basic draws a line connecting the center of the circle to the negative end point. For example, the following procedure draws a pie with a slice removed.

```
Private Sub Form_Click ()
   Const PI = 3.14159265
   Circle (3500, 1500), 1000, , -PI / 2, -PI / 3
End Sub
```

> **Note** The formula for converting from degrees to radians is to multiply degrees by Pi/180.

Drawing Ellipses

The aspect ratio of a circle controls whether or not it appears perfectly round (a circle) or elongated (an ellipse). The complete syntax for the Circle method is:

[*object*.]**Circle** [**Step**](*x*, *y*), *radius*, [*color*], [*start*], [*end*] [, *aspect*]

The *start* and *end* arguments are optional, but the commas are necessary if you want to skip arguments. For example, if you include the *radius* and *aspect* arguments, but *no color, start*, or *end* argument, you must add four successive commas to indicate that you're skipping the three arguments:

```
Circle (1000, 1000), 500, , , , 2
```

The *aspect* argument specifies the ratio of the vertical to horizontal dimensions. Here, *aspect* is a positive floating-point number. This means you can specify integer or fractional expressions, but not negative values. Large values for *aspect* produce ellipses stretched out along the vertical axis, while small values for *aspect* produce ellipses stretched out along the horizontal axis. Since an ellipse has two radii — one horizontal x-radius and one vertical y-radius — Visual Basic applies the single argument *radius* in a Circle statement to the longer axis. If *aspect* is less than one, *radius* is the x-radius; if *aspect* is greater than or equal to one, *radius* is the y-radius.

> **Note** The *aspect* argument always specifies the ratio between the vertical and horizontal dimensions in terms of true physical distance. To ensure that this happens (even when you use a custom scale), the radius is specified in terms of horizontal units.

The following procedure illustrates how different *aspect* values determine whether Circle uses the *radius* argument as the x-radius or the y-radius of an ellipse:

```
Private Sub Form_Click ()
' Draw solid ellipse.
   FillStyle = 0
   Circle (600, 1000), 800, , , , 3
' Draw empty ellipse.
   FillStyle = 1
   Circle (1800, 1000), 800, , , , 1 / 3
End Sub
```

The output is shown in Figure 12.17.

Figure 12.17 Ellipses drawn with the Circle method

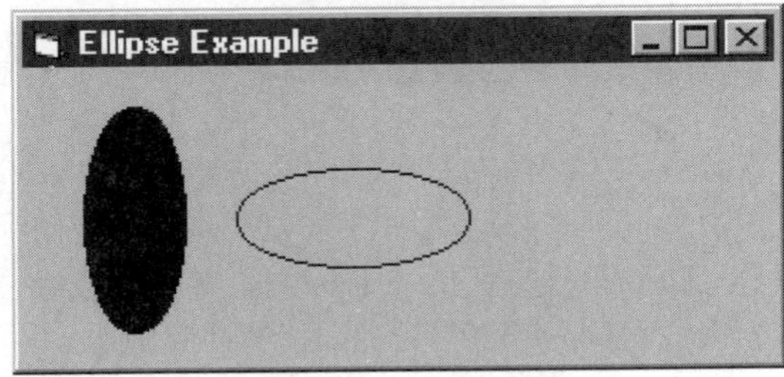

For More Information For more information about drawing circles and arcs, see "Drawing Circles" earlier in this chapter.

Painting Graphics at Arbitrary Locations

You can paint graphics at arbitrary locations on a form, on a picture box, and to the Printer object using the PaintPicture method. The syntax for the PaintPicture method is:

[*object.*]**PaintPicture** *pic*, *destX*, *destY*[, *destWidth*[, *destHeight*[, *srcX* _

[, *srcY*[, *srcWidth*[, *srcHeight*[, *Op*]]]]]]]

The destination *object* is the form, picture box, or Printer object where the *pic* picture is rendered. If *object* is omitted, the current form is assumed. The *pic* argument must be a Picture object, as from the Picture property of a form or control.

The *destX* and *destY* arguments are the horizontal and vertical locations where the picture will be rendered in the ScaleMode of *object*. The *destWidth* and *destHeight* arguments are optional and set the width and height with which the picture will be rendered in the destination *object*.

The *srcX* and *srcY* arguments are optional and define the x-coordinate and y-coordinate of the upper-left corner of a clipping region within *pic*.

The optional *Op* argument defines a raster operation (such as AND or XOR) that is performed on the picture as it is being painted on the destination *object*.

The PaintPicture method can be used in place of the BitBlt Windows API function to perform a wide variety of bit operations while moving a rectangular block of graphics from one position to any other position.

For example, you can use the PaintPicture method to create multiple copies of the same bitmap, and tile them on a form. Using this method is faster than moving picture controls on a form. The following code tiles 100 copies of a picture control and flips every picture horizontally by supplying a negative value for *destWidth*.

```
For i = 0 To 10
   For j = 0 To 10
      Form1.PaintPicture picF.Picture, j * _
         picF.Width, i * picF.Height, _
         picF.Width, -picF.Height
Next j, i
```

For More Information See "PaintPicture Method" in the *Microsoft Visual Basic 6.0 Language Reference*.

Specifying Line Width

The DrawWidth property specifies the width of the line for output from the graphics methods. The BorderWidth property specifies the outline thickness of line and shape controls.

The following procedure draws lines of several different widths.

```
Private Sub Form_Click ()
   DrawWidth = 1
   Line (100, 1000)-(3000, 1000)
   DrawWidth = 5
   Line (100, 1500)-(3000, 1500)
   DrawWidth = 8
   Line (100, 2000)-(3000, 2000)
End Sub
```

The results are shown in Figure 12.18.

Figure 12.18 The effects of changing the DrawWidth property

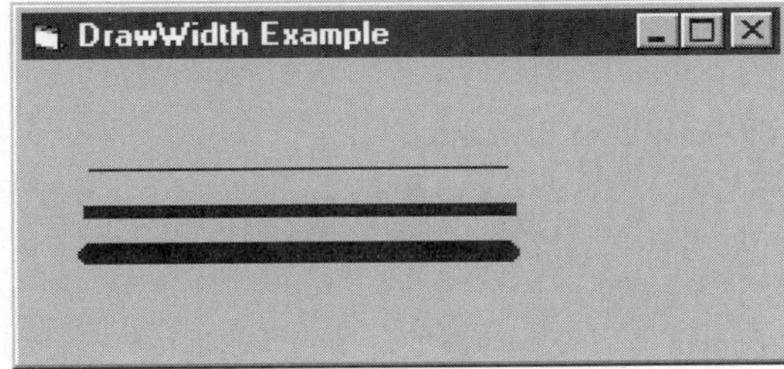

Figure 12.19 shows three shape controls with different BorderWidth values.

Figure 12.19 The effects of changing the BorderWidth property

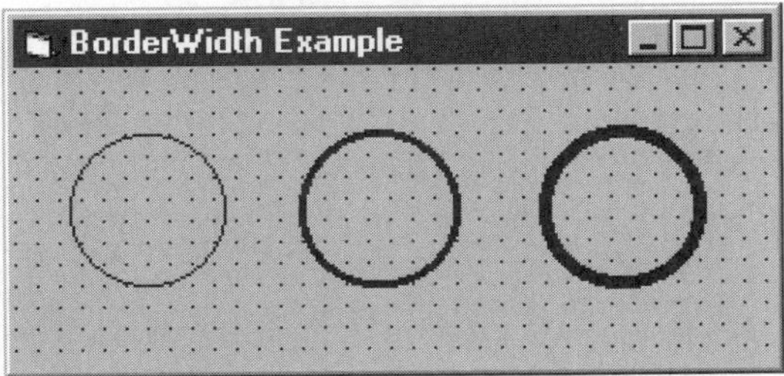

Specifying Solid or Broken Lines

The DrawStyle property specifies whether the lines created with graphics methods are solid or have a broken pattern. The BorderStyle property of a shape control serves the same function as the DrawStyle property, but applies to a variety of objects.

Note The BorderStyle property of a shape control serves a different purpose and uses different settings from the BorderStyle property in other controls and in forms. The BorderStyle property of a shape or line control serves a different purpose and uses different settings from the BorderStyle property on other objects. For shape and line controls, the BorderStyle property works like the DrawStyle property as described in this section. For forms and other controls, the BorderStyle property determines whether the control or form has a border and if so, whether the border is fixed or sizable.

Solid and Inside Solid Styles

The inside solid style (DrawStyle or BorderStyle = 6) is nearly identical to the solid style. They both create a solid line. The difference between these settings becomes apparent when you use a wide line to draw a box or a shape control. In these cases, the solid style draws the line half inside and half outside the box or shape. The inside solid style draws the line entirely inside the box or shape. See "Drawing Boxes," earlier in this chapter, to see how to draw a box.

The following procedure demonstrates all of the supported settings of the DrawStyle property by creating a loop in which the setting goes from 0 to 6, one step at a time. The results are shown in Figure 12.20.

```
Private Sub Form_Click ()
   Dim I As Integer, Y As Long
   For I = 0 To 6
      DrawStyle = I
      Y = (200 * I) + 1000
      Line (200, Y)-(2400, Y)
   Next I
End Sub
```

Figure 12.20 The effects of changing the DrawStyle property

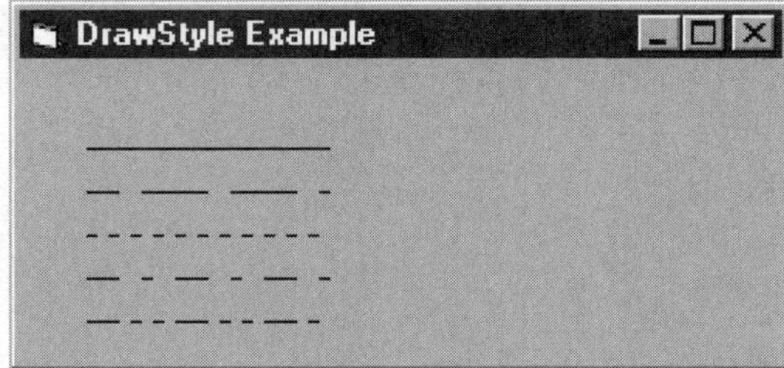

For More Information See "DrawStyle Property" or "BorderStyle Property" in the *Microsoft Visual Basic 6.0 Language Reference*.

Controlling Display Using DrawMode

The DrawMode property determines what happens when you draw one pattern on top of another. Although changing the DrawMode property usually has some effect (especially with color systems), it is often not necessary to use this property when you are drawing on a blank or pure white background, or on a background of undifferentiated color.

You can set DrawMode to a value from 1 to 16. Common settings appear in the following table.

Setting	Description
4	Not Copy Pen. Draws the inverse of the line pattern, regardless of what is already there.
7	Xor Pen. Displays the difference between the line pattern and the existing display, as explained later in this section. Drawing an object twice with this mode restores the background precisely as it was.
11	No operation. In effect, this turns drawing off.
13	Copy Pen (default). Applies the line's pattern, regardless of what is already there.

For More Information See "DrawMode Property" in the *Microsoft Visual Basic 6.0 Language Reference*.

The Xor Pen

A DrawMode setting of 7 is useful for animation. Drawing a line twice restores the existing display precisely as it was before the line was drawn. This makes it possible to create one object that "moves over" a background without corrupting it, because you can restore the background as you go. Most modes are not guaranteed to preserve the old background.

For example, the following code moves a circle every time the mouse is clicked. No matter what pattern was underneath the circle, it gets restored.

```
Private Sub Form_Click ()
   ForeColor = 255 : DrawMode = 7
   Circle (CurrentX, CurrentY), 1000
   CurrentX = CurrentX + 220
   CurrentY = CurrentY + 220
   Circle (CurrentX, CurrentY), 1000
End Sub
```

The Xor Pen draw mode (and most of the other DrawMode settings) works by comparing each individual pixel in the draw pattern (called the "Pen") and the corresponding pixel in the existing area (called the "Destination"). On monochrome systems, the pixel is turned either on or off, and Visual Basic performs a simple logical comparison: It turns a pixel on if either the Pen or Destination pixel is on, but not if both are on.

In color systems, each pixel is assigned a color value. For DrawMode settings such as Xor Pen, Visual Basic compares each corresponding pair of pixels in the Pen and Destination and performs a binary (bitwise) comparison. The result determines the color value of the resulting pixel, as shown in Figure 12.21.

Figure 12.21 Using the Xor Pen to set the binary value of a pixel in a line

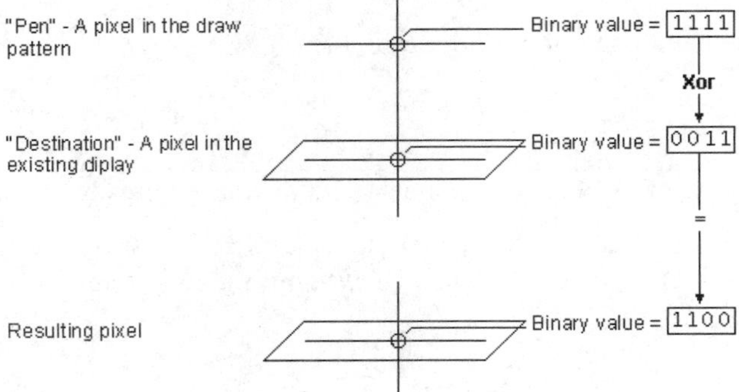

Creating Graphics When a Form Loads

When creating graphics that appear on a form when it loads, consider placing the graphics methods in the Form_Paint event. Form_Paint graphics will get repainted automatically in every paint event. If you place graphics in the Form_Load event, set the AutoRedraw property on the form to True. In this case, Form_Load should show the form, then draw the graphics. Remember, forms are not visible during the Form_Load event. Because Visual Basic does not process graphics methods on a form that is not visible, graphics methods in the Form_Load event are ignored unless AutoRedraw is set to True.

Working with Color

Visual Basic uses a consistent system for all color properties and graphics methods. A color is represented by a Long integer, and this value has the same meaning in all contexts that specify a color.

Specifying Colors at Run Time

There are four ways to specify a color value at run time:

- Use the RGB function.
- Use the QBColor function to choose one of 16 Microsoft QuickBasic colors.
- Use one of the intrinsic constants listed in the Object Browser.
- Enter a color value directly.

This section discusses how to use the RGB and QBColor functions as simple ways to specify color. See "Using Color Properties" later in this chapter for information on using constants to define color or directly entering color values.

Using the RGB Function

You can use the RGB function to specify any color.

To use the RGB function to specify a color

1. Assign each of the three primary colors (red, green, and blue) a number from 0 to 255, with 0 denoting the least intensity and 255 the greatest.
2. Give these three numbers as input to the RGB function, using the order red-green-blue.
3. Assign the result to the color property or color argument.

Every visible color can be produced by combining one or more of the three primary colors. For example:

```
' Set background to green.
Form1.BackColor = RGB(0, 128, 0)
' Set background to yellow.
Form2.BackColor = RGB(255, 255, 0)
' Set point to dark blue.
PSet (100, 100), RGB(0, 0, 64)
```

For More Information For information on the RGB function, see "RGB Function" in the *Microsoft Visual Basic 6.0 Language Reference*.

Using Color Properties

Many of the controls in Visual Basic have properties that determine the colors used to display the control. Keep in mind that some of these properties also apply to controls that aren't graphical. The following table describes the color properties.

Property	Description
BackColor	Sets the background color of the form or control used for drawing. If you change the BackColor property after using graphics methods to draw, the graphics are erased by the new background color.
ForeColor	Sets the color used by graphics methods to create text or graphics in a form or control. Changing ForeColor does not affect text or graphics already created.
BorderColor	Sets the color of the border of a shape control.
FillColor	Sets the color that fills circles created with the Circle method and boxes created with the Line method.

For More Information For detailed descriptions of these color properties, see "BackColor, ForeColor Properties," "BorderColor Property," and "FillColor Property" in the *Microsoft Visual Basic 6.0 Language Reference*.

Defining Colors

The color properties can use any of several methods to define the color value. The RGB function described in "Working with Color," earlier in this chapter, is one way to define colors. This section discusses two more ways to define colors:

- Using defined constants
- Using direct color settings

Using Defined Constants

You don't need to understand how color values are generated if you use the intrinsic constants listed in the Object Browser. In addition, intrinsic constants do not need to be declared. For example, you can use the constant vbRed whenever you want to specify red as a color argument or color property setting:

```
BackColor = vbRed
```

Using Direct Color Settings

Using the RGB function or the intrinsic constants to define color are indirect methods. They are indirect because Visual Basic interprets them into the single approach it uses to represent color. If you understand how colors are represented in Visual Basic, you can assign numbers to color properties and arguments that specify color directly. In most cases, it's much easier to enter these numbers in hexadecimal.

The valid range for a normal RGB color is 0 to 16,777,215 (&HFFFFFF&). Each color setting (property or argument) is a 4-byte integer. The high byte of a number in this range equals 0. The lower 3 bytes, from least to most significant byte, determine the amount of red, green, and blue, respectively. The red, green, and blue components are each represented by a number between 0 and 255 (&HFF).

Consequently, you can specify a color as a hexadecimal number using this syntax:

```
&HBBGGRR&
```

The *BB* specifies the amount of blue, *GG* the amount of green, and *RR* the amount of red. Each of these fragments is a two-digit hexadecimal number from 00 to FF. The median value is 80. Thus, the following number specifies gray, which has the median amount of all three colors:

```
&H808080&
```

Setting the most significant bit to 1 changes the meaning of the color value: It no longer represents an RGB color, but an environment-wide color specified through the Windows Control Panel. The values that correspond to these system-wide colors range from &H80000000 to &H80000015.

Note Although you can specify over 16 million different colors, not all systems are capable of displaying them accurately. For more information on how Windows represents colors, see "Working with 256 Colors," later in this chapter.

Using System Colors

When setting the colors of controls or forms in your application, you can use colors specified by the operating system instead of specific color values. If you specify system colors, when users of your application change the values of system colors on their computers, your application automatically reflects the user-specified color values.

Each system color has both a defined constant and a direct color setting. The high byte of direct color settings for system colors differs from those of normal RGB colors. For RGB colors, the high byte equals 0 whereas for system colors the high byte equals 8. The rest of the number refers to a particular system color. For example, the hexadecimal number used to represent the color of an active window caption is &H80000002&.

When you select color properties at design time with the Properties window, selecting the System tab lets you choose system settings, which are automatically converted into the hexadecimal value. You can also find the defined constants for system colors in the Object Browser.

Working with 256 Colors

Visual Basic supports 256 colors on systems with video adapters and display drivers that handle 256 or more colors. The ability to display 256 simultaneous colors is particularly valuable in multimedia applications or applications that need to display near-photographic-quality images.

You can display 256-color images and define up to 256 colors for graphics methods in:

- Forms
- Picture boxes
- Image controls (display images only)

Note Support for 256 colors does not apply to Windows metafiles. Visual Basic displays metafiles using the default palette of 16 VGA colors.

Color Palettes

Color palettes provide the basis for 256-color support in Visual Basic applications. In discussing palettes, it's important to understand the relationship between different palette types. The *hardware palette* contains 256 entries defining the actual RGB values that will be displayed on screen. The *system halftone palette* is a predefined set of 256 RGB values made available by Windows itself. A *logical palette* is a set of up to 256 RGB values contained within a bitmap or other image.

Windows can draw using the 256 colors in the hardware palette. Twenty of these 256 colors, called *static colors*, are reserved by the system and cannot be changed by an application. Static colors include the 16 colors in the default VGA palette (the same as the colors defined by Visual Basic's QBColor function), plus four additional shades of gray. The system halftone palette always contains these static colors.

The foreground window (the window with focus) determines the 236 nonstatic colors in the hardware palette. Each time the hardware palette is changed, all background windows are redrawn using these colors. If the colors in a background window's logical palette don't perfectly match those currently in the hardware palette, Windows will assign the closest match.

Displaying 256-Color Images

Forms, picture boxes, and image controls automatically display images in 256 colors if the user's display hardware and software can support that many colors on screen. If the user's system supports fewer colors than the image, then Visual Basic will map all colors to the closest available.

On true-color (16-million color) displays, Visual Basic always uses the correct color. On monochrome or 16-color displays, Visual Basic will dither background colors and colors set with the FillColor property. *Dithering* is a process used to simulate colors not available from the video adapter and display driver.

Drawing with Color Palettes

With 256-color video drivers, you can use up to 256 colors with graphics methods. By default, the 256 colors available in Visual Basic are those in the system halftone palette. Although you can specify an exact color using the RGB function, the actual color displayed will be the closest match from the halftone palette, as shown in Figure 12.22.

Figure 12.22 Color matching from a specified color to the display

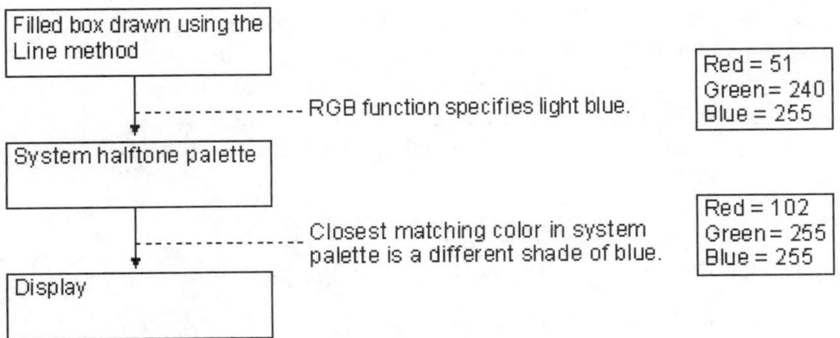

Although the default palette for Visual Basic is the system halftone palette, you can also control the display of colors with the PaletteMode and Palette properties of forms, user controls, and user documents. In this case, the color match is much the same, except that colors will be matched to the closest color in the hardware palette.

Managing Multiple Color Palettes

When you work with color palettes, keep in mind that many displays can display only 256 colors simultaneously on the screen.

This limitation becomes important when you use more than one color palette in your application. For example, on a single form, you might display a 256-color bitmap in an image control while displaying a second image in a picture box. If the logical palettes of these two images don't contain exactly the same 256 colors, Windows must decide which logical palette places its colors in the hardware palette first. Remember: The hardware palette determines what actually appears on the screen.

A similar situation occurs when your Visual Basic application has two or more forms with differing logical palettes. As each form receives focus, its logical palette controls the hardware palette. This can often result in a less than optimal display on 256-color systems. As a Visual Basic programmer, you can control the hardware palette by using the PaletteMode property.

The PaletteMode Property

When designing applications that may run on 256-color systems, you can control the way that Windows chooses the display colors by setting the PaletteMode property of a form, user control, or user document. (User controls and user documents are only available in the Professional and Enterprise editions.) All controls contained on the form, user control, or user document will be displayed based on the PaletteMode. The following table shows the available PaletteMode settings:

Mode	Constant	Applies to
Halftone	vbPaletteModeHalftone	Forms, User Controls, User Documents
UseZOrder	vbPaletteModeUseZOrder	Forms, User Controls, User Documents
Custom	vbPaletteModeCustom	Forms, User Controls, User Documents
Container	vbPaletteModeContainer	User Controls
None	vbPaletteModeNone	User Controls
Object	vbPaletteModeObject	ActiveX designers that contain a palette

The PaletteMode property only applies to 256-color displays. On high-color or true-color displays, color selection is handled by the video driver using a palette of 32,000 or 16 million colors respectively. Even if you're programming on a system with a high-color or true-color display, you still may want to set the PaletteMode, because many of your users may be using 256-color displays.

The PaletteMode property can be set at design time through the Properties window, or changed at run time via code. The Palettes sample application demonstrates the effects of displaying images with different palettes using several different PaletteMode settings.

Note For previous versions of Visual Basic, PaletteMode corresponded to UseZOrder.

Halftone PaletteMode

The default mode for forms and user documents is Halftone. In this mode, any controls, images contained on the form, or graphics methods draw using the system halftone palette.

Halftone mode is a good choice in most cases because it provides a compromise between the images in your form, and colors used in other forms or images. It may, however, result in a degradation of quality for some images. For example, an image with a palette containing 256 shades of gray may lose detail or display unexpected traces of other colors.

UseZOrder PaletteMode

Z-order is a relative ordering that determines how controls overlap each other on a form. When the PaletteMode of the form with the focus is set to UseZOrder, the palette of the topmost control always has precedence. This means that each time a new control becomes topmost (for instance, when you load a new image into a picture box), the hardware palette will be remapped. This will often cause a side effect known as palette flash: The display appears to flash as the new colors are displayed, both in the current form and in any other visible forms or applications.

Although the UseZOrder setting provides the most accurate color rendition, it comes at the expense of speed. Additionally, this method can cause the background color of the form or of controls that have no image to appear dithered. Setting the PaletteMode to UseZOrder is the best choice when accurate display of the topmost image outweighs the annoyance of palette flash, or when you need to maintain backward compatibility with earlier versions of Visual Basic.

Custom PaletteMode

If you need more precise control over the actual display of colors, you can use a 256-color image to define a custom palette. To do this, assign a 256-color image (.bmp, .cur, .ico, .dib, or .gif) to the Palette property of the form and set the PaletteMode property to Custom. The bitmap doesn't have to be very large; even a single pixel can define up to 256 colors for the form or picture box. This is because the logical palette of a bitmap can list up to 256 colors, regardless of whether all those colors appear in the bitmap.

As with the default method, colors that you define using the RGB function must also exist in the bitmap. If the color doesn't match, it will be mapped to the closest match in the logical palette of the bitmap assigned to the Palette property.

To set the Custom PaletteMode at run time, add the following code to the Form_Load event (assuming that the image containing your chosen palette has been assigned to a Image control named Image1):

```
' Assign the palette from Image1 to the form.
Form1.Palette = Image1.Picture
' Use the Custom mode.
Form1.PaletteMode = vbPaletteModeCustom
```

Alternatively, you can use the Picture object to achieve the same effect without the extra Image control:

```
Dim objPic As Picture
Set objPic = LoadPicture(App.Path & "\Pastel.bmp")
' Assign picture object's palette to the form.
Form1.Palette = objPic
' Use the Custom mode.
Form1.PaletteMode = vbPaletteModeCustom
```

The Custom PaletteMode is your best choice when you want to maintain a uniform palette throughout your application.

> **Note** Using the Custom PaletteMode can also improve the performance of your application in cases where you aren't using any 256-color graphics. If you set the PaletteMode of a form to Custom and leave the Palette property blank, your form will load faster because no palette matching will occur.

For More Information To learn more about the Picture object, see "Using the Picture Object," later in this chapter.

Other Palette Modes

Two additional PaletteMode settings are available when creating user controls: Container and None. The Container mode maps the palette of the user control and any contained controls to the ambient palette of the container (form or user document) at run time. If the container doesn't supply an ambient palette, the Halftone mode will be invoked. Because you may not know in advance where your user control may be deployed, this mode can prevent your control from conflicting with other palette handling methods.

The None mode does just what you might expect: It eliminates palette handling altogether. When creating a user control that doesn't display images or graphics, setting PaletteMode to None improves performance by eliminating the added overhead of handling palette messages.

Using Relative Palette Colors

When designing for 256 color displays, some colors may appear dithered. This can make text and other graphic elements difficult to read. By specifying a relative palette color, Visual Basic will display the closest undithered approximation of a specified color on 256 color displays while still displaying the exact color at higher color depths.

To force Visual Basic to use the closest solid, rather than dithered, color for a given property, put a 2 in the high order byte of the color property. For example, to force a form's background to be a solid light orange you could use the following code:

```
Private Function PaletteRGB(RGB As Long) As Long
   PaletteRGB = &H02000000 Or RGB
End Function
```

If you set this at design time:

```
Form1.BackColor = &H00C0E0FF&  'dithered light orange
```

And add the following to the Form_Click event:

```
Private Sub Form_Click()
   Form1.BackColor = PaletteRGB(Form1.BackColor)
End Sub
```

At run-time when the form is clicked the backcolor will change to a solid, rather than dithered, shade. It is now using the closest color out of the halftone palette. This effect may not be visible on systems running at a color depth greater than 256 colors.

Using the Picture Object

The Picture object is similar in some respects to the Printer object — you can't see it, but it's useful nonetheless. You could think of the Picture object as a invisible picture box that you can use as a staging area for images. For example, the following code loads a Picture object with a bitmap and uses that bitmap to set the Picture property of a picture box control:

```
Private Sub Command1_Click()
   Dim objPic As Picture
   Set objPic = LoadPicture("Butterfly.bmp")
   Set Picture1.Picture = objPic
End Sub
```

The Picture object supports bitmaps, GIF images, JPEG images, metafiles, and icons.

Using Arrays of Picture Objects

You can also use an array of Picture objects to keep a series of graphics in memory without using a form that contains multiple picture box or image controls. This is convenient for creating animation sequences or other applications where rapid image changes are required. Declare the array at the module level:

```
Dim objPics(1) As Picture
```

Add the following code to the Form_Load event:

```
' Load bitmaps int the Picture object array.
Set objPics(0) = LoadPicture("Butterfly1.bmp")
Set objPics(1) = LoadPicture("Butterfly2.bmp")
```

Then in Timer event you can cycle the images:

```
Static intCount As Integer
If intCount = 0 Then
   intCount = 1
Else
   intCount = 0
End If
' Use the PaintPicture method to display the bitmaps
'  on the form.
PaintPicture objPics(intCount), 0, 0
```

By adding a loop to increment the x and y coordinates, you could easily make the butterfly bitmaps "fly" across the form.

Using the Picture Object Instead of the Windows API

There are lots of things you can do with bitmaps, icons, or metafiles in the Windows API, but the Picture object already does most of them for you. This means that you are better off using the Picture object instead of the Windows API whenever possible. The Picture object also allows you to use .jpg and .gif files, whereas the Windows API does not.

There is no direct relationship between a Picture.Handle and a PictureBox.hDC. The hDC property of the picture box is the handle provided by the operating system to the device context of the picture box control. The Handle property of the Picture object is actually the handle of the GDI object that is contained in the Picture object.

There are now two completely different ways to paint graphics on a window (or blit). You can use BitBlt or StretchBlt on the hDC of an object, or you can use the PaintPicture method on the Picture object or property. If you have an Image control, you can only use PaintPicture because Image controls do not have an hDC.

For More Information For more information about the Windows API, see Part 4, "Accessing DLLs and the Windows API" in the *Microsoft Visual Basic 6.0 Component Tools Guide* volume of the *Microsoft Visual Basic 6.0 Reference Library*.

Printing

Printing is one of the most complex tasks a Windows – based application performs. Good results depend on all parts of the process working together. Poor results can arise from problems in your application, variations in printer drivers, or limited printer capabilities. Although it is a good idea to test your application with commonly used printers and printer drivers, you can't test all the possible combinations users may have.

Printing from your application involves these three components:

- The code in your application that starts the printing process.
- The printer drivers installed on both your system and the systems of users of your application.
- The capabilities of the printers available to users of your application.

The code in your application determines the type and quality of print output available from your application. But the users' printer drivers and printers also impact print quality. This section deals with enabling printing from a Visual Basic application. For information on printing from the Visual Basic development environment, see "Printing Information in the Immediate Window" in Chapter 13, "Debugging Your Code and Handling Errors."

Printing from an Application

Visual Basic provides three techniques for printing text and graphics.

- You can produce the output you want on a form and then print the form using the PrintForm method.
- You can send text and graphics to a printer by setting the default printer to a member of the Printers collection.
- You can send text and graphics to the Printer object and then print them using the NewPage and EndDoc methods.

This section examines the advantages and disadvantages of these three approaches.

Using the PrintForm Method

The PrintForm method sends an image of the specified form to the printer. To print information from your application with PrintForm, you must first display that information on a form and then print that form with the PrintForm method. The syntax is as follows:

[*form*.]**PrintForm**

If you omit the form name, Visual Basic prints the current form. PrintForm prints the entire form, even if part of the form is not visible on the screen. If a form contains graphics, however, the graphics print only if the form's AutoRedraw property is set to True. When printing is complete, PrintForm calls the EndDoc method to clear the printer.

For example, you could send text to a printer by printing it on a form and then calling PrintForm with the following statements:

```
Print "Here is some text."
PrintForm
```

The PrintForm method is by far the easiest way to print from your application. Because it may send information to the printer at the resolution of the user's screen (typically 96 dots per inch), results can be disappointing on printers with much higher resolutions (typically 300 dots per inch for laser printers). The results may vary depending on objects on your form.

For More Information See "PrintForm Method" in the *Microsoft Visual Basic 6.0 Language Reference*.

Using the Printers Collection

The Printers collection is an object that contains all the printers that are available on the operating system. The list of Printers are the same as those available in the Print Setup dialog box or the Windows Control Panel. Each printer in the collection has a unique index for identification. Starting with 0, each printer in the collection can be referenced by its number.

Regardless of which printing method you use, all printed output from a Visual Basic application is directed to the Printer object, which initially represents the default printer specified in the Windows Control Panel. However, you can set the default printer to any one member in the Printers collection.

To select the printer from the collection, use the following syntax:

Set Printer = Printers(*n***)**

The following statements print the device names of all the printers on the operating system to the Immediate window:

```
Private Sub Command1_Click()
Dim x As Printer
   For Each x In Printers
      Debug.Print x.DeviceName
   Next
End Sub
```

> **Note** You cannot create new instances of the Printer object in code, and you cannot directly add or remove printers from the Printers collection. To add or remove printers on your system, use the Windows Control Panel.

Using the Printer Object

The Printer object is a device-independent drawing space that supports the Print, PSet, Line, PaintPicture, and Circle methods to create text and graphics. You use these methods on the Printer object just as you would on a form or picture box. The Printer object also has all the font properties described earlier in this chapter. When you finish placing the information on the Printer object, you use the EndDoc method to send the output to the printer. When applications close, they automatically use the EndDoc method to send any pending information on the Printer object.

The Printer object provides the best print quality across a variety of printers because Windows translates text and graphics from the device-independent drawing space of the Printer object to best match the resolution and abilities of the printer. You can also print multiple-page documents by using the NewPage method on the Printer object.

The main drawback to using the Printer object is the amount of code required to get the best results. Printing bitmaps on the Printer object also takes time and can therefore slow the performance of the application.

Printing with the Printer Object

There are several ways to place text and graphics on the Printer object. To print with the Printer object, do any of the following:

- Assign the specific member of the Printers collection to the Printer object if you want to print to a printer other than the default printer.
- Put text and graphics on the Printer object.
- Print the contents of the Printer object with the NewPage or EndDoc method.

Printer Object Properties

The properties of the Printer object initially match those of the default printer set in the Windows Control Panel. At run time, you can set any of the Printer object properties, which include: PaperSize, Height, Width, Orientation, ColorMode, Duplex, TrackDefault, Zoom, DriverName, DeviceName, Port, Copies, PaperBin, and PrintQuality. For more details and syntax for these methods, see the *Microsoft Visual Basic 6.0 Language Reference*.

If the TrackDefault property is True and you change the default printer in the Windows Control Panel, the Printer object property values will reflect the properties of the new default printer.

You cannot change some properties in the middle of a page once a property has been set. Changes to these properties will only affect subsequent pages. The following statements show how you can print each page using a different print quality:

```
For pageno = 1 To 4
   Printer.PrintQuality = -1 * pageno
   Printer.Print "The quality of this page is"; pageno
   Printer.NewPage
Next
```

Print quality values can range from –4 to –1, or a positive integer corresponding to the print resolution in dots per inch (DPI). For example, the following code would set the printer's resolution to 300 DPI:

```
Printer.PrintQuality = 300
```

For More Information For information on the Printer object properties, see the appropriate property in the *Microsoft Visual Basic 6.0 Language Reference*.

> **Note** The effect of Printer property values depends on the driver supplied by the printer manufacturer. Some property settings may have no effect, or several different property settings may all have the same effect. Settings outside the accepted range may or may not produce an error. For more information on specific drivers, see the manufacturer's documentation.

Scale Properties

The Printer object has these scale properties:

- ScaleMode
- ScaleLeft and ScaleTop
- ScaleWidth and ScaleHeight
- Zoom

The ScaleLeft and ScaleTop properties define the x- and y-coordinates, respectively, of the upper-left corner of a printable page. By changing the values of ScaleLeft and ScaleTop, you can create left and top margins on the printed page. For example, you can use ScaleLeft and ScaleTop to center a printed form (PFrm) on the page using these statements:

```
Printer.ScaleLeft = -((Printer.Width - PFrm.Width) / 2)
Printer.ScaleTop = -((Printer.Height - PFrm.Height) _
   / 2)
```

Many printers support the Zoom property. This property defines the percentage by which output is scaled. The default value of the Zoom property is 100, indicating that output will be printed at 100 percent of its size (actual size). You can use the Zoom property to make the page you print smaller or larger than the actual paper page. For example, setting Zoom to 50 makes your printed page appear half as wide and half as long as the paper page. The following syntax sets the Zoom property to half the size of the default Printer object:

```
Printer.Zoom = 50
```

Positioning Text and Graphics

You can set CurrentX and CurrentY properties for the Printer object, just as you can for forms and picture boxes. With the Printer object, these properties determine where to position output on the current page. The following statements set drawing coordinates to the upper-left corner of the current page:

```
Printer.CurrentX = 0
Printer.CurrentY = 0
```

You can also use the TextHeight and TextWidth methods to position text on the Printer object. For more information on using these text methods, see "Displaying Print Output at a Specific Location," earlier in this chapter.

Printing Forms on the Printer Object

You may want your application to print one or more forms along with information on those forms, especially if the design of the form corresponds to a printed document like an invoice or a time card. For the easiest way to do this, use the PrintForm method. For the best quality on a laser printer use the Print and graphics methods with the Printer object. Keep in mind that using the Printer object takes more planning, because you must recreate the form on the Printer object before you print.

Recreating a form on the Printer object may also require recreating:

- The outline of the form, including title and menu bars.
- The controls and their contents, including text and graphics.
- The output of graphics methods applied directly to the form, including the Print method.

The extent to which you recreate these elements on the Printer object depends on your application and how much of the form you need to print.

Recreating Text and Graphics on a Form

When creating text and graphics on a form using the Print, Line, Circle, PaintPicture, or PSet methods, you may also want a copy of this output to appear on the Printer object. The easiest way to accomplish this is to write a device-independent procedure to recreate the text and graphics.

For example, the following procedure uses the PaintPicture method to print a form or control's Picture property to any output object, such as a printer or another form:

```
Sub PrintAnywhere (Src As Object, Dest As Object)
   Dest.PaintPicture Src.Picture, Dest.Width / 2, _
      Dest.Height / 2
   If Dest Is Printer Then
      Printer.EndDoc
   End If
End Sub
```

You then call this procedure and pass it the source and destination objects:

```
PrintAnywhere MyForm, Printer
PrintAnywhere MyForm, YourForm
```

For More Information For more information, see "Print Method," "Line Method," "Circle Method," "Pset Method," or "PaintPicture Method" in the *Microsoft Visual Basic 6.0 Language Reference*.

Printing Controls on a Form

The Printer object can receive the output of the Print method and the graphics methods (such as the Line or PSet method). But you cannot place controls directly on the Printer object. If your application needs to print controls, you must either write procedures that redraw each type of control you use on the Printer object, or use the PrintForm method.

Printing the Contents of the Printer Object

Once you have placed text and graphics on the Printer object, use the EndDoc method to print the contents. The EndDoc method advances the page and sends all pending output to the spooler. A *spooler* intercepts a print job on its way to the printer and sends it to disk or memory, where the print job is held until the printer is ready for it. For example:

```
Printer.Print "This is the first line of text in _
   a pair."
Printer.Print "This is the second line of text in _
   a pair."
Printer.EndDoc
```

Note Visual Basic automatically calls EndDoc if your application ends without explicitly calling it.

Creating Multiple-Page Documents

When printing longer documents, you can specify in code where you want a new page to begin by using the NewPage method. For example:

```
Printer.Print "This is page 1."
Printer.NewPage
Printer.Print "This is page 2."
Printer.EndDoc
```

Canceling a Print Job

You can terminate the current print job by using the KillDoc method. For example, you can query the user with a dialog box to determine whether to print or terminate a document:

```
Sub PrintOrNot()
   Printer.Print "This is the first line to _
      illustrate KillDoc method"
   Printer.Print "This is the second line to _
      illustrate KillDoc method"
   Printer.Print "This is the third line to _
      illustrate KillDoc method"
```

```
   If vbNo = MsgBox("Print this fine document?", _
         vbYesNo) Then
      Printer.KillDoc
   Else
      Printer.EndDoc
   End If
End Sub
```

If the operating system's Print Manager is handling the print job, the KillDoc method deletes the entire job you sent to the printer. However, if the Print Manager is not controlling the print job, page one may have already been sent to the printer, and will be unaffected by KillDoc. The amount of data sent to the printer varies slightly among printer drivers.

Note You cannot use the KillDoc method to terminate a print job that was initiated with the PrintForm method.

Trapping Printer Errors

Trappable run-time errors may occur while printing. The following table lists some examples that may be reported:

Error number	Error message
396	**Property cannot be set within a page.** This error occurs when the same property is set differently on the same page.
482	**Printer Error.** Visual Basic reports the error whenever the printer driver returns an error code.
483	**Printer driver does not support the property.** This error occurs when attempting to use a property that is not supported by the current printer driver.
484	**Printer driver unavailable.** This error occurs when the WIN.INI printer information is missing or insufficient.

Note Printer errors do not always occur immediately. If a statement causes a printer error, the error may not be raised until execution of the next statement that addresses that printer.

For More Information For a detailed discussion on run-time errors, see Chapter 13, "Debugging Your Code and Handling Errors."

CHAPTER 13

Debugging Your Code and Handling Errors

No matter how carefully crafted your code, errors can (and probably will) occur. Ideally, Visual Basic procedures wouldn't need error-handling code at all. Unfortunately, sometimes files are mistakenly deleted, disk drives run out of space, or network drives disconnect unexpectedly. Such possibilities can cause run-time errors in your code. To handle these errors, you need to add error-handling code to your procedures.

Sometimes errors can also occur within your code; this type of error is commonly referred to as a *bug*. Minor bugs — for example, a cursor that doesn't behave as expected — can be frustrating or inconvenient. More severe bugs can cause an application to stop responding to commands, possibly requiring the user to restart the application, losing whatever work hasn't been saved.

The process of locating and fixing bugs in your application is known as *debugging*. Visual Basic provides several tools to help analyze how your application operates. These debugging tools are particularly useful in locating the source of bugs, but you can also use the tools to experiment with changes to your application or to learn how other applications work.

This chapter shows how to use the debugging tools included in Visual Basic and explains how to handle *run-time errors* — errors that occur while your code is running and that result from attempts to complete an invalid operation.

Contents

- Error Handling with ActiveX Components
- Approaches to Debugging
- Avoiding Bugs
- Design Time, Run Time, and Break Mode
- Using the Debugging Windows
- Using Break Mode
- Running Selected Portions of Your Application
- Monitoring the Call Stack
- Testing Data and Procedures with the Immediate Window
- Special Debugging Considerations
- Tips for Debugging

Sample Application: Errors.vbp

Many of the code samples in this chapter are taken from the Errors.vbp sample application. You'll find this sample application listed in the Samples directory.

How to Handle Errors

Ideally, Visual Basic procedures wouldn't need error-handling code at all. Reality dictates that hardware problems or unanticipated actions by the user can cause run-time errors that halt your code, and there's usually nothing the user can do to resume running the application. Other errors might not interrupt code, but they can cause it to act unpredictably.

For example, the following procedure returns true if the specified file exists and false if it does not, but doesn't contain error-handling code:

```
Function FileExists (filename) As Boolean
   FileExists = (Dir(filename) <> "")
End Function
```

The Dir function returns the first file matching the specified file name (given with or without wildcard characters, drive name, or path); it returns a zero-length string if no matching file is found.

The code appears to cover either of the possible outcomes of the Dir call. However, if the drive letter specified in the argument is not a valid drive, the error "Device unavailable" occurs. If the specified drive is a floppy disk drive, this function will work correctly only if a disk is in the drive and the drive door is closed. If not, Visual Basic presents the error "Disk not ready" and halts execution of your code.

To avoid this situation, you can use the error-handling features in Visual Basic to intercept errors and take corrective action. (Intercepting an error is also known as *trapping* an error.) When an error occurs, Visual Basic sets the various properties of the error object, Err, such as an error number, a description, and so on. You can use the Err object and its properties in an error-handling routine so that your application can respond intelligently to an error situation.

For example, device problems, such as an invalid drive or an empty floppy disk drive, could be handled by the following code:

```
Function FileExists (filename) As Boolean
   Dim Msg As String
   ' Turn on error trapping so error handler responds
   ' if any error is detected.
   On Error GoTo CheckError
      FileExists = (Dir(filename) <> "")
      ' Avoid executing error handler if no error
      ' occurs.
      Exit Function

CheckError:         ' Branch here if error occurs.
   ' Define constants to represent intrinsic Visual
   ' Basic error codes.
   Const mnErrDiskNotReady = 71, _
   mnErrDeviceUnavailable = 68
   ' vbExclamation, vbOK, vbCancel, vbCritical, and
   ' vbOKCancel are constants defined in the VBA type
   ' library.
   If (Err.Number = MnErrDiskNotReady) Then
      Msg = "Put a floppy disk in the drive "
      Msg = Msg & "and close the door."
      ' Display message box with an exclamation mark
      ' icon and with OK and Cancel buttons.
      If MsgBox(Msg, vbExclamation & vbOKCancel) = _
      vbOK Then
         Resume
      Else
         Resume Next
      End If
   ElseIf Err.Number = MnErrDeviceUnavailable Then
      Msg = "This drive or path does not exist: "
      Msg = Msg & filename
      MsgBox Msg, vbExclamation
      Resume Next
   Else
      Msg = "Unexpected error #" & Str(Err.Number)
      Msg = Msg & " occurred: " & Err.Description
      ' Display message box with Stop sign icon and
      ' OK button.
```

```
      MsgBox Msg, vbCritical
      Stop
   End If
   Resume
End Function
```

In this code, the Err object's Number property contains the number associated with the run-time error that occurred; the Description property contains a short description of the error.

When Visual Basic generates the error "Disk not ready," this code presents a message telling the user to choose one of two buttons — OK or Cancel. If the user chooses OK, the Resume statement returns control to the statement at which the error occurred and attempts to re-execute that statement. This succeeds if the user has corrected the problem; otherwise, the program returns to the error handler.

If the user chooses Cancel, the Resume Next statement returns control to the statement following the one at which the error occurred (in this case, the Exit Function statement).

Should the error "Device unavailable" occur, this code presents a message describing the problem. The Resume Next statement then causes the function to continue execution at the statement following the one at which the error occurred.

If an unanticipated error occurs, a short description of the error is displayed and the code halts at the Stop statement.

The application you create can correct an error or prompt the user to change the conditions that caused the error. To do this, use techniques such as those shown in the preceding example. The next section discusses these techniques in detail.

For More Information See "Guidelines for Complex Error Handling" in "Error-Handling Hierarchy," later in this chapter, for an explanation of how to use the Stop statement.

Designing an Error Handler

An *error handler* is a routine for trapping and responding to errors in your application. You'll want to add error handlers to any procedure where you anticipate the possibility of an error (you should assume that any Basic statement can produce an error unless you explicitly know otherwise). The process of designing an error handler involves three steps:

1. Set, or *enable*, an error trap by telling the application where to branch to (which error-handling routine to execute) when an error occurs.

   The On Error statement enables the trap and directs the application to the label marking the beginning of the error-handling routine.

   In the Errors.vpb sample application, the FileExists function contains an error-handling routine named `CheckError`.

2. Write an error-handling routine that responds to all errors you can anticipate. If control actually branches into the trap at some point, the trap is then said to be *active*.

   The `CheckError` routine handles the error using an If...Then...Else statement that responds to the value in the Err object's Number property, which is a numeric code corresponding to a Visual Basic error. In the example, if "Disk not ready" is generated, a message prompts the user to close the drive door. A different message is displayed if the "Device unavailable" error occurs. If any other error is generated, the appropriate description is displayed and the program stops.

3. Exit the error-handling routine.

   In the case of the "Disk not ready" error, the Resume statement makes the code branch back to the statement where the error occurred. Visual Basic then tries to re-execute that statement. If the situation has not changed, then another error occurs and execution branches back to the error-handling routine.

   In the case of the "Device unavailable" error, the Resume Next statement makes the code branch to the statement following the one at which the error occurred.

Details on how to perform these steps are provided in the remainder of this topic. Refer to the FileExists function example as you read through these steps.

Setting the Error Trap

An error trap is enabled when Visual Basic executes the On Error statement, which specifies an error handler. The error trap remains enabled while the procedure containing it is active — that is, until an Exit Sub, Exit Function, Exit Property, End Sub, End Function, or End Property statement is executed for that procedure. While only one error trap can be enabled at any one time in any given procedure, you can create several alternative error traps and enable different ones at different times. You can also disable an error trap by using a special case of the On Error statement — On Error GoTo 0.

To set an error trap that jumps to an error-handling routine, use a On Error GoTo *line* statement, where *line* indicates the label identifying the error-handling code. In the FileExists function example, the label is `CheckError`. (Although the colon is part of the label, it isn't used in the On Error GoTo *line* statement.)

For More Information For more information about disabling error handling, see "Turning Off Error Handling," later in this chapter.

Writing an Error-Handling Routine

The first step in writing an error-handling routine is adding a line label to mark the beginning of the error handling routine. The line label should have a descriptive name and must be followed by a colon. A common convention is to place the error-handling code at the end of the procedure with an Exit Sub, Exit Function, or Exit Property statement immediately before the line label. This allows the procedure to avoid executing the error-handling code if no error occurs.

The body of the error handling routine contains the code that actually handles the error, usually in the form of a Case or If…Then…Else statement. You need to determine which errors are likely to occur and provide a course of action for each, for example, prompting the user to insert a disk in the case of a "Disk not ready" error. An option should always be provided to handle any unanticipated errors by using the Else or Case Else clause — in the case of the FileExists function example, this option warns the user then ends the application.

The Number property of the Err object contains a numeric code representing the most recent run-time error. By using the Err object in combination with the Select Case or If...Then...Else statement, you can take specific action for any error that occurs.

> **Note** The string contained in the Err object's Description property explains the error associated with the current error number. The exact wording of the description may vary among different versions of Microsoft Visual Basic. Therefore, use `Err.Number`, rather than `Err.Description`, to identify the specific error that occurred.

Exiting an Error-Handling Routine

The FileExists function example uses the Resume statement within the error handler to re-execute the statement that originally caused the error, and uses the Resume Next statement to return execution to the statement following the one at which the error occurred. There are other ways to exit an error-handling routine. Depending on the circumstances, you can do this using any of the statements shown in the following table.

Statement	Description
Resume [0]	Program execution resumes with the statement that caused the error or the most recently executed call out of the procedure containing the error-handling routine. Use it to repeat an operation after correcting the condition that caused the error.
Resume Next	Resumes program execution at the statement immediately following the one that caused the error. If the error occurred outside the procedure that contains the error handler, execution resumes at the statement immediately following the call to the procedure wherein the error occurred, if the called procedure does not have an enabled error handler.
Resume *line*	Resumes program execution at the label specified by *line*, where *line* is a line label (or nonzero line number) that must be in the same procedure as the error handler.
Err.Raise Number:= *number*	Triggers a run-time error. When this statement is executed within the error-handling routine, Visual Basic searches the calls list for another error-handling routine. (The *calls list* is the chain of procedures invoked to arrive at the current point of execution. See the section, "Error-Handling Hierarchy," later in this chapter.)

The Difference Between Resume and Resume Next Statements

The difference between Resume and Resume Next is shown in Figure 13.1.

Figure 13.1 Program flow with Resume and Resume Next

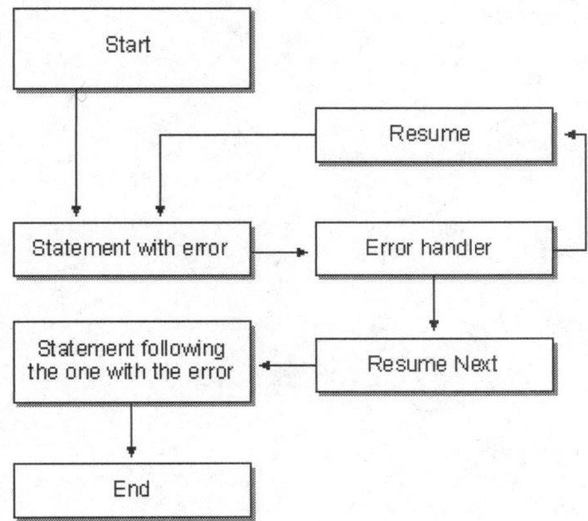

Generally, you would use Resume whenever the error handler can correct the error, and Resume Next when the error handler cannot. You can write an error handler so that the existence of a run-time error is never revealed to the user or to display error messages and allow the user to enter corrections.

For example, the Function procedure in the following code example uses error handling to perform "safe" division on its arguments without revealing errors that might occur. The errors that can occur when performing division are:

Error	Cause
"Division by zero"	Numerator is nonzero, but the denominator is zero.
"Overflow"	Both numerator and denominator are zero (during floating-point division).
"Illegal procedure call"	Either the numerator or the denominator is a nonnumeric value (or can't be considered a numeric value).

In all three cases, the following Function procedure traps these errors and returns Null:

```
Function Divide (numer, denom) as Variant
   Dim Msg as String
   Const mnErrDivByZero = 11, mnErrOverFlow = 6
   Const mnErrBadCall = 5
   On Error GoTo MathHandler
      Divide   = numer / denom
      Exit Function
```

```
MathHandler:
   If Err.Number = MnErrDivByZero Or _
   Err.Number = ErrOverFlow _
   Or Err = ErrBadCall Then
      Divide = Null   ' If error was Division by
                      ' zero, Overflow, or Illegal
                      ' procedure call, return Null.
   Else
      ' Display unanticipated error message.
      Msg = "Unanticipated error " & Err.Number
      Msg = Msg & ": " & Err.Description
      MsgBox Msg, vbExclamation
   End If          ' In all cases, Resume Next
                   ' continues execution at
   Resume Next     ' the Exit Function statement.
End Function
```

Resuming Execution at a Specified Line

Resume Next can also be used where an error occurs within a loop, and you need to restart the operation. Or, you can use Resume *line*, which returns control to a specified line label.

The following example illustrates the use of the Resume *line* statement. A variation on the FileExists example shown earlier, this function allows the user to enter a file specification that the function returns if the file exists.

```
Function VerifyFile As String
   Const mnErrBadFileName = 52, _
   mnErrDriveDoorOpen = 71
   Const mnErrDeviceUnavailable = 68, _
   mnErrInvalidFileName = 64
   Dim strPrompt As String, strMsg As String, _
   strFileSpec As String
   strPrompt = "Enter file specification to check:"
StartHere:
   strFileSpec = "*.*"   ' Start with a default
                         ' specification.
   strMsg = strMsg & vbCRLF & strPrompt
   ' Let the user modify the default.
   strFileSpec = InputBox(strMsg, "File Search", _
   strFileSpec, 100, 100)
   ' Exit if user deletes default.
   If strFileSpec = "" Then Exit Function
   On Error GoTo Handler
      VerifyFile = Dir(strFileSpec)
      Exit Function
```

```
Handler:
   Select Case Err.Number   ' Analyze error code and
                            ' load message.
      Case ErrInvalidFileName, ErrBadFileName
         strMsg = "Your file specification was "
         strMsg = strMsg & "invalid; try another."
      Case MnErrDriveDoorOpen
         strMsg = "Close the disk drive door and "
         strMsg = strMsg & "try again."
      Case MnErrDeviceUnavailable
         strMsg = "The drive you specified was not "
         strMsg = strMsg & "found. Try again."
      Case Else
         Dim intErrNum As Integer
         intErrNum = Err.Number
         Err.Clear          ' Clear the Err object.
         Err.Raise Number:= intErrNum' Regenerate
                                     ' the error.
   End Select
   Resume StartHere   ' This jumps back to StartHere
                      ' label so the user can try
                      ' another file name.
End Function
```

If a file matching the specification is found, the function returns the file name. If no matching file is found, the function returns a zero-length string. If one of the anticipated errors occurs, a message is assigned to the `strMsg` variable and execution jumps back to the label `StartHere`. This gives the user another chance to enter a valid path and file specification.

If the error is unanticipated, the Case Else segment regenerates the error so that the next error handler in the calls list can trap the error. This is necessary because if the error wasn't regenerated, the code would continue to execute at the `Resume StartHere` line. By regenerating the error you are in effect causing the error to occur again; the new error will be trapped at the next level in the call stack.

For More Information For more details, see "Error Handling Hierarchy," later in this chapter.

> **Note** Although using Resume *line* is a legitimate way to write code, a proliferation of jumps to line labels can render code difficult to understand and debug.

Error Handling Hierarchy

An *enabled* error handler is one that was activated by executing an On Error statement and hasn't yet been turned off — either by an On Error GoTo 0 statement or by exiting the procedure where it was enabled. An *active* error handler is one in which execution is currently taking place. To be active, an error handler must first be enabled, but not all enabled error handlers are active. For example, after a Resume statement, a handler is deactivated but still enabled.

When an error occurs within a procedure lacking an enabled error-handling routine, or within an active error-handling routine, Visual Basic searches the calls list for another enabled error-handling routine. The calls list is the sequence of calls that leads to the currently executing procedure; it is displayed in the Call Stack dialog box. You can display the Call Stack dialog box only when in break mode (when you pause the execution of your application), by selecting the View, Call Stack menu item or by pressing CTRL+L.

Searching the Calls List

Suppose the following sequence of calls occurs, as shown in Figure 13.2:

1. An event procedure calls Procedure A.
2. Procedure A calls Procedure B.
3. Procedure B calls Procedure C.

Figure 13.2 A sequence of calls

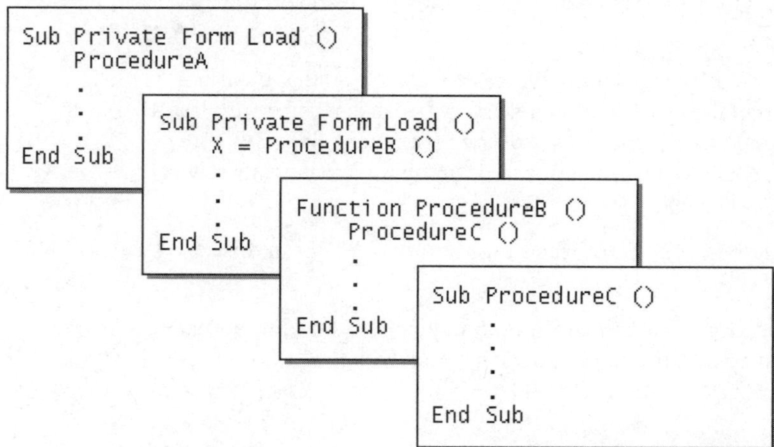

While Procedure C is executing, the other procedures are pending, as shown in the calls list in the Call Stack dialog box.

For More Information For more information, see "Monitoring the Call Stack," later in this chapter.

Figure 13.3 shows the calls list displayed in the Call Stack dialog box.

Figure 13.3 The calls list when procedures are pending

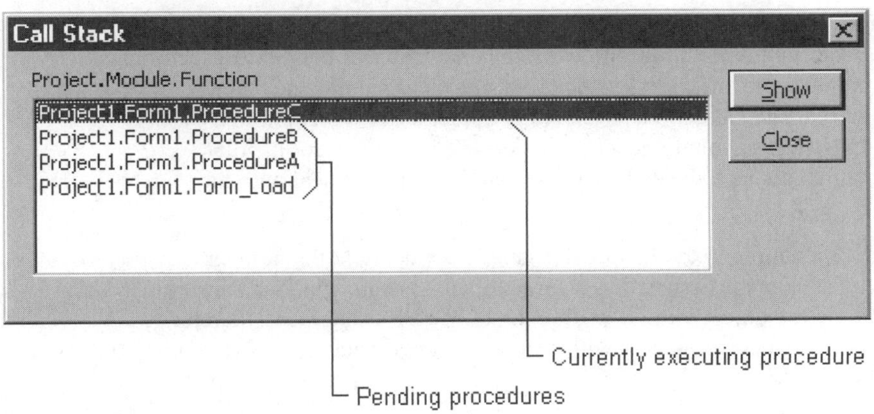

If an error occurs in Procedure C and this procedure doesn't have an enabled error handler, Visual Basic searches backward through the pending procedures in the calls list — first Procedure B, then Procedure A, then the initial event procedure (but no farther) — and executes the first enabled error handler it finds. If it doesn't encounter an enabled error handler anywhere in the calls list, it presents a default unexpected error message and halts execution.

If Visual Basic finds an enabled error-handling routine, execution continues in that routine as if the error had occurred in the same procedure that contains the error handler. If a Resume or a Resume Next statement is executed in the error-handling routine, execution continues as shown in the following table.

Statement	Result
Resume	The call to the procedure that Visual Basic just searched is re-executed. In the calls list given earlier, if Procedure A has an enabled error handler that includes a Resume statement, Visual Basic re-executes the call to Procedure B.
Resume Next	Execution returns to the statement following the last statement executed in that procedure. This is the statement following the call to the procedure that Visual Basic just searched back through. In the calls list given earlier, if Procedure A has an enabled error handler that includes a Resume Next statement, execution returns to the statement after the call to Procedure B.

Notice that the statement executed is in the procedure *where the error-handling procedure is found*, not necessarily in the procedure where the error occurred. If you don't take this into account, your code may perform in ways you don't intend. To make the code easier to debug, you can simply go into break mode whenever an error occurs, as explained in the section, "Turning Off Error Handling," later in this chapter.

If the error handler's range of errors doesn't include the error that actually occurred, an unanticipated error can occur within the procedure with the enabled error handler. In such a case, the procedure could execute endlessly, especially if the error handler executes a Resume statement. To prevent such situations, use the Err object's Raise method in a Case Else statement in the handler. This actually generates an error within the error handler, forcing Visual Basic to search through the calls list for a handler that can deal with the error.

In the VerifyFile procedure example in the Errors.vbp sample application, the number originally contained in `Err.Number` is assigned to a variable, `intErrNum`, which is then passed as an argument to the Err object's Raise method in a Case Else statement, thereby generating an error. When such an error occurs within an active error handler, the search back through the calls list begins.

Allocating Errors to Different Handlers

The effect of the search back through the calls list is hard to predict, because it depends on whether Resume or Resume Next is executed in the handler that processes the error successfully. Resume returns control to the most recently executed call out of the procedure containing the error handler. Resume Next returns control to whatever statement immediately follows the most recently executed call out of the procedure containing the error handler.

For example, in the calls list shown in Figure 13.3, if Procedure A has an enabled error handler and Procedure B and C don't, an error occurring in Procedure C will be handled by Procedure A's error handler. If that error handler uses a Resume statement, upon exit, the program continues with a call to Procedure B. However, if Procedure A's error handler uses a Resume Next statement, upon exit, the program will continue with whatever statement in Procedure A follows the call to Procedure B. In both cases the error handler does not return directly to either the procedure or the statement where the error originally occurred.

Guidelines for Complex Error Handling

When you write large Visual Basic applications that use multiple modules, the error-handling code can get quite complex. Keep these guidelines in mind:

- While you are debugging your code, use the Err object's Raise method to regenerate the error in all error handlers for cases where no code in the handler deals with the specific error. This allows your application to try to correct the error in other error-handling routines along the calls list. It also ensures that Visual Basic will display an error message if an error occurs that your code doesn't handle. When you test your code, this technique helps you uncover the errors you aren't handling adequately. However, in a stand-alone .exe file, you should be cautious: If you execute the Raise method and no other procedure traps the error, your application will terminate execution immediately, without any QueryUnload or Unload events occurring.
- Use the Clear method if you need to explicitly clear the Err object after handling an error. This is necessary when using inline error handling with On Error Resume Next. Visual Basic calls the Clear method automatically whenever it executes any type of Resume statement, Exit Sub, Exit Function, Exit Property, or any On Error statement.
- If you don't want another procedure in the calls list to trap the error, use the Stop statement to force your code to terminate. Using Stop lets you examine the context of the error while refining your code in the development environment.

  Caution Be sure to remove any Stop statements before you create an .exe file. If a stand-alone Visual Basic application (.exe) encounters a Stop statement, it treats it as an End statement and terminates execution immediately, without any QueryUnload or Unload events occurring.
- Write a fail-safe error-handling procedure that all your error handlers can call as a last resort for errors they cannot handle. This fail-safe procedure can perform an orderly termination of your application by unloading forms and saving data.

For More Information See "Testing Error Handling by Generating Errors," "Inline Error Handling," and "Design Time, Run Time, and Break Mode," later in this chapter.

Testing Error Handling by Generating Errors

Simulating errors is useful when you are testing your applications, or when you want to treat a particular condition as being equivalent to a Visual Basic run-time error. For example, you might be writing a module that uses an object defined in an external application, and want errors returned from the object to be handled as actual Visual Basic errors by the rest of your application.

In order to test for all possible errors, you may need to generate some of the errors in your code. You can generate an error in your code with the Raise method:

object.**Raise** *argumentlist*

The *object* argument is usually Err, Visual Basic's globally defined error object. The *argumentlist* argument is a list of named arguments that can be passed with the method. The VerifyFile procedure in the Errors.vbp sample application uses the following code to regenerate the current error in an error handler:

```
Err.Raise Number:=intErrNum
```

In this case, `intErrNum` is a variable that contains the error number which triggered the error handler. When the code reaches a Resume statement, the Clear method of the Err object is invoked. It is necessary to regenerate the error in order to pass it back to the previous procedure on the call stack.

You can also simulate any Visual Basic run-time error by supplying the error code for that error:

```
Err.Raise Number:=71 ' Simulate "Disk Not Ready" error.
```

Defining Your Own Errors

Sometimes you may want to define errors in addition to those defined by Visual Basic. For example, an application that relies on a modem connection might generate an error when the carrier signal is dropped. If you want to generate and trap your own errors, you can add your error numbers to the vbObjectError constant.

The vbObjectError constant reserves the numbers ranging from its own offset to its offset + 512. Using a number higher than this will ensure that your error numbers will not conflict with future versions of Visual Basic or other Microsoft Basic products. ActiveX controls may also define their own error numbers. To avoid conflicts with them, consult the documentation for controls you use in your application.

To define your own error numbers, you add constants to the Declarations section of your module:

```
' Error constants
Const gLostCarrier = 1 + vbObjectError + 512
Const gNoDialTone = 2 + vbObjectError + 512
```

You can then use the Raise method as you would with any of the intrinsic errors. In this case, the description property of the Err object will return a standard description — "Application-defined or object defined error." To provide your own error description, you will need to add it as a parameter to the Raise method.

For More Information To learn more about generating your own error, see "Raise Method," in the *Microsoft Visual Basic 6.0 Language Reference* volume of the *Microsoft Visual Basic 6.0 Reference Library.*

Inline Error Handling

You may be accustomed to programming in a language that doesn't raise exceptions — in other words, it doesn't interrupt your code's execution by generating exceptions when errors occur, but instead records errors for you to check later. The C programming language works in this manner, and you may sometimes find it convenient to follow this practice in your Visual Basic code.

When you check for errors immediately after each line that may cause an error, you are performing *inline error handling*. This topic explains the different approaches to inline error handling, including:

- Writing functions and statements that return error numbers when an error occurs.
- Raising a Visual Basic error in a procedure and handling the error in an inline error handler in the calling procedure.
- Writing a function to return a Variant data type, and using the Variant to indicate to the calling procedure that an error occurred.

Returning Error Numbers

There are a number of ways to return error numbers. The simplest way is to create functions and statements that return an error number, instead of a value, if an error occurs. The following example shows how you can use this approach in the FileExists function example, which indicates whether or not a particular file exists.

```
Function FileExists (p As String) As Long
   If Dir (p) <> " " Then
      FileExists = conSuccess   ' Return a constant
                                ' indicating the
   Else                         ' file exists.
      FileExists = conFailure   ' Return failure
                                ' constant.
   End If
End Function

Dim ResultValue As Long
ResultValue = FileExists ("C:\Testfile.txt")
If ResultValue = conFailure Then
    .
    .  ' Handle the error.
    .
Else
    .
    .  ' Proceed with the program.
    .
End If
```

The key to inline error handling is to test for an error immediately after each statement or function call. In this manner, you can design a handler that anticipates exactly the sort of error that might arise and resolve it accordingly. This approach does not require that an actual run-time error arise. This becomes useful when working with API and other DLL procedures which do not raise Visual Basic exceptions. Instead, these procedures indicate an error condition, either in the return value, or in one of the arguments passed to the procedures; check the documentation for the procedure you are using to determine how these procedures indicate an error condition.

Handling Errors in the Calling Procedure

Another way to indicate an error condition is to raise a Visual Basic error in the procedure itself, and handle the error in an inline error handler in the calling procedure. The next example shows the same FileExists procedure, raising an error number if it is not successful. Before calling this function, the On Error Resume Next statement sets the values of the Err object properties when an error occurs, but without trying to execute an error-handling routine.

The On Error Resume Next statement is followed by error-handling code. This code can check the properties of the Err object to see if an error occurred. If `Err.Number` doesn't contain zero, an error has occurred, and the error-handling code can take the appropriate action based on the values of the Err object's properties.

```
Function FileExists (p As String)
   If Dir (p) <> " " Then
      Err.Raise conSuccess   ' Return a constant
                             ' indicating the
   Else                      'file exists.
      Err.Raise conFailure   ' Raise error number
                             ' conFailure.
   End If
End Function

Dim ResultValue As Long
On Error Resume Next
ResultValue = FileExists ("C:\Testfile.txt")
If Err.Number = conFailure Then
   .
   .  ' Handle the error.
   .
Else
   .
   .  ' Continue program.
   .
End If
```

The next example uses both the return value and one of the passed arguments to indicate whether or not an error condition resulted from the function call.

```
Function Power (X As Long, P As Integer, _
ByRef Result As Integer)As Long
   On Error GoTo ErrorHandler
   Result = x^P
   Exit Function
ErrorHandler:
   Power = conFailure
End Function

' Calls the Power function.
Dim lngReturnValue As Long, lngErrorMaybe As Long
lngErrorMaybe = Power (10, 2, lngReturnValue)
If lngErrorMaybe Then
   .
   .  ' Handle the error.
   .
Else
   .
   .  ' Continue program.
   .
End If
```

If the function was written simply to return either the result value or an error code, the resulting value might be in the range of error codes, and your calling procedure would not be able to distinguish them. By using both the return value and one of the passed arguments, your program can determine that the function call failed, and take appropriate action.

Using Variant Data Types

Another way to return inline error information is to take advantage of the Visual Basic Variant data type and some related functions. A Variant has a tag that indicates what type of data is contained in the variable, and it can be tagged as a Visual Basic error code. You can write a function to return a Variant, and use this tag to indicate to the calling procedure that an error has occurred.

The following example shows how the Power function can be written to return a Variant.

```
Function Power (X As Long, P As Integer) As Variant
   On Error GoTo ErrorHandler
   Power = x^P
   Exit Function

ErrorHandler:
    Power = CVErr(Err.Number)      ' Convert error code to
                                   ' tagged Variant.
End Function
```

```
' Calls the Power function.
Dim varReturnValue As Variant
varReturnValue = Power (10, 2)
If IsError (varReturnValue) Then
    .
    .  ' Handle the error.
    .
Else
    .
    .  ' Continue program.
    .
End If
```

Centralized Error Handling

When you add error-handling code to your applications, you'll quickly discover that you're handling the same errors over and over. With careful planning, you can reduce code size by writing a few procedures that your error-handling code can call to handle common error situations.

The following FileErrors function procedure shows a message appropriate to the error that occurred and, where possible, allows the user to choose a button to specify what action the program should take next. It then returns code to the procedure that called it. The value of the code indicates which action the program should take. Note that user-defined constants such as MnErrDeviceUnavailable must be defined somewhere (either globally, or at the module level of the module containing the procedure, or within the procedure itself). The constant vbExclamation is defined in the Visual Basic (VB) object library, and therefore does not need to be declared.

```
Function FileErrors () As Integer
   Dim intMsgType As Integer, strMsg As String
   Dim intResponse As Integer
   ' Return Value    Meaning
   ' 0               Resume
   ' 1               Resume Next
   ' 2               Unrecoverable error
   ' 3               Unrecognized error
   intMsgType = vbExclamation
   Select Case Err.Number
      Case MnErrDeviceUnavailable ' Error 68.
         strMsg = "That device appears unavailable."
         intMsgType = vbExclamation + 4
      Case MnErrDiskNotReady       ' Error 71.
         strMsg = "Insert a disk in the drive "
         strMsg = strMsg & "and close the door."
         intMsgType = vbExclamation + 4
```

```
      Case MnErrDeviceIO    ' Error 57.
         strMsg = "Internal disk error."
         intMsgType = vbExclamation + 4
      Case MnErrDiskFull    ' Error 61.
         strMsg = "Disk is full. Continue?"
         intMsgType = vbExclamation + 3
      ' Error 64 & 52.
      Case ErrBadFileName, ErrBadFileNameOrNumber
         strMsg = "That filename is illegal."
         intMsgType = vbExclamation + 4
      Case ErrPathDoesNotExi       ' Error 76.
         strMsg = "That path doesn't exist."
         intMsgType = vbExclamation + 4
      Case ErrBadFileMode       ' Error 54.
         strMsg = "Can't open your file for that "
         strMsg = strMsg & "type of access."
         intMsgType = vbExclamation + 4
      Case ErrFileAlreadyOpen   ' Error 55.
         strMsg = "This file is already open."
         intMsgType = vbExclamation + 4
      Case ErrInputPastEndOfFile   ' Error 62.
         strMsg = "This file has a nonstandard "
         strMsg = strMsg & "end-of-file marker, "
         strMsg = strMsg & "or an attempt was made "
         strMsg = strMsg & "to read beyond "
         strMsg = strMsg & "the end-of-file marker."
         intMsgType = vbExclamation + 4
      Case Else
         FileErrors = 3
         Exit Function
   End Select
   intResponse = MsgBox (strMsg, intMsgType, _
   "Disk Error")
   Select Case intRresponse
      Case 1, 4    ' OK, Retry buttons.
         FileErrors = 0
      Case 5       ' Ignore button.
         FileErrors = 1
      Case 2, 3    ' Cancel, End buttons.
         FileErrors = 2
      Case Else
         FileErrors = 3
   End Select
End Function
```

This procedure handles common file and disk-related errors. If the error is not related to disk Input/Output, it returns the value 3. The procedure that calls this procedure should then either handle the error itself, regenerate the error with the Raise method, or call another procedure to handle it.

Note As you write larger applications, you'll find that you are using the same constants in several procedures in various forms and modules. Making those constants public and declaring them in a single standard module may better organize your code and save you from typing the same declarations repeatedly.

You can simplify error handling by calling the FileErrors procedure wherever you have a procedure that reads or writes to disk. For example, you've probably used applications that warn you if you attempt to replace an existing disk file. Conversely, when you try to open a file that doesn't exist, many applications warn you that the file does not exist and ask if you want to create it. In both instances, errors can occur when the application passes the file name to the operating system.

The following checking routine uses the value returned by the FileErrors procedure to decide what action to take in the event of a disk-related error.

```
Function ConfirmFile (FName As String, _
Operation As Integer) As Integer
' Parameters:
' Fname: File to be checked for and confirmed.
' Operation: Code for sequential file access mode
' (Output, Input, and so on).
' Note that the procedure works for binary and random
' access because messages are conditioned on Operation
' being <> to certain sequential modes.
' Return values:
' 1   Confirms operation will not cause a problem.
' 0   User decided not to go through with operation.
   Const conSaveFile = 1, conLoadFile = 2
   Const conReplaceFile = 1, conReadFile = 2
   Const conAddToFile = 3, conRandomFile = 4
   Const conBinaryFile = 5
   Dim intConfirmation As Integer
   Dim intAction As Integer
   Dim intErrNum As Integer, varMsg As Variant

   On Error GoTo ConfirmFileError ' Turn on the error
                                  ' trap.
   FName = Dir(FName)             ' See if the file exists.
   On Error GoTo 0                ' Turn error trap off.
   ' If user is saving text to a file that already
   ' exists...
   If FName <> "" And Operation = conReplaceFile Then
      varMsg = "The file " & FName &
      varMsg = varMsg & "already exists on " & vbCRLF
      varMsg = varMsg & "disk. Saving the text box "
      varMsg = varMsg & & vbCRLF
      varMsg = varMsg & "contents to that file will "
      varMsg = varMsg & "destroy the file's current "
      varMsg = varMsg & "contents, " & vbCRLF _
```

```
    varMsg = varMsg & "replacing them with the "
    varMsg = varMsg & "text from the text box."
    varMsg = varMsg & vbCRLF & vbCRLF
    varMsg = varMsg & "Choose OK to replace file, "
    varMsg = varMsg & "Cancel to stop."
    intConfirmation = MsgBox(varMsg, 65, _
    "File Message")
' If user wants to load text from a file that
' doesn't exist.
ElseIf FName = "" And Operation = conReadFile Then
    varMsg = "The file " & FName
    varMsg = varMsg & " doesn't exist." & vbCRLF
    varMsg = varMsg & "Would you like to create and
    varMsg = varMsg & "then edit it?" & vbCRLF
    varMsg = varMsg & vbCRLF & "Choose OK to "
    varMsg = varMsg & "create file, Cancel to stop."
    intConfirmation = MsgBox(varMsg, 65, _
    "File Message")
' If FName doesn't exist, force procedure to return
' 0 by setting
' intConfirmation = 2.
ElseIf FName = "" Then
    If Operation = conRandomFile Or _
    Operation = conBinaryFile Then
        intConfirmation = 2
    End If
' If the file exists and operation isn't
' successful,
' intConfirmation = 0 and procedure returns 1.
End If
' If no box was displayed, intConfirmation = 0;
' if user chose OK, in either case,
' intConfirmation = 1 and ConfirmFile should
' return 1 to confirm that the intended operation
' is OK. If intConfirmation > 1, ConfirmFile should
' return 0, because user doesn't want to go through
' with the operation...
If intConfirmation > 1 Then
    ConfirmFile = 0
Else
    ConfirmFile = 1
    If Confirmation = 1 Then
        ' User wants to create file.
        If Operation = conLoadFile Then
            ' Assign conReplaceFile so caller will
            ' understand action that will be taken.
            Operation = conReplaceFile
        End If
```

```
            ' Return code confirming action to either
            ' replace existing file or create new one.
         End If
      End If
   Exit Function
   ConfirmFileError:
   intAction = FileErrors
      Select Case intAction
         Case 0
            Resume
         Case 1
            Resume Next
         Case 2
            Exit Function
         Case Else
            intErrNum = Err.Number
            Err.Raise Number:=intErrNum
            Err.Clear
      End Select
End Function
```

The ConfirmFile procedure receives a specification for the file whose existence will be confirmed, plus information about which access mode will be used when an attempt is made to actually open the file. If a sequential file is to be saved (conReplaceFile), and a file is found that already has that name (and will therefore be overwritten), the user is prompted to confirm that overwriting the file is acceptable.

If a sequential file is to be opened (conReadFile) and the file is not found, the user is prompted to confirm that a new file should be created. If the file is being opened for random or binary access, its existence or nonexistence is either confirmed (return value 1) or refuted (return value 0). If an error occurs in the call to Dir, the FileErrors procedure is called to analyze the error and prompt the user for a reasonable course of action.

Turning Off Error Handling

If an error trap has been enabled in a procedure, it is automatically disabled when the procedure finishes executing. However, you may want to turn off an error trap in a procedure while the code in that procedure is still executing. To turn off an enabled error trap, use the On Error GoTo 0 statement. Once Visual Basic executes this statement, errors are detected but not trapped within the procedure. You can use On Error GoTo 0 to turn off error handling anywhere in a procedure — even within an error-handling routine itself.

For example, try single stepping, using Step Into, through a procedure such as this:

```
Sub ErrDemoSub ()
   On Error GoTo SubHandler ' Error trapping is
                              ' enabled.
      ' Errors need to be caught and corrected here.
      ' The Kill function is used to delete a file.
      Kill "Oldfile.xyz"
   On Error GoTo 0    ' Error trapping is turned off
                       ' here.
      Kill "Oldfile.xyz"
   On Error GoTo SubHandler ' Error trapping is
                              ' enabled again.
      Kill "Oldfile.xyz"
   Exit Sub
SubHandler:        ' Error-handling routine goes here.
   MsgBox "Caught error."
   Resume Next
End Sub
```

For More Information To learn how to use the Step Into feature, see "Running Selected Portions of Your Application," later in this chapter.

Debugging Code with Error Handlers

When you are debugging code, you may find it confusing to analyze its behavior when it generates errors that are trapped by an error handler. You could comment out the On Error line in each module in the project, but this is also cumbersome.

Instead, while debugging, you could turn off error handlers so that every time there's an error, you enter break mode.

To disable error handlers while debugging

1. From the **Code** window context menu (available by right-clicking on the Code window), choose **Toggle**.
2. Select the **Break on All Errors** option.

With this option selected, when an error occurs anywhere in the project, you will enter break mode and the Code window will display the code where the error occurred.

If this option is not selected, an error may or may not cause an error message to be displayed, depending on where the error occurred. For example, it may have been raised by an external object referenced by your application. If it does display a message, it may be meaningless, depending on where the error originated.

Error Handling with ActiveX Components

In applications that use one or more objects, it becomes more difficult to determine where an error occurs, particularly if it occurs in another application's object. For example, Figure 13.4 shows an application that consists of a form module, that references a class module, that in turn references a Microsoft Excel Worksheet object.

Figure 13.4 Regenerating errors between forms, classes, and ActiveX components

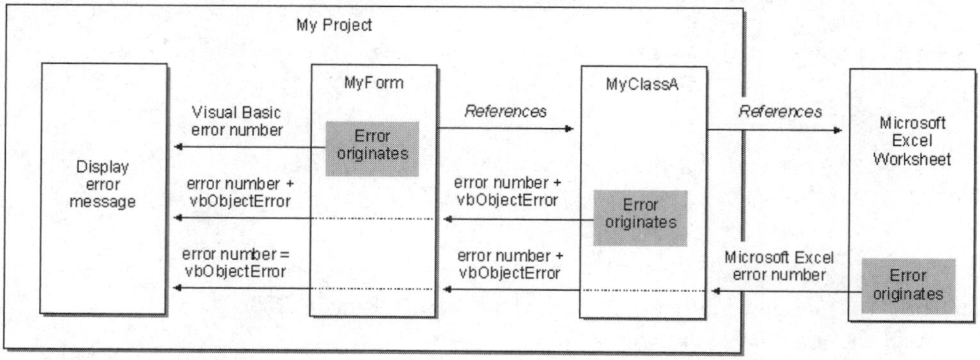

If the Worksheet object does not handle a particular error arising in the Worksheet, but regenerates it instead, Visual Basic will pass the error to the referencing object, MyClassA. When an error is raised in an external object and it is untrapped, it will be raised in the procedure that called the external object.

The MyClassA object can either handle the error (which is preferable), or regenerate it. The interface specifies that any object regenerating an error that arises in a referenced object should not simply propagate the error (pass the error code), but should instead remap the error number to something meaningful. When you remap the error, the number can either be a number defined by Visual Basic that indicates the error condition, if your handler can determine that the error is similar to a defined Visual Basic error (for instance, overflow or division by zero), or an undefined error number. Add the new number to the intrinsic Visual Basic constant vbObjectError to notify other handlers that this error was raised by your object.

Whenever possible, a class module should try to handle every error that arises within the module itself, and should also try to handle errors that arise in an object it references that are not handled by that object. However, there are some errors that it cannot handle because it cannot anticipate them. There are also cases where it is more appropriate for the referencing object to handle the error, rather than the referenced object.

When an error occurs in the form module, Visual Basic raises one of the predefined Visual Basic error numbers.

Note If you are creating a public class, be sure to clearly document the meaning of each non-Visual Basic error-handler you define. (Public classes cannot be created in the Learning Edition.) Other programmers who reference your public classes will need to know how to handle errors raised by your objects.

When you regenerate an error, leave the Err object's other properties unchanged. If the raised error is not trapped, the Source and Description properties can be displayed to help the user take corrective action.

Handling Errors in Objects

A class module could include the following error handler to accommodate any error it might trap, regenerating those it is unable to resolve:

```
MyServerHandler:
   Select Case ErrNum
      Case 7    ' Handle out-of-memory error.
         .
         .
         .
      Case 440     ' Handle external object error.
         Err.Raise Number:=vbObjectError + 9999
      ' Error from another Visual Basic object.
      Case Is > vbObjectError and Is < vbObjectError _
      + 65536
         ObjectError = ErrNum
      Select Case ObjectError
         ' This object handles the error, based on
         ' error code documentation for the object.
         Case vbObjectError + 10
         .
         .
         .
         Case Else
            ' Remap error as generic object error and
            ' regenerate.
            Err.Raise Number:=vbObjectError + 9999
         End Select
      Case Else
         ' Remap error as generic object error and
         ' regenerate.
         Err.Raise Number:=vbObjectError + 9999
   End Select
   Err.Clear
   Resume Next
```

The `Case 440` statement traps errors that arise in a referenced object outside the Visual Basic application. In this example, the error is simply propagated using the value 9999, because it is difficult for this type of centralized handler to determine the cause of the error. When this error is raised, it is generally the result of a fatal automation error (one that would cause the component to end execution), or because an object didn't correctly handle a trapped error. Error 440 shouldn't be propagated unless it is a fatal error. If this trap were written for an inline handler as discussed in "Inline Error Handling," earlier in this chapter, it might be possible to determine the cause of the error and correct it.

The statement

```
Case Is > vbObjectError and Is < vbObjectError + 65536
```

traps errors that originate in an object within the Visual Basic application, or within the same object that contains this handler. Only errors defined by objects will be in the range of the vbObjectError offset.

The error code documentation provided for the object should define the possible error codes and their meaning, so that this portion of the handler can be written to intelligently resolve anticipated errors. The actual error codes may be documented without the vbObjectError offset, or they may be documented after being added to the offset, in which case the Case Else statement should subtract vbObjectError, rather than add it. On the other hand, object errors may be constants, shown in the type library for the object, as shown in the Object Browser. In that case, use the error constant in the Case Else statement, instead of the error code.

Any error not handled should be regenerated with a new number, as shown in the Case Else statement. Within your application, you can design a handler to anticipate this new number you've defined. If this were a public class (not available in the Learning Edition), you would also want to include an explanation of the new error-handling code in your application's documentation.

The last Case Else statement traps and regenerates any other errors that are not trapped elsewhere in the handler. Because this part of the trap will catch errors that may or may not have the vbObjectError constant added, you should simply remap these errors to a generic "unresolved error" code. That code should be added to vbObjectError, indicating to any handler that this error originated in the referenced object.

Debugging Error Handlers in ActiveX Components

When you are debugging an application that has a reference to an object created in Visual Basic or a class defined in a class module, you may find it confusing to determine which object generates an error. To make this easier, you can select the Break in Class Module option on the General tab of the Options dialog box (available from the Tools menu). With this option selected, an error in a class module or an object in another application or project that is running in Visual Basic will cause that class to enter the debugger's break mode, allowing you to analyze the error. An error arising in a compiled object will not display the Immediate window in break mode; rather, such errors will be handled by the object's error handler, or trapped by the referencing module.

For More Information For a thorough discussion of the Break in Class Module option, see "Debugging Class Modules" in Chapter 9, "Programming with Objects."

Approaches to Debugging

The debugging techniques presented in this chapter use the analysis tools provided by Visual Basic. Visual Basic cannot diagnose or fix errors for you, but it does provide tools to help you analyze how execution flows from one part of the procedure to another, and how variables and property settings change as statements are executed. Debugging tools let you look inside your application to help you determine what happens and why.

Visual Basic debugging support includes breakpoints, break expressions, watch expressions, stepping through code one statement or one procedure at a time, and displaying the values of variables and properties. Visual Basic also includes special debugging features, such as edit-and-continue capability, setting the next statement to execute, and procedure testing while the application is in break mode.

For More Information For a quick overview of Visual Basic debugging, see "Tips for Debugging," later in this chapter.

Kinds of Errors

To understand how debugging is useful, consider the three kinds of errors you can encounter:

- Compile errors
- Run-time errors
- Logic errors

Compile Errors

Compile errors result from incorrectly constructed code. If you incorrectly type a keyword, omit some necessary punctuation, or use a Next statement without a corresponding For statement at design time, Visual Basic detects these errors when you compile the application.

Compile errors include errors in syntax. For example, you could have a statement as follows:

```
Left
```

Left is a valid word in the Visual Basic language, but without an object, it doesn't meet the syntax requirements for that word (*object*.Left). If you have selected the Auto Syntax Check option in the Editor tab on the Options dialog box, Visual Basic will display an error message as soon as you enter a syntax error in the Code window.

To set the Auto Syntax Check option

1. From the **Tools** menu, select **Options**, and click the **Editor** tab on the **Options** dialog box.
2. Select **Auto Syntax Check**.

For More Information See the section "Avoiding Bugs," later in this chapter, for other techniques to use to avoid errors in your code.

Run-Time Errors

Run-time errors occur while the application is running (and are detected by Visual Basic) when a statement attempts an operation that is impossible to carry out. An example of this is division by zero. Suppose you have this statement:

```
Speed = Miles / Hours
```

If the variable `Hours` contains zero, the division is an invalid operation, even though the statement itself is syntactically correct. The application must run before it can detect this error.

For More Information You can include code in your application to trap and handle run-time errors when they occur. For information on dealing with run-time errors, see "How to Handle Errors," earlier in this chapter.

Logic Errors

Logic errors occur when an application doesn't perform the way it was intended. An application can have syntactically valid code, run without performing any invalid operations, and yet produce incorrect results. Only by testing the application and analyzing results can you verify that the application is performing correctly.

How Debugging Tools Help

Debugging tools are designed to help you with:

- Logic and run-time errors.
- Observing the behavior of code that has no errors.

For instance, an incorrect result may be produced at the end of a long series of calculations. In debugging, the task is to determine what and where something went wrong. Perhaps you forgot to initialize a variable, chose the wrong operator, or used an incorrect formula.

There are no magic tricks to debugging, and there is no fixed sequence of steps that works every time. Basically, debugging helps you understand what's going on while your application runs. Debugging tools give you a snapshot of the current state of your application, including:

- Appearance of the user interface (UI).
- Values of variables, expressions, and properties.
- Active procedure calls.

The better you understand how your application is working, the faster you can find bugs.

For More Information For more details on viewing and testing variables, expressions, properties, and active procedure calls, see "Testing Data and Procedures with the Immediate Window" and "Monitoring the Call Stack," later in this chapter.

The Debug Toolbar

Among its many debugging tools, Visual Basic provides several buttons on the optional Debug toolbar that are very helpful. Figure 13.5 shows these tools. To display the Debug toolbar, right-click on the Visual Basic toolbar and select the Debug option.

Figure 13.5 The Debug toolbar

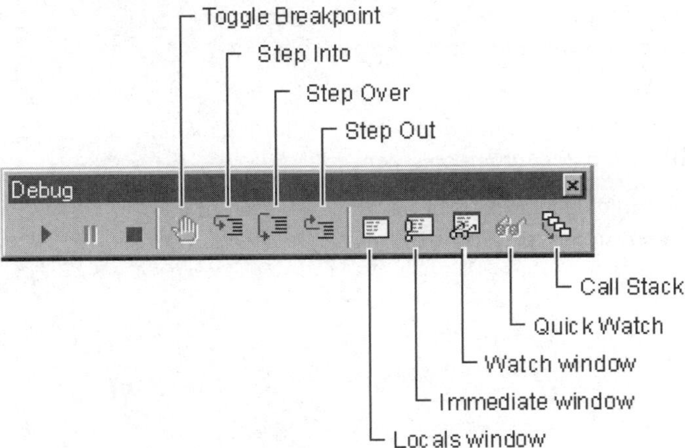

The following table briefly describes each tool's purpose. The topics in this chapter discuss situations where each of these tools can help you debug or analyze an application more efficiently.

Debugging tool	Purpose
Breakpoint	Defines a line in the Code window where Visual Basic suspends execution of the application.
Step Into	Executes the next executable line of code in the application and steps into procedures.
Step Over	Executes the next executable line of code in the application without stepping into procedures.
Step Out	Executes the remainder of the current procedure and breaks at the next line in the calling procedure.
Locals Window	Displays the current value of local variables.
Immediate Window	Allows you to execute code or query values while the application is in break mode.
Watch window	Displays the values of selected expressions.
Quick Watch	Lists the current value of an expression while the application is in break mode.
Call Stack	While in break mode, presents a dialog box that shows all procedures that have been called but not yet run to completion.

For More Information The debugging tools are only necessary if there are bugs in your application. See the next section, "Avoiding Bugs."

Avoiding Bugs

There are several ways to avoid creating bugs in your applications:

- Design your applications carefully by writing down the relevant events and the way your code will respond to each one. Give each event procedure and each general procedure a specific, well-defined purpose.
- Include numerous comments. As you go back and analyze your code, you'll understand it much better if you state the purpose of each procedure in comments.
- Explicitly reference objects whenever possible. Declare objects as they are listed in the Classes/Modules box in the Object Browser, rather than using a Variant or the generic Object data types.

- Develop a consistent naming scheme for the variables and objects in your application. For more information, see Appendix B, "Visual Basic Coding Conventions."
- One of the most common sources of errors is incorrectly typing a variable name or confusing one control with another. You can use Option Explicit to avoid misspelling variable names. For more information on requiring explicit variable declaration, see "Introduction to Variables, Constants, and Data Types" in Chapter 5, "Programming Fundamentals."

Design Time, Run Time, and Break Mode

To test and debug an application, you need to understand which of three modes you are in at any given time. You use Visual Basic at design time to create an application, and at run time to run it. This chapter introduces *break mode*, which suspends the execution of the program so you can examine and alter data.

Identifying the Current Mode

The Visual Basic title bar always shows you the current mode. Figure 13.6 shows the title bar for design time, run time, and break mode.

Figure 13.6 Identifying the current mode with the Visual Basic title bar

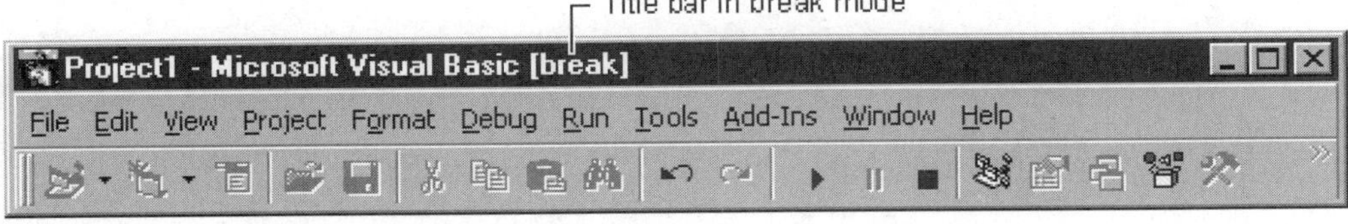

The characteristics of the three modes are listed in the following table.

Mode	Description
Design time	Most of the work of creating an application is done at design time. You can design forms, draw controls, write code, and use the Properties window to set or view property settings. You cannot use the debugging tools, except for setting breakpoints and creating watch expressions. From the Run menu, choose Start, or click the Run button to switch to run time. If your application contains code that executes when the application starts, choose Step Into from the Run menu (or press F8) to place the application in break mode at the first executable statement.
Run time	When an application takes control, you interact with the application the same way a user would. You can view code, but you cannot change it. From the Run menu, choose End, or click the End button to switch back to design time.
Break mode	From the Run menu, choose Break, click the Break button, or press CTRL+BREAK to switch to break mode. Execution is suspended while running the application. You can view and edit code (choose Code from the View menu, or press F7), examine or modify data, restart the application, end execution, or continue execution from the same point. You can set breakpoints and watch expressions at design time, but other debugging tools work only in break mode. See "Using Break Mode," later in this chapter.

Using the Toolbar to Change Modes

The toolbar provides three buttons that let you change quickly from one mode to another. These buttons appear in Figure 13.7.

Figure 13.7 Start, Break, and End buttons on the toolbar

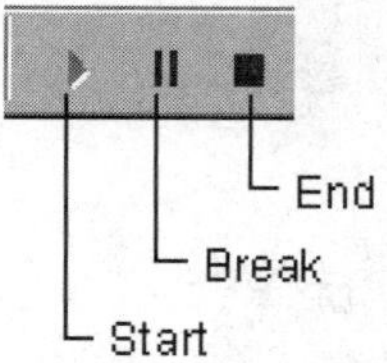

Whether any of these buttons is available depends on whether Visual Basic is in run-time mode, design-time mode, or break mode. The following table lists the buttons available for different modes.

Mode	Toolbar buttons available
Design time	Start
Run time	Break, End
Break	Continue, End (in break mode, the Start button becomes the Continue button)

Using the Debugging Windows

Sometimes you can find the cause of a problem by executing portions of code. More often, however, you'll also have to analyze what's happening to the data. You might isolate a problem in a variable or property with an incorrect value, and then have to determine how and why that variable or property was assigned an incorrect value.

With the debugging windows, you can monitor the values of expressions and variables while stepping through the statements in your application. There are three debugging windows: the Immediate window, the Watch window, and the Locals window

- The *Immediate window* shows information that results from debugging statements in your code, or that you request by typing commands directly into the window.

Figure 13.8 The Immediate window

For More Information To learn more about the Immediate window, see "Testing Data and Procedures with the Immediate Window" later in this chapter.

- The *Watch window* shows the current *watch expressions*, which are expressions whose values you decide to monitor as the code runs. A *break expression* is a watch expression that will cause Visual Basic to enter break mode when a certain condition you define becomes true. In the Watch window, the Context column indicates the procedure, module, or modules in which each watch expression is evaluated. The Watch window can display a value for a watch expression only if the current statement is in the specified context. Otherwise, the Value column shows a message indicating the statement is not in context. To access the Watch window, select Watch Window from the View menu. Figure 13.9 shows the Watch window.

Figure 13.9 The Watch window

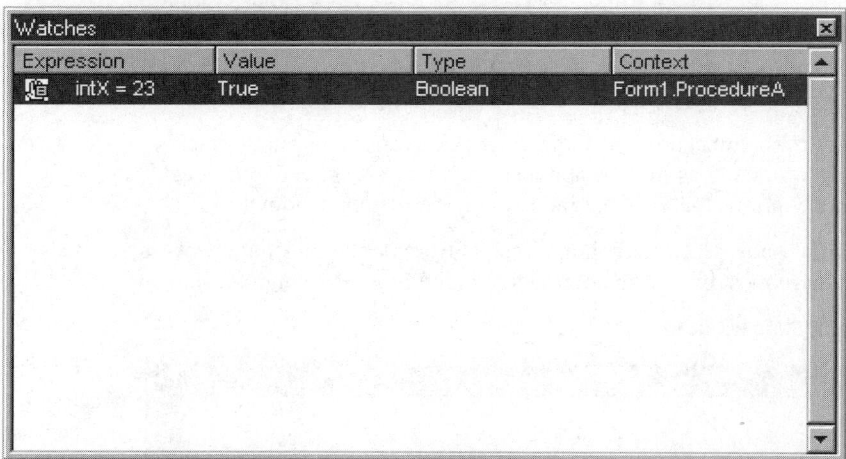

For More Information To learn more about the Watch window, see "Monitoring Data with Watch Expressions" later in this chapter.

- The *Locals window* shows the value of any variables within the scope of the current procedure. As the execution switches from procedure to procedure, the contents of the Locals window changes to reflect only the variables applicable to the current procedure. To access the Locals window, select Locals Window from the View menu. Figure 13.10 shows the Locals window.

Figure 13.10 The Locals window

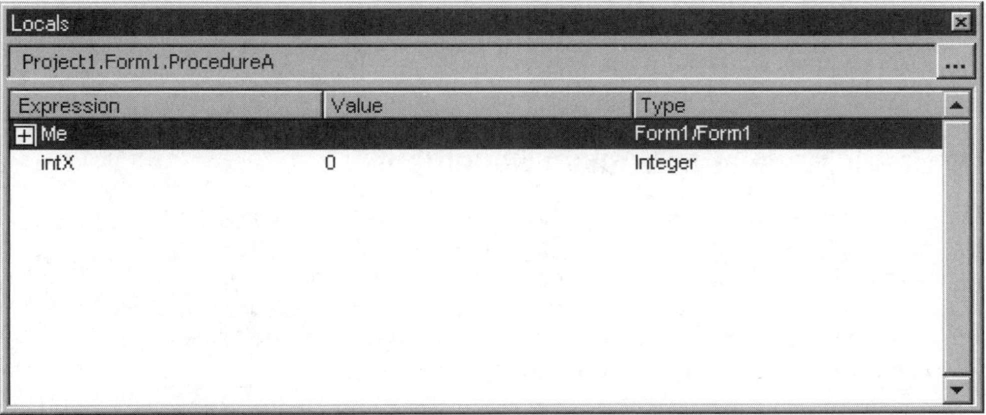

The current procedure and form (or module) determine which variables can be displayed according to the scoping rules presented in "Understanding the Scope of Variables" in Chapter 5, "Programming Fundamentals." For example, suppose the Immediate window indicates that Form1 is the current form. In this case, you can display any of the form-level variables in Form1. You can also use `Debug.Print` to examine local variables of the procedure displayed in the Code window. (You can always examine the value of a public variable.) For more information about printing information in the Immediate window, see "Testing data and Procedures with the Immediate Window," later in this chapter.

Using Break Mode

At design time, you can change the design or code of an application, but you cannot see how your changes affect the way the application runs. At run time, you can watch how the application behaves, but you cannot directly change the code.

Break mode halts the operation of an application and gives you a snapshot of its condition at any moment. Variable and property settings are preserved, so you can analyze the current state of the application and enter changes that affect how the application runs. When an application is in break mode, you can:

- Modify code in the application.
- Observe the condition of the application's interface.
- Determine which active procedures have been called.
- Watch the values of variables, properties, and statements.
- Change the values of variables and properties.
- View or control which statement the application will run next.

- Run Visual Basic statements immediately.
- Manually control the operation of the application.

  Note You can set breakpoints and watch expressions at design time, but other debugging tools work only in break mode.

Entering Break Mode at a Problem Statement

When debugging, you may want the application to halt at the place in the code where you think the problem might have started. This is one reason Visual Basic provides breakpoints and Stop statements. A *breakpoint* defines a statement or set of conditions at which Visual Basic automatically stops execution and puts the application in break mode without running the statement containing the breakpoint. See "Using Stop Statements," later in this chapter, for a comparison of Stop statements and breakpoints.

You can enter break mode manually if you do any of the following while the application is running:

- Press CTRL+BREAK.
- Choose Break from the Run menu.
- Click the Break button on the toolbar.

It's possible to break execution when the application is idle (when it is between processing of events). When this happens, execution does not stop at a specific line, but Visual Basic switches to break mode anyway.

You can also enter break mode automatically when any of the following occurs:

- A statement generates an untrapped run-time error.
- A statement generates a run-time error and the Break on All Errors error trapping option has been selected.
- A break expression defined in the Add Watch dialog box changes or becomes true, depending on how you defined it.
- Execution reaches a line with a breakpoint.
- Execution reaches a Stop statement.

Fixing a Run-Time Error and Continuing

Some run-time errors result from simple oversights when entering code;these errors are easily fixed. Frequent errors include misspelled names and mismatched properties or methods with objects — for example, trying to use the Clear method on a text box, or the Text property with a file list box. Figure 13.11 shows a run-time error message.

Figure 13.11 Run-time errors halt execution

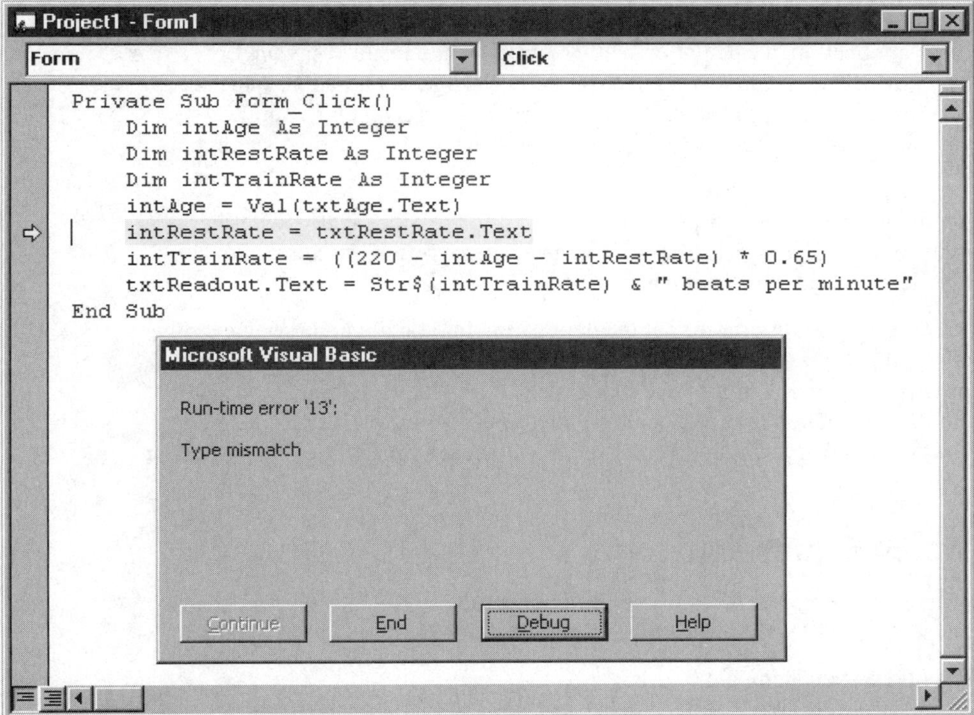
Project1 - Form1
Form
Click
Private Sub Form_Click()
Dim intAge As Integer
Dim intRestRate As Integer
Dim intTrainRate As Integer
intAge = Val(txtAge.Text)
intRestRate = txtRestRate.Text
intTrainRate = ((220 - intAge - intRestRate) * 0.65)
txtReadout.Text = Str$(intTrainRate) & " beats per minute"
End Sub
Microsoft Visual Basic
Run-time error '13':
Type mismatch
Continue
End
Debug
Help

Often you can enter a correction and continue program execution with the same line that halted the application, even though you've changed some of the code. Simply choose Continue from the Run menu or click the Continue button on the toolbar. As you continue running the application, you can verify that the problem is fixed.

If you select Break on All Errors from the Default Error Trapping State option group on the General tab on the Options dialog box (available from the Tools menu), Visual Basic disables error handlers in code, so that when a statement generates a run-time error, Visual Basic enters break mode. If Break on All Errors is not selected, and if an error handler exists, it will intercept code and take corrective action.

> **Note** When you change the Default Error Trapping State option via the Options dialog box, this setting becomes the default for all subsequent sessions of VB. To change error handling for just the current session, select Toggle from the code window context menu to open a submenu that allows selection of the break mode.

Some changes (most commonly, changing variable declarations or adding new variables or procedures) require you to restart the application. When this happens, Visual Basic presents a message that asks if you want to restart the application.

Monitoring Data with Watch Expressions

As you debug your application, a calculation may not produce the result you want or problems might occur when a certain variable or property assumes a particular value or range of values. Many debugging problems aren't immediately traceable to a single statement, so you may need to observe the behavior of a variable or expression throughout a procedure.

Visual Basic automatically monitors watch expressions — expressions that you define — for you. When the application enters break mode, these watch expressions appear in the Watch window, where you can observe their values.

You can also direct watch expressions to put the application into break mode whenever the expression's value changes or equals a specified value. For example, instead of stepping through perhaps tens or hundreds of loops one statement at a time, you can use a watch expression to put the application in break mode when a loop counter reaches a specific value. Or you may want the application to enter break mode each time a flag in a procedure changes value.

Adding a Watch Expression

You can add a watch expression at design time or in break mode. You use the Add Watch dialog box (shown in Figure 13.12) to add watch expressions.

Figure 13.12 The Add Watch dialog box

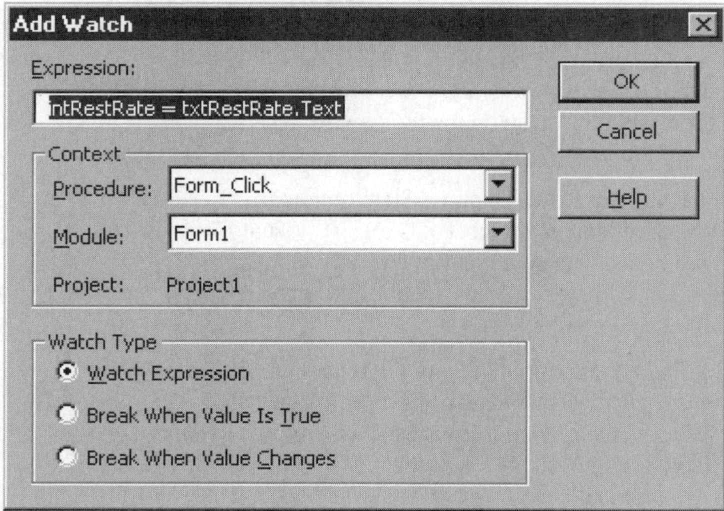

The following table describes the Add Watch dialog box.

Component	Description
Expression box	Where you enter the expression that the watch expression evaluates. The expression is a variable, a property, a function call, or any other valid expression.
Context option group	Sets the scope of variables watched in the expression. Use if you have variables of the same name with different scope. You can also restrict the scope of variables in watch expressions to a specific procedure or to a specific form or module, or you can have it apply to the entire application by selecting All Procedures and All Modules. Visual Basic can evaluate a variable in a narrow context more quickly.
Watch Type option group	Sets how Visual Basic responds to the watch expression. Visual Basic can watch the expression and display its value in the Watch window when the application enters break mode. Or you can have the application enter break mode automatically when the expression evaluates to a true (nonzero) statement or each time the value of the expression changes.

To add a watch expression

1. From the **Debug** menu, choose **Add Watch**.
2. The current expression (if any) in the Code Editor will appear in the **Expression** box on the **Add Watch** dialog box. If this isn't the expression you want to watch, enter the expression to evaluate in the **Expression** box.
3. If necessary, set the scope of the variables to watch.

   If you select the **Procedure** or **Module** option under **Context**, select a procedure, form, or module name from the appropriate list box.
4. If necessary, select an option button in the **Watch Type** group to determine how you want Visual Basic to respond to the watch expression.
5. Choose **OK**.

   Note You can also add an expression by dragging and dropping from the Code Editor to the Watch window.

Editing or Deleting a Watch Expression

The Edit Watch dialog box, shown in Figure 13.13, lists all the current watch expressions. You can edit and delete any watch listed in the Watch window.

Figure 13.13 The Edit Watch dialog box

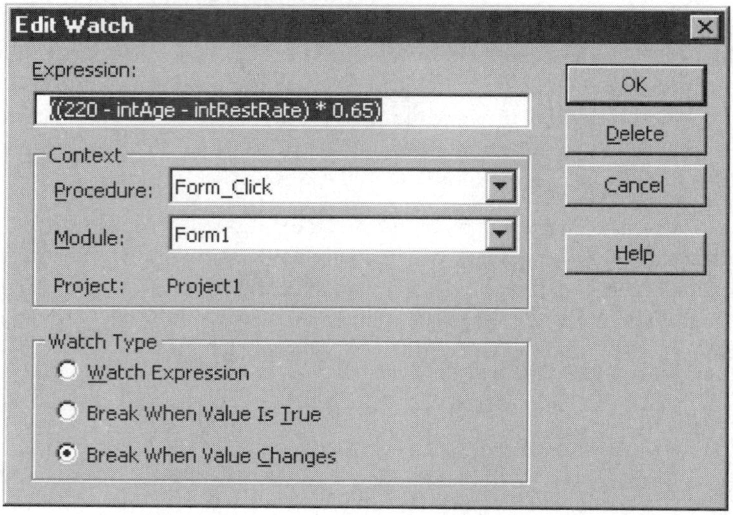

To edit a watch expression

1. In the Watch window, double click the watch expression you want to edit.

   – or –

   Select the watch expression you want to edit and choose **Edit Watch** from the **Debug** menu.
2. The **Edit Watch** dialog box is displayed and is identical to the **Add Watch** dialog box except for the title bar and the addition of a Delete button.
3. Make any changes to the expression, the scope for evaluating variables, or the watch type.
4. Choose **OK**.

To delete a watch expression

In the **Watch** window, select the watch expression you want to delete.

- Press the DELETE key.

Identifying Watch Types

At the left edge of each watch expression in the Watch window is an icon identifying the watch type of that expression. Figure 13.14 defines the icon for each of the three watch types.

Figure 13.14 Watch type icons

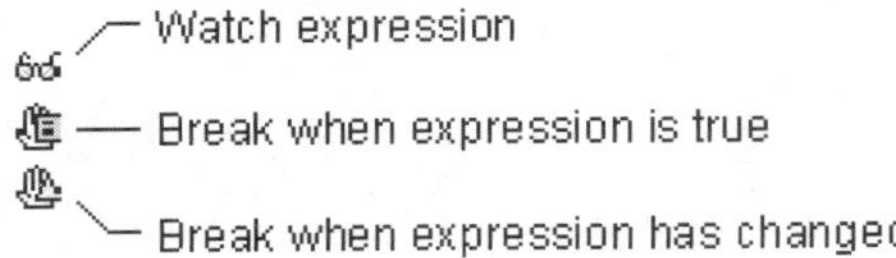

Using Quick Watch

While in break mode, you can check the value of a property, variable, or expression for which you have not defined a watch expression. To check such expressions, use the Quick Watch dialog box, shown in Figure 13.15.

Figure 13.15 The Quick Watch dialog box

The Quick Watch dialog box shows the value of the expression you select from the Code window. To continue watching this expression, click the Add button; the Watch window, with relevant information from the Quick Watch dialog box already entered, is displayed. If Visual Basic cannot evaluate the value of the current expression, the Add button is disabled.

To display the Quick Watch dialog box

1. Select a watch expression in the Code window.
2. Click the **Quick Watch** button on the **Debug** toolbar. (To display the Debug toolbar, right-click on the Visual Basic toolbar and select the **Debug** option.)

   – or –

   Press SHIFT+F9.

   – or –

   From the **Debug** menu, choose **Quick Watch**.
3. If you want to add a watch expression based on the expression in the **Quick Watch** dialog box, choose the **Add** button.

Using a Breakpoint to Selectively Halt Execution

At run time, a breakpoint tells Visual Basic to halt just before executing a specific line of code. When Visual Basic is executing a procedure and it encounters a line of code with a breakpoint, it switches to break mode.

You can set or remove a breakpoint in break mode or at design time, or at run time when the application is idle.

To set or remove a breakpoint

1. In the Code window, move the insertion point to the line of code where you want to set or remove a breakpoint.

   – or –

   Click in the margin on the left edge of the Code window next to the line where you want to set or remove a breakpoint.
2. From the **Debug** menu, choose **Toggle Breakpoint**.

   – or –

   Click the **Toggle Breakpoint** button on the **Debug** toolbar. (To display the Debug toolbar, right-click on the Visual Basic toolbar and select the **Debug** option.)

   – or –

   Press F9.

When you set a breakpoint, Visual Basic highlights the selected line in bold, using the colors that you specified on the Editor Format tab of the Options dialog box, available from the Tools menu.

For example, Figure 13.16 shows a procedure with a breakpoint on the fifth line. In the Code window, Visual Basic indicates a breakpoint by displaying the text on that line in bold and in the colors specified for a breakpoint.

Figure 13.16 A procedure halted by a breakpoint

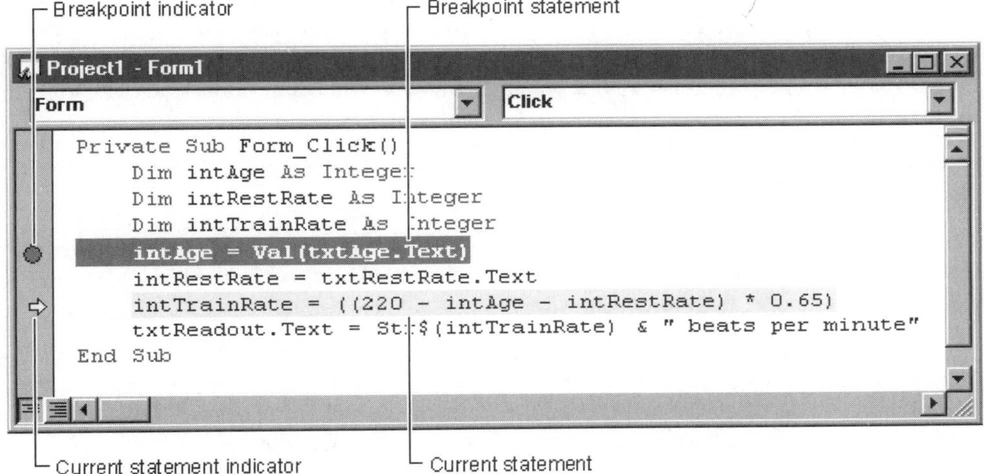
Breakpoint indicator
Breakpoint statement
Project1 - Form1
Form
Click
Private Sub Form_Click()
Dim intAge As Integer
Dim intRestRate As Integer
Dim intTrainRate As Integer
intAge = Val(txtAge.Text)
intRestRate = txtRestRate.Text
intTrainRate = ((220 - intAge - intRestRate) * 0.65)
txtReadout.Text = Str$(intTrainRate) & " beats per minute"
End Sub
Current statement indicator
Current statement

Identifying the Current Statement

In Figure 13.16, a rectangular highlight surrounds the seventh line of code. This outline indicates the *current statement*, or next statement to be executed. When the current statement also contains a breakpoint, only the rectangular outline highlights the line of code. Once the current statement moves to another line, the line with the breakpoint is displayed in bold and in color again.

To specify the color of text of the current statement

1. From the **Tools** menu, choose **Options** and click the **Editor Format** tab on the **Options** dialog box.
2. Under **Code Colors**, select **Execution Point Text**, and set the **Foreground**, **Background**, and **Indicator** colors.

Examining the Application at a Breakpoint

Once you reach a breakpoint and the application is halted, you can examine the application's current state. Checking results of the application is easy, because you can move the focus among the forms and modules of your application, the Code window, and the debugging windows.

A breakpoint halts the application just before executing the line that contains the breakpoint. If you want to observe what happens when the line with the breakpoint executes, you must execute at least one more statement. To do this, use Step Into or Step Over.

> **Note** Although it's possible to set a breakpoint in a MouseMove event procedure or in a Timer event, this can cause unexpected results. The normal flow of events is disrupted when entering break mode; single-stepping through the code from within these procedures may present different behavior than that which would occur in run mode.

For More Information See the section, "Running Selected Portions of Your Application," later in this chapter.

When you are trying to isolate a problem, remember that a statement might be indirectly at fault because it assigns an incorrect value to a variable. To examine the values of variables and properties while in break mode, use the Locals window, Quick Watch, watch expressions, or the Immediate window.

For More Information To learn how to use the Immediate window to test the values of properties and variables, see "Testing Data and Procedures with the Immediate Window," later in this chapter. To learn more about watch expressions, see "Monitoring Data with Watch Expressions," earlier in this chapter.

Using Stop Statements

Placing a Stop statement in a procedure is an alternative to setting a breakpoint. Whenever Visual Basic encounters a Stop statement, it halts execution and switches to break mode. Although Stop statements act like breakpoints, they aren't set or cleared the same way.

> **Caution** Be sure to remove any Stop statements before you create an .exe file. If a stand-alone Visual Basic application (.exe) encounters a Stop statement, it treats it as an End statement and terminates execution immediately, without any QueryUnload or Unload events occurring.

> **Note** It's usually better to use the Assert method rather than a Stop statement. The Assert method halts execution only when a specified condition isn't met; unlike the Stop statement, calls to the Assert method are automatically removed when the application is compiled. For more information, see "Verifying Your Code with Assertions," later in this chapter.

Remember that a Stop statement does nothing more than temporarily halt execution, while an End statement halts execution, resets variables, and returns to design time. You can always choose Continue from the Run menu to continue running the application.

For More Information See "How to Handle Errors," earlier in this chapter, for an example that uses the Stop statement.

Running Selected Portions of Your Application

If you can identify the statement that caused an error, a single breakpoint might help you locate the problem. More often, however, you know only the general area of the code that caused the error. A breakpoint helps you isolate that problem area. You can then use Step Into and Step Over to observe the effect of each statement. If necessary, you can also skip over statements or back up by starting execution at a new line.

Step Mode	Description
Step Into	Execute the current statement and break at the next line, even if it's in another procedure.
Step Over	Execute the entire procedure called by the current line and break at the line following the current line.
Step Out	Execute the remainder of the current procedure and break at the statement following the one that called the procedure.

Note You must be in break mode to use these commands. They are not available at design time or run time.

Using Step Into

You can use Step Into to execute code one statement at a time. (This is also known as single stepping.) After stepping through each statement, you can see its effect by looking at your application's forms or the debugging windows.

To step through code one statement at a time

- From the **Debug** menu, choose **Step Into**.

  – or –

  Click the **Step Into** button on the **Debug** toolbar. (To display the Debug toolbar, right-click on the Visual Basic toolbar and select the **Debug** option.)

  – or –

  Press F8.

When you use Step Into to step through code one statement at a time, Visual Basic temporarily switches to run time, executes the current statement, and advances to the next statement. Then it switches back to break mode.

Note Visual Basic allows you to step into individual statements, even if they are on the same line. A line of code can contain two or more statements, separated by a colon (:). Visual Basic uses a rectangular outline to indicate which of the statements will execute next. Breakpoints apply only to the first statement of a multiple-statement line.

Using Step Over

Step Over is identical to Step Into, except when the current statement contains a call to a procedure. Unlike Step Into, which steps into the called procedure, Step Over executes it as a unit and then steps to the next statement in the current procedure. Suppose, for example, that the statement calls the procedure SetAlarmTime:

```
SetAlarmTime 11, 30, 0
```

If you choose Step Into, the Code window shows the SetAlarmTime procedure and sets the current statement to the beginning of that procedure. This is the better choice only if you want to analyze the code within SetAlarmTime.

If you use Step Over, the Code window continues to display the current procedure. Execution advances to the statement immediately after the call to SetAlarmTime, unless SetAlarmTime contains a breakpoint or a Stop statement. Use Step Over if you want to stay at the same level of code and don't need to analyze the SetAlarmTime procedure.

You can alternate freely between Step Into and Step Over. The command you use depends on which portions of code you want to analyze at any given time.

To use Step Over

- From the **Debug** menu, choose **Step Over**.

  – or –

  Click the **Step Over** button on the **Debug** toolbar. (To display the Debug toolbar, right-click on the Visual Basic toolbar and select the **Debug** option.)

  – or –

  Press SHIFT+F8.

Using Step Out

Step Out is similar to Step Into and Step Over, except it advances past the remainder of the code in the current procedure. If the procedure was called from another procedure, it advances to the statement immediately following the one that called the procedure.

To use Step Out

- From the **Debug** menu, choose **Step Out**.

  – or –

  Click the **Step Out** button on the **Debug** toolbar. (To display the Debug toolbar, right-click on the Visual Basic toolbar and select the **Debug** option.)

  – or –

  Press CTRL+SHIFT+F8.

Bypassing Sections of Code

When your application is in break mode, you can use the Run To Cursor command to select a statement further down in your code where you want execution to stop. This lets you "step over" uninteresting sections of code, such as large loops.

To use Run To Cursor

1. Put your application in break mode.
2. Place the cursor where you want to stop.
3. Press CTRL+F8.

   – or –

   From the **Debug** menu, choose **Run To Cursor**.

Setting the Next Statement to Be Executed

While debugging or experimenting with an application, you can use the Set Next Statement command to skip a certain section of code — for instance, a section that contains a known bug — so you can continue tracing other problems. Or you may want to return to an earlier statement to test part of the application using different values for properties or variables.

With Visual Basic, you can set a different line of code to execute next, provided it falls within the same procedure. The effect is similar to using Step Into, except Step Into executes only the next line of code in the procedure. By setting the next statement to execute, you choose which line executes next.

To set the next statement to be executed

1. In break mode, move the insertion point (cursor) to the line of code you want to execute next.
2. From the **Debug** menu, choose **Set Next Statement**.
3. To resume execution, from the **Run** menu, choose **Continue**.

   – or –

   From the **Debug** menu, choose **Run To Cursor**, **Step Into**, **Step Over**, or **Step Out**.

Showing the Next Statement to Be Executed

You can use Show Next Statement to place the cursor on the line that will execute next. This feature is convenient if you've been executing code in an error handler and aren't sure where execution will resume. Show Next Statement is available only in break mode.

To show the next statement to be executed

1. While in break mode, from the **Debug** menu, choose **Show Next Statement**.
2. To resume execution, from the **Run** menu, choose **Continue**.

   – or –

   From the **Debug** menu, choose **Run To Cursor**, **Step Into**, **Step Over**, or **Step Out**.

Monitoring the Call Stack

The Call Stack dialog box shows a list of all active procedure calls. *Active procedure calls* are the procedures in the application that were started but not completed.

The Call Stack dialog box helps you trace the operation of an application as it executes a series of nested procedures. For example, an event procedure can call a second procedure, which can call a third procedure — all before the event procedure that started this chain is completed. Such nested procedure calls can be difficult to follow and can complicate the debugging process. Figure 13.17 shows the Call Stack dialog box.

> **Note** If you put the application in break mode during an idle loop, no entries appear in the Call Stack dialog box.

Figure 13.17 The Call Stack dialog box

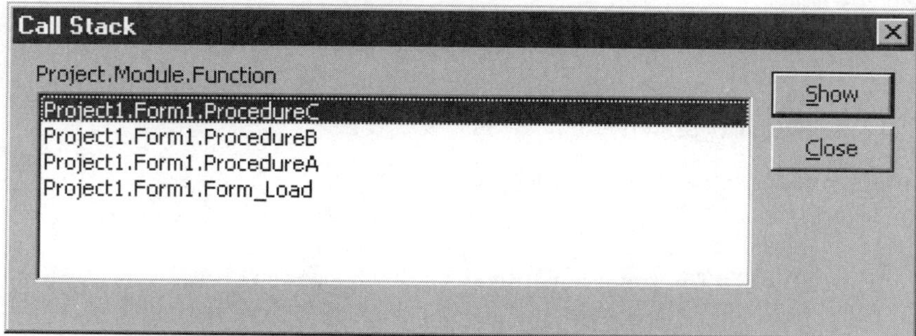

You can display the Call Stack dialog box only when the application is in break mode.

To display the Call Stack dialog box

- From the **View** menu, choose **Call Stack**.

  – or –

  Click the **Call Stack** button on the **Debug** toolbar. (To display the Debug toolbar, right-click on the Visual Basic toolbar and select the **Debug** option.)

  – or –

  Press CTRL+L.

  – or –

  Click the button next to the Procedure box in the **Locals** window.

Tracing Nested Procedures

The Call Stack dialog box lists all the active procedure calls in a series of nested calls. It places the earliest active procedure call at the bottom of the list and adds subsequent procedure calls to the top of the list.

The information given for each procedure begins with the module or form name, followed by the name of the called procedure. Because the Call Stack dialog box doesn't indicate the variable assigned to an instance of a form, it does not distinguish between multiple instances of forms or classes. For more information on multiple instances of a form, see Chapter 9, "Programming with Objects," and "Multiple-Document Interface (MDI) Applications" in Chapter 6, "Creating a User Interface."

You can use the Call Stack dialog box to display the statement in a procedure that passes control of the application to the next procedure in the list.

To display the statement that calls another procedure in the Calls Stack dialog box

1. In the **Call Stack** dialog box, select the procedure call you want to display.
2. Choose the **Show** button.

   The dialog box is closed and the procedure appears in the Code window.

The cursor location in the Code window indicates the statement that calls the next procedure in the Call Stack dialog box. If you choose the current procedure in the Call Stack dialog box, the cursor appears at the current statement.

Checking Recursive Procedures

The Call Stack dialog box can be useful in determining whether "Out of stack space" errors are caused by recursion. *Recursion* is the ability of a routine to call itself. You can test this by adding the following code to a form in a new project:

```
Sub Main()
   Static intX As Integer
   intX = intX + 1
   Main
End Sub

Private Sub Form_Click()
   Main
End Sub
```

Run the application, click the form, and wait for the "Out of stack space" error message. Choose the Debug button, and then choose Call Stack on the View menu. You'll see multiple calls to the Main procedure, as shown in Figure 13.18.

Figure 13.18 The Call Stack dialog box lists a recursive procedure

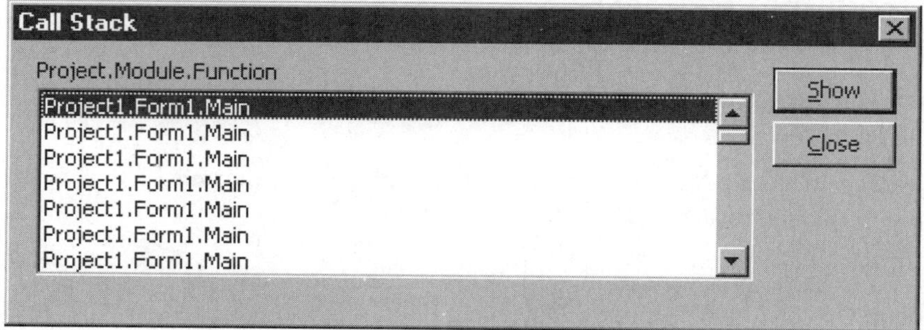

As a double check, highlight `intX` in the Code window, and choose Quick Watch from the Debug menu. The value for `intX` is the number of times the Main procedure executed before the break.

Testing Data and Procedures with the Immediate Window

Sometimes when you are debugging or experimenting with an application, you may want to execute individual procedures, evaluate expressions, or assign new values to variables or properties. You can use the Immediate window to accomplish these tasks. You evaluate expressions by printing their values in the Immediate window.

Printing Information in the Immediate Window

There are two ways to print to the Immediate window:

- Include `Debug.Print` statements in the application code.
- Enter Print methods directly in the Immediate window.

These printing techniques offer several advantages over watch expressions:

- You don't have to break execution to get feedback on how the application is performing. You can see data or other messages displayed as you run the application.
- Feedback is displayed in a separate area (the Immediate window), so it does not interfere with output that a user sees.
- Because you can save this code as part of the form, you don't have to redefine these statements the next time you work on the application.

Printing from Application Code

The Print method sends output to the Immediate window whenever you include the Debug object prefix:

Debug.Print [*items*][;]

For example, the following statement prints the value of `Salary` to the Immediate window every time it is executed:

```
Debug.Print "Salary = "; Salary
```

This technique works best when there is a particular place in your application code at which the variable (in this case, `Salary`) is known to change. For example, you might put the previous statement in a loop that repeatedly alters `Salary`.

> **Note** When you compile your application into an .exe file, `Debug.Print` statements are removed. Thus, if your application only uses `Debug.Print` statements with strings or simple variable types as arguments, it will not have any `Debug.Print` statements. However, Visual Basic will not strip out function calls appearing as arguments to `Debug.Print`. Thus, any side-effects of those functions will continue to happen in a compiled .exe file, even though the function results are not printed.

For More Information See "Debug Object," in the *Microsoft Visual Basic 6.0 Language Reference.*

Printing from Within the Immediate Window

Once you're in break mode, you can move the focus to the Immediate window to examine data.

To examine data in the Immediate window

1. Click the Immediate window (if visible).

   – or –

   From the **View** menu, choose **Immediate Window**.

   Once you have moved focus to the Immediate window, you then can use the Print method without the Debug object.

2. Type or paste a statement into the Immediate window, and then press ENTER.

   The Immediate window responds by carrying out the statement, as shown in Figure 13.19.

Figure 13.19 Using the Print method to print to the Immediate window

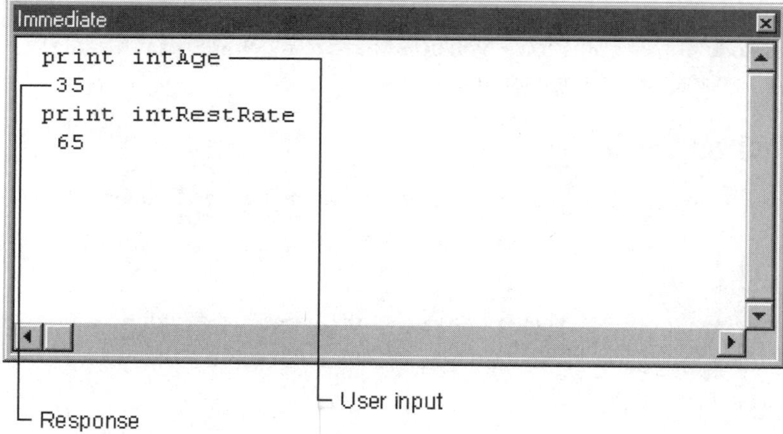

A question mark (?) is useful shorthand for the Print method. The question mark means the same as Print, and can be used in any context where Print is used. For example, the statements in Figure 13.19 could be entered as shown in Figure 13.20.

Figure 13.20 Using a question mark instead of the Print method

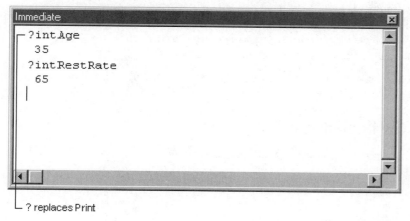

Printing Values of Properties

You can evaluate any valid expression in the Immediate window, including expressions involving properties. The currently active form or module determines the scope. If the execution halts within code that is attached to a form or class, you can refer to the properties of that form (or one of its controls) and make the reference to the form implicit with statements like the following:

```
? BackColor
? Text1.Height
```

Assuming that Text1 is a control on the currently active form, the first statement prints the numeric value of the current form's background color to the Immediate window. The second statement prints the height of Text1.

If execution is suspended in a module or another form, you must explicitly specify the form name as follows:

```
? Form1.BackColor
? Form1.Text1.Height
```

> **Note** Referencing an unloaded form in the Immediate window (or anywhere else) loads that form.

For More Information To learn about changing properties and values in the Immediate window, see the next section, "Assigning Values to Variables and Properties."

Assigning Values to Variables and Properties

As you start to isolate the possible cause of an error, you may want to test the effects of particular data values. In break mode, you can set values with statements like these in the Immediate window:

```
BackColor = 255
VScroll1.Value = 100
MaxRows = 50
```

The first statement alters a property of the currently active form, the second alters a property of `VScroll1`, and the third assigns a value to a variable.

After you set the values of one or more properties and variables, you can continue execution to see the results. Or you can test the effect on procedures, as described in the next section, "Testing Procedures with the Immediate Window."

Testing Procedures with the Immediate Window

The Immediate window evaluates any valid Visual Basic executable statement, but it doesn't accept data declarations. You can enter calls to Sub and Function procedures, however, which allows you to test the possible effect of a procedure with any given set of arguments. Simply enter a statement in the Immediate window (while in break mode) as you would in the Code window. For example:

```
X = Quadratic(2, 8, 8)
DisplayGraph 50, Arr1
Form_MouseDown 1, 0, 100, 100
```

When you press the ENTER key, Visual Basic switches to run time to execute the statement, and then returns to break mode. At that point, you can see results and test any possible effects on variables or property values.

Scope applies to procedure calls just as it does to variables. You can call any procedure within the currently active form. You can always call a procedure in a module, unless you define the procedure as Private, in which case you can call the procedure only while executing in the module.

For More Information Scope is discussed in "Introduction to Variables, Constants, and Data Types" in Chapter 5, "Programming Fundamentals."

Viewing and Testing Multiple Instances of Procedures

You can use the Immediate window to run a procedure repeatedly, testing the effect of different conditions. Each separate call of the procedure is maintained as a separate instance by Visual Basic. This allows you to separately test variables and property settings in each instance of the procedure. To see how this works, open a new project and add the following code to the form module:

```
Private Sub Form_Click()
   AProcedure
End Sub

Sub AProcedure()
   Dim intX As Integer
   intX = 10
   BProcedure
End Sub

Sub BProcedure()
   Stop
End Sub
```

Run the application and click the form. The Stop statement puts Visual Basic into break mode and the Immediate window is displayed. Change the value of `intX` to 15 in the procedure "AProcedure," switch to the Immediate window, and type the following:

```
AProcedure
```

This calls the procedure "AProcedure" and restarts the application. If you switch to the Immediate window and run "AProcedure" again, and then open the Call Stack dialog box, you'll see a listing much like the one in Figure 13.21. Each separate run of the program is listed, separated by the `[<Debug Window>]` listing.

Figure 13.21 The Call Stack dialog box shows multiple instances of procedures

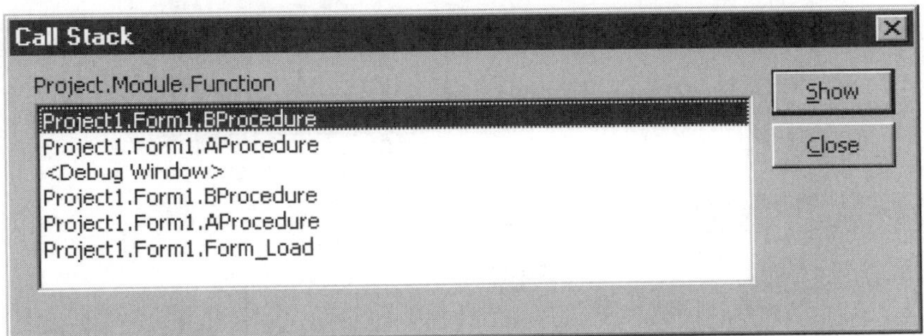

Visual Basic maintains a listing of the procedures executed by each command from the Immediate window. Newer listings are at the top of the list. You can use the Call Stack dialog box to select any instance of a procedure, and then print the values of variables from that procedure in the Immediate window.

For example, if you double-click the earliest instance of "AProcedure" and use the Immediate window to print the value of `intX`, it will return 10, as shown in Figure 13.22. If you changed the value of `intX` to 15 for the second run of the "AProcedure," that value is stored with the second instance of the procedure.

Figure 13.22 Printing the values of variables in the Immediate window

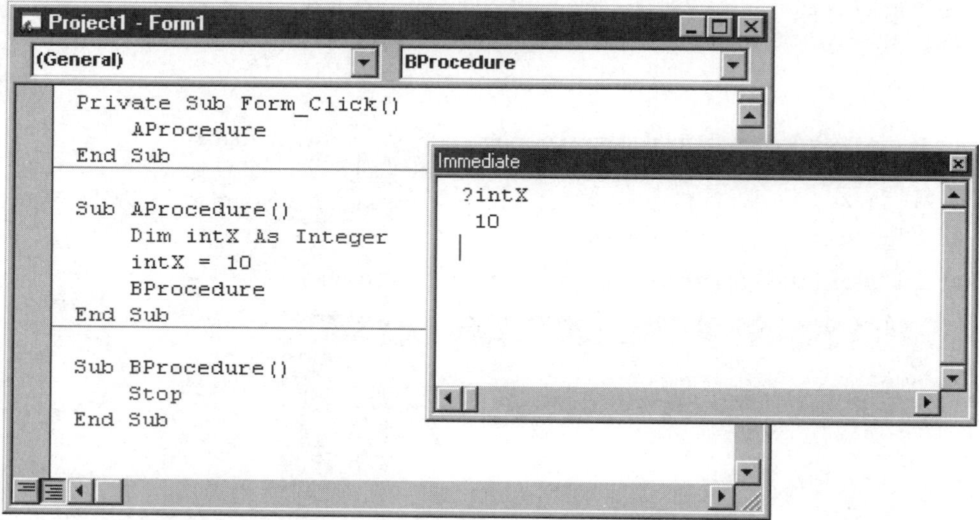

Note Although most statements are supported in the Immediate window, a control structure is valid only if it can be completely expressed on one line of code; use colons to separate the statements that make up the control structure. The following For loop is valid in the Immediate window:

```
For I = 1 To 20 : Print 2 * I : Next I
```

Checking Error Numbers

You can use the Immediate window to display the message associated with a specific error number. For example, enter this statement in the Immediate window:

```
error 58
```

Press ENTER to execute the statement. The appropriate error message is displayed, as shown in Figure 13.23.

Figure 13.23 Displaying error messages from the Immediate window

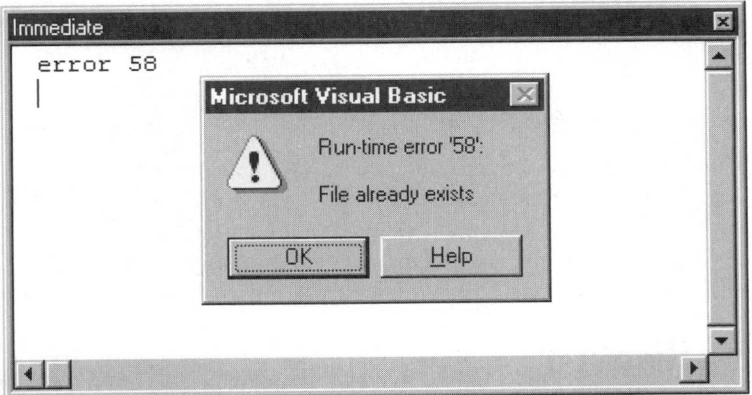

Tips for Using the Immediate Window

Here are some shortcuts you can use in the Immediate window:

- You can use Data Tips to inspect the value of a variable or object. Data Tips are similar to ToolTips except that they display the current value when the mouse is held over a variable or object property in the Code Window in Break mode. The display of Data Tips is limited to variables and objects that are currently in scope.
- Data Tips are also available in the Immediate window in Break mode. Unlike the Code Editor, the Immediate window will display values for object properties regardless of scope if a fully qualified object name is provided. For example, a Data Tip would always be displayed for Form1.Text1.Width, but not for Text1.Width unless Text1 was currently in scope.
- Once you enter a statement, you can execute it again by moving the insertion point back to that statement and pressing ENTER anywhere on the line.
- Before pressing ENTER, you can edit the current statement to alter its effects.
- You can use the mouse or the arrow keys to move around in the Immediate window. Don't press ENTER unless you are at a statement you want to execute.
- CTRL+HOME will take you to the top of the Immediate window; CTRL+END will take you to the bottom.
- The HOME and END keys move to the beginning and end of the current line.

  Note Although you will primarily use the Immediate window in Break mode, it is also possible to use the Immediate window in Design mode. This capability is provided in order to debug ActiveX components within the design environment. Using the Immediate window at Design time for a Standard project type may cause unexpected results.

Special Debugging Considerations

Certain events that are a common part of using Microsoft Windows can pose special problems for debugging an application. It's important to be aware of these special problems so they don't confuse or complicate the debugging process.

If you remain aware of how break mode can put events at odds with what your application expects, you can usually find solutions. In some event procedures, you may need to use `Debug.Print` statements to monitor values of variables or properties instead of using watch expressions or breakpoints. You may also need to change the values of variables that depend on the sequence of events. This is discussed in the following topics.

Breaking Execution During MouseDown

If you break execution during a MouseDown event procedure, you may release the mouse button or use the mouse to do any number of tasks. When you continue execution, however, the application assumes that the mouse button is still pressed down. You don't get a MouseUp event until you press the mouse button down again and then release it.

When you press the mouse button down during run time, you break execution in the MouseDown event procedure again, assuming you have a breakpoint there. In this scenario, you never get to the MouseUp event. The solution is usually to remove the breakpoint in the MouseDown procedure.

Breaking Execution During KeyDown

If you break execution during a KeyDown procedure, similar considerations apply. If you retain a breakpoint in a KeyDown procedure, you may never get a KeyUp event. (KeyDown and KeyUp are described in Chapter 11, "Responding to Mouse and Keyboard Events.")

Breaking Execution During GotFocus or LostFocus

If you break execution during a GotFocus or LostFocus event procedure, the timing of system messages can cause inconsistent results. Use a `Debug.Print` statement instead of a breakpoint in GotFocus or LostFocus event procedures.

Modal Dialogs and Message Boxes Suppress Events

The development environment cannot raise events while a modal form or message box is displayed, because of potential conflicts in the debugger. Therefore, events are suppressed until the modal form or message box is dismissed.

Important Suppression of events only happens in the development environment. Once a project is compiled, events will be raised even when a modal form or message box is displayed.

Some example scenarios in which this can occur:

- A form with a Timer control on it is running in the development environment. Selecting Options from the Tools menu will open the Options dialog box, which is modal. Until the dialog is dismissed, the Timer control's Timer event will not be raised.
- An instance of a UserControl with a Timer control on it is placed on a form at design time. (The timer may be used to make the control appear animated; this effect can occur even in design mode, because controls can execute code at design time.) Selecting Add Class Module from the Project menu will open the Add Class Module dialog, which is modal. The Timer control's Timer event will be suppressed until the dialog is dismissed.
- A UserDocument contains a Timer control, and a command button that displays a message box. If the UserDocument is being debugged using Internet Explorer, pressing the button to display the message box will cause the Timer control's Timer event to be suppressed until the message box is dismissed.

Testing and Using Command-Line Arguments

You can choose to have your application use command-line arguments, which provide data to your application at startup. The user can enter them by choosing the operating environment's Run command, and then typing arguments after the application name. You can also use command-line arguments when creating an icon for the application.

For example, suppose you create an alarm clock application. One of the techniques for setting the alarm time is to let the user type in the selected time directly. The user might enter the following string in the Run dialog box:

```
Alarm 11:00:00
```

The Command function returns all arguments entered after the application name (in this case, Alarm). The Alarm application has only one argument, so in the application code, you can assign this argument directly to the string that stores the selected time:

```
AlarmTime = Command
```

If Command returns an empty string, there are no command-line arguments. The application must either ask for the information directly or select a default action.

To test code that uses Command, you can specify sample command-line arguments from within the Visual Basic environment. The application evaluates sample command-line input the same way it does if the user types the argument.

To set sample command-line arguments

1. From the **Project** menu, choose **Properties**.
2. Click the **Make** tab on the **Project Properties** dialog box.
3. Enter the sample arguments in the **Command Line Arguments** field. (Do not type the name of the application itself.)
4. Choose **OK**.
5. Run the application.

For More Information See "Command Function" in the *Microsoft Visual Basic 6.0 Language Reference* volume of the *Microsoft Visual Basic 6.0 Reference Library*.

Removing Debugging Information Before Compiling

If you do not want debugging statements included in the application you distribute to users, use conditional compilation to conveniently delete these statements when the Make EXE File command is used.

For example:

```
Sub Assert(Expr As Boolean, Msg As String)
   If Not Expr Then
      MsgBox Msg
   End If
End Sub

Sub AProcedure(intX As Integer)
   # If fDebug Then
      Assert intX < 10000 and intX > 0, _
      "Argument out of range"
   # End If
      ' The code can now assume the correct value.
End Sub
```

Because the call to the Assert procedure is conditionally compiled, it is only included in the .exe file if fDebug is set to True. When you compile the distribution version of the application, set fDebug to False. As a result, the .exe file will be as small and fast as possible.

> **Note** Since the release of Visual Basic version 5.0, it is no longer necessary to create your own Assert procedures. The Debug.Assert statement performs the same function and is automatically stripped from the compiled code. See the next section, "Verifying Your Code with Assertions," for more information.

Verifying Your Code with Assertions

Assertions are a convenient way to test for conditions that should exist at specific points in your code. Think of an Assert statement as making an assumption. If your assumption is True, the assertion will be ignored; if your assumption is False, VB will bring it to your attention.

In Visual Basic, assertions take the form of a method: the Assert method of the Debug object. The Assert method takes a single argument of the type Boolean which states the condition to be evaluated. The syntax for the Assert method is as follows:

Debug.Assert(*boolean expression***)**

A Debug.Assert statement will never appear in a compiled application, but when you're running in the design environment it causes the application to enter break mode with the line containing the statement highlighted (assuming that the expression evaluates to False). The following example shows the Debug.Assert statement:

```
Debug.Assert Trim(CustName) <> "John Doe"
```

In this case, if the CustName is John Doe, the application will enter break mode; otherwise the execution will continue as usual. Using Debug.Assert is similar to setting a watch with the Break When Value Is True option selected, except that it will break when the value is false.

Using Compile on Demand

Compile on Demand and Background Compile are related features that allow your application to run faster in the development environment. It's possible that using these features may hide compile errors in your code until you make an exe for your entire project. Both features are turned on by default, and they can be turned on or off on the General tab of the Options dialog box available from the Tools menu.

Compile on Demand allows your application, in the development environment, to compile code only as needed. When Compile on Demand is on and you choose Start from the Run menu (or press the F5 key), only the code necessary to start the application is compiled. Then, as you exercise more of your application's capabilities in the development environment, more code is compiled as needed.

Background Compile allows Visual Basic at run time in the development environment to continue compiling code if no other actions are occurring.

With these features turned on, some code may not be compiled when a project is run in the development environment. Then, when you choose to Make EXE file (or turn off Compile on Demand), you may see new and unexpected errors as that code is newly compiled.

There are three techniques you can use at development milestones, or any other time, to flush out any errors hidden by using Compile on Demand.

- Turn Compile on Demand off and then run the application. This forces Visual Basic to check the entire application for compile errors.
- Make an executable with your project. This will also force Visual Basic to check the entire application for compile errors.
- Choose Start With Full Compile from the Run menu.

Tips for Debugging

There are several ways to simplify debugging:

- When your application doesn't produce correct results, browse through the code and try to find statements that may have caused the problem. Set breakpoints at these statements and restart the application.
- When the program halts, test the values of important variables and properties. Use Quick Watch or set watch expressions to monitor these values. Use the Immediate window to examine variables and expressions.
- Use the Break on All Errors option to determine where an error occurred. To temporarily change this option, select Toggle from the Code window context menu, then toggle the option from the submenu. Step through your code, using watch expressions and the Locals window to monitor how values change as the code runs.
- If an error occurs in a loop, define a break expression to determine where the problem occurs. Use the Immediate window together with Set Next Statement to re-execute the loop after making corrections.
- If you determine that a variable or property is causing problems in your application, use a Debug.Assert statement to halt execution when the wrong value is assigned to the variable or property.
- To set the error trapping state that Visual Basic defaults to at the beginning of any debugging session, open the Options dialog box (available from the Tools menu), select the General tab, and set the Default Error Trapping State option. Visual Basic will use this setting the next time you start it, even if the setting was entered for another project.

Occasionally you may encounter a bug that's especially difficult to track down. Don't panic — here are some things that you can do:

- First and foremost, make a backup. This is the point at which even experienced programmers frequently lose many hours of work. When you experiment, it is far too easy to accidentally overwrite or delete necessary sections of code.

- Use the debugging facilities built in to Visual Basic. Attempt to identify the line or lines of code generating the error. Isolate the code. If you can isolate the problem to one block of code, try to reproduce the same problem with this block of code separated from the rest of your program. Select the code, copy it, start a new project, paste the code into the new project, run the new project, and see if the error still occurs.
- Create a log file. If you cannot isolate the code or if the problem is erratic or if the problem only happens when compiled, then the debugging facility of Visual Basic will be less effective. In these situations you can create a log file which records the activity of your program. This will allow you to progressively isolate the location of the suspect code. Call the following procedure from various points in your program. You should pass in a string of text which indicates the current location of the code executing in your program.

```
Sub LogFile (Message As String)
   Dim LogFile As Integer
   LogFile = FreeFile
   Open "C:\VB\LogFile.Log" For Append As #LogFile
   Print #LogFile, Message
   Close #LogFile
End Sub

Sub Sub1 ()
   '...
   Call LogFile("Here I am in Sub1")
   '...
End Sub
```

- Simplify the problem. If possible, remove any third party controls and custom controls from your project. Replace them with Visual Basic standard controls. Eliminate any code that does not seem to relate to the problem.
- Reduce the search space. If you cannot resolve the problem with any of the above methods, then it is time to eliminate all other non-Visual Basic causes from the problem search space. Copy your AUTOEXEC.BAT and CONFIG.SYS files to backup files. Comment out any and all drivers and programs from these two files that are not absolutely essential to running your program under Windows. Change your Windows video driver to the standard Windows VGA driver. Shut down Windows and reboot your machine. This will eliminate the possibility that there is some other program or driver which is interfering with your program.
- If you cannot locate a solution and are unable to isolate or resolve the problem with any of these methods, it's time to look for help. See the technical support documentation.

For More Information Breakpoints are described in "Using a Breakpoint to Selectively Halt Execution" earlier in this chapter. Read more about Watch expressions in "Monitoring Data with Watch Expressions." The Immediate window is discussed in "Testing Data and Procedures with the Immediate Window." See "Verifying Your Code with Assertions" for more about the Assert method of the Debug object.

CHAPTER 14

Processing Drives, Folders, and Files

When programming in Windows, it's very important to have the ability to add, move, change, create, or delete folders (directories) and files, and get information about and manipulate drives.

Visual Basic allows you to process drives, folders, and files in two different ways: through traditional methods such as the Open statement, Write#, and so forth, and through a new set of tools, the File System Object (FSO) object model.

Contents

Introduction to the File System Object Model

A new feature for Visual Basic is the File System Object (FSO) object model, which provides an object-based tool for working with folders and files. This allows you to use the familiar `object.method` syntax with a rich set of properties, methods, and events to process folders and files, in addition to using the traditional Visual Basic statements and commands.

The FSO object model gives your applications the ability to create, alter, move, and delete folders, or to detect if particular folders exist, and if so, where. It also enables you to gain information about folders, such as their names, the date they were created or last modified, and so forth.

The FSO object model makes processing files much easier as well. When processing files, your primary goal is to store data in a space- and resource-efficient, easy-to-access format. You need to be able to create files, insert and change the data, and output (read) the data. While you can store data in a database, such as Jet or SQL, it adds a significant amount of overhead to your application. For many reasons, you may not want to have such an overhead, or your data access requirements may not require all the extra features associated with a full-featured database. In this case, storing your data in a binary or text file is the most efficient solution.

The FSO object model, which is contained in the Scripting type library (Scrrun.Dll), supports text file creation and manipulation through the TextStream object. It does not as yet, however, support the creation or manipulation of binary files. To manipulate binary files, use the Open command with the Binary flag. Full information on how to manipulate binary files is contained in "Using Binary File Access," later in this chapter.

The File System Objects

The FSO object model has these objects:

Object	Description
Drive	Allows you to gather information about drives attached to the system, such as how much room is available, what its share name is, and so forth. Note that a "drive" isn't necessarily a hard disk. It can be a CD-ROM drive, a RAM disk, and so forth. Also, drives aren't required to be physically attached to the system; they can be also be logically connected through a LAN.
Folder	Allows you to create, delete, or move folders, plus query the system as to their names, paths, and so on.
Files	Allows you to create, delete, or move files, plus query the system as to their names, paths, and so on.
FileSystemObject	The main object of the group, full of methods that allow you to create, delete, gain information about, and generally manipulate drives, folders, and files. Many of the methods associated with this object duplicate those in the other objects.
TextStream	Enables you to read and write text files.

For information about the various properties, methods, and events in the FSO object model, use the Object Browser in Visual Basic (press F2) and look at the Scripting type library.

Programming in the FSO Object Model

Programming in the FSO object model involves three main tasks:

- Using the CreateObject method, or dimension a variable as a FileSystemObject object to create a FileSystemObject object.
- Using the appropriate method on the newly-created object.
- Accessing the object's properties.

The FSO object model is contained in a type library called Scripting, which is located in the file Scrrun.Dll. If you don't already have a reference to it, check Microsoft Scripting Runtime in the References dialog available from the Properties menu. You can then use the Object Browser to view its objects, collections, properties, methods, and events, as well as its constants.

Creating a FileSystemObject Object

The first step is to create a FileSystemObject object to work with. You can do this in two ways:

- Dimension a variable as type FileSystemObject object:

  ```
  Dim fso As New FileSystemObject
  ```

- Use the CreateObject method to create a FileSystemObject object:

  ```
  Set fso = CreateObject("Scripting.FileSystemObject")
  ```

  In the above syntax, Scripting is the name of the type library, and FileSystemObject is the name of the object which you want to create an instance of.

  Note The first method works only in Visual Basic, while the second method works either in Visual Basic or VBScript.

Using the Appropriate Method

The next step is to use the appropriate method of the FileSystemObject object. For example, if you want to *create* a new object, you can use either CreateFolder or CreateTextFile. (The FSO object model doesn't support the creation or deletion of drives.)

If you want to delete objects, you can use the DeleteFile and DeleteFolder methods of the FileSystemObject object, or the Delete method of the File and Folder objects.

Using the appropriate methods, you can also copy and move files and folders.

Note that some functionality in the FileSystemObject object model is redundant. For example, you can copy a file using either the CopyFile method of the FileSystemObject object, or you can use the Copy method of the File object. The methods work the same. Both exist to give you maximum programming flexibility.

Accessing Existing Drives, Files, and Folders

To gain access to an *existing* drive, file, or folder, use the appropriate "get" method of the FileSystemObject object:

- GetDrive
- GetFolder
- GetFile

For example:

```
Dim fso As New FileSystemObject, fil As File
Set fil = fso.GetFile("c:\test.txt")
```

Note, however, that you don't need to use the "get" methods for newly-created objects, since the "create" functions already return a handle to the newly-created object. For example, if you create a new folder using the CreateFolder method, you don't then need to use the GetFolder method to access its properties, such as Name, Path, Size, and so forth. Just set a variable to the CreateFolder function to gain a handle to the newly-created folder, then access its properties, methods, and events:

```
Private Sub Create_Folder()
   Dim fso As New FileSystemObject, fldr As Folder
   Set fldr = fso.CreateFolder("C:\MyTest")
   MsgBox "Created folder: " & fldr.Name
End Sub
```

Accessing the Object's Properties

Once you have a handle to an object, you can access its properties. For example, say you want to obtain the name of a particular folder. First you create an instance of the object, then you get a handle to it with the appropriate method (in this case, the GetFolder method, since the folder already exists):

```
Set fldr = fso.GetFolder("c:\")
```

Now that you have a handle to a Folder object, you can check its Name property:

```
Debug.Print "Folder name is: "; fldr.Name
```

If you want to find out the last time a file was modified, use the following syntax:

```
Dim fso As New FileSystemObject, fil As File
Set fil = fso.GetFile("c:\detlog.txt")  ' Get a File object to query.
Debug.Print "File last modified: "; fil.DateLastModified ' Print info.
```

Working with Drives and Folders

With the FSO object model you can work with drives and folders programmatically just as you can in the Windows Explorer interactively. You can copy and move folders, get information about drives and folders, and so forth.

Getting Information About Drives

The Drive object allows you to gain information about the various drives attached to a system, either physically or over a network. Its properties allow you to obtain information about:

- The total size of the drive in bytes (TotalSize property)
- How much space is available on the drive in bytes (AvailableSpace or FreeSpace properties)
- What letter is assigned to the drive (DriveLetter property)
- What type of drive it is, such as removable, fixed, network, CD-ROM, or RAM disk (DriveType property)
- The drive's serial number (SerialNumber property)
- The type of file system the drive uses, such as FAT, FAT32, NTFS, and so forth (FileSystem property)
- Whether a drive is available for use (IsReady property)
- The name of the share and/or volume (ShareName and VolumeName properties)
- The path or root folder of the drive (Path and RootFolder properties)

Example Usage of the Drive Object

The example below shows how to use the Drive object to gather information about a drive. Remember that you won't see a reference to an actual Drive object in the following code; rather, you use the GetDrive method to get a reference to an existing Drive object (in this case, `drv`):

```
Private Sub Command3_Click()
   Dim fso As New FileSystemObject, drv As Drive, s As String
   Set drv = fso.GetDrive(fso.GetDriveName("c:"))
   s = "Drive " & UCase("c:") & " - "
   s = s & drv.VolumeName & vbCrLf
   s = s & "Total Space: " & FormatNumber(drv.TotalSize / 1024, 0)
   s = s & " Kb" & vbCrLf
   s = s & "Free Space: " & FormatNumber(drv.FreeSpace / 1024, 0)
   s = s & " Kb" & vbCrLf
   MsgBox s
End Sub
```

Using CurDir, ChDrive, ChDir, or App.Path

If you use the CurDir function, the ChDrive and ChDir statements, or the Path property (App.Path), be aware that they may return a UNC path (that is, \\Server\Share…) rather than a drive path (such as E:\Folder), depending on how you run your program or project.

App.Path returns a UNC path:

- When you run a project after loading it from a network share, even if the network share is mapped to a drive letter.
- When you run a compiled executable file from a network share (but only if it is run using a UNC path).

ChDrive cannot handle UNC paths, and thus raises an error when App.Path returns one. You can handle this error by adding On Error Resume Next before the ChDrive statement, or by testing the first two characters of App.Path to see if they are backslashes:

```
On Error Resume Next
ChDrive App.Path
ChDir App.Path
```

This modification handles all cases in which the program is started from Windows using a UNC path (for example, in the Run dialog accessed from the Start menu), because Windows sets the current directory to a UNC path. ChDir handles changes between UNC paths correctly. (The failure of ChDrive can be ignored, because there is no drive letter for a UNC path.)

However, the above code above won't work if you run the program by entering a UNC path at MS-DOS command prompt. This is because the command prompt always has a drive path for the current directory, so CurDir is set to a drive path. ChDir does not raise an error, but it fails to change the directory from a drive path to a UNC path. The only workaround for this situation is to locate a local drive that's mapped to the share specified in the UNC path, or to use network commands to create such a mapping.

If the project is loaded into the Visual Basic IDE from a network share — either a UNC path or a mapped drive path — then App.Path returns a UNC path when the project is run and ChDrive fails and raises an error. ChDir doesn't raise an error, but the directory is not changed. The only workaround is to manually set the drive and directory:

```
Const PROJECTSHARE = "E:\VBPROJ\MYPROJECT"
#Const Debug = True
#If Debug Then
   ChDrive PROJECTSHARE
   ChDir PROJECTSHARE
#Else
   On Error Resume Next
   ChDrive App.Path
   ChDir App.Path
#End If
```

If more than one person might open the project on the network share, a DOS environment variable can be used to allow each person to have their own mapping for the share:

```
#Const Debug = True
#If Debug Then
   ChDrive Environ("MYPROJECTDIR")
   ChDir Environ("MYPROJECTDIR")
#Else
   On Error Resume Next
   ChDrive App.Path
   ChDir App.Path
#End If
```

The value of MYPROJECTDIR specifies the mapped drive letter and the path, for example:

```
SET MYPROJECTDIR=M:\VBProj\MyProject
```

Working with Folders

This list shows common folder tasks and the methods for doing them:

Task	Method
Create a folder	FileSystemObject.CreateFolder
Delete a folder	Folder.Delete or FileSystemObject.DeleteFolder
Move a folder	Folder.Move or FileSystemObject.MoveFolder
Copy a folder	Folder.Copy or FileSystemObject.CopyFolder
Retrieve the name of a folder	Folder.Name
Find out if a folder exists on a drive	FileSystemObject.FolderExists
Get an instance of an existing Folder object	FileSystemObject.GetFolder
Find out the name of a folder's parent folder	FileSystemObject.GetParentFolderName
Find out the path of system folders	FileSystemObject.GetSpecialFolder

Example

This example demonstrates usage of the Folder and FileSystemObject objects to manipulate folders and gain information about them:

```
Private Sub Command10_Click()
   ' Get instance of FileSystemObject.
   Dim fso As New FileSystemObject, fldr As Folder, s As String
   ' Get Drive object.
   Set fldr = fso.GetFolder("c:")
   ' Print parent folder name.
   Debug.Print "Parent folder name is: " & fldr
   ' Print drive name.
   Debug.Print "Contained on drive " & fldr.Drive
   ' Print root file name.
   If fldr.IsRootFolder = True Then
      Debug.Print "This folder is a root folder."
   Else
      Debug.Print "This folder isn't a root folder."
   End If
   ' Create a new folder with the FileSystemObject object.
   fso.CreateFolder ("c:\Bogus")
   Debug.Print "Created folder C:\Bogus"
   ' Print the base name of the folder.
   Debug.Print "Basename = " & fso.GetBaseName("c:\bogus")
   ' Get rid of the newly-created folder.
   fso.DeleteFolder ("c:\Bogus")
   Debug.Print "Deleted folder C:\Bogus"
End Sub
```

Working with Files

You can work with files in Visual Basic by using the new object-oriented FSO objects such as Copy, Delete, Move, and OpenAsTextStream, among others, or by using the older existing functions such as Open, Close, FileCopy, GetAttr, and so forth. Note that you can move, copy, or delete files regardless of their file type.

For more information on usage of the older existing functions, see "Processing Files with Older File I/O Statements and Functions" in this chapter. The rest of this section describes using the new FSO objects, methods, and properties to work with files.

There are two major categories of file manipulation:

- Creating, adding, or removing data, and reading files
- Moving, copying, and deleting files

Creating Files and Adding Data with File System Objects

There are three ways to create a sequential text file (sometimes referred to as a "text stream"). One way is to use the CreateTextFile method. To create an empty text file:

```
Dim fso As New FileSystemObject, fil As File
Set fil = fso.CreateTextFile("c:\testfile.txt", True)
```

> **Note** The FSO object model does not yet support the creation of random or binary files. To create random and binary files, use the Open command with either the Random or Binary flag. Full information on how to manipulate random and binary files is contained in "Using Random File Access" and "Using Binary File Access," later in this chapter.

Another way is to use either the OpenTextFile method of the FileSystemObject object with the ForWriting flag set:

```
Dim fso As New FileSystemObject, ts As New TextStream
Set ts = fso.OpenTextFile("c:\test.txt", ForWriting)
```

Or you can use the OpenAsTextStream method with the ForWriting flag set:

```
Dim fso As New FileSystemObject, fil As File, ts As TextStream
Set fso = CreateObject("Scripting.FileSystemObject")
fso.CreateTextFile ("test1.txt")
Set fil = fso.GetFile("test1.txt")
Set ts = fil.OpenAsTextStream(ForWriting)
```

Adding Data to the File

Once the text file is created, you can add data to it in three steps:

1. Open the text file for the writing of data.
2. Write the data.
3. Close the file.

To open the file, you can use either of two methods: the OpenAsTextStream method of the File object, or the OpenTextFile method of the FileSystemObject object.

To write data to the open text file, use either the Write or WriteLine methods of the TextStream object. The only difference between Write and WriteLine is that WriteLine adds newline characters to the end of the specified string.

If you want to add a newline to the text file, use the WriteBlankLines method.

To close an open file, use the Close method of the TextStream object.

Here's an example of how to open a file, use all three write methods to add data to the file, then close the file:

```
Sub Create_File()
   Dim fso, txtfile
   Set fso = CreateObject("Scripting.FileSystemObject")
   Set txtfile = fso.CreateTextFile("c:\testfile.txt", True)
   txtfile.Write ("This is a test. ") ' Write a line.
   ' Write a line with a newline character.
   txtfile.WriteLine("Testing 1, 2, 3.")
   ' Write three newline characters to the file.
   txtfile.WriteBlankLines(3)
   txtfile.Close
End Sub
```

Reading Files with File System Objects

To read data from a text file, use the Read, ReadLine, or ReadAll methods of the TextStream object:

Task	Method
Read a specified number of characters from a file	Read
Read an entire line (up to, but not including, the newline character)	ReadLine
Read the entire contents of a text file	ReadAll

If you use the Read or ReadLine method and you want to skip to a particular portion of data, you can use the Skip or SkipLine method.

The resulting text of the read methods is stored in a string which can be displayed in a control, parsed by string operators (such as Left, Right, and Mid), concatenated, and so forth.

> **Note** The vbNewLine constant contains a character or characters (depending on the operating system) to advance the cursor to the beginning of the next line (carriage-return/linefeed). Be aware that the ends of some strings may have such nonprinting characters.

Example

```
Sub Read_Files()
   Dim fso As New FileSystemObject, txtfile, _
      fil1 As File, ts As TextStream
   Set txtfile = fso.CreateTextFile("c:\testfile.txt", True)
   MsgBox "Writing file"
   ' Write a line.
   Set fil1 = fso.GetFile("c:\testfile.txt")
```

```
    Set ts = fil1.OpenAsTextStream(ForWriting)
    ts.Write "Hello World"
    ts.Close
    ' Read the contents of the file.
    Set ts = fil1.OpenAsTextStream(ForReading)
    s = ts.ReadLine
    MsgBox s
    ts.Close
End Sub
```

Moving, Copying, and Deleting Files

The FSO object model has two methods each for moving, copying, and deleting files:

Task	Method
Move a file	File.Move or FileSystemObject.MoveFile
Copy a file	File.Copy or FileSystemObject.CopyFile
Delete a file	File.Delete or FileSystemObject.DeleteFile

Example

This example creates a text file in the root directory of drive C, writes some information to it, moves it to a directory called \tmp, makes a copy of it in a directory called \temp, then deletes the copies from both directories.

To run this example, make sure that you have directories named \tmp and \temp in the root directory of drive C.

```
Sub Manip_Files()
    Dim fso as New FileSystemObject, txtfile, fil1, fil2
    Set txtfile = fso.CreateTextFile("c:\testfile.txt", True)
    MsgBox "Writing file"
    ' Write a line.
    txtfile.Write ("This is a test.")
    ' Close the file to writing.
    txtfile.Close
    MsgBox "Moving file to c:\tmp"
    ' Get a handle to the file in root of C:\.
    Set fil1 = fso.GetFile("c:\testfile.txt")
    ' Move the file to \tmp directory.
    fil1.Move ("c:\tmp\testfile.txt")
    MsgBox "Copying file to c:\temp"
    ' Copy the file to \temp.
    fil1.Copy ("c:\temp\testfile.txt")
```

```
    MsgBox "Deleting files"
    ' Get handles to files' current location.
    Set fil1 = fso.GetFile("c:\tmp\testfile.txt")
    Set fil2 = fso.GetFile("c:\temp\testfile.txt")
    ' Delete the files.
    fil1.Delete
    fil2.Delete
    MsgBox "All done!"
End Sub
```

Processing Files with Older File I/O Statements and Functions

Ever since the first version of Visual Basic, files have been processed using the Open statement and other related statements and functions (listed below). These mechanisms will eventually be phased out in favor of the FSO object model, but they are fully supported in Visual Basic 6.0.

If you can design your application to use database files, you will not need to provide direct file access in your application. The data control and bound controls let you read and write data to and from a database, which is much easier than using direct file-access techniques.

However, there are times when you need to read and write to files other than databases. This set of topics shows how to process files directly to create, manipulate, and store text and other data.

File Access Types

By itself, a *file* consists of nothing more than a series of related bytes located on a disk. When your application accesses a file, it must assume what the bytes are supposed to represent (characters, data records, integers, strings, and so on).

Depending upon what kind of data the file contains, you use the appropriate file access type. In Visual Basic, there are three types of file access:

- Sequential — For reading and writing text files in continuous blocks.
- Random — For reading and writing text or binary files structured as fixed-length records.
- Binary — For reading and writing arbitrarily structured files.

Sequential access is designed for use with plain text files. Each character in the file is assumed to represent either a text character or a text formatting sequence, such as a newline character (NL). Data is stored as ANSI characters. It is assumed that a file opened for *random access* is composed of a set of identical-length *records*. You can employ user-defined types to create records made up of numerous fields — each can have different data types. Data is stored as binary information.

Binary access allows you to use files to store data however you want. It is similar to random access, except there are no assumptions made about data type or record length. However, you must know precisely how the data was written to the file to retrieve it correctly.

For More Information To learn more about file access types, see "Using Sequential File Access," "Using Random File Access," and "Using Binary File Access," later in this chapter.

File Access Functions and Statements

The following functions are used with all three types of file access:

Dir	FileLen	LOF
EOF	FreeFile	Seek
FileCopy	GetAttr	SetAttr
FileDateTime	Loc	

The following table lists all of the file access statements and functions available for each of the three types of direct file access.

Statements & Functions	Sequential	Random	Binary
Close	X	X	X
Get		X	X
Input( )	X		X
Input #	X		
Line Input #	X		
Open	X	X	X
Print #	X		
Put		X	X
Type...End Type		X	
Write #	X		

For More Information For additional information on file access functions and statements, look up the function or statement topic in the index.

Using Sequential File Access

It is recommended that you use File System Objects to create text files, but this information is provided in case you need to use the older text file creation methods.

Sequential access works best when you want to process files consisting only of text, such as the files created with a typical text editor — that is, files in which data is *not* divided into a series of records. Sequential access may not be well suited for storing long series of numbers, because each number is stored as a character string. A four-digit number would require 4 bytes of storage instead of the 2 bytes it requires to store the same number as an integer.

Opening Files for Sequential Access

When you open a file for sequential access, you open it to perform one of the following operations:

- Input characters from a file (Input)
- Output characters to a file (Output)
- Append characters to a file (Append)

To open a file for sequential access, use the following syntax for the Open statement:

Open *pathname* **For** [**Input** | **Output** | **Append**] **As** *filenumber* [**Len** = *buffersize*]

When you open a sequential file for Input, the file must already exist; otherwise, an error occurs. When you try to open a nonexistent file for Output or Append, however, the Open statement creates the file first and then opens it.

The optional Len argument specifies the number of characters to buffer when copying data between the file and your program.

After opening a file for an Input, Output, or Append operation, you must close it, using the Close statement, before reopening it for another type of operation.

Editing Files Opened for Sequential Access

If you want to edit a file, first read its contents to program variables, then change the variables, and finally, write the variables back to the file. The following sections discuss how to edit records opened for sequential access.

Reading Strings from Files

To retrieve the contents of a text file, open the file for sequential Input. Then use the Line Input #, Input( ), or Input # statement to copy the file into program variables.

Visual Basic provides statements and functions that will read and write sequential files one character at a time or one line at a time.

For example, the following code fragment reads a file line by line:

```
Dim LinesFromFile, NextLine As String

Do Until EOF(FileNum)
   Line Input #FileNum, NextLine
   LinesFromFile = LinesFromFile + NextLine + Chr(13) + Chr(10)
Loop
```

Although Line Input # recognizes the end of a line when it comes to the carriage return-linefeed sequence, it does not include the carriage return-linefeed when it reads the line into the variable. If you want to retain the carriage return-linefeed, your code must add it.

You can also use the Input # statement, which reads a list of numbers and/or string expressions written to the file. For example, to read in a line from a mailing list file, you might use the following statement:

```
Input #FileNum, name, street, city, state, zip
```

You can use the Input function to copy any number of characters from a file to a variable, provided the variable is large enough. For example, the following code uses Input to copy the specified number of characters to a variable:

```
LinesFromFile = Input(n, FileNum)
```

To copy an entire file to a variable, use the InputB function to copy bytes from a file to a variable. Since the InputB function returns an ANSI string, you must use the StrConv function to convert the ANSI string to a UNICODE string as follows:

```
LinesFromFile = StrConv(InputB(LOF(FileNum), FileNum), vbUnicode)
```

Writing Strings to Files

To store the contents of variables in a sequential file, open it for sequential Output or Append, and then use the Print # statement. For example, a text editor might use the following line of code to copy the contents of a text box into a file:

```
Print #FileNum, TheBox.Text
```

Visual Basic also supports the Write # statement, which writes a list of numbers and/or string expressions to a file. It automatically separates each expression with a comma and puts quotation marks around string expressions:

```
Dim AnyString As String, AnyNumber As Integer

AnyString = "AnyCharacters"
AnyNumber = 23445
Write #FileNum, AnyString, AnyNumber
```

This code segment writes two expressions to the file specified by `FileNum`. The first contains a string and the second contains the number 23445. Therefore, Visual Basic writes the following characters (including all punctuation) to the file:

```
"AnyCharacters",23445
```

Note If you are using Write # and Input # with sequential access, consider using random or binary access instead, because they are better suited to record-oriented data.

For More Information For additional information on sequential file access, see "Open Statement" in the *Microsoft Visual Basic 6.0 Language Reference* volume of the *Microsoft Visual Basic 6.0 Reference Library*.

Using Random File Access

The File System Object model does not provide random file creation or access methods. If you need to create or read random files, this information will help you do so.

The bytes in random-access files form identical records, each containing one or more fields. A record with one field corresponds to any standard type, such as an integer or fixed-length string. A record with more than one field corresponds to a user-defined type. For example, the Worker Type defined below creates 19-byte records that consist of three fields:

```
Type Worker
   LastName As String * 10
   Title As String * 7
   Rank  As String * 2
End Type
```

Declaring Variables

Before your application opens a file for random access, it should declare all variables required to handle data from the file. This includes user-defined types, which correspond to records in the file, as well as standard types for other variables that hold data related to processing a file opened for random access.

Defining Record Types

Before opening a file for random access, define a type that corresponds to the records the file does or will contain. For example, an Employee Records file could declare a user-defined data type called `Person` as follows:

```
Type Person
   ID                  As Integer
   MonthlySalary       As Currency
   LastReviewDate      As Long
   FirstName           As String * 15
```

```
   LastName          As String * 15
   Title             As String * 15
   ReviewComments    As String * 150
End Type
```

Declaring Field Variables in a Type Definition

Because all records in a random-access file must have the same length, it is often useful for string elements in a user-defined type to have a fixed length, as shown in the `Person` type declaration above, where, for instance, `FirstName` and `LastName` have a fixed length of 15 characters.

If the actual string contains fewer characters than the fixed length of the string element to which it is written, Visual Basic fills the trailing spaces in the record with blanks (character code 32). Also, if the string is longer than the field size, it is truncated. If you use variable-length strings, the total size of any record stored with Put or retrieved with Get must not exceed the record length specified in the Open statement's Len clause.

Declaring Other Variables

After defining a type that corresponds to a typical record, declare any other variables that your application needs to process a file opened for random access. For example:

```
' A record variable.
Public Employee As Person
' Tracks the current record.
Public Position As Long
' The number of the last record in the file.
Public LastRecord As Long
```

Opening Files for Random Access

To open a file for random access, use the following syntax for the Open statement:

Open *pathname* [**For Random**] **As** *filenumber* **Len** = *reclength*

Because Random is the default access type, the For Random keywords are optional.

The expression Len = *reclength* specifies the size of each record in bytes. Note that every string variable in Visual Basic stores a Unicode string and that you must specify the byte length of that Unicode string. If *reclength* is less than the actual length of the record written to the file, an error is generated. If *reclength* is greater than the actual length of the record, the record is written, although some disk space may be wasted.

You could use the following code to open a file:

```
Dim FileNum As Integer, RecLength As Long, Employee As Person

' Calculate the length of each record.
RecLength = LenB(Employee)
' Get the next available file number.
FileNum = FreeFile
' Open the new file with the Open statement.
Open "MYFILE.FIL" For Random As FileNum Len = RecLength
```

Editing Files Opened for Random Access

If you want to edit a random access file, first read records from the file into program variables, then change the values in the variables, and finally, write the variables back into the file. The following sections discuss how to edit files opened for random access.

Reading Records into Variables

Use the Get statement to copy records into variables. For instance, to copy a record from the Employee Records file into the `Employee` variable, you could use the following code:

```
Get FileNum, Position, Employee
```

In this line of code, `FileNum` contains the number that the Open statement used to open the file; `Position` contains the record number of the record to copy; and `Employee`, declared as user-defined type `Person`, receives the contents of the record.

Writing Variables to Records

Use the Put statement to add or replace records into files opened for random access.

Replacing Records

To replace records, use a Put statement, specifying the position of the record you want to replace; for example:

```
Put #FileNum, Position, Employee
```

This code will replace the record number specified by `Position`, with the data in the `Employee` variable.

Adding Records

To add new records to the end of a file opened for random access, use the Put statement shown in the preceding code fragment. Set the value of the `Position` variable equal to one more than the number of records in the file. For example, to add a record to a file that contains five records, set `Position` equal to 6.

The following statement adds a record to the end of the file:

```
LastRecord = LastRecord + 1
Put #FileNum, LastRecord, Employee
```

Deleting Records

You could delete a record by clearing its fields, but the record would still exist in the file. Usually you don't want empty records in your file, because they waste space and interfere with sequential operations. It is better to copy the remaining records to a new file, and then delete the old file.

To remove a deleted record in a random-access file

1. Create a new file.
2. Copy all the valid records from the original file into the new file.
3. Close the original file and use the Kill statement to delete it.
4. Use the Name statement to rename the new file with the name of the original file.

For More Information For additional information on random file access, see "Open Statement" in the *Microsoft Visual Basic 6.0 Language Reference*.

Using Binary File Access

The File System Object model does not provide binary file creation or access methods. If you need to create or read binary files, this information will help you do so.

Binary access gives you complete control over a file, because the bytes in the file can represent anything. For example, you can conserve disk space by building variable-length records. Use binary access when it is important to keep file size small.

> **Note** When writing binary data to a file, use a variable that is an array of the Byte data type, instead of a String variable. Strings are assumed to contain characters, and binary data may not be properly stored in String variables.

Opening a File for Binary Access

To open a file for binary access, use the following syntax for the Open statement:

Open *pathname* **For Binary As** *filenumber*

As you can see, Open for binary access differs from Open for random access in that Len = *reclength* is not specified. If you include a record length in a binary-access Open statement, it is ignored.

Storing Information in Variable-Length Fields

To best appreciate binary access, consider a hypothetical Employee Records file. This file uses fixed-length records and fields to store information about employees.

```
Type Person
   ID               As Integer
   MonthlySalary    As Currency
   LastReviewDate   As Long
   FirstName        As String * 15
   LastName         As String * 15
   Title            As String * 15
   ReviewComments   As String * 150
End Type
```

Regardless of the actual contents of the fields, every record in that file takes 209 bytes.

You can minimize the use of disk space by using binary access. Because this doesn't require fixed-length fields, the type declaration can omit the string length parameters.

```
Type Person
   ID               As Integer
   MonthlySalary    As Currency
   LastReviewDate   As Long
   FirstName        As String
   LastName         As String
   Title            As String
   ReviewComments   As String
End Type

Public Empl As Person    ' Defines a record.
```

Each employee record in the Employee Records file now stores only the exact number of bytes required because the fields are variable-length. The drawback to binary input/output with variable-length fields is that you can't access records randomly — you must access records sequentially to learn the length of each record. You can seek directly to a specified byte position in a file, but there is no direct way to know which record is at which byte position if the records are of variable length.

For More Information For additional information on binary file access, see "Open Statement" in the *Microsoft Visual Basic 6.0 Language Reference*.

CHAPTER 15

Designing for Performance and Compatibility

In an ideal world, every user of your applications would have a computer with the fastest possible processor, plenty of memory, unlimited drive space, and a blazingly fast network connection. Reality dictates that for most users, the actual performance of an application will be constrained by one or more of the above factors. As you create larger and more sophisticated applications, the amount of memory the applications consume and the speed with which they execute become more significant. You may decide you need to *optimize* your application by making it smaller and by speeding calculations and displays.

As you design and code your application, there are various techniques that can be used to optimize the performance. Some techniques can help to make your application faster; others can help to make it smaller. In this chapter you will learn some of the more common optimization tricks that you can use in your own applications.

Visual Basic shares most of its language features with Visual Basic for Applications, which is included in Microsoft Office and many other applications. Visual Basic, Scripting Edition (VBScript), a language for Internet scripting, is also a subset of the Visual Basic language. If you're also developing in Visual Basic for Applications or VBScript, you'll probably want to share some of your code between these languages.

This chapter discusses the differences between the three versions of the Visual Basic language and provides some tips for creating portable code.

Contents

Sample Application: Optimize.vbp

Many of the optimization techniques in this chapter are illustrated in the Optimize.vbp sample application which is listed in the Samples directory.

Understanding Optimization

Optimization could be thought of as both a science and an art. The science is the techniques of optimization; the art is determining where and when optimizations should be applied. By definition, optimization is "the process of producing more efficient (smaller and/or faster) programs through selection and design of data structures, algorithms, and instruction sequences."

It is a common misconception that optimization is a process that takes place at the end of the development cycle. To create a truly optimized application, you must be optimizing it while you are developing it. You choose your algorithms carefully, weighing speed against size and other constraints; you form hypotheses about what parts of your application will be fast or slow, large or compact; and you test those hypotheses as you go.

The first step in the process of optimization is determining your goal. You can optimize your program for many different characteristics:

- Real speed (how fast your application actually calculates or performs other operations).
- Display speed (how fast your application paints the screen).
- Perceived speed (how fast your application appears to run; this is often related to display speed but not always to real speed).
- Size in memory.
- Size of graphics (this directly affects size in memory, but often has additional ramifications when working in Microsoft Windows).

Rarely, however, can you optimize for multiple characteristics. Typically, an approach that optimizes size compromises on speed; likewise, an application that is optimized for speed is often larger than its slower counterpart. For this reason, recommended optimization techniques in one area may directly contradict suggestions in another.

It's important to note that optimization is not always completely beneficial. Sometimes the changes you make to speed up or trim down your application result in code that is harder to maintain or debug. Some optimization techniques contradict structured coding practice, which may cause problems when you try to expand your application in the future or incorporate it into other programs.

In designing an optimization strategy for your application there are three things to consider: knowing what to optimize, knowing where to optimize, and knowing when to stop.

Knowing What to Optimize: Understanding the Real Problem

If you don't start with a clear goal in mind, you can waste a lot of time optimizing the wrong things. Your goal should be based on the needs and expectations of the user. For example, speed might be a major concern for calculating sales tax in a point-of-sale application, whereas application size would be most important for an application that will be downloaded via the Internet. The key to developing a good optimization strategy is to understand the real problem that the optimization will address.

Although your optimization strategy will target a specific goal, it helps to think about optimization throughout the development process. When writing code, you can learn a lot by simply stepping through your code and thinking carefully about what's actually happening. You may forget that setting properties causes events to occur, and if there is a lot of code in those event procedures, an innocuous line of code can cause a tremendous delay in your program. Even if your primary goal is size, speed optimizations can sometimes be implemented without adding to code size.

Knowing Where to Optimize: Maximum Benefit with Minimum Effort

If you're like most developers, you can't afford the time to optimize everything in your application. It's sometimes useful to think of having an "optimization budget." After all, added time equates to added development cost. Where can you spend your time to get a maximum return on your investment? Obviously you want to focus on the areas that seem to be the slowest or fattest, but to maximize the results of your efforts, you want to concentrate on code where a little work will make a lot of difference.

For example, if speed is your primary goal, the bodies of loops are usually a good place to start. Whenever you speed up the operations inside a loop, that improvement is multiplied by the number of times the loop is executed. For loops with a large number of iterations, just one less string operation in the body can make a big difference. The same principle applies to frequently called subroutines as well.

Knowing When to Stop: Weighing the Results

Sometimes things aren't worth optimizing. For example, writing an elaborate but fast sorting routine is pointless if you're only sorting a dozen items. It's possible to sort things by adding them to a sorted list box and then reading them back out in order. With large numbers of items this is horribly inefficient, but if there aren't a lot of items it is just as quick as any other method, and the code is admirably simple (if a bit obscure).

There are other cases where optimization is wasted effort. If your application is ultimately bound by the speed of your disk or network, there is little you can do in your code to speed things up. Instead you need to think about ways to make these delays less problematic for your users: progress bars to tell them your code isn't simply hung, caching data so they see the delays less often, yielding so that they can use other programs while they wait, and so on.

For More Information See "Interrupting Background Processing" in Chapter 11, "Responding to Mouse and Keyboard Events."

Optimizing for Speed

Speed is often a major determining factor in a user's overall impression of and satisfaction with an application. Unfortunately, many of the things that influence the speed of an application are beyond your control as a programmer: the speed of the processor, the lack of adequate memory, or the speed of data connections. For this reason, it's often necessary to optimize your application so that it will run faster (or at least appear to run faster).

Optimizations for speed can be divided into three general categories: real speed (the actual time spent performing calculations and executing code), display speed (the time spent displaying graphics or painting the screen), and perceived speed (how fast your application appears to run). The types of optimizations that you will actually use depend on the type and purpose of the application — not all optimizations are appropriate or beneficial in all cases.

As with any type of optimization, you need to weigh the potential benefit against the cost. It doesn't make much sense to spend hours optimizing a routine that is rarely called. Determine the areas where speed improvements will affect (and be noticed by) the most users, such as the initial load time for the application.

Optimizing Code

Unless you're doing tasks like generating fractals, your applications are unlikely to be limited by the actual processing speed of your code. Typically other factors — such as video speed, network delays, or disk activities — are the limiting factor in your applications. For example, when a form is slow to load, the cause might be the number of controls and graphics on the form rather than slow code in the Form_Load event. However, you may find points in your program where the speed of your code is the gating factor, especially for routines that are called frequently. When that's the case, there are several techniques you can use to increase the real speed of your applications:

- Avoid using Variant variables.
- Use Long integer variables and integer math.
- Cache frequently used properties in variables.
- Use module-level variables instead of Static variables.

- Replace procedure calls with inline code.
- Use constants whenever possible.
- Pass arguments with ByVal instead of ByRef.
- Use typed optional arguments.
- Take advantage of collections.

Even if you're not optimizing your code for speed, it helps to be aware of these techniques and their underlying principles. If you get in the habit of choosing more efficient algorithms as you code, the incremental gains can add up to a noticeable overall improvement in speed.

Avoid Using Variant Variables

The default data type in Visual Basic is Variant. This is handy for beginning programmers and for applications where processing speed is not an issue. If you are trying to optimize the real speed of your application, however, you should avoid Variant variables. Because Visual Basic converts Variants to the appropriate data type at run time, operations involving other simple data types eliminate this extra step and are faster than their Variant equivalents.

A good way to avoid Variants is to use the Option Explicit statement, which forces you to declare all your variables. To use Option Explicit, check the Require Variable Declaration check box on the Editor tab of the Options dialog box, available from the Tools menu.

Be careful when declaring multiple variables: If you don't use the As *type* clause, they will actually be declared as Variants. For example, in the following declaration, X and Y are variants:

```
Dim X, Y, Z As Long
```

Rewritten, all three variables are Longs:

```
Dim X As Long, Y As Long, Z As Long
```

For More Information To learn more about Visual Basic data types, see "Data Types" in Chapter 5, "Programming Fundamentals."

Use Long Integer Variables and Integer Math

For arithmetic operations avoid Currency, Single, and Double variables. Use Long integer variables whenever you can, particularly in loops. The Long integer is the 32-bit CPU's native data type, so operations on them are very fast; if you can't use the Long variable, Integer or Byte data types are the next best choice. In many cases, you can use Long integers when a floating-point value might otherwise be required. For example, if you always set the ScaleMode property of all your forms and picture controls to either twips or pixels, you can use Long integers for all the size and position values for controls and graphics methods.

When performing division, use the integer division operator (\) if you don't need a decimal result. Integer math is always faster than floating-point math because it doesn't require the offloading of the operation to a math coprocessor. If you do need to do math with decimal values, the Double data type is faster than the Currency data type.

The following table ranks the numeric data types by calculation speed.

Numeric data types	Speed
Long	Fastest
Integer	
Byte	
Single	
Double	
Currency	Slowest

Cache Frequently Used Properties in Variables

You can get and set the value of variables faster than those of properties. If you are getting the value of a property frequently (such as in a loop), your code runs faster if you assign the property to a variable outside the loop and then use the variable instead of the property. Variables are generally 10 to 20 times faster than properties of the same type.

Never get the value of any given property more than once in a procedure unless you know the value has changed. Instead, assign the value of the property to a variable and use the variable in all subsequent code. For example, code like this is very slow:

```
For i = 0 To 10
   picIcon(i).Left = picPallete.Left
Next I
```

Rewritten, this code is much faster:

```
picLeft = picPallete.Left
For i = 0 To 10
      picIcon(i).Left = picLeft
Next I
```

Likewise, code like this . . .

```
Do Until EOF(F)
   Line Input #F, nextLine
   Text1.Text = Text1.Text + nextLine
Loop
```

. . . is much slower than this:

```
Do Until EOF(F)
   Line Input #F, nextLine
   bufferVar = bufferVar & nextLine & vbCrLf
Loop
Text1.Text = bufferVar
```

However, this code does the equivalent job and is even faster:

```
   Text1.Text = Input(F, LOF(F))
```

As you can see, there are several methods for accomplishing the same task; the best algorithm is also the best optimization.

This same technique can be applied to return values from functions. Caching function return values avoids frequent calls to the run-time dynamic-link library (DLL), Msvbvm60.dll.

Use Module-level Variables Instead of Static Variables

While variables declared as Static are useful for storing a value over multiple executions of a procedure, they are slower than local variables. By storing the same value in a module-level variable your procedure will execute faster. Note, however, that you will need to make sure that only one procedure is allowed to change the module-level variable. The tradeoff here is that your code will be less readable and harder to maintain.

Replace Procedure Calls with Inline Code

Although using procedures makes your code more modular, performing each procedure call always involves some additional work and time. If you have a loop that calls a procedure many times, you can eliminate this overhead by removing the procedure call and placing the body of the procedure directly within the loop. If you place the same code inline in several loops, however, the duplicate code increases the size of your application. It also increases the chances that you may not remember to update each section of duplicate code when you make changes.

Likewise, calling a procedure that resides in the same module is faster than calling the same module in a separate .BAS module; if the same procedure needs to be called from multiple modules this gain will be negated.

Use Constants Whenever Possible

Using constants makes your application run faster. Constants also make your code more readable and easier to maintain. If there are strings or numbers in your code that don't change, declare them as constants. Constants are resolved once when your program is compiled, with the appropriate value written into the code. With variables, however, each time the application runs and finds a variable, it needs to get the current value of the variable.

Whenever possible, use the intrinsic constants listed in the Object Browser rather than creating your own. You don't need to worry about including modules that contain unused constants in your application; when you make an .exe file, unused constants are removed.

Pass Unmodified Arguments with ByVal Instead of ByRef

When writing Sub or Function procedures that include unmodified arguments, it is faster to pass the arguments by value (ByVal) than to pass them by reference (ByRef). Arguments in Visual Basic are ByRef by default, but relatively few procedures actually modify the values of their arguments. If you don't need to modify the arguments within the procedure, define the them as ByVal, as in the following example:

```
Private Sub DoSomething(ByVal strName As String, _
ByVal intAge As Integer)
```

Use Typed Optional Arguments

Typed optional arguments can improve the speed of your Sub or Function calls. In prior versions of Visual Basic, optional arguments had to be Variants. If your procedure had ByVal arguments, as in the following example, the 16 bytes of the Variant would be placed on the stack.

```
Private Sub DoSomething(ByVal strName As String, _
Optional ByVal vntAge As Variant, _
Optional ByVal vntWeight As Variant)
```

Your function uses less stack space per call, and less data is moved in memory, if you use typed optional arguments:

```
Private Sub DoSomething(ByVal strName As String, _
Optional ByVal intAge As Integer, _
Optional ByVal intWeight As Integer)
```

The typed optional arguments are faster to access than Variants, and as a bonus, you'll get a compile-time error message if you supply information of the wrong data type.

Take Advantage of Collections

The ability to define and use collections of objects is a powerful feature of Visual Basic. While collections can be very useful, for the best performance you need to use them correctly:

- Use For Each...Next rather than For...Next.
- Avoid using Before and After arguments when adding objects to a collection.
- Use keyed collections rather than arrays for groups of objects of the same type.

Collections allow you to iterate through them using an integer For...Next loop. However, the For Each...Next construct is more readable and in many cases faster. The For Each...Next iteration is implemented by the creator of the collection, so the actual speed will vary from one collection object to the next. However, For Each...Next will rarely be slower than For...Next because the simplest implementation is a linear For...Next style iteration. In some cases the implementor may use a more sophisticated implementation than linear iteration, so For Each...Next can be much faster.

It is quicker to add objects to a collection if you don't use the Before and After arguments. Those arguments require Visual Basic to find another object in the collection before it can add the new object.

When you have a group of objects of the same type, you can usually choose to manage them in a collection or an array (if they are of differing types, a collection is your only choice). From a speed standpoint, which approach you should choose depends on how you plan to access the objects. If you can associate a unique key with each object, then a collection is the fastest choice. Using a key to retrieve an object from a collection is faster than traversing an array sequentially. However, if you do not have keys and therefore will always have to traverse the objects, an array is the better choice. Arrays are faster to traverse sequentially than collections.

For small numbers of objects, arrays use less memory and can often be searched more quickly. The actual number where collections become more efficient than arrays is around 100 objects; however, this can vary depending on processor speed and available memory.

For More Information See "Using Collections as an Alternative to Arrays" in Chapter 8, "More About Programming."

Measuring Performance

Determining the best algorithm for a given situation isn't always obvious. Sometimes you'll want to test your hypotheses; this can be easily done by creating a simple application to measure performance, as shown below. The Optimize.vbp sample application also contains examples of several different test scenarios.

To create a performance testing application

1. Open a new .exe project.
2. Create a form with two command buttons: Command1 and Command2.
3. In the Command1_Click Event add the following code:

```
Private Sub Command1_Click()
   Dim dblStart As Double
   Dim dblEnd As Double
   Dim i as Long

   dblStart = Timer      ' Get the start time.
```

```
      For i = 0 To 9999
         Routine to test' Enter your routine here.
      Next

      dblEnd = Timer        ' Get the end time.

      Debug.Print dblEnd - dblStart   ' Display the
                                   ' elapsed time.
   End Sub
```

4. Add the same code to the Command2_Click event, substituting the second version of your routine inside the loop.
5. Run the application and monitor the results in the Immediate window.

This example uses the default property of Visual Basic's Timer class to time the execution of the routine within the loop. By placing your code inside the loop for each command button, you can quickly compare the performance of two algorithms. The code can be within the loop or can be a call to other procedures.

You may need to experiment with different values for the upper bounds of the loop counter, especially for fast routines. Make sure that you run each version several times to get an average; results can vary from one run to the next.

You can also optimize your application by increasing data access speed.

Optimizing Display Speed

Because of the graphical nature of Microsoft Windows, the speed of graphics and other display operations is crucial to the *perceived speed* of the application. The faster forms appear and paint, the faster your application will seem to the user. There are several techniques you can use to speed up the apparent speed of your application, including:

- Set the ClipControls property of containers to False.
- Use AutoRedraw appropriately.
- Use image controls instead of picture box controls.
- Hide controls when setting properties to avoid multiple repaints.
- Use Line instead of PSet.

Set the ClipControls Property of Containers to False

Unless you are using graphics methods (Line, PSet, Circle, and Print), you should set ClipControls to False for the form and for all frame and picture box controls (it may cause unpredictable results if your code includes graphics methods that draw behind other controls). When ClipControls is False, Visual Basic doesn't overpaint controls with the background before repainting the controls themselves. On forms that contain a lot of controls, the resulting speed improvements are significant.

For More Information See "Layering Graphics with AutoRedraw and ClipControls" in Chapter 12, "Working with Text and Graphics."

Use AutoRedraw Appropriately

When AutoRedraw is set to True for a form or control, Visual Basic maintains a bitmap to repaint that form or control. Although this improves the speed of simple repaints (for example, when the form or control is revealed after a window that covers it is removed), it slows graphics methods. Visual Basic has to perform the graphics methods on the AutoRedraw bitmap and then copy the entire bitmap to the screen. This process also consumes a considerable amount of memory.

If your application generates complex graphics but doesn't change them frequently, setting AutoRedraw to True is appropriate. But if your application draws graphics that must change frequently, you will get better performance if you set AutoRedraw to False and perform the graphics methods for the form or control in the Paint event.

For More Information See "Layering Graphics with AutoRedraw and ClipControls" in Chapter 12, "Working with Text and Graphics."

Use Image Controls Instead of Picture Box Controls

This optimization improves the speed and minimizes the size of your application; use it whenever possible. When you are simply displaying pictures and reacting to click events and mouse actions on them, use the image control instead of the picture box. Don't use a picture box unless you need the capabilities only the picture box provides, such as graphics methods, the ability to contain other controls, or dynamic data exchange (DDE).

Hide Controls When Setting Properties to Avoid Multiple Repaints

Every repaint is expensive. The fewer repaints Visual Basic must perform, the faster your application will appear. One way to reduce the number of repaints is to make controls invisible while you are manipulating them. For example, suppose you want to resize several list boxes in the Resize event for the form:

```
Sub Form_Resize ()
Dim i As Integer, sHeight As Integer
   sHeight = ScaleHeight / 4
   For i = 0 To 3
      lstDisplay(i).Move 0, i * sHeight, _
      ScaleWidth, sHeight
   Next
End Sub
```

This creates four separate repaints, one for each list box. You can reduce the number of repaints by placing all the list boxes within a picture box, and hiding the picture box before you move and size the list boxes. Then, when you make the picture box visible again, all of the list boxes are painted in a single pass:

```
Sub Form_Resize ()
Dim i As Integer, sHeight As Integer
   picContainer.Visible = False
   picContainer.Move 0, 0, ScaleWidth, ScaleHeight
   sHeight = ScaleHeight / 4
   For i = 0 To 3
      lstDisplay(i).Move 0, i * sHeight, _
      ScaleWidth, sHeight
   Next
   picContainer.Visible = True
End Sub
```

Note that this example uses the Move method instead of setting the Top and Left properties. The Move method sets both properties in a single operation, saving additional repaints.

Use Line Instead of PSet

The Line method is faster than a series of PSet methods. Avoid using the PSet method and batch up the points into a single Line method. Shape and line controls are appropriate for simple graphical elements that rarely change; complex graphics, or graphics that change rapidly, are generally best handled with graphics methods.

Optimizing Perceived Speed

Often the subjective speed of your application has little to do with how quickly it actually executes its code. To the user, an application that starts up rapidly, repaints quickly, and provides continuous feedback feels "snappier" than an application that just "hangs up" while it churns through its work. You can use a variety of techniques to give your application that "snap":

- Keep forms hidden but loaded.
- Preload data.
- Use timers to work in the background.
- Use progress indicators.
- Speed the start of your application.

Keep Forms Hidden but Loaded

Hiding forms instead of unloading them is a trick that has been around since the early days of Visual Basic 1.0, but it is still effective. The obvious downside to this technique is the amount of memory the loaded forms consume, but it can't be beat if you can afford the memory cost and making forms appear quickly is of the highest importance.

Preload Data

You can also improve the apparent speed of your application by prefetching data. For example, if you need to go to disk to load the first of several files, why not load as many of them as you can? Unless the files are extremely small, the user is going to see a delay anyway. The incremental time spent loading the additional files will probably go unnoticed, and you won't have to delay the user again.

Use Timers to Work in the Background

In some applications you can do considerable work while you are waiting for the user. The best way to accomplish this is through a timer control. Use static (or module-level) variables to keep track of your progress, and do a very small piece of work each time the timer goes off. If you keep the amount of work done in each timer event very small, users won't see any effect on the responsiveness of the application and you can prefetch data or do other things that further speed up your application.

For More Information To learn more about the timer control, see " Using the Timer Control" in Chapter 7, "Using Visual Basic's Standard Controls." For a discussion of background processing, see "Interrupting Background Processing" in Chapter 11, "Responding to Mouse and Keyboard Events."

Use Progress Indicators

When you can't avoid a long delay in your program, you need to give the user some indication that your application hasn't simply hung. Windows 95 uses a standard progress bar to indicate this to users. You can use the ProgressBar control in the Microsoft Windows Common Controls included with the Professional and Enterprise editions of Visual Basic. Use DoEvents at strategic points, particularly each time you update the value of the ProgressBar, to allow your application to repaint while the user is doing other things.

At the very least, you should display the wait cursor to indicate the delay by setting the form's MousePointer property to vbHourglass (11).

Speed the Start of Your Application

Apparent speed is most important when your application starts. Users' first impression of the speed of an application is measured by how quickly they see something after clicking on its name in the Start menu. With the various run-time DLLs that need to be loaded for Visual Basic for Applications, ActiveX controls, and so forth, some delay is unavoidable with any application. However, there are some things you can do to give a response to the user as quickly as possible:

- Use Show in the Form_Load event.
- Simplify your startup form.
- Don't load modules you don't need.
- Run a small Visual Basic application at startup to preload the run-time DLLs.

Use Show in the Form_Load Event

When a form is first loaded, all of the code in the Form_Load event occurs before the form is displayed. You can alter this behavior by using the Show method in the Form_Load code, giving the user something to look at while the rest of the code in the event executes. Follow the Show method with DoEvents to ensure that the form gets painted:

```
Sub Form_Load()
   Me.Show              ' Display startup form.
   DoEvents             ' Ensure startup form is painted.
   Load MainForm        ' Load main application fom.
   Unload Me         ' Unload startup form.
   MainForm.Show        ' Display main form.
End Sub
```

Simplify Your Startup Form

The more complicated a form is, the longer it takes to load. Keep your startup form simple. Most applications for Microsoft Windows display a simple copyright screen (also known as a splash screen) at startup; your application can do the same. The fewer controls on the startup form, and the less code it contains, the quicker it will load and appear. Even if it immediately loads another, more complicated form, the user will know that the application has started.

For large applications you may want to preload the most commonly used forms at startup so that they can be shown instantly when needed. A satisfying way to do this is to display a progress bar in your startup form and update it as you load each of the other forms. Call DoEvents after loading each form so that your startup form will repaint. Once all the important forms have been loaded, the startup form can show the first one and unload itself. Of course, each form you preload will run the code in its Form_Load event, so take care that this doesn't cause problems or excessive delays.

Don't Load Modules You Don't Need

Visual Basic loads code modules on demand, rather than all at once at startup. This means that if you never call a procedure in a module, that module will never be loaded. Conversely, if your startup form calls procedures in several modules, then all of those modules will be loaded as your application starts up, which slows things down. You should therefore avoid calling procedures in other modules from your startup form.

Run a Small Visual Basic Application at Startup to Preload the Run-time DLLs

A large part of the time required to start a Visual Basic application is spent loading the various run-time DLLs for Visual Basic, ActiveX, and ActiveX controls. Of course, if these are already loaded, none of that time need be spent. Thus, users will see your application start up faster if there is another application already running that uses some or all of these DLLs.

One way to significantly improve the startup performance of your applications is to provide another small, useful application that the user always runs. For example, you might write a small application to display a calendar and install it in the startup group for Windows. It will then load automatically on system startup, and while it is useful in itself, it also ensures that the various Visual Basic run-time DLLs are loaded.

Finally, with the Professional and Enterprise editions of Visual Basic you can divide your application into a main skeleton application and several component executables or DLLs. A smaller main application will load faster, and it can then load the other parts as needed.

Optimizing for Size

In the past, available memory and system resources were often limiting factors in designing an application. With 32-bit operating systems, such as Windows 95 and Windows NT, these factors are rarely a concern for most Visual Basic programmers. However, there are a number of scenarios where minimizing the size of an application is still important.

Size is extremely important for applications that will be downloaded from the Internet or transferred as attachments to e-mail. For those not fortunate enough to have high-speed data connections, transferring a 1-megabyte file could take an hour or more. In addition to the .exe file, many applications will require additional .dll or .ocx files, adding to the size (and time) of the download. In these scenarios, you would want to optimize your application's size on disk.

Even if users won't be downloading your application, it's usually a good idea to make your application as compact as possible. Smaller applications load faster, and because they consume less memory, you can run additional applications at the same time. You can often improve performance by optimizing your application's size in memory.

Reducing Code Size

When reducing the size of an application is important, there are a number of techniques that you can apply to make your code more compact. In addition to reducing the application's size in memory, most of these optimizations will also reduce the size of the .exe file. As an additional benefit, a smaller application will load faster.

Most size optimization techniques involve eliminating unnecessary elements from your code. Visual Basic automatically eliminates certain elements when you compile your application. There is no reason to restrict the length or number of the following elements:

- Identifier names
- Comments
- Blank lines

None of these elements affect the size of your application in memory when it is running as an .exe file.

Other elements, such as variables, forms, and procedures,do take up space in memory. It is usually best to streamline these. There are several techniques you can use to reduce the memory your application occupies when it is running as an .exe file. These techniques can reduce code size:

- Reduce the number of loaded forms.
- Reduce the number of controls.
- Use labels instead of text boxes.
- Keep data in disk files or resources and load only when needed.
- Organize your modules.
- Consider alternatives to Variant data types.
- Use dynamic arrays and erase to reclaim memory.
- Reclaim space used by strings or object variables.
- Eliminate dead code and unused variables.

Reduce the Number of Loaded Forms

Each loaded form, whether visible or not, consumes a significant amount of memory (which varies with the number and types of controls on the form, the size of bitmaps on the form, and so on). Load forms only when you need to display them, and unload them (rather than hide them) when you no longer need them. Remember that any reference to properties, methods, or controls on a form, or a form variable declared with New, causes Visual Basic to load the form.

When you unload a form using the Unload method, only a portion of the memory occupied by the form is released. To free all memory, invalidate the reference to the form by using the Nothing keyword:

```
Set Form = Nothing
```

Reduce the Number of Controls

When designing your application, try to place as few controls on a form as possible. The actual limit depends on the type of controls as well as available system, but in practice, any form with a large number of controls will perform slowly. A related technique is to use control arrays where possible, rather than putting a large number of controls of the same type on a form at design time.

For More Information To learn more about control arrays, see "Working with Control Arrays" in Chapter 7, "Using Visual Basic's Standard Controls."

Use Labels Instead of Text Boxes

Label controls use fewer Windows resources than text boxes do, so you should use labels in place of text boxes whenever possible. For example, if you need a hidden control on a form for storing text, it is more efficient to use a label.

Even a data entry form that requires numerous text fields can be optimized using this technique. You can create a label for each field and use a single text box for input, moving it to the next label's location in the LostFocus event:

```
Private Sub Label1_LostFocus()
   ' Update Label1
   Label1.Caption = Text1.Text
   ' Move the Textbox over the next label
   Text1.Move Label2.Left, Label2.Top
   ' Update Text1 contents
   Text1.Text = Label2.Caption
End Sub
```

You can make a label look like a text box by setting the BackColor and BorderStyle properties. Although this technique requires more code, it can significantly reduce resource usage for a form that contains numerous fields.

Keep Data in Disk Files or Resources and Load Only When Needed

Data you place directly into your application at design time (as properties or as literal strings and numbers in your code) increases the memory the application consumes at run time. You can reduce memory by loading the data from disk file or resources at run time. This is particularly valuable for large bitmaps and strings.

For More Information For information on adding resources to your application, see "Working With Resource Files" in Chapter 8, "More About Programming."

Organize Your Modules

Visual Basic loads modules on demand — that is, it loads a module into memory only when your code calls one of the procedures in that module. If you never call a procedure in a particular module, Visual Basic never loads that module. Placing related procedures in the same module causes Visual Basic to load modules only as needed.

Consider Alternatives to Variant Data Types

The Variant data type is extremely flexible, but it is also larger than any of the other data types. When you must squeeze every last byte out of your application, consider replacing Variant variables, and especially arrays of Variant variables, with other data types.

Each Variant takes 16 bytes, compared to 2 for an Integer or 8 for a Double. Variable-length String variables use 4 bytes plus 1 byte per character in the string, but each Variant containing a string takes 16 bytes plus 1 byte per character in the string. Because they are so large, Variant variables are particularly troublesome when used as local variables or arguments to procedures, because they quickly consume stack space.

In some cases, however, using other data types forces you to add more code to compensate for the loss of flexibility that the Variant data type provides, resulting in no net reduction in size.

Use Dynamic Arrays and Erase to Reclaim Memory

Consider using dynamic arrays instead of fixed arrays. When you no longer need the data in a dynamic array, use Erase or ReDim Preserve to discard unneeded data, and reclaim the memory used by the array. For example, you can reclaim the space used by a dynamic array with the following code:

```
Erase MyArray
```

Whereas Erase completely eliminates the array, ReDim Preserve makes the array smaller without losing its contents:

```
ReDim Preserve MyArray(10, smallernum)
```

Erasing a fixed-size array will not reclaim the memory for the array — it simply clears out the values of each element of the array. If each element was a string, or a Variant containing a string or array, then erasing the array would reclaim the memory from those strings or Variants, not the memory for the array itself.

Reclaim Space Used by Strings or Object Variables

The space used by (nonstatic) local string and array variables is reclaimed automatically when the procedure ends. However, global and module-level string and array variables remain in existence for as long as your program is running. If you are trying to keep your application as small as possible, you should reclaim the space used by these variables as soon as you can. You reclaim string space by assigning the zero-length string to it:

```
SomeStringVar = ""    ' Reclaim space.
```

Similarly, you can reclaim some (but not all) of the space used by an object variable by setting it to Nothing. For example, to remove a Recordset object variable:

```
Private rs As New RecordSet

   ...                  ' Code to initialize and use recordset would go here
   rs.Close             ' Close the recordset
   Set rs = Nothing     ' Set the object reference to Nothing
```

If you don't explicitly set an object reference to Nothing, a reference to the object will remain in memory until the application is terminated; for an application that uses a lot of objects this can quickly consume your available memory and slow the application.

You can also reclaim space by unloading forms and setting them to Nothing rather than simply hiding them when they are no longer needed.

Eliminate Dead Code and Unused Variables

As you develop and modify your applications, you may leave behind *dead code* — entire procedures that are not called from anywhere in your code. You may also have declared variables that are no longer used. Although Visual Basic does remove unused constants, it does not remove unused variables and dead code when you create an .exe. Consider reviewing your code to find and remove unused procedures and variables. For example, Debug.Print statements, while ignored in the run-time .exe, are sometimes present in the .exe file.

Debug.Print statements with strings or variables as arguments are not compiled when you create an .exe. However, where Debug.Print statements have a function call as an argument, the Debug.Print statement itself is ignored by the compiler, but the function call is compiled. Then, when the application is run, the function is called but the return is ignored. Because functions that appear as arguments to Debug.Print will take up space and cycle time in an .exe, it may be beneficial to delete these statements before you make an .exe.

Use the Find command on the Edit menu to search for references to a particular variable. Or, if you have Option Explicit statements in each of your modules, you can quickly discover if a variable is used in your application by removing or commenting out its declaration and running the application. If the variable is used, Visual Basic will generate an error. If you don't see an error, the variable was not used.

For More Information To learn more about the Debug.Print statement, see "Printing Information in the Immediate Window" in Chapter 13, "Debugging Your Code and Handling Errors."

Cutting Back on Graphics

Graphics (pictures and graphics methods) can consume a lot of memory. To some extent, this is unavoidable: Graphics contain a lot of information, so they tend to be large. But in many cases, you can reduce the impact that graphics have on the size of your application by applying some of the following techniques:

- Use the image control to display bitmaps.
- Load bitmaps from files as needed and share pictures.
- Use the PaintPicture method.
- Free the memory used by graphics.
- Use rle-format bitmaps or metafiles.

Use the Image Control to Display Bitmaps

The picture controls in many Visual Basic applications exist merely to be clicked or to be dragged and dropped. If this is all you're doing with a picture control, you are wasting a lot of Windows resources. For these purposes, image controls are superior to picture controls. Each picture control is an actual window and uses significant system resources. The image control is a "lightweight" control rather than a window and doesn't use nearly as many resources. In fact, you can typically use five to 10 times as many image controls as picture controls. Moreover, image controls repaint faster than picture controls. Only use a picture controls when you need a feature only it provides, such as dynamic data exchange (DDE), graphics methods, or the ability to contain other controls.

Load Bitmaps from Files As Needed and Share Pictures

When you set a Picture property at design time, you add the picture to the form and thereby increase the memory the form consumes at run time. You can reduce memory consumption by storing pictures in a resource file and using the LoadResPicture function to load them at run time. If you never use all the pictures associated with a form at the same time, this technique saves memory over storing all the pictures in controls on the form. It can speed up form load because not all the pictures need to be loaded before the form can be shown.

You can share the same picture between multiple picture controls, image controls, and forms. If you use code like this you only maintain one copy of the picture:

```
Picture = LoadPicture("C:\Windows\Chess.bmp")
Image1.Picture = Picture   ' Use the same picture.
Picture1.Picture = Picture ' Use the same picture.
```

Contrast that with this code, which causes three copies of the bitmap to be loaded, taking more memory and time:

```
Picture = LoadPicture("C:\Windows\Chess.bmp")
Image1.Picture = LoadPicture("C:\Windows\Chess.bmp")
Picture1.Picture = LoadPicture("C:\Windows\Chess.bmp")
```

Similarly, if you load the same picture into several forms or controls at design time, a copy of that picture is saved with each form or control. Instead, you could place the picture in one form and then share it with the other forms and controls as described above. This makes your application both smaller (because it doesn't contain redundant copies of the picture) and faster (because the picture doesn't have to be loaded from disk multiple times).

Use the PaintPicture Method

Rather than placing bitmaps in controls, you can use the PaintPicture method to display bitmaps anywhere on forms. This is particularly useful when you want to tile a bitmap repeatedly across a form: You only need to load the bitmap once, but you can use PaintPicture to draw it multiple times.

Free the Memory Used by Graphics

When you are no longer using a picture in the Picture property of a form, picture box, or image control, set the Picture property to Nothing to empty it:

```
Set Picture1.Picture = Nothing
```

If you use the Image property of a picture box or form, Visual Basic creates an AutoRedraw bitmap (even if the AutoRedraw property for that form or picture box is False). When you have finished using the Image property, you can reclaim the memory used by this bitmap by using the Cls method before setting AutoRedraw to False. For example, the following code reclaims the memory used by the Image property for a control called mypic:

```
mypic.AutoRedraw = True ' Turn on AutoRedraw bitmap.
mypic.Cls               ' Clear it.
mypic.AutoRedraw = False  ' Turn off bitmap.
```

Use Rle-Format Bitmaps or Metafiles

Although the default picture format is the bitmap (.bmp), Visual Basic can also utilize other graphics file formats. Several painting and graphics programs allow you to save bitmaps in a standard compressed bitmap format called Run Length Encoded (.rle). Rle bitmaps can be several times smaller than their uncompressed counterparts, particularly for bitmaps that contain large swatches of solid color, and they aren't appreciably slower to load or display. Using metafiles (.wmf) can produce even greater savings — 10 times or more in some cases. Try to use metafiles at their normal size: they are much slower to paint when they have to be stretched larger or smaller.

You can also use .gif and .jpg formats. They are generally much smaller; however there is some tradeoff in image quality and loading speed.

Segmented Applications

Visual Basic enables you to think about the architecture of your application in new ways. Instead of a single, monolithic executable, you can write an application that consists of a core front-end executable supported by a number of ActiveX components. This approach offers several significant optimization benefits:

- The components are loaded on demand and can be unloaded when no longer needed.
- Cross-process components can be 32-bit executables on Windows 95 or Windows NT, even if other parts of the application are 16-bit components.
- Remote components can use the resources of other machines on the network.

In addition, the components can be debugged independently and reused in other applications. This may not improve the speed of your application, but it may improve your speed in creating the next one.

To determine how to best optimize your application by segmenting it, you must evaluate the kinds of components you can create and how they fit into your application. There are three kinds of components you can create with the Professional or Enterprise editions of Visual Basic:

- Cross-process
- In-process
- Remote

These three kinds are not exclusive: You could use all three in a single application. But from the standpoint of optimizing your application, they each have very different characteristics.

For More Information Component creation is discussed in depth in the *Microsoft Visual Basic 6.0 Component Tools Guide* volume of the *Microsoft Visual Basic 6.0 Reference Library* included with the Professional and Enterprise editions of Visual Basic.

Cross-Process Components

A cross-process component is an executable program that offers its services to other programs. Like all executables, it starts up and runs with its own stack in its own process space; thus, when a application acting as a client uses one of the objects provided by a component, the operation crosses from the client's process space to the component's — hence the name. Cross-process components offer some valuable features when compared to the other types:

- Asynchronous operation ("threads").
- Untrapped errors in the component won't cause the calling application to crash.
- Interoperability between 16-bit and 32-bit applications.

Of these, the first and the last points are of particular interest from an optimization standpoint.

Because a cross-process component is a separate program, it can operate asynchronously with the component acting as a client. It has a separate "thread" that multitasks with the client program (technically speaking this is not a thread but a separate process; however, conceptually the two are equivalent). The two programs can communicate and share objects, but they run independently. This is particularly useful when your application needs to perform some operation that takes a long time. The client can call the component to perform the operation and then continue responding to the user.

Even if your application will run on a 32-bit system, you may not be able to make it 32-bit immediately if you rely on legacy 16-bit applications or components. However, if you segment your application using cross-process components, you can mix and match 16-bit and 32-bit components. This allows you to incrementally take advantage of 32-bit features and performance while preserving your investment in 16-bit components.

For all their strengths, cross-process components have a significant disadvantage: performance. This manifests itself in a couple of ways:

- Startup speed
- Cross-process call overhead

A cross-process component is an executable created with Visual Basic, so the same startup issues related to application startup also apply. The good news is that if you are calling a cross-process component written in Visual Basic from another Visual Basic program, almost all the support DLLs will already be loaded. This greatly reduces the time required to start the component. Many components are smaller than your average Visual Basic application, with few or no forms to load, which again improves load time. Nevertheless, a cross-process component will always be slower to start than an in-process component.

Once it is running, a cross-process component suffers from its very nature: Every interaction with the component is a cross-process call. Crossing process boundaries takes a lot of CPU cycles. So every reference to an object from the cross-process component is much more expensive than an equivalent reference to an object in the client application itself or an in-process component. Reducing the number of cross-process calls in your code can reduce the impact of the cross-process call overhead.

In-Process Components

An in-process component offers its services to other programs within their process space. Compared to cross-process components, in-process components offer two advantages:

- Improved load time
- No cross-process overhead

With an in-process component, no new process needs to be created and no run-time DLLs need to be loaded. This can make an in-process component considerably quicker to load compared to an equivalent cross-process component.

Because it is in-process, there is no cross-process overhead when referring to the methods or properties on an object supplied by the component. Objects from the component operate with the same efficiency as objects within the client application itself.

Remote Components

The Enterprise Edition of Visual Basic enables you to create remote components that execute on a separate machine elsewhere on the network. Although network overhead will inevitably exact a toll on application performance, you can make up for it by using the resources of additional CPUs. This is particularly true when you work with a remote component that is operating on data that is local to the machine containing the component. Since this data would have to be fetched across the network anyway, a component operating on it locally and returning only the results across the network can actually be more efficient.

For example, you might write an object in a component that can search for files matching a specified criteria on the local hard disk. By making this a remote component and placing a copy on each machine on the network, you could write a distributed file-finder program that searches all the network components in parallel, using all those CPU resources.

Optimizing Objects

As you use more and more objects in your Visual Basic applications, optimizing your use of those objects becomes more and more important. There are several key techniques to making the most efficient use of objects:

- Use early binding.
- Minimize the dots.

- Use Set and With...End With.
- Minimize cross-process calls.

In Visual Basic, referencing another application's object in your code (by getting or setting an object's property, or executing one of its methods) constitutes a cross-process call. Cross-process calls are expensive and you should try to avoid them if you are concerned about optimizing your application.

Early Binding vs. Late Binding

Visual Basic can use objects more efficiently if it can early bind them. An object can be early bound if you supply a reference to a type library containing the object, and you declare the type of the object:

```
Dim X As New MyObject
```

Or, equivalently:

```
Dim X As MyObject
Set X = New MyObject
```

Early binding enables Visual Basic to do most of the work of resolving the definition of the object at compile time rather than at run time, when it impacts performance. This also allows Visual Basic to check the syntax of properties and methods used with the object and report any errors.

If Visual Basic cannot bind an object early, it must bind it late. Late binding objects is expensive: At compile time you get no error checking, and each reference at run time requires at least 50% more work by Visual Basic.

Generally, you should always early bind objects if possible. The only times you should have to declare a variable As Object is if you do not have a type library for the object in question, or you need to be able to pass any kind of object as an argument to a procedure.

For More Information To learn more about early binding, see "Speeding Object References" in Chapter 10, "Programming with Components."

Minimize the Dots

When referencing other applications' objects from Visual Basic, you use the dot syntax "." to navigate an object's hierarchy of collections, objects, properties, and methods. It is not uncommon to create very lengthy navigation strings. For example:

```
' Refers to cell A1 on Sheet1 in the first workbook
' of an Microsoft Excel spreadsheet.
Application.Workbooks.Item(1).Worksheets.Item_
("Sheet1").Cells.Item(1,1)
```

In addition to being a rather lengthy string to type, this line of code is fairly difficult to read — and it is extremely inefficient.

When calling an object from Visual Basic, each "dot" requires Visual Basic to make multiple calls.

To write the most efficient applications, minimize the use of dots when referencing an object.

You can usually minimize the dots by analyzing the objects and methods available to you. For example, the above line of code can be shortened by removing the Item method (this is the default method for collections anyway, so you'll rarely use it in code) and by using the more efficient Range method:

```
' Refers to cell A1 on Sheet1 in the first workbook
' of an Microsoft Excel spreadsheet.
Application.Workbooks(1).Worksheets("Sheet1")_
.Range("A1")
```

You can shorten this even further by rewriting the code so that it refers to the active sheet in the active workbook, instead of a specific sheet in a specific workbook:

```
' Refers to cell A1 on the active sheet in the
' active workbook.
Range("A1")
```

Of course, the above example assumes it's OK to refer to cell A1 of any sheet that happens to be active.

Use Set and With...End With

Using the Set statement also allows you to shorten navigation strings and gives you a bit more control over your code. The following example uses the Dim and Set statements to create variables that refer to frequently used objects:

```
Dim xlRange As Object
Set xlRange = Application.ActiveSheet.Cells(1,1)
xlRange.Font.Bold = True
xlRange.Width = 40
```

Visual Basic provides the With...End With construct to set an implied object within code:

```
With Application.ActiveSheet.Cells(1,1)
   .Font.Bold = True
   .Width = 40
End With
```

Minimize Cross-Process Calls

If you are using a cross-process ActiveX component, you can't completely avoid making cross-process calls. However, there are several ways to minimize the number of cross-process calls you need to make. If possible, do not reference objects inside a For...Next loop. Cache values in variables and use the variables in loops. If you have to call a large number of methods on an object, you can greatly improve the performance of your application by moving the code into the component. For example, if the component is Word or Microsoft Excel, you can put a looping macro in a template in Word or a looping procedure into module in Microsoft Excel. You then call the macro or procedure from Visual Basic, which is a single call that launches a looping operation within the component.

If you are writing components, you can design the objects in the component to be efficient by reducing the cross-process calls required to perform an operation. For example, when you have several interrelated properties, implement a method with several arguments — one for each property. Calling the method requires a single cross-process call regardless of how many arguments it has, whereas setting each property requires a separate cross-process call. Likewise, if you anticipate that the component acting as a client will want to call your component in a loop (for example, to sum or average all the values in a list property), you can improve performance by providing methods that do the looping within your object and return the appropriate value.

For More Information Component creation is discussed in depth in the *Microsoft Visual Basic 6.0 Component Tools Guide* included with the Professional and Enterprise editions of Visual Basic.

Compiled vs. Interpreted Applications

By default, applications created in Visual Basic are compiled as interpreted or p-code executables. At run time, the instructions in the executables are translated or interpreted by a run-time dynamic-link library (DLL). The Professional and Enterprise editions of Visual Basic include the option to compile a native code .exe. In many cases, compiling to native code can provide substantial gains in speed over the interpreted versions of the same application; however, this is not always the case. The following are some general guidelines regarding native-code compilation.

- Code that does a lot of primitive operations on hard-typed, nonstring variables will yield a maximum ratio of generated native code to displaced p-code operations. Complex financial calculations or fractal generation, therefore, would benefit from native code.
- Computationally intensive programs, or programs that shuffle a lot of bits and bytes around within local data structures, will gain very visibly with native code.
- For many programs, especially those doing a lot of Windows API calls, COM method calls, and string manipulations, native code will not be much faster than p-code.

- Applications that consist primarily of functions from the Visual Basic for Applications run-time library are not going to see much if any advantage from native code, because the code in the Visual Basic for Applications run-time library is already highly optimized.
- Code that involves a lot of subroutine calls relative to inline procedures is also unlikely to appear much faster with native code. This is because all the work of setting up stack frames, initializing variables, and cleaning up on exit takes the same time with both the p-code engine and generated native code.

Note that any calls to objects, DLLs or Visual Basic for Applications run-time functions will negate the performance benefits of native code. This is because relatively little time is spent executing code — the majority of time (usually around 90–95%) is spent inside forms, data objects, Windows .dlls, or the Visual Basic for Applications run time, including intrinsic string and variant handling.

In real-world tests, client applications typically spent about 5% of their total execution time executing the p-code. Hence, if native code was instantaneous, using native code for these programs would provide at most a 5% performance improvement.

What native code does is to enable programmers to write snippets of code or computationally intensive algorithms in Basic that were never possible before because of performance issues. Enabling these "snippets" to run much faster can also improve the responsiveness of certain portions of an application, which improves the perceived performance of the overall application.

For More Information To learn more about native-code compilation, see "Compiling Your Project to Native Code" in Chapter 8, "More About Programming."

Compatibility with Other Microsoft Applications

Visual Basic is the senior member of the family of Visual Basic products that includes Visual Basic for Applications and Visual Basic, Scripting Edition (VBScript). While most of the code that you write in Visual Basic can be shared with applications written in Visual Basic for Applications or VBScript, there are some exceptions.

Compatibility with Visual Basic for Applications

Visual Basic for Applications is a single, common application scripting language and environment that users and developers can leverage across their Windows desktop. Visual Basic for Applications is included in Microsoft Office and other Microsoft applications. It is also licensed to other software vendors and included in a wide range of products.

Visual Basic for Applications, contained in Vba6.dll, is the underlying language engine for Visual Basic. This library contains all of the language elements that are shared by Visual Basic for Applications and Visual Basic. You can view the elements by selecting VBA from the Library listbox in the Object Browser. Code written in Visual Basic for Applications is portable to Visual Basic with the following limitations: Visual Basic for Applications code that refers to application-specific elements (such as an Microsoft Excel worksheet) may be ported, provided that they contain a fully qualified reference and provided that the referenced application exists on the target machine.

Elements specific to Visual Basic, such as forms and intrinsic controls, are contained in the type library Vb6.olb (which is also visible in the Object Browser). In general, code written in Visual Basic is portable to Visual Basic for Applications as long as it doesn't reference these elements.

For More Information To learn more about Visual Basic for Applications, visit the Microsoft Web site at http://www.microsoft.com. To learn more about referencing objects, see "Creating a Reference to an Object" in Chapter 10, "Programming with Components." To learn more about native-code compilation, see "Compiling Your Project to Native Code" in Chapter 8, "More About Programming."

Compatibility with Visual Basic Scripting Edition

Visual Basic Scripting edition (VBScript) is designed to be hosted within an Internet browser, such as the Microsoft Internet Explorer or other, third-party browsers. VBScript is a lightweight and extremely fast language engine designed specifically for environments like the Internet, intranets, or the World Wide Web. VBScript leverages the strengths of Visual Basic and enables developers to use their Visual Basic development knowledge to quickly create solutions for the Internet or World Wide Web.

VBScript supports a subset of the Visual Basic for Applications language syntax. Visual Basic Scripting edition does not include an IDE like that found in Microsoft Visual Basic, because it is designed to be a lightweight language engine that can be shared across different platforms. You can write VBScript code in Visual Basic's Code Editor, but you can't run or test the application in the Visual Basic IDE.

Because VBScript is a cross-platform development language, some of the elements of the Visual Basic for Applications language are not included. These include any file input/output functions, intrinsic constants, intrinsic data types, and so forth. When porting code from Visual Basic to VBScript, it's important to review your code for unsupported elements.

For More Information To learn more about Visual Basic, Scripting Edition, including a list of supported language elements, visit the Microsoft Web site at http://www.microsoft.com.

CHAPTER 16

International Issues

If you are planning to distribute your Visual Basic application to an international market, you can reduce the amount of time and code necessary to make your application as functional in its foreign market as it is in its domestic market. This chapter introduces key concepts and definitions for developing international applications with Visual Basic, presents a localization model, and emphasizes the advantages of designing software for an international market.

This chapter also discusses guidelines for writing Visual Basic code that results in a flexible, portable, and truly international application. A section is devoted to writing Visual Basic code that handles the specific aspects of the double-byte character set (DBCS) used on East Asian versions of Windows.

Contents

Sample Application: Atm.vbp

Some of the code examples in this chapter are taken from the Automated Teller Machine (Atm.vbp) sample, which is listed in the Samples directory.

International Software Definitions

Before you start developing international software, you should know some fundamental terms.

International Software

International software is software that is marketable worldwide. A software product is international only if it is as functional in its foreign market as it is in its domestic market. For more information about how to localize your application, see "Designing International Software," later in this chapter.

Locale

A *locale* describes the user's environment — the local conventions, culture, and language of the user's geographical region. A locale is made up of a unique combination of a *language* and a *country*. Two examples of locales are: English/U.S. and French/Belgium.

A language might be spoken in more than one country; for instance, French is spoken in France, Belgium, Canada, and many African nations. While these countries share a common language, certain national conventions (such as currencies) vary among countries. Therefore, each country represents a unique locale. Similarly, one country might have more than one official language. Belgium has three — French, Dutch, and German. Therefore, Belgium has three distinct locales. For more information about locale-specific settings, see "General Considerations When Writing International Code," later in this chapter.

Localization

Localization is the process by which an application is adapted to a locale. It involves more than just literal, word-for-word translation of these resources — it is the meaning that must be communicated to the user. For more information about how to localize your application, see "Designing International Software," later in this chapter.

String Resources

String resources refers to all the text that appears in the application's user interface. They include, but are not limited to, menus, dialog boxes, and informational, alert, and error messages. If an application will be used in a locale other than the one in which it was developed, these resources will have to be translated, or localized.

For More Information For definitions of East Asian terminology, see "ANSI, DBCS, and Unicode: Definitions" later in this chapter. For more information about string resources and resource files, see "Using Resource Files for Localization," later in this chapter.

Designing International Software

It is a lot more efficient to design your application with localization in mind, following an approach that separates string resources from code, than to revise your finished application to make it international later in the development process.

Advantages of Designing International Software

There are four primary advantages to designing and implementing your Visual Basic application so that it is sensitive and appropriate to international conventions, foreign data, and format processing:

- You can launch your Visual Basic application onto the market more rapidly. No additional international development is needed once the initial version of the product is complete.
- You use resources more efficiently. Adding international support to your finished Visual Basic application may make it less stable. More development and testing resources would be required than if the same support had been implemented as part of the original development process.
- If the international version of your Visual Basic application is built from the same set of sources as the version in which you originally developed your application, only isolated modules need international attention, thus making it easier and less expensive to maintain code while including international support. See "Using Resource Files for Localization" later in this chapter.
- Developing an international version of your application becomes easy. For instance, you can develop an English-language version of your application that runs in a German operating environment without rewriting code. You only need to customize the user interface. See "Designing an International-Aware User Interface," later in this chapter.

Localization Model

Any application that will be localized represents two conceptual blocks: a *code block* and a *data block*. Figure 16.1 represents the data block as the "user interface component" and the code block as the "application component."

Figure 16.1 The data block and code block make up a localized product

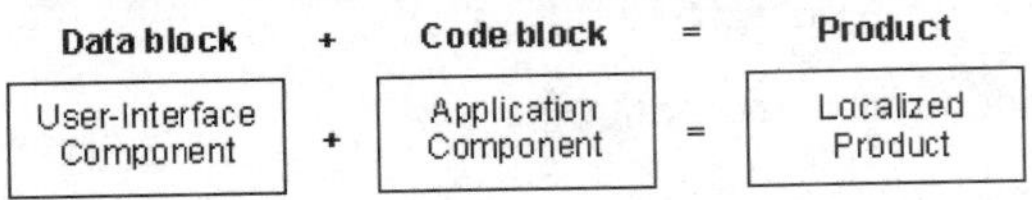

The data block contains all the user-interface string resources but no code. Conversely, the code block contains only the application code that is run for all locales. This Visual Basic code handles the string resources and the locale-specific settings. "Writing International Code in Visual Basic," later in this chapter, provides details on how to write Visual Basic code that handles locale-specific settings, such as dates, currencies, and numeric values and separators.

In theory, you can develop a localized version of your Visual Basic application by changing only the data block. The code block for all locales should be the same. Combining the data block with the code block results in a localized version of your application. The keys to successful international software design are the separation of the code and data blocks and the ability for data to be accurately read by your Visual Basic application, regardless of the locale.

Although it may be more work for the person writing the Visual Basic application, no user-interface elements should be present in the Visual Basic code. Instead, the string resources should be placed in a separate file, from which they will be loaded at run time. This file is called a *resource file* (.res), which is a file that contains all the strings, bitmaps, and icons that are localized. For more information about resource files, see "Using Resource Files for Localization," later in the chapter.

The teams working on localizing the application should work exclusively on the resource file to develop all the different language versions of the application. This approach has the following advantages:

- **Efficiency**. Developing a new international version of the application only involves creating a new international resource file because each version has the same code block. This streamlines the creation of multiple language versions of your Visual Basic application.
- **Greater security**. Whether you decide to localize your application in-house or to use an external company, you won't need to access source code to develop international versions of your application. This approach will also lower the amount of testing needed for the international version.
- **Better localization**. By placing all string resources in one file, you ensure a more efficient localization process and reduce the chance of leaving some strings unlocalized.

The following table lists some factors to consider when designing your Visual Basic application.

Factor	Item
Language	Strings in the user interface (menus, dialog boxes, and error messages)
	Printed and online documentation
Locale-specific settings	Date/time formats (separators, order of day/month/year)
	Number formats (decimal and thousand separators)
	Currency formats (symbol and format)
	Sort order and string comparison

The first factor, language, is addressed primarily in the design phase of your Visual Basic application. See "Designing an International-Aware User Interface" for more information. The second factor, locale-specific settings, is discussed in "Writing International Code in Visual Basic" and "International Sort Order and String Comparison," later in this chapter.

Using Resource Files for Localization

A resource file is a useful mechanism for separating localizable information from code in Visual Basic.

Note You can have only one resource file in your project. If you attempt to add more than one resource file, Visual Basic generates an error message.

Advantages of Storing Strings in Resource Files

When you are writing Visual Basic code, you can use the LoadResString, LoadResPicture, and LoadResData functions in place of references to string literals, pictures, and data. Storing such elements in a resource file offers two benefits:

- Performance and capacity are increased because strings, bitmaps, icons, and data can be loaded on demand from the resource file, instead of all being loaded at once when a form or a module is loaded.
- The resources that need to be translated are isolated in one resource file. There is no need to access the source code or recompile the application.

To create a resource file

1. Select **Add New Resource File** from the **Project** menu.

   Note This command is only available when the Resource Editor Add-In is loaded. To load the Resource Editor Add-In, select **Add-In Manager** from the **Add-Ins** menu. In the **Add-In Manager** dialog box, select **VB6 Resource Editor** and check the **Loaded/Unloaded** box.

2. In the **Open A Resource File** dialog box, enter a name for the resource file. The resource file will be added to the **Related Documents** node in **the Project Explorer**.

   Note You can also add an existing resource file to your project. Note, however, that any changes you make to an existing resource file may affect another application that uses it.

Visual Basic recognizes resource files by the .res file name extension. If the resource file does not have the appropriate file name extension, Visual Basic won't load it. Conversely, if any file uses the .res file name extension, Visual Basic interprets that it is a resource file when adding it to the project. If the file does not follow the standard format for a resource file, Visual Basic generates an error message the first time you attempt to use the resource file support functions (LoadResString, LoadResPicture, and LoadResData), or when you try to make an .exe file. Visual Basic will generate the same error message if you try to add a 16-bit resource file to a project.

The .res file, before and after you compile the .exe file, is a standard *Windows resource file*, which means the resources contained in the file can be loaded in any standard Windows-based resource editor.

To edit a resource file

1. Select **Resource Editor** from the **Tools** menu.

   Note This command is only available when the Resource Editor Add-In is loaded. To load the Resource Editor Add-In, select **Add-In Manager** from the **Add-Ins** menu. In the **Add-In Manager** dialog box, select **VB6 Resource Editor** and check the **Loaded/Unloaded** box.

2. Select a button from the **Resource Editor Toolbar** to edit an existing resource or add a new one. To learn more about editing resources, see the Resource Editor Add-In documentation.

Locking Resource Files

Visual Basic uses file locking on the .res file to prevent problems with multiple applications trying to use the file at the same time. Visual Basic will lock the .res file whenever:

- Visual Basic is in run mode or break mode.
- You create an .exe file.

For More Information For an example of how a resource file can be used to create an application that works in several locales, see "The Automated Teller Machine Sample Application," later in this chapter. For background information about programming with resource files, see "Working with Resource Files" in Chapter 8, "More About Programming."

The Automated Teller Machine Sample Application

This sample application has been designed to illustrate support for resource files in Visual Basic. The application contains three forms, a standard module, and a resource file. When you run the Automated Teller Machine (Atm.vbp) sample application, an opening screen lets you perform a bank transaction in one of several languages, including German, French, Italian, and Spanish.

The following code from the FrmInput.frm file loads resources stored in the Atm32.res file, which contains the localized strings for all languages.

```
Sub Form_Load()
   imgFlag = LoadResPicture(I, vbResBitmap)
   Caption = LoadResString(I)
   lblPINCode = LoadResString(1 + I)
   fraAccount = LoadResString(2 + I)
   optChecking.Caption = LoadResString(3 + I)
   optSavings.Caption = LoadResString(4 + I)
   lblAmount = LoadResString(5 + I)
   cmdOK.Caption = LoadResString(6 + I)
   SetCursor cmdOK
End Sub
```

```
Sub cmdOK_click()
    ' Display a process message.
    MsgBox LoadResString(7 + I)
    frmAmountWithdrawn.Show vbModal
    Unload Me
End Sub
```

At run time, this code reads the appropriate section of the resource file, based on an offset that is initialized when the user makes a language selection in the opening screen. The *offset* is a public variable declared in the standard module that indicates how far from a starting point a particular item is located. In the ATM sample application, the offset variable is `I`.

In the resource file, resource identifiers 16 through 47 are reserved for English, 48 through 79 are reserved for French, 80 through 111 are reserved for German, and so on. Each language contains the localized entries that make up the data block of the sample application. This block currently contains the eleven resources that are particular to each language.

This sample application, which contains several data blocks, introduces an alternative to a language-specific resource file using only one data block. Depending on the nature of the application you are developing, you may consider using one resource file per language version of your application or a single resource file containing all the localized data blocks.

The design of the Automated Teller Machine sample application presents several advantages beyond the ones outlined earlier in the chapter:

- The application can grow in scope by providing service in more languages. Simply add the same data block to the resource file and localize it as needed. If you decide to add a language, you may have to add a button to the opening screen.
- The application can grow in size if you want to extend your application by, for instance, allowing the ATM users to make deposits. Simply allow for wider identifier ranges (160 for example) for each language in the resource file. Currently, the identifiers range from 16 to 47, 48 to 79, and so on.

For More Information See "LoadResString Function," "LoadResPicture Function," and "LoadResData Function" in the *Microsoft Visual Basic 6.0 Language Reference* volume of the *Microsoft Visual Basic 6.0 Reference Library*. For information on resource files, see "Working with Resource Files" in Chapter 8, "More About Programming," and Chapter 15, "Designing for Performance and Compatibility."

Designing an International-Aware User Interface

Because text tends to grow when you localize an application, you should pay special attention when designing the following user interface (UI) components:

- Messages
- Menus and dialog boxes
- Icons and bitmaps
- Access and shortcut keys

Messages

English text strings are usually shorter than localized text strings in other languages. The following table shows the additional average growth for strings, based on initial length. This data is drawn from past Visual Basic localization projects and describes an average growth rate.

English length (in characters)	Additional growth for localized strings
1 to 4	100%
5 to 10	80%
11 to 20	60%
21 to 30	40%
31 to 50	20%
Over 50	10%

When designing the interface, consider these growth ratios and allow for text to wrap to more lines as the messages get longer.

Menus and Dialog Boxes

As with messages, menus and dialog boxes may grow when the application is localized. Consider the two following identical dialog boxes in the Automated Teller Machine sample application. You can see that extra space was allocated in the dialog box to allow for text expansion. Figure 16.2 shows the English dialog box, while Figure 16.3 shows the Spanish dialog box. Knowing that text can grow, plan your interface so that controls don't have to be resized or other elements redesigned when localized.

Figure 16.2 English input dialog box in the ATM sample application

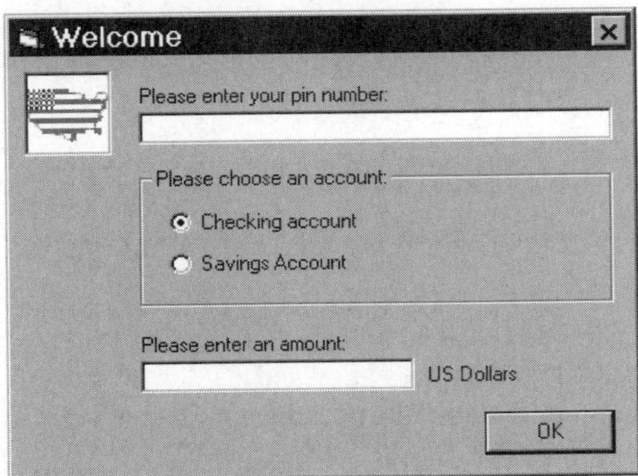

Figure 16.3 Spanish input dialog box in the ATM sample application

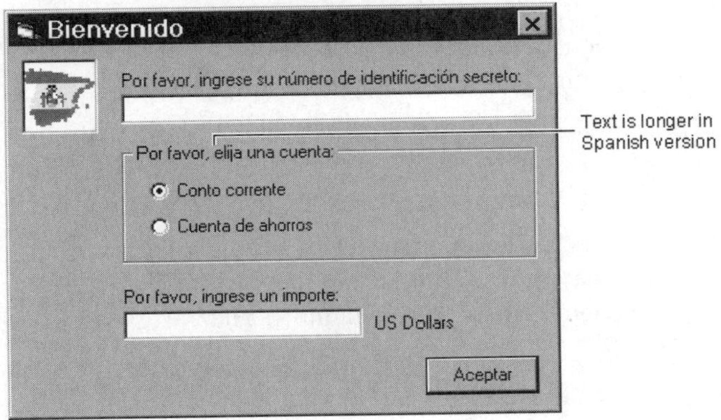

In menus and dialog boxes, avoid crowding status bars. Even abbreviations might be longer or simply not exist in other languages.

Icons and Bitmaps

Icons and bitmaps are usually used to depict a certain functionality without using text. Consider the following rules when working with icons and bitmaps:

- Avoid using bitmaps that are not an international standard. The following bitmaps represent a mailbox in the United States, but many users from other locales will not recognize it.

- Avoid using bitmaps that contain text. They take time to redraw, and text growth might also become an obstacle, as illustrated in the following icons.

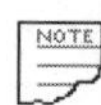

- Make sure that bitmaps or icons are culturally sensitive. What may be acceptable in one locale may be inappropriate or offensive in another.

Access and Shortcut Keys

Different locales have different keyboard layouts. Not all characters exist in all keyboard layouts. When developing your Visual Basic application, make sure all access-key and shortcut-key combinations you assign can be reproduced with international keyboards. One simple method to verify that your keyboard assignments work properly for the locales you are targeting is to choose the desired keyboard layout from your Windows Control Panel, along with keyboard layout pictures (which some reference manuals contain), and try the access-key and shortcut-key combinations.

Because certain access-key and shortcut-key combinations are not available for certain locales or because they are reserved for system use by some editions of Windows, it is best to avoid them when developing your Visual Basic application. Here are some examples of characters to avoid:

@ $ { } [ ] \ ~ | ^ ' < >

One way to work around this limitation is to use numbers and function keys (F1, F2, etc.) instead of letters in shortcut-key combinations. These may be less intuitive but they will not require any localization, because virtually all keyboard layouts include numbers and function keys.

> **Note** DBCS characters cannot be used as access or shortcut keys.

General Considerations When Writing International Code

When you're developing an application that will be localized — whether you're programming with Visual Basic or another tool — you must take into account differences between languages. You should identify the strings that need to be localized, allow for strings to grow, and avoid the pitfalls of string concatenation.

Hard-Coded Localizable Strings

The localization model presented in "Designing International Software" introduced the concepts of data block and code block. When building the resource files containing all the localizable strings, it is important to include *only* the strings that need to be localized. Any item that does not need to be partially or entirely localized can be hard-coded. Conversely, it is also fundamental to make sure all the resources that need to be localized are actually present in these resource files.

Buffer Sizes

If you are declaring a buffer size based on the expected length of a string or word, make sure this buffer can accommodate larger words and strings. See "Designing an International-Aware User Interface," for average growth rates of translated strings. The buffer size you declare in your Visual Basic code must account for this increase.

Consider the following example. Your Visual Basic declares a 2-byte buffer size for the word "OK." In Spanish, however, the same word is translated as "Aceptar," which would cause your program to overflow. Identical considerations apply for double-byte characters. Refer to "Issues Specific to the Double-Byte Character Set (DBCS)," later in this chapter for more information about DBCS.

String Concatenation

When you try to reduce the size of a string, one possible approach is string concatenation. This method allows you to use the same resource in several strings. However, there are some dangers when using this approach. Consider the following example:

English	French
String1: one after the other	String1: un après l'autre
String2: The controls will be deleted.	String2: Les contrôles seront supprimés.
String3: The forms will be deleted.	String3: Les feuilles seront supprimées.

Taken separately, String1, String2, and String3 can be easily localized. If your code performs String2 + String1 or String3 + String1, the resulting English string would look fine. The localized strings, however, are likely to be wrong. In the French column, for instance, String3 + String1 would be wrong because in French grammar, forms (feuilles) is a feminine word, thus String1 should be "une après l'autre" and not "un après l'autre." The same situation will be true in many other foreign languages. The only way to avoid this is to keep String2 and String1, and String3 and String1, together in the resource file.

In the above example, the order of the words that make up the sentence is the same in English and in French. However, the order is generally not the same in these two languages, or many other foreign languages. (For example, in both German and Japanese the verb generally appears at the end of the sentence.) The following example illustrates this situation:

English	French
String1: DLL	String1: DLL
String2: Missing Data Access	String2: Accès aux données manquante
String3: Missing OLE	String3: OLE manquante

If your code performs String2 + String1 and String3 + String1, localized versions will be broken because the order of the two strings produces a message that does not make any sense. One possible solution is to simply add String1 to String2 and String3 directly in the resource file and remove String1.

Another possible solution is presented in the following table:

English	French
String2: Missing Data Access '|1'	String2: '|1' d'accès aux données manquant
String3: Missing OLE '|1'	String3: '|1' OLE manquant

In this case, the localizer can identify '|1' as a placeholder and make the necessary changes in the resource file to reflect the appropriate way to build a sentence for the localized language.

Finally, it is also important to know that words or sentences that appear identical in English may need to be translated into different words or sentences when localized. Consider the following example:

English	French
String1: Setup program	String1: Programme d'installation
String2: String1 did not complete successfully.	String2: String1 a échoué.

In the English version, String1 is used as the setup program banner. It is also used as part of an error message in String2. In the French version, String1 worked perfectly as the stand-alone banner string. However, it needed to become "Le programme d'installation" to be used with String2.

Writing International Code in Visual Basic

Preparing a product for use in other locales implies more than just translating text messages. The product must support national conventions and provide country-specific support for numbers. In order to know how to work with different dates, currencies, and numeric values and separators, you have to understand the distinction Visual Basic makes between system locale and code locale.

System Locale vs. Code Locale

The *system locale* is the locale of the user who runs your program — it is used as a reference for user input and output and uses Control Panel settings provided by the operating system. The *code locale* is always English/U.S. in Visual Basic, regardless of which international version you use. Code locale determines the programming language and all the locale-specific settings.

Date

In Visual Basic, never type dates as strings in your code. Entering dates in code in the format #month/day/year# ensures that the date will be interpreted correctly in any system locale. Because Visual Basic allows only English/U.S. as a programming locale, the date will be the same to a user wherever your application is run.

For example, if a user enters 8/2/97 in an input dialog box,

```
CDate ("8/2/97")
```

returns the following results, based on the system locale:

Operating system	Output
French/France	`08/02/97` (= February 8, 1997)
English/U.S.	`8/2/97` (= August 2, 1997)

Conversely, if you enter 8/2/97 in code,

```
CDate (#8/2/97#)
```

returns the results in the following table, based on the code locale:

Operating system	Output
French/France	`02/08/97` (= August 2, 1997)
English/U.S.	`8/2/97` (= August 2, 1997)

If the user is in France and enters 8/2/97, the application will interpret this date as February 8, 1997, because the date format in France is day/month/year. If a user in the United States enters the same string, the application will understand August 2, 1997, because the date format is month/day/year.

Currency

Avoid typing currencies as strings in your code. For example, the following code does not run in any locale except those where the dollar sign ($) is the currency symbol.

```
Money = "$1.22"
NewMoney = CCur(Money)
```

If you run this code example in the French/France locale, where "F" is the currency symbol, Visual Basic will generate a "Type mismatch" error message, because $ is not recognized as a currency symbol in that locale. Instead, simply use numbers, as shown in the following example. Use a period as a decimal separator, because the code locale for Visual Basic is always English/U.S. The following code will run correctly, regardless of the user's locale.

```
Money = 1.22
NewMoney = CCur(Money)
```

Numeric Values and Separators

In the United States, the period (.) is used as the decimal separator. In several European countries, however, the comma (,) is used as the decimal separator. Similarly, in the United States, a comma is used as the thousands separator to isolate groups of three digits to the left of the decimal separator. In several European countries, a period or a space is used for this purpose. The following table lists some examples of different number formats:

Countries	Number formats
U.S.	1,234,567.89 1,234.56 .123
France	1 234 567,89 1 234,56 0,123
Italy	1.234.567,89 1.234,56 0,123

Note In Visual Basic, the Str and Val functions always assume a period is the decimal separator. In a majority of locales, this assumption is not valid. Instead, use the CStr, CDbl, CSng, CInt, and CLng functions to provide international conversions from any other data type to the data type you need. These functions use the system locale to determine the decimal separator.

For More Information See the next section, "Locale-Aware Functions," for more information about the Print and Format functions. See "CStr Function," "CSng Function," and "CInt Function," and, in Appendix E, "Type Conversion Functions." All references are in the *Microsoft Visual Basic 6.0 Language Reference*.

Locale-Aware Functions

Each locale has different conventions for displaying dates, time, numbers, currency, and other information. It is not necessary to know all the conventions of your users' locales. In Visual Basic, many functions use the user's system locale, which uses the Control Panel settings provided by the operating system to automatically determine the conventions at run time. These functions are called *locale-aware* functions.

Print Method

Even though the Print method provides little flexibility for different output formats, it does use the user's system locale. In the following example, dates are printed using the correct short date format, numbers are printed with the correct decimal separator, and currencies are printed with the correct symbol:

```
MyDate = #11/24/1997#
MyNumber = 26.5
Money = 1636.32
MyMoney = Format(Money, "###,###.##")
Debug.Print MyDate, MyNumber, MyMoney
```

When this code is run in an English/U.S. locale, the following output appears in the Immediate window:

```
11/24/1997  26.5  1,636.32
```

When this code is run in a German/Germany locale, the following output appears in the Immediate window:

```
24/11/1997  26,5  1.632,32
```

For More Information See "Print Method" in the *Microsoft Visual Basic 6.0 Language Reference*.

Format Function

The Format function can accept format codes, but format codes always produce the same type of output regardless of the user's locale. For example, the format code "mm-dd-yy" is not appropriate for a user in Belgium, where the day precedes the month.

For more flexibility, the Format function also provides named formats that will automatically determine which conventions to use at run time, including General Date, Long Date, Short Date, and Long Time. Using named formats produces output that is based on the user's system locale. The named formats can even generate output in the user's native language, including the names of months and days of the week. The following example illustrates this:

```
MyDate = #8/22/1997 5:22:20 PM#
NewDate1 = Format(MyDate, "Medium Date")
NewDate2 = Format(MyDate, "Short Date")
NewDate3 = Format(MyDate, "Long Date")
NewDate4 = Format(MyDate, "General Date")
Debug.Print NewDate1, NewDate2, NewDate3, NewDate4
```

When this code is run in an English/U.S. locale, the following output appears in the Immediate window:

```
22-Aug-97 8/22/97    Monday, August 22, 1997   8/22/97 5:22:20 PM
```

When this code is run in a French/France locale, the following output appears in the Immediate window:

```
22-août-97  22/08/97    lundi 22 août 1997     22/08/97 17:22:20f
```

For More Information See "Format Function" in the *Microsoft Visual Basic 6.0 Language Reference*.

International Sort Order and String Comparison

String comparison is widely used in Visual Basic. Using this functionality, however, may yield incorrect results if you overlook certain programming requirements.

Sorting Text

Sorting text means ordering text according to language conventions. Format and font are irrelevant to the sorting process because both involve presentation rather than content. At first glance, sorting text looks simple: *a* precedes *b*, *b* precedes *c*, and so on. However, there are many languages that have more complex rules for sorting. Correct international sorting is not always a simple extension of sorting English text, and it requires a different understanding of the sorting process.

Correct international sorting can imply *context-sensitive sorting*. Character contraction and expansion are the two important areas of context-sensitive sorting.

- *Character contraction* occurs when a two-character combination is treated as a single, unique letter. For example, in Spanish the two-character combination *ch* is a single, unique letter and sorts between *c* and *d*.
- *Character expansion* occurs in cases where one letter represents one character, but that one character sorts as if it were two. For example, *ß* (eszett) is equivalent to *ss* in both German/Germany and German/Switzerland locales. However, *ß* is equivalent to *sz* in the German/Austria locale.

Before implementing the sorting order, you must consider code pages. A *code page* is an ordered character set that has a numeric index (code point) associated with each character. Because there are various code pages, a single code point might represent different characters in different code pages. While most code pages share the code points 32 through 127 (ASCII character set), they differ beyond that. Typically, the ordering of any additional letters in these code pages is not alphabetic.

For More Information See "DBCS Sort Order and String Comparison," later in this chapter, for more information about working with East Asian languages.

String Comparison in Visual Basic

String comparison rules are different for each locale. Visual Basic provides a number of tools, such as Like and StrComp, which are locale-aware. To use these effectively, however, the Option Compare statement must first be clearly understood.

Comparing Strings with the Option Compare Statement

When using this statement, you must specify a string comparison method: either Binary or Text for a given module. If you specify Binary, comparisons are done according to a sort order derived from the internal binary representations of the characters. If you specify Text, comparisons are done according to the case-insensitive textual sort order determined by the user's system locale. The default text comparison method is Binary.

In the following code example, the user enters information into two input boxes. The information is then compared and sorted in the appropriate alphabetic order.

```
Private Sub Form_Click ()
Dim name1 As String, name2 As String
   name1 = InputBox("Enter 1st hardware name here:")
   name2 = InputBox("Enter 2nd hardware name here:")
If name1 < name2 Then
   msg = " ' " & name1 & " ' comes before ' " & _
   name2 & " ' "
Else
   msg = " ' " & name2 & " ' comes before ' " & _
   name1 & " ' "
End If
   MsgBox msg
End Sub
```

If this code is run in an English/U.S. locale, the message box will contain the following output if the user enters `printer` and `Screen`:

```
'Screen' comes before 'printer'
```

This result is based on the fact that the default text-comparison method is Binary. Because the internal binary representation of uppercase *S* is smaller than the one for lowercase *p*, the conditional statement Screen < printer is verified. When you add the Option Compare Text statement in the Declarations section of a module, Visual Basic compares the two strings on a case-insensitive basis, resulting in the following output:

```
'printer' comes before 'Screen'
```

If this code is run in a French/Canada locale, the message box will contain the following output if the user enters `imprimante` and `écran`:

```
'imprimante' comes before 'écran'
```

Similarly, if you add the Option Compare Text statement to your code, the two terms will appear in the right order — that is, écran will precede `imprimante`. In addition to being case insensitive, the comparison takes into account the accented characters, such as *é* in French, and places it right after its standard character — in this case, *e*, in the sorting order.

If the user had entered `ecran` and `écran`, the output would be:

```
'ecran' comes before 'écran'
```

For More Information See "Option Compare Statement" in the *Microsoft Visual Basic 6.0 Language Reference*.

Comparing Strings with the Like Operator

You can use the Like operator to compare two strings. You can also use its pattern-matching capabilities. When you write international software, you must be aware of pattern-matching functions. When character ranges are used with Like, the specified pattern indicates a range of the sort ordering. For example, under the Binary method for string comparison (by default or by adding Option Compare Binary to your code), the range [A–C] would miss both uppercase accented *a* characters and all lower-case characters. Only strings starting with A, B, and C would match. This would not be acceptable in many languages. In German, for instance, the range would miss all the strings beginning with *Ä*. In French, none of the strings starting with *À* would be included.

Under the Text method for string comparison, all the accented *A* and *a* characters would be included in the interval. In the French/France locale, however, strings starting with *Ç* or *ç* would not be included, since *Ç* and *ç* appear after *C* and *c* in the sort order.

Using the [A–Z] range to check for all strings beginning with an alphabetic character is not a valid approach in certain locales. Under the Text method for string comparison, strings beginning with *Ø* and *ø* would not be included in the range if your application is running in a Danish/Denmark locale. Those two characters are part of the Danish alphabet, but they appear after Z. Therefore, you would need to add the letters after Z. For example, `Print "øl" Like "[A-Z]*"` would return False, but `Print "øl" Like "[A-ZØ]*"` would return True with the Option Compare Text statement.

Comparing Strings with the StrComp Function

The StrComp function is useful when you want to compare strings. It returns a value that tells you whether one string is less than, equal to, or greater than another string. The return value is also based on the string comparison method (Binary or Text) you defined with the Option Compare statement. StrComp may give different results on the strings you compare, depending on the string comparison method you define.

For More Information See "DBCS Sort Order and String Comparison," later in this chapter, for more information about comparing strings in East Asian languages. See also "StrComp Function" in the *Microsoft Visual Basic 6.0 Language Reference*.

International File Input/Output

Locale is also an important consideration when working with file input and output in Visual Basic. Both the Print # and Write # statements can be used to work with data files, but they have distinct purposes.

Print

The Print # statement puts data into a file as the data is displayed on the screen, in a locale-aware format. For instance, date output uses the system Short Date format, and numeric values use the system decimal separator.

The Input # statement cannot read locale-aware data in Visual Basic that has been written to a file with the Print # statement. To write locale-independent data that can be read by Visual Basic in any locale, use the Write # statement instead of the Print # statement.

Write

Like the Print # statement, the Write # statement puts data into a file in a fixed format, which ensures that the data can be read from the file in any locale when using the Input # statement. For instance, dates are written to the file using the universal date format, and numeric values are written to the file using the period as the decimal separator. In the following code example, a date and a numeric value are written to a file with the Write # statement. The same file is reopened later, its content is read with the Input # statement, and the results are printed in the Immediate window. The Long Date information is drawn from the system locale:

```
Dim MyDate As Date, NewDate As Date
Dim MyNumber As Variant
   MyDate = #8/2/67#
   MyNumber = 123.45
Open "Testfile" for Output As #1
   Write #1, MyDate, MyNumber
Close #1

Open "Testfile" for Input As #1
   Input #1, MyDate, MyNumber
   NewDate = Format(Mydate, "Long Date")
Debug.Print NewDate, MyNumber
Close #1
```

When you run this code in an English/U.S. locale, the following output appears in the Immediate window:

```
Wednesday, August 02, 1967  123.45
```

When you run this code in a French/France locale, the following output appears in the Immediate window:

```
mercredi 2 août 1967        123,45
```

In both locales, the output is accurate — that is, the information was stored and retrieved properly using the Write # and Input # statements.

For More Information For background information on processing files, see "Working With Files" in Chapter 14, "Processing Drives, Folders, and Files." See also "Print # Statement" or "Write # Statement" in the *Microsoft Visual Basic 6.0 Language Reference.*

Locale-Aware SQL Queries Based on Dates

As explained in "Writing International Code in Visual Basic," different countries have different date formats. If your application performs a comparison between two dates, date literals must be stored in a unique format to ensure a reliable comparison, regardless of a user's locale. In Visual Basic, the database engine stores a date/time value as a DateSerial value, which is represented by an 8-byte floating-point number, with the date as the integral portion and the time as the fractional portion. This approach is completely locale-independent and will let you perform date/time comparisons using the international date/time formats.

Structured Query Language (SQL) is an ANSI standard with which Visual Basic complies. Dates are saved in tables and databases using the English/U.S. format (month/day/year). This format was also adopted for the Microsoft Jet database engine. Queries that use these fields may return the wrong records or no records at all if a non-U.S. date format is used.

This constraint also applies to the Filter property, to the FindFirst, FindNext, FindPrevious, and FindLast methods of the Recordset object, and to the WHERE clause of an SQL statement.

Using DateSerial and DateValue

There are two functions you can use to handle the limitations of the SQL standard. Avoid using date/time literals in your code. Instead, consider using the DateValue or the DateSerial functions to generate the date you want. The DateValue function uses the system's Short Date setting to interpret the string you supply; the DateSerial function uses a set of arguments that will run in any locale. If you are using date/time literals in your SQL query or with the Filter property, you have no choice but to use the English/U.S. format for date and time.

The following examples illustrate how to perform a query based on a date. In the first example, a non-U.S. date format is used. The Recordset returned is empty because there is a syntax error in the date expression:

```
Dim mydb As Database
Dim myds As Recordset

Set mydb = OpenDatabase("MyDatabase.mdb")
' Table that contains the date/time field.
Set myds = mydb.OpenRecordset("MyTable,dbopenDynaset")
' The date format is dd/mm/yy.
myds.FindFirst "DateFiled > #30/03/97#"
' A data control is connected to mydb.
Data1.Recordset.Filter = "DateFiled = #30/03/97#"
```

```
mydb.Close
myds.Close
```

The following example, however, will work adequately in any locale because the date is in the appropriate format:

```
Dim mydb As Database
Dim myds As Recordset

Set mydb = OpenDatabase("MyDatabase.mdb")
' Table that contains the date/time field.
Set myds = mydb.OpenRecordset("MyTable, dbopenDynaset")

myds.FindFirst "DateFiled > #03/30/97#"  ' Date format
                                          ' is mm/dd/yy.

' A data control is connected to mydb.
Data1.Recordset.Filter = "DateFiled = _
DateValue(""" & DateString & """)"

mydb.Close
myds.Close
```

Issues Specific to the Double-Byte Character Set (DBCS)

The *double-byte character set* (DBCS) was created to handle East Asian languages that use ideographic characters, which require more than the 256 characters supported by ANSI. Characters in DBCS are addressed using a 16-bit notation, using 2 bytes. With 16-bit notation you can represent 65,536 characters, although far fewer characters are defined for the East Asian languages. For instance, Japanese character sets today define about 12,000 characters.

In locales where DBCS is used — including China, Japan, Taiwan, and Korea — both single-byte and double-byte characters are included in the character set. The single-byte characters used in these locales conform to the 8-bit national standards for each country and correspond closely to the ASCII character set. Certain ranges of codes in these single-byte character sets (SBCS) are designated as *lead bytes* for DBCS characters. A consecutive pair made of a lead byte and a trail byte represents one double-byte character. The code range used for the lead byte depends on the locale.

Note DBCS is a different character set from Unicode. Because Visual Basic represents all strings internally in Unicode format, both ANSI characters and DBCS characters are converted to Unicode and Unicode characters are converted to ANSI characters or DBCS characters automatically whenever the conversion is needed. You can also convert between Unicode and ANSI/DBCS characters manually. For more information about conversion between different character sets, see “DBCS String Manipulation Functions,” later in this chapter.

When developing a DBCS-enabled application with Visual Basic, you should consider:

- Differences between Unicode, ANSI, and DBCS.
- DBCS sort orders and string comparison.
- DBCS string manipulation functions.
- DBCS string conversion.
- How to display and print fonts correctly in a DBCS environment.
- How to process files that include double-byte characters.
- DBCS identifiers.
- DBCS-enabled events.
- How to call Windows APIs.

Tip Developing a DBCS-enabled application is good practice, whether or not the application is run in a locale where DBCS is used. This approach will help you develop a flexible, portable, and truly international application. None of the DBCS-enabling features in Visual Basic will interfere with the behavior of your application in environments using exclusively single-byte character sets (SBCS), and the size of your application will not increase because both DBCS and SBCS use Unicode internally.

For More Information For limitations on using DBCS for access and shortcut keys, see "Designing an International-Aware User Interface," earlier in this chapter.

ANSI, DBCS, and Unicode: Definitions

Visual Basic uses Unicode to store and manipulate strings. Unicode is a character set where 2 bytes are used to represent each character. Some other programs, such as the Windows 95 API, use ANSI (American National Standards Institute) or DBCS to store and manipulate strings. When you move strings outside of Visual Basic, you may encounter differences between Unicode and ANSI/DBCS. The following table shows the ANSI, DBCS, and Unicode character sets in different environments.

Environment	Character set(s) used
Visual Basic	Unicode
32-bit object libraries	Unicode
16-bit object libraries	ANSI and DBCS
Windows NT API	Unicode
Automation in Windows NT	Unicode
Windows 95 API	ANSI and DBCS
Automation in Windows 95	Unicode

ANSI

ANSI is the most popular character standard used by personal computers. Because the ANSI standard uses only a single byte to represent each character, it is limited to a maximum of 256 character and punctuation codes. Although this is adequate for English, it doesn't fully support many other languages.

DBCS

DBCS is used in Microsoft Windows systems that are distributed in most parts of Asia. It provides support for many different East Asian language alphabets, such as Chinese, Japanese, and Korean. DBCS uses the numbers 0–128 to represent the ASCII character set. Some numbers greater than 128 function as *lead-byte characters*, which are not really characters but simply indicators that the next value is a character from a non-Latin character set. In DBCS, ASCII characters are only 1 byte in length, whereas Japanese, Korean, and other East Asian characters are 2 bytes in length.

Unicode

Unicode is a character-encoding scheme that uses 2 bytes for *every* character. The International Standards Organization (ISO) defines a number in the range of 0 to 65,535 (2^{16}–1) for just about every character and symbol in every language (plus some empty spaces for future growth). On all 32-bit versions of Windows, Unicode is used by the Component Object Model (COM), the basis for OLE and ActiveX technologies. Unicode is fully supported by Windows NT. Although both Unicode and DBCS have double-byte characters, the encoding schemes are completely different.

Character Code Examples

Figure 16.4 shows an example of the character code in each character set. Note the different codes in each byte of the double-byte characters.

Figure 16.4 Character codes for "A" in ANSI, Unicode, and DBCS

A	ANSI character "A"	&H41	
A	Unicode character "A"	&H41	&H00
Ａ	DBCS character that represents a Japanese wide-width "A"	&H82	&H60
Ａ	Unicode wide-width "A"	&H21	&HFF

DBCS Sort Order and String Comparison

You need to be aware of the issues when sorting and comparing DBCS text, because the Option Compare Text statement has a special behavior when used on DBCS strings. When you use the Option Compare Binary statement, comparisons are made according to a sort order derived from the internal binary representations of the characters. When you use Option Compare Text statement, comparisons are made according to the case-insensitive textual sort order determined by the user's system locale.

In English "case-insensitive" means ignoring the differences between uppercase and lowercase. In a DBCS environment, this has additional implications. For example, some DBCS character sets (including Japanese, Traditional Chinese, and Korean) have two representations for the same character: a narrow-width letter and a wide-width letter. For example, there is a single-byte "A" and a double-byte "A." Although they are displayed with different character widths, Option Compare Text treats them as the same character. There are similar rules for each DBCS character set.

You need to be careful when you compare two strings. Even if the two strings are evaluated as the same using Like or StrComp, the exact characters in the strings can be different and the string length can be different, too.

For More Information For general information about comparing strings with the Option Compare statement, see "International Sort Order and String Comparison," earlier in this chapter.

DBCS String Manipulation Functions

Although a double-byte character consists of a lead byte and a trail byte and requires two consecutive storage bytes, it must be treated as a single unit in any operation involving characters and strings. Several string manipulation functions properly handle all strings, including DBCS characters, on a character basis.

These functions have an ANSI/DBCS version and a binary version and/or Unicode version, as shown in the following table. Use the appropriate functions, depending on the purpose of string manipulation.

The "B" versions of the functions in the following table are intended especially for use with strings of binary data. The "W" versions are intended for use with Unicode strings.

Function	Description
Asc	Returns the ANSI or DBCS character code for the first character of a string.
AscB	Returns the value of the first byte in the given string containing binary data.
AscW	Returns the Unicode character code for the first character of a string.
Chr	Returns a string containing a specific ANSI or DBCS character code.
ChrB	Returns a binary string containing a specific byte.

Function	Description
ChrW	Returns a string containing a specific Unicode character code.
Input	Returns a specified number of ANSI or DBCS characters from a file.
InputB	Returns a specified number of bytes from a file.
InStr	Returns the first occurrence of one string within another.
InStrB	Returns the first occurrence of a byte in a binary string.
Left, Right	Returns a specified number of characters from the right or left sides of a string.
LeftB, RightB	Returns a specified number of bytes from the left or right side of a binary string.
Len	Returns the length of the string in number of characters.
LenB	Returns the length of the string in number of bytes.
Mid	Returns a specified number of characters from a string.
MidB	Returns the specified number of bytes from a binary string.

The functions without a "B" or "W" in this table correctly handle DBCS and ANSI characters. In addition to the functions above, the String function handles DBCS characters. This means that all these functions consider a DBCS character as one character even if that character consists of 2 bytes.

The behavior of these functions is different when they're handling SBCS and DBCS characters. For instance, the Mid function is used in Visual Basic to return a specified number of characters from a string. In locales using DBCS, the number of *characters* and the number of *bytes* are not necessarily the same. Mid would only return the number of characters, not bytes.

In most cases, use the character-based functions when you handle string data because these functions can properly handle ANSI strings, DBCS strings, and Unicode strings.

The byte-based string manipulation functions, such as LenB and LeftB, are provided to handle the string data as binary data. When you store the characters to a String variable or get the characters from a String variable, Visual Basic automatically converts between Unicode and ANSI characters. When you handle the binary data, use the Byte array instead of the String variable and the byte-based string manipulation functions.

For More Information See the *Microsoft Visual Basic 6.0 Language Reference* for the appropriate function.

If you want to handle strings of binary data, you can map the characters in a string to a Byte array by using the following code:

```
Dim MyByteString() As Byte
' Map the string to a Byte array.
MyByteString = "ABC"
' Display the binary data.
```

```
For i = LBound(MyByteString) to UBound(MyByteString)
   Print Right(" " + Hex(MyByteString(i)),2) + " ,";
Next
Print
```

DBCS String Conversion

Visual Basic provides several string conversion functions that are useful for DBCS characters: StrConv, UCase, and LCase.

StrConv Function

The global options of the StrConv function are converting uppercase to lowercase, and vice versa. In addition to those options, the function has several DBCS-specific options. For example, you can convert narrow letters to wide letters by specifying vbWide in the second argument of this function. You can convert one character type to another, such as hiragana to katakana in Japanese. StrConv enables you to specify a LocaleID for the string, if different than the system's LocaleID.

You can also use the StrConv function to convert Unicode characters to ANSI/DBCS characters, and vice versa. Usually, a string in Visual Basic consists of Unicode characters. When you need to handle strings in ANSI/DBCS (for example, to calculate the number of bytes in a string before writing the string into a file), you can use this functionality of the StrConv function.

Case Conversion in Wide-Width Letters

You can convert the case of letters by using the StrConv function with vbUpperCase or vbLowerCase, or by using the UCase or LCase functions. When you use these functions, the case of English wide-width letters in DBCS are converted as well as ANSI characters.

Font, Display, and Print Considerations in a DBCS Environment

When you use a font designed only for SBCS characters, DBCS characters may not be displayed correctly in the DBCS version of Windows. You need to change the Font object's Name property when developing a DBCS-enabled application with the English version of Visual Basic or any other SBCS-language version. The Name property determines the font used to display text in a control, in a run-time drawing, or during a print operation. The default setting for this property is MS Sans Serif in the English version of Visual Basic. To display text correctly in a DBCS environment, you have to change the setting to an appropriate font for the DBCS environment where your application will run. You may also need to change the font size by changing the Size property of the Font object. Usually, the text in your application will be displayed best in a 9-point font on most East Asian platforms, whereas an 8-point font is typical on European platforms.

These considerations apply to printing DBCS characters with your application as well.

How to Avoid Changing Font Settings

If you do not have any DBCS-enabled font or do not know which font is appropriate for the target platform, there are several options for you to work around the font issues.

In the Traditional Chinese, Simplified Chinese, and Korean versions of Windows, there is a system capability called *Font Association*. With Korean Windows, for example, Font Association automatically maps any English fonts in your application to a Korean font. Therefore, you can still see Korean characters displayed, even if your application uses English fonts. The associated font is determined by the setting in \HKEY_LOCAL_MACHINE\System\CurrentControlSet\control\fontassoc \Associated DefaultFonts in the system registry of the run-time platform. With Font Association supported by the system, you can run your English application on a Chinese or Korean platform without changing any font settings. Font Association is not available on other platforms, such as Japanese Windows.

Another option is to use the System or FixedSys font. These fonts are available on every platform. Note that the System and FixedSys fonts have few variations in size. If the font size you set at design time (with the Size property of the Font object) for either of these fonts does not match the size of the font on the user's machine, the setting may be ignored and the displayed text truncated.

How to Change the Font at Run Time

Even though you have the options above, these solutions have restrictions. Here is an example of a global solution to changing the font in your application at run time. The following code, which works in any language version of Windows, applies the proper font to the Font object specified in the argument.

```
Private Const DEFAULT_CHARSET = 1
Private Const SYMBOL_CHARSET = 2
Private Const SHIFTJIS_CHARSET = 128
Private Const HANGEUL_CHARSET = 129
Private Const CHINESEBIG5_CHARSET = 136
Private Const CHINESESIMPLIFIED_CHARSET = 134
Private Declare Function GetUserDefaultLCID Lib "kernel32" () As Long

Public Sub SetProperFont(obj As Object)
   On Error GoTo ErrorSetProperFont
   Select Case GetUserDefaultLCID
   Case &H404 ' Traditional Chinese
      obj.Charset = CHINESEBIG5_CHARSET
      obj.Name = ChrW(&H65B0) + ChrW(&H7D30) + ChrW(&H660E) _
       + ChrW(&H9AD4)    'New Ming-Li
      obj.Size = 9
```

```
    Case &H411 ' Japan
       obj.Charset = SHIFTJIS_CHARSET
       obj.Name = ChrW(&HFF2D) + ChrW(&HFF33) + ChrW(&H20) + _
        ChrW(&HFF30) + ChrW(&H30B4) + ChrW(&H30B7) + ChrW(&H30C3) + _
        ChrW(&H30AF)
       obj.Size = 9
    Case &H412 'Korea UserLCID
       obj.Charset = HANGEUL_CHARSET
       obj.Name = ChrW(&HAD74) + ChrW(&HB9BC)
       obj.Size = 9
    Case &H804 ' Simplified Chinese
       obj.Charset = CHINESESIMPLIFIED_CHARSET
       obj.Name = ChrW(&H5B8B) + ChrW(&H4F53)
       obj.Size = 9
    Case Else   ' The other countries
       obj.Charset = DEFAULT_CHARSET
       obj.Name = ""    ' Get the default UI font.
       obj.Size = 8
    End Select
    Exit Sub
ErrorSetProperFont:
    Err.Number = Err
End Sub
```

You can modify this sample code to make the font apply to other font settings, such as printing options.

Processing Files That Use Double-Byte Characters

In locales where DBCS is used, a file may include both double-byte and single-byte characters. Because a DBCS character is represented by two bytes, your Visual Basic code must avoid splitting it. In the following example, assume Testfile is a text file containing DBCS characters.

```
' Open file for input.
Open "TESTFILE" For Input As #1

' Read all characters in the file.
Do While Not EOF(1)
   MyChar = Input(1, #1)' Read a character.
   ' Perform an operation using Mychar.
Loop
Close #1                       ' Close file.
```

When you read a fixed length of bytes from a binary file, use a Byte array instead of a String variable to prevent the ANSI-to-Unicode conversion in Visual Basic.

```
Dim MyByteString(0 to 4) As Byte

Get #1,, MyByteString
```

When you use a String variable with Input or InputB to read bytes from a binary file, Unicode conversion occurs and the result is incorrect.

Keep in mind that the names of files and directories may also include DBCS characters.

For More Information For background information on file processing, see "Working With Files" in Chapter 14, "Processing Drives, Folders, and Files." For information on the Byte data type, see "Data Types" in Chapter 5, "Programming Fundamentals."

Identifiers in a DBCS Environment

DBCS characters are not supported in any of the following identifiers:

- Public procedure names
- Public variables
- Public constants
- Project name (as specified in the Project Properties dialog box)
- Class names (Name property of a class module, a user control, a property page, or a user document)

DBCS-Enabled KeyPress Event

The KeyPress event can process a double-byte character code as one event. The higher byte of the *keyascii* argument represents the lead byte of a double-byte character, and the lower byte represents the trail byte.

In the following example, you can pass a KeyPress event to a text box, whether the character you input is single-byte or double-byte.

```
Sub Text1_KeyPress (KeyAscii As Integer)
   Mychar = Chr(KeyAscii)
   ' Perform an operation using Mychar.
End Sub
```

For More Information See "KeyPress Event" in the *Microsoft Visual Basic 6.0 Language Reference*.

Calling Windows API Functions

Many Windows API and DLL functions return size in bytes. This return value represents the size of the returned string. Visual Basic converts the returned string into Unicode even though the return value still represents the size of the ANSI or DBCS string. Therefore, you may not be able to use this returned size as the string's size. The following code gets the returned string correctly:

```
buffer = String(145, Chr(" "))
   ret = GetPrivateProfileString(section, _
   entry, default, buffer, Len(buffer)-1, filename)
   retstring = Left(buffer, Instr(buffer, Chr(0))-1))
```

For More Information For more information, see "Accessing the Microsoft Windows API" in Part 4, "Accessing DLLs and the Windows API" of the *Microsoft Visual Basic 6.0 Component Tools Guide* volume of the *Microsoft Visual Basic 6.0 Reference Library*, available in the Professional and Enterprise editions.

Visual Basic Bidirectional Features

Visual Basic is bidirectional (also known as "BiDi")-enabled. "Bidirectional" is a generic term used to describe software products that support Arabic and other languages which are written right-to-left. More specifically, bidirectional refers to the product ability to manipulate and display text for both left-to-right and right-to-left languages. For example, displaying a sentence containing words written in both English and Arabic requires bidirectional capability.

Microsoft Visual Basic includes standard features to create and run Windows applications with full bidirectional language functionality. However, these features are operational only when Microsoft Visual Basic is installed in a bidirectional 32-bit Microsoft Windows environment, such as Arabic Microsoft Windows 95. Other bidirectional 32-bit Microsoft Windows environments are available as well.

The RightToLeft property has been added to forms, controls, and other Visual Basic objects to provide an easy mechanism for creating objects with bidirectional characteristics. Although RightToLeft is a part of every Microsoft Visual Basic installation, it is operational only when Microsoft Visual Basic is installed in a bidirectional 32-bit Microsoft Windows environment.

Bidirectional Features documentation describes all Microsoft Visual Basic bidirectional features. You can find this information under Additional Information under Reference in the Visual Basic table of contents. Click the See Also under the title of this topic to go directly to the overview topic.

For compatibility with Microsoft Visual Basic 4.0, two versions of the 32-bit Grid control (Grid32.ocx) are included with Microsoft Visual Basic 6.0 but not installed. Both are located in the \Tools folder of the product media. The standard and bidirectional versions are located in the \Controls and \Controls\Bidi subfolders, respectively.

CHAPTER 17

Distributing Your Applications

After you create a Visual Basic application, you may want to distribute it to others. You can freely distribute any application you create with Visual Basic to anyone who uses Microsoft Windows. You can distribute your applications on disk, on CDs, across networks, or over an intranet or the Internet.

When you distribute an application, there are two steps you must go through:

- Packaging — you must package your application files into one or more .cab files that can be deployed to the location you choose, and you must create setup programs for certain types of packages. A *.cab file* is a compressed file that is well suited to distribution on either disks or the Internet.
- Deployment — you must move your packaged application to the location users can install it from. This may mean copying the package to floppy disks or to a local or network drive, or deploying the package to a Web site.

You can use two tools to package and distribute your applications: the Package and Deployment Wizard (formerly the Setup Wizard), or the Setup Toolkit provided with your Visual Basic installation. The Package and Deployment Wizard automates many of the steps involved in distributing applications by presenting you with choices about how you want to configure your .cab files. The Setup Toolkit lets you customize some of what happens during the installation process.

Contents

The Package and Deployment Wizard

The Visual Basic Package and Deployment Wizard helps you create .cab files for your application, group them into a unit, or *package*, that contains all information needed for installation, and deliver those packages to end users. You can use Visual Basic's Package and Deployment Wizard to create packages that are distributed on floppy disks, CDs, a local or network drive, or the Web. The Package and Deployment Wizard automates much of the work involved in creating and deploying these files.

The Package and Deployment Wizard offers three options

- The Package option helps you package a project's files into a .cab file that can then be deployed, and in some cases creates a setup program that installs the .cab files. The wizard determines the files you need to package and leads you through all the choices that must be made in order to create one or more .cab files for your project.
- The Deploy option helps you deliver your packaged applications to the appropriate distribution media, such as floppies, a network share, or a Web site.
- The Manage Scripts option lets you view and manipulate the scripts you have saved from previous packaging and deployment sessions in the wizard. Each time you use the wizard, you save a script that contains all the choices you made. You can reuse these scripts in later sessions if you want to use similar settings and make the same choices as you did previously.

For More Information See "Application Packaging with the Wizard," later in this chapter, for more information about packaging your projects and for more information on deploying an application to the Web or another destination. See "Managing Wizard Scripts," later in this chapter, for more information on how to create and use scripts.

The Package and Deployment Wizard vs. the Setup Toolkit Project

The Package and Deployment Wizard walks you through creating and distributing professional setup programs for your Visual Basic applications. In addition to creating .cab files for your application, the wizard also creates the application's setup program by compiling the Setup Toolkit project installed with Visual Basic. The setup program is called setup1.exe.

In most cases, the Package and Deployment Wizard is the best way to create and distribute your application's setup1.exe program. However, if you want your application's setup program to use features not provided by the Package and Deployment Wizard, you can do so by modifying the Setup Toolkit project. Like any other Visual Basic project, the forms, code, and functionality of this project can be modified or enhanced.

> **Note** The Package and Deployment Wizard and the Setup Toolkit create setup programs and distribution media only for Visual Basic applications. To create setup programs for other Windows-based applications, use the setup toolkit provided with that development product or in the Microsoft Windows SDK.

For More Information For more information on using the toolkit project to package and deploy your applications, see "The Setup Toolkit," later in this chapter.

Starting the Package and Deployment Wizard

The Visual Basic Package and Deployment Wizard makes it easy for you to create the necessary .cab files and setup programs for your application. Like other wizards, the Package and Deployment Wizard prompts you for information so that it can create the exact configuration you want.

There are three ways you can start the Package and Deployment Wizard:

- You can run it from within Visual Basic as an add-in. If you run the wizard as an add-in, you must first set the necessary references in the Add-In Manager to load the wizard. When you use the wizard as an add-in, Visual Basic assumes that you want to work with the project you currently have open. If you want to work with another project, you must either open that project before starting the add-in, or use the wizard as a stand-alone component.
- You can run it as a stand-alone component from outside the development environment. When you run the wizard as a stand-alone component, you are prompted to choose the project on which you want to work.
- You can start it in silent mode by launching it from a command prompt. See "Running the Wizard in Silent Mode" in this topic for more information.

After you start the wizard, a series of screens prompt you for information about your project and let you choose options for the package. Each screen explains how it is to be used, including which information is optional, and what information must be entered before you can move to the next screen. If you find that you need more information on any screen, press F1 or click the Help button.

> **Note** You should save and compile your project before running the Package and Deployment Wizard.

In most cases, the Package and Deployment Wizard is all you need to create a package that is ready for deployment. However, if you want to customize your packaging process further or provide functionality not supported by the Package and Deployment Wizard, you can modify the Setup Toolkit Project.

To start the Package and Deployment Wizard from within Visual Basic

1. Open the project you want to package or deploy using the wizard.

   Note If you are working in a project group or have multiple projects loaded, make sure that the project you want to package or deploy is the current project before starting the wizard.

2. Use the Add-In Manager to load the Package and Deployment Wizard, if necessary: Select **Add-In Manager** from the **Add-Ins** menu, select **Package and Deployment Wizard** from the list, then click **OK**.
3. Select **Package and Deployment Wizard** from the **Add-Ins** menu to launch the wizard.
4. On the main screen, select one of the following options:
   - If you want to create a standard package, Internet package, or dependency file for the project, click **Package**.
   - If you want to deploy the project, click **Deploy**.
   - If you want to view, edit, or delete scripts, click **Manage Scripts**.

   For an introduction to these options, see "The Package and Deployment Wizard."
5. Proceed through the wizard screens.

To start the Package and Deployment Wizard as a stand-alone component

1. If the project you want to package is open, save it and close Visual Basic.
2. Click the **Start** button, and then click **Package and Deployment Wizard** from the Visual Basic submenu.
3. In the **Project** list on the initial screen, choose the project you want to package.

   Note You can click **Browse** if your project is not in the list.

4. On the main screen, select one of the following options:
   - If you want to create a standard package, Internet package, or dependency file for the project, click **Package**.
   - If you want to deploy the project, click **Deploy**.
   - If you want to view, edit, or delete scripts, click **Manage Scripts**.
5. Proceed through the wizard screens.

Running the Wizard in Silent Mode

Using scripts, you may package and deploy your project files in *silent mode.* In silent mode, the wizard runs without your having to attend it to make choices and move through screens. The wizard packages and deploys your project using the settings contained in a script.

Silent mode is especially useful if you are packaging and deploying as part of a batch process. For example, early in the development of your project, you may use the Package and Deployment Wizard to package your project and deploy it to a test location. You can later create a batch file to perform the same packaging and deployment steps periodically as you update your project.

To package and deploy in silent mode

1. Open an MS-DOS prompt.
2. Type the name of the wizard executable, pdcmdln.exe, followed by the path and file name of your Visual Basic project, and the appropriate command line arguments, as shown in the following example:

```
PDCmdLn.exe C:\Project1\Project1.vbp /p "Internet Package"
   /d Deployment1 /l "C:\Project1\Silent Mode.log"
```

Note You can perform packaging and deployment in a single silent session by specifying both the /p and the /d arguments, as shown in the example above. Otherwise, use either /p or /d.

Argument	Description
/p ***packagingscript***	Type **/p** followed by the name of a previously saved packaging script to package the project silently according to the specified script.
/d ***deploymentscript***	Type **/d** followed by the name of a previously saved deployment script to deploy the project silently according to the specified script.
/l ***path***	Specifies that the wizard should store all output from the wizard, such as error messages and success reports, to a file rather than displaying them on the screen. Type **/l** followed by the path and file name of a file in which output should be stored. If the file does not exist, the wizard creates it.

Note Any file or script name that includes spaces should be enclosed in quotation marks, as shown in the example above.

For More Information See the next section, "Application Packaging with the Wizard," for instructions on how to use the wizard to package your project. See "Application Deployment with the Wizard" for instructions on how to use the wizard to deploy your projects. See "Modifying the Setup Project," later in this chapter, for more information on customizing the installation process.

Application Packaging with the Wizard

Application packaging is the act of creating a package that can install your application onto the user's computer. A *package* consists of the .cab file or files that contain your compressed project files and any other necessary files the user needs to install and run your application. These files may include setup programs, secondary .cab files, or other needed files. The additional files vary based on the type of package you create.

You can create two kinds of packages — standard packages or Internet packages. If you plan to distribute on disk, floppy, or via a network share, you should create a *standard package* for your application. If you plan to distribute via an intranet or Internet site, you should create an *Internet package*.

In most cases, you will package your applications using the Package and Deployment Wizard, which is provided with Visual Basic. You can package applications manually, but the wizard provides valuable shortcuts and automates some of the tasks you would have to perform yourself in a manual packaging session.

> **Note** In addition, you can use the Setup Toolkit and the Package and Deployment Wizard together. You can modify the Setup Toolkit project to customize your setup programs and add features that the Package and Deployment Wizard does not provide, then use the wizard to package and deploy the application.

In addition to creating standard and Internet packages, you can also use the packaging portion of the Package and Deployment Wizard to create dependency files. Dependency files list the run-time components that must be distributed with your application's project files.

> **Important** Any time you create a package, you should be sure that the version number for your project has been set on the Make tab of the Project Properties dialog box. This is especially important if you are distributing a new version of an existing application: Without the appropriate change in version numbers, the end user's computer may determine that critical files do not need to be updated.

For More Information For a more detailed explanation of standard packages and their contents, see "Standard Packages," See "Internet Packages," for more information about Internet packages and their contents. See "Using the Package and Deployment Wizard with the Setup Toolkit," for more information on using the two tools together to create customized setup programs. See "Dependency Files" for an explanation of the contents of a dependency file. All references are later in this chapter.

Files You Are Allowed to Distribute

You can freely distribute any application or component that you create with Visual Basic. In addition to an executable (.exe) file, your application might require other files, such as DLLs, ActiveX controls (.ocx files), or bitmaps (.bmp files).

You can legally distribute sample application files and any files that were originally copied to the \Icons subdirectory of the \Visual Studio\Common\Graphics directory when you first installed Visual Basic on your system. Microsoft makes no warranty, express or implied, regarding the merchantability or fitness of these applications, nor does Microsoft assume any obligation or liability for their use.

If you have purchased the Professional or Enterprise Edition of Visual Basic, you can also distribute any files originally copied to the \Visual Studio\Common\Graphics and \Program Files\Common Files\ODBC subdirectories.

> **Note** You may also be able to distribute other ActiveX controls, .exe files, and DLLs that you have purchased. Consult the manufacturer's license agreement for each of the files you plan to distribute to determine whether you have the right to distribute the file with your application.

Overall Steps in the Packaging Process

Regardless of the type of package you create or the tool you use to create it, there are certain steps that must be taken.

> **Note** The Package and Deployment Wizard performs many of these steps for you automatically.

1. **Determine the type of package you want to create**. You can create a standard package for Windows-based programs that will be distributed on disk, on CD, or over a network; or you can create an Internet package for programs that will be distributed on the Web. You can also choose to create only a dependency file.
2. **Determine the files you need to distribute**. The wizard must determine the project files and dependent files for your application before it can create the package. *Project files* are the files included in the project itself — for example, the .vbp file and its contents. *Dependent files* are run-time files or components your application requires to run. Dependency information is stored in the vb6dep.ini file, or in various .dep files corresponding to the components in your project.
3. **Determine where to install files on the user's machine**. Program and setup files are usually installed into a subdirectory of the Program Files directory, while system and dependent files are usually installed into the \Windows\System or \Winnt\System32 directory. Your setup program must take this into account and determine where to install each file.
4. **Create your package**. The wizard creates the package and the setup program (setup1.exe) for it, referencing all necessary files. The end result of this step is one or more .cab files and any necessary setup files.
5. **Deploy your package**. The deployment process involves creating your distribution media and copying all necessary files to the location from which users can access it. For information on deployment, see "Application Deployment with the Wizard," later in this chapter.

For More Information For a full list of common run-time, setup, and dependency files, see "Files You Need to Distribute," later in this chapter. See "Dependency Files," later in this chapter, for more information on creating a .dep file.

Packaging Features

Using the Package and Deployment Wizard, you can easily create a professional setup program for your application or deploy an Internet application to the Web. The wizard performs these steps during the packaging process:

- **Automatic inclusion of your application's main setup program (setup1.exe)**. The wizard adds the Setup Toolkit application, Setup1.exe, to the package. This file is the main installation program for your application.
- **Automatic creation of your application's .cab files**. The Package and Deployment Wizard can create a single .cab file or multiple .cab files for your application.
- **Script-based sessions**. You can select a script from another packaging session with the same project if you want to use the same or very similar settings as you move through the wizard. This can save you significant time. In addition, you can use a previously saved script to package a project in silent mode. This is especially useful as part of a batch compilation process.
- **Optional creation of dependency files**. Dependency files identify the run-time files that must be included with your application when it is distributed.
- **Automatic support for data access, Remote Automation, and DCOM features**. The wizard automatically determines whether your project includes functionality that changes the setup process. For example, if you include certain types of data access, Remote Automation, or DCOM features, you may need to include drivers or other files in your package. The wizard checks your projects and displays screens that allow you to specify the appropriate options in these cases.
- **Shared file capability**. The wizard allows you to install some files as shared files. This means that the files will not be removed from the system during an uninstall if other applications are using them.
- **Alternate file locations for Internet packages**. In Internet packages, the wizard allows you to specify whether dependency files should be included in the setup program or downloaded from an alternate Web site.
- **Safety settings for Internet packages**. If you do not use the IObjectSafety interface in your project, the Package and Deployment Wizard lets you mark components in your application as safe.
- **Custom destination locations for each file in the project**. Most files have a default location to which they are installed, depending on whether they are project files or system files. You can change these locations if you want to install the files to a different location.

For More Information See "Deployment Features," later in this chapter, for more information on features of the Package and Deployment Wizard.

Standard Packages

A standard package is a package that is designed to be installed by a setup.exe program, rather than through the downloading of a .cab file from a Web site. You create standard packages for Windows-based applications that will be distributed through disks, CD, or a network share.

When you create a standard package, you must carefully consider the distribution method you plan to use prior to creating your package. If you plan to use floppies, you must usually create multiple .cab files that can be placed onto several disks, rather than one large .cab file. An option in the Package and Deployment Wizard lets you specify whether you want one or multiple .cab files and the .cab size to use (1.44 MB, 1.2 MB, etc.). If you select multiple .cab files, the wizard splits your application files into several sets that do not exceed the indicated size.

> **Important** Even if the application you plan to distribute on floppy disks is small enough to fit on a single disk when packaged into one large .cab file, you should still choose the multiple .cab option so that you have access to the floppy disk deployment process later in the wizard. In this case, only one .cab file will be created.

If you're planning to deploy to a network or local share, to CDs, or to a Web site, you can create either one large .cab file or multiple smaller .cab files.

Parts of a Standard Package

There are several files that are always part of your standard packages. These include:

- **The setup.exe file**. Setup.exe acts as a pre-installation executable. Setup.exe is the first thing run on the user's machine in the installation process, and it performs necessary processing that must occur before the main installation takes place.
- **The setup1.exe file**. Setup1.exe acts as the main setup program for your application.
- **All required support files**. Support files are stored in the \Support subdirectory, beneath the directory in which the package was created. In addition to the setup.exe and setup1.exe files, this directory contains the files necessary to customize the .cab files for the application if the users so desire.
- **The .cab files for your application.** Both Internet and Windows-based applications are packaged into .cab files prior to distribution. A .cab file takes the place of what was, in previous versions of Visual Basic, a long list of compressed application files. All of those files are now contained within the .cab. You can have a single .cab for your application, or you can create multiple .cabs for floppy disk delivery.

Note If your application will be run on a bidirectional (BiDi) operating system, you will need to manually include the vbame.dll file in the Setup.lst created by the Package and Deployment Wizard. You can do this by adding the file at the Included Files screen when running the Package and Deployment Wizard, by editing the Setup.lst directly, or by adding an entry for vbame.dll to the vb6dep.ini file so that it will be automatically added to the Setup.lst whenever you run the Package and Deployment Wizard.

Data Access Features

If your application uses one of Visual Basic's data access technologies, such as Data Access Objects (DAO), ActiveX Data Objects (ADO), or Remote Data Objects (RDO), the Package and Deployment Wizard performs two additional steps during the packaging process:

- If your application uses ADO, OLEDB, or ODBC components, the wizard automatically adds a file called mdac_typ.exe to the list of files to include in your package. Mdac_type.exe is a self-extracting executable that installs all of the necessary components you need for your data access technology.
- The wizard prompts you to choose the appropriate data access option when your application includes DAO features. You choose the appropriate method — ISAM-based, ODBCDirect, ODBC through Jet, etc.

Remote Automation and DCOM Features

If your application utilizes remote code components (formerly called OLE servers), you need to create two packages for the application: a setup program for the client, and one for the server. You can use the Package and Deployment Wizard to package the application, simply by running it twice on the same project group — once on the client project, and once on the server project.

Before you package either the client or the server, you must make sure that you have created the necessary remote support (.vbr) files for the project and placed them in the same directory where the .vbp file for the project is located.

To create support for Remote Automation or DCOM

1. Open the project group in Visual Basic and select the project that will act as the server.
2. Select **Project Properties** from the **Project** menu. Select the **Components** tab of the **Project Properties** dialog box and check the **Remote Server Files** option.

   When you compile the project with this option selected, the .vbr file is created automatically.

Registry Files

If your project references any .reg or .vbl files, you will see an additional screen in the wizard where you can specify how this registry information should be treated. You can choose to simply copy the registry files to the end user's computer, or you can have the system store the information in the registry and automatically register it on the end user's computer.

Missing or Outdated Files

As you move through the wizard, a series of dialogs may appear if any files needed by your application are missing or if any files have missing or outdated dependency information. You can either choose to proceed without the dependency information for the component, locate the missing files, or permanently mark a file as requiring no dependencies.

Internet Packages

Internet packages are .cab-based setup programs that are designed to be downloaded from a Web site. Internet Explorer uses a process known as Internet Component Download to install your Internet application. The Package and Deployment Wizard automatically includes information needed for this process in the packages it creates.

There are several types of Visual Basic applications or components that can be packaged for Internet deployment, including:

- ActiveX controls (.ocx files) that are displayed on a Web page.
- ActiveX .exe or .dll files, designed to run on the client or the Web server.
- ActiveX documents, that are displayed in place of a Web page.
- DHTML applications, client-based applications that link HTML pages to Visual Basic code through the use of Dynamic HTML.
- IIS applications, server-based applications that link HTML pages to an object called a webclass. The webclass intercepts server requests from the browser and responds to them with Visual Basic code.

For More Information Extensive information about the Internet Component Download process can be found in Chapter 4, "Downloading ActiveX Components," in Part 5, "Building Internet Applications" in the *Microsoft Visual Basic 6.0 Component Tools Guide* volume of the *Microsoft Visual Basic 6.0 Language Reference Library.*

Parts of an Internet Package

There are several files that are always part of your Internet packages. These include:

- **The primary .cab file for your application**. The primary .cab file for Internet packages is used as the setup program for your application. The primary .cab file includes project components, such as the executable or DLL for your application or your .ocx file for controls, an .inf file referencing secondary cabs and containing safety and registry information, and all required dependency files that are not in secondary .cabs.
- **All required support files**. Support files for an Internet application may include HTML files, Active Server Pages (.asp) files, graphics files in a variety of formats, or other files your application must access to run.
- **Any secondary .cab files for your application**. In addition to project files, applications often reference several run-time components, such as the Visual Basic run-time DLL, individual ActiveX controls, and data access objects. If these components are available online in prepackaged .cab files, you can reference those .cab files in your primary .cab, rather than shipping the files yourself.

Secondary .cab files provide an efficient way to ensure that the user has the most current version of components. If a newer version of a component in a secondary .cab file becomes available on the external Web site, users who download your application will receive the updated version automatically.

> **Note** If you cannot or do not want your application setup to require a connection to the Internet, you may place the secondary .cab files on a server within your intranet. An intranet server often provides for faster downloading and allows users to download from a secure network.

How Internet Component Download Works

After you package your Internet application or component for download, you deploy it to a specific location on a Web server, from which users can access it. Usually, your package is referenced as part of an existing Web page — that is, your control or other component is hosted by a Web page.

When a user accesses the Web page that hosts your package, the system downloads your package to the user's computer. The package is verified for safety, unpacked, registered, installed, and *then* activated. All of this occurs in the background and is controlled by the browser.

The Package and Deployment Wizard plays two parts in the process described above:

1. It packages your component and its associated files into a compressed (.cab) file that the browser uses to download your component. The Package and Deployment Wizard determines which files your project needs to run, gathers those files, compresses them into a .cab file, and generates the HTML that points to your component.
2. It deploys your packaged files to the Web server location of your choice. For more information on deploying your Internet component download package, see "Application Deployment with the Wizard," later in this chapter.

Safety Issues

When you prepare Internet applications and components for download, you must package them into a file that can be delivered to the user through a browser. In addition, you must perform a few precautionary steps to ensure users that your application will not harm their computers. These steps can include:

- Digitally signing your components so that users can verify the contents of the component and identify you as the software's source.
- Setting safety levels to vouch that your components will not damage users' computers or corrupt their data.
- Arranging for licensing of any components that require it. When you add an ActiveX control to a Web page, you are distributing it to any users who download the control from the page. Unless you license the control, there is little to prevent an end user from taking your control and using it in their own applications. The license acts as a kind of copyright for your control, preventing unauthorized use.

Safety settings can be made within the Package and Deployment Wizard. When you work with an Internet package, a screen in the wizard asks you to verify safety settings. This screen appears lists only the objects in your project that do not implement a safety interface called IObjectSafety.

> **Note** Signing and licensing must be done outside of the packaging process. You should arrange licensing for any components before you package the component. Digital signing can be done after you package the application — the Package and Deployment Wizard reserves space within the .cab file for information about the digital signature.

For More Information See "Steps to Prepare your Component for Download" in Chapter 4, "Downloading ActiveX Components," in Part 5, "Building Internet Applications" of the *Microsoft Visual Basic 6.0 Component Tools Guide* for detailed explanations of component safety, licensing, and signing. See "Setting Safety Levels for ActiveX Components" in Chapter 4, "Downloading ActiveX Components," in Part 5, "Building Internet Applications" of the *Microsoft Visual Basic 6.0 Component Tools Guide,* for more information on the IObjectSafety interface.

Dependency Files

A dependency (.dep) file contains information about the run-time requirements of an application or component — for example, which files are needed, how they are to be registered, and where on the user's machine they should be installed. You can create .dep files for standard projects in all versions of Visual Basic. If you have the Professional or Enterprise edition of Visual Basic, you can create .dep files for ActiveX controls, ActiveX documents, and other ActiveX components.

The Package and Deployment Wizard uses .dep files when it packages your applications. It scans all available dependency information for the application to build a comprehensive list of information about the run-time files the application needs, then builds installation information from that list. For a standard package, the information from the .dep files is written to a Setup.lst file that is stored outside the packaged .cab file. For an Internet package, the .dep file information is written to an .inf file that is stored within the packaged .cab file.

When you package a component, you have the option of creating a .dep file to accompany it when it is deployed. You would do this if you have created a component you want to distribute with dependency information. It is recommended that you package and deploy your component before you package and deploy your dependency file, so that the packaging portion of the wizard knows the source location of the component that the dependency file references.

Types of Dependency Files

In Visual Basic, dependency information is stored in files generated by the Package and Deployment Wizard or created manually by you. There are two types of files that can contain dependency information:

- Component .dep files — a .dep file lists files needed by a particular control or component. The Package and Deployment Wizard uses this file when it creates the setup program. In addition, the wizard can create this type of .dep file for you.
- The VB6dep.ini file — a list of dependency files for the entire Visual Basic development environment.

When you run the Package and Deployment Wizard, it looks for dependency information in .dep files and in vb6dep.ini. If dependency information cannot be found for a component in either location, the wizard notifies you of the missing dependency information. You can ignore this omission or correct the problem by creating the appropriate dependency files.

> **Note** If you ignore the omission, your program may not function properly after installation. If, however, you are certain that a dependent file will already be loaded on the user's machine, you may ignore the warning and proceed.

Component Dependency Files

A .dep file lists all the files required by a particular component. When you purchase or use a component from a vendor, you receive a .dep file from them. For example, all of the ActiveX controls shipped with Visual Basic have a companion .dep file. These .dep files list all of the dependent files used by the control, plus version and registry information.

You should generate a .dep file for any component that you create in Visual Basic if that component may be used in another project. The information from the .dep file for each component in a project is combined to form the project's dependency information. If you do not create a .dep file for your component, the dependency information for any projects in which it is used may be incorrect.

The VB6dep.ini File

The VB6dep.ini file provides the Package and Deployment Wizard with an all-purpose list of dependencies and references used by Visual Basic. This list is created when you install Visual Basic and resides in the \Wizards\PDWizard subdirectory of the main Visual Basic directory.

Missing Dependency Information

The Package and Deployment Wizard will inform you if dependency information is missing for a component in your project. There are three ways you can add the necessary dependency information:

- Edit the vb6dep.ini file to manually add an entry for a particular component.
- Create a .dep file for the component with the Package and Deployment Wizard.
- Contact the component's vendor and request a .dep file.

Application Deployment with the Wizard

Application deployment is the act of moving your packaged application to either the distribution media you have chosen or to a Web site from which it can be downloaded. There are two ways you can deploy your Visual Basic application:

- You can use the Deployment portion of the Package and Deployment Wizard to deploy your application to floppy disks, a local or network drive, or to a Web site.
- You can manually copy files to disks or shares, or you can manually publish files to the appropriate Web location.

The Package and Deployment Wizard provides shortcuts and automatically performs some of the same tasks you would have to perform if you manually deployed your application.

Overall Steps in the Deployment Process

Whether you deploy your packages with the Package and Deployment Wizard by hand, there are certain steps that must be taken.

1. **Create a package for deployment**. This can be either a single .cab file or a series of .cab files, depending on how you plan to distribute the application.
2. **Identify the package you want to deploy**. You can choose any valid package for the selected project.
3. **Choose a deployment method**. You can deploy your application to the Internet, to floppy disks, or to a directory on a local or network drive.
4. **Choose the files to deploy**. If you are deploying to the Internet, you can add and remove files from the list of files to be deployed.
5. **Determine the destination for deployed files**. For Internet deployment, this involves specifying a Web site to which the package should be deployed. For directory deployment, this means indicating the drive location to which the package should be deployed. For floppy disk deployment, this means choosing the appropriate floppy drive.
6. **Deploy your package**. If you are using the Package and Deployment Wizard, the wizard handles this process for you. If not, you must copy the files to the appropriate locations on your shared or local drive, or publish your files to the Web.

Deployment Features

Using the Package and Deployment Wizard, you can easily copy your packaged applications to the appropriate location. The Package and Deployment Wizard performs these steps, with your input, during the deployment process:

- **Choice of deployment methods**. You can choose to deploy to floppy disks, a local or network drive, or an intranet or Internet site.
- **Script-based sessions.** You can select a script from another deployment session for the same project if you want to use the same or very similar settings as you move through the wizard. This can save you significant time.
- **Automatic access to Web Publishing technology**. Web Publishing technology makes it easy to publish files to an intranet or Internet site.

For More Information For more information on Web publishing see "Internet Tools and Technologies" in the *Internet Client SDK,* online. For more features of the wizard, see "Packaging Features," earlier in this chapter.

Deploying Your Application

The wizard offers you a choice between deploying to the Web using Web Publishing technology, or deploying to floppies or a directory on a local or network drive.

Deploying to Floppy Disks, Directories, and CDs

You can deploy to floppy disks using the Package and Deployment Wizard only if you have created a standard package using the Multiple Cabs option. This options ensures that your package consists of multiple .cab files or of a single .cab that is smaller than the size of a disk. The system gives you the option of formatting each disk before you copy your .cab files to it. You do not have to format the disk, but you must use empty disks for this deployment process.

If you choose to deploy to a directory, the system prompts you to pick a local or network directory into which your files will be copied. You can then either direct your users to access the setup program for your application from that location, or you can move your files onto CD-ROMs.

> **Note** If you have a writable CD drive, you may be able to copy your files directly to that drive using the deployment portion of the wizard, rather than deploying to a directory and then copying the files to your CDs.

Deploying to the Web

You can deploy any package, whether it is a standard or Internet package, to the Web. When you choose Web Publishing as your deployment method, the system considers the project folder to be the *local base folder* for your deployment. The local base folder is used to determine how files and directories should be copied to the Web site you choose. Files and directories that are within the local base directory will be deployed to the Web server with the same directory structure as the base directory.

> **Note** By default, the wizard does not deploy source files from within the project directory or the \Support subdirectory. The packaging portion of the wizard creates the \Support directory and places files in it that can be used to recreate your .cab files.

Managing Wizard Scripts

When you work in the Package and Deployment Wizard, you can create and store scripts. A *script* is a record of the selections you made in a packaging or deployment session. Creating a script retains these selections so that you can apply them to future sessions in the wizard for the same project. Using scripts can save you significant time in your packaging and deployment sessions. In addition, you can use scripts to package and deploy your applications in silent mode.

Each time you package or deploy a project, Visual Basic stores information about that session as a script. All scripts for a project are stored in a special file within the application's project directory. You can view the full list of scripts for the current project by using the Manage Scripts option in the Package and Deployment Wizard. This option lets you:

- View a list of all packaging or deployment scripts.
- Rename a script.
- Create a copy of a script with a new name.
- Delete a script that you no longer need.

Caution If you remove a packaging script, the deployment portion of the Package and Deployment Wizard will no longer recognize the package created from that script as one that it can deploy. You will then have to repackage the file in order to be able to deploy it. Delete only those scripts you are certain you no longer need.

To view a list of scripts

1. Start the wizard, and then select **Manage Scripts** from the main screen.

   Important If you have started the wizard as a stand-alone application, you must choose the Visual Basic project you want before selecting Manage Scripts.

2. Choose the appropriate panel for the scripts you want to view.

The Setup Toolkit

The Setup Toolkit is a project installed with Visual Basic that is used by the Package and Deployment Wizard when it creates a setup program. The Setup Toolkit project contains the forms and code that the application's setup program uses to install files onto the user's computer. When you use the Package and Deployment Wizard, the wizard includes the setup1.exe file that the Setup Toolkit project creates. This file is used as the application's main installation file.

Note There are two setup programs involved in the installation process — setup.exe and setup1.exe. The setup.exe program performs pre-installation processing on the user's computer, including installing the setup1.exe program and any other files needed for the main installation program to run. Only setup1.exe is customizable through the Setup Toolkit.

In addition to playing a supporting role in the process of creating a setup program, the Setup Toolkit can be used to modify the screens seen in the installation process, or to create a setup program directly. You might create a custom setup program if you need to add additional functionality not supported by the wizard to your installation sequence.

The Setup Toolkit project resides in the \Wizards\PDWizard\Setup1 subdirectory of the main Visual Basic directory.

Caution The files in this project are the same files used by the output of the Package and Deployment Wizard. Do not modify them without making a backup copy in another directory first. If you modify setup1.exe, subsequent setup programs created by the Package and Deployment Wizard will use the modified version.

You use the Setup Toolkit by loading the Setup1.vbp file into Visual Basic and making modifications to the appearance or functionality of the project. In doing so, you may need to manually go through the steps that the Package and Deployment Wizard would otherwise do for you. The following sections describe steps in the process and explain how to determine which files you need to include in your setup, how to create a Setup.lst, how to create distribution media, and how to test your setup.

Overall Steps to Modify the Package and Deployment Wizard

When you modify the Setup Toolkit with the intention of changing the output created by the Package and Deployment Wizard, you follow these steps:

1. Modify the Setup Toolkit project to contain any new prompts, screens, functions, code, or other information you want to include. When you are finished, compile the project to create setup1.exe.
2. Run the Package and Deployment Wizard, following the prompts on each screen, to create your distribution media.

Overall Steps to Create a Custom Setup Program

When you create a setup program manually using the Setup Toolkit rather than the Package and Deployment Wizard, you must follow these steps:

1. If necessary, modify the Setup Toolkit project to contain any new prompts, screens, functions, code, or other information you want to include.
2. Determine the files you want to distribute, including all run-time, setup, and dependency files.
3. Determine where to install the files on the users' computers.
4. Manually create your Setup.lst file to reflect the names and installation locations of all files that must be included for your project.
5. Determine how you will be distributing files.
6. Create the .cab files for your project using the Makecab utility.

   Tip You can use the Package and Deployment Wizard to create your .cab files, then modify the .cab files manually. When the wizard creates your .cab files, it creates a .ddf file and a batch file in the \Support subdirectory of your project directory. To modify the .cab files, edit the .ddf file, then run the batch file provided. The batch file in turn will run Makecab.exe to recreate your .cab files.

7. Create the setup1.exe for your project by compiling the Setup Toolkit project with your changes.

8. Copy your files to the distribution media, or manually publish your files to the Web site using the Web Publishing Wizard, available in the ActiveX SDK.

For More Information For more information on using the Web Publishing Wizard, see "Internet Tools and Technologies" in the *Internet Client SDK,* online. See the next section, "Modifying the Setup Project," for more information on modifying the Setup Toolkit project. See "Files you Need to Distribute" and "Where to Install Files on the User's Machine" for more information on how to place files on the user's computer, and "Manually Creating Distribution Media" for more information on copying your files to the appropriate media, all later in this chapter.

Modifying the Setup Project

You can modify the Setup1.vbp project if you want to add new screens, prompts, or events to the installation sequence created by the Package and Deployment Wizard. You write code in the setup program just as you would in any other Visual Basic program. A number of function calls are available that are especially useful in setup routines.

Some examples of situations in which you might modify the Setup Toolkit project include:

- You need to add special user prompts during installation.
- You want to create a customized look and feel for your setup program.
- You want to display billboards during installation. Billboards present information about your product's features, service and support, registration, and other related information.
- You want to use your own compression utility to copy your application's files to the distribution media.

  Important Because the Package and Deployment Wizard uses the files in the Setup Toolkit project, you should always make a backup of the project before making any changes. In addition, you should back up the full contents of the Setup1 directory.

To modify the Setup Toolkit project

1. Create a backup of \Wizards\PDWizard\setup1.exe and all contents of the \Wizards\PDWizard\Setup1 directory before making any changes.

2. Open the setup1.vbp project from the \Wizards\PDWizard\Setup1 directory.

3. Make any changes to the code, forms, or modules in this project.

4. Save the project and compile it to create setup1.exe.

5. If you are using the Package and Deployment Wizard to package your application, launch the Package and Deployment Wizard and create a package for your application.

6. If you are creating your own custom setup package, continue through the steps outlined in "The Setup Toolkit."

   Important Any time you create a package, using either the Package and Deployment Wizard or the Setup Toolkit project, you should be sure that the version numbers for your project have been set on the Make tab of the Project Properties dialog box in Visual Basic. This is especially important if you are distributing a new version of an existing application — without the appropriate change in version numbers, the end user's computer may determine that critical files do not need to be updated.

Files You Need to Distribute

The first step in creating a custom setup program is to determine which files to distribute. All Visual Basic applications need a minimum set of files, referred to as *bootstrap files*, that are needed before your application can be installed. In addition, all Visual Basic applications require application-specific files, such as an executable file (.exe), data files, ActiveX controls, or .dll files.

There are three main categories of files needed to run and distribute your application:

- Run-time files
- Setup files
- Application-specific files

Run-Time Files

Run-time files are files your application must have in order to work correctly after installation. These files are needed by all Visual Basic applications. The following are the run-time files for Visual Basic projects:

- Msvbvm60.dll
- Stdole2.tlb
- Oleaut32.dll
- Olepro32.dll
- Comcat.dll
- Asyncfilt.dll
- Ctl3d32.dll

While these files are needed by all Visual Basic applications, they may not be necessary for every type of installation package. For example, when creating an Internet package, the Package and Deployment Wizard assumes that any computer capable of performing an Internet download already has all of these files except for Msvbvm60.dll. Therefore this is the only run-time file that the wizard includes in an Internet package.

Note Run-time files can be further classified by their installation location. See "Where to Install Files on the User's Machine" for more information.

Setup Files for Standard Packages

Setup files are all of the files required to set up your standard application on the user's machine. These include the setup executables (setup.exe and setup1.exe), the setup file list (Setup.lst), and the uninstall program (st6unst.exe).

Visual Basic applications that are designed to be distributed on disk, on CD, or from a network location use the same setup files, regardless of whether you use the Package and Deployment Wizard or the Setup Toolkit to create your setup programs. These files are listed below.

File name	Description
setup.exe	Program that the user runs to pre-install the files that are needed for your application to be installed on the user's machine. For example, the setup.exe file installs the setup1.exe file, the Visual Basic run-time DLL, and other files without which the rest of the setup process cannot run.
setup1.exe	The setup program for your Visual Basic application. This executable file is generated by the Setup Toolkit and included in the package by the Package and Deployment Wizard. You can rename this file as long as the new name is reflected in the Setup.lst file.
Setup.lst	Text file that contains installation instructions and lists all the files to be installed on the user's machine.
Vb6stkit.dll	Library containing various functions used in Setup1.exe.
St6unst.exe	Application removal utility.

Note Applications designed to be delivered over the Internet generally do not use any of these files. See "Internet Packages" earlier in this chapter for more information on the files involved in Internet delivery.

Application Dependencies

In order to run your application, end users will need certain files in addition to the common run-time files and special setup files. Many of these files will be obvious to you: the executable file, any data files, and any ActiveX controls that you used. The less obvious files are your project's other dependent files. For example, some of the ActiveX controls used by your project may in turn require other files. One of the tasks of the Package and Deployment Wizard is to determine the complete list of such required files.

For More Information See "Dependency Files," earlier in this chapter, for information on using the Package and Deployment Wizard to create dependency files for your application.

Where to Install Files on the User's Machine

Before writing your setup program, you must determine where to install all of the necessary files on the user's machine. You record this information in your Setup.lst file. See "Manually Editing a Setup.lst File" in this chapter for more information on how to record this information in the file.

The files required by your application can be divided into several categories.

- Program-specific files — files your application requires to run and that are not used by other applications.
- Shared files — files used by your application but also accessed by other applications on the user's machine.
- Remote Automation server components — files necessary for Remote Automation or DCOM functionality.

Each type of file is best installed in a different location.

Program Files

Program files are files your application must have in order to run and that are useful only in the context of your application — for example, the application's .exe file and its required data files.

Program files should be installed in the application directory that the user specifies during installation. Code in Setup1.vbp demonstrates how to write files to this location. By default, the Setup Toolkit uses the \Program Files directory as the root location to install applications onto Windows 95 or later and Windows NT systems. For example, Setup1 suggests that Project1 be installed in the \Program Files\Project1 directory.

> **Caution** When installing a file on the user's machine, you should not copy an older version of the file over a new version. The CopyFile function in Setup1.bas uses the VerInstallFile API function to copy files to the user's machine. VerInstallFile will *not* overwrite an existing file with an older version.

Shared Application Files

Shared application files are files that can be used by more than one application on the system. For example, several different vendors may ship applications that use the same ActiveX control. If you create an application that uses the control, you should indicate in your installation program that the control's .ocx file is designed to be shared.

Shared files must be installed in a location that allows other applications to access the them. In most cases, this is \Program Files\Common Files for Windows 95 and Windows NT 4.0 or later.

When an end user uninstalls your application, the system only removes a shared file if there are no other applications that could use the file.

Remote Automation Components

Install Remote Automation server components to the \Windows\System or \Winnt\System32 directory. This ensures that your applications use the most current Remote Automation server components.

> **Tip** You can use the $(WinSysPath) installation macro to ensure that these files are installed in the correct directory.

Manually Editing a Setup.lst File

If you use the Package and Deployment Wizard, the wizard creates the Setup.lst file automatically. You can edit the file manually after creation if you need to customize it.

The Setup.lst file describes all the files that must be installed on the user's machine for your application and contains crucial information for the setup process. For example, the Setup.lst file tells the system the name of each file, where to install it, and how it should be registered. There are five sections to the Setup.lst file:

- The BootStrap section — lists the core information about the application, such as the name of the main setup program for the application, the temporary directory to use during the installation process, and the text in the startup window that appears during installation.
- The BootStrap Files section — lists all files required by the main installation file. Normally, this includes just the Visual Basic run-time files.
- The Setup1 Files section — lists all other files required by your application, such as .exe files, data, and text.
- The Setup section — contains information needed by other files in the application.
- The Icon Groups section — contains information about the groups your installation process will create. Each member of this section has a correlating section containing the icons to be created in that group.

For More Information See "Format of the Bootstrap and Setup1 Files Sections," later in this chapter, for information on the syntax for these sections.

The BootStrap Section

The BootStrap section contains all the information the setup.exe file needs to set up and launch the main installation program for your application.

> **Note** Remember that there are two setup programs for your installation: setup.exe, which is a pre-installation program, and setup1.exe, which is compiled from the Setup Toolkit. The BootStrap section provides instructions to the setup.exe file.

The BootStrap section contains the following components:

Component	Description
SetupTitle	The title to show in the dialog box that appears as setup.exe is copying files to your system.
SetupText	The text to show within the dialog box that appears as setup.exe is copying files to your system.
CabFile	The name of the .cab file for your application, or the name of the first .cab file for your application if your package has multiple .cab files.
Spawn	The name of the application to launch when setup.exe finishes processing. In most instances, this will be the setup1.exe file.
TmpDir	The location you wish to use for the temporary files generated during the installation process.
Uninstall	The name of the application to use as an uninstall program. In general, this is st6unst.exe, which is automatically packaged into all packages created with the wizard.

The BootStrap Files Section

The BootStrap Files section lists all the files that must be loaded on the user's machine before your application and dependency files can be loaded. These pre-install, or *bootstrap*, files include the core files required to run any Visual Basic application, such as the Visual Basic run-time DLL (Msvbvm60.dll). The setup program installs these files prior to installing and launching the main installation program.

The following example shows entries in a typical BootStrap Files section:

```
[Bootstrap Files]
File1=@Msvbvm60.dll,$(WinSysPathSysFile),$(DLLSelfRegister),
➥ 1/23/98 9:43:25 AM,1457936,6.0.80.23

File2=@OleAut32.dll,$(WinSysPath),$(DLLSelfRegister),
➥ 1/21/98 11:08:26 PM,571152,2.30.4248.1

File3=@OlePro32.dll,$(WinSysPathSysFile),$(DLLSelfRegister),
➥ 1/21/98 11:08:27 PM,152336,5.0.4248.1
```

The Setup1 Files Section

The Setup1 Files section contains all the other files required by your application, such as your .exe file, data, text, and dependencies. The setup program installs these files after it installs the core files listed in the Bootstrap Files section.

The following example shows entries in a typical Setup1 Files section:

```
[Setup1 Files]
File1=@LotsAControls.exe,$(AppPath),$(EXESelfRegister),,1/26/98 3:43:48 PM,7168,1.0.0.0

File2=@mscomctl.ocx,$(AppPath),$(DLLSelfRegister),,1/23/98 9:43:40 AM,1011472,6.0.80.23
```

The Setup Section

The Setup section of the Setup.lst file is simply a list of information used by other parts of the installation process. The following table lists the information contained in the Setup section.

Component	Description
Title	The name of the application as it will appear in the splash screen during installation, in the program groups on the Start menu, and in the program item name.
DefaultDir	The default installation directory. The user can specify a different directory during the installation process.
ForceUseDefDir	If left blank, the user is prompted for an installation directory. If set to 1, the application is automatically installed to the directory specified by “DefaultDir” in Setup.lst.
AppToUninstal	The name you wish to see as your application in the Add/Remove Programs utility in Control Panel.
AppExe	The name of your application’s executable file, such as Myapp.exe.

The IconGroups Section

The IconGroups section contains information about the Start menu program groups created by the installation process. Each program group to be created is first listed in the IconGroups section, then assigned an individual section (Group0, Group1, Group2, etc.) that contains information about icons and titles for that group. Groups are numbered sequentially starting at zero.

The following example shows entries in a typical IconGroups section and related subsections:

```
[IconGroups]
Group0=MyTestEXE
Group1=Group1

[MyTestExe]
Icon1=my.exe
Title1=MyTestExe

[Group1]
Icon1=ReadMe.txt
Title1=ReadMe
Icon2=my.hlp
Title2=Help
```

Format of the Bootstrap and Setup1 Files Sections

The Bootstrap Files and Setup1 Files sections of the Setup.lst file contain a complete list of the files that the setup programs (setup.exe and setup1.exe) need to install on the user's computer. Each file is listed individually, on its own line, and must use the following format:

File*x*= *file*,*install*,*path*,*register*,*shared*,*date*,*size*[,*version*]

Part	Meaning
File*x*	A keyword that must appear at the beginning of each line. *X* is a sequence number, starting at 1 in each section and moving in ascending order. You cannot skip values.
File	The name of the file as it will appear after installation on the user's computer. This is usually the same as the Install argument. If you want this file to be extracted from a cab, place an @ at the beginning of the name (for example, @my.exe).
Install	The name of the file as it appears on any distribution media.

Part	Meaning
Path	The directory to which the file should be installed. Either an actual directory path, a macro indicating a user-specified path, or a combination of the two. See "Path Argument Macros in Setup.lst Files," later in this chapter, for more information on the available macros.
Register	A key that indicates how the file is to be included in the user's system registry. See "Registry Keys in Setup.lst Files," later in this chapter, for more information.
Shared	Specifies that the file should be installed as shared.
Date	The last date on which the file was modified, as it would appear in Windows Explorer. This information helps you to verify that you have the correct versions of the files on the setup disks.
Size	The file size as it would appear in Windows Explorer. The setup program uses this information to calculate how much disk space your application requires on the user's machine.
Version	An optional internal version number of the file. Note that this is not necessarily the same number as the display version number you see by checking the file's properties.

Path Parameter Macros in Setup.lst Files

The *Path* argument in the Setup.lst file represents the location to which the file should be installed. The value used for this argument is either an actual path or a macro indicating a path specified by the user. The following tables list the macros that can be used in the installation.

Macro	Installs a file in this directory	Valid for this section
$(WinSysPath)	\Windows\System (Windows 95 or later) \Winnt\System32 (Windows NT)	Setup1 Files and Bootstrap Files
$(WinSysPathSysFile)	\Windows\System (Windows 95 or later) \Winnt\System32 (Windows NT) The file is installed as a system file and is not removed when the application is removed.	Setup1 Files only
$(WinPath)	• \Windows (Windows 95 or later) • \Winnt (Windows NT)	Setup1 Files and BootStrap Files
$(AppPath)	The application directory specified by the user, or the *DefaultDir* value specified in the Setup section.	Setup1 Files only
$(AppPath)\Samples	\Samples, beneath the application directory.	Setup1 Files only

Macro	Installs a file in this directory	Valid for this section
path (for example, c:\\)	The directory identified by *path* (not recommended).	Setup1 Files only
$(CommonFiles)	\Program Files\Common Files\ Often combined with a subdirectory, as in $(CommonFiles)\My Company\My Application.	Setup1 Files only
$(CommonFilesSys)	$(CommonFiles)\System	Setup1 Files only
$(ProgramFiles)	\Program Files	Setup1 Files only

Registry Keys in Setup.lst Files

The Register key in the Setup.lst file indicates how the file should be registered on the user's computer. You can indicate that the file does not need to be registered, or indicate one of several registry options for files that do need registration.

The following table lists the possible keys.

Register Key	Meaning
(no key)	The file does not contain linked or embedded objects and does not need to be registered.
$(DLLSelfRegister)	The file is a self-registering .dll, .ocx, or any other .dll file with self-registering information.
$(EXESelfRegister)	The file is an ActiveX .exe component created in Visual Basic, or any other .exe file that supports the /RegServer and /UnRegServer command-line switches.
$(TLBRegister)	The file is a type library file and should be registered accordingly.
$(Remote)	The file is a remote support file (.vbr) and should be registered accordingly.
Filename.reg	The file is a component you distribute that needs to be registered but does not provide self-registration. This key indicates a .reg file that contains information that needs to be updated in the system registry. The .reg file must also be added to your Setup.lst file and installed.

The *filename*.reg key is not the recommended method of getting registration information into the registry. Registry entries added in this manner cannot be automatically uninstalled with the Application Removal program.

Specifying Remote Server Components in the Setup.lst File

If you use remote server components in your applications, you must place an entry in the Setup1 Files section marking a file as a remote server component and specifying connection information. This information is used by the Client Registration utility to register the Remote Automation server.

The following example shows how you specify remote server components:

```
File1=@LotsAControls.vbr,$(WinSysPath),$(Remote),,1/26/98 3:43:48 PM,1024,1.0.0.0
File2=@Server2.vbr,$(WinSysPath),$(Remote),,1/23/98 9:43:40 AM,1024,6.0.80.23
Remote1="Schweizer","ncacn_ip_tcp",1,RA
Remote2=,,1,DCOM
```

The Remote*x* entry consists of the server address, network protocol, and authentication information, separated by commas. You must also specify whether the component is to be used in a Remote Automation or DCOM environment using the *RA* or *DCOM* arguments.

Manually Creating Distribution Media

There are several ways you can distribute your application — on floppy or compact discs, over a network, or on a Web site. As part of the deployment process, you must copy your packaged files onto the distribution media you plan to use.

> **Note** If you package and deploy your files using the Package and Deployment Wizard, these steps are not necessary because the wizard will create your disks, network location, or Internet component download distribution media for you automatically.

You can use any of the following methods when you manually create distribution media:

- If you plan to distribute on floppies, you must copy files onto the disks in a specific order. You must place the setup.exe and Setup.lst files onto the first disk, followed by all the files in the Bootstrap Files section of your project's Setup.lst file, then place other .cab files onto the remaining disks.
- To distribute on a network share, you simply copy your packaged files to the appropriate location, using Windows Explorer, a command prompt, or some other method.
- To distribute on CD, you simply copy your files to the CDs.
- To distribute on the Internet, you copy your Internet package to the appropriate Web site, using the Web Publishing Wizard, available in the *ActiveX SDK*.

For More Information For more information on creating a Web publishing site using the Web Publishing Wizard, see "Internet Tools and Technologies" in the *Internet Client SDK*, online.

Creating Distribution Media

You can create your distribution media after you have determined the files to include in your setup program, created the Setup.lst file, compressed any necessary files, and decided how to lay out files on the media:

- If you are using floppy disks for your distribution, you need to copy the files to one or more disks.
- If you are using another mechanism, such as CDs or a network location, you need to copy your files to the appropriate location or staging area for CD production.
- For Internet or intranet delivery, you need to publish your files to the appropriate Web site, after formatting them for Internet component download.

Creating Distribution Disks

It is a good practice to label your distribution disks with the number and name of the disk and instructions for setting up your application. Repeat this installation message on each of the distribution disks. After your disks are labeled, you are ready to copy your files to the distribution disks.

To create distribution disks

1. Copy the pre-installation files listed below onto the first disk:
   - Setup.exe
   - Setup.lst
2. Copy the remaining bootstrap .cab files onto the rest of the first disk and any subsequent disks that are needed.
3. After all bootstrap .cab files are copied, copy the rest of your .cab files onto the necessary disks.

Manually Deploying to a Web Site

If you want to manually deploy your application or component to a site on the Web, you can use the Web Publishing Wizard to deploy your packaged files to the appropriate location. The Web Publishing Wizard is available on the Microsoft Web site at www.microsoft.com, and is also installed with Internet Explorer 4.*x*.

For More Information See "Internet Tools and Technologies" in the *Internet Client SDK* for more information on the Web Publishing Wizard. See "Manually Creating Distribution Media" earlier in this chapter for information about deciding how to place your files on the disks.

Using the Package and Deployment Wizard with the Setup Toolkit

In addition to using the Setup Toolkit project to create your own custom setup project, you can use the Setup Toolkit project in conjunction with the Package and Deployment Wizard. In this case, you use the Setup Toolkit project to customize the screens or other parts of the installation sequence, then use the wizard to create and deploy the package for the application. The wizard compiles the Setup Toolkit project and creates the setup1.exe program for the application.

For example, you might use the Setup Toolkit and the Package and Deployment Wizard together to add dialog boxes to the installation program, prompting the user to specify whether to install optional features in your application. For example, you may have an online Help file that some users would rather not install. You can add as many installation options as you want.

To add an installation option to your setup program

1. In the Setup1.vbp project, edit the code for the Form_Load event in the setup1.frm form. To add functionality, you add code after the code block calls the ShowBeginForm function (Sub ShowBeginForm).

   The following shows an example of how you would add a dialog box that asks if the user wants to install optional files:

   ```
   Dim LoadHelp As Integer
   LoadHelp = MsgBox ("Do you want to install Help? ", vbYesNo)
   If LoadHelp = vbYes Then
      CalcDiskSpace "Help"
   EndIf
   ' Block of code containing cIcons = CountIcons(strINI FILES)
   If LoadHelp = vbYes Then
      cIcons = CountIcons("Help")
   EndIf
   ' Block of code containing CopySection strINI_FILES.
   If LoadHelp = vbYes Then
      CopySection "Help"
   EndIf
   ' Block of code containing CreateIcons, strINI FILES, strGroupName
   ```

2. Close Setup1.frm, save the form and the Setup Toolkit project, and compile to create the Setup1.exe file.
3. Run the **Package and Deployment Wizard**, and select **Package** from the main screen.
4. Proceed through the wizard, making the appropriate choices. For the example shown above, you would make sure that all optional files the user could choose to install in your custom dialog box were listed in the Add and Remove screen.

5. Once you are done with the Package and Deployment Wizard, generate the distribution media.
6. Make any necessary changes to the Setup.lst file. In the example above, you would add a new section with a section you used in the CopySection section of your code. In this case, your section would look something like this:

   ```
   [Help]
   File1=MyApp.HL1,MyApp.HLP,$(AppPath),,,10/12/96,2946967,0.0.0
   ```

7. Deploy and test your package.

When the user runs the installation program for the example shown in this procedure, the setup program copies all the BootStrap files to the user's machine and then prompts the user to indicate whether to install the Help files. If the user chooses Yes, the CalcDiskSpace statement determines whether there is sufficient disk space on the user's machine for the Help files. The program then installs all of the files listed with the Setup1 Files section in Setup.lst.

Next, the program tests the LoadHelp flag again. If the user chose to install the Help files, Setup1.exe next executes the CopySection statement for the Help files, and installs the files listed in the [Help] section of Setup.lst.

For More Information See "The Package and Deployment Wizard," earlier in this chapter, for more information on features of the wizard.

Testing Your Setup Program

After you have completed the packaging process and produced distribution media for your application, you must test your setup program. Be sure to test your setup program on a machine that does not have Visual Basic or any of the ActiveX controls required by your application. You should also test your setup on all applicable operating systems.

To test your floppy disk-based or CD-based setup program

1. Insert the first disk or the CD in the appropriate drive.
2. In Windows 95 and Windows NT 4.0 or later, from the **Start** menu, choose **Run**, and type:

   ***drive*:\setup**

   – or –

   Double-click **Setup.exe** from the disk drive.
3. When the installation finishes, run the installed program to be sure it behaves as expected.

To test your network drive-based setup program

1. From another computer on the same network as the distribution server, connect to the server and directory containing your distribution files.
2. In the distribution directory, double-click the **Setup.exe** file.
3. When the installation finishes, run the installed program to be sure it behaves as expected.

To test your Web-based setup program

1. Deploy your package to a Web server.
2. Access the Web page from which your application's .cab file can be referenced. Download will begin automatically, and you will receive prompts asking you if you want to proceed.
3. When the installation finishes, run the installed program to be sure it behaves as expected.

Allowing the User to Remove Your Application

When the user installs your application, the setup program copies the application-removal utility St6unst.exe to the \Windows or \Winnt directory. Each time you use the Visual Basic setup program to install an application, an application removal log file (St6unst.log) is generated in the application's installation directory. The .log file contains entries indicating:

- Directories created during installation.
- Files installed and their location. This list contains all of the files in the setup program, even if some files were not installed on the user's machine because a newer version of the same file already existed. The log file indicates whether the file was a shared file and if so, whether it replaced the existing file.
- Registry entries created or modified.
- Links and Start menu entries created with Windows 95 and Windows NT 4.0 or later.
- Self-registered .dll, .ex, or .ocx files.

In Windows 95 and Windows NT 4.0 or later, the setup program adds the application removal utility to the list of registered applications displayed in the Add/Remove Programs section of Control Panel. End users should use Add/Remove Programs to uninstall the application.

> **Caution** It is important to make sure that you have correctly set options for any files that should be shared, either by adding the files to the Shared Files screen in the Package and Deployment Wizard, or by indicating the installation location for the file as a shared file directory. If you accidentally install a file that should be shared without the correct settings, users will be able to remove it when they uninstall your application, which may cause problems for other applications on your system.

In the event of a failed or canceled installation, the application-removal utility automatically removes all of the directories, files, and registration entries that the setup program created in the installation attempt.

With Windows 95 or later and Windows NT, shared files are reference-counted in the registry. For example, a shared file used by three applications will have a reference count of three. When you remove an application that uses a shared file, the reference count for the shared file decreases by one. When the count for the file reaches zero, the user will be prompted for final removal of that item.

Situations in Which the Application Removal Utility Might Fail

For the application-removal utility to properly uninstall your application, the log file and registry entries created by the setup program must be accurate and unchanged from the time of installation.

The Application Removal utility might fail or work incorrectly if any of the following situations exists:

- The end user copied shared files manually. In this case, reference counting is not updated in the registry, so the system cannot correctly judge when to remove the file.
- The end user deletes installed files or an application directory rather than using the application-removal utility. This deletes the log file, so that application removal is impossible. In addition, it makes it impossible to remove system registry entries for program files, DLLs, or .ocx files in the application directory because these files must be run in order to be removed.
- A setup program for an application that is not compliant with Windows 95 installs the same shared files as does your application.
- A shared file is installed into a different directory than the one in which it already exists on the hard drive.
- The end user installs the same Visual Basic application in two different directories. Not only will the first installation no longer work, but the application removal scenarios will clash. The end user should always remove the first installation before installing an application in a different directory.
- The end user deletes the application setup log (St6unst.log). Without the application setup log file, the application-removal utility has no installation information and will fail.

Some of these scenarios could degrade the installed file-registry correspondence, cause the Application Removal utility to prematurely reach a zero-reference count for a particular file, and subsequently ask if this file could be deleted. If a file is prematurely deleted, it could cause other applications to cease functioning or function incorrectly due to missing file dependencies, missing components, and so on.

Distributing Localized ActiveX Controls

In most ways, distributing localized ActiveX controls is no different from distributing the original version. A problem may arise, however, if a new version of the control is released and distributed on the Web with another application.

ActiveX controls shipped with Visual Basic are automatically translated, or localized, into the correct language for the version of Visual Basic you own. For example, in the Japanese version of Visual Basic, controls are available in Japanese and are ready for distribution in that language. When you distribute these controls, the Package and Deployment Wizard must determine the necessary files to package with them.

> **Note** This topic applies only to the ActiveX controls distributed with Visual Basic. It does not apply to user controls created with Visual Basic unless they contain a Visual Basic ActiveX control.

Visual Basic's localized ActiveX controls have two parts:

- The .ocx file for the control, which acts as the code block for the control. The same .ocx file is used for every language version of Visual Basic.
- The satellite DLL file, which contains the localized strings for the control. This acts as the data block for the control. The satellite DLL varies between versions, according to the language version of Visual Basic you have purchased.

The Package and Deployment Wizard automatically includes the correct satellite DLL when you package an application that contains a localized Visual Basic ActiveX control. When the end user downloads the application, the correct satellite DLL is installed on their computer.

If a new version of the control is distributed on the Internet, the .ocx file and the satellite DLL will be out of sync unless the new, localized satellite DLL is also downloaded with the second application. When that happens, the end user may suddenly find that the strings for the new control are either wrong or are in English, because the .ocx defaults to using the English strings (which are always available in the .ocx file) when the compatible satellite DLL is not found. To alleviate this problem, you should instruct end users to download the latest version of the satellite DLL from www.microsoft.com/vstudio/.

For More Information See "Designing International Software" in Chapter 16, "International Issues," for an explanation of code blocks and data blocks.

APPENDIX A

Visual Basic Specifications, Limitations, and File Formats

This appendix describes the system requirements, limitations on a Visual Basic project, the types of files that my be included in your Visual Basic project, and descriptions of the form (.frm) and project (.vbp) files.

Note While many of these limitations are described in terms of a specific number, keep in mind that other conditions (such as available memory and system resources) may impose a restriction before the specified limit is reached.

Contents

System Requirements for Visual Basic Applications

The following hardware and software is required for Visual Basic applications:

- Pentium 90MHz or higher microprocessor.
- VGA 640x480 or higher-resolution screen supported by Microsoft Windows.
- 24MB RAM for Windows 95, 32MB for Windows NT.
- Microsoft Windows NT 3.51 or later, or Microsoft Windows 95 or later.
- Microsoft Internet Explorer version 4.01 or later. (version 4.01 Service Pack 1 or later for DHTML application developers, and 4.x for end users of these applications).

- Disk space requirements:
  - Standard Edition: typical installation 48MB, full installation 80MB.
  - Professional Edition: typical installation 48MB, full installation 80MB.
  - Enterprise Edition: typical installation 128MB, full installation 147MB.
  - Additional components (if required): MSDN (for documentation): 67MB, Internet Explorer 4.x: approximately 66MB.
- CD-ROM (no MS-DOS support assumed).

Project Limitations

A single project can contain up to 32,000 "identifiers" (any nonreserved keyword), which include, but are not limited to, forms, controls, modules, variables, constants, procedures, functions, and objects. Note that the actual number of identifiers is limited to available memory.

Variable names in Visual Basic can be no longer than 255 characters, and the names of forms, controls, modules, and classes cannot be longer than 40 characters. Visual Basic imposes no limit on the actual number of distinct objects in a project.

Control Limitations

Each nongraphical control (all the controls except shape, line, image, and label) uses a window. Each window uses system resources, limiting the total number of windows that can exist at one time. The exact limit depends on the available system resources and the type of controls used.

To reduce consumption of system resources, use the shape, line, label, and image controls instead of picture box controls to create or display graphics.

Total Number of Controls

The maximum number of controls allowed on a single form depends on the type of controls used and available system resources. However, there is a fixed limit of 254 control names per form. A control array counts only once toward this limit because all the controls in the array share a single control name.

The limit on control array indexes is 0 to 32,767 on all versions.

If you layer controls on top of each other, such as using several frame controls within other frames, Visual Basic will generally accept no more than 25 levels of nested controls.

Limitations for Particular Controls

The following table lists property limitations that apply to particular controls in Visual Basic.

Property	Applies to	Limitation
List and ListCount	List box and combo box controls	Maximum number of items is 32K; the limit on the size of each item is 1K (1024 bytes).
Text	Text box control	Limited to 64K.
Caption	Label control	Limited to 1024 bytes.
	Command button, check box, frame, and option button controls	Limited to 255 characters. Any caption over these limits is truncated. Captions on custom control properties are limited to 32K.
	Menu control	Limited to 235 characters.
Tag	All controls	Limited only by available memory.
Name	All controls	Limited to 40 characters.

Note In Visual Basic, control property names are limited to 30 characters.

Code Limitations

The amount of code that can be loaded into a form, class, or standard module is limited to 65,534 lines. A single line of code can consist of up to 1023 bytes. Up to 256 blank spaces can precede the actual text on a single line, and no more than twenty-five line-continuation characters (_) can be included in a single logical line.

Procedures, Types, and Variables

There is no limit on the number of procedures per module. Each procedure can contain up to 64K of code. If a procedure or module exceeds this limit, Visual Basic generates a compile-time error. If you encounter this error, you can avoid it by breaking extremely large procedures into several smaller procedures, or by moving module-level declarations into another module.

Visual Basic uses tables to store the names of identifiers (variables, procedures, constants, and so on) in your code. Each table is limited to 64K.

DLL Declare Table

Each form and code module uses a table that contains a structure describing a DLL entry point. Each structure uses approximately 40 bytes, with a total restricted size of 64K, resulting in roughly 1,500 declarations allowed per module.

Project-Name Table

The entire application uses a single table that contains all names. These include:

- Constant names
- Variable names
- User-defined — type definition names
- Module names
- DLL-procedure declaration names

The project name table is unlimited in total size, but is limited to a total of 32K case-sensitive unique entries. If the limit is reached, reuse private identifiers in different modules to limit the number of unique entries to 32K.

Import Table

Every reference to an identifier in a different module creates an entry in the Import Table. Each such entry is a minimum of 24 bytes and is restricted to 64K, resulting in roughly 2,000 references per module.

Module-Entries Table

This table accepts up to 125 bytes per module, with a total limit of 64K, resulting in about 400 modules per project.

Data Limitations

The following limitations apply to variables in the Visual Basic language.

Form, Standard, and Class Module Data

The data segment (that is, the data defined in the Declarations section) of the VBA module of any form or module in Visual Basic can be up to 64K. This data segment contains the following data:

- Local variables declared with Static.
- Module-level variables other than arrays and variable-length strings.
- 4 bytes for each module-level array and variable-length string.

Procedures, Types, and Variables

If a procedure or module exceeds the 64K code limit, Visual Basic generates a compile-time error.

If you define a procedure that has more than 64K of local variables defined, you get the error "Too many local nonstatic variables."

If you define a module that has more than 64K of module-level variables defined, or if you define a User-Defined Type larger than 64K, you get the error "Fixed or static data can't be larger than 64K."

If you encounter this error, you can avoid it by breaking extremely large procedures into several smaller procedures, or by moving module-level declarations into another module.

An array declared as a variable doesn't contribute to the entire size of the array; only the array descriptor counts toward the 64K limit. So it is acceptable, for example, to have a declaration such as `Dim x(1000000) As Byte` either in a procedure or at module level. Out of memory problems occur, however, if you declare a large, fixed-size array in a record, then declare instances of those records as variables.

User-Defined Types

No variable of a user-defined type can exceed 64K, although the sum of variable-length strings in a user-defined type may exceed 64K (variable-length strings occupy only 4 bytes each in the user-defined type; the actual contents of a string are stored separately). User-defined types can be defined in terms of other user-defined types, but the total size of the types cannot exceed 64K.

Stack Space

Arguments and local variables in procedures take up stack space at run time. Module-level and static variables do not take up stack space because they are allocated in the data segment for forms or modules. Any DLL procedures you call use this stack while they are executing.

Visual Basic itself uses some of the stack for its own purposes, such as storing intermediate values when evaluating expressions.

Total available stack size for Visual Basic is one megabyte (1MB) per thread. A stack may grow beyond this, however, if there is adjacent free memory.

For More Information For tips on conserving stack space, see Chapter 15, "Designing for Performance and Compatibility."

System Resource Limitations

Some limitations on Visual Basic, and the applications you create with it, are imposed by Microsoft Windows. These limitations may change when you install a different version of Microsoft Windows.

Windows Resources

Every open window uses some system resources (data areas used by Microsoft Windows). If you run out of system resources, the run-time error "Windows is running low on available resources" occurs. You can check the percentage of system resources remaining by choosing About from the Help menu in the Program Manager or File Manager in Windows NT 3.51, or, in Windows 95 and Windows NT 4.0, by choosing About in the Windows Explorer Help menu. Applications can also call the Windows API GetFreeSystemResources to reclaim system resources, close windows (such as open forms and Code windows, as well as windows in other applications), and exit running applications.

Project File Formats

Microsoft Visual Basic utilizes and creates a number of files at both design and run time. Which files will be required by your project or application depends upon its scope and functionality.

Project File Extensions

Visual Basic produces a number of files when you create and compile a project. These can be categorized as follows: design-time, miscellaneous development, and run-time.

Design time files are the building blocks of your project: basic modules (.bas) and form modules (.frm), for example.

Miscellaneous files are produced by various processes and functions of the Visual Basic development environment: Package and Deployment Wizard dependency files (.dep), for example.

Design-time and Miscellaneous Files

The following table lists all the design-time and miscellaneous other files that may be produced when you develop an application:

Extension	Description
.bas	Basic module
.cls	Class module
.ctl	User Control file
.ctx	User Control binary file
.dca	Active Designer cache
.ddf	Package and Deployment Wizard CAB information file

Extension	Description
.dep	Package and Deployment Wizard dependency file
.dob	ActiveX document form file
.dox	ActiveX document binary form file
.dsr	Active Designer file
.dsx	Active Designer binary file
.dws	Deployment wizard script file
.frm	Form file
.frx	Binary form file
.log	Log file for load errors
.oca	Control TypeLib cache file
.pag	Property page file
.pgx	Binary property page file
.res	Resource file
.tlb	Remote Automation TypeLib file
.vbg	Visual Basic group project file
.vbl	Control licensing file
.vbp	Visual Basic project file
.vbr	Remote Automation registration file
.vbw	Visual Basic project workspace file
.vbz	Wizard launch file
.wct	WebClass HTML template

Run-Time Files

When you compile your application, all the necessary design-time files are included in the run-time executable files. Run-time files are listed in the following table:

Extension	Description
.dll	In-process ActiveX component
.exe	Executable file or ActiveX component
.ocx	ActiveX control
.vbd	ActiveX document state file
.wct	WebClass HTML template

Form Structures

While many of the files in a typical Visual Basic project are in a binary format and are readable only by specific processes and functions of Visual Basic or your application, the form (.frm) and project (.vbp) files are saved as ASCII text. These are readable in a text viewer (Notepad for instance).

The following sections describe the design- and run-time files in a typical Visual Basic project and the format of the form (.frm) and project (.vbp) files.

Visual Basic form (.frm) files are created and saved in ASCII format. The structure of a form consists of:

- The version number of the file format.
- A block of text containing the form description.
- A set of form attributes.
- The Basic code for the form.

The form description contains the property settings of the form. Blocks of text that define the properties of controls on the form are nested within the form. Controls contained within other controls have their properties nested within the text of the container. Figure A.1 illustrates the structure of the form description.

Figure A.1 Structure of the form description

```
Version 6.00
Begin VB.Form formname

   Form Properties
   Begin VB.controltype controlname

      Control Properties
      Begin VB.controltype controlname

           Control Properties

      End

      Begin VB.controltype controlname

           Control Properties

      End

   End

End
Attributes

Basic code for this form begins here.
```

Printing Form Descriptions

If you want to print a form description, you can do so without having to save the form.

To print a form description

1. From the **File** menu, choose **Print**.
2. Select the **Form As Text** check box, and choose **OK** to print the form description.

Version Number

The version number for forms created with Visual Basic is 6.00. If the version number is omitted from the form, an error is generated. When you load a Visual Basic application that has a version number less than 6.00, a warning dialog box appears informing you that the file will be saved in the new format.

Form Description

The form description starts with a Begin statement and ends with an End statement. The syntax of the Begin statement is:

Begin VB.{**Form**|**MDIForm**} *formname*

The End statement determines where the form description ends and the set of form attributes begins. Without the End statement, Visual Basic tries to read the attributes as if it were describing controls and properties of the form, thus producing errors.

Between the Begin Form and End statements are the properties of the form itself, followed by descriptions of each control on the form. Figure A.2 shows the nested structure of the form description in greater detail.

Figure A.2 Nested structure of the form description

```
Version 6.00
Begin VB.Form MyForm1
    BackColor = &H00FF0000&
    Caption = "Form1"
    Height = 6684
    Left = 828
    .
    .
    .
    Begin VB.Frame Frame1
       Caption = "Frame1"
       Height = 1692
       .
       .
       .
       Begin VB.CommandButton MyButton
          Caption = "Start"
          Height = 372
          .
          .
          .
       End
    End
End

Control blocks
```

Control Blocks

A *control block* consists of the text in the form description that defines the properties of an individual control. Like the form description itself, control blocks start with a Begin statement and end with an End statement. The syntax for a Begin statement of a control block is as follows:

Begin *controlclass.controltype controlname*

The properties for the control appear between the Begin statement and the End statement.

Control-Block Order

The order of the control blocks determines the z-order of the controls. *Z-order* is a relative ordering that determines how controls overlap each other on a form. The first control in the form description establishes the bottom of the z-order. Controls that appear later in the form description are higher in the z-order and therefore overlap controls that are lower in the z-order.

Embedded Control Blocks

Some controls can contain other controls. When a control is contained within another control, its control block is embedded in the control block of the container. You can embed control blocks inside:

- Frames
- Picture boxes
- Menus
- Custom controls, depending on their purpose

Embedded controls are commonly used to place option buttons inside a frame. Visual Basic must have all the information necessary for a container before adding any contained controls, so properties for a control must come before any embedded control blocks. Visual Basic ignores any properties within a control block that appear after embedded control blocks.

Menu Controls

Menu controls must appear together at the end of the form description, just before the Attributes section begins. When Visual Basic encounters a menu control during the loading of an ASCII form, it expects to find all the menu controls together. Once it detects a nonmenu control following one or more menu controls, Visual Basic assumes there are no more menu controls on the form and ignores any other menu controls it encounters during the loading of that form.

Shortcut Keys

Shortcut keys are keys you use to activate a menu control. The ASCII form uses the same syntax as the SendKeys statement to define key combinations: "+" = SHIFT, "^" = CTRL, and "{F*n*}" = function key where *n* is the key number. Alphabetic characters represent themselves. Shortcut key syntax is:

```
Shortcut = ^{F4}      ' <CTRL><F4>
```

Note Top-level menus cannot have a shortcut key.

For More Information See "SendKeys Statement," online.

Comments in the Form Description

You can add comments to the form description. The single quotation mark (') is the comment delimiter.

> **Caution** Comments and formatting in the form description are not retained when you save the form in Visual Basic. However, comments and indents in the code section of the form file are preserved.

Form Description Properties

When Visual Basic saves a form, it arranges the properties in a default ordering. However, you can list properties in any order when creating a form.

Any property you don't list is set to its default value when loaded. When Visual Basic saves a form, it includes only those properties that do not use default values as their settings. Each control determines whether or not all of its properties are saved, or only those whose values are different from the default settings.

Syntax

Use this syntax to define properties in the form description:

property = *value*

Text property values must appear within double quotation marks. Boolean properties have a value of –1 for True and 0 for False. Visual Basic interprets any value other than –1 or 0 as True. Properties with listed values include their numeric value with the description of the value included as a comment. For example, the BorderStyle property appears like this:

```
BorderStyle = 0       ' None
```

Binary Property Values

Some controls have properties that have binary data as their values, such as the Picture property of picture box and image controls or certain properties of custom controls. Visual Basic saves all binary data for a form in a binary data file separate from the form.

Visual Basic saves the binary data file in the same directory as the form. The binary data file has the same file name as the form, but it has an .frx filename extension. Visual Basic reads the binary data file when loading the form. The binary data file (.frx) must be available to the form when Visual Basic loads it. If you share forms with others that use a binary data file, be sure to provide the binary data file (.frx) as well as the form (.frm).

Properties having binary data as their values appear in the form as a reference to a byte offset in the binary data file. For example, the value of a Picture property appears like this in a form description:

```
Begin VB.Image imgDemo
   Picture = "Myform.frx":02EB
End
```

The property listing means that the binary data that defines the Picture property of this control begins at byte 2EB (hex) in the file Myform.frx.

Icon Property

The value of the Icon property in a form depends on which icon is used for the form. The following table lists Icon property values and how those properties appear in a form.

Icon property setting	ASCII form contents
The default icon	No reference to the Icon property
(None)	`Icon = 0`
Any icon other than the default icon	Byte offset reference to the binary data file. For example: `Icon = "Myform.frx":0000`

TabIndex Property

If the TabIndex property is not specified, Visual Basic assigns the control the earliest possible location in the tab order once all other controls load.

Units of Measurement

Control sizes, *x* and *y* coordinates, and other property values using units of measurement are expressed in twips. When a control uses a scale mode other than twips, Visual Basic converts the twip values in the ASCII form to the units of measurement specified by the control's ScaleMode property when loading the form.

Color Values

Color values appear as RGB values. For example, the ForeColor property appears like this:

```
ForeColor = &H00FF0000&
```

Visual Basic can also read QBColor values, converting them to RGB when loading the form. ASCII forms using QBColor values must use this syntax:

ForeColor = QBColor(*qbcolor***)**

where *qbcolor* is a value from 0 to 15.

Note that the *qbcolor* argument corresponds to the color values used by graphics statements in other versions of Basic, such as Visual Basic for MS-DOS, Microsoft QuickBasic, and the Microsoft Basic Professional Development System.

Property Objects

Some property objects, such as the Font object, appear as a separate block, showing all of the settings for the various properties of the object. These blocks are enclosed in BeginProperty and EndProperty statements of the following form:

BeginProperty *propertyname*

property1 = value1
property2 = value2

EndProperty

Basic Code

The Basic code appears in the form immediately after the Attributes section following the last End statement in the form description. Statements in the Declarations section of a form appear first, followed by event procedures, general procedures, and functions.

Sample ASCII Form

Figure A.3 shows the Blanker.frm form from the Blanker sample application.

Figure A.3 Sample form from Blanker.vbp sample application

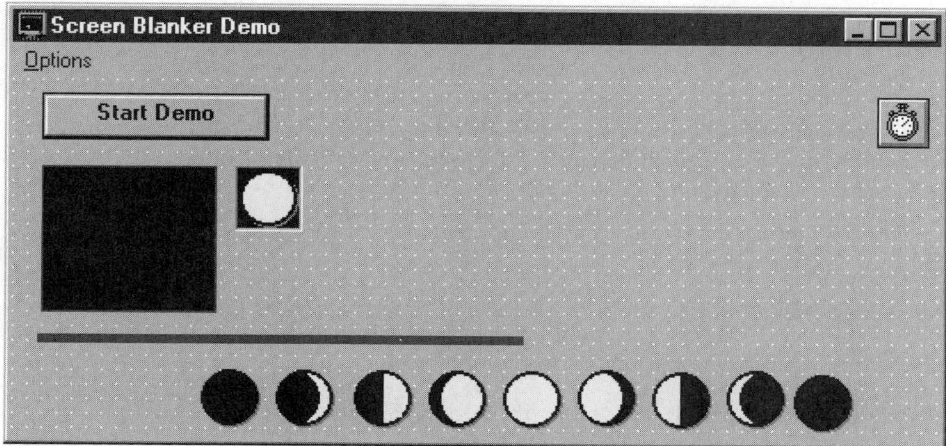

Here is part of the Blanker form saved in Visual Basic. Portions of the form removed to save space are indicated by a vertical ellipsis.

```
VERSION 6.00
Begin VB.Form DemoForm
   BackColor = &H00000000&
   Caption = "Screen Blanker Demo"
   ClientHeight = 960
   ClientLeft = 1965
   ClientTop = 1965
   ClientWidth = 7470
   ForeColor = &H00000000&
   Begin Property Font
      name = "MS Sans Serif"
      charset = 0
      .
      .
      .
   End Property
   Height = 5115
   Icon = "Blanker.frx":0018
   Left = 900
   LinkMode = 1                    ' Source
   LinkTopic = "Form1"
   ScaleHeight = 4425
   ScaleWidth = 7470
   Top = 1335
   Width = 7590
   Begin VB.Timer Timer1
      Interval = 1
      Left = 6960
      Top = 120
   End
   Begin VB.CommandButton cmdStartStop
      BackColor = &H00000000&
      Caption = "Start Demo"
      Default = -1
      Height = 390
      Left = 240
      TabIndex = 0
      Top = 120
      Width = 1830
   End
```

```
      Begin VB.PictureBox picBall
         AutoSize = -1             ' True
         BackColor = &H00000000&
         BorderStyle = 0           ' None
         ForeColor = &H00FFFFFF&
         Height = 465
         Left = 1800
         Picture = "Blanker.frx":0788
         ScaleHeight = 465
         ScaleWidth = 465
         TabIndex = 1
         Top = 720
         Visible = 0               ' False
         Width = 465
      End
      .
      .
      .
      Begin VB.Menu mnuOption
         Caption = "&Options"
         Begin VB.Menu mnuLineCtlDemo
            Caption = "&Jumpy Line"
            Checked = -1           ' True
         End
         Begin VB.Menu mnuCtlMoveDemo
            Caption = "Re&bound"
         End
         .
         .
         .
         Begin VB.Menu mnuExit
            Caption = "E&xit"
         End
      End
   End
   .
   .
   .
   Attribute VB_Name = "DemoForm"
   Attribute VB_Creatable = False
   Attribute VB_Exposed = False
   Dim Shared FrameNum
   Dim Shared XPos
   Dim Shared YPos
   Dim Shared DoFlag
   Dim Shared Motion
   .
   .
   .
```

```
Sub CircleDemo ()
   Dim Radius
   R = 255 * Rnd
   G = 255 * Rnd
   B = 255 * Rnd

   XPos = ScaleWidth / 2
   YPos = ScaleHeight / 2
   Radius = ((YPos * 0.9) + 1) * Rnd
   Circle (XPos, YPos), Radius, RGB (R, G, B)
End Sub
.
.
.
Private Sub Timer1_Timer ()
.
.
.
End Sub
```

Form File Loading Errors

When Visual Basic loads a form into memory, it first converts the form to binary format. When you make changes to the form and save the changes, Visual Basic rewrites the file in ASCII format.

When Visual Basic encounters an error while loading a form, it creates a log file and reports that error in the log file. Visual Basic adds error messages to the log file each time it encounters an error in the form. When the form load is finished, Visual Basic displays a message that tells you an error log file was created.

The log file has the same filename as the form file but with a .log filename extension. For example, if errors occurred when loading Myform.frm, Visual Basic would create a log file named Myform.log. If you reload Myform.frm later and errors continue to occur when loading the form, Visual Basic replaces the previous Myform.log file.

Form Load Error Log Messages

The following error messages can appear in an error log file. Note that these error messages deal only with problems that can occur when Visual Basic loads the form description. They do not indicate any problems that can exist in event procedures, general procedures, or any other part of the Basic code.

Cannot load Menu menuname.

This message appears if Visual Basic finds a menu control whose parent menu is defined as a menu separator. Menu controls that act as parents for menu controls in a submenu cannot be menu separators. Visual Basic does not load the menu control.

This message also appears if Visual Basic finds a menu control whose parent menu has its Checked property set to True. Menu controls that act as parents for menu controls in a submenu cannot be checked. Visual Basic does not load the menu control.

Cannot set Checked property in Menu menuname.

This message appears if Visual Basic finds a top-level menu control with its Checked property set to True. Top-level menus cannot have a checkmark. Visual Basic loads the menu control, but doesn't set its Checked property.

Cannot set Shortcut property in menuname.

This message appears if Visual Basic finds a top-level menu control with a shortcut key defined. Top-level menus cannot have a shortcut key. Visual Basic loads the menu control, but doesn't set the Shortcut property.

Class classname in control controlname is not a loaded control class.

This message appears if Visual Basic finds a class name it doesn't recognize.

Control controlname could not be loaded.

This message appears if Visual Basic encounters an unknown type of control in the form description. Visual Basic creates a picture box to represent the unknown control, giving that picture box any valid properties from the unknown control description. When this message appears, a number of invalid property errors are likely to follow.

Control controlname has a quoted string where the property name should be.

This message appears if Visual Basic finds text inside quotation marks instead of a property name, which you do not place inside quotation marks. For example:

```
"Caption" = "Start Demo"
```

In this case, the property name Caption should not have been enclosed in quotation marks. Visual Basic ignores the line in the form description that produced this error.

The control name controlname is invalid.

This message appears if the name of a control is not a valid string in Visual Basic. Visual Basic will not load the control.

Control name too long; truncated to controlname.

This message appears if Visual Basic finds a control name longer than 40 characters. Visual Basic loads the control, truncating the name.

Did not find an index property and control controlname already exists. Cannot create this control.

This message appears if Visual Basic finds a control without an index that has the same name as a previously loaded control. Visual Basic doesn't load the control.

Form formname could not be loaded.

This message appears if Visual Basic encounters the end of file unexpectedly or if the first Begin statement is missing.

The Form or MDIForm name formname is not valid; cannot load this form.

This message appears if the name of a form is not a valid string in Visual Basic. Visual Basic will not load the form.

Valid strings must start with a letter; can include only letters, numbers and underscores; and must have 40 or fewer characters.

The property name propertyname in control controlname is invalid.

This message appears if the name of a property is not a valid string in Visual Basic or is longer than 30 characters. Visual Basic will not set the property.

Property propertyname in control controlname could not be loaded.

This message appears if Visual Basic encounters an unknown property. Visual Basic skips this property when loading the form.

Property propertyname in control controlname could not be set.

This message appears if Visual Basic cannot set the property of the specified control as indicated by the form description.

Property propertyname in control controlname had an invalid value.

This message appears if Visual Basic encounters an invalid value for a property. Visual Basic changes the property value to the default value for that property.

Property propertyname in control controlname has an invalid file reference.

This message appears if Visual Basic couldn't use a file name reference. This will happen if the referenced file (probably a binary data file for the form) is not found at the specified directory.

Property propertyname in control controlname has an invalid property index.

This message appears if Visual Basic finds a property name with a property index greater than 255. For example:

```
Prop300 = 5436
```

Visual Basic ignores the line in the form description that produced this error.

Property propertyname in control controlname has an invalid value.

This message appears if Visual Basic finds a property with a value that is not correct for that control. For example:

```
Top = Cahr(22)    ' Really wanted Char(22).
```

Visual Basic sets the property with its default value.

Property propertyname in control controlname must be a quoted string.

This message appears if Visual Basic finds a property value without quotation marks that should appear inside quotation marks. For example:

```
Caption = Start Demo
```

Visual Basic ignores the line in the form description that produced this error.

Syntax error: property propertyname in control controlname is missing an '='.

This message appears if Visual Basic finds a property name and value without an equal sign between them. For example:

```
Text     "Start Demo"
```

Visual Basic doesn't load the property.

For More Information Additional information on errors encountered during form load is available by clicking the Help button in the error dialog box or by pressing F1.

Project File (.vbp) Format

Visual Basic always saves project files (.vbp) in ASCII format. The project file contains entries that reflect settings for your project. These include the forms and modules in your project, references, miscellaneous options that you have chosen to control compilation, etc.

Here is what a .vbp file might look like. This project includes modules saved with the class and file and names shown in the table below.

Module type	Class name	File name
MDI form	Aform	A_Form.frm
Form	Bform	B_Form.frm
Standard module	Cmodule	C_Module.bas
Class module	Dclass	D_Class.cls

```
Type=Exe
Form=B_Form.frm
Reference=*\G{00020430-0000-0000-C000-
000000000046}#2.0#0#..\..\..\WINDOWS\SYSTEM\STDOLE2.TLB#OLE Automation
Form=A_Form.frm
Module=CModule; C_Module.bas
Class=DClass; D_Class.cls
Startup="BForm"
Command32=""
Name="Project1"
HelpContextID="0"
CompatibleMode="0"
MajorVer=1
```

```
MinorVer=0
RevisionVer=0
AutoIncrementVer=0
ServerSupportFiles=0
VersionCompanyName="Microsoft"
CompilationType=0
OptimizationType=0
FavorPentiumPro(tm)=0
CodeViewDebugInfo=0
NoAliasing=0
BoundsCheck=0
OverflowCheck=0
FlPointCheck=0
FDIVCheck=0
UnroundedFP=0
StartMode=0
Unattended=0
ThreadPerObject=0
MaxNumberOfThreads=1
```

Entries are added to the .vbp when you add forms, modules, components, etc. to your project. Entries are also added when you set options for your project. Many of these options are set using the Project Properties dialog box.

For More Information Press F1 to get explanations of the options that can be chosen in the Project Properties dialog box.

APPENDIX B

Visual Basic Coding Conventions

This appendix presents a set of suggested coding conventions for Visual Basic programs.

Coding conventions are programming guidelines that focus not on the logic of the program but on its physical structure and appearance. They make the code easier to read, understand, and maintain. Coding conventions can include:

- Naming conventions for objects, variables, and procedures.
- Standardized formats for labeling and commenting code.
- Guidelines for spacing, formatting, and indenting.

In the sections that follow, each of these areas are discussed, along with examples of good usage.

Contents

Why Coding Conventions?

The main reason for using a consistent set of coding conventions is to standardize the structure and coding style of an application so that you and others can easily read and understand the code.

Good coding conventions result in precise, readable, and unambiguous source code that is consistent with other language conventions and as intuitive as possible.

Minimal Coding Conventions

A general-purpose set of coding conventions should define the minimal requirements necessary to accomplish the purposes discussed above, leaving the programmer free to create the program's logic and functional flow.

The object is to make the program easy to read and understand without cramping the programmer's natural creativity with excessive constraints and arbitrary restrictions.

To this end, the conventions suggested in this appendix are brief and suggestive. They do not list every possible object or control, nor do they specify every type of informational comment that could be valuable. Depending on your project and your organization's specific needs, you may wish to extend these guidelines to include additional elements, such as:

- Conventions for specific objects and components developed in-house or purchased from third-party vendors.
- Variables that describe your organization's business activities or facilities.
- Any other elements that your project or enterprise considers important for clarity and readability.

For more information For information about restrictions on naming procedures, variables, and constants, see "Code Basics" in Chapter 5, "Programming Fundamentals."

Object Naming Conventions

Objects should be named with a consistent prefix that makes it easy to identify the type of object. Recommended conventions for some of the objects supported by Visual Basic are listed below.

Suggested Prefixes for Controls

Control type	Prefix	Example
3D Panel	pnl	pnlGroup
ADO Data	ado	adoBiblio
Animated button	ani	aniMailBox
Check box	chk	chkReadOnly
Combo box, drop-down list box	cbo	cboEnglish
Command button	cmd	cmdExit
Common dialog	dlg	dlgFileOpen
Communications	com	comFax
Control (used within procedures when the specific type is unknown)	ctr	ctrCurrent
Data	dat	datBiblio
Data-bound combo box	dbcbo	dbcboLanguage

Control type	Prefix	Example
Data-bound grid	dbgrd	dbgrdQueryResult
Data-bound list box	dblst	dblstJobType
Data combo	dbc	dbcAuthor
Data grid	dgd	dgdTitles
Data list	dbl	dblPublisher
Data repeater	drp	drpLocation
Date picker	dtp	dtpPublished
Directory list box	dir	dirSource
Drive list box	drv	drvTarget
File list box	fil	filSource
Flat scroll bar	fsb	fsbMove
Form	frm	frmEntry
Frame	fra	fraLanguage
Gauge	gau	gauStatus
Graph	gra	graRevenue
Grid	grd	grdPrices
Hierarchical flexgrid	flex	flexOrders
Horizontal scroll bar	hsb	hsbVolume
Image	img	imgIcon
Image combo	imgcbo	imgcboProduct
ImageList	ils	ilsAllIcons
Label	lbl	lblHelpMessage
Lightweight check box	lwchk	lwchkArchive
Lightweight combo box	lwcbo	lwcboGerman
Lightweight command button	lwcmd	lwcmdRemove
Lightweight frame	lwfra	lwfraSaveOptions
Lightweight horizontal scroll bar	lwhsb	lwhsbVolume
Lightweight list box	lwlst	lwlstCostCenters
Lightweight option button	lwopt	lwoptIncomeLevel

Control type	Prefix	Example
Lightweight text box	lwtxt	lwoptStreet
Lightweight vertical scroll bar	lwvsb	lwvsbYear
Line	lin	linVertical
List box	lst	lstPolicyCodes
ListView	lvw	lvwHeadings
MAPI message	mpm	mpmSentMessage
MAPI session	mps	mpsSession
MCI	mci	mciVideo
Menu	mnu	mnuFileOpen
Month view	mvw	mvwPeriod
MS Chart	ch	chSalesbyRegion
MS Flex grid	msg	msgClients
MS Tab	mst	mstFirst
OLE container	ole	oleWorksheet
Option button	opt	optGender
Picture box	pic	picVGA
Picture clip	clp	clpToolbar
ProgressBar	prg	prgLoadFile
Remote Data	rd	rdTitles
RichTextBox	rtf	rtfReport
Shape	shp	shpCircle
Slider	sld	sldScale
Spin	spn	spnPages
StatusBar	sta	staDateTime
SysInfo	sys	sysMonitor
TabStrip	tab	tabOptions
Text box	txt	txtLastName
Timer	tmr	tmrAlarm
Toolbar	tlb	tlbActions

Control type	Prefix	Example
TreeView	tre	treOrganization
UpDown	upd	updDirection
Vertical scroll bar	vsb	vsbRate

Suggested Prefixes for Data Access Objects (DAO)

Use the following prefixes to indicate Data Access Objects.

Database object	Prefix	Example
Container	con	conReports
Database	db	dbAccounts
DBEngine	dbe	dbeJet
Document	doc	docSalesReport
Field	fld	fldAddress
Group	grp	grpFinance
Index	ix	idxAge
Parameter	prm	prmJobCode
QueryDef	qry	qrySalesByRegion
Recordset	rec	recForecast
Relation	rel	relEmployeeDept
TableDef	tbd	tbdCustomers
User	usr	usrNew
Workspace	wsp	wspMine

Some examples:

```
Dim dbBiblio As Database
Dim recPubsInNY As Recordset, strSQLStmt As String
Const DB_READONLY = 4        ' Set constant.
'Open database.
Set dbBiblio = OpenDatabase("BIBLIO.MDB")
' Set text for the SQL statement.
strSQLStmt = "SELECT * FROM Publishers WHERE _
   State = 'NY'"
' Create the new Recordset object.
Set recPubsInNY = db.OpenRecordset(strSQLStmt, _
   dbReadOnly)
```

Suggested Prefixes for Menus

Applications frequently use many menu controls, making it useful to have a unique set of naming conventions for these controls. Menu control prefixes should be extended beyond the initial "mnu" label by adding an additional prefix for each level of nesting, with the final menu caption at the end of the name string. The following table lists some examples.

Menu caption sequence	Menu handler name
File Open	mnuFileOpen
File Send Email	mnuFileSendEmail
File Send Fax	mnuFileSendFax
Format Character	mnuFormatCharacter
Help Contents	mnuHelpContents

When this naming convention is used, all members of a particular menu group are listed next to each other in Visual Basic's Properties window. In addition, the menu control names clearly document the menu items to which they are attached.

Choosing Prefixes for Other Controls

For controls not listed above, you should try to standardize on a unique two or three character prefix for consistency. Use more than three characters only if needed for clarity.

For derived or modified controls, for example, extend the prefixes above so that there is no confusion over which control is really being used. For third-party controls, a lower-case abbreviation for the manufacturer could be added to the prefix. For example, a control instance created from the Visual Basic Professional 3D frame could uses a prefix of fra3d to avoid confusion over which control is really being used.

Constant and Variable Naming Conventions

In addition to objects, constants and variables also require well-formed naming conventions. This section lists recommended conventions for constants and variables supported by Visual Basic. It also discusses the issues of identifying data type and scope.

Variables should always be defined with the smallest scope possible. Global (Public) variables can create enormously complex state machines and make the logic of an application extremely difficult to understand. Global variables also make the reuse and maintenance of your code much more difficult.

Variables in Visual Basic can have the following scope:

Scope	Declaration	Visible in
Procedure-level	'Private' in procedure, sub, or function	The procedure in which it is declared
Module-level	'Private' in the declarations section of a form or code module (.frm, .bas)	Every procedure in the form or code module
Global	'Public' in the declarations section of a code module (.bas)	Everywhere in the application

In a Visual Basic application, global variables should be used only when there is no other convenient way to share data between forms. When global variables must be used, it is good practice to declare them all in a single module, grouped by function. Give the module a meaningful name that indicates its purpose, such as Public.bas.

It is good coding practice to write modular code whenever possible. For example, if your application displays a dialog box, put all the controls and code required to perform the dialog's task in a single form. This helps to keep the application's code organized into useful components and minimizes its run-time overhead.

With the exception of global variables (which should not be passed), procedures and functions should operate only on objects passed to them. Global variables that are used in procedures should be identified in the declaration section at the beginning of the procedure. In addition, you should pass arguments to subs and functions using ByVal, unless you explicitly need to change the value of the passed argument.

Variable Scope Prefixes

As project size grows, so does the value of recognizing variable scope quickly. A one-letter scope prefix preceding the type prefix provides this, without greatly increasing the size of variable names.

Scope	Prefix	Example
Global	g	gstrUserName
Module-level	m	mblnCalcInProgress
Local to procedure	None	dblVelocity

A variable has global scope if it is declared Public in a standard module or a form module. A variable has *module-level* scope if declared Private in a standard module or form module, respectively.

> **Note** Consistency is crucial to productive use of this technique; the syntax checker in Visual Basic will not catch module-level variables that begin with "p."

Constants

The body of constant names should be mixed case with capitals initiating each word. Although standard Visual Basic constants do not include data type and scope information, prefixes like i, s, g, and m can be very useful in understanding the value and scope of a constant. For constant names, follow the same rules as variables. For example:

```
mintUserListMax    'Max entry limit for User list
                   '(integer value,local to module)
gstrNewLine        'New Line character
                   '(string, global to application)
```

Variables

Declaring all variables saves programming time by reducing the number of bugs caused by typos (for example, aUserNameTmp vs. sUserNameTmp vs. sUserNameTemp). On the Editor tab of the Options dialog, check the Require Variable Declaration option. The Option Explicit statement requires that you declare all the variables in your Visual Basic program.

Variables should be prefixed to indicate their data type. Optionally, especially for large programs, the prefix can be extended to indicate the scope of the variable.

Variable Data Types

Use the following prefixes to indicate a variable's data type.

Data type	Prefix	Example
Boolean	bln	blnFound
Byte	byt	bytRasterData
Collection object	col	colWidgets
Currency	cur	curRevenue
Date (Time)	dtm	dtmStart
Double	dbl	dblTolerance
Error	err	errOrderNum
Integer	int	intQuantity
Long	lng	lngDistance
Object	obj	objCurrent
Single	sng	sngAverage

Data type	Prefix	Example
String	str	strFName
User-defined type	udt	udtEmployee
Variant	vnt	vntCheckSum

Descriptive Variable and Procedure Names

The body of a variable or procedure name should use mixed case and should be as long as necessary to describe its purpose. In addition, function names should begin with a verb, such as InitNameArray or CloseDialog.

For frequently used or long terms, standard abbreviations are recommended to help keep name lengths reasonable. In general, variable names greater than 32 characters can be difficult to read on VGA displays.

When using abbreviations, make sure they are consistent throughout the entire application. Randomly switching between Cnt and Count within a project will lead to unnecessary confusion.

User-Defined Types

In a large project with many user-defined types, it is often useful to give each such type a three-character prefix of its own. If these prefixes begin with "u," they will still be easy to recognize quickly when you are working with a user-defined type. For example, "ucli" could be used as the prefix for variables of a user-defined Client type.

Structured Coding Conventions

In addition to naming conventions, structured coding conventions, such as code commenting and consistent indenting, can greatly improve code readability.

Code Commenting Conventions

All procedures and functions should begin with a brief comment describing the functional characteristics of the procedure (what it does). This description should not describe the implementation details (how it does it) because these often change over time, resulting in unnecessary comment maintenance work, or worse yet, erroneous comments. The code itself and any necessary inline comments will describe the implementation.

Arguments passed to a procedure should be described when their functions are not obvious and when the procedure expects the arguments to be in a specific range. Function return values and global variables that are changed by the procedure, especially through reference arguments, must also be described at the beginning of each procedure.

Procedure header comment blocks should include the following section headings. For examples, see the next section, "Formatting Your Code."

Section heading	Comment description
Purpose	What the procedure does (not how).
Assumptions	List of each external variable, control, open file, or other element that is not obvious.
Effects	List of each affected external variable, control, or file and the effect it has (only if this is not obvious).
Inputs	Each argument that may not be obvious. Arguments are on a separate line with inline comments.
Returns	Explanation of the values returned by functions.

Remember the following points:

- Every important variable declaration should include an inline comment describing the use of the variable being declared.
- Variables, controls, and procedures should be named clearly enough that inline commenting is only needed for complex implementation details.
- At the start of the .bas module that contains the project's Visual Basic generic constant declarations, you should include an overview that describes the application, enumerating primary data objects, procedures, algorithms, dialogs, databases, and system dependencies. Sometimes a piece of pseudocode describing the algorithm can be helpful.

Formatting Your Code

Because many programmers still use VGA displays, screen space should be conserved as much as possible while still allowing code formatting to reflect logic structure and nesting. Here are a few pointers:

- Standard, tab-based, nested blocks should be indented four spaces (the default).
- The functional overview comment of a procedure should be indented one space. The highest level statements that follow the overview comment should be indented one tab, with each nested block indented an additional tab. For example:

```
'*****************************************************
' Purpose:  Locates the first occurrence of a
'           specified user in the UserList array.
' Inputs:
'  strUserList(): the list of users to be searched.
'  strTargetUser: the name of the user to search for.
' Returns:  The index of the first occurrence of the
'           rsTargetUser in the rasUserList array.
'           If target user is not found, return -1.
'*****************************************************

Function intFindUser (strUserList() As String, strTargetUser As _
   String)As Integer
   Dim i As Integer          ' Loop counter.
   Dim blnFound As Integer   ' Target found flag.
   intFindUser = -1
   i = 0
   While i <= Ubound(strUserList) and Not blnFound
      If strUserList(i) = strTargetUser Then
         blnFound = True
         intFindUser = i
      End If
   Wend
End Function
```

Grouping Constants

Variables and defined constants should be grouped by function rather than split into isolated areas or special files. Visual Basic generic constants should be grouped in a single module to separate them from application-specific declarations.

& and + Operators

Always use the **&** operator when linking strings and the **+** operator when working with numerical values. Using the **+** operator to concatenate may cause problems when operating on two variants. For example:

```
vntVar1 = "10.01"
vntVar2 = 11
vntResult = vntVar1 + vntVar2  'vntResult = 21.01
vntResult = vntVar1 & vntVar2  'vntResult = 10.0111
```

Creating Strings for MsgBox, InputBox, and SQL Queries

When creating a long string, use the underscore line-continuation character to create multiple lines of code so that you can read or debug the string easily. This technique is particularly useful when displaying a message box (MsgBox) or input box (InputBox) or when creating an SQL string. For example:

```
Dim Msg As String
Msg = "This is a paragraph that will be " _
& "in a message box. The text is" _
& " broken into several lines of code" _
& " in the source code, making it easier" _
& " for the programmer to read and debug."
MsgBox Msg

Dim QRY As String
QRY = "SELECT *" _
& " FROM Titles" _
& " WHERE [Year Published] > 1988"
TitlesQry.SQL = QRY
```

APPENDIX C

Native Code Compiler Switches

Microsoft Visual Basic allows you to compile your applications to fast, efficient native code, using the same optimizing back-end compiler technology as Microsoft Visual C++. Native code compilation provides several options for optimizing and debugging that aren't available with p-code. These options are traditionally called "switches," because each option can be turned on or off.

This appendix documents the native code compiler options, which appear on the Compile tab of the Project Properties dialog box, available on the Project menu. For more information about native code, see "Compiling Your Project to Native Code" in Chapter 8, "More About Programming."

Contents

- Optimize for Fast Code
- Optimize for Small Code
- No Optimizations
- Favor Pentium Pro
- Create Symbolic Debug Info
- Assume No Aliasing
- Remove Array Bounds Checks
- Remove Integer Overflow Checks
- Remove Floating-Point Error Checks
- Remove Safe Pentium FDIV Checks
- Allow Unrounded Floating-Point Operations

Optimize for Fast Code

Maximizes the speed of compiled executable files by instructing the compiler to favor speed over size.

When the compiler translates Visual Basic statements into machine code, there are often many different sequences of machine code that can correctly represent a given statement or construct. Sometimes these differences offer trade-offs of size versus speed. Selecting this option ensures that when the compiler recognizes such alternatives it will always generate the fastest code sequence possible, even when that may increase the size of the compiled program.

Optimize for Small Code

Minimizes the size of compiled executable files by instructing the compiler to favor size over speed.

When the compiler translates Visual Basic statements into machine code, there are often many different sequences of machine code that can correctly represent a given statement or construct. Sometimes these differences offer trade-offs of size versus speed. Selecting this option ensures that when the compiler recognizes such alternatives it will always generate the smallest code sequence possible, even when that may decrease the execution speed of the compiled program.

No Optimizations

Turns off all optimizations.

With this option selected, the compiler generates code that is significantly slower and larger than if optimization for fast or small code is selected.

Favor Pentium Pro

Optimizes code generation to favor the Pentium Pro (P6) processor. Code generated with this option will still run on earlier processors, but less efficiently.

The Pentium Pro microprocessor architecture allows certain code generation strategies that can substantially improve efficiency. However, code created using these strategies does not perform as well on 80386- and 80486-based or Pentium computers. Therefore, you should only use this option if all or most of the machines your program will run on use the Pentium Pro.

Create Symbolic Debug Info

Generates symbolic debug information in the compiled executable file.

Programs compiled to native code using this option can be debugged using Visual C++ (5.0 or later) or another compatible debugger. Setting this option will generate a .pdb file with the required symbol information for use with compatible symbolic debuggers.

Assume No Aliasing

Tells the compiler that your program does not use aliasing.

An alias is a name that refers to a memory location that is already referred to by a different name. This occurs when using ByRef arguments that refer to the same variable in two ways. For example:

```
Sub Foo(x as integer, y as integer)
   x = 5 ' Code is referring to the same variable
         ' (the local z in Main)
   y = 6 ' via two different names, x and y.
End Sub
Sub Main
   Dim z as integer
   Foo z,z
End Sub
```

Using this option allows the compiler to apply optimizations it couldn't otherwise use, such as storing variables in registers and performing loop optimizations. However, you should be careful not to check this option if your program passes arguments ByRef, since the optimizations could cause the program to execute incorrectly.

Remove Array Bounds Checks

Turns off error checking for valid array indexes and the correct number of dimensions of the array.

By default Visual Basic makes a check on every access to an array to determine if the index is within the range of the array. If the index is outside the bounds of the array, an error is returned. Selecting this option will turn off this error checking, which can speed up array manipulation significantly. However, if your program accesses an array with an index that is out of bounds, invalid memory locations may be accessed without warning. This can cause unexpected behavior or program crashes.

Remove Integer-Overflow Checks

Turns off error checking to insure that numeric values assigned to integer variables are within the correct range for the data types.

By default in Visual Basic, a check is made on every calculation to a variable with an integer-style data type (Byte, Integer, Long, and Currency) to be sure that the resulting value is within range of that data type. If the value is of the wrong magnitude, an error will occur. Selecting this option will turn off this error checking, which can speed up integer calculations. If data type capacities are overflowed, however, no error will be returned and incorrect results may occur.

Remove Floating-Point Error Checks

Turns off error checking to insure that numeric values assigned to floating-point variables are within the correct range for the data types, and that division by zero or other invalid operations do not occur.

By default in Visual Basic, a check is made on every calculation to a variable with a floating point data types (Single and Double) to be sure that the resulting value is within range of that data type. If the value is of the wrong magnitude an error will occur. Error checking is also performed to determine if division by zero or other invalid operations are attempted. Selecting this option turns off this error checking which can speed up floating point calculations. If data type capacities are overflowed, however, no error will be returned and incorrect results may occur.

Remove Safe Pentium FDIV Checks

Turns off the generation of special code to make floating point division safe on Pentium processors with the floating-point division (FDIV) bug.

The native code compiler automatically adds extra code for floating-point operations to make these operations safe when run on Pentium processors that have the FDIV bug. Selecting this option produces code that is smaller and faster, but which may in rare cases produce slightly incorrect results on Pentium processors with the FDIV bug.

Allow Unrounded Floating-Point Operations

Allows the compiler to compare the results of floating-point expressions without first rounding those results to the correct precision.

Floating-point calculations are normally rounded off to the correct degree of precision (Single or Double) before comparisons are made. Selecting this option allows the compiler do floating-point comparisons before rounding, when it can do so more efficiently. This improves the speed of some floating-point operations; however, this may result in calculations being maintained to a higher precision than expected, and two floating-point values that might be expected to compare equal might not.

In general this option should not be used if you perform equality comparisons directly on the results of floating-point computations. For example:

```
Dim Q As Single

Q = <floating-point computation>
  ...
If Q = <floating-point computation> then
  ...
End If
```

If the option is set, the comparison of Q will be made with the result of the floating-point expression, which will likely have higher precision than that of a Single, so the comparison may fail. If the option is not set, the result of the floating-point expression will be rounded to the appropriate precision (Single) before the comparison, then the comparison will succeed.

APPENDIX D

Adding Help to Your Application

No matter how well crafted the application, at some point most users are going to have questions about how to use it. Unless you're going to be there to answer their questions in person, the best way to handle this is by providing a Help file for the application.

Visual Basic provides support for two different Help systems: the traditional Windows Help system (WinHelp), and the newer HTML Help. This appendix covers the steps necessary to add either WinHelp or HTML Help to your application, pointing out the few differences between the two where applicable. What it doesn't cover is how to author a Help file — there are numerous authoring tools available that can help you to do that.

Contents

Adding Support for Help

Adding support for Help to your Visual Basic application is really quite simple. All you need to do is set one property, HelpFile (and, of course, write and compile a Help file), to display Help when the user presses the F1 key or requests Help from a menu. An additional property, HelpContextID, can be set to provide a contextual Help topic for any user interface element in your application. The process of hooking up Help is essentially the same for both WinHelp and HTML Help.

The HelpFile Property

The HelpFile property of the App object is used to specify the file name of the Help file for your application. It requires a valid WinHelp (.hlp) or HTML Help (.chm) file. If the file doesn't exist, an error will occur.

To set the HelpFile property

1. Select **Project Properties** from the **Project** menu to open the **Project Properties** dialog box.
2. In the **Help File Name** field of the **General** tab, enter the path and file name for your application's Help file (.hlp or .chm).

You can also set the HelpFile programmatically. The following code would specify an HTML Help file that resides in the same directory as the application's executable file:

```
Private Sub Form_Load()
   App.HelpFile = App.Path & "\foo.chm"
End Sub
```

The ErrObject object also has a HelpFile property, allowing you to specify a different Help file for error messages. For example, if you have several applications that share the same error messages, you can put Help for the error messages in a single Help file that can be called by the Err.Helpfile property in each application.

The HelpContextID Property

The HelpContextID property is used to link a user interface element (such as a control, form, or menu) to a related topic in a Help file. The HelpContextID property must be a Long that matches the Context ID of a topic in a WinHelp (.hlp) or HTML Help (.chm) file.

For example, you might enter 10000 in the HelpContextID property of a TextBox. When the user selects the TextBox and presses F1, Visual Basic searches for a topic with a Context ID of 10000 in the Help file specified in the application's HelpFile property. If its found, a Help window will open and display the topic; if not, an error will occur and the Help file's default topic will be displayed.

You should use a unique HelpContextID to match each Help topic in your Help file. In some cases, you may want to assign the same HelpContextID for several objects if the objects share a common Help topic.

You don't necessarily have to enter a HelpContextID for every control on a form. If the user presses F1 on a control with a HelpContextID of 0 (the default), Visual Basic will search for a valid HelpContextID for the control's container.

To assign a HelpContextID for a control or form

1. Select the control or form for which you want to enter a HelpContextID.
2. Double-click HelpContextID in the Properties window and enter a valid Long integer.

   Keep track of the value that you enter so that you can use the same value for the context ID of the associated Help topic.

   Note For the CommonDialog control and possibly for some other controls, the name of this property is HelpContext instead of HelpContextID.

To assign a HelpContextID for a menu

1. Select **Menu Editor** from the **Tools** menu.
2. Choose the menu item for which you want to enter a HelpContextID.
3. Enter a valid Long in the Select the HelpContextID box.

   Keep track of the value that you enter so that you can use the same value for the context ID of the associated Help topic.

The HelpContextID can also be entered programmatically as follows:

```
Private Sub Form_Load()
   Command1.HelpContextID = 12345
   MenuHelp.HelpContextID = 23456
   Err.HelpContext = 34567
End Sub
```

> **Tip** If you have more than a few Help topics, it may help to establish a numbering scheme before you start entering HelpContextID's. Assign a different range of numbers for each form or major element in your application, for example, 1000–1999 for the first form, 2000–2999 for the second, and so forth.

Adding Support for What's This Help

Visual Basic allows you to easily add What's This Help to your applications. What's This Help provides quick access to Help text in a popup window without the need to open the Help viewer. It is typically used to provide simple assistance for user interface elements such as data entry fields. Visual Basic supports What's This Help topics in both WinHelp (.hlp) and HTML Help (.chm) files.

Setting the WhatsThisHelp property of a form to True enables What's This Help. When What's This Help is enabled, context-sensitive Help for the form is disabled.

To enable What's This Help for a form

1. With the form selected, double-click the WhatsThisHelp property in the Properties window to set it to **True**.
2. Set the following properties to add a What's This button to the title bar of the form:

Property	Setting
BorderStyle	1 – Fixed Single or 2 – Sizable
MaxButton	False
MinButton	False
WhatsThisButton	True

Note A form can't have a What's This Help button if it has Minimize and Maximize buttons. As an alternative to the settings shown above, you can also set the BorderStyle property to 3 – Fixed Dialog, since a fixed dialog doesn't have Minimize and Maximize buttons.

3. Select each control for which you want to provide What's This Help and assign a unique value to the WhatsThisHelpID property of the control.

   Keep track of the value that you enter so that you can use the same value for the context ID of the associated Help topic.

   Important To implement What's This Help in HTML Help, all What's This Help topics must be contained in a Cshelp.txt file that is compiled into the .chm file. For more information, see the documentation for your HTML Help authoring tool.

You can also enable What's This Help without using a What's This button by setting the WhatsThisHelp property of the form to True and invoking the WhatsThisMode method of a form or the ShowWhatsThis method of a control.

Distributing Help with Your Application

The final step in adding Help to your application is making sure that it gets into the hands of the end user. The requirements for distributing Help with your application differ slightly for WinHelp versus HTML Help.

Distributing WinHelp

Since every Windows system already has the Windows Help Viewer installed, the only thing you need to distribute is the Help file (.hlp) itself. The Package and Deployment Wizard will automatically add a dependency for the Help file referenced by your application. If you're creating setup by another means, you'll need to make sure that the .hlp file is included and installed to the right location (usually in the same directory as the application or the \Windows\Help directory.)

Distributing HTML Help

HTML Help is a relatively new technology, hence you can't assume that every user will have the files needed to view HTML Help. The Package and Deployment Wizard will add a dependency for the HTML Help file (.chm) referenced by your application; but it may not add all dependencies for the HTML Help viewer files. You will need to modify your setup to include these files. Consult the documentation for your HTML Help authoring tool for more information on which files are required in a given situation.

Index

A

B

C

D

E

G

J

K

L

N

O

P

Q

R

S

U

W

X

Y

Z

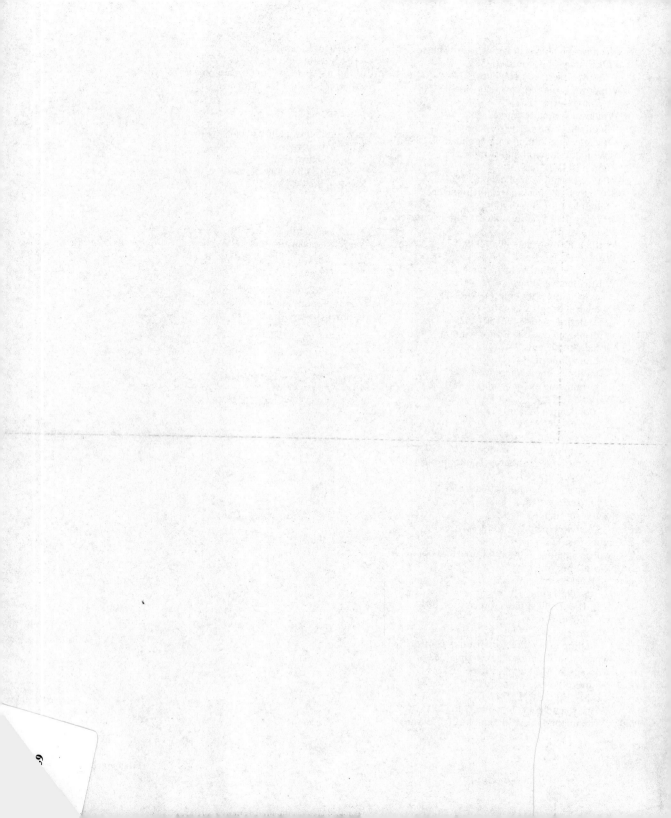